THE PRACTICE OF MODERN INTERNAL AUDITING

Appraising Operations for Management

LAWRENCE B. SAWYER

THE PRACTICE OF MODERN

Appraising Operations for Management

LAWRENCE B. SAWYER

THE INSTITUTE OF INTERNAL AUDITORS, INC.

INTERNAL AUDITING

This text by Lawrence B. Sawyer — attorney, accountant, Certified Internal Auditor, and businessman — is based on his **30** years' experience as a working internal auditor in both business and government.

THE PRACTICE OF MODERN INTERNAL AUDITING

Appraising Operations for Management

Library of Congress Catalog Card Number 72-96691

This book was set in Century Expanded by Typo-Graphics, Inc. and printed by Vaughan Printers, Inc. The designer was Wayne Hovis; the drawings were done by Wayne Hovis, Robert Sigo and Billy Welch of Art Services of Orlando. The editor and publication supervisor was Cissie Cooper.

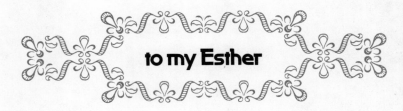

to my Esther

preface

Modern internal auditing — used here to mean the comprehensive review and appraisal of the diverse operations of an organization as a service to management — has been dealt with extensively, particularly since it started being called management or operational auditing. Many publications by both theorists and practitioners alike have analyzed it and dissected it. Much has been said on what it is and how it differs from the traditional compliance auditing.

But my experience in teaching and training internal auditors and in discussing internal auditing with students and faculty has impelled the conclusion that not enough has been said about "how to do it." The theory has been explored extensively. The practice has been dealt with sketchily and in fragments.

To remedy that defect, then, is the purpose of this book; a book that can be used by the student, by both the novice and the experienced practitioner, and by those in management whom the auditing organization serves; a book that can be used as a guide to the actual practice of modern internal auditing and as a means of measuring the capabilities and the accomplishments of auditing organizations.

It has been said that modern internal auditing differs from the classical compliance auditing in that it requires a different stance and a different state of mind — but that it is still basically auditing, for does it not function by evaluating internal control systems and testing transactions? True. But the different stance and the different state of mind call for different techniques and different methods to accomplish the auditor's objectives. The analysis of an expense account bears little resemblance to the analysis of an engineering department or an advertising department. The corrective action required for account misclassifications is vastly different from the action needed to improve the system of control over a company's proprietary rights or its budgeting for television advertising.

The need for a guide to convey these newly developed methods and techniques has become increasingly pressing as internal auditing has been adopted and is being practiced in more and more companies throughout the world. Yet it is unfortunately true that many companies which have embraced modern auditing with the hope that it will provide for them the control and information that they feel have been lacking, have become sorely disappointed with the results. The reason is often painfully simple. The people they have hired to perform modern auditing have not had the necessary experience and have not been able to obtain help in developing that experience from existing books on the subject.

It is axiomatic that internal auditing is not bought by management. It must be sold to management. It is also axiomatic that the auditor cannot ask management what it expects of him. Management usually does not really know. The experienced auditor must tell management what he has to offer. And then he must produce and prove his worth. He must sell his product with each audit project he completes. He must produce an audit package that is professional, useful, and technically correct. And he will be allowed few mistakes.

In this book we shall seek to help him avoid such mistakes; for the emphasis will be on "how to." We shall offer practical guides on the primary aspects of modern internal auditing and on the internal auditing organization which seeks to practice it.

Looking at the other side of the coin, management must know what standards to apply to its own auditing organization, what it should expect in the form of audit service, and what is required to upgrade its audit staff and the audit program. I hope this book will provide the yardstick for such measurements.

We shall be concerned with how to establish the auditing organization and how to sell its services to management . . . how to obtain and train a competent staff . . . how to set forth the audit goals, as well as corollary goals for expanding the audit function, with management's blessing and involvement . . . how to make meaningful assignments of audit projects and keep them under control . . . how to develop significant information from preliminary surveys as a start to or as a substitute for detailed testing . . . how to develop useful audit programs that are tailored to the needs of the individual project and keyed to the objectives of the activities reviewed . . . how to use advanced sampling techniques in the audit . . . how to perform audits of and with the computer . . . how to develop facts and supporting evidence during the field work . . . how to prepare useful, economical, and explicit working papers to document the results of the audit . . . how to plan and prepare the internal audit report so that it can fill the needs of all levels of readers . . . how to obtain auditee participation and understanding through the draft review conference, and how to make internal audits productive by ensuring prompt action to strengthen weaknesses and adopt recommendations . . . how to let management know what internal auditing is accomplishing for it in such a way as to promote a proper understanding of the internal auditor's indispensable function in the overall management process.

With a solid understanding of these techniques, both by the auditor and those he serves, modern internal auditing has a good chance of being firmly and permanently installed in its proper place in the councils of executive management. Without it, management may become disenchanted and ask for the return of the classical, pedestrian "bean counting" to which it was accustomed.

Lawrence B. Sawyer

acknowledgements

A book that sets out to span the spectrum of modern internal auditing, a book that seeks to give space to diverse practices, a book that essays to take the picture of a profession in the full rush of its burgeoning growth — a book that tries to do all these things, must depend on many contributors if the picture is to be taken with a wide-angle lens and with reasonable fidelity.

I am deeply and humbly grateful, therefore, to those practitioners throughout the internal auditing profession who gave unstintingly of ideas, suggestions, and examples that helped widen my horizons during my research and compilation of information. Not all the examples proferred have been incorporated into this book. But each one helped open a broader vista of the practice of modern internal auditing.

There is no one "right" way to staff an organization, develop auditors, prepare programs, do field work, deal with people, report audit results, or communicate with executive management. That is why I have selected examples from many different disciplines. One practice or procedure may be right for this organization and wrong for that one. Some examples shown in this book might suit one practitioner and not another. No attempt was made to provide an encyclopedia of forms and methods. But those displayed and discussed may act as a spur to adapt them to or devise them for some particular needs.

For their valuable contributions to this book I am much indebted to such organizations as American Greetings Corporation, American Institute of Certified Public Accountants, American Oil Company, American United Life Insurance Company, California Institute of Technology, Canadian Institute of Chartered Accountants, Defense Contract Audit Agency, Eastman Kodak Co., Ford Motor Company, General Electric Company, Honeywell, Inc., International Business Machines Corporation, International Society for General Semantics, Kennecott Copper Corporation, Jones & Laughlin Steel Corporation, Lockheed Aircraft Corporation, Pacific Northwest Bell Telephone Company, Sperry Rand Corporation, Springs Mills, Inc., State of Wisconsin Legislative Audit Bureau, Teachers Insurance and Annuity Association of America, Thiokol Chemical Corporation, Union Carbide Corporation — Nuclear Division, U. S. Air Force Auditor General, U. S. Department of Agriculture, U. S. Department of Health, Education and Welfare, U. S. General Accounting Office, University of Alabama, Virginia Polytechnic Institute and State University, Wells Fargo Bank, and Weyerhaeuser Company.

My very special thanks go to Donald E. Dooley, Dr. Frederic E. Mints, and Duane E. Wilson — three of the most respected names in internal auditing — who reviewed the manuscript and extended expert guidance and wise counsel.

Some of the chapters needed technical help. For his valuable aid in correcting, amending, and expanding on the chapter on computer auditing and for his meticulous review of the chapter on sampling, I extend my heartfelt gratitude to William F. Wilkerson and his associates at the U. S. Department of Health, Education and Welfare. And for his welcome review of the chapter on reports, I am grateful indeed to Dr. William C. Himstreet.

I owe a debt of gratitude to three mentors who demonstrated abundantly and successfully to me how to practice the difficult art-science of auditing for management: Paul E. Heeschen, Charles N. Inman, and Dr. Frederic E. Mints.

Every work needs fine tuning. I was fortunate to be the beneficiary of the sound judgment and exquisite craftsmanship of Arthur A. Dickerman, who smoothed the rough spots and placed an unerring finger on the pesky errors that plague the harried author.

And for his steadfast support and his high standards, my respect and regards to Stuart C. Dew.

Many authors, including this one, have found themselves stuck dead center in the slough of despond — unable to move. For the ever-present encouragement and fierce loyalty that helped me get moving again, and for her fine professionalism in editing this book, I give my fond thanks to Cissie Cooper.

And to the one who suffered with me all the way through, who typed my murky drafts, and whose canny sense with words and logic helped me from committing more than my share of blunders — to my Esther, as always, my love.

LBS

contents

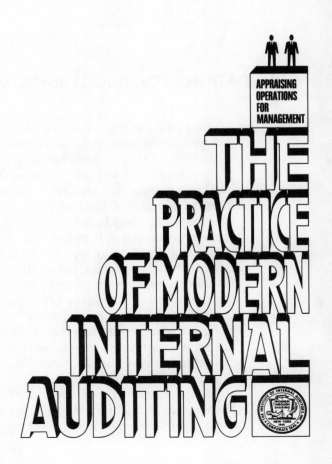

APPRAISING
OPERATIONS
FOR
MANAGEMENT

THE
PRACTICE
OF MODERN
INTERNAL
AUDITING

THE INSTITUTE OF INTERNAL AUDITORS
PROGRESS THROUGH SHARING
NEW YORK
CORPORATE SEAL

one

ESTABLISHING THE AUDITING ORGANIZATION

FOUNDATIONS FOR SUCCESSFUL INTERNAL AUDITING

Successful internal auditing is constructed on a foundation of technical excellence. But the structure must be firmly buttressed — on the one side by demonstrated acceptance and support at the highest levels in the enterprise; on the other by continued, imaginative service to management. Each of the two buttresses is an integral member of the structure. Let one weaken and the structure may tilt, ready to fall at the first hard blow from the winds of retrenchment and cost reduction.

These axioms apply equally to the auditor seeking to provide the full benefits of internal auditing to his company and to the manager who is aware of these benefits but who is not yet obtaining them from his auditing organization. The enterprising auditor must bring home to management the value of the service he can render in a proper climate and environment. The enlightened manager can obtain these unique services if he knows what to demand of his director of auditing and what modern internal auditing is capable of doing for him.

Both the auditor and the manager must understand that although technical ability may get the audit job done professionally, the auditor's conclusions and recommendations may lie impotent and ignored in his carefully prepared audit report. Proper standing in the enterprise, however, reinforced by management support, gives the job and the report full force and effect. And innovative, well-considered service to the decision-makers in the company — at all levels — develops willing customers for the audit function, while providing the internal auditor with entree into every area of the enterprise and a seat in the councils of executive management.

Accepted standing in the organization is essential for another reason as well: It is the guarantee of independence. And for the auditing function to be effective, it must be independent of the activities it audits.

Total independence is as elusive as a perfect vacuum. Complete independence implies freedom from all dependency — including financial dependency. Hence, as long as the auditing department is a part of the enterprise and receives its life support from the enterprise, it must relinquish some independence. The auditor's goal, therefore, is to achieve the greatest amount of practical independence in the real world situation in which he finds himself — independence which will protect him from having to compromise his audit objectives.

Independence, however, is more than a slogan or shibboleth. It is the climate which the auditing organization needs to live and breathe and function. Internal auditing is a professional activity.

Its purpose is to make professional judgments. It therefore demands the highest type of judicial detachment, integrity, and objectivity.[1]

These attributes atrophy in the absence of practical independence. Thus, the utter essentiality of a reporting status that permits the maintenance of objectivity and removes the auditor from effective dependence upon the people whose activities he audits.

Management has begun to recognize that need for independence. This is demonstrated by the results of a recent survey[2] which showed that in about 10 years the percentage of auditing organizations reporting to a vice president or higher rose from 30% to 47%. The ultimate, of course, is for the auditing organization to report to the board.[3] This is desirable but — unlike banks, where the director of auditing usually reports to the board — is not always achievable. The minimum requirement is for the auditing organization to report to an officer whose own status is such that he can command prompt and proper consideration of the auditor's opinions and recommendations. Preferably, that officer should be a member of the board; ideally, a member of the board's auditing committee.

But in any event, auditing management should have access to the board. Obtaining that access calls for salesmanship, backed by imaginative service. The sales campaign may be a long and arduous one, but it will be worth the effort. And with a proper campaign, the sale is sure to be consummated; for the auditor has a product which the board will want to buy: an objective view of the company . . . a professional diagnosis of its health . . . a unique focus on its maladies, both existing and incipient, which often do not appear in the other reporting mechanisms provided to the board.

That same salesmanship can be used to provide information to executive management. And as management becomes accustomed to new forms of reports and diagnoses, it will become dependent

---

[1]Smith, N.A., "Achieving the Objectives of Internal Auditing," *The Internal Auditor*, May/June 1970, p. 65.

[2]*Survey of Internal Auditing, 1968.* Research Committee Report No. 15, The Institute of Internal Auditors, p. 13.

[3]Throughout this book I shall use the terms "company" or "Board of Directors" when referring to an organizational entity or to the highest councils of management in such an entity. These terms are used for convenience. For "company" one can just as well read "government agency," "nonprofit organization" or any other operating entity to which internal auditing might apply. Similarly, "Board of Directors" can be read as "partners," "chief administrative officer," "commissioners" or any other final authority to which an organization or agency is responsible.

upon them, look forward to them, make use of them, and elevate the director of auditing to a position as a member of the *executive* management team.

How does the auditor accomplish this feat of being made a part of the highest levels of management? First, he must influence executive management to establish his status in the clearest possible terms. Second, he must provide management with significant, interesting, and usable information which compels attention and demonstrates the value of the auditing organization.

We shall talk about the first in the following subsection. We shall leave the second to the final chapter in this book.

PREPARING THE FUNCTIONS AND RESPONSIBILITY STATEMENT

Most companies maintain a set of statements which establish the authority and responsibility of the major positions in the organization. These become the charters under which each organization operates. In them is set forth, for the rest of the company to see, how executive management regards the purpose, mission, and authority of each major function within the company. The auditor should make certain, therefore, that the charter for his position is one within whose framework he can function with the degree of independence that can guarantee objectivity.

The statement must be carefully drafted so that it affords the auditor all the authority he needs, yet does not assign responsibility which he cannot conceivably carry out. It should not restrict the auditor to matters of accounting and finance. On the other hand, it should not require him to provide opinions on the effectiveness of functions of a highly technical nature. For this reason, many such statements place stress on the review of management controls, rather than on the appraisal of performance. The competent internal auditor is capable of reviewing administrative and management controls over any activity within the company. This ability clearly cannot extend to the evaluation of performance of professional or technical activities calling for specialized study and knowledge to carry out. At the same time, of course, he should not be debarred from evaluating effective performance of those administrative activities where he can be a competent judge.

A specimen functions and responsibility statement — a composite of several such statements — is shown in Exhibit 1-1.

Exhibit 1-1.   THE DIRECTOR OF AUDITING STATEMENT OF AUTHORITY AND RESPONSIBILITY

Authority

The director of auditing is authorized to direct a broad, comprehensive program of internal auditing within the company. Internal auditing examines and evaluates the adequacy and effectiveness of the systems of management control provided by the company to direct its activities toward the accomplishment of its objectives in accordance with company policies and plans. In accomplishing his activities, the director of auditing and his representatives are authorized to have full, free, and unrestricted access to all company functions, records, property, and personnel.

Responsibility

The director of auditing is responsible for:

■ Establishing policies for the auditing activity and directing its technical and administrative functions.

■ Developing and executing a comprehensive audit program for the evaluation of the management controls provided over all company activities.

■ Examining the effectiveness of all levels of management in their stewardship of company resources and their compliance with established policies and procedures.

■ Recommending improvement of management controls designed to safeguard company resources, promote company growth, and ensure compliance with government laws and regulations.

■ Reviewing procedures and records for their adequacy to accomplish intended objectives, and appraising policies and plans relating to the activity or function under audit review.

■ Authorizing the publication of reports on the results of audit examinations, including recommendations for improvement.

■ Appraising the adequacy of the action taken by operating management to correct reported deficient conditions; accepting adequate corrective action; continuing reviews with appropriate management personnel on action he considers inadequate until there has been a satisfactory resolution of the matter.

■ Conducting special examinations at the request of management, including the reviews of representations made by persons outside the company.

DEVISING THE MANAGEMENT DIRECTIVE

Management support must be proclaimed clearly and categorically in the company's highest policy statement. Without management support the auditor is an ineffectual instrument. Since the auditor obtains action on his findings and recommendations through audit reports, the authority to issue them and to expect prompt, effective action must have the unequivocal sanction of executive management. In unmistakable terms, all levels of the company must be given to understand that any unresolved matters reported by the auditor must be responded to. And the response must be made to an officer with authority to insist upon it.

The management directive must be quite specific, setting time limits for the submission of replies to unresolved matters. It must be equally specific about the auditor being the judge of the adequacy of the reply.

Exhibit 1-2. COMPANY POLICY

It is the policy of the company to provide an internal auditing organization as a means of supplying management personnel at all levels with information to control the operations for which they are responsible. The vice president-administration is assigned responsibility for the internal auditing program and will see that:

■ Organizations within the company are reviewed at appropriate intervals to determine whether they are effectively carrying out their functions of planning, accounting, custody, and control in accordance with management instructions, policies, and procedures and in a manner that is consonant both with company objectives and with high standards of administrative practice.

■ The results of the examinations made by the auditors, the opinions which they form, and the recommendations which they make are promptly reported to management personnel who should be informed or who should take appropriate action.

■ Any plans or actions taken to correct reported conditions are evaluated for satisfactory disposition of audit findings and, if the disposition is considered unsatisfactory, to see that further discussions are held to achieve satisfactory disposition.

The director of auditing and his staff of auditors shall have full, free, and unrestricted access to all company activities, records, property, and personnel.

The division manager is responsible for seeing that corrective action on reported deficient conditions is either planned or taken within 30 days from receipt of a report disclosing those conditions. He is also responsible for seeing that a written report of action planned or completed is sent to the vice president-administration. If a plan for action is reported, a second report shall be made promptly upon completion of the plan.

Such a directive is the underpinning for the internal auditing organization. Without it, auditing becomes a matter of grace, to be accepted or rejected by operating management. With it, auditing becomes a matter of right, binding upon operating management and ensuring action when action is called for. This right must be earned, of course; but the opportunity to earn it will not exist in the absence of a clear mandate from the highest executive level of the company setting forth its support of the audit effort.

Exhibit 1-2, which accomplishes the objectives just discussed, is a composite of several different policy statements.

WRITING JOB DESCRIPTIONS

Statements of function and responsibility and management directives set the stage for the director of auditing. They provide the arena in which he will function. But he cannot function at optimal levels without the right staff. His staff must therefore have adequate status in the company in terms of salary grades. In most companies the salary grades are established by salary review boards who make their determinations by reviewing job descriptions.

The job descriptions for the various levels of audit staff may make or break the auditing organization. Modern internal auditing demands the highest level of audit effort. Only the best auditors are able to accomplish it successfully and carry out the promise that is held forth to management by the progressive director of auditing. It has been abundantly demonstrated that it is much better to perform the internal auditing function with fewer competent staff auditors than with many mediocre ones. Indeed, the function will just plain not be accomplished without men of intelligence, imagination, and initiative — to say nothing of understanding and the ability to deal with others. And such men come high in the market place.

For this reason the job descriptions should be drafted with care. They should set forth requirements capable of being accomplished by the best auditors, not by the average auditors. Such descriptions will warrant the assignment of salary grades which will attract the best men, not only from the market place but from within the company itself.

In relatively large auditing organizations, with far-flung operations and locations, the hierarchy of jobs is usually somewhat as follows:

1. Director of Auditing
2. Audit Managers

3. Audit Supervisors
4. Senior Auditors
5. Associate Auditors (sometimes called semi-seniors)
6. Assistant Auditors (sometimes called junior auditors)

A typical description of the director's function has been shown in Exhibit 1-1. Examples of job descriptions for the remaining positions, each a composite of several, are shown in Exhibits 1-3a, 1-3b, 1-3c, 1-3d, and 1-3e.

Exhibit 1-3a. POSITION DESCRIPTION
INTERNAL AUDITING — MANAGER

Purpose

■ To administer the internal auditing activity of an assigned location.

■ To develop a comprehensive, practical program of audit coverage for the assigned location.

■ To obtain accomplishment of the program in accordance with acceptable audit standards and stipulated schedules.

■ To maintain effective working relations with executive and operating management.

Authority and Responsibility

Within the general guidelines provided by the director of auditing:

■ Prepares a comprehensive, long-range program of audit coverage for the location to which he is assigned.

■ Identifies those activities subject to audit coverage, evaluates their significance, and assesses the degree of risk inherent in the activity in terms of cost, schedule, and quality.

■ Establishes the departmental structure.

■ Obtains and maintains an audit staff capable of accomplishing the internal audit function.

■ Assigns audit areas, staff, and budget to supervisory auditors.

■ Develops a system of cost and schedule control over audit projects.

■ Establishes standards of performance and, by review, determines that performance meets the standards.

■ Provides executive management within the assigned location with reports on audit coverage and the results of the audit activity, and interprets those results so as to improve the audit program and the audit coverage.

■ Establishes and monitors accomplishment of objectives directed toward increasing his department's ability to serve management.

Exhibit 1-3b. POSITION DESCRIPTION
INTERNAL AUDITING — SUPERVISOR

Purpose
- To develop a comprehensive, practical program of audit coverage for assigned areas of audit.
- To supervise the activities of auditors assigned to the review of various organizational and functional activities.
- To ensure conformance with acceptable audit standards, plans, budgets, and schedules.
- To maintain effective working relations with operating management.
- To provide for and conduct research; develop manuals and training guides.

Authority and Responsibility
Under the general guidance of the manager of Internal Auditing:
- Supervises the work of auditors engaged in the reviews of organizational and functional activities.
- Provides a comprehensive, practical program of annual audit coverage within general areas assigned by the manager of Internal Auditing.
- Determines areas of risk and appraises their significance in relation to operational factors of cost, schedule, and quality. Classifies audit projects as to degree of risk and significance and as to frequency of audit coverage.
- Provides for flexibility in his program so as to be responsive to management's special needs.
- Schedules projects and staff assignments so as to comply with management's needs, within the scope of the department's overall program.
- Coordinates the program with the company's public accountant.
- Reviews and approves the purpose, scope, and audit approach of each audit project for his assigned areas of audit cognizance.
- Directs audit projects to see that professional standards are maintained in the planning and execution and in the accumulation of evidentiary data.
- Counsels and guides auditors to see that the approved audit objectives are met and that adequate, practical coverage is achieved.
- Reviews and edits audit reports and, in company with the auditor-in-charge for the assigned project, discusses the reports with appropriate management.
- Presents oral briefings to branch-level management.
- Provides for and performs research on audit techniques.
- Provides formal plans for the recruiting, selecting, training, evaluating, and supervising of staff personnel.
- Develops manuals and other training aids.
- Accumulates data, maintains records, and prepares reports on the administration of audit projects and other assigned activities.
- Assists in evaluating overall results of the internal audits.
- Identifies factors causing deficient conditions and recommends courses of action to improve the conditions, including special surveys and audits.
- Provides for a flow of communication from operating management to the manager and to the director of auditing.

Exhibit 1-3c. POSITION DESCRIPTION
INTERNAL AUDITOR — SENIOR

Purpose

- To conduct reviews of assigned organizational and functional activities. ᾽
- To evaluate the adequacy and effectiveness of the management controls over those activities.
- To determine whether organizational units in the company are performing their planning, accounting, custodial, or control activities in compliance with management instructions, applicable statements of policy and procedures, and in a manner consistent with both company objectives and high standards of administrative practice.
- To plan and execute audits in accordance with accepted standards.
- To report audit findings and to make recommendations for correcting unsatisfactory conditions, improving operations, and reducing cost.
- To perform special reviews at the request of management.
- To direct the activities of assistants.

Authority and Responsibility

Under the general guidance of a supervising auditor:

- Surveys functions and activities in assigned areas to determine the nature of operations and the adequacy of the system of control to achieve established objectives.
- Determines the direction and thrust of the proposed audit effort.
- Plans the theory and scope of the audit, and prepares an audit program.
- Determines the auditing procedures to be used, including statistical sampling and the use of electronic data processing equipment.
- Identifies the key control points of the system.
- Evaluates a system's effectiveness through the application of his knowledge of business systems, including financial, manufacturing, engineering, procurement, and other operations, and his understanding of auditing techniques.
- Recommends necessary staff required to complete the audit.
- Performs the audit in a professional manner and in accordance with the approved audit program.
- Obtains, analyzes, and appraises evidentiary data as a basis for an informed, objective opinion on the adequacy and effectiveness of the system and the efficiency of performance of the activities being reviewed.
- Directs, counsels, and instructs staff assistants assigned to the audit, and reviews their work for sufficiency of scope and for accuracy.
- Makes oral or written presentations to management during and at the conclusion of the examination, discussing deficiencies and recommending corrective action to improve operations and reduce cost.
- Prepares formal written reports, expressing opinions on the adequacy and effectiveness of the system and the efficiency with which activities are carried out.
- Appraises the adequacy of the corrective action taken to improve deficient conditions.

Exhibit 1-3d. POSITION DESCRIPTION
INTERNAL AUDITOR — ASSOCIATE

Purpose

■ To conduct or assist in conducting reviews of assigned organizational and functional activities.

■ To evaluate the adequacy and effectiveness of the management controls over those activities.

■ To determine whether organizational units in the company are performing their planning, accounting, custodial, or control activities in compliance with management instructions, applicable statements of policy and procedures, and in a manner consistent with both company objectives and high standards of administrative practice.

■ To plan and execute complete reviews of limited audit assignments, or conduct reviews of portions of extensive audit assignments, in accordance with accepted professional standards.

■ To report audit findings and to make recommendations for the correction of unsatisfactory conditions, improvements in operations, and reductions in cost.

■ To perform or to assist in the performance of special reviews at the request of management.

■ To direct, when applicable, the activities of assistants.

Authority and Responsibility

Under the guidance of a supervising or senior internal auditor:

■ Surveys functions and activities in assigned areas to determine the nature of operations and the adequacy of the system of control to achieve established objectives.

■ Determines or assists in determining the direction and thrust of the proposed audit effort.

■ Plans or assists in planning the theory and scope of the audit, and prepares or assists in preparing an audit program.

■ Determines or assists in determining the audit procedures to be used.

■ Identifies the key control points of the system.

■ Performs the audit in a professional manner and in accordance with the approved audit program.

■ Obtains, analyzes, and appraises evidentiary data as a basis for an informed, objective opinion on the adequacy and effectiveness of the system and the efficiency of performance of the activities being reviewed.

■ Makes, or assists in making, oral or written presentations to management during and at the conclusion of the examination, discussing deficiencies, recommending corrective action, and suggesting improvements in operations and reductions in cost.

■ Prepares formal written reports, as requested, expressing opinions on the adequacy and effectiveness of the system and the efficiency with which activities are carried out.

■ Appraises, or assists in appraising, the adequacy of the corrective action taken to improve deficient conditions.

Exhibit 1-3e. POSITION DESCRIPTION
INTERNAL AUDITOR — ASSISTANT

Purpose

■ To verify and analyze transactions and representations while conducting reviews of assigned organizational and functional activities.

■ To evaluate the adequacy and effectiveness of the management controls over those activities.

■ To assist in determining whether organizational units in the company are performing their planning, accounting, custodial, or control activities in compliance with management instructions, applicable statements of policy and procedures, and in a manner consistent with both company objectives and high standards of administrative practice.

■ To prepare working papers showing the results of the audit examination.

■ To report audit findings on the results of the review of assigned segments of the audit and to make recommendations for the correction of unsatisfactory conditions, improvements in operations, and reductions in cost.

■ To assist in the performance of special reviews at the request of management.

Authority and Responsibility

Under the direct supervision of a senior internal auditor:

■ Assists in planning work on assigned segments of the audit.

■ Assists in determining records or activities to analyze, the extent of tests to apply and the working papers to prepare.

■ Assists in performing the audit in accordance with the approved program and in a professional manner.

■ Recommends the means of obtaining, analyzing, and evaluating evidentiary data as a basis for an informed, objective opinion on the adequacy and effectiveness of the system of control and on the efficiency of performance of the activities being reviewed.

■ Reviews transactions, documents, records, reports, and methods for accuracy and effectiveness.

■ Prepares acceptable working papers which record and summarize data on the assigned audit segment.

■ Holds preliminary discussions of apparent deficiencies with operating personnel to verify facts and to obtain explanations of and reasons for such apparent deficiencies.

DEVELOPING THE AUDIT MANUALS

The audit manuals constitute the voice of the director of auditing. They tell his people how he regards his responsibilities to management and how he would like them carried out. They provide for stability, continuity, standards of acceptable performance, and the means of coordinating the efforts of a number of persons or of various units within the auditing organization. But in modern internal auditing the director is faced with a dilemma. On the one hand, he sees the desirability of providing instruction and achieving some optimal level of uniformity in his organization. On the other, he sees the possibility, through his pronouncements, of inhibiting imagination and innovative auditing.

Despite the dangers of stifling independent thinking, however, the staff needs guidance (1) to prevent individuals from going off in different directions, (2) to establish standards that lift the level of performance, and (3) to provide assurance that the auditing department's final product meets the director's requirements.

The auditing department's statements of policies and procedures must provide instructions and guidelines in several different areas. For convenience, this body of instruction may be divided into the following groupings:

- Technical functions — seeing that the job of conducting internal audits meets acceptable standards of coverage.
- Administrative functions — seeing that the internal audit department, as a group of individuals, runs smoothly.
- Miscellaneous functions — providing answers to the complete spectrum of day-to-day problems of the auditing department, as they arise.

The audit manuals are a mirror of the life style and philosophy of the individual audit department and its chief officer. Each manual, therefore, in each auditing organization, will be uniquely structured to carry out the ideas of the individual who charts the department's course. This book can provide guidelines, however, to assure reasonably adequate coverage.

Technical Functions

The technical audit manual will offer a guide to the performance of an internal audit. Without limiting the matters that may properly be included, the following subjects should probably be discussed.

Objectives of the audit. Establish the perimeters around the audit project so that an audit program can be written which will delineate the audit area and prevent wandering off into avenues that are irrelevant to the central theme of the audit.

Theory of the audit. Establish the idea of the audit approach. Shall it be a review of an organization or of a function? What is the auditor trying to establish or accomplish? Is the idea to make a survey with little testing, or is it to select certain suspected activities for detailed examination? Is the auditor seeking to determine the degree to which the existing structure is effective or does he want to know whether established procedures are being carried out?

Scope of the audit. Establish the matters which should be reviewed in all examinations. For example, have responsibilities been adequately assigned? Is authority commensurate with responsibility? Have organizational or functional objectives been set? Do reports to higher management show progress in meeting established objectives? Are methods and procedures designed to facilitate meeting those objectives? Are objectives actually being met? Does management have a self-checking system to highlight deviations from acceptable performance?

Preliminary reviews. Provide guides on the matters to be considered in the initial phase of the audit: The review of prior working papers, the research of internal auditing literature on the activity to be reviewed, and the examination of organization charts and relevant company directives.

Preliminary discussions. Indicate the levels of management at which preliminary discussions should be held, the nature of the assistance the auditor may offer to management, and the explanations he should make of the audit objectives, approaches, and programs.

Preliminary surveys. Indicate the nature of the preliminary survey, the kind of information to be obtained, the ways in which it can be obtained, and the uses to which the information should be put. (A more detailed analysis of the function of the preliminary survey will be made in a succeeding chapter.)

Audit programs. Show the requirements for each individual audit program to be tailored to the particular assignment and to determine operating objectives and related controls; and show the detail with which the programs shall be prepared.

Budgets and schedules. Describe the controls to be exercised over the audit project to assure compliance with budget and schedule constraints.

Working papers. Establish standards for working papers, for methods of summarizing data, and for indexing and cross-referencing worksheets.

Draft reviews with auditees. Set forth policies on reviews of findings, obtaining corrective action, the evidence of corrective action needed to close a finding, and the levels at which findings should be discussed.

Report writing. Provide guidelines on the format of reports, their length, the philosophy of reporting (problems only, or comprehensive analysis of the activity reviewed), and the levels of management to which the reports are directed.

Replies to reports. Provide instruction on how to deal with replies, what action to take if they are not acceptable, and how to close reports on which the replies are found to be acceptable.

Administrative Functions

Another volume of instructions is needed to provide guidance on those matters which are related to the business of performing internal audits, but which are not an actual part of performing the audit function. A separate manual, usually referred to as the administrative manual, facilitates revisions and is easier to handle. If it is combined with the audit manual it tends to become unwieldy. The administrative manual often takes the form of a compilation of staff memos, each of which can be issued or revised whenever considered desirable. Some of the matters which may be the subject of staff memos are as follows:

A. Office Administration
   1. Organization of the audit department
   2. Audit office filing system
   3. Reference library
   4. Supplies
   5. Time reports
   6. Housekeeping
   7. Security requirements
   8. Miscellaneous correspondence
   9. Periodic administrative reports

B. Personnel
   1. Personnel records
   2. Travel instructions and expense reports
   3. Staff evaluations
   4. Incentive awards
   5. Reporting injuries
   6. Jury duty
   7. Military duty

C. **Audit Projects**
 1. Assignment of the audit project
 2. Human relations — dealing with the auditee
 3. Permanent files for audit projects
 4. Budget estimates for audit projects
 5. Requests for program revisions or budget adjustments
 6. Uses of statistical sampling
 7. Uses of electronic data processing on audit projects
 8. Safeguarding working papers
 9. Destroying working papers
 10. Exit interviews with auditees
 11. Closing audit projects

D. **Audit Reports**
 1. Interim or progress reports
 2. Supervisory review of audit reports
 3. Proofreading, reference-checking, and processing final reports
 4. Distribution of audit reports
 5. Requests for copies of audit reports

Miscellaneous Functions

Auditors, like most other employees, are bombarded with many instructions — over and above those appearing in the technical and administrative manuals. These instructions may amplify, explain, or restrict statements in those manuals or they may cover matters not quite germane to the information in technical and administrative regulations. But whatever their relationship, these instructions come out in an unending stream.

Usually, they appear in memoranda, formal or informal, from the director's office. And since they were created by the same pen that wrote or approved the manuals, they have the same force and effect and require the same adherence.

Unfortunately, miscellaneous instructions, like comets, usually blaze across the departmental sky and then fall to rest in some correspondence file. There they lie, quiescent, to be revived only when they have been violated and are used to bludgeon the violator, or when they are vaguely remembered and take hours to locate. All such instructions, therefore, should be kept in an organized manner, capable of ready retrieval, in a "Miscellaneous Manual."

The manual should be thoughtfully compiled and maintained, so that (1) only matters of continuing significance are included; (2) it is periodically and formally updated to incorporate new information and to delete superseded instructions; (3) the referencing system provides for easy revisions, additions, and deletions; and (4) the index is complete, easy to maintain, and facilitates prompt retrieval of information.

Clearly, each audit department's Miscellaneous Manual must be different, and no strict format or table of contents can be devised to be universally applicable. One for a manufacturing company would bear no recognizable relationship to one for an insurance company, for instance. But the following example of a table of contents will provide some guidance for the preparation of such a manual — a manual which can save untold hours of searching and assure closer adherence to the director's instructions:

MISCELLANEOUS MANUAL

Contents

A. Our Organization
   1. Internal Auditing in Our Company
   2. Structure of Our Organization
   3. Our Responsibilities and Authority
   4. Our Interface with Other Organizations

B. Our Program
   1. Planning Our Program
   2. Cooperating with Our Public Accountants
   3. Coordinating with Our Security Department
   4. Reviewing Our Audit Program with Management

C. Our Auditing Methods and Techniques
   1. Areas of Risk
   2. Using Electronic Data Processing
   3. Using Statistical Sampling
   4. Discussing the Program with the Auditee
   5. Discussing Deficiencies with the Auditee
   6. Audit Time Spans and Budgets
   7. Cost Reduction Suggestions
   8. Recommendations for Improved Operations
   9. Audit Time Spans
   10. Determining Causes for Deficiencies
   11. Reviewing Draft Reports with Auditees

D. **Audit Reports**
 1. Format of Regular Reports
 2. Format of Special Reports
 3. Distribution of Audit Reports
 4. Replies to Audit Reports
 5. Classifying Deficiency Findings

E. **Coordinating Among Units**
 1. Audits Performed Concurrently
 2. Exchange of Audit Programs
 3. Exchange of Research Information
 4. Uniformity of Audit Programs

F. **Reports of Audit Activity**
 1. Monthly Reports
 2. Quarterly Reports
 3. Annual Reports

G. **Miscellaneous**
 1. Professional Activities
 2. Budgets
 3. Change of Status Notices
 4. Travel

Each memorandum or instruction is separately numbered according to the system set out above. For example, a memorandum providing information on how to budget for research projects might be numbered G.2.1. A subsequent memorandum setting forth budgeting for employee indoctrination might be numbered G.2.2, and so forth.

SELLING MODERN INTERNAL AUDITING TO MANAGEMENT

Successful selling, as every successful salesman knows, is bottomed on two firm requirements: Know your product. Know your customer. The salesman must know every element of his product, and which features make the product most salable. And he must know who his customer is and what his customer wants.

That is not quite as simple as it may sound, in terms of internal auditing. The product will vary with the experience, tenure, and sophistication of the auditing personnel. And the customer — the real customer; namely, executive management, those who guide the destiny of the entire enterprise — must be carefully wooed and cultivated as a part of a long-range, studied sales effort.

A major objective of the auditing organization is to be accepted as a full member in the councils of executive management . . . treated with respect as the provider of a product that is valuable, desirable, and unobtainable elsewhere . . . turned to automatically when problems within the auditor's purview arise . . . and looked to for current information on the state and effectiveness of the company's operating controls.

The auditor's sales campaign must be aggressive and dynamic. For executive management rarely singles out the auditor — he must step forward and parade his wares. Yet the campaign must not be founded on puffery or seller's talk; for let but a single hasty promise go unfulfilled, and management may become disillusioned and frustrate future sales campaigns.

Selling modern internal auditing must start with a salable product. That product is the ability of the auditing organization to perform competently and professionally. Every audit performed in the traditional, financial area must be thorough and sound. Each auditor must, as an emissary of his department, function as a professional man. Each audit report should carry the imprint of professional quality in terms of both form and substance. No document should go out over the director's signature that is not of a caliber that is equal to what goes out over the signature of the company's chief executive officer.

Management thus learns to expect and be confident of a high level of professionalism in the traditional financial audits and in the auditor's reports. Having merited management's confidence, the auditor can begin to give special character and scope to his audits — even in the financial areas. The audits can start to adopt a management viewpoint.

For example, in a traditional financial audit it is characteristic to determine whether discounts are being taken and the extent to which they are lost, and to make a comparison between lost discounts during current and prior accounting periods. These are serious matters, of course, but they are pedestrian, unexciting, and little deserving of high level attention. The final report on such an audit will go no higher than to the chief accountant and would be routinely filed and forgotten.

But what if the auditor applied management thinking to his examination? For example: Why are discounts being lost? How are lost discounts affected by Accounting Department workload, Receiving Department delays, or the Purchasing Department's failure to get purchasing documents to Receiving in time? Are payments to obtain discounts scheduled too far in advance of the discount dates, thereby adversely affecting cash flow? Would it be possible to save money by paying interest on borrowed funds to pay bills within discount periods? Should it be company policy to take discounts, whether they are literally earned or not, and refund the amounts only to the suppliers who complain?

When the auditor is able to discuss matters such as these in his reports, then higher management gets interested. Aware of this interest, the auditor can and should improve the product's package. For example, he can attach to his report charts and graphs that dramatically highlight his findings. Where a number of branches are involved, he can show the effect of the activities of an upstream organization upon a downstream organization. He can, from his advantageous position, determine where there are breakdowns in communication or where information or reports available in one organization may be of use in another.

He has the opportunity, while still hanging on to what he may regard as his lifeline, which is attached to his natural base in Finance — at least for a while — to move surefootedly into operating organizations, and to disclose an understanding of operating problems as well as financial problems. At the same time, he can trace the accounting systems and records to their diverse sources, where they become palpable things and living people instead of digits and data.

When the controller becomes aware of this new capability, right under his nose, he may start asking for studies in areas outside his authority, but within his concern . . . like asking for a determination as to whether the work-in-process accounts fairly reflect the cost of items actually in process in the shop. In that situation, one financial auditor, by carefully dipping his toe into the operational sea, began a long and successful journey into modern internal auditing.[4]

The auditor found that the only way to obtain the information needed to satisfy the controller's question was through the production control records. The auditor was led to a searching and complete investigation of the whole spectrum of production control documents and reports and was able to learn how to grapple with factory operations. The auditor learned there was no reason for fears or trepidation. The problems were the same in operations as in finance. The question was still "do the records fairly reflect?" and "can management rely on the information contained in the operating reports prepared from those records?" The principles of verification, analysis, and appraisal are the same for physical

---

quantities as they are for dollars and cents.

In the initial attempts at modern internal auditing, as contrasted with compliance auditing — the pedestrian determination of whether people follow instructions — the audit report should carefully explain the bases on which the audit opinions rest. There is little doubt in the mind of the controller that the auditor is competent to determine whether the balances in subsidiary accounts are in agreement with the balance in the control account, for example. But this freedom from doubt is not necessarily shared by the chief engineer, to pick just one non-financial manager. So in his audit report the auditor has a selling job to do before his findings will be fully accepted. Thought and care, however, will achieve the desired result.

For instance, in an audit of controls over the accuracy of engineering drawings, the auditor can readily determine what controls are generally considered acceptable to carry out the objective of achieving error-free drawings.[5] These controls may be assumed to include such matters as:

- An engineering handbook, setting forth company practices, policies, and approved methods.
- An independent group of drawing checkers to verify the accuracy of the drawings and to recommend changes.
- An approval system calling for signatures of responsible engineering supervisors or consultants on all drawings before their release.
- A system of feedback, from the factory, of all drawing errors found there while the factory workers are trying to build the products from the drawings.

If the audit report sets forth these widely accepted standards and, for example, shows (1) that the auditor checked a representative number of handbooks against a master handbook for currency and accuracy; (2) that he checked a representative number of drawings for evidence of check and correction of errors; (3) that he also checked those drawings for required signatures; and (4) that he determined what action was being taken to evaluate and make use of feedback information — then engineering management will listen attentively to what the auditor has to say. And the auditor will have successfully carried out a significant sales campaign.

---

[5]Mosher, Jack A., "Auditing the Quality of Engineering Drawings," *The Internal Auditor*, Fall 1964, p. 16.

SUMMARY

Modern internal auditing, to be successful, must be grounded on management support and acceptance and on imaginative service to management. Also, it must have a reporting status in the company that ensures proper consideration of the findings and recommendations developed by the auditor. To this end, the internal auditor's charter must set forth explicitly his broad authority and correlative responsibility; the management directive must spell out clearly the requirement for prompt and responsive replies to his audit reports; and the auditor's job description must call for the efforts of superior people, not average ones. Audit manuals should supply standards and guidelines, not detailed instructions. The auditor must mount a continuing campaign to sell his product to executive management; and the product he sells must be of the quality that will capture and keep management's interest.

SELECTING AND DEVELOPING THE STAFF

THE NEED FOR A SUPERIOR STAFF

The vision of the director of auditing and the high expectations of management are merely wistful wishes without the right staff to do the job. The dreams of improved and varied services to management through modern internal auditing turn into nightmares if the people who prepare the audit programs, do the questing and the questioning, make the appraisals, and offer the recommendations are not up to the demands that modern internal auditing makes of its practitioners.

What is more, internal auditing is not static. It is expanding under our very eyes. The subjects under review grow more difficult with each audit, as management uses more modern techniques with every passing day. And as management relies more upon the auditor, it gets more insistent for greater depth and breadth to the audit approach.

So, the business of selecting the right people, orienting them, training them, promoting their development, and evaluating them accurately, must occupy much of the director's thoughts and energies. In this chapter we shall explore these matters in some detail.

HOW TO SELECT INTERNAL AUDITORS

To build a superior staff, one first must know the standards for excellence. Modern internal auditing, with its demands for intelligence, technical competence, and the ability to deal with people at all levels of the company, sets high standards for its practitioners.

Those standards should never be compromised. The organizations being audited judge all of internal auditing by the individual auditors they deal with. The audit team should, therefore, include those who will perpetuate the image that the director of auditing wishes to project throughout the enterprise. It is far, far better to be understaffed than to hire a single man who can tear down in one assignment what took years for the rest of the team to build.

For these reasons, when the director makes his personnel selections, he must consider two attributes: Professional ability and certain qualities of character.

Education is the first building block. Some say that a knowledge of accounting is not essential. I disagree. It will be a long time before top management accepts the theory that their auditors need not know accounting, and management would be shocked to find one who was unaware of the basics of accounting theory. By and large, then, the prospective auditor should have a bachelor's degree preferably with a knowledge of basic accounting at least. It is highly desirable that he also have a master's degree in business administration. Of help to him and the auditing organization would be courses in the humanities and the behavioral sciences, because he will be dealing more with people than with numbers. It is essential, however, that he be mathematically literate and that he have a grounding both in statistical theory and application, and a working knowledge of electronic data processing. All of these are the tools of modern management — and the modern internal auditor must be able to grip the same tools with equal dexterity.

The qualities of character constitute the other building block — qualities to meet the demands made by modern internal auditing. Such qualities include adaptability, understanding, and determination, among many others. For example:

Adaptability is needed to cope with the diversity of internal auditing . . . the ability to accommodate to the ever-changing environment the auditor meets in his varied assignments . . . the facility to readily absorb the argot and jargon that the activity being audited has spawned, together with the ability to translate what he has learned into plain English . . . the agility required to react quickly to new problems, new product lines, new management viewpoints, and new company objectives.

Understanding is needed because the auditor is constantly dealing with people . . . the ability to grasp what makes them react favorably or with hostility . . . the empathy that enables the auditor to comprehend their problems and to walk in their shoes for a while . . . the sensitivity to what frustrates them . . . the perception of how they feel about their jobs, their managers, and their company . . . the tact that enables him to ask productive questions without raising the hackles of the person being questioned.

Determination is needed to deal with difficult problems and to trudge unblazed paths . . . the resistance to pressures that would sway the auditor from his goals . . . the insistence that he and he alone must satisfy his own internal monitor before he stops his pursuit of the answers to his questions . . . the willingness to work as hard and as long as is necessary to establish the facts and to document them so that they will be impregnable to attack.

The knowledge that his professional opinion is a solemn affirmation demands integrity, independence, objectivity, and responsibility . . . the reputation for dealing only in facts . . . for placing the facts in perspective . . . for being able to evaluate objectively the materiality of his findings . . . for having no axe to grind save that which hews to the line and strikes only for the greater good of the entire enterprise . . . for being absolutely trustworthy . . . for being a completely responsible individual, because he has it within his power to do irreparable injury through his citations of deficiencies and his assessments of blame.

Round these qualities out with the ability to communicate, both orally and in writing, a strong messianic fervor about his profession that sells both him and his product, and the imagination and initiative that find new ways of attacking old problems — and the compleat internal auditor begins to emerge.

Where does one look for this paragon ? There are many sources[1].

Universities and Colleges

Here one obtains the raw material and forms it into the desired likeness. But obtaining the likely graduate calls for long-range programs. The director of auditing, or one of his people who is personable, enthusiastic, and speaks well before an audience, should be on a continuing program of speeches to students. There is enough excitement, adventure, and chance for advancement in the profession to form the core of an absorbing sales talk. The speaking program should be of long range if it is to produce results, and it should be pursued even during those periods when staff positions are completely filled.

Certified Public Accountants

Young accountants who have put in an apprenticeship with a public accounting firm, looking for new and exciting opportunities, who are tired of dealing with the ancient history of accounts and transactions, and who might find playing a constructive role in the future more to their taste, can be fine prospects. They can be readily sold on the more solid prospects of modern internal auditing than on the oft disheartening position of controller in a small company. And an excellent sales approach is to cite those managers and executives in the company who reached their present positions from the springboard of internal auditing. The attention of the young CPA can be attracted by advertisements in the leading accounting journals.

Within the Company

Here the director of auditing has an excellent start. He is in a position to get a first-hand look at the prospect in actual operation. And the prospect already has a working knowledge of the company's policies, methods, products, and management. The audit staff should be asked to be constantly alert to people who have the basic equipment and who should be approached — through established channels, of course — for an interview.

[1]Evans, E. R., "Managing The Internal Audit Function," *The Internal Auditor*, January/February 1970, p. 14.

The Institute of Internal Auditors

The Internal Auditor, The Institute of Internal Auditors' journal, takes advertisements for auditors and has the advantage of being delivered to some 10,000 internal auditors throughout the world.

★ ★ ★

Having attracted the prospect, what then? There are two steps that should be taken: First, interviewing; second, testing.

Interviews

The interview should be a well-planned, well-organized affair. The prospect's résumé and application should be carefully read and his references should be called. Calling the reference is better than writing to him. A former employer will be more free and candid on the telephone than on imperishable paper.

The interview should be set for a time when the pressure of other work will not interfere. The director of auditing should screen the prospect first. If he seems to be a likely candidate, some of his staff supervisors should interview him also.

Interviewing is an art and takes practice to develop. It should be a two-way street: The interviewer tells about the job, the company, the opportunities, and the nature of the work. The interviewee tells about himself.

Some people, when interviewed, need to be drawn out; some need to be guided. Questions to ask include:

■ What were some of the assignments you conducted?
■ How did you approach them?
■ What kind of reports did you write?
■ How have you kept up your education?
■ Why do you want to make a change?
■ What do you like about internal auditing?
■ What don't you like about it?
■ What kind of assignment do you like best?
■ What are your hobbies?
■ What are your personal goals?

Keep records of all interviews. And keep the records in an organized manner so that they can be used readily to compare the qualities and qualifications of different candidates for the same position. Exhibit 2-1a is an example of an applicant interview record. Exhibit 2-1b gives definitions of the qualities being explored and rated.

Exhibit 2-1a.—INTERVIEW RATING SHEET

Name _____ Age _____

Degrees _____

Last two employers _____

_____

Schools _____

_____

Certifications _____

Will Travel? _____

	0	2	4	6	8	10
Attitude						
Appearance						
Maturity						
Sociability						
Self-Expression						
Motivation						
Intelligence						
Persuasiveness						
Self-Confidence						
Interest						
Potential						
Overall Evaluation						

Should we test this applicant? _____

Should we make him an offer? _____

If so, for what position? _____

Comments _____

_____

_____

Interviewer _____

Date _____

Testing

With so much hanging in the balance, the director of auditing needs every edge he can get in deciding whether or not to hire a prospect. Only time will disclose whether the decision to hire was correct. And there are no standard tests, at this writing, for internal auditors — certainly none like those given to doctors, lawyers, pharmacists, and accountants. But several tests have been developed independently by some auditing organizations to give an insight into the prospect's writing ability and thought processes.

Exhibit 2-1b. INTERVIEW RATING SHEET —
DEFINITIONS

Rating Factors

Attitude — Outlook in general

Appearance — Physical appearance, neatness, dress, posture

Maturity — Behavior and apparent emotional stability

Sociability — Apparent ability to get along with others; warmth, response

Self-expression — Ability to express thoughts clearly, concisely, effectively

Motivation — Drive, initiative, enthusiasm, energy, desire to succeed

Intelligence — Mental ability, judgment, alertness, organization of thoughts

Persuasiveness — Ability to influence others

Self-confidence — Poise, interest in challenge

Interest — Indication of sincere interest in internal auditing and our company

Potential — Your impression of the applicant's potential for a management position

Overall Evaluation — Your general impression of the applicant

Rating Scores

10 — Outstanding.	Exceptional, clearly superior; applicable only in rare instances
8 — Excellent.	Considerably above average, definitely stands out, makes immediate and lasting impression
6 — Satisfactory Plus.	Well above average, a potential asset to the company
4 — Satisfactory.	Normal for a person of his age, experience and education
2 — Satisfactory Minus.	A marginal rating; doesn't quite meet minimum standards
0 — Unsatisfactory.	Unsuitable for our work

It should be pointed out that many directors of auditing are opposed to such tests. Others, however, have used them with a fair degree of success and have validated them by comparing the grades on the tests with the evaluations subsequently given to the same employees on job rating sheets. These comparisons have shown reasonable correlations between test scores and the later evaluations.

For the tests to be effective, the prospect should not be able to see them in advance. It would be unwise, therefore, to use the exact tests printed in a book of general circulation, such as this. Thus, each test should be separately developed by the auditing organization itself. For this reason we have developed some ideas and truncated examples for the preparation of such tests, rather than providing complete copies of those in actual use.

1. Test of writing ability

Provide the applicant with a statement of an audit situation and ask him to write a report in a prescribed format, setting forth, for example, (a) background information, (b) the purpose of the audit, (c) the scope of the audit, (d) the auditor's opinion, and (e) the recommendations for corrective action. Examples of two such audit situations might be as follows:

- Envelopes are opened in the mail room by any one of several mail room employees. All remittances are placed in a box until the end of the day. At that time they are placed in an interdepartmental envelope and sent by company mail to the cashier.
- Buyers in the Purchasing Department are permitted to develop their own lists of prospective bidders, prepare the requests for bids, mail them directly to the bidders being solicited, and receive the completed bids directly from the mail room.

The instructions to the applicant should tell him to write his report in nontechnical terms which would be plain to a manager who has no accounting or purchasing background. He should also be told that his report will be evaluated according to standards of clarity, coherence (how it hangs together), structure, and the use of appropriate language.

Evaluating and grading such tests present a problem, because there are no simple mathematical criteria to rely upon. Some measure of objectivity can be obtained, however, by assigning maximum numerical grades for each of the four standards and permitting two or more people to rate the test results independently of each other. The grading criteria might be as follows:

Standard	Maximum value	Grade
Clarity	40	_____
Coherence	35	_____
Structure	15	_____
Words	10	_____
Totals	100	_____

2. Test of ability to organize thoughts

Provide the applicant with a series of about 25 statements about an audit problem. The statements are numbered sequentially, but their logical order has been scrambled. Ask the applicant to rearrange the statements in a reasonable order under headings which have been provided. The headings may be Purpose, Scope, Control Findings, Performance Findings, Opinion, and Recommendations. An abbreviated example of the hashed statements is shown in Exhibit 2-2a. The solution is shown in Exhibit 2-2b.

Exhibit 2-2a. TEST OF ABILITY TO ORGANIZE THOUGHTS

INSTRUCTIONS: Insert in the spaces provided, the proper numbers in their proper order.

Purpose	Scope	Control Findings	Performance Findings	Opinion	Recommendations
( )	( )	( )	( )	( )	( )
( )	( )	( )	( )	( )	( )
( )	( )	( )	( )	( )	( )
( )	( )	( )	( )	( )	( )
( )	( )	( )	( )	( )	( )

(1) We also recommended that supervisors periodically check manuals to make sure they are kept up to date.
(2) It is also our opinion that the system was working as intended except for the fact that some manuals were not up to date.
(3) Our test of the checked drawings showed that they had all been signed off by engineering supervisors before release.
(4) We reviewed systems and procedures by reading instructions and interviewing engineering personnel.
(5) Our test of the error reports showed them to be accurate and timely.
(6) We found an adequate supply of drafting manuals for all engineers, but 20% of the manuals were not up to date.
(7) We also set out to determine whether the system was working as intended.
(8) We set out to evaluate the adequacy of the system of control over the accuracy of engineering drawings.
(9) Our test of 100 drawings showed that they had all been verified by drawing checkers.
(10) We also found that all drawings must be verified by drawing checkers for accuracy.
(11) We found that after checking, the drawings must be reviewed by engineering supervisors before release.
(12) It is our opinion that the control system was adequate.
(13) We found that a drafting manual had been developed to provide detailed instructions to engineering draftsmen.
(14) We examined 100 engineering drawings in detail.
(15) Management had developed a system of reporting the number of drawing errors based on complaints from the production organization.
(16) We recommended that all manuals be brought up to date promptly.

Exhibit 2-2b. SOLUTION TO TEST OF ABILITY TO ORGANIZE THOUGHTS

Purpose

(8) We set out to evaluate the adequacy of the system of control over the accuracy of engineering drawings.

(7) We also set out to determine whether the system was working as intended.

Scope

(4) We reviewed systems and procedures by reading instructions and interviewing engineering personnel.

(14) We examined 100 engineering drawings in detail.

Control Findings

(13) We found that a drafting manual had been developed to provide detailed instructions to engineering draftsmen.

(10) We also found that all drawings must be verified by drawing checkers for accuracy.

(11) We found that after checking, the drawings must be reviewed by engineering supervisors before release.

(15) Managment had developed a system of reporting the number of drawing errors based on complaints from the production organization.

Performance Findings

(6) We found an adequate supply of drafting manuals for al! engineers, but 20% of the manuals were not up to date.

(9) Our test of 100 drawings showed that they had all been verified by drawing checkers.

(3) Our test of checked drawings showed that they had all been signed off by engineering supervisors before release.

(5) Our test of the error reports showed them to be accurate and timely.

Opinion

(12) It is our opinion that the control system was adequate.

(2) It is also our opinion that the system was working as intended except for the fact that some manuals were not up to date.

Recommendations

(16) We recommended that all manuals be brought up to date promptly.

(1) We also recommended that supervisors periodically check manuals to make sure they are kept up to date.

The tests can be graded by deducting from the perfect score of 100, two points each for every statement shown in wrong sequence under the correct heading, and four points each for every statement shown under the wrong heading.

3. Test of ability to differentiate between fact and conjecture

A fact is something that has actual existence, something that can be inferred with certainty, a proposition that is verified or verifiable. A conjecture is something suggesting insufficient evidence for it to be regarded as a fact. The auditor who cannot distinguish between the two needs help, because adducing facts, appraising them, and drawing conclusions from facts — not just making conjectures — are the heart and marrow of his work.

The biggest roadblocks to appraising the truth or falsity of a proposition are taking things for granted, jumping to conclusions, and accepting plausible appearance for hard fact. The inexperienced auditor — and quite often the old hand — may accept appearance for substance and come to improper conclusions. There is a subtle little test — full of pitfalls for the unwary — that can be devised both to trip up the conclusion jumper and to provide some good education for any auditor. It brings home sharply that what appears factual on the surface is but a signal to an experienced auditor to ask more questions.

This test can be developed along the lines as set forth in Exhibit 2-3. A score of 85% or better would be excellent, 75%, Good; 60%, Fair; 50%, Poor; and less than that, Unsatisfactory. The example shown just has five comments or questions. In practice it is well to have two or three situations presented with at least 25 or 30 questions in total.

HOW TO PROVIDE ORIENTATION

Orientation, as distinguished from training, means pointing the new auditor in the right direction. The first days in a new organization can be traumatic. The new man wants to like and respect his new environment. He wants to feel that the people around him know what they are doing and that he can learn from them.

He wants to feel comfortable in his new job and in his new department, and his senses will be especially heightened to any ineptness or uncertainty. When he has been around a while, waiting for something to do is no great strain; he knows how to occupy himself. But in his first day or days, any delay, confusion, or lack of organization will be accentuated and will create an undesirable reaction.

Exhibit 2-3. DISTINGUISHING BETWEEN FACT AND CONJECTURE
(The instructions and the test are as follows. In this example, the answers are shown in parentheses after each comment.)

How to Take the Test

Shown below is a statement which you are to assume is completely true, although some parts are deliberately vague; so read the statement carefully. You may look back at the statement any time during the test.

Read the comments about the statement. Next to each comment indicate whether it is True (T), False (F), or Questionable (Q). Circle the letter you consider applicable. Circle T or F if you're quite sure of them. Circle Q if you are doubtful about the comment.

Answer each comment in turn. Do not change your answers once they are made.

Statement

XYZ Corporation's Purchase Order 30305, dated May 15, 1971, was issued to the ABC Company for 10 castings at $10 each. The owner of the ABC Company is a brother of Joe Blow, XYZ Corporation's casting buyer.

Comments

1. An order for 10 castings was placed with ABC Company on 5/15/71. (This is questionable, since we know only the date of the purchase order, not when the order was placed. It could have been placed by telephone at an earlier date.) **T F Q**
2. Joe Blow and the owner of ABC Company are brothers. (This is true, being categorically stated.) **T F Q**
3. Joe Blow gave an order to his brother. (This is questionable; while Joe Blow was the castings buyer, the order could possibly have been placed by someone else—Joe might have been on vacation.) **T F Q**
4. Purchase Order 30503 is dated May 15, 1971. (This is questionable. The purchase order in the statement, which is numbered 30305, is dated May 15, 1971. We don't know the date of Purchase Order 30503, which may or may not be May 15, 1971.) **T F Q**
5. The value of Purchase Order 30305 is $100, without considering discount terms. (This is true.) **T F Q**

Orientation of the new employee should therefore be carefully planned and structured. One of the people in the auditing organization — with a strong teacher instinct — should be assigned the task of introducing the new auditor to his surroundings and guiding him through the maze of new requirements. And this mentor should be thoroughly prepared with a specific program and with well-designed materials to do the job with ease and confidence.

Generally, the period of orientation should take at least three or four days and should be organized into four phases:

- Introduction to the staff
- Discussion
- Reading
- Feedback

There should be a liberal portion of each, so spaced that the new man is neither confused nor bored. Many organizations, unfortunately, sit the new man behind a mountain of organization charts, manuals, directives, and books, and then leave him to his own devices until he is completely bored and disenchanted and his head is crammed with a welter of unabsorbed information.

First off, after the new auditor has been cleared through the personnel routines, he should have an unhurried chat with the director of auditing who should seek to set the new employee at ease. Thereafter, he should be shown to his desk by his mentor so that he has a feeling of permanence and a home base. Then he should have a tour of introductions to other staff people, with the mentor briefly telling the old hands about the new auditor's background.

The mentor should bring the new auditor into his office, provide him with copies of audit manuals, staff instructions, and other necessary tools, and give him a brief preview of what the next few days will bring. At that point it is well to determine what personal business the employee will have to take care of as a result of the change to his new job and, perhaps, new locality. Provision should be made for any needed time off. Those matters should be discussed at the outset so that they will not weigh on the employee's mind and distract him from his orientation.

The breadth and intensity of the orientation will, of course, depend on the new auditor's prior experience. The mentor should be conversant with that experience. Clearly, an employee transferred from within the company, a newly graduated student, and an experienced auditor from another company all require different handling in their orientation.

An orientation guide, providing general information about the company and the auditing organization, can be an important tool in furnishing general information that can be referred to as needed. Such a guide should be made available immediately to the new auditor so as to provide answers to many questions formulated and still unformulated in his mind. Each company must develop its own, of course; but to assist in its development, an outline of such a guide is shown in Exhibit 2-4.

Exhibit 2-4. ORIENTATION GUIDE
(The following outline provides a framework for the development of an orientation guide to be provided each new auditor.)

Purpose

1. To orient you, as a new member of the Internal Auditing
   staff, to your new environment.
2. To guide you through a review of pertinent administrative
   and technical matters before we assign you to an audit
   examination.

Organization

Company
   Provide an overview of the company organization and the
names of key management people.

Internal Auditing
   Show where Internal Auditing stands in the organization.
Supply the names of the people most closely related to the
audit function.

Administration

Hours of Work	Nature of Company Directives
Daily Notification of Location	Administrative Manual
Delivery of Paychecks	Audit Manual
Time Reports	Supplies
Security Matters	Desk Assignments

Benefits

Vacations	Military Leave
Sick Leave	Retirement Plan
Holidays	Insurance
Jury Duty	

The mentor needs a formal program of his own to help him
remember all the matters he should cover during the orientation.
Exhibit 2-5 is an example of such a program.

The technical matters discussed in the orientation are certainly
a necessary part of the internal auditor's education. Of equal importance, however, not only to the novice but the seasoned practitioner, is an understanding of human relations. In the following
section is a brief survey of behavioral patterns with which all
internal auditors should be familiar.

Exhibit 2-5. PROGRAM FOR THE ORIENTATION AND TRAINING OF NEW EMPLOYEES

The orientation of new staff auditors is being accomplished through a proper combination of reading, listening, and doing. The first few days of the auditor's orientation should be given over largely to the first two. He will get to the "doing" on his initial audit projects.

At the outset, give the new auditor a copy of an orientation guide which provides general information about the company and the auditing organization.

The program provided here will supplement the orientation guide and help the training supervisor give the new auditor additional information on general administrative matters and on the more technical aspect of the auditing approach. The program should be supplemented by any additional information considered desirable.

The orientation will take anywhere from three to five days, depending on the individual's background. The oral instructions and any tours provided should be interspersed between periods of reading so as to give some variety to the orientation period.

The discussion outline is as follows:

A. *The Internal Auditing Organization*
1. Introduce the new auditor to the rest of the staff.
2. Discuss the auditing organization's objectives and how they are implemented. Specifically cover opportunities for promotion and inform him of the company's policies in management selection.
3. Supply the employee with his copies of applicable manuals. Have him scan the manuals to familiarize himself with their contents.
4. Discuss:
   ■ The job duties and responsibilities of all members of Internal Auditing — from the director of auditing to the assistant auditor. Provide the new auditor with a copy of his own job description and answer any questions he may have about it.
   ■ Discuss standards as they relate to audit coverage, audit examinations, administrative records and reports, and communications.
5. Explain how the audit work is controlled:
   ■ The long-range program.
   ■ The basis for programmed jobs: (a) areas which, by experience, require close review, (b) chart of accounts, (c) needs of management, and (d) other.
   ■ Discuss the various periodic reports to management.
   ■ Discuss job assignments.
6. Review the contents of the department's library with the new auditor.

B. *The Company*
1. Have the employee attend any special orientation classes provided by the company to all new employees.
   ■ Answer any questions raised by the new auditor as a result of the class instruction.
   ■ Provide a tour of the plant, supplementing if necessary the tour given during the company-provided classes.

Exhibit 2-5. (Cont.)

2. Have the new auditor scan:
   - Organization charts
   - General information on the company
   - The latest corporate annual report
3. Acquaint the new auditor with the general ledger, subsidiary ledgers, and journal vouchers. Show him the chart and text of accounts.
4. Acquaint him with the work order system and with overhead accumulation and distribution.
5. Introduce him to management personnel with whom he may have contact on the job.

C. *Internal Auditing*
1. Bring to the new auditor's attention:
   - *Basic Internal Auditing Principles and Techniques,* by John B. Thurston.
   - *Operational Auditing Handbook*, by Bradford Cadmus.
   - Reference file of *The Internal Auditor,* the *Bibliography of Internal Auditing* and the supplements, and the Research Reports, issued by The Institute of Internal Auditors.
2. Have the new auditor read pertinent articles in *The Internal Auditor* and other periodicals which relate to modern auditing in general.
3. Review the steps taken in planning an audit project.
   - Explain the use of standard forms used in the organization.
   - Explain the preliminary research undertaken, such as the use of the permanent file, the master program, organization charts, procedure manuals, and prior working papers.
   - Explain how and when the audit program should be prepared, emphasizing the identification of the activity's major objectives, plans, and controls.
   - Discuss the survey approach to audits, flow charting, and sampling.
4. Lead the new auditor through a selected set of working papers, showing him how the material is organized and how it is used to support the audit report.
5. Discuss the preparation of a segment of working papers, which will normally include:
   - General Information: Include applicable directives, procedures, practices, work flow (supported by flow charts), statistics, key controls.
   - Purpose: The purpose should tie into the program and, if necessary, expand upon it. Try to cover cost, quality, and timeliness.
   - Scope: Show just what was done in the audit and give the source of the information and data.
   - Findings: These are the facts that are to be evidenced by the schedules documenting the audit tests. The findings should be responsive to the questions raised in the purpose. There may be several findings for one purpose.

Exhibit 2-5. (Cont.)

■ Opinions: These are the conclusions that are based on the findings. There should be an "Opinion" for each "Purpose." The opinions should be specific; either favorable or unfavorable. "No exceptions" will not suffice.

■ Test
work sheets: The work sheets should support the findings. They should indicate scope and sufficiency of test or the reasons why tests were limited. They should be summarized, so that the reviewer has no difficulty tracing the findings to the detail in the test schedules. Use copies of client's records, reports, tabulations, etc., whenever possible to avoid unnecessary copying.

6. Discuss deficiency findings. They should be thoroughly documented. The documentary evidence should show:

■ Just what is wrong.

■ Whether the deficiency violates some directive or is just poor administrative practice.

■ The significance of the deficiency and what effect it will have if it goes uncorrected.

■ What evidence has been adduced to prove the existence and extent of the deficiency.

■ Who or what is responsible.

■ Whether the deficiency relates to control, performance, or both.

■ The basic cause behind the deficient condition.

■ What corrective action the auditor suggests.

■ The client's opinion about the deficiency and what he proposes to do to correct it.

7. Provide the new auditor with copies of typical reports and explain the various report sections and their purpose and the different formats that are used.

8. Discuss procedures in reviewing report drafts.

9. Discuss responsibilities for the evaluation of corrective action and the closure of audit projects.

D. *Evaluation and Follow-up*

1. The supervisor in charge of orientation should keep in touch with the new auditor as he starts on audit projects to see if he needs answers to any of the questions that come up during actual work on the job.

2. In about a month the supervisor should have a session with the new auditor, going over again the matters covered in this program and reinforcing those matters that may have been forgotten. One technique would be to use this program as a questionnaire to raise issues for the auditor to discuss or answer.

HUMAN RELATIONS

The Need for Understanding

Modern internal auditing, to a great extent, means dealing with people. The internal auditor deals with people at all levels of the company, from managers to hourly workers. He is the representative of the auditing department, and how he acts will largely affect how people will regard the department. He must be equipped with some understanding of people, of management styles, of problems in communication, and of the techniques of listening and obtaining information.

In the next few pages we shall briefly cover some of the principles of human relations that are important to the auditor. The new practitioner may not appreciate the significance of the principles and how to apply them until he actually goes out into the field and deals with people face to face — but he should be exposed to the principles early and be aware of their importance to his job. And the experienced practitioner would do well to review them from time to time.

Management Style

As a member of the management team, the auditor must have a good grasp of what the behavioral scientists have uncovered about management style. This style has taken some dramatic shifts since the manager was the supreme autocrat some 75 years ago. Many factors have influenced management style: greater security for employees through union and government protection, greater independence on the part of the worker, greater enlightenment on the part of management, cultural changes, and increased emphasis and focus by behavioral scientists on determining what motivates employees to achieve their greatest potential — and what does not.

The styles which have evolved and which are still evolving have an effect on the auditor's behavior and practice. As just one example, when dealing with an autocratic manager, the auditor must be completely aware that any action to correct a deficiency and any suggestion to improve operations must be discussed and cleared with him. Any agreements at lower levels may easily be overridden; they just will not count.

Thus, the auditor should understand the various styles that exist today, what these styles depend on, what performance may be expected to result under particular styles, and how employees react to them. This understanding should be reflected in the "theory of the audit" — the particular thrust and emphasis of the audit — and in the audit program.

While some of these styles are rooted in history and others are just appearing on the horizon, all of them may be found to coexist in varying shades in the same company, depending on the make-up of the individual managers and the needs and motivations of the employees. The names given to these styles by some behavioral scientists are:[2]

- ■ Autocratic
- ■ Custodial
- ■ Supportive
- ■ Collegial

Although we recognize there are shades and gradations in these styles — indeed the same individual may have more than one style in his make-up — nevertheless, it is useful to define each in turn, showing why the auditor should be aware of them and how they may affect his audit approach.

The autocratic style.   This style has been in existence the longest. It is a throwback, and it depends on power, pure and simple. It is founded on complete authority in the manager and unquestioning obedience in his people. Employees working under this style become dependent upon management, and they seldom think for themselves. Management takes the position that employees work only because they have to and that they must be driven to perform.

Performance is usually minimal, and good morale is deemed to have been achieved if the employee assents unprotestingly to management's orders. The style still exists today — in varying degrees — especially in low-grade, low-paying jobs where the employees give minimal effort for bare subsistence. It is the Theory X, made popular by Douglas McGregor, who saw it as the conventional view of management. Indeed, in managing certain types of effort this style may still be appropriate.

When the auditor sees this style, anywhere up the chain of command, he must be prepared to find lack of independence in subordinates and the fear of taking any action which might conflict with management's views. The auditor will want to find clear instructions, tight controls, and a rigid approval system; for in their absence effective performance is unlikely. He should be prepared to clear all findings with the autocrat, for there rests the last word.

---

[2]Davis, Dr. Keith, "Evolving Models of Organizational Behavior," *The Internal Auditor*, November/December 1968, p. 27.

The custodial style. This style was the first break from the autocratic one. It sought to improve productivity through material rewards to the employee and to a greater dependency on the part of the employee. Management listened to the industrial relations specialists and became obsessed with the need for a "happy shop."

Happiness was nurtured by additional fringe benefits and group security plans. The autocratic, masculine manager gave way to the maternal organization. This change occurred during the depression of the 1930s and during and after World War II when fringe benefits became the goals to be developed by employers, unions, and the government. The economic rewards and the security blanket were offered in return for gratitude and hoped-for improved productivity.

The employee turns his dependency from the autocratic manager to the maternal organization. He is happier than he was under the autocrat, but there is nothing here to inspire him to greater heights. The custodial style gives him subsistence and security, but not motivation or self-actualization. Yet the custodial style will persist so long as employees see their job as a means toward an economic end and managers are unable to kindle motivational fires in their people.

When the auditor encounters the custodial style, he will find that the best sales talk for changes or corrections is laced with assurances that life will be made easier or better. He should also be alert to the fact that the "country club" atmosphere is not necessarily conducive to high productivity ... that perhaps management, in concert with its people, needs to set realistic goals and to measure itself against them.

The supportive style. This style depends on leadership. It is founded on management support and the motivation of employees to greater productivity.

The employee is no longer pushed, or urged forward with an economic carrot — he is now awakened to his potentials; he sees himself as participating in the setting of goals.

The supportive style arose in the 1940s and began to replace the custodial style when behavioral science research showed that happiness through security alone did not necessarily equate with productivity. The supportive style depends on management providing a climate for its people to increase their capacity. It is founded on the theory that most people want to work and to do a good job, if only management will bring out their inherent desires and capabilities and will show them that productivity can give greater satisfaction than passive contentment.

The employee begins to identify his own goals with those of the organization. He finds his drives awakened; his performance and his job are an important part of his life, rather than a mere source of sustenance or security. This attitude is reflected in McGregor's "Theory Y."

In this climate, the auditor is well advised to take both management and employees into his confidence at the outset of the audit and throughout its course. He can sell his audit recommendations by showing that they will improve productivity and help achieve organizational goals.

The collegial style (group of colleagues). This style is founded on contribution by all members of the team. Each is an equal contributor, respected for his contributions. Management, instead of being autocratic, and demanding obedience; or custodial, and supplying security; or supportive, and providing leadership — is just one of the contributors and is respected, like any other competent colleague, for its contribution.

The collegial style is still on the horizon, but it is looming larger and larger, particularly in certain professional activities. It depends on the ability of management to develop a feeling of equal participation among the colleagues — with each participant offering something of value, and feeling that he himself is also valued.

Management's role is one of integration rather than command or leadership. The employee responds to this climate with a feeling of responsibility. The result is self actualization rather than motivation which carries certain overtones of manipulation by the leader. The product will be true enthusiasm for the job, a sense of fulfillment and recognition.

The auditor's reaction to such a style would be to adapt to it. He should present himself as another contributor. He should offer his recommendations and suggestions as contributions to the greater good of the organization. Indeed, in such an atmosphere of dedication and cooperation, the auditor would probably find himself imbued with the same enthusiasm as his auditees.

Communication

The modern internal auditor, much more than the financial auditor, works with people. He often walks uncharted paths and needs to ask the way as he goes along. He needs cooperation from the auditee or his audit may well be frustrated by incomplete information, inaccurate data, or warped perspectives.

Some auditors can obtain this cooperation through force of personality or through an empathetic attitude that invariably draws people out — makes them want to unburden themselves or tell all. Others cannot. Yet those others can achieve the same or similar results through study and understanding. But all auditors, both the empathetic and the diffident, should have a clear understanding of the art and science of communication — what opens the channels, and what closes them down.

First and foremost, let there be no misunderstanding: The auditor is often feared. He represents in the minds of many of the auditees — both the managers and their people — a critic, a threat to security, and an unknown quantity that can adversely affect an individual's status, well-being, and his very job.

The auditor's first task, then, is to allay the fear. If he does not, communications are completely blocked. He may speak but the auditee will not listen; he may ask for help but the auditee will not respond. Yet there are steps that can be taken and there are qualities that can be developed which will help open communications and keep them open.

First, there must be complete candor. Let the auditee know what to expect. This goes a long way to smooth down the hackles that were raised at the mere mention of auditor. Consider the doctor who is about to inject a patient with some medical drug. He says, "You'll feel the prick of the needle; it will hurt a bit, but not much. Then you'll feel a warmth throughout your body. Your mouth will get dry, and you'll feel a tingling in your finger tips. In 5 minutes, all of this will subside, and you'll feel as before." With that preparation, the patient, usually with interest rather than fear, will mentally check off the described symptoms as they occur. If they happen precisely as predicted, he has no fear; and he admiringly regards the doctor as a fine fellow and splendid physician. If, on the other hand, without warning a red film obstructs his vision — something the doctor had expected but had not mentioned — the patient becomes fearful, apprehensive, and resentful. Rapport is ruptured; trust is shattered. The doctor becomes an object of fear.

This is not a fanciful analogy; and the auditor would do well to keep it in mind. In the absence of suspected fraud and except for surprise cash audits, there is no earthly reason why there cannot be complete candor and rapport from the very outset of the audit until its conclusion.

The relationship of complete candor starts very early when the long-range audit program is discussed with branch and executive management. By and large, it should be continued immediately upon the assignment of the audit project to the auditor. First, the auditor in charge, or his supervisor, should notify appropriate line management of the assignment, explaining that the job is a regular part of the total audit process. In the telephone call to the manager directly in charge of the activity under audit, the auditor should set up a meeting to engage in preliminary discussions. By the time that meeting comes to pass, any initial shock will have had a chance to dissipate.

In advance of this meeting, the auditor should develop sufficient information — which we shall discuss later in the chapter on preliminary surveys — to be able to speak with reasonable facility about the activity.

At this meeting, the groundwork is laid for the rapport that should exist for the duration of the audit project. In technical areas, the auditor will explain candidly that he is no technical expert on the activities for which the manager is responsible, but that he is an expert on control. He will point out that his report will provide an opinion directed toward the adequacy of the controls and that performance generally will be measured in relation to the effectiveness of such controls.

All questions of significance, the auditor assures the manager, will be discussed during the course of the examination. When appropriate, informal interim reports will be provided. The object is not to parade errors, but to identify matters which prevent the orderly functioning of the activity and create barriers to effective accomplishment of established goals. If there are problems with interfacing organizations, the auditor would like to know about them, because with his own wide-ranging movements about the company he might be able to alleviate or obtain solutions to the problems.

After his discussion with the manager, the auditor will ask to take a tour of the facility and to be introduced to the manager's staff. The auditor's attitude should be friendly, courteous, and open. He may not have these qualities inherently, but he can develop them. It is all a matter of attitude. Those qualities will emerge if he says to himself: "I am not a cop. I am not an investigator. I am not an efficiency expert. I am an auditor. And I am a guest in their house. I shall be courteous. I shall treat people with respect. And I shall regard my examination as a community effort, for the greater good of the department and the company." Then, when he has convinced himself that this is the attitude which will contribute most to the success of his own audit objectives, it will show in his bearing, his demeanor, and his communication with people.

Barriers to communication. Throughout his dealings with people, the auditor should keep in mind the attitudes and the words that will block communication and those that will aid communication. Knowing that he represents a threat in the mind of the auditee, he must constantly be on his guard to allay fears, not increase them. When the auditee first encounters the auditor, the thoughts often uppermost in his mind are how to impress the auditor, how to evade an anticipated attack, and how to escape any punishment that the auditor's disclosures may bring to pass. The auditee's behavior is defensive; and it will remain defensive until the auditor, deliberately but tactfully, erodes the barriers that defensiveness raises.[3]

What then are the aids to communication — to that subtle business of transferring from one mind to another, thoughts, facts, and impressions, without filtering them, without being evasive, and without subterfuge? The auditor needs those aids, because he cannot function without asking questions; and any question can be considered an implied threat. Yet, if he is aware of what is destructive and what is constructive to communication, he can breach the barriers to communications. Here are some of the ways:[4]

■ The auditor, in seeking information, should not sit in judgment. He is not a judge. He is not a prosecutor. He is a fellow employee trying to get facts. An evaluative, judgmental attitude is quickly detected by the auditee and puts him on his guard — raises his defenses. When the auditor asks "Why did you do that?" the defenses become hard and unbreakable.

On the other hand, when the auditor shows in his questions and in his attitude that he is genuinely requesting information, seeking only for the truth, and needing help to find it, the defenses drop. Instead of "Why did you do that?" the auditor should ask "How is this done?" "How does it help you to do it this way?" "What would happen if it were done another way?"

■ The auditor's attitude in asking questions should not be that of the cold inquisitor. People do not relate to inquisitors. They rarely want to help inquisitors. They raise barriers to the questions of inquisitors. Even "How is that done?" when asked in a cold, detached, or neutral tone, evokes little helpful response.

---

[3]Finke, D. B., "The Audit Interview: Key to Successful Evaluation," *The Internal Auditor*, July/August 1968, p. 39.

[4]Gibbs, Jack R., "Defensive Communication," *A Review of General Semantics, Vol. XXII, No. 2*, June 1965, p. 221, International Society for General Semantics.

But an attitude of empathy will get the right response. An attitude that clearly says "I know you have an important job. I know that there are frustrations that come with the job. I know there are difficulties you must overcome. Tell me about them. I shall understand. I sympathize. Maybe together we can come up with some answers. Don't fear me. I just want to know how things are done so that I can help. If I see something that needs looking at, we'll discuss it openly and together." But the auditor had better honestly feel what he says or it won't come through as empathy. It will come through as strategy and manipulation. And his hearer will sense it; the barriers to communication will go up.

■ The auditor is undoubtedly a superior human being; he couldn't perform difficult audits unless he were bright, quick, and perceptive. But let any feeling of superiority show in his attitude and he will obtain resentment, not communication. Superiority in the sender implies that the receiver is less worthy, that the sender needs no help, that he is in competition rather than in partnership. The receiver then closes his mind to the sender's message or he forgets it and concentrates on competing instead of supplying information.

In contrast, the offer of a problem-solving partnership builds the receiver's self-esteem. He now wishes to contribute, to help in accomplishing the partnership goals. While there may be obvious differences in ability and status between the auditor and the auditee — the sender and the receiver — an atmosphere is engendered which makes those differences unimportant.

■ The auditor who carries an air of dogmatism and certainty meets rigid defenses in the auditee. The dogmatic auditor is telling, not asking. The auditee sees the auditor as exercising control — and most people find control repugnant — particularly from one who is not their supervisor. If there ever is a time for certainty it is not in the preliminary discussion. This is the learning period, not the assertive period.

If the auditor, on the other hand, conveys the feeling of open-mindedness, of willingness to hear opposing views out, willingness to experiment with his own ideas and not be rigid or prejudiced in his conceptions, the barriers to communication crumble, and the channels of information start flowing freely and fully.

Listening. Having opened the channels of communication, the auditor must now be able to absorb what he hears. He will be doing a great deal of listening in his audit; and he will be doing a great deal of forgetting as well. One source of utter frustration in an audit of an activity that is completely new to the auditor is his realization that he cannot remember all that he hears and that he may have to ask the same question of the same individual several times.

The difficulty varies, of course, with the familiarity the auditor has of this or similar activities. Hearing and absorbing information successfully are dependent on the mental associations the auditor is able to make. If the area has some familiarity, or if the auditor has studied the particular "language" of the activity, there are a number of associations or "hooks" on which the new information can be hung. If the activity is completely new, then the words he hears may have little meaning to him. He must then rely on various devices to assist him. One of these is an informal questionnaire. The other is developing good listening techniques.

It has been demonstrated that a listener generally retains only about one half of what he hears. After a few months he will be lucky to have retained 25 per cent of that. And these levels of learning are achieved only when conditions are perfect.

Conditions are rarely perfect, however. There are external distractions: noise, activity, and other conversations in the vicinity. There are internal distractions as well: The mind may wander because of personal problems or because of the inability of the speaker to hold the listener's attention. The speaker may arouse emotions and prejudices which block the listening process. Finally, the listener may be so busy developing rebuttals, bringing up his own experiences, or trying to impress the speaker, that he hasn't heard a thing.

But there are methods which the listener can adopt which will produce good listening habits.[5] First, the listener must understand that his listening rate is much greater than the speaker's speaking rate. Most people speak at a rate of about 125 words a minute — but our minds work at a far greater rate. As a result, unless we discipline ourselves, our minds will wander. To counteract this tendency, the listener should try these techniques:

■ The listener should not only hear the spoken words but also think ahead of the speaker, trying to anticipate what he's leading to and what will be the conclusions that can be drawn. This keeps the listener's mind on track and makes the listening more interesting.

[5]Nichols, Dr. Ralph G., "Listening is Good Business," *The Internal Auditor,* March/April 1970, p. 41.

▪ The listener should seek the evidence the speaker has or has not adduced to support his comments or buttress the points he is trying to make. This will form the basis for intelligent and relevant questions which will expand on the speaker's thoughts and make them easier to recall.

▪ The listener should mentally summarize what has gone before. If there appear to be any gaps in his recollection of what has been said, he may ask for a reprise which will aid in the absorption of the information.

▪ The listener should look directly at the speaker, observe his facial expressions, gestures, tone, and posture so as to focus on the nonverbal communications, which are sometimes more important than the verbal ones. This also tends to keep the mind tethered to the subject and to improve recall.

And, as we have pointed out before, the listener should withhold evaluation, because a judgmental attitude can be a severe block to communication.

HOW TO PROVIDE CONTINUING TRAINING

Orientation is not the same as training. Orientation assumes the ability to do the job the man was hired for; it merely adjusts him to his new surroundings so that he can adapt his abilities to new requirements and a changed environment, effectively, efficiently, and with the least amount of trauma.

Training provides a man with new abilities — abilities to do his own job better or help him handle a new job. Internal auditors have a particular need for training — as distinguished from orientation — when they come directly from school or from another discipline, like public accounting, or disciplines even less kindred to internal auditing.

Auditors also need training for the next job . . . from assistant to auditor-in-charge . . . from auditor-in-charge to supervisor . . . from supervisor to manager . . . from manager to director of auditing.

Training Assistant Auditors

The assistant has the greatest need for training. In many cases he will be learning a brand new job — not just adding to previously acquired information. His ways are not yet set; his areas of ignorance more likely exceed his areas of knowledge of the job — yet he is a valuable resource that must be carefully developed and protected.

He should not be pushed beyond his capabilities, lest he do harm to himself, his assignment, and his organization. Yet he must not be assigned exclusively to the dreary pedestrianism of detailed verification lest he become bored and dull.

At the very outset, he should be assigned to those senior auditors — auditors-in-charge — who are known to be masters of their art and who are willing to tend and nurture this valuable asset. These seniors, who have been auditors-in-charge for considerable periods, should be permitted some training budget so that they will be willing to take the time to teach, to evaluate, and, if necessary, to insist on a particular set of working papers being done over or a particular test extended.

Besides teaching the fundamentals, the auditor-in-charge should let the assistant feel he is a part of the team by having him read the audit program and by explaining the objectives of the particular activity under review as well as the objectives of the audit itself. At the other end of the assignment, or during its course, the assistant should be invited to attend conferences with client personnel to discuss audit findings. This will let the assistant see first hand how important it is to develop the facts fully and to assess their significance maturely.

The assistant should be exposed to variety, and should be placed with seniors of differing bents and approaches. During this time, his course should be recorded so that the director of auditing will be aware of the assistant's experience and experiences, as a basis for more difficult or more varied assignments.

The assistant's progress should be evaluated from time to time; and just as soon as it is propitious, he should be given a job of his own, to try his wings and to be master of his own efforts. He should not be pushed beyond his capacity. The mastery of the mechanics, at this point, is more important than innovative auditing and sparks of inventiveness. His job should be pretty well circumscribed so that he will not be forced into the agony of decisions as to whether to run down this new avenue or that. For example, good initial assignments are follow-up audits of significant deficiency findings reported in prior audits. Here the trail has been blazed — the prior working papers fully chart the course and set forth the audit objectives and boundaries at the outset.

The assistant's first jobs must be closely supervised to make sure the mechanics have indeed been mastered. For when the auditor moves on into uncharted waters, after his apprenticeship, it is often the mastery of mechanics — the ability to accumulate and array data professionally and to draw conclusions logically — that will be his sextant and get him to port without foundering.

After assignments of increasing difficulty have been accomplished successfully, the assistant can, without fear on his own part and on the part of management, be promoted to senior auditor.

Training Senior Auditors and Supervisors

Each auditing organization needs a formal program of training for the next higher position. There are at least two reasons: First, the staff personnel should be able to see physical evidence that they are being given the opportunity to show their capacity for more responsible work and to move up through the ranks. Second, no organization, including the auditing department, should leave itself open to catastrophe through the sudden loss of the "indispensable" man. Someone, and preferably more than one, should be able to step into a vacancy with the least trauma and the least dislocation of routines.

Over and above the general training program for the staff as a whole, the continuing program should provide for senior auditors to be assigned for predetermined periods to supervisory positions and for supervisors to be assigned to manager positions. Through these training assignments the staff man learns the nuts and bolts of the next higher job. Management evaluates his ability to take over. He himself develops confidence that he can do the job; or, on the other hand, may decide that the higher job is not for him.

During these training periods, when the supervisory ranks are swelled temporarily, one of the senior supervisors may be relieved of some of his regular assignments, for two purposes: (1) to act as mentor to the supervisory trainee; and (2) to perform research on audit methods, techniques, and practices; to make reviews of working papers, reports, and executed forms to see whether procedures are generally being followed; or to develop new manuals or training aids.

Similarly, during the period when one of the supervisors is in management training, the manager may take on long-range projects on the direction and function of the entire auditing organization and — during the six-month "sabbatical" — take a good hard look at himself and his department to determine whether it is doing the job it is supposed to be doing or whether new approaches and areas should be explored.

Through such training systems, the director of auditing can develop "back-up" charts which he can submit to executive management to show that his organization is not encrusted with the mold of inaction, but rather is a viable entity, ready to withstand the onslaughts which may be brought about by personnel losses.

HOW TO PROMOTE CONTINUING EDUCATION

Too many people — auditors included — entertain the naive notion that education is something that happens to the very young in a schoolroom. The constant winds of change should dispel that foggy notion; but apathy and lack of direction can be a frustrating and formidable barrier.

The torrents of technological changes in the business community should make it abundantly clear that the auditor must learn to breast the tide of new knowledge or remain high, dry, and desiccated on the shore. And for those staff people incapable of self-renewal, audit management owes itself and them the duty of getting them immersed in the waters of continued learning.

Internal auditing especially — this relatively young and growing product of business needs — must keep current with the same changes that management itself must cope with. And there is no excuse for a progressive auditing organization that does not have formal, continuing programs of education for its staff people. There are many forms this education can take. Let us explore some of them.

Individual Study

The professional man must continue his formal education as long as he keeps alive in his profession. When he stops learning, his professional life starts to atrophy. The modern internal auditor — like the modern business manager he serves — is fast becoming a generalist in a world of specialists. And new ideas and theories in all aspects of the management sciences are the sustenance on which he feeds so as to remain strong enough to keep pace with the management for which he is the "eyes and ears."

New ideas and theories found in professional journals give him a taste and a hint. But it is only in formal university courses that he will get a full meal that he can convert into the useful muscle that will help him stay at the top of his profession. Every auditor should, now and again, take a formal course in a university, if one is available, or in a correspondence course if the university is not reasonably close by. There is a discipline about formal university courses — with their homework, supervision, and grades — which induces an extra effort that reading alone does not always do.

But it is like anything else in the world of business and government. When the staff man sees that his management regards such instruction as important, he will start considering the possibilities seriously. But how can the staff be motivated to take courses?

The "self-starter" has his own internal motivation and desire for self-renewal. Others need help and direction.

Management can take these steps:

- Make available in the office catalogues of extension courses from all local universities.

- Let it be known that an MBA carries a higher price tag than a BA or BS.

- Ask each staff man, at the beginning of each year, to complete a written statement of what he proposes to do to improve his knowledge.

- Discuss with each staff man his own long-range and short-range plans for self-renewal.

- Post lists of staff people taking courses, and of those who have completed them.

- Put the names of members of the auditing organization on lists of those to be considered for management training courses sponsored by the company.

- Let it be understood throughout the auditing department that the company thinks highly of, and provides opportunities for, those people who continue their education.

Not only will such courses benefit the individual, he can then pass on some of this knowledge as a teacher of others through staff meetings.

Staff Meetings

There are different types of staff meetings, each with different purposes. They can be used to communicate or reinforce routine administrative matters, to teach new techniques, and to let off steam.

As administrative controls within the auditing organization proliferate, it is helpful to have meetings to reinforce an understanding of existing instructions and to explain the purpose of new ones. The meetings are good forums for upgrading the staff's knowledge of bread-and-butter topics, such as report writing, audit programming, and the like.

As the use of more complex matters becomes significant, the meetings can become classrooms to teach such techniques as the use of the computer in statistical sampling, model building, and probability theory.

The staff meetings can be used as safety valves. Under careful supervision, the staff people can be given an opportunity to be heard on such matters as administrative procedures that are not working, promotion possibilities, salaries, administrative detail, lack of communication, and the many other things that are best not permitted to fester. Ground rules should be set early for such meetings. People should be asked well in advance of the meeting to develop specific questions, and — important — several searching, and even impertinent, questions should be "planted" so as to remove inhibitions on the part of others who may be fearful of posing their own questions.

Staff meetings should be programmed formally. A certain amount of budget should be allotted to developing and attending the meetings. Dates for the meetings and the assignments to conduct them should be established at the time the year's audit program is established.

A double return can be obtained from staff meetings by assigning each one to one or more staff men to research the subject, develop the lesson plan or presentation, and lead the meeting. In this way their capacities are broadened both in terms of the subject itself and in learning to deal with audiences — particularly audiences who are prone to ask hard questions.

Each assignment should be given a specific budget so that the project does not get out of hand. Also, a supervisor should be assigned so that the staff people have someone to consult with, to remove road blocks, and unobstrusively to make sure that the objectives will be met.

Some of the topics that might be considered for staff meetings are:

- Audit programming
- Working paper presentation
- Outlining reports
- Developing deficiency findings
- Describing interesting deficiency findings
- Selecting samples
- Determining confidence levels and precision ranges
- Deciding on the sampling techniques to use under different circumstances
- Surveys vs. detailed examinations
- Standards of acceptable evidence of corrective action
- New company products
- New company systems
- Presentations by other company personnel

The Institute of Internal Auditors

The Institute, like any other professional organization, provides opportunities for continued education. *The Internal Auditor*, The Institute's technical journal, is a primary source of information on management auditing. Its Research Bulletins are well-stocked warehouses of information and instruction on particular phases of the auditor's work. The Institute's educational arm, the Cadmus Education Foundation (CEF), is the chief source of education on matters relating expressly to modern internal auditing, providing seminars and study courses in a broad spectrum of subjects which include EDP, statistical sampling, and staff improvement. In time, CEF will provide a selection of correspondence courses on auditing subjects.

Attendance at local chapter meetings of The Institute offers opportunities to hear speakers on auditing and related topics. The interchange at the meeting's social hour can often provide an opportunity to unearth a nugget of information that can be of value on an ongoing audit project or that can give a new slant on an old problem.

The local chapter also can offer balm for that managerial itch — a balm that cannot always be found at the office. Working as a committee chairman or an officer adds stature to the individual, provides him with the opportunity to make management decisions and try out new ideas, and gives him a widening circle of professional colleagues.

Institute relations need not be suspended because of travel. Auditors about to go on travel status should consult The Institute's *Directory of Membership*. It will show those chapters closest to the temporary duty station and the dates and places of chapter meetings.

Here again, audit management must take the initiative — to plant the idea, to urge participation, to set examples, to show management approval of participation in The Institute, and to provide the necessary time and support.

Research

Research is a form of education with many side benefits. It differs from structured classroom education where often the student merely regurgitates what the teacher has fed him. In research the student obtains fulfillment from what he has accomplished. Too, the result of his work transcends the numerical grade given in the classroom and provides a tangible product — sometimes one that is unique. Where a class grade is soon forgotten and is at most of benefit or value only to the student, the research report completed outside the classroom and for satisfaction, not for credit, may be of lasting value and of benefit to others. Moreover, the researcher may become both student and teacher.

The auditing department, like any other aggressive enterprise, should foster research in its own field — both to widen its own vistas and to increase the capacities of its people. And as in any other effort of the department, the director of auditing should give research projects the dignity and support of regularly planned programs.

Provision for specific research projects should be made in the annual program. Research projects should be given project numbers and project budgets. Researchers should be selected from among the staff with a view toward their natural proclivities and in consideration of how the research will benefit them.

Research projects can be assigned to individuals or teams. Teams should be led by staff people with the demonstrated or the potential ability to motivate themselves and others. The keynote is professionalism in approach and execution, with close management involvement to ensure a professional product.

Having selected their topics, the researchers should then present, for management approval, their research objectives, milestones by which to measure progress, and an estimate of the end result of the research — be it a report, a program, or a suggested course of action. Man-hours expended should be charged against the project, and requests for any extensions of time and budget should be made as formal as those for normal audit projects.

Research can be original — the development of brand new ideas — or it can constitute the accumulation and arraying of information to determine whether the old ways are still valid. Research topics can cover any aspect of audit activity, for example:

- EDP Applications to Audit Processes
- Advanced Program Techniques for Operational Audits
- Simulation and Game Theory as Audit Tools
- Advanced Working Paper Techniques
- Methods of Evaluating Human Resources
- Analysis of Audit Report Techniques
- How Best to Audit the Procurement Activity
- Development of a Style Manual for Auditors
- Adapting Operations Research Techniques to Audit Needs

A description of an actual research project, with some excerpts from the research report, is shown in Exhibit 2-6.

Exhibit 2-6. RESEARCH REPORT ON AUDITS OF PROCUREMENT

Foreword

Procurement accounts for the majority of all company expenditures. These expenditures are committed by a large number of people working in many diverse procurement activities. Complete examinations of such activities and of the work of all the people currently is clearly infeasible. Accordingly, the audit effort must be directed toward those areas where there is the greatest risk of potential exposure to the loss or dissipation of company resources as a result of improper procurement activities.

To that end, we established a research project to determine how we could accomplish optimum coverage of the procurement activity, by identifying actual or potential risks and indicating the related controls.

Purpose and Scope

The objectives of the research project were (1) to identify the areas of major risk inherent in the procurement process, and (2) to suggest possible means of control designed to protect against such risks.

To accomplish our purpose, we used the "brainstorming" technique. The members of the research committee assembled for brainstorming sessions to list various risks, both actual and potential, that may be encountered in the procurement process. For each risk we attempted to suggest some form of control to provide protection against inadequate or improper procurement action.

We then sorted the various risk areas by major groups, and for each group we set forth the objectives of the activities and sufficient general information to give some background on how they function.

Results of Research

Our research resulted in eight groupings and four subgroupings of risk areas and associated control. The groupings are identified as follows:

   I Bidding Procedures
   II Noncompetitive Procurements
   III Decentralized Ordering and Receiving Areas
      A. Procurement Activities at Outlying Locations
      B. Direct Deliveries of Purchased Materials and Supplies
      C. Nonstocked Inventory Plan
      D. Shipments of Company-Owned Materials from Suppliers to Third Parties.
   IV Outside Production
   V Blanket Purchase Orders
   VI Purchase Order Changes
   VII Procurements Paid for from Imprest Funds
   VIII Time and Material and Labor Hour Procurements

Lists of the risk areas and the suggested controls are included. Risk areas include not only actual risks ("Selection of an unqualified supplier") but also areas of potential risk ("Sole source procurement"). For simplicity we have designated them all as "risk areas." It will be observed that the same risk areas may appear more than once, in different groupings, since the identical risk can be equally applicable to two or more different groups. The same is true of the related controls.

We have concluded that the review and evaluation of these risk areas represent the least amount of audit effort that should be expended in examining pro-

Exhibit 2-6. (Cont.)

curement activities. We wish to emphasize that the lists should not be used as check sheets which will completely satisfy audit objectives because (1) there is no substitute for imaginative, innovative auditing; (2) the lists and the associated general information which were prepared as of the date of this research report are almost certain to change with the passage of time because of the advent of new circumstances, procedures, and systems; and (3) it is a virtual impossibility to succeed in listing every conceivable risk area inherent in so broad and complex an activity as procurement.

Properly used, however, the lists should represent reasonably satisfactory audit guidelines and should provide assurance of at least minimum audit coverage within the procurement organizations assigned for audit.

I Bidding Procedures

Purpose of Activity

To obtain, through competitive means, required materials, supplies, and services at the most favorable terms, giving due regard to quality, price, and schedule.

General Information

To provide assurance that materials and services will be obtained at acceptable prices on schedule from qualified suppliers, the following controls are provided by established written procedures:

- It is the policy of the Procurement Division to solicit competitive bids for all items to be purchased except under specified conditions when the solicitation of bids is considered to be impractical.
- In general, written quotations are to be obtained from all prospective suppliers. Written quotations are to be obtained without exception in connection with all procurements over $10,000.
- For procurements estimated to be in excess of $1,000, prior written supervisory approval is to be obtained of the prospective bidders.
- Buyers are to show on the applicable procurement request the number of bids solicited, whether the bids obtained were oral or written, and, when competitive bids are not obtained, the reasons for not obtaining them.
- Written quotations are to be obtained from the suppliers on Requests for Quotation (RFQ) forms whenever practicable, and are to be controlled by the responsible purchasing agents.
- Buyers are to select the lowest bidder capable of performing the desired work on schedule, and they are to provide adequate reasons for not selecting the low bidder.

Because of numerous pressures of varying kinds, there often is an inducement to circumvent established procedures. The circumventions may often be found in the following risk areas.

Risk Areas	*Suggested Controls*
1. Incomplete or poor initial selection of proposed sources of supply.	1. The review and approval of bidders' lists by procurement supervisors and by Quality Control and Finance personnel before completing and mailing the RFQ's.

Exhibit 2-6. (Cont.)

2. Authority for the same group both to select proposed suppliers and to type and mail the RFQs.

3. Authority for the buying group which originated the RFQs to receive the bids directly from the mail room or from the supplier.

4. The receipt from suppliers of bids on other than company RFQ forms.

5. The acceptance of oral, non-RFQ types of bids.

6. Awards based on fewer than three bids.

7. Awards to other than low bidders.

8. The disclosure of bid information received from some suppliers to other, favored suppliers.

9. The pitting of favored suppliers against only those suppliers known to submit high bids.

10. The submission to nonfavored suppliers of specifications, or other matters, which affect cost, that are more stringent than those submitted to favored suppliers.

11. The communication of extension of bid periods or changes in RFQs only to favored suppliers.

12. Collusive bidding among suppliers available or selected to bid.

---

2. The typing and mailing of RFQs by an organization other than the buying group.

3. The receipt and retention of bids until the closing date, by an organization other than the buying group.

4. The analysis of terms and conditions to detect any conditions of sale which may conflict with "Terms and Conditions of Purchase."

5. The review and approval of the use of this type of bid by appropriate supervision.
The review and approval of the proposed sources of supply.
The requirement that suppliers submit written confirmation of bids.
The review of RTP and bid award by appropriate management level.

6. The provision for written explanations and justifications of awards based on fewer than three bids, and review of those reasons by appropriate supervision.

7. The provision for written justifications and for supervisory approvals.

8. Bids remain sealed until opening in the presence of witnesses.

9. Supervisory review and evaluation of list of bidders.

10. Data assembled, compared, and mailed by an organization (other than the buying group).

11. Extensions or changes typed and mailed by some organization (other than the buying group) that handled the original RFQs.

12. Estimates from using organizations of what are reasonable prices.
Review of trade periodicals for what are going prices.
Communication by procurement supervision with their counterparts in kindred companies to see what others are paying.

The research resulted in a new approach to the audit of procurement activities. The auditing organization felt that the audit procedures in use were bogging the auditor down in a welter of detail. He was so busy examining individual transactions that he lost sight of the significant risk areas and control points in the procurement activities. The researchers approached the project with the theory that inadequacies discovered in transactions could result merely in the correction of certain symptoms, while weaknesses in controls over significant risk areas could, if undetected, result in serious systemic maladies.

By means of brainstorming sessions,[6] attended by the members of the research team which was composed of supervisors and staff auditors who had had considerable experience in procurement audits, risk areas were identified and the control measures to look for or insist on were suggested. Exhibit 2-6 shows the research report's sections on Foreword, Purpose and Scope, and Results of Research, as well as the detailed section on bidding activities.

Educating for the Future

The internal auditor can expect to become more and more involved in the scientific methods which managers are beginning to turn to for aid in making business decisions. And where management goes, the internal auditor should be prepared to follow. Thus, scientific method is one of the subjects that should be on the internal auditor's curriculum for continuing education.

The field of scientific method — quantitative techniques — is often referred to by the term operations research, or OR. OR makes use of mathematical and statistical models which are used in decision-making—models that are simulations of the real thing.

A model is a depiction of the interrelationships among recognized factors. In business, models depict the whole business or any part of it. For example, the balance sheet and the income statement may be considered models. The balance sheet is a "static" model representing the listing of the assets and liabilities of the business.

---

[6]Brainstorming is a form of group creative thinking on an assigned topic. The atmosphere is relaxed. All ideas are welcome. No ideas are held up to the harsh, inhibiting light of criticism since, on the one hand, critical analysis tends to cut off the creative process and, on the other, a ludicrous or impractical idea may trigger a useful one. The evaluation of the ideas is left for later.

Brainstorming can fail its objective, however, if the problem to which solutions are sought has not been precisely determined and defined. It is of little value to develop brilliant solutions to problems that are not causing the difficulties that need correcting.

The income statement is a "dynamic" model of the stream of income and expense flowing through the business. Other models may include the entire accounting system, the production control system, the quality control system, organization charts, and plant layout. So the model concept is not really new. We have long used depictions to represent — not to be — the real thing. What is new is the myriad of variations — including statistical and mathematical models — that we are beginning to see.

OR usually calls for:

- An identification and definition of the central problem;
- An overall systems approach;
- Teams representing various disciplines — mathematicians, statisticians, engineers and, as time goes on, knowledgeable internal auditors; and
- The use of mathematical and statistical models as the means of analysis.

Operations research was born during World War II. Teams of mathematicians, statisticians, physicists, chemists, and military men pooled their talents to solve problems that would not yield to experience and intuition. These problems required a disciplined, structured approach. They included the search for optimum convoy sizes, repair schedules for airplane engines, and the deployment of ships to avoid or reduce losses from enemy attack.

With the advent of digital computer techniques, the vast number of calculations sometimes required in OR permitted it to become a practical tool for management. The manager found that he could use it as a disciplined means for discovering feasible alternatives, evaluating them, and selecting the best alternative.

OR is essentially a planning tool — not a means of control. Control is less significant since even poor decisions can sometimes be efficiently carried out. An obsolete piece of machinery can be used superbly — through proper scheduling, maintenance, repair, and crutching by other machines — yet the overall costs might far exceed the cost of replacing it.

When done accurately and properly, OR can replace intuition, business folklore, and guessing with the collection and appraisal of enormous numbers of interrelated and relevant factors. For example, OR can provide answers to:

- The best allocation of facilities to products.
- The best geographical location of warehouses.
- The most economical size for inventories.

- The proper size of territories that salesmen should cover.
- The number of salesmen to employ.
- The price to bid on a specific contract.
- When to replace a fleet of trucks.
- The effect of lowered or raised prices.
- Projected sales for the next month or the next year.

As managers become more and more mathematically literate, the auditor may become increasingly involved in scientific methods. He may be called upon by management to evaluate a proposed OR application. Or he may find it necessary to analyze the propriety of an OR application which was used as the basis for a course of action.

Many of these OR methods are far over the horizon; but the modern internal auditor should be prepared to recognize them when he encounters them and be able to put some of them to practical use. We shall touch briefly on some of the OR techniques in this chapter, and where appropriate we shall point out some of the uses to which they can be applied.

Probability Theory. This theory refers to the probability that some event will occur or to the frequency with which an event will occur in an infinite number of trials. The expected ratio of the probable occurrences, on the one hand, to the total trials, on the other, may be based on data obtained from experience.

The probability ratio is a percentage between zero at one end (impossibility) and unity (certain). For example, the probability that the sun will rise in the east is certainty (unity) or 1. The probability that it will set in the east is impossibility or 0. The probability that the sun rising in the east will be obscured by clouds is somewhere in between.

Probability theory may be used to refine estimates of revenues and costs for many managerial decisions. It is also the basis for the sampling plans and techniques used in audit tests. See Chapter 7.

Regression Analysis. Simple and multiple regression analysis are methods of expressing mathematically the relationship between the data for two or more variables. The method of least squares is the most popular way of determining the equation which best fits the data at hand. This is a mathematical tool for studying the relationship between variables to make more valid projections — in other words, to predict the expected. Regression analysis describes the relationships mathematically; it does not tell *why* the relationships exist.

Internal auditors may use regression analysis to analyze projected general and administrative rates through the use of EDP programs geared to multiple regression analysis. A discussion of this statistical method, as well as a description of a time-shared computer program to deal with regression analysis problems, will be found in Volume 3 of the "Mathematics for Management Series," *Statistical Inference,* by Springer, Herlihy, Mall, and Beggs, Richard D. Irwin, Inc., Homewood, Illinois, 1966.

PERT/CPM. These methods are forms of network analysis. PERT stands for Program Evaluation and Review Techniques. CPM stands for Critical Path Method. PERT breaks down a project into a set of events and arranges them in a logical network. CPM differs from PERT in that (1) it is built up for jobs or activities instead of events, and (2) it makes no allowance for uncertainty in the estimates of events. Network methods help management to:

■ Plan a complex project.

■ Schedule jobs or events in a workable sequence.

■ Redeploy manpower to provide as nearly as possible a level work force.

■ Reschedule to compensate for delays and bottlenecks.

■ Determine the cost-time tradeoff (what it will cost to save or make up time).

■ Determine the probability of meeting a specified date (or finding the date which there is some specified probability of meeting).

CPM has been used to schedule the field work on complex audit jobs requiring the efforts of many auditors. It can provide the audit manager with a means of directing and coordinating the many segments of the field work.

Linear Programming. This is the language of activities. It describes how these activities use available resources to accomplish assigned tasks. Linear programming also describes how these activities function within the limitations of time and space. The term linear comes from the linear algebraic equations used to describe programs and schedules. It is used in planning such things as production schedules, transportation and traffic, personnel assignments, and salary levels.

Monte Carlo Method. This method has been termed the unsophisticated mathematician's friend. It can be adapted to many situations as long as alternatives can be quantitatively specified. It is a form of simulation — the use of mathematical models — which seeks to solve such business problems as:

- How many telephone trunk lines should be provided?
- How many repairmen should be hired to keep production machinery operating at a maximum profit level?
- How many repair parts of each kind should be kept in inventory?
- What is the potential profit or loss from a revised production system?

Inventory Theory. This theory provides a language to describe a system which is subject to a pattern of demand and is capable of building up supplies. The demands may vary. The supply may be subject to delays and uncertainties. The inventory may be depleted by deterioration and obsolescence. Management cost will include cost of shortages, cost of replenishment, and cost of holding the inventory.

Studies of inventories have made it possible to predict demands on inventory within statistical limits and to estimate the net costs of adopting various inventory policies, even when there are many kinds of inventory, seasonal fluctuations, and unpredictable demands. Inventory theory is not restricted to inventories alone. It may also be applied to staffing, manloading, parking facilities, and cash flows.

Queuing Theory. This theory provides the language for describing a system of service units. It describes how customers arrive for service, how service meets requirements in terms of average service time and variations in service time, how long customers may have to wait, and how long the service may be idle. It has been used quite successfully in devising methods of speeding up lines of customers waiting to be served by tellers at banks.

Sensitivity Analysis. This method is used in relation to linear programming. In formulating and solving linear programming problems, one makes certain assumptions, at least initially. It is assumed that all values of the coefficients are derived from the analysis of data and that they represent *average* values or *best estimate* values. Accordingly, it is important to analyze the *sensitivity* of the solution to variations in these coefficients or in the estimates of these coefficients. Stated another way, one seeks to determine the ranges of variation of the coefficients over which the solution will remain optimal. Sensitivity studies of this sort are known as parametric linear programming.

Game Theory.   This theory is used to establish a basis for decision. It takes into account the consequences of the action by one party upon the actions of an opponent who is choosing from among alternatives. Game theory goes beyond the classical theory of probability, which is limited to pure chance. In game theory, strategic aspects are stressed; that is, aspects controlled by the participants. It is therefore well adapted to the study of competition where there are present several common factors, such as conflicting interests, incomplete information, the interplay of rational decisions, and chance.

Dynamic Programming.   This is what is termed a "maximization theory." It is used where a whole series of states or actions take place and where a decision in each state is dependent on the decision made in the preceding state. It permits one to determine mathematically the period-by-period consequences of decisions.

It can be used to calculate the desirability of incurring temporary losses for the sake of long term gains. For example, through dynamic programming one could calculate the benefits of expending large sums on research and development and incurring losses during immediate periods in the hope of making much greater profits in later periods.

Exponential Smoothing.   This technique is used to correlate later values with earlier ones in the same series. It is used to base predictions on past observations, giving the greatest weight to the latest observations. It can be applied to determining the production of optimum lot sizes to meet forecasted sales.

HOW TO EVALUATE STAFF AUDITORS

People engaged in every form of endeavor need evaluation to let them know how they are doing. To be effective, these evaluations should be frank, fair, frequent, and friendly. And since not all evaluators have the proper combinations of honesty and tact — the ability to get the truth across while still maintaining good relations — the evaluation program should be carefully structured so as to provide some assurance that all evaluations will be carried out according to an established, consistent, and well-understood pattern.

Internal auditing provides special problems in evaluating staff people. No two projects that the staff man carries out or assists in are the same. Some projects do not even stretch a man's abilities. Others may turn out to be beyond an individual's potential or experience. Still other projects, which had previously been performed in a pedestrian and unimaginative fashion, may be raised to unsuspected heights because of an auditor's novel approach or innovative methods. All these factors should be considered in structuring the evaluation system so as to be fair to the employee and to his department.

To measure anything reasonably well, of course, requires objective standards and consistent methods of gauging performance. Also, in aid of personnel relations, all who will be measured should be fully aware of the standards and the methods. Thus, the policy or program should be clearly set forth in a staff memorandum or directive. The instructions should make clear what is considered excellent, adequate, or unsatisfactory performance. The instructions should also establish when and how often the evaluations will be made and how they will be used.

The size of the auditing organization also has a significant bearing on how the evaluation program will be structured. A director of auditing with a half dozen staff people should have no difficulty making personal and even unstructured evaluations. A large organization, with several supervisors and a large number of in-charge auditors and assistants, presents impediments to close contact between the staff man and the director. Here it is the supervisors who have the personal contact with the auditors-in-charge, while the latter have the contact with their assistants. And the greater the number of supervisors, the more remote the possibility that all evaluations in the department will be carried out in the same way.

Thus, when the director of auditing does all the evaluations himself, he can be completely open with his staff men about precisely how he rated them. When staff men are subject to the review of different supervisors or auditors-in-charge during the year, the director should be careful about letting the evaluators be the last word. Hence, it would be preferable for the evaluations of an individual by more than one supervisor or auditor-in-charge to be combined and weighted by the director and then discussed with the individuals at appropriate periods. Different supervisors and different auditors-in-charge will most likely have varying standards, likes, dislikes, and prejudices. These qualities should be neutralized by having a single spokesman for the department in this always delicate yet essential aspect of personnel relations.

One program that has worked reasonably well — no one method is perfect where souls are being bared — provides the following pattern:

■ At the conclusion of each audit assignment, the auditor-in-charge prepares a rating sheet for each of his assistants, and the supervisor prepares one for the auditor-in-charge. A rating for each assignment is necessary because of the variations among assignments. The actual numerical or adjectival ratings are not discussed, but a dialogue is conducted on the strengths and weaknesses observed on that particular project.

This dialogue can work well or poorly, depending on how it is approached. An often successful ploy is for the evaluator to open the conversation by asking the staff man how he thought he performed, what he felt he did well, what he felt he did poorly, what he learned from the job, and what areas of improvement he sees for himself. These dialogues are valuable because it is cruel to a man to permit him to go to another audit assignment unaware of certain defects that adversely affect his performance, and which will continue to plague his work unless he can identify his weaknesses and make a conscious effort toward improvement.

The supervisor or auditor-in-charge owes it to his subordinate to help him identify his weaknesses. He also owes it to the man to use tact and sympathy. Thus, to lead the man's self-evaluation toward the known defects can probably accomplish the most good. Most people like to talk about themselves, and getting the staff man to do the exploring himself can accomplish the objectives of the dialogue with the least amount of abrasion.

■ At the end of a 6-month or 12-month period, the director of auditing combines the various ratings for each staff man and discusses the results with him. In some organizations the periodic discussions are held when the salary adjustments are made. The purpose is to bring home the significance of the rating. In other organizations the periodic discussions are held separately from the salary adjustment interviews. In this view, the emphasis is placed on improving the auditor, not on rewarding or punishing him.

These ratings and interviews are of extreme importance to the individual. In very large organizations, they may be the only time during the year when the staff man has a chance for an eye-to-eye colloquy with the director. They should be carried out in an unhurried atmosphere and be pervaded by a deep and sincere interest in the man's problems, goals, and aspirations, and in his program to work them out.

In filling out rating sheets, the evaluator should seek to maintain a distinction between accomplishments and traits. While both are significant, each has a different function. The rating of accomplishments should apply to the particular project completed, since each project has different problems. The evaluation of traits deals with the qualities that the auditor carries with him through his working life. Traits are harder to evaluate since the evaluator is applying subjective standards. But it is well for the director of auditing to be aware of significant traits since they may affect his decisions about an auditor.

For example, a project which will require contacts at high levels in the company should not be assigned to an auditor who is expert at his profession but not personable or articulate. Similarly, if possible, a project which requires a large number of assistants should not be assigned to an auditor who does not possess qualities of leadership.

Numerous forms of rating sheets are in use. Several of them, which provide for evaluations of both accomplishments and traits, have been reproduced in Exhibits 2-7 and 2-8.

Exhibits 2-7a and 2-7b provide numerical ratings on a large variety of subjects and qualities, with adjectival ratings to give meaning to the numbers. Exhibit 2-7a is a rating sheet for an assistant auditor. Exhibit 2-7b is a rating sheet for an in-charge auditor. Numerical ratings provide for quantitative comparisons among different auditors. The qualities being appraised on these sheets are self-explanatory. These forms also provide for an evaluation of the difficulty of the job: Class A is for a relatively simple job. Class B is for a job of normal difficulty. Class C is for a job of exceptional difficulty. These factors can be used to adjust total scores. Five per cent is deducted for easy jobs and added for difficult ones.

Exhibit 2-8a is a rating form which provides adjectival ratings only. The same form is used both for assistants and for auditors-in-charge. Certain of the factors may be marked NA (not applicable), however, when appropriate to distinguish between the two. Exhibit 2-8b provides explanations for the performance factors.

Exhibit 2-7a. STAFF RATING FORM — ASSISTANT AUDITORS

Total Score _____

Name: _____ Period: From _____ To _____

Job No.: _____ Job Title: _____

Class (A B C) _____ Signature: _____ Date: _____

Planning and Organizing	Excellent	Very Good	Good	Fair	Unsatis- factory
1. Understanding of the procedures and problems relating to the audit segments assigned to him.	80	72	64	48	32
2. Conformance to the instructions provided by the auditor-in-charge and by the departmental manuals — yet questioning what seems illogical or unreasonable in the instructions.	60	54	48	36	24
3. Organizing and programming the work assigned to him so as to provide for coverage of the key control points in proper depth.	60	54	48	36	24
Totals	200	180	160	120	80

Field Work					
4. Accuracy of working papers — computations, references, statistical analyses.	90	81	72	54	36
5. Thoroughness of examination — yet knowing when to suggest discontinuance of the investigations.	90	81	72	54	36
6. Appropriateness of tests to the transactions reviewed.	60	54	48	36	24
7. Adequacy of documentation for work performed — showing nature, scope, and results of examination.	60	54	48	36	24
8. Completion of required field work — leaving no loose ends.	40	36	32	24	16
9. Summarization of findings — to facilitate review.	40	36	32	24	16
10. Evaluation of findings in forming opinion — use of judgment in assessing significance.	60	54	48	36	24
11. Care in preparing and organizing working papers — properly indexed, cross-referenced, initialed, dated.	60	54	48	36	24
Totals	500	450	400	300	200

Exhibit 2-7a. (Cont.)

Oral Expression	Excellent	Very Good	Good	Fair	Unsatis-factory
12. Clarity and conciseness of oral expression.	60	54	48	36	24
13. Effectiveness	40	36	32	24	16
Totals	100	90	80	60	40

Writing Ability

	Excellent	Very Good	Good	Fair	Unsatis-factory
14. Use of clear, concise, and appropriate language in working paper comments and in summaries and write-ups.	90	81	72	54	36
15. Organization of written material.	60	54	48	36	24
Totals	150	135	120	90	60

Administration

	Excellent	Very Good	Good	Fair	Unsatis-factory
16. Meeting the budget and the schedule for the work assigned to him.	50	45	40	30	20
Grand Totals	1,000	900	800	600	400

General Characteristics

(Place check mark under appropriate adjectival rating)

	Excellent	Very Good	Good	Fair	Unsatis-factory
17. Alertness, energy, and initiative.	—	—	—	—	—
18. Pleasantness, open-mindedness, tact, and cooperativeness.	—	—	—	—	—
19. Work habits — diligent application of effort to the job, and observation of company working hours.	—	—	—	—	—

Readiness for In-Charge Work

	Excellent	Very Good	Good	Fair	Unsatis-factory
20. Ability to carry out work successfully with only general supervision.	—	—	—	—	—

Additional Comments

Discuss specific attributes which require strengthening so as to improve this man's ability to handle in-charge assignments:

Exhibit 2-7b. STAFF RATING FORM — IN-CHARGE AUDITORS

Total Score _____

Name: _____ Period: From _____ To _____

Job No.: _____ Job Title: _____

Class (A B C) _____ Signature: _____ Date: _____

Planning	Excellent	Very Good	Good	Fair	Unsatis-factory
1. Understanding of procedures and problems relating to the activity under examination—awareness of objectives of activity under review, and relationship of those objectives to company objectives.	40	36	32	24	16
2. Coverage in the audit program of all key control points — giving proper weight and emphasis to most significant control points.	50	45	40	30	20
3. Nature of planned tests — use of imagination and economy.	30	27	24	18	12
4. Extent of planned tests—use of appropriate sampling techniques.	30	27	24	18	12
Totals	150	135	120	90	60
Field Work					
5. Completion of required field work — coverage of all programmed steps; adequate reasons to eliminate steps.	20	18	16	12	8
6. Accuracy of working papers —computations, references, statistical analyses.	70	63	56	42	28
7. Thoroughness of examination — yet knowing when to discontinue investigations.	70	63	56	42	28
8. Appropriateness of tests to the transactions reviewed.	40	36	32	24	16
9. Adequacy of documentation for work performed — showing nature, scope, and results of examination.	45	41	36	27	18
10. Summarization of findings — to facilitate review.	25	22	20	15	10
11. Evaluation of findings in forming opinion — judgment in assessing significance of findings.	65	59	52	39	26
12. Working paper preparation and organization — properly indexed, cross-referenced, initialed, dated.	40	36	32	24	16
Totals	375	338	300	225	150

Exhibit 2-7b. (Cont.)

Report Draft	Excellent	Very Good	Good	Fair	Unsatis- factory
13. Adequacy of support for report state- ments—ability of findings to withstand successful attack.	60	54	48	36	24
14. Proper treatment of findings according to relative significance—giving greater weight and space to more serious findings.	60	54	48	36	24
15. Organization — presenting material in a logical and orderly sequence.	50	45	40	30	20
16. Compliance with departmental instruc- tions on reporting — following rules laid down in departmental manuals.	40	36	32	24	16
17. Clarity and appropriateness of report language — making findings clear to nontechnical reader.	50	45	40	30	20
18. Accuracy in preparation and review to eliminate errors	40	36	32	24	16
Totals	300	270	240	180	120
Oral Communication					
19. Clarity and conciseness	60	54	48	36	24
20. Persuasiveness	40	36	32	24	16
Totals	100	90	80	60	40
Administration					
21. Meeting budget	40	36	32	24	16
22. Meeting schedule	35	31	28	21	14
Totals	75	67	60	45	30
Grand Totals	1,000	900	800	600	400

General Characteristics

(Place check mark under appropriate adjectival rating)

23. Alertness, energy, and initiative.	—	—	—	—	—
24. Pleasantness, open-mindedness, tact, and cooperativeness	—	—	—	—	—
25. Work habits — diligent application of effort to the job, and observation of company working hours	—	—	—	—	—

Additional Comments

Exhibit 2-8a. STAFF PERFORMANCE APPRAISAL

Name _____ Assistant ☐ Auditor in Charge ☐
Assignment _____ Period Covered _____
Overall rating for this   Desirability on Another Assignment:
assignment   Desirable   _____
                                                         Acceptable   _____
                                                         Prefer Another Staff Member _____

Performance Factors*

	NA	S−	S	S+	E	O
Quantity of Work						
Quality of Work						
Knowledge of Auditing						
Auditing Aptitude						
Problem Analysis						
Decision-Making						
Planning						
Follows Instructions						
Communications: Oral						
Written						

Personal Characteristics*

	NI	FA
Creativity		
Initiative		
Persistence		
Ability to work with others		
Judgment		
Adaptability		
Persuasiveness		
Leadership		
Self Confidence		
Attitude		

*See general instructions, Exhibit 2-8b, for definitions and rating terms

Attributes: Circle up to five adjectives which best describe the staff member's outstanding personal characteristics. They may be desirable and/or undesirable qualities. Extra blanks are provided for adjectives which you consider more descriptive.

aggressive	enthusiastic	lazy	self-assured
articulate	erratic	loud	shallow
careless	excitable	mature	sloppy
casual	flexible	naive	steady
cautious	flippant	neat	taciturn
clumsy	gullible	observant	tenacious
conceited	imaginative	officious	vacillating
deliberate	immature	open-minded	verbose
discreet	impulsive	overbearing	vigorous
discriminating	inarticulate	plodding	vulgar
dogmatic	indifferent	presumptuous	witty
dull	indiscreet	prim	_____
eager	inflexible	pushy	_____
energetic	inquisitive	resourceful	_____

Counseling: The completed appraisal report is confidential and should not be shown or read to the staff member even though it is required that his performance on each assignment be discussed with him. Discuss the staff member's performance on each assignment with him during the course of the examination and in summary form at the end of the assignment. Please answer Yes, No, or Not Applicable (N/A) to these questions:

Exhibit 2-8a. (Cont.)

Have you discussed with the staff member at a meeting for that purpose: (1) Good work he had done? _____ (2) Poor performance? _____ (3) Correctable deficiencies? _____ (4) Means of correcting deficiencies?_____ Give the date of the meeting _____.

Matters discussed with staff member and his reaction:

_____

_____

_____

_____

_____

Comments: Comment on exceptionally outstanding performance or unsatisfactory ratings, as well as qualities not covered elsewhere. Do not include comments that are only a restatement of the various ratings: Specific illustrations are always more helpful than remarks of a general nature. Be concise.

_____

_____

_____

_____

_____

_____

_____   _____
             Signature   Date

Exhibit 2-8b.

General Instructions: The purpose of the staff performance appraisal form is to obtain information on the level of work the audit staff member is qualified to perform as well as on his prospects for advancement. The appraisal report is necessary for knowledgeable decisions on adjustments of compensation and on promotions, as well as a means of summarizing information to assist in effectively counseling and training the staff member. The completed appraisal report is confidential and should not be shown or read to the staff member, even though it is required that his performance on the assignment be discussed with him. There is a difference between discussion of performance and reporting, since the latter includes grading and evaluating, while the former does not.

Exhibit 2-8b. (Cont.)
DEFINITIONS
Rating Factors

Performance Factors

Quantity of work - Accomplishments measured against the requirements of his position; results measured against objectives. Timely completion of work for which he is responsible.

Quality of work - The degree of excellence of the end results; thoroughness, accuracy, and overall caliber of completed assignments, including adequacy and clarity of working papers.

Knowledge of auditing - Does he understand basic auditing principles and company operational policies and procedures?

Auditing aptitude - Does he understand audit program objectives, and does he have the ability to analyze the systems of control to be audited?

Problem analysis - Does he recognize problems and does he break problem situations into essential parts logically and systematically? Does he gather facts and get beneath the surface to discover their full meaning?

Decision-making - Does he screen facts, get to the heart of the problem, and make sound and timely decisions?

Planning - Does he plan his work systematically and practically, and does he establish logical priorities to do a more efficient audit job?

Follows instructions - Does he have the ability to follow instructions exactly and conscientiously; is he proficient in comprehending instructions?

Communication skills - Does he express his point of view clearly, logically, and convincingly in written and oral communications; and does he keep his superior currently informed?

Personal Characteristics

Creativity - Ability to apply imagination and originality to the job to develop new and improved procedures or applications.

Initiative - Is he a self-starter?

Persistence - Is he persevering? Does he pursue goals resolutely? Is he not easily deterred from attaining his objectives?

Ability to work with others - Ability to get along with people. Is he tactful and diplomatic and aware of the effect he has on others?

Judgment - Ability to comprehend all facets of a problem and assign proper values to each consideration in arriving at a decision.

Adaptability - Ability to adjust to change and to meet new situations.

Persuasiveness - Ability to influence others.

Leadership - Ability to motivate subordinates and associates to action.

Self-Confidence - Ability to remain at ease, self-assured, and poised.

Attitude - Enthusiasm for his job, loyalty to the company, and the ability to accept constructive criticism.

Exhibit 2-8b. (Cont.)

Rating Terms

Performance Factors

O	- Outstanding	Exceptional, superior; would apply only in rare instances
E	- Excellent	Considerably above average; stands out; demonstrates rare ability
S+	- Satisfactory Plus	Above average
S	- Satisfactory	Exhibits an acceptable degree of performance under strong direction
S-	- Satisfactory Minus	A marginal rating; does not meet minimum accepted standards
NA	- Not Acceptable	

Personal Characteristics

NI	- Needs Improvement	Definite improvement required to reach normally accepted standards.
FA	- Fully Acceptable	Meets normally accepted standards in all respects.

SUMMARY

The compleat internal auditor combines technical competence and education with qualities of adaptability, understanding, determination, integrity, independence, objectivity, and responsibility. He may be recruited from universities and colleges, from the ranks of CPAs, from within the company, and from practicing internal auditors. The recruitment program should include polished interviewing techniques and practical testing methods. The new auditor should be provided with a comprehensive orientation program that will ease his transition into the department. Adequate service to management requires a continuing training program to keep the staff abreast of new management methods and new auditing techniques. These techniques can be developed within the auditing organization through an imaginative research program. The director of auditing should provide a well-structured program of employee evaluation to keep the auditor informed of his progress, his strong points, and those shortcomings that need attention.

PREPARING LONG-RANGE
PROGRAMS

THE NEED FOR PLANNING AND FOR MANAGEMENT INVOLVEMENT

A good long-range audit program is an instrument of many uses. It is the auditor's guide . . . it is the support for his budget request . . . it is a way of involving management in the audit plans and obtaining its commitment to the scope of the audit . . . it is the standard by which the auditor measures his accomplishments . . . it is a visible sign to management that the audit activity is under competent control . . . and it is a notice to the external auditors of proposed coverage.

Long-range programs are also needed to set non-auditing objectives for upgrading the ability to make broader, deeper, more meaningful audits and to provide a better service to management.

The Program as a Guide

The long-range program, by spelling out in detail the audit projects to be carried out, gives evidence of coverage of key functions at planned intervals. It provides assurance that no significant auditable area has been overlooked.

The program also simplifies the job of assigning work to the staff. Without a detailed program, the audit effort can be a haphazard groping, a repeated exercise in responding to random requests or making last-minute decisions on "what do we do next."

In large audit organizations, the program can be allocated equitably to different supervisors or audit managers. They in turn can assign projects to their staff people in a logical order. Also, the well-constructed program, stretching out for two, three or five years, can provide an air of permanence to the audit organization. It is evidence of long-term planning and the continued existence of the audit effort. Above all, it is a tangible demonstration of the place of the auditing function as the keystone in the company's structure of internal control.

In smaller organizations it relieves the director of auditing from constantly having to make decisions on audit coverage. It permits him to make those decisions and settle his program problems — with provision for flexibility, of course — in advance of the year's work.

The Program as a Justification for Budget

The long-range program should be specific. It should parse out in detail each audit project to be performed, while still providing for the unknown and the unanticipated. Each project listed should indicate through its title the nature of the audit to be performed and should provide an estimate of the time required.

The sum total of the allotted time for the current year is a simple demonstration of the number of auditors needed. The sum total of man-days for each of subsequent years is a projection of changes or of continuity of staff levels. The program, therefore, when accepted by executive management, becomes a commitment to the number of auditors authorized. Simple arithmetic rather than rhetoric sustains the director's request for maintaining or increasing staff levels. And the accepted man-days, together with provision for administrative expense, travel expense, and related costs, represent management's approved budget for the audit organization.

The approved program provides an additional and subtle function. It defends against one of the internal auditor's constant fears — being requested to perform extraneous functions . . . to be at the beck and call of middle management for fire-fighting duties. When the audit program is accepted, it is tacit acknowledgment by management at the executive levels that the auditor's primary function is to carry out audit and not line activities. When such line activities become essential under emergency conditions, then the auditor can properly request top management's approval before carrying them out.

The Program as a Means of Obtaining Management Participation

All long-range programs should be reviewed up through the policy-making level of the company.

The program reviews with management people at the higher operating levels in the company provide them with a preview of the audit coverage in the areas of their responsibility. During these reviews the manager is given an opportunity to discuss each project and to comment on whether the scheduling is appropriate in the light of the company's present or projected activities; whether other projects — different from those listed — should be covered; whether some of the projects listed require less or no coverage; what difficulties the auditor should anticipate; what specific problems management would like to see considered; and what the thrust of a particular audit should be.

When an operating manager accepts the program he is in effect committed to it, and he has provided the auditor entree to the organizations under his control and authority to subject them to the audits planned. The auditor then enters those areas and carries on his audit work with the full support of higher management; indeed, almost as a matter of contract with management.

The Program as a Means of Establishing Standards

The program gives the director of auditing a yardstick by which to measure his own accomplishments and the accomplishments of each of his audit managers. Current reports of work completed — in terms of man-days — provide a means of showing management whether the director has done what he intended to do. The comparison of man-days budgeted with man-days expended shows the degree of realization of his goals. For example, overruns of budgeted man-days on audit projects can point to deficiencies either in budgeting or in accomplishment and can indicate the need for improvement in one or the other. They may be indicators that the budgets were unrealistic or that the audit projects were inadequately planned or programmed. The analysis of the variances can provide information to help in future programming or to point to needed changes in audit approach.

Further, in large auditing organizations, the program can be used to measure the competence of audit managers or supervisors. At the beginning of the year the program may be divided among supervisors, and staff auditors may be assigned to them for specified periods. The performance of the supervisor in carrying out his allotted programs with the staff assigned is one indicator of his ability.

The Program as a Means of Control

Executives are strongly trending toward scientific management. They are becoming more and more imbued with the concepts of objective- and goal-oriented administration, with adequate planning, and with sound administrative policies. Management expects that all entities within its purview will also operate in an organized, well-administered manner.

Hence, the well-structured, well-considered, long-range program, with periodic reports to show that the program is not just window dressing but a real management tool, is one of the benchmarks of a well-controlled audit organization. It shows a setting of clear and quantifiable objectives. It implies a firm agreement with management in those objectives. Thus, when the cost-reduction itch starts, when ill-conceived and ineffective functions are subjected to the analytical glare of executive management, then the well-developed program of audits may be one of the reasons for keeping the auditing department from being reduced or eliminated.

The Program as Notice to the External Auditor

The external auditor usually structures his own audit verification effort to take into account the system of internal control.

The long-range audit program provides him with insight as to how internal control is being monitored, how the keystone of internal control — the internal audit — is operating, and permits him to pattern his own program so as to complement or coincide with the internal audit program.

Through prearrangement, specific internal audit projects may be so scheduled that they will provide the external auditor with adequate assurances and permit him to limit his own tests of internal control. This form of cooperation may provide for welcome reductions in the cost of the external audit[1].

THE STRUCTURE OF THE LONG-RANGE PROGRAM

The infinite variety of company structures and purposes makes a common program for all an impossibility. No two companies are truly alike; in fact, most are quite different. Thus no two programs can be alike. While production control may be of great significance to one company, it may be nonexistent in another. Inventory control will patently be more important to a retail store than it would be to an insurance company.

Hence, while no one long-range program will have universal applicability, an organized approach can meet the needs of many. Exhibit 3-1 gives the outline of a long-range program which provides a structure that can be adapted to most companies. In addition to the bare outline, a number — certainly nowhere near all — of potential areas of coverage are shown.

The program is divided into major areas of review. This program covers a five-year span. That span could be two, three, or four years, depending on the number of years between particular audits. If no area of coverage remains unreviewed for more than three years, then a longer span for a long-range program may not be applicable. Whatever the span, however, the program should be reevaluated every year to account for changes in company structure, product lines, and audit emphasis.

The first two columns in the program show, by project number and report date, the last time that the particular audit was performed. The third column lists the identification numbers of the applicable permanent or master program files. The fourth column describes the area of coverage. The fifth column shows the evaluation of the project in terms of urgency, from 1 (extreme urgency) to 5 (least urgency). The sixth column shows the frequency with which the audits should be made: every 1, 2, 3, 4, or 5 years. The next five columns show the years in which the audits should be made and the number of man-days allotted to each project.

In most cases, the budgets are for specific projects. In others, as in reviews of EDP activities or follow-up reviews, lump sum budgets are set out to be expended as circumstances warrant during the year.

---

[1]Abbott, J. W., "The External Auditor - Colleague or Rival," *The Internal Auditor*, Winter 1964, p. 34.

Exhibit 3-1 has been compressed to make it easier to understand and to make it applicable to a greater variety of companies. For example, in some companies, procurement, which is shown only as one line in the exhibit, could very easily be expanded to include such matters as material requirements, shortage controls, scrap disposition, selection of suppliers, documentation of purchases, administration of subcontracts, and so forth.

An alternative program format is shown in Exhibit 3-2. This suggested program, even more truncated for purposes of illustration, suggests using a three-year span, but allocates the coming year's budget to each of the four quarters. This program format provides for spelling out deferred projects and the time allocated to those projects. Thus, management obtains visibility on those areas of audit coverage which cannot be included in the three-year cycle in the light of current audit department budgets.

The allocated man-days, the scheduled frequencies, and the classification of priorities in the two programs illustrated should not be regarded as suggestions for actual use. They are all purely fictitious. Each audit organization must decide for itself what priorities to assign to its audit projects and how many days to allocate to those projects.

PROGRAM BUDGETS

One approach to budgeting is to start with the authorized level of audit personnel. Multiply that number by the available man-hours in the year. This base must then be reduced by vacation time, sick leave, employee training, staff meetings and the like. The remainder is available for audit work.

This remainder is broken down into programmed and nonprogrammed work. The amount of nonprogrammed work is set aside — based on past experience, discussions with management, or the best available forecasts — for special requests from management, follow-up of prior deficiencies, reviews of especially sensitive activities, research, and the like.

What time remains is allotted to specific audit assignments. The budget assigned to each audit project is in essence what the director of auditing can afford to spend (or cannot afford *not* to spend) on the particular audit. Some budgets are developed intuitively. Intuition is a personal matter incapable of precise analysis. But past experience can be recorded and preserved on a simple form.

The form should be completed at the conclusion of each regularly programmed audit assignment. It should be prepared by the person in the best position to provide the information; namely, the auditor

Exhibit 3-1. LONG-RANGE AUDIT PROGRAM: FIVE-YEAR SPAN

Audit Proj. No.	Rep't Date	Perm. File No.	Audit Project	Class	Freq.	1973	1974	1975	1976	1977
			MARKETING							
64-20	1-70	M-1	Advertising Dep't.	3	3	40			40	
70-18	2-71	M-2	Sales Dep't. — Product A	3	3		50			50
71-25	3-72	M-3	Sales Dep't. — Product B	3	3			50		
70- 2	4-70	M-4	Branch X	3	3	30			30	
71- 4	5-71	M-5	Branch Y	3	3		30			30
71- 7	6-72	M-6	Branch Z	3	3			30		
68- 9	7-68	M-7	Customer Service Dep't.	4	5	40				
71- 8	8-71	M-8	Contract Administration	2	3		40			40
			Total			110	120	80	70	120
			INDUSTRIAL RELATIONS							
70-13	9-70	IR-1	Safety Dep't.	3	3	30			30	
69-19	10-69	IR-2	Personnel Records	4	4	40				40
72-20	12-72	IR-3	Employment	3	3			30		
			Total			70	—	30	30	40
			ENGINEERING							
69-15	1-70	E-1	Research and Development	2	3	50			50	
71-13	2-72	E-2	Drawings — Quality	2	2		60		60	
10-20	3-71	E-3	Drawings — Schedule	2	3		50			50
71- 2	4-71	E-4	Technical Information and Data	3	4			50		
69- 5	5-70	E-5	Engineering Files	4	5			50		
			Total			50	110	100	110	50
			MANUFACTURING OPERATIONS							
70- 4	6-70	MO-1	Manufacturing Engineering	3	5			50		
72- 1	7-72	MO-2	Procurement	1	1	100	100	100	100	100
70- 9	8-70	MO-3	Quality Control	2	3	60			60	
71- 5	9-71	MO-4	Production Control	2	3		50			50
71-12	10-71	MO-5	Material Control	2	2	50		50		50
72-13	11-72	MO-6	Stores	2	3			40		
69-22	12-69	MO-7	Scheduling	3	4	30				30
70-17	1-71	MO-8	Receiving	3	4			40		
71-20	2-72	MO-9	Tooling	2	4				50	
71-22	3-72	MO-10	Time Studies	4	5					**50**
70- 3	4-70	MO-11	Traffic	3	4		**50**			
71- 6	5-71	MO-12	Shipping	3	5				**30**	
			Total			240	200	280	240	280

Calendar Year / Man-Days

No.	Ref	Date								
ACCOUNTING										
72-5	A-1	6-72	Budgets and Forecasts	1	1	40	40	40	40	40
72-4	A-2	7-72	Cost Distribution	2	2		50		50	
72-6	A-3	8-72	Inventories	2	2	30	40		40	
70-11	A-4	9-70	Timekeeping	3	3	50		50	30	50
71-3	A-5	10-71	Payroll	2	2	30	30	30		30
72-12	A-6	11-72	Billing	1	1	50		50	30	50
71-9	A-7	12-71	Accounts Payable	2	2		50			
71-19	A-8	1-72	Accounts Receivable	2	2		40		50	
71-21	A-9	2-72	General Accounting	3	3					40
			Total			200	250	170	240	210
FINANCE										
71-1	F-1	3-71	Mail Room	2	2	40	30	40	30	40
72-3	F-2	4-72	Cash Receipts	1	1	30	30	30	20	30
72-2	F-3	5-72	Cash Disbursements	1	1	30	20	20	30	20
70-7	F-4	6-70	Credit	3	2	20	20		30	
72-7	F-5	7-72	Cash Planning	2	2					
69-12	F-6	8-69	Insurance	2	2					
			Total			120	100	90	110	90
ELECTRONIC DATA PROCESSING										
72-8	EDP-1	8-72	Installation	1	1	50	50	50	50	50
72-9	EDP-2	9-72	Maintenance	1	1	50	50	50	50	40
			Total			100	100	100	100	90
FUNCTIONAL EXAMINATIONS										
71-14	FE-1	10-71	Conflict of Interest							
72-11	FE-2	11-72	Rotation of Employees in Key Positions	3	2					
70-16	FE-3	12-70	Incorporation of Engineering Changes	3	2	40	50	70	40	50
			Total			40	50	70	40	50
SPECIAL EXAMINATIONS										
Various	SE-1		Special Management Requests	1	1	100	100	100	100	100
Various	SE-2		Follow-up Audits	1	1	50	50	50	50	50
Various	SE-3		Audits of Suppliers	1	1	100	100	100	100	100
Various	SE-4		Sensitive Control Areas	1	1	50	50	50	50	50
			Total			300	300	300	300	300
			Grand Total			1230	1230	1220	1240	1240

Exhibit 3-2. LONG-RANGE AUDIT PROGRAM: THREE-YEAR SPAN

Perm. File No.	Subject	Audit Freq. (Yrs)	Last Audit Date	Man-days Sch.	Man-days Act.	1973 (Quarters) 1	2	3	4	1974	1975	Defer
	Area A											
A-1	Subject 1	3	5/71	20	22					20		
A-2	Subject 2	2	4/71	20	15		15					
A-3	Subject 3	3	4/72	10	11							10
	Area B											
B-1	Subject 1	2	11/71	25	31				30			
B-2	Subject 2	3	6/72	25	26						25	
B-3	Subject 3	1	2/72	35	32			30				
	Area C											
C-1	Subject 1	1	4/72	20	24		20					
C-2	Subject 2	3	1/72	25	20							20
C-3	Subject 3	2	2/71	35	25	40						
	Area D											
D-1	Subject 1	3	10/70	10	11				10			
D-2	Subject 2	3	6/72	25	35						30	
D-3	Subject 3	2	10/72	40	39					40		
	Misc.			50	60		15	15	15	15	60	
	Special Mgm't Requests			40	80		20	20	20	20	80	

in charge of that assignment. For at that point he knows more about that audit activity than anyone else.

The auditor should record on the form his conclusions as to (1) the significance of the job (should it be repeated and, if so, how soon); (2) whether the job is important enough to stand on its own feet, or whether it can be combined with one or more other jobs; (3) whether the audit thrust should be altered on future jobs; (4) what is a reasonable budget for the job, either as a survey or as a full-scale audit assignment; (5) what parts of the job absolutely must be done to protect the company and what parts can be slighted with impunity; and (6) what parts of the job should be followed up before the next regularly scheduled assignment. Exhibit 3-3 is one example of such a form.

The executed form should be kept in the permanent file as assistance (1) to the auditor who next does the job, and (2) to the director of auditing or the audit managers in developing their long-range program.

Exhibit 3-3. AUDIT ANALYSIS

Question	Answer (Give reasons)
1. Should this audit project be repeated?	
2. If the answer is **yes** —	
a. How soon?	
b. Should it be combined with another project?	
c. What budget is recommended:	
(1) As a full-scale project?	
(2) As a survey?	
3. What parts of the audit project —	
a. Should be scheduled for an interim examination?	
b. Must be covered or warrant special attention in future examinations?	
c. Should be eliminated in future examinations?	
4. What suggestions do you have for the auditor making the next examination in this area?	

_____   _____
Auditor in Charge   Date

ACTIVITIES NEEDING SPECIAL AUDIT EMPHASIS

Certain activities within a company are particularly susceptible to improprieties, manipulation, or significant loss. These activities are usually of serious concern to executive management. They should be of equal concern to the auditor. Like weak links in a chain, they are most susceptible to failure. Then, when breakdown occurs, the manager's lifted eyebrow is invariably turned toward the auditor. And the auditor who has failed to foresee the potential difficulty has no one but himself to blame.

Each company has its peculiar problem areas. Only that company's auditors can isolate and pinpoint them. These areas deserve special consideration and special assurance to management that they are being given proper audit scrutiny. These areas should be researched and listed, and the list should be regularly reviewed and revised as circumstances change.

Once identified, the sensitive areas should be interwoven into the fabric of the regular audit program and audited when the related activity is covered. An audit of deliveries by-passing the Receiving Department — often particularly susceptible to fraud — can be performed as a part of the Receiving Department audit. But the inherent dangers are· such as to demand special assurances that direct deliveries are not overlooked in the regular Receiving audit. Other areas may be covered in special audits.

Exhibit 3-4 is an example of a listing of "Activities Requiring Special Audit Emphasis." It includes sensitive control areas common to many companies. It can be expanded or revised to include areas peculiar to particular companies. The exhibit lists the activities — whose titles make them self-explanatory — the permanent file most applicable to that activity, the latest audit report (audit project number and report date) and the period scheduled for the next review. This period may coincide with the regular audit, or it may represent special scheduling for an interim or follow-up review.

The listing should be reviewed with management at the same time as the long-range program is reviewed. This will offer management an opportunity to add to the list, to be made aware of the special audit coverage, and to be alerted to the penalties of reducing the audit scope.

NONAUDITING LONG-RANGE OBJECTIVES

An audit organization is no different from any other business entity: It grows or it atrophies. It cannot tie its life line to past experience alone. The rest of the company, to be successful, is learning, adapting, expanding, and testing new ideas. The director of auditing cannot do less if he is adequately to serve his profession, his company, and his people.

Admittedly, it is hard to fit nonauditing objectives into a busy and sometimes backbreaking audit schedule. But there is no choice. It is a case of improve or perish. And somehow, some way, there are always means by which that schedule can accommodate more; especially when the need is understood — when the potential benefits are brought home to the audit group.

But such objectives must be more than wishful dreams. They must be implemented through quantifiable goals. They must call for enumerated tasks. They must result in set schedules. They must be controlled. And of equal importance, they must be keyed to certain continuing objectives that will lift the auditor out of his daily routine and out of himself — show him that he can make himself better than he thinks he is.

First, then, comes the setting of these continuing objectives — objectives that persist as long as the auditing organizations shall continue — a guiding star by which to steer the audit craft. These objectives must be set by the director of auditing and should reflect his own philosophy of what he considers most significant to the growth of his organization. The objectives should be high-minded and should make mind-stretching demands.

It would not be amiss to key these objectives to the trinity of aims mentioned in the first paragraph of this section: profession, company, people. Thus, the continuing objectives may be stated as follows:

- To make the auditing organization the leader in the profession.
- To expand the service to management.
- To help the individual auditor achieve greater dimension and stature.

All nonauditing development projects should be keyed to these fundamental objectives. In this way the development program has form and structure, and it will be balanced among plans that concern each of the three objectives.

Obviously, the director of auditing will have a selling job to do. He is asking his people to take on additional work. He is hoping the work will be done to some extent on their own time. He would like to see a personal commitment that can evoke the kind of effort and dedication that will accomplish the impossible and produce a superb product. He foresees his people marching to the same drums that beat in his own brain and developing a sense of pride and

Exhibit 3-4. ACTIVITIES REQUIRING SPECIAL AUDIT EMPHASIS

Activity	Applicable Permanent File	Latest Report	Scheduled for Next Review
Marketing			
No charge sales	M-2	70-18, 2-71	1974
	M-3	71-25, 3-72	1975
Industrial Relations			
Authority to drive into plant	IR-1	70-13, 9-70	1973
Vehicle inspection — entering and leaving plant	IR-1	70-13, 9-70	1973
Control of master keys	IR-1	70-13, 9-70	1973
Conflict of interest	IR-2	69-19, 10-69	1973
Wage and salary adjustments	IR-2	69-19, 10-69	1973
Engineering			
Company proprietary data	E-1	69-15, 1-70	1973
Designation of sole procurement source	E-4	71-2, 4-71	1975
Preparation of restrictive specifications	E-4	71-2, 4-71	1975
Manufacturing Operations			
Deliveries by-passing Receiving Department	MO-8	70-17, 1-71	1975
Scrap and salvage	MO-5	71-12, 10-71	1973
Control over selection of suppliers	MO-2	71-1, 7-72	1973
Control over purchase order changes	MO-2	72-1, 7-72	1973
Transportation and routing of materials	MO-11	70-3, 4-70	1974
Supplies susceptible to pilferage	MO-6	72-13, 11-72	1975

Accounting

Approval and payment of overtime	A-5	71-3, 10-71	1973
Payrolls	A-5	71-3, 10-71	1973
Bank reconciliations	A-9	71-21, 2-72	1974
Employee bonuses	A-5	71-3, 10-71	1973
Credit memo forms	A-6	72-12, 11-72	1973
Executive-approved invoices	A-7	71-9, 12-71	1973
Payments to suppliers	A-7	71-9, 12-71	1973
Accounts payable check mailing	A-7	71-9, 12-71	1973
Fixed assets	A-9	71-21, 2-72	1974

Finance

Blank, void, and mutilated checks	F-3	72-2, 5-72	1973
Undelivered checks	F-3	72-2, 5-72	1973
Facsimile signature plate	F-3	72-2, 5-72	1973
Cashier's funds	F-3	72-2, 5-72	1973
Petty cash funds	F-3	72-2, 5-72	1973
Cash receipts	F-2	72-3, 4-72	1973
Credit approvals	F-4	70-7, 6-70	1973
Travelers checks	F-3	72-2, 5-72	1973
Metered postage	F-1	71-1, 3-71	1973

Other

Rotation and vacations of employees in key control positions	SE-4	71-25, 3-72	1974

achievement that money itself cannot buy.

But whether these projects are undertaken through persuasion, cajolery, or outright directive, they must be undertaken ... they must be a part of the long-range program. Resting on laurels is a debilitating posture.

There is no end to the development projects that can be pursued. Each year the director of auditing should ask his own people which projects they wish to undertake. Proposals for new projects should be carefully screened to avoid duplication, frivolous excursions into unreality, exercises not worth the effort, or projects having no reasonable relation to the continuing objectives.

Once approved, each project should be carefully controlled. The proposal should be accompanied by a schedule of specific milestones and a set of standards by which to measure accomplishments. Such standards or units of measurement might be a research report, or a new manual, or a new pro forma program. Or they might be the number of audit projects in which a particular new technique is to be employed.

Development projects should be keyed to the needs of each individual audit organization. The examples that follow are merely some ideas of the projects that can be scheduled, relating them to the three prime objectives and showing the standards or units of measurement that can be applied:

Project	Due date	Standard of measurement
1. To make the auditing organization the best in the profession.		
A. Expand the use of EDP in making sample selections	Dec. 19XX	5 audits
B. Experiment with oral presentations and visual aids	Dec. 19XX	10 audits
C. Develop a style manual for report writing	Dec. 19XX	Completed manual
D. Experiment with the use of questionnaires to obtain data for audit examinations	Nov. 19XX	Two proposed questionnaires

Project	Due date	Standard of measurement
E. Establish dollar budget controls over various phases of audit examinations and reporting	June 19XX	Research report
2. Expand the service to management		
A. Develop or improve a system of classifying deficiency findings to afford management a basis for broad, corrective action, throughout the company, through analysis of causes	July 19XX	List of deficiency causes
B. Develop or improve an annual summary report to management on the adequacy and effectiveness of its controls, based on audits made during the year	Nov. 19XX	Pro forma report
C. Perform research into the needs of various levels of management for audit assistance	June 19XX	Research report
D. Develop or improve summary reports to management on audit results accumulated by families of jobs	June 19XX	Two proposed summaries
E. Develop or improve a system of reporting significant findings in common areas as an aid to management in perceiving potential deficiencies, their causes, and the results if uncorrected	Dec. 19XX	Ten significant findings

Project	Due date	Standard of measurement
3. Help auditors achieve greater dimension and stature		
A. Encourage auditors to take outside courses	Dec. 19XX	Completion of 10 courses
B. Encourage participation in the professional organization of internal auditors	June 19XX	Two new members One chapter officer One international officer
C. Develop or improve a program of counseling with staff auditors on their future education and training	Dec. 19XX	Annual counseling with all staff auditors
D. Establish and hold training programs for auditors on such subjects as:		

- ■ Use of EDP in audits
- ■ Statistical sampling
- ■ Report writing
- ■ Flowcharting
- ■ Audit programming
- ■ Oral presentations
- ■ Visual aids
- ■ Referencing reports
- ■ Office regulations

Each quarter, or at least semiannually, the director of auditing should receive status reports of these projects. When the projects are completed, appropriate recognition should be accorded those who accomplished their objectives. Also, the annual or semiannual reports to management on audit accomplishments should give prominent place to these accomplishments as well. The last chapter of·this book contains examples of such reports.

REVIEWS WITH MANAGEMENT

The audit program has significance to management to the extent that management becomes involved in its development. Reviewing the proposed program with management obtains both its involvement and its blessing. The review meetings provide for an interchange of ideas and an understanding of management's problems and needs.

These reviews should be undertaken first at the branch or division level; that is, in terms of Exhibit 3-1, they would be undertaken with the directors or vice presidents of Marketing, Industrial Relations, Engineering, Operations, Accounting, and Finance.

The audit representatives should prepare well for the reviews. They should provide copies of the program for each functional organization. They should come prepared to answer the questions that are bound to be asked and to take notes of the suggestions which the branch or division director makes. A record of these suggestions should be deposited in the appropriate permanent or master file.

In preparation for the meeting, the audit representatives should accumulate copies of all relevant audit reports. In addition, they should prepare brief notes of the audit objectives of each of the audit projects. In this way, they will have at their fingertips the answer to such questions as "What problems did you encounter the last time in the audit of personnel records?" or "How do you propose to examine the accuracy of engineering drawings?"

In addition, the audit representatives should inquire as to what impact new programs will have on branch activities; what aspect of current programs cause the director the most problems, and which programs appear to be phasing out and do not warrant audit attention. Finally, the audit representatives should solicit advice from the branch director as to the scheduling of the audits within his branch; which projects should be postponed — which projects should be advanced.

After the reviews at the branch level, the proposed program should be adjusted to accommodate the needs of management or to reflect new information obtained. At that point, it should be discussed with the top company executives, at the company president level, or with the audit committee of the board of directors. A summary of the program should be prepared to support the request for audit budget for the forthcoming year.

The presentation at the summit can be sparked by visual aids summarizing the last year's results, the proposed audit effort for the coming year, and the number of auditors required to accomplish the work.

COORDINATION WITH OTHER CONTROL AGENCIES IN THE COMPANY

Internal auditing does not stand alone as a monitor of control. In all large companies there are other agencies which may be equally concerned with matters of control. Their interest may have a more technical aspect; but it may complement the internal auditor's interests in the administrative aspects of control.

The security department is concerned with control over irregularities. The quality control department is concerned with control over product reliability and conformance to specifications. The safety department is concerned with control over accident prevention. The industrial engineering organization is concerned with control over operating practices and procedures. Depending on the nature of the company, other agencies may have comparable control functions.

Achieving Coordination

The internal auditing department should keep an open line of communications to these agencies in planning its audits. Valuable information can be obtained, either to reduce any possibility of duplicate surveillance or to point to areas where special audit emphasis may be warranted.

There are many ways in which this coordination can be accomplished. The following approaches are representative.

Security.   Hold periodic meetings with security personnel. Keep them informed of the ongoing audit projects. Solicit their suggestions on where manipulations or other improprieties have occurred or can occur. Offer to assist in reviewing records relating to ongoing security investigations; the auditor usually can locate the records more readily and accumulate the data more easily. Ask to be kept informed of ongoing investigations which indicate the possibility of control breakdowns.

Quality Control.   Exchange programs and reports with the quality control agency. Seek to be kept informed of repetitive defects in suppliers' goods or in-house manufactured products; there may be administrative control weaknesses contributing to the difficulties.

Safety.   Establish arrangements with the agency concerned with safety so that suspected dangers encountered in the audit can be immediately reported for investigation. And provide for feedback showing the nature of the corrective action.

Industrial Engineering. Provide for a pattern of preliminary discussions with the industrial engineers before engaging in audits in production areas. Clear any findings and recommendations with the industrial engineers when areas within their cognizance are involved. With their technical expertise they may be able to point to matters which the auditor may have overlooked in his findings and recommendations.

SUMMARY

The long-range audit program is a useful instrument that helps the director of auditing justify budgets, obtain management participation, establish standards for realization of audit goals, control the audit effort, show management what will and what will not be covered, and assist the external auditor in developing his own program.

There are many ways of structuring the program, but it is important to carry allotments of budget down to the individual audit projects. Each audit project should be considered in terms of its relationship to the entire audit effort. Projects should be evaluated in terms of their relative significance. This can be accomplished intuitively or on the basis of past experience.

Included in the program and made an integral part of it should be coverage of sensitive areas which experience teaches are subject to breakdown in control or to manipulation.

Along with the audit objectives, the director of auditing should establish long-term goals for improving the audit organization and its people and for constant upgrading of its service to management.

Reviewing the program with management affords an opportunity to determine management's needs, to obtain its involvement in the audit program, and to highlight the auditor's service to management.

Coordinating audit plans with other control agencies in the company can add breadth and depth to the audit scope. These agencies include Security, Quality Control, Safety, and Industrial Engineering.

four ■

STARTING, PLANNING AND
CONTROLLING THE AUDIT PROJECT

AUDIT ASSIGNMENTS

A well-controlled, well-structured internal audit project has a far better chance of meeting its goals than one that is haphazard and formless. True, the internal audit demands creative thinking and calls for the auditor to beat new paths and stretch old boundaries. But without control of budget and schedule and without clearly defined guides to get it going, the project tends to languish; it suffers from lack of discipline.

Discipline, from without and within, is the hallmark of the professional. His profession's stated criteria impose certain disciplines. His own well-developed standards provide the rest. These disciplines include a clear understanding of the value of the audit project in relation to the needs of the company. They also include an understanding of the value of timeliness and of the staleness of yesterday's news.

The long-range program has allotted a budget and schedule to the audit project assigned to the auditor. These budgets and schedules are part of the audit organization's master plan. They were set in contemplation of the value of the project to the company and the timing most suitable to the company. The auditor must therefore fit his own audit budget and schedule into the plans mapped out by the master program.

In this chapter, then, we shall discuss the very initial steps in assigning and planning of the audit project: controlling the audit projects, meeting budgets and schedules, dealing with budget revisions, providing for progress reports on the job, maintaining an overview of the projects in process, reviewing permanent files, and devising ways of reminding the auditor of what he should do to launch a project on its way.

CONTROLLING AUDIT PROJECTS

The first step in controlling any audit project is "getting it on the books." This is no different from establishing a work order to authorize approved work and to permit the expenditure of money and effort on such work. A simple form, controlled by a register, should be devised for the purpose.

The form might show the number and title of the project; the assigned budget; the name of the auditor-in-charge, his assistants, and his supervisor; and such other information that may be considered necessary. The register will control the assignment of project numbers and will provide a historical record of projects for ready reference. The register will remain under the control of the office secretary; copies of assignment records will be distributed to the auditor-in-charge, his supervisor, and the office file.

There is a tendency, in devising forms like these, to provide for every conceivable contingency. The forms then get complicated and forbidding. Some of the called-for information gets omitted, and the system collapses of its own weight. Worst of all, uncorrected neglect of any prescribed procedure tends to heap contempt on other procedures, resulting in incomplete records and tending to impair office administration. Exhibit 4-1 is a simple assignment record which provides essentially all the information needed to authorize a project.

Exhibit 4-1. PROJECT ASSIGNMENT ORDER

Title _____ In Charge _____

Project No. _____ Supervisor _____

Permanent File No. _____ Start Date _____

Programmed
Frequency _____

Programmed
Budget _____

Approved Budget _____
(After audit program approved)

Accounts to be Analyzed: _____

Reports to be Reviewed: _____

Special Instructions: _____

Authorized by _____

Date _____

Each audit organization will determine its own system of project numbering. A logical system will provide a simple means of showing the kind of project, the year, and the number of each project within each year's series. For example:

R7X-1   The first "regular" project specifically included in the long-range audit program for the year 197X.

M7X-2   The second project which was specifically requested by management during 197X.

S7X-3   The third special examination — not included in the long-range program — undertaken by the auditing organization because of special needs due to unexpected circumstances.

I7X-4   The fourth interim project, conducted between regularly programmed reviews. Interim reviews are designed to determine whether key controls or sensitive areas reviewed at intervals of two or more years are continuing to function as intended.

FU7X-5   The fifth follow-up project established to determine whether corrected deficiencies have recurred and whether the corrective action that had been instituted is still effective.

Res7X-1   The first research project of the year 197X undertaken to carry out plans for developing and expanding the effectiveness of the auditing organization.

Separate series of projects provide for more precise control over the audit organization's budget. For example, man-days expended on regular projects can be compared with the annual budget for those projects. The same is true for the budgets established for management requests, special work, research, and the rest. The means by which such accomplishments can be reported to management will be discussed in the final chapter of this book.

PROJECT BUDGETS AND SCHEDULES

Creative souls abhor control. Modern internal auditing is largely a creative activity. The auditors engaged in that activity sometimes argue that budget and schedule constraints stifle creativity. Nonsense. Any business activity functions only so long as there are funds to pay for it. And every activity has its price tag. Even pure research in a company engaged in scientific projects must be granted a budget and must have progress evaluated. True, the budgets may require adjustment when new conditions surface. Also true, however, is that the project may be eliminated or halted when the budget limitations are reached and no return can be foreseen.

In all audit activities, individual project budgets and schedules are essential. Without them there is a tendency to dawdle; a tendency to give equal weight to all segments of an audit — instead of determining which segments are the most significant and warrant the most attention; and a tendency to spend inordinate lengths of time to "tie up loose ends."

Accordingly, budgets and schedules on all assigned projects must become a normal way of life. And such controls, to be effective, must include a current recording and reporting system. The system should provide for:

■ A way for the auditor-in-charge to allot budget to the various segments of his audit project and to keep a record of the time spent on those segments.

■ A way for each staff man to report time charges during the current period — usually a month.

■ A way for the auditing department to report currently — usually monthly — on the status of all its current audit projects.

Exhibit 4-2 is a suggested work sheet for controlling individual project budgets. It is kept in the working papers and provides for allocating the entire budget to the various segments of the project from initial planning through completion of the final report.

Exhibit 4-2. TIME RECORD

Project No. _____

TIME CHARGES IN HOURS FOR WEEK ENDED:

W/P Ref.		Budget Orig.	Budget Rev.	Total Act'l	First Week	Week	Cum.	Week	Cum.	Week	Cum.	Week	Cum.	Week	Cum.	Week	Cum.	Week	Cum.	Week	Cum.
	Planning																				
	Field Work																				
	Total Field Work																				
	Report Writing																				
	Client Review																				
	Project Closure																				
	Total																				

Exhibit 4-3 is a suggested time report for every employee in the department. The report provides for an accounting for each hour in the work week. It provides for both programmed and nonprogrammed work and for vacations, holidays, and sick leave.

Exhibit 4-4 is a suggested monthly report which lists each project open at the end of the month, the budget allotted to it, the actual charges, the estimated date for completion of the field work and the estimated date for the release of the final report. The auditor-in-charge should make his initial estimate of field work completion at least by the midpoint of his audit.

BUDGET REVISIONS

While control through budgets is essential, that control should not be so rigid as to be self-defeating. The thrust of the internal audit is such that it cannot be reduced to a mechanical exercise. New projects, not previously undertaken, are constantly added to the program. And each old project either is attacked somewhat differently from the last or faces changes in organization or activity. Thus the budget system requires some flexibility without relinquishing formal control.

The rules for budget revision should be reasonable and simple. Yet, at the same time, they should not represent a cloak for incompetence or poor planning. Thus, budget adjustments should be entertained as soon as it is determined that the audit project undertaken is not the same as the project planned in the long-range program. By and large, then, budgets should generally be appraised for potential revision — either up or down — immediately after the preliminary survey and the preparation of the audit program.

The preliminary survey, discussed in detail in the chapter that follows, establishes the subject of the review, the theory of the audit approach, and the structure of the project. If the survey discloses new activities — different from those contemplated when the audit project was first programmed — appropriate budget adjustments should be requested and authorized. If the activities remain the same, any budget overruns that do occur should be explained, but not glossed over by extending the allotted budget.

For example, the present auditor-in-charge may have uncovered substantial deficiencies which required extended investigation. Or he may have been saddled with assistants whose work had to be done over or who required considerable attention. Or his audit tests may have required expansion to satisfy him of the reliability of

Exhibit 4-3. TIME REPORT

Name _____

Period Ended _____

Programmed Work:		W/E					W/E						W/E						W/E						W/E						W/E					
Proj. No.	Title	M	T	W	T	F	S	M	T	W	T	F	S	M	T	W	T	F	S	M	T	W	T	F	S	M	T	W	T	F	S	M	T	W	T	F	S
Non-Programmed Work:																																						
Abandoned projects																																						
Follow-up on completed proj.																																						
Special Investigations (Desc.)																																						
Other (Describe)																																						
Other Working Time:																																						
New employee training																																						
Staff meetings and training																																						
Research (Describe)																																						
Proofreading																																						
Supervisory and Adminis.																																						
IIA																																						
Secretarial and clerical																																						
Non-Working Time:																																						
Vacations																																						
Sick leave																																						
Approved time off																																						
Leave without pay																																						
Holidays																																						
Totals																																						

Exhibit 4-4. STATUS OF CURRENT PROJECTS AND PERSONNEL ASSIGNMENTS MONTH ENDED JANUARY 31, 197X

Personnel Assigned		Man-Days			Due Date	
Supervisor A Project		Budget	To Date	To Complete	Field Work Completion	Report Issue
Auditor 1 Project title		50	40	10	2-5-7X	
Ass't. A Project Number (date started)						
Auditor 2 Project title Project Number (date started)		35	31	4	1-29-7X	2-15-7X
Auditor 3 Project title Project Number (date started)		45	10	35	(1)	-
Supervisor B etc.						

(1) Not yet determined

his findings. These matters, while legitimately taking more time, have no effect on the basic element in the long-range audit program . . . the activities subject to review remain the same.

In effect, therefore, decisions to revise budgets should be made in terms of the long-term program. The difficulties normally inherent in an internal audit project are simply a matter for consideration in evaluating the auditor's accomplishments on that job. Accordingly, requests for budget revisions should clearly spell out the structural changes in the subject under review and should provide estimates of the additional time occasioned by those changes.

Similarly, where the survey and the resulting audit program indicate that coverage can profitably be restricted or reduced, prompt downward adjustments should be made at that point. It would be naive to assume that the auditor-in-charge will proceed with alacrity to offer to relinquish some of his treasured budget. Clearly, his job will be made easier if he can carry on a reduced audit with an unreduced allotment of man-days. But in order to evaluate his efforts, the budget should represent the time allotted for a reasonably proficient auditor to accomplish a particular examination. Accordingly, the supervisor or the audit manager should review the results of the survey and the proposed audit program to determine whether budget reductions as well as increases are in order.

INTERIM PROGRESS REPORTS

While more formal reports of progress will be prepared monthly or quarterly, the supervisor or audit manager cannot wait that long to know how his projects are proceeding. The supervisor or manager who is suddenly caught by surprise when the budget has been used up or the schedule has slipped — and the project is nowhere near completion — must turn his criticism inward.

The supervisor must function under the same rules that he expects operating managers to follow. Reduced to their essentials — and perhaps oversimplified — the guideposts of the good manager read: "Feedback," "Follow-up," and "No Surprises." Hence, the supervisor should expect from the auditors under his supervision a simple weekly report which provides this information. Exhibit

---

Exhibit 4-5. WEEKLY STATUS REPORT

Week ended_____

Audit Project _____

	Man-Days
Budget	_____
Prior week's cumulative total	_____
This week's total	_____
This week's cumulative total	_____
Budget still available	_____
Required to complete	_____

Audit Segments Over Budget

	Man-Days	
Segment	Budgeted	Over
1.	____	____
2.	____	____
3.	____	____

Action Required to Recover

1.

2.

3.

Potential Problems

_____
Auditor-in-Charge

Note: Submit this report to the supervisor by 10 a.m. each Monday.

4-5 is an example. It is designed to show the allotted budget, the man-days used through the prior week, the man-days used in the week just ended, and the anticipated man-days required to finish the job.

The form provides, also, for comments on anticipated problems and information on when assistants will be released. The latter information is quite important. It helps reduce assistants' stand-by time. The proper timing of assignments for assistants is a perennial problem; and the sooner the person in charge of assignments is aware of the release of an assistant, the better he can schedule the assignments.

SCHEDULE BOARDS

Scheduling staff assignments is not a simple chore at best. Slipped project schedules, unanticipated interruptions, and special requests from management complicate an already difficult task. Also, trying to get a clear picture of the current and downstream assignments of 20 or 30 auditors can boggle the mind. The project scheduler is well advised, therefore, to obtain some mechanical aid that is flexible and easy to keep up to date.

One device is a large cork board which makes use of assignment slips and numbered tack heads to show at a glance precisely what the scheduled assignments are for periods up to a year. Exhibit 4-6 pictures such a board — curtailed for greater clarity by showing only the month of January.

On the board that is illustrated, all the auditors in charge and all the assistants are grouped separately in alphabetical order. The supervisors are shown at the bottom of the board on differently colored slips of paper to differentiate the jobs which are under their supervision.

The entire board covers a period of a year, and each of the small squares represents one week. The scheduled assignments for each auditor-in-charge are written on cardboard strips of the same color as that assigned to the supervisor of the job. Each assistant is assigned a number and is represented by a broad-headed tack bearing that number. A string suspended vertically across the board — moved each week — indicates the current week.

To simplify explanations, Exhibit 4-6 shows the status of jobs for only one of the supervisors, Underwood. His jobs are written on blue cardboard slips. The note on Exhibit 4-6 explains the assignments.

Exhibit 4-6. ASSIGNMENT BOARD

JANUARY

Auditors in Charge
Astor
Burdick
Carson
Donald
Evans
Fields
Graham
Hoyt
Iverson
Johnson
King
Harmon

Assistants
1. Anderson
2. Burns
3. Chandler
4. Davis

	① • Interim Rev. of Stores (2) • ①		
• Receiving (6-4) •			
		③	③
• Res. and Develop. (6-4)			
④	④		④
• Quality Control (7-5)	Ⓥ	Ⓥ	
Ⓥ	Ⓥ		
		Ⓥ	Ⓥ
(Blue) UNDERWOOD	(Green) VICTOR	(Yellow) WALTERS	

Note:
Astor is working on a 2-week-long interim review of stores

- - -

Carson's Receiving project is carried over from a prior year and has 3 weeks to go. The 50-day budget is divided into 6 weeks for Carson and 4 weeks for his assistant, Anderson, whose number ① appears above the weeks he still will work on the project.

Fields' project on R and D starts in the second week in January. The project extends into February, which is not shown in this illustration.

- - -

Johnson's project began during the first week in January and extends into February.

- - -

Harmon, King, and Burns are scheduled for vacations, as indicated by the V's on the heads of the pins in the board.

PERMANENT FILES

Permanent files for internal audits will vary to some extent from those used in financial audits. In financial audits there is generally a consistent pattern in the conduct of the audit and the evaluation of the accounting data. The pattern in operating departments may not be that consistent.

Operating departments are often subject to constant flux and change in their activities. Product lines change. As one activity becomes reduced it may warrant consolidation with another. Organizations become restructured to accommodate changing conditions. The emphasis that had been given to a particular function yesterday may be entirely different from what is called for today.

Accordingly, the permanent files should be useful, but economical. They should not be cluttered with matters that will not be of help either in the current audit or in planning the long-range program. Some of the matters that can be useful are as follows:

Prior Audit Reports and Replies

Copies of all prior audit reports and replies provide a historical record of deficiencies, recommendations, and corrective action taken or proposed. They are a good index of the audit approaches taken in prior years, the audit emphasis, and the audit findings. Where the record indicates a continuing trend of satisfactory opinions, in toto or in part, the current audit programs may be structured to reduce audit emphasis accordingly. Continuing difficulties, on the other hand, would be a signal for increased emphasis.

Audit Reports from Other Company Divisions or Branch Offices

In multi-divisional audit organizations, where each issues its own audit reports under its own long-range program, copies of such reports give added insight into methods of attacking particular audit problems. Each internal auditor has his own techniques, preferences, and strengths; and each can learn from the work of another. Unique deficiencies unearthed in one division may hint of audit techniques that may not have been considered at other divisions.

Records of Reviews with Higher Management

The long-range program reviews that are held with higher management often throw a sharp light on the needs and problems of management. They can sometimes illuminate the dark corners of an audit subject and provide the auditor with a means of offering an improved service to management. Copies of the records of these reviews constitute an important part of the permanent file.

Post-Audit Reviews

These reviews (see Exhibit 3-3, the Audit Analysis form) provide conclusions and recommendations on audit approaches by the individual most qualified to make them — the auditor-in-charge who just completed the audit of the subject under consideration. His recommendations — if the current organization chart or other information indicates they are still relevant — provide helpful guides for the current program.

Auditors' Comments

All auditors, as a part of their current reviews, learn of matters which are of interest to the audit organization but which may not be germane to their own current audit purposes. Where such matters speak of emergent circumstances, they may warrant the immediate opening of a special project or the expansion of a current one. But if the demand is not immediate, the matter should be informally recorded and the record made a part of the permanent file of the appropriate audit project.

Records of Accounts and Reports

In many audit organizations, a copy of the chart of accounts is referenced to appropriate audit projects. In this way, there is assurance that the operating matters relating to these accounts will be covered in the long-range program or the accounts will be analyzed, if appropriate. Each permanent file, therefore, should contain a reference to the related accounts.

Also, management looks to the auditor to assure it of the validity and reliability of the management reports on which it leans in making its day-to-day decisions. Errors or improprieties in such reports can have serious repercussions if they contribute to incorrect decisions. Such reports should be reviewed by the auditor — to the extent he considers it necessary — when he engages in the audit of the particular activity. Records of these reports should likewise be referenced in the appropriate permanent files.

Miscellaneous Matters

There is considerable diversity of opinion among directors of auditing on what belongs in a permanent file. The miscellaneous matters which follow were taken from responses to our inquiries concerning program or permanent file material. They are indicative, in some ways, of how closely the auditing organization follows operating matters.

- ▪ A copy of each program and the related questionnaires applicable to a particular audit project, just so long as those programs and questionnaires remain applicable.

■ Organization charts, which are to be replaced or corrected as changes occur.

■ Contracts with labor unions; and copies of long-term contracts — such as those with concessionaires.

■ Flowcharts and descriptions of operations and of significant equipment and facilities.

■ Records of wage earners' incentive plans.

■ Lists of departments or cost centers, to help in the long-range planning and to assure coverage periodically.

■ Historical financial information.

■ Basic directives or instructions applicable to specific locations or activities.

■ Important correspondence specifically related to the audit project.

■ Summaries of audit time, segregated by subject matter and program sections, as an aid in planning future audits.

■ Summaries of periods (weeks, months, or quarters) test checked, to avoid repeating the same periods in subsequent audits.

■ Summaries of operating routines, highlighting internal control points.

■ Schedules of accounts receivable write-offs for use in future verifications.

■ Descriptions of major credit problems for use in future audit examination.

■ Photographs of locations, copies of price lists and sales brochures, and plats of plant layouts.

■ The latest 12-month financial and operations reports for each location.

■ For separately incorporated components: copies or digests of articles of incorporation; by-laws; minutes of board meetings; minutes of stockholders' meetings; capital stock authorizations; abstracts of changes in surplus accounts; abstracts of title to property; records of the last examination of public records for transfers of title; registration of mortgages, judgments, liens, and other relevant records of judicial proceedings; lists of lands and buildings; reconciliations of changes in surplus with earnings reported for tax purposes; descriptions of pending tax assessments; and claims for tax refunds.

PRELIMINARY PLANNING OF AUDIT PROJECTS

Between the time the auditor receives his assignment and the time he starts his preliminary survey, there are many things he can do to lay the foundations for the project and properly organize his work. The experienced auditor probably does it routinely from habit, although the habits he has developed may not be the best ones. The novice tends to do a great deal of fumbling in an internal audit before he gets down to actual surveys and examinations.

This initial period can be either disheartening or productive, depending on how well the auditor is guided through the preliminary phases of the audit project. And while each internal audit is likely to be different from the others, there are many initial steps that are common to all. These steps should be set forth in a reminder list that will ease the launching of the job and tend to break the natural inertia that takes place between the end of the last audit and the start of a new one.

The reminder list is in no way designed to inhibit initiative or creativity. It will merely make the planning easier. Without such a list, the auditor has a tendency to say "where do I start?" or "what do I do next?" and spends a good deal of time asking himself those questions. With it he can rapidly perform the necessary mechanical chores needed to get the project going in an organized fashion and gradually ease into the survey with a minimum of false starts. Besides, it will help him to organize his working papers more methodically and make the subsequent audit steps easier to perform.

Exhibit 4-7 is an example of such a reminder list. We shall discuss it in detail shortly; but even before he follows the instructions called for in the list, the auditor can take a few initial steps that give him the feeling of having made tangible inroads into the planning phase of the audit.

The very first thing the auditor should do is to prepare a table of contents for the first part of his working papers. This will discipline him into making provision for certain matters to be covered as the job progresses, and to establish his working paper references. This table of contents — and the documents and records to which they refer — will be applicable with little variation in most internal audit projects. An example is set forth as follows, together with explanatory comments in parentheses:

Table of Contents

Subject	Working paper reference
Referenced report draft	A-1
(Copy of the draft from which the final report was prepared, with marginal references to the applicable supporting working papers.)	
Report outline	A-2
(The skeletal structure of the proposed report, to be reviewed by the supervisor before the report is drafted.)	
Review notes	A-3
(Notes on reviews of report drafts with the audited management personnel.)	
Assignment sheet	A-4
(See Exhibit 4-1, Project Assignment Order.)	
Notes from permanent file	A-5
(Notes inserted in the permanent file, since the last audit, to indicate areas to be covered, problems encountered, people to talk to, etc.)	
Audit instructions	A-6
(Notes on discussions with the supervisor or audit manager on the conduct of the audit.)	
Prior audit report and replies	A-7
(Removed from the permanent file for ready reference during the audit examination.)	
Time record	A-8
(Record of time budgeted and used. See Exhibit 4-2)	
Project reminder list	A-9
(List of steps to take in performing the audit project. See Exhibit 4-7)	
Notes on preliminary contacts	A-10
(Record of discussions with or telephone calls to management personnel telling them of the proposed audit project.)	
Organization charts	A-11
(Copies of the major organization charts covering the audit area.)	
Policy statements, directives, procedures	A-12

Subject	Working paper reference
Tentative audit program	A-13

Tentative audit program — A-13
(Primarily, a brief record of the intended purpose, scope, and theory of the proposed audit and a preliminary assessment of its thrust and course.)

Audit program — A-14
(The formal audit program, prepared after the preliminary survey.)

Summary of prior audit findings and suggestions — A-15
(A list of all such matters brought out by the prior audit. The purpose is to determine whether corrective action has been effective or whether deficient conditions have recurred.)

Glossary of terms and abbreviations — A-16
(Each activity in a company has its own jargon. The auditor will pick up their terms or abbreviations and sprinkle them throughout his working papers. A glossary is needed for the uninitiated reviewer of the papers.)

Questionnaires and responses — B-1
(Formal or informal lists of questions asked of or mailed to the auditees, and the answers.)

Volume statistics — B-2
(Data showing the volume of transactions or other values relevant to the audit.)

Flow charts — B-3
(New or updated charts — charts from prior audits can be used, either intact or with some updating.)

Records of Audit Findings — B-4
(Reports of each individual deficiency finding and records of corrective action taken.)

Miscellaneous — B-5
(Any other information not relevant to individual audit segments or tests.)

AUDIT PROJECT REMINDER LIST

Because of the host of matters requiring attention to get many audit projects under way, it is desirable to have them conveniently listed so that they are not overlooked. Certainly, such lists are not intended to replace the auditor's ingenuity or imagination. On the other hand, there is no need for him to try to recall all the steps when a convenient list can readily accomplish the purpose.

The needs of different companies will be satisfied only by lists tailored to their individual activities and methods. And so no general list will be applicable to every company or operating entity. Nevertheless, a guide to the preparation of such a list is set forth as Exhibit 4-7.

The sample list is divided into three parts. The first part (Exhibit 4-7a) covers the planning phase and is relevant to the matters just listed in the pro forma table of contents for working papers. The second part covers certain matters, common to most projects, which would arise during the field work. The third part relates to the preparation of the audit report and the closing of the project. These last steps will be discussed in more detail in a subsequent chapter.

COST REDUCTIONS

There can be little doubt that cost reductions are close and dear to the heart of executive management. If a report of the correction of a serious deficiency ranks in the management mind at 7 on a scale of 10, then a solid cost reduction will rank at the very top or mighty close to it.

Some of the auditor's cost reductions will emerge from a combination of an existing condition, good luck, and a sparkle of insight. These events, however, like comets, flash but rarely across the auditor's sky. Yet this does not mean that cost reductions must always await a fortuitous union of occurrences. They can be hunted systematically, if the hunter knows where and how to look.

In many instances, cost reductions come about simply because a methodical man looked hard at a piece of equipment, a form, an EDP-prepared report, a manually prepared report, or a register, and then said to himself:

■ How can these activities be simplified?
■ How can this process be improved?
■ How can this form be combined with another?
■ How can this flow of work be rerouted?
■ How can this step be abolished entirely?
■ How can this amount of copying be done away with?

Exhibit 4-7a. AUDIT PROJECT REMINDER LIST

	Completed	
Planning	(x)	(NA)

1. Permanent file reviewed for:
   a. Audit Analysis sheet (Exhibit 3-3) of prior examination
   b. Prior audit report and related replies _____
   c. Notes and comments _____
2. Prepared a summary of the prior deficiencies and suggestions _____
3. Obtained Project Assignment Order (Exhibit 4-1) _____
4. Reviewed related reports from other audit organizations within the company _____
5. Reviewed the *Bibliography of Internal Auditing* for articles or research publications touching on the subject to be reviewed _____
6. Interviewed manager of organization(s) to be audited _____
7. Analyzed applicable organization charts, procedural instructions, and directives _____
8. Conducted preliminary survey _____
9. Prepared the audit program, making provision, where applicable, for
   a. Examination of assigned ledger accounts _____
   b. Review of applicable management reports _____
   c. Determination whether EDP reports received by the organization are needed _____
   d. Determination whether input provided to Data Processing by the organization is accurate, authentic, and timely _____
   e. Consideration of factors affecting income and other taxes _____
   f. Allocation of project man-days to audit program segments _____
   g. Use of statistical sampling _____
   h. Plans for issuance of interim reports _____
   i. Review of compliance with record retention provisions and security regulations _____
   j. Use of flow charts to evaluate control system _____
10. Reviewed audit program and this check list with the supervisor _____

_____	_____
Date	Supervisor

Exhibit 4-7b. AUDIT PROJECT REMINDER LIST

	Completed	
	(x)	(NA)

Field Work
1. Posted project time record each day and reported time each week to the supervising auditor
2. Forecasted calendar date of field work completion at mid-point of the field work
3. Discussed with client management personnel their availability for review of findings and of draft reports so as to anticipate vacations and other absences

Final
1. Completed record of audit findings and report outline, and reviewed them with the supervising auditor
2. Prepared report draft and cross-referenced it to the working papers
3. Transferred appropriate records to the permanent file
4. Prepared Audit Analysis sheet (Exhibit 3-3)
5. Described matters for consideration in other audit projects in writing and placed notes of such matters in the appropriate permanent files
6. Scheduled reviews of the draft report with client personnel
7. Confirmed status of completed and open deficiency findings either by test or by review with client personnel
8. Performed final verification of the draft report, as modified by reviews with client or otherwise, before submitting it for final typing
9. Prepared staff rating forms for assistants and reviewed them with the supervising auditor
10. Examined prior audit working papers and suggested to supervising auditor which should be retained and which destroyed
11. Completed current audit working papers and submitted them to the supervising auditor before filing them
12. Placed record of open findings in a follow-up file so that they would be monitored until considered closed
13. Returned all documents taken from office files to those files

---

Date   Auditor-in-Charge

The results of consistent, organized, methodical attacks on waste and duplication far exceed the rare flashes of genius. Thus, educating the staff to direct its efforts and attention to those records and activities where excessive cost may exist can have long-range benefits — for the company, and for the auditor in the eyes of management.

One such way is through a reminder list, to be used in each appropriate audit. An example of such a list is shown as Exhibit 4-8.

| Exhibit 4-8. REMINDER LIST FOR COST REDUCTION (Indicate Matters Reviewed) | | | | | | | |
Records	Elimi-nate	Combine	Sim-plify	Improve	Re-route	Elim. Copying	W/P Ref.
Forms							
Tabulated reports							
Manually prepared reports							
Logs and registers							
Equipment usage							

RECORDS OF IMPRESSIONS

Still another list is included in the auditor's catalogue of reminders. It helps provide a special service to management — information which will not ordinarily appear in the auditor's formal report. It is a record of the auditor's observations and impressions gained during the audit. An example of such a form is shown as Exhibit 4-9.

The information recorded on the form does not constitute the usual, objective compilation of well-documented facts. It is valuable nevertheless. Its value lies in the fact that management is concerned not only with the hard facts of the audit; it is also concerned about its people. The auditor is in an especially advantageous position to provide such information.

Exhibit 4-9. RECORD OF IMPRESSIONS

Audit Project   Title

Organization Audited

This record will serve to document your impressions of certain aspects of the organization you have reviewed. Complete it after each audit. Use it for each organization substantially involved in a functional review of many organizations. We plan to summarize the data so as to determine whether there are any general trends or problems throughout the company which should be brought to management's attention. Thus, unless there is an impression which directly relates to a specific deficiency finding, do not discuss the record with client personnel. If you feel you do not have sufficient information to answer a question, so state beneath each question.

Exhibit 4-9. (Cont.)

Yes or No

1. **Employee Morale**
   a. Do employees seem to have a good attitude toward their fellow employees, their jobs, their supervisors, and the company? _____
   b. Do they accept their assignments readily? _____
   c. Do they appear to support departmental and company goals? _____

2. **Working Habits**
   a. Do people appear to be working at a reasonable tempo? _____
   b. Do they apear to be conducting an excessive amount of personal business at work?
   c. Are working hours, lunch hours, and coffee breaks observed? _____
   d. Is supervision sympathetic toward employee complaints? Is supervision willing to take appropriate corrective action? _____
   e. Does the manager seem to keep employees informed? _____

3. **Organization and Staffing**
   a. Does the organization seem to be well organized to accomplish objectives? _____
   b. Are tasks segregated properly? _____
   c. Does work appear to flow in an orderly and economical manner?
   d. Do employees appear to be working within their job classifications? _____
   e. Do new employees appear to be receiving sufficient orientation and training? _____

4. **Supervision**
   a. Do supervisors appear to know their jobs, and do they have the respect of their employees? _____
   b. Do supervisors seem to be exercising control and providing direction to employees? _____

5. **Interface with Other Organizations**
   a. Does the organization seem to communicate effectively with interfacing organizations? _____
   b. Are there any obvious conflicts? _____
   c. Does there seem to be evidence of genuine cooperation? _____

6. **Working Areas**
   a. Do working areas seem to be properly laid out and maintained? _____
   b. Do location, noise levels, lighting, temperature, and housekeeping seem adequate and lend themselves to an effective operation? _____
   c. Does machinery and equipment seem to be properly maintained? _____
   d. Do employees seem to have adequate equipment? _____

In the following space explain any adverse ratings. If specific deficiency findings appear relevant to any of the adverse ratings, reference them.

_____   _____   _____
Supervisor   Auditor-in-Charge   Date

Very often, poor performance cannot be traced solely to inoperative controls or inadequate instructions. It can sometimes be the result of slovenly habits, poor morale, inappropriate organizational structure or work flow, indifferent supervision, clashes with interfacing organizations, badly maintained facilities and equipment, and general environment. Such inadequacies can have a profound effect on production. And where conditions like these exist, the auditor has a duty to bring them to management's attention.

Obviously, this concept involves some delicate and sensitive balances. The impressions should not be recorded lightly. They should be based on more than one fleeting observation. And they should not be broadcast to line personnel, because the practice could easily evoke the cry of "company spy."

On the other hand, when the defects are the direct cause of reportable deficiencies — and can be readily demonstrated — they should be promptly discussed with line management, along with the objectively established deficiency. But in general these reports should not be presented individually to higher management. Rather, they should be summarized periodically to determine whether they represent undesirable trends throughout the organization — symptoms of a general malaise deserving special attention to improve employee relations and working conditions.

These reports should be handled with discretion; but properly used, they can perform a special service for management.

FRAUD

The auditor has no responsibility for detecting fraudulent acts. But the sad fact is that when fraud is discovered by someone other than the auditor, management will almost invariably ask, "Where were the auditors?" While the auditor cannot reasonably be considered to be an *insurer* against fraud, his examinations should be made with due professional skill and care. This includes requisite knowledge and training in his field. It is well for the director of auditing, therefore, to equip his staff with information that will alert them to known indicators of fraud. He will then be on record as having taken prudent and reasonable steps to educate his staff to the danger signals that can warn of the possibility of fraud.

Two exhibits have been provided for this purpose. Exhibit 4-10 is a list of signals that point toward the possibility of embezzlement. Exhibit 4-11 is a list of common forms of fraud. Each staff auditor should become familiar with them. No such lists can be all-inclusive; but they are indicative.

Exhibit 4-10. DANGER SIGNS THAT POINT
TOWARD THE POSSIBILITY
OF EMBEZZLEMENT

■ Regularly borrowing small amounts from fellow employees.

■ Placing undated or post-dated checks in change funds.

■ Requesting people to "hold" the maker's checks.

■ Issuing personal checks that are cashed by the company and returned by the bank for reasons indicating irregularity.

■ Being responsible for collectors or creditors appearing at the place of business.

■ Making excessive use of the telephone to stall creditors.

■ Making it a practice to cover up inefficiencies, or to plug figures.

■ Criticizing others unfairly, in an attempt to divert suspicion.

■ Placing unauthorized I.O.U.'s in change funds, or prevailing upon people in authority to accept I.O.U.'s for small, short-term loans.

■ Answering audit questions with unreasonable explanations.

■ Becoming annoyed at reasonable questions.

■ Excessive gambling losses; and gambling in any form.

■ Drinking excessively, nightclubbing, or associating with questionable characters.

■ Acquiring through "business" channels expensive automobiles and extravagant household furnishings.

■ Explaining a higher standard of living as money left from an estate.

■ Refusing to leave the custody of records during the day; working overtime regularly.

■ Refusing to take vacations or accept promotions.

■ Suffering extended illnesses or being affected by illness in the family without a reasonable plan for paying the medical bills.

■ Associating with and being entertained by a member of a supplier's staff.

■ Carrying an unusually large bank balance, or making heavy purchases of securities.

■ Bragging about exploits, and/or carrying unusual amounts of cash.

■ Rewriting records under the guise of neatness.

When fraud is suspected, the auditor is best advised to consult with the security people who are equipped by training and experience to obtain statements and confessions without laying the company open to suits for such matters as false imprisonment, slander, and defamation of character.

Exhibit 4-11. COMMON FORMS OF FRAUD

■ Pilfering stamps.
■ Stealing merchandise, tools, supplies, and equipment.
■ Removing small amounts from cash funds and registers.
■ Failing to record sales of merchandise, and pocketing the cash.
■ Creating overages in cash funds and registers by under-recording.
■ Overloading expense accounts or diverting advances to personal use.
■ Lapping collections on customers' accounts.
■ Pocketing payments on customers' accounts, issuing receipts on scraps of paper or in self-designed receipt books.
■ Collecting an account, pocketing the money, and charging it off; collecting charged-off accounts and not reporting the collections.
■ Charging customers' accounts with cash stolen from the accounts.
■ Issuing credit for false customer claims and returns.
■ Failing to make bank deposits daily, or depositing only part of the money.
■ Altering dates on deposit slips to cover stealing.
■ Making round sum deposits — attempting to catch up by the end of the month.
■ Carrying fictitious extra help on payrolls, or increasing rates or hours.
■ Carrying employees on the payroll beyond the actual severance dates.
■ Falsifying additions to payrolls; withholding unclaimed wages.
■ Destroying, altering, or voiding cash sales tickets and pocketing the cash.
■ Withholding cash sales amounts by using false charge accounts.
■ Recording unwarranted cash discounts.
■ Increasing amounts of petty cash vouchers and/or totals in accounting for disbursements.
■ Using personal expenditure receipts to support false paid-out items.
■ Using carbon copies of previously used original vouchers, or using a properly approved voucher of a prior period by changing the date.
■ Paying false invoices, either self-prepared or obtained through collusion with suppliers.
■ Increasing the amounts of suppliers' invoices through collusion.
■ Charging personal purchases to the company through the misuse of purchase orders.

Exhibit 4-11. (Cont.)

- Billing stolen merchandise to fictitious accounts.
- Shipping stolen merchandise to an employee or relative's home.
- Falsifying inventories to cover thefts or delinquencies.
- Seizing checks payable to the company or to suppliers.
- Raising canceled bank checks to agree with fictitious entries.
- Inserting fictitious ledger sheets.
- Causing erroneous footings of cash receipts and disbursements books.
- Deliberately confusing postings to both control and detail accounts.
- Selling waste and scrap and pocketing the proceeds.
- Selling door keys or combinations to safes or vaults.
- Creating credit balances on ledgers and converting the differences to cash.
- Falsifying bills of lading and splitting the revenue with the carrier.
- Obtaining unprotected blank checks and forging the signature.
- Permitting special prices or privileges to customers, or granting business to favored suppliers, for "kickbacks."

SUMMARY

Audit projects require management control and guidance to keep them on track and on target, and to alert audit supervision to any impending difficulties. Some of the means of control are:

- Project assignment orders to authorize the individual projects and to "get them on the books."
- Assigned budgets and schedules, and a means for reporting against them.
- A formal system of authorizing budget revisions.
- Weekly reports of progress.
- Visible records of the status of current projects and those that are imminent, to simplify the auditing organization's assignment chores.
- Economical and helpful permanent files.
- Guides and reminder lists to the preliminary planning of audit projects.
- Reminder lists to make sure that all basic and routine matters are expeditiously handled, and that all matters of interest to management will not be overlooked.

PERFORMING THE PRELIMINARY SURVEY

THE PURPOSE OF THE PRELIMINARY SURVEY

Simply stated, the purpose of the preliminary survey is familiarization. But familiarization for the auditor is different from familiarization for the casual observer. The auditor must not only view the scene and read the words — he must hear the music too. He must do more than observe the flow of work. He must perceive the true objectives ... he must pinpoint the key controls ... he must understand the management style ... he must test the quality of the employees. Only then will he be able to determine significant control points, develop a thoughtful audit program, deploy his audit efforts economically, and form a firm foundation for the examination that follows.

Inadequate familiarization can result in a lack of understanding of what the audit assignment really is; in an inept audit program; in spending too much time on one activity and too little on another; in overemphasizing the insignificant; in not understanding the information he is garnering; in not understanding the people he must deal with and therefore not being able to deal with them — in short, in frustration.

Where a poor survey, or no survey at all, can result in a poor audit or a wasted one, a good survey may not only insure an intelligent audit examination — but may also sometimes be sufficient to substitute for many parts of the detailed examination. Yet the preliminary survey is very often given short shrift by the auditor. And more's the pity, because it is one of the most useful and incisive tools available to cut through the mystifying mass of detail that blocks a clear view of the audit objectives, and to get the audit job started quickly and in the right direction.

Many operations in large companies are extremely complex. Often, the people engaged in an activity can spend years working on it without truly understanding all its facets — much less the interface between such facets and those of companion activities. Clearly, then, the auditor who seeks not only to understand the activity but also to evaluate it and suggest improvements has a baffling path to follow. And the path gets rockier and thornier as business activities get more complex . . . as the computer injects its ubiquitous tentacles into the scene . . . as managers learn to use more sophisticated management techniques, such as operations research and statistical inference . . . as the external environment, such as legal restrictions, political atmosphere, ecology, public relations, employee relations, market conditions, changing technology, safety requirements, and stockholders' concern impinge on the internal operation of the activity . . . as management styles change and as middle management turns and twists to keep pace with new executive postures.

It is a baffling path indeed. A forbidding one. And the human mind, with its limitations on absorbing and remembering, is boggled by the mass of information, nuances, relationships, causes, and effects that must be gathered, sorted out, absorbed, and put to practical use. But no mass of data has yet been accumulated that cannot be given some semblance of order and in some way be arrayed, summarized, and evaluated — if done in a logical, organized, and methodical manner. And that is what the preliminary survey is all about: Collect data, array it, summarize it, evaluate it, and put it to use in developing an audit program.

Put in simpler terms, the preliminary survey answers these questions about an activity for the auditor:[1]

- ■ What is the job?
- ■ Who does it?
- ■ Why is it done?
- ■ How is it done?

And throughout, he must learn to understand the people doing the work and the managers who seek to lead them.

To develop this information accurately, completely, and economically, there are certain qualities and abilities that the auditor should have or acquire:

- ■ He must be able to equip himself for the preliminary survey so as to be in a position to ask intelligent questions and develop suitable questionnaires.
- ■ He must be able to set a cooperative, participative tone for the audit during his first meeting.
- ■ He must have a clear understanding of the information he needs, the sources for that information, and how to obtain it.
- ■ He should be adept at the technique of flowcharting so as to draw pictures of complex operations which narrative descriptions would not convey.
- ■ He must have an understanding of objective-oriented management, because without clear-cut objectives, activities may drift and flounder; and if the auditor does not understand the activity's objectives, his audit may also drift and flounder.
- ■ He must understand the theory of control — and its anatomy, with all its diverse forms.
- ■ He must know how to assess the background and training of the people that staff the activity under review.
- ■ He must be able to extract from the ore he has mined those risks that lie beneath the surface of an activity or are implicit in its operations.

These are the subjects we shall explore in the remainder of this chapter.

---

[1]Inman, C. N., "Managerial Auditing of Operations," *The Internal Auditor* June 1958, p. 50.

PREPARATION FOR THE PRELIMINARY SURVEY

Get what's important and get it fast. That is the essence of a good preliminary survey. Focus on the highlights; the detail will come later. Get the view from the skies; not from the ground. The purpose of the preliminary survey will be frustrated by a laborious, time-consuming reading and digesting of manuals, job instructions, and reports.

The auditor's office review, after he has been given his assignment and made a start on organizing his working papers (Chapter 4) should provide enough insight about the activity he will audit so as to enable him to ask reasonably intelligent questions. Nobody expects the auditor to be an expert on the activity's affairs at the outset; but he is expected to have a general familiarity of where it stands in the company hierarchy and what it is supposed to be doing.

The result of the office review will be a brief questionnaire to guide the auditor's discussions with the auditee-manager. The questionnaire can readily be developed from the following records:

■ The permanent file
■ The prior audit report
■ Management's charter for the activity to be reviewed

From this material the auditor can devise questions to suit his audit objectives and to pose to the auditee-manager at their first meeting. But let haste not interfere with the orderly listing of questions; for without a methodical guide, the conversation will ramble, the manager's time will be wasted, and the first impression the manager receives will be one of disorganization. A useful form for this questionnaire — which is in effect an agenda for the meeting — is the "split page," with questions on the left-hand side and space for the jotted responses on the right. The pages can then be placed in the working papers without recopying them. Some of the questions that can be asked, depending on the audit purpose, are:

1. How many sections within your activity?
2. How many people?
3. What activities do you carry out?
4. Which activities do you consider:
   a. The most important?
   b. The most troublesome?
5. How do you exercise control over your organization?
6. What control reports do you receive from your own people?
7. What standards have you set for your people?
8. How do you train your people?

9. How do you evaluate their performance ?
10. How do the supervisors help to improve
    employee performance ?
11. Is there a high turnover rate ?
12. How do you set priorities for your work ?
13. What is the extent and nature of your backlog ?
14. To whom do you report ?
15. What reports do you prepare for your own management ?
    How often ?
16. What organizations do you interface with ?
17. What kind of feedback do you get from them ?
18. What major changes have occurred since the last audit ?
19. What is the status of the deficiency findings last reported ?
20. What areas do you think need the most attention ?

This informal questionnaire may be expanded or contracted, according to the circumstances. The nature of the questions will vary, depending on whether the proposed audit is organizational (completely within a single organizational unit) or functional (following a function from beginning to end and crossing organizational lines). In the organizational audit, people-oriented questions will predominate. In the functional audit, the questions will deal more with work flow, interface with other organizations, and feedback.

Formal questionnaires, transmitted in advance of the auditor's arrival, may sometimes be useful. They can provide ample preparation for the auditor's arrival. They can involve the auditee's supervisory personnel in the audit — a sort of collegial approach. They can give management personnel an opportunity to take a good hard look at themselves; since, if it is properly prepared, the questionnaire can be a good self-evaluation form. It can provide substantial economies, since the leg work will have been mainly done by those most competent to do it rapidly, and the auditor need but analyze the answers and the supporting data and then ask amplifying questions of the auditee personnel.

Such questionnaires may be sent out under the cover of a memorandum signed by the executive, located at the company headquarters, to whom the off-site manager reports. This will obtain the involvement of executive management and will add a touch of authority to the request. The memorandum should be drafted by the auditor for the signature of the executive. The memorandum will introduce the auditor or audit team, give the time of arrival, ask for cooperation, and let it be known that the questions should not only be answered fully and openly but should be supported by copies of relevant reports and other pertinent documents, to await the arrival of the auditor.

A copy of a sample transmittal memorandum is shown in Exhibit 5-1. A copy of a sample questionnaire for an off-base manufacturing plant — whose accounting records are, in the main, handled by the headquarters office — is shown in Exhibit 5-2a-d.

Exhibit 5-1.

To: Manager, Plant X
From: Vice President, Off-Site Plants
Subject: Audit of Plant X Activities

The Internal Auditing Department is planning to perform its periodic audit of activities at Plant X in the very near future. The audit will take about 10 days and will be performed by two auditors; John A. Smith is the auditor-in-charge, and William B. Jones will assist him.

The auditors will arrive at Plant X on or about November 9. Mr. Smith will call you a few days before his arrival to tell you the exact date.

To save the time of both the auditors and your staff, they have developed a set of questionnaires which should elicit a good deal of the information they will need. If the answers to the questions could be prepared in advance of their visit, it would simplify the audit and reduce the length of the auditors' stay at Plant X.

The questions are divided into the areas of Administration, Manufacturing Services, Production, and Quality Control — conforming to the Plant X organization — and so can be assigned to several people for response, thereby reducing the burden on any one individual. The auditors have asked that you attach any relevant reports and records to the answered questions to illustrate the documentation being used.

Hold the answered questions pending the auditors' visit. After they have had an opportunity to review the replies and the supporting documentation, please assign someone to provide them with a "walk-through" of the Plant X facility, to answer any further questions they may have, and to assist them through the remainder of their audit.

I shall appreciate your according full cooperation to the auditors and providing them with any assistance they may need.

Vice President, Off-Site Plants

cc: J. A. Smith

Exhibit 5-2a. CONTROL QUESTIONNAIRE

Administration

■ What means are used for recording employees' attendance?

■ What means are used for recording employees' time charges?

■ What means of monitoring are used to ensure the accuracy of the attendance records and time charges?

■ How are attendance and labor hours balanced?

■ What is the basis for redistributing labor charges from pool work orders to ultimate work orders?

■ What methods are used to control payments to suppliers?

■ What methods are used to safeguard assets and facilities?

■ How are the entrance and exit of personnel controlled?

■ How are the entrance and exit of materials controlled?

■ How are valuable documents controlled?

■ How is the need for repetitive reports determined?

■ How are telephone and telegram expenses controlled?

■ How are files kept up to date?

■ How are insurable values determined?

Exhibit 5-2b. CONTROL QUESTIONNAIRE

Production Services

■ What methods are used to schedule and control the manufacture of assemblies?

■ How are behind-schedule conditions determined and reported?

■ What assurance is provided that current, accurate planning documents (shop orders, tool orders, etc.) are used?

■ What provision is made that the latest blueprints will be used?

■ What are the methods used to forecast needs for component parts and other materials and supplies?

■ What provision is made for scheduling and taking cycle inventories?

■ What methods are used to evaluate employee productivity?

■ What provisions have been made to procure materials and services at the most favorable prices?

■ What provisions have been made to account for and safeguard severable fixed assets?

Exhibit 5-2b. (Cont.)
- What provisions have been made for issuing, safeguarding, and accounting for standard tools and supplies?
- What provisions have been made to identify tools?
- How are tools inventoried?
- What provision has been made for preventive and corrective maintenance? Is there a planned program?
- What means are used to control vehicles and gasoline and to provide for appropriate maintenance?
- What provisions have been made for the detection, accumulation, and disposition of scrapped and surplus materials?

Exhibit 5-2c. CONTROL QUESTIONNAIRE

Production
- What means are used to ensure the prompt shipment of completed assemblies?
- What methods are used to expedite the receipt of parts and the reporting of parts shortages?
- What means are used to maintain parts and stock bins?
- What provision has been made to detect the excess usage of material?
- What are the methods employed to control high-value stock levels?

Exhibit 5-2d. CONTROL QUESTIONNAIRE

Quality Control
- What methods are used in the inspection of assemblies to assure compliance with quality standards and engineering drawings and specifications?
- What records of rejection are maintained?
- What are the procedures for reviewing and evaluating discrepant parts and materials?
- What provision has been made for the inspection of production tooling?
- How are production and inspection stamps controlled?
- What provision has been made for the certification of gauges and equipment?

Some companies use such questionnaires in advance of undertaking large operational reviews. Although the questionnaires are sometimes considered to constitute an onerous task by the recipient, the auditor's position is that the auditee-manager should have the requested information readily at hand in order to be able to manage his activities effectively. Exhibit 5-3a is an example of such a questionnaire for a purchasing department. Exhibit 5-3b covers a marketing department.

Exhibit 5-3a. DETAILED QUESTIONNAIRE FOR PURCHASING OPERATIONS

■ What proportion of the company's purchases are "off the shelf" items, and what proportion are made to the company's design?

■ What procedures have been developed for conducting surveys of supplier operations and claims?

■ What procedures have been developed to cover negotiations with suppliers?

■ Which purchase negotiations, if any, have been delegated to other company organizations?

■ What means are used to follow up on supplier deliveries? What authority does the buyer have to expend additional funds to expedite delayed deliveries?

■ What kind of regular reports does the Purchasing Department issue on its follow-up activities?

■ How does the Purchasing Department judge the quality of supplier performance? What standards of performance have been set?

■ What steps are taken to develop alternatives to sole source suppliers?

■ What controls have been installed to make sure that the company receives credit for short shipments, rejected parts and materials, etc.?

■ What procedures have been developed on purchase order documentation?

■ What approvals are required before a purchase order may be issued?

■ Are there any reciprocal agreements with certain suppliers? If so, which suppliers, and what are the agreements?

■ What procedures govern supplier overshipments?

■ What procedures apply when invoice and purchase order prices differ?

■ What procedures apply when suppliers ship in advance of requested dates?

■ How are price and source files kept up to date?

■ How does the Purchase Department participate in "make or buy" decisions?

■ What are the procedures for controlling, recording, and recalling company-owned tools supplied to suppliers, or made by suppliers and held at their plants?

■ What termination procedures have been developed for canceled orders?

■ What reports are prepared on the amounts of orders issued to various suppliers?

■ How is the Purchasing Department Manual kept up to date?

Exhibit 5-3a. (Cont.)

- What has been the ratio of Purchasing Department employees to total company employees during the past three years?
- What has been the volume of purchases per Purchasing Department employee during the past three years?
- What Purchasing Department training programs are in effect?
- What is the policy towards encouraging purchasing personnel to attend technical seminars and conferences?
- To what extent has the Purchasing Department cooperated with suppliers to have them undertake cost reduction and value engineering programs of their own?
- What are the three most important problems facing the company — from the Purchasing manager's viewpoint?
- What type of assistance is received from corporate headquarters?
- What additional type of assistance would the department like to receive?

Exhibit 5-3b. DETAILED QUESTIONNAIRE FOR MARKETING OPERATIONS

- List the major products sold and their approximate share of the market.
- Give your ideas about each product's future.
- Who are the company's major customers, and what kind of products are sold to each?
- To what extent does the company use dealers, agents, and distributors?
- Who are the strongest competitors in the company's major product lines?
- What was the sales and profit trend over the past three years, by important territorial, product, and customer groups?
- Does marketing management systematically and regularly compare sales forecasts with performance, and attempt to determine the reason for the differences?
- What kind of regular and current reports are prepared for marketing management which compare actual sales and profits with forecasted sales and profits for each marketed item?
- What market analysis functions are now in use?
- Which of the company's product lines have required the most intensive marketing effort? Why?
- To what extent has intensive marketing effort on weak product lines paid off in improved profitability?
- How is your advertising program coordinated with other selling efforts?
- On what basis is the overall advertising budget allocated so as to —
  a. Control spending for highest total profitability?
  b. Allow monthly comparisons between actual expenditures and budgeted expenditures?

Exhibit 5-3b. (Cont.)

■ How is the company's catalog kept up to date?
■ What training programs does the Marketing Department have in effect?
■ How are prices set on company products?
■ How are prices set on spare parts?
■ What latitude do salesmen have in setting prices?
■ How is the performance of salesmen measured?
■ How frequently are the regular marketing publications issued, and to whom are they distributed?
■ What analyses are made of sales returns to determine causes?
■ What is the approximate number and approximate value of items that are shipped but not billed?
■ What is Marketing's procedure to review sales stock for excess and obsolete parts?
■ What are the amounts of inventory write-offs for excess and obsolete inventory for the past three years?
■ Do salesmen set delivery schedules? If so, on what basis?
■ To whom has the Marketing Manual been distributed?
■ What procedures are followed to see that the Marketing Manual is kept up to date?
■ What written procedures have been developed for internal departmental operations?
■ What approvals are required to initiate changes in sales policies and procedures?
■ What are the two or three most important problems facing the company — from the Marketing manager's viewpoint?
■ What types of marketing assistance does the department receive from corporate headquarters?
■ What additional assistance would it like to have?

PRELIMINARY MEETING

The preliminary meeting will most likely set the tone for the audit. That tone should be one of cooperation. The auditor should be open and candid about his audit objectives. His questions should be posed in the tone of a seeker of information, not an inquisitor. No disputes, discords, or challenges should mar this first meeting. By and large the auditee-manager wishes only to be treated fairly and viewed objectively, have findings placed in proper perspective, and make sure that all deficiencies encountered will be reviewed with him. The auditor should adopt this as his purpose as well.

After the preliminary discussion, the auditor will make certain requests to facilitate his review:

■ A desk or desks for him and his assistants

■ A file cabinet or drawer for his working papers

■ Copies of organizational charts, manuals, job instructions, and reports

■ Access to the correspondence files

The auditor may ask to be introduced to the manager's supervisors and to be advised as to sources for additional material and information. The manager may wish the auditor to deal directly with him, or he may assign a supervisor for that purpose.

One final gesture on the part of the auditor, at the conclusion of the meeting, can cement a participative, collegial relationship which can go a long way toward removing the preconception auditees often harbor about auditors. The gesture and the related technique have been tried and they work well. The auditor can ask for another meeting, to take place after his preliminary survey and the preparation of the audit program. The purpose of the meeting would be threefold. The auditor will:

1. Give a brief report of the initial audit impressions.

2. Explain what he now conceives to be the objectives of the activities under review. (A clear understanding of these objectives is central to an effective audit — and the auditor and the auditee should come to an agreement on this understanding of objectives and how they fit into the company objectives.)

3. Set forth the general thrust of the audit program.

Many misunderstandings can be resolved and many fears can be allayed at such a meeting.

OBTAINING INFORMATION

What Information to Obtain

The preliminary survey will move along rapidly and systematically if the auditor has a clear idea of what he wants. Here, in essence, are the records and the information he will need:

■ **The charter for the activity**

He will want copies of management's policy statements, directives, statements of function and responsibility, and delegations of authority.

But beyond obtaining the written word, the auditor will be focussing on the objectives of the activity — what its mission really is, not necessarily what is set forth in the official record.

Official records can sometimes be window dressing, or they may not have kept pace with changing times and changing aims. In a subsequent part of this chapter we shall discuss more fully the subject of objectives.

■ **The organization of the activity**

The auditor will want to obtain material on the activity's organization, with special emphasis on the functions under review. The material and information may include:

1. Organization charts
2. Position of the organization in the company structure
3. Nature, size, and location of subsidiary organizations
4. Interfacing organizations and their relationship to the activity under review

■ **Financial information**

The auditor will want to obtain information on assets, investments, and other financial data, including the location and nature of assets.

■ **Operating instructions**

During the preliminary survey, the auditor should not make detailed studies of operating instructions, but should obtain copies of them. Detailed analyses at this time can be inefficient, since the auditor will not be able to appreciate their relevance and significance until he has begun his in-depth studies.

■ **Operating methods**

The auditor will want to get a picture of the flow of records and data. One of the best ways is through flow charts. Flow charts can be simple or detailed, depending on the auditor's needs. But a ready facility with flowcharting can provide useful pictures of the operations and can pinpoint gaps in the flow or highlight the risk areas.

A detailed discussion of flow charts will be found later in this chapter.

■ **Problem areas**

During the survey, the auditor should keep in mind the problems mentioned by the auditee-manager and the deficiency findings discussed in prior audit reports. He will want to focus on the controls which have been designed to alleviate the difficulties or reduce the risks.

■ **Matters of management interest**

The auditor will be interested in exploring the areas mentioned during the discussions with management on the long-range program, as being of concern to them.

Sources of Information

Some of the sources of information are:

■ Discussions with supervision and employees engaged in the activity under review

■ Discussions with managers in the downstream and upstream organizations

■ Correspondence files

■ Reports submitted to and by the auditee-manager

■ Budgets

■ Statements of short-range and long-range objectives, and the reports issued to show accomplishment of those objectives

■ Procedural manuals

■ Reports by government control agencies — state and federal

Physical Inspections

Physical inspections should be in two phases:

First, the auditor should make a tour of the facilities to obtain a better understanding, in general terms, of plant layout and facilities. This will be a bird's eye view — a frame of reference for the policies, procedures, and organization chart. At this point, people are met, introductions are made, and questions are asked. Some of the questions may be:

■ Is the work coming to you on schedule, and is it of acceptable quality?

■ Are there any informal or formal reports of difficulties encountered with the work received?

■ What problems are being experienced?

■ Has corrective action proved successful?

■ How is the activity controlled?

In relatively simple operations, this tour may be enough of an inspection. In complex operations, the auditor may find it necessary to go on to a second phase.

The second phase may be used in conjunction with preparing flow charts, which we shall discuss later in this chapter. This type of inspection may be regarded as a "walk-through" of transactions relating to the activity under audit, from their inception to the time they are concluded or leave the area.

The walk-through is an especially good way of confirming work-flow and document-processing. Often, oral explanations and even written directions are confusing or even just wishful thinking. But by walking the document through the process cycle, the auditor can make sure that purported process and control points are in existence and are really ᴏperating. The auditor should not walk through every type of document processed by the auditee organization, but just those he feels are really significant in terms of the organization's chief objectives. The results of his walk-throughs may readily be documented on flow charts.

FLOWCHARTING

Flowcharting is a combination of science and art. But chiefly it is an art. And like most arts, it takes time to develop a facility for it. Some people take to flowcharting readily and do well with it. To others it is a dreary chore. But with practice it can become a useful instrument for all auditors. It provides a visual grasp of the system and a means for analyzing complex operations that cannot be achieved by detailed narratives.

Formal flowcharting should be standardized in an auditing department. All the auditors should use the same templates and follow the same basic instructions. It is usually helpful to coordinate flowcharting techniques with the external auditor — the independent accountant — so that each can use the work of the other.

Exhibit 5-4 shows certain standardized flow chart symbols, and a legend describing each. These symbols will be used for formal flow charts.

Not all flow charts, however, need be detailed, formal, and extensive. The auditor may find his needs satisfied by a simple layout that will give him an easily read overview of the system. Exhibit 5-5 provides the key steps involved in the process that starts with the procurement and ends with the storage of purchased materials. This may be adequate in some circumstances.

On the other hand, the system under review may be so complex or so fraught with risk that a detailed and formal flow chart is needed to ensure exact knowledge of every step of the way.

Exhibit 5-6 depicts a formal flow chart of a direct delivery system. This system is part of the receiving operation. But because materials by-pass the normal receiving routines, with their usual safeguards, and are delivered by suppliers directly to the using departments, the system presents certain risks. Therefore, it is beneficial to the auditor to know every part of the delivery routine and to identify the control points and the risk areas.

Exhibit 5-4. STANDARD FLOW CHART SYMBOLS

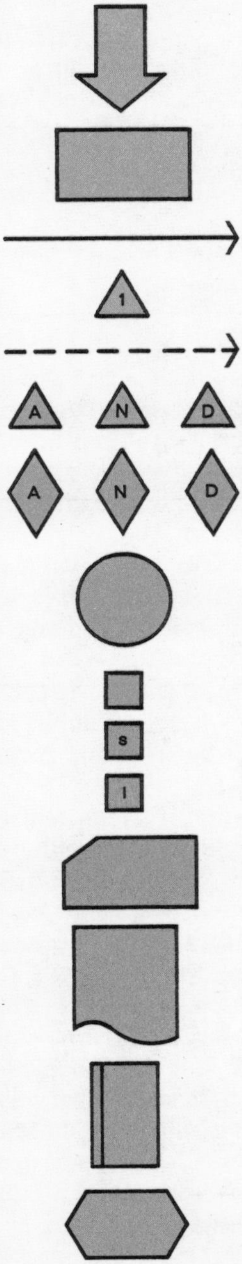

Starting point in the flow of documents

Document

Direction in the flow of a document

Control point

Direction in the flow of information

Permanent file of documents, **A**lphabetically, **N**umerically, and by **D**ate

Temporary file of documents, **A**lphabetically, **N**umerically and by **D**ate

Operation or action

Document destroyed

Document signed

Document initialed

Punch card

Report or computer printout

Book or ledger

Source of postings to general ledger

Exhibit 5-5. INFORMAL FLOW CHART
Procurement of Materials

PURCH. DEPT.	RECEIVING DEPT.			A/C PAYABLE	INSPECTION	STORES
	OFFICE	DOCK	HOLD AREA			
Purchase Orders and changes are prepared and sent to: 1. Supplier 2. Accounts Payable 3. Receiving Dep't. 4. Buyer 5. Purchasing Files	The master P.O. is held in temporary files awaiting receipt of materials and shipping notice. Upon receipt of shipping notice, the receiving information is added to the ditto master of the P.O. to create the Receiving Memo.	Materials and shipping notice are received. The S/N is sent to Receiving Office. The materials are sent to the hold area.	Materials are held until the Receiving Memo is prepared. Thereupon the materials are sent to Inspection.	Evidence of receipt is matched with copy of P.O. No invoice is required. If match is satisfactory, payment to supplier is approved.	Material is inspected. Unsatisfactory material is sent to hold area. Satisfactory material is sent to stores.	Materials are stored awaiting requisitions from using departments.

Exhibit 5-6 shows the flow of documents and material from the point at which the using department orders the material, through procurement, receipt, documentation of receipt, and processing for payment.

Besides picturing the processing of documentation, the flow chart brings into sharper focus the key controls on which the auditor should concentrate his tests. Based on an analysis of the chart, he can pinpoint the controls. An analysis of Exhibit 5-6 can show him the importance of the following matters:

- The control over procurement and direct delivery stamps should be operating and effective. If any individual in the company could avail himself of those stamps, he could easily subvert the system to his own use.

- The system of checking the approval signatures through review in a control agency will help prevent the unauthorized use of the direct delivery system.

- Packing slips signed by the same employee who is authorized to issue or approve requests to purchase defeat the assurances gained by a division of authority.

- Payments to suppliers should not be made without evidence of actual receipt. Otherwise, collusion between a supplier and an employee is made easy.

- An accurate commitment record is a strong control over the determination of cash needs and overextending the capacity of a supplier, as determined by the Credit Department.

- Check signing should be separated from the authority to consummate the commitment for which the check is issued.

- Delays in processing documents can have an adverse effect on earned discounts; and the surest way to accelerate the processing flow is to show the managers responsible just how their organizations are preventing prompt payment.

- Similarly, reports on violations of rules relating to direct deliveries will have a salutary effect on compliance with the rules.

Exhibit 5-6. FORMAL FLOW CHART
Processing Direct Deliveries

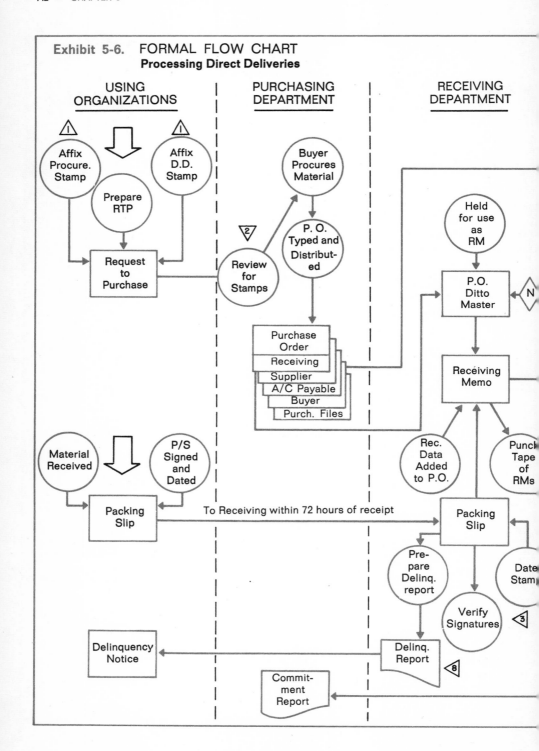

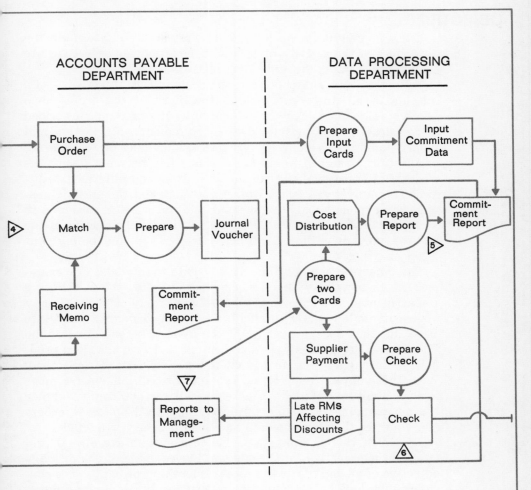

ACCOUNTS PAYABLE DEPARTMENT

DATA PROCESSING DEPARTMENT

Key Controls:

1. Stamps controlled by registers in Purch. Department. Only authorized Departments and personnel may validate RTPs or use D.D. system.

2. Unvalidated requests are returned to requesters.

3. Improperly approved P/S's challenged.

4. Payments not made without proof of receipt. Invoices not required.

5. Record of commitments helps establish cash needs.

6. Check signed in Finance Department (not on chart) where it is mailed to supplier.

7. Reports to cognizant managers on unearned discounts monitors timeliness of processing P.O.'s, P/S's, RMs and payments to suppliers.

8. Reports warn that D.D. privileges may be withdrawn.

Abbreviations:

D D — Direct Delivery
P O — Purchase Order
P/S — Packing Slip
RM — Receiving Memo
RTP — Request to Purchase

OBJECTIVES

Every preliminary survey should first seek to determine the objectives of the activity under audit. Unless those objectives are clearly understood, the audit may miss its mark.

Taking a clear, sharp picture of the activity's objectives — its mission within the company — is the mark of the professional auditor. He is not swayed or influenced by the functions described in job descriptions or published in statements of function and responsibility. These may be obsolete or they may be self-serving declarations designed to elevate status. They may not get to the marrow of the activity. Also, the auditor should differentiate between objectives and goals. Objectives represent the entity's mission or purpose. Goals are measurable units to be achieved in meeting the objectives. For example, service is an objective of the gas company. Installing 1,000 new gas ovens in the coming year is a goal.

The objective is more difficult to isolate than goals. For example, the statement of function may declare that the Purchasing Department shall issue approved purchase orders on the authority of properly validated requirements from using organizations. Quite true. But that does not really hit the mark. The objective of the Purchasing Department, plain and simple, is to get the right product, at the right price, in the right quantity, at the right time. With those objectives in mind, the auditor will make a far more incisive audit than if he were merely seeking to determine whether the department was issuing properly approved purchase orders and whether the requirements had been properly validated.

Moreover, the controls applicable to a system are directly related to the objectives of the system. For example, if the primary objective of an activity is to process something promptly, the controls devised should be centered on ensuring timeliness and meeting established schedules. If, on the other hand, the objective is precision, with timeliness secondary, the controls should be concerned with accuracy and adherence to established standards.

Hence, throughout his survey, the auditor should be sorting out in his mind exactly what the objectives are and what goals the auditee organization is or should be working toward. He should seek to find out:

■ Whether formal statements of objectives have been prepared.

■ Whether these objectives are in consonance with company objectives — the entity's grand design.

■ Whether all who will be affected by the objectives participated in setting them.

■ Whether the objectives are known to all who will participate in their achievement.

■ Whether the objectives realistically consider the activity's available resources.

■ Whether the objectives will run the activity aground on the shoals of external constraints and controls.

■ Whether established goals will motivate people to reach beyond what they think is their grasp.

■ Whether the goals are measurable.

■ Whether periodic, formal reports are being prepared to show how well the objectives are being achieved and the goals are being met.

■ Whether both objectives and goals are periodically reevaluated and redefined.

CONTROL

Of all the keys on the auditor's ring, his knowledge of control is the most useful, the most reliable, and the most universal. It is his master key, the "Open Sesame" that unlocks any door in the company. For every managed activity is managed through administrative control. Hence, as an auditor for management, he must understand administrative control in all its forms and aspects. And he must apply this understanding in every audit assignment.

He must understand the nature of the control with which executive management is concerned. He must see the relationship of control to the other key executive functions of planning and organizing.

He must also understand the nature of the control with which line management and line supervision are concerned and how these people establish the means to carry out their objectives.

Control has been variously defined. To accountants and auditors, one of the most authoritative definitions is that given by the American Institute of Certified Public Accountants in its "Statements of Auditing Procedures, No. 29":

"Internal control comprises the plan of organization and all of the coordinate methods and measures adopted within a business to safeguard its assets, check the accuracy and reliability of its accounting data, promote operational efficiency, and encourage adherence to prescribed managerial policies."

The American Institute then goes on to define accounting and administrative controls in the following paragraphs:

"Accounting controls comprise the plan of organization and all methods and procedures that are concerned mainly with, and relate directly to, the safeguarding of assets and the reliability of the financial records. They generally include such controls as the systems of authorization and approval, separation of duties concerned with record keeping and accounting reports from those concerned with operations of asset custody, physical controls over assets, and internal auditing.

"Administrative controls comprise the plan of organization and all methods and procedures that are concerned mainly with operational efficiency and adherence to managerial policies and usually relate only indirectly to the financial records. They generally include such controls as statistical analyses, time and motion studies, performance reports, employee training programs, and quality controls."

Control does not exist in a vacuum. It has meaning and relevance only when it is designed to see to it that a management purpose is carried out or a management objective is met. Also, a control is not a faceless, formless thing; it is a physical device which performs an observable function. Thus, I like to see a definition which clearly comes to grips with the concept of objectives, on the one hand, and the physical means on the other . . . which also clearly shows that "control" can be a verb or a noun — each with its own meaning. In this view, the following definition is appropriate:[2]

"Control comprises all the means devised in a company to direct, restrain, govern, and check upon its various activities for the purpose of seeing that company objectives are met. The means of control include, but are not limited to, form of organization, policies, systems, procedures, instructions, standards, committees, charts of account, forecasts, budgets, schedules, reports, records, check lists, methods, devices, and internal auditing."

This definition does not differentiate among "management control," "executive control," "internal control," and "administrative (or operational) control." There seems to be no need for any differentiation, since any differences that exist in the means of control are attributable to the nature of the objectives sought to be achieved — not from any variations in the application of the concept of control.

---

[2]Sawyer, L. B., "The Anatomy of Control," *The Internal Auditor,* Spring 1964, p. 15.

Management control and executive control are concerned with carrying out broad company-wide purposes and plans. Internal control and administrative control are concerned with carrying out operating purposes and plans. The means of control used are those which fit the established objectives.

Management control relies on long-range plans, budgets and forecasts, broad policy statements, organization charts, statements of function and responsibility, and internal auditing.

Internal control and administrative control rely on systems of authorization and approval, separation of duties, departmental budgets and forecasts, job assignment sheets, reports, production schedules, manuals, performance standards, logs, registers, charts, forms, records, and check lists.

There is an interrelationship among the three key management functions of planning, organizing, and controlling. There is an interplay of action among them; and an integrated, well-functioning entity comes into being when each is in harmony with the others. This interplay can be perceived by examining the hierarchy of business controls that will usually exist in these functions.

Planning

Planning, in essence, defines what should be done, how, where, and when it should be done, and who should do it. When management plans, it:

- Sets objectives and goals and devises broad plans to carry them out.
- Assigns the necessary responsibility to carry out the plans and meet the objectives and goals.
- Sees to it that there is continuity for the plans.
- Periodically reappraises the objectives and plans in the light of observed results and changing conditions.

Organizing

Having planned, management must now supply and deploy the resources needed to carry out its plans. The function of organizing is concerned with providing the capital, plant, people, and materials needed to achieve the objectives. It is also concerned with setting guidelines within which the plans should be followed. When management organizes, it establishes a structure and a system whose purpose it is to:

- Achieve its objectives.

- Discharge the assigned responsibility for carrying out established plans.

- Maintain the needed continuity of organization and responsibility.

- Periodically reappraise the structure and the system to ensure their continued effectiveness.

Controlling

With objectives set and an organization formed, management must now see that they *are* carried out, effectively and efficiently. Management does this through control. When management exercises its function of control, it is constraining and regulating action in accordance with the requirements of the plans for the accomplishment of its objectives. Management achieves and maintains control by:

- Setting basic standards for cost, quality, and timeliness.

- Maintaining and adjusting these standards to meet changing conditions.

- Training personnel to meet the standards.

- Devising a system of approvals, or checks and balances, to maintain control over operations.

- Making sure that standards are met.

- Monitoring all on-going processes.

- Devising optimum systems of records and reports.

With the concept of control and its interrelated functions in mind, the auditor is in a position to apply his own standards to existing control systems as he reviews a functional or organizational activity. When he observes that any of these means of control are missing or are weak, he can perceive potential risks that should alert him to perform in-depth examinations.

Some standards which the auditor may use are as follows:

1. Preparing: Has management provided all the needed resources to carry out a particular company objective ?

2. Scheduling: Have definite schedules been devised and milestones set to establish when or at what rate the principal phases of the objectives will be achieved?

3. Coordinating: When interdependent activities are concerned with the achievement of a particular objective, has provision been made to coordinate their activities ?

4. Directing: Have proper instructions been provided to explain the objectives and to give the necessary instruction on what steps shall be taken to accomplish them ?

5. Obtaining Feedback: Has a feedback system been devised so that management can tell whether actual results agree with planned results, and can decide whether there is need for improvement ?

6. Achieving Improvement: Is management monitoring the on-going process so as to act promptly in removing any interference with plans and to modify them to meet changing conditions ?

The auditor has reason for concern when the system he reviews does not include these safeguards. They are highly significant to the proper functioning of any organizational unit, and we shall therefore explore them in greater depth in Chapter 9, "Field Work."

Routine vs. Operating Controls

In looking at controls, the auditor should keep his eyes raised. He should be concerned with the objectives and related controls that are of greatest concern to executive management. Certainly, he has a responsibility for the adequacy and effectiveness of the system of internal check, and he will not overlook shoddy controls in traditional areas of audit concern. But that should not keep his gaze riveted to the ground, looking for lost coins when there is gold to be mined in the hills.

Using some commonplace examples, let us see the difference between the financial and the management approach in activities concerned with cash, accounts receivable, and inventories:

Internal Check	Management Control
Cash	
Establish a record of cash received, at the earliest possible moment. Establish appropriate safeguards to see that records are properly maintained.	Provide for timely forecasts of cash needs. Provide for the investment of any funds temporarily in excess of immediate requirements.
Accounts Receivable	
See that receivables ledgers are controlled by general ledger accounts. Prove their agreement currently.	Provide for aging of receivables and for reports to management on their collectibility.
Inventory	
Inventories should be maintained in storerooms under the centralized control of responsible individuals.	Provide for reports to management of inventories on hand and for the coordination between sales forecasts and inventories so that proper planning may be made for the manufacturing requirements and for optimal levels of investments in inventories.

Now let us go beyond the traditional audit areas to one which is not often under audit scrutiny: research and development. But here too, the auditor who is well-grounded in the concept of control can ask incisive and penetrating questions on administrative control:

■ How is all the work on research and development projects authorized ?

■ How is such work budgeted ?

■ How are actual expenditures and budgeted costs compared ?

■ Does management receive progress reports on each research and development project ?

■ Are provisions made for adequate, technical diaries and logs to record activities and to permit another technician to take over if the current technician suddenly becomes unavailable ?

- What provisions are made to see to it that the projects funded are actually the projects carried out ?
- What contributions has research and development made ?

PEOPLE

People are the backbone of every organization. Good controls, in and of themselves, are powerless to carry on an activity successfully in the face of poor personnel. The auditor cannot avoid considering the people engaged in an activity while he is examining the activity itself.

For this reason, the preliminary survey should include a review of personnel records and practices. This review may not permit the auditor to make definitive determinations, but it may raise danger signals and influence the audit program. Here are some of the things the auditor might try to find out:

- Has there been a rapid turnover of personnel ?
- Is the organization peopled with new and inexperienced personnel ?
- Is the educational background appropriate for the kind of work being performed ?
- Does an adequate training program exist for new employees ?
- Is there a mix of ages, or at some time in the near future will the staff be decimated by retirements?
- Does each key position, including the manager's, have a back-up in the event of disability or retirement ?
- Is there a system of rotation so that a person knows more than one job ?
- Is there a formal system of in-job training for higher-level positions ?
- Are people kept informed of what is going on in the company ?
- Is the requirement to take vacations enforced so that improper practices are not kept hidden ?

The answers he obtains through these questions may have a significant effect on the size of the samples the auditor will examine during the field work part of his audit. When the answers indicate a satisfactory condition, the auditor may reduce the high levels of sample reliability which he might otherwise demand from his test results; in other words, he may be justified in examining smaller samples. Where his survey indicates unsatisfactory personnel practices, the auditor may have to make his tests more rigorous, expand his samples, and be on the look-out for ineffective, inefficient job performance.

RISKS

One of the important functions of the preliminary survey is to supply information for the audit program — a program which will provide the greatest return for the expenditure of the audit effort. When it is properly performed, the survey should give the auditor all the insight he needs to prepare a thoughtful, effective program.

The survey may show that some activities are under strict and rigorous control, with adequate management surveillance — the best kind of control. It would be inefficient to spend much time in making extensive tests to confirm what already appears to be a well-functioning operation.

Other activities may seem suspect — fraught with risk. If a weakness detected during the survey seems clear enough, it should be discussed then and there with the auditee-manager. If he agrees with the finding and offers to take corrective action, further audit effort would seem pointless. If the manager remains unconvinced and needs proof, the auditor should schedule a purposive test — rather than a random sample — to support the existence and significance of the weakness he feels sure exists.

His survey may indicate other risks. Flow charts may highlight key control points which need more thorough investigation to establish the degree of effectiveness and efficiency of performance. Downstream departments may point to inadequate output from the audited department. Inquiries and reviews of files may disclose other indicators. Some of these, listed at random, are:

- Customer complaints
- Poor inventory turnover ratios
- Prolonged poor quality from suppliers
- Delays between the time of receipt of unsatisfactory materials and the issuing of debit memos
- Increases in the volume of returns and allowances
- Critical field service reports
- Excessive rework costs

Thus, the preliminary survey, with its overview of the entire operation — instead of a nibbling at corners — provides a firm foundation for the preparation of a thoughtful audit program that concentrates on those matters which are of chief interest to management:

1. Are the key risk areas being monitored?
2. Are inadequate controls and ineffective, inefficient performance being brought to light and corrected?

SUMMARY

The preliminary survey charts the course for the audit. It sometimes can provide a clear enough view of operations to warrant eliminating some tests traditionally considered essential. The time spent on the preliminary survey, therefore, is usually well repaid with a more economical audit.

In the preliminary survey, the auditor gets to know the people, to understand the operations, and to focus on objectives, controls, and risks. Thus, he is equipped to perform an audit that is intelligent, effective, and efficient — not just a haphazard trawling in unknown waters.

Performing a successful preliminary survey takes training and practice. But the auditor who has developed an understanding of what to look for, where to look for it, and how to document the results of his search, will be able to draw a clear map to guide him toward his audit goals.

AUDIT
PROGRAMS

INTRODUCTION

An audit program is a detailed plan of action for an audit examination. It is as important to an auditor as a map is to a navigator.

With a good program, an average but conscientious auditor will at the very least make a sound audit. A superb auditor will make a superb and comprehensive audit. Without a program, the audit examination may be a thrashing about in uncharted waters. The superb auditor, by dint of his imagination and experience, may still perform some excellent work; but his overall effort and results may be formless, aimless, and uncontrolled. The average auditor, without a program to show him the way, may get bogged down in a swamp of minutiae without ever seeing some of the real points of interest in the audit assignment.

A good program is a guide, a lifeline, and a means of self control for the auditor. Apart from keeping him on track, it will help keep him on budget and on schedule; and it will alert him to the need to reevaluate his game plan when some aspect of the audit may require expansion — giving him reason to reduce other aspects to compensate.

In audits of operations which may vary from year to year or from branch office to branch office, the audit program can rarely be of the pro forma type — one that has been prepared in advance and used over and over. It usually must be tailored to particular circumstances.

On the other hand, there are some functions which continue year after year, in pretty much the same manner. Also, there may be conditions under which substantially the same operations are carried out with much the same objectives in many company branches. In such circumstances, the pro forma program — sometimes disparagingly termed the "canned" program — saves time, assures uniformity, and provides for all needed coverage.

We shall discuss both types.

WHAT THE PROGRAM SHOULD INCLUDE

The Theory of the Audit

Deliberation and early program development are needed to evolve what the lawyers call "the theory of the case." It is the particular thrust, method, slant, and concept which the lawyer will use in trying a law suit. In the same way, the auditor needs to develop the theory of the audit. That theory can be the central theme of the audit — all the audit steps being just variations.

The theory of the audit will vary, depending on the auditor's background and predilections, the style of the operating manager, and the particular weight given certain operations at the time of the audit.

Some auditors may be accounting oriented; others may be scientific management oriented. Whatever their special bent, it will affect their audit thrust — the theory of their audit.

Then again, some operating managers may be technicians who were graduated from the ranks because of technical competence and not because of administrative talent; others may be good administrators, well versed in practices of control, follow-up, feed-back, and periodic verifications of what their people are doing from day to day.

Finally, some activities in an organization or function appear more important at one time of year or at one stage of a project than another. Engineering is stressed early in the project; final inspection at a later point.

But all these things will affect the thrust of the audit, and they emphasize the need for early programming.

As an example of the "theory of the audit" take the examination of a payroll. We shall discuss two approaches — one pedestrian, another imaginative. In neither example have we tried to be exhaustive — merely to provide indications of different audit theories. The pedestrian theory of the audit would include the following steps:

1. Review internal checks designed to:
   a. Prevent improper additions of names to the payroll and the prompt deletion of the names of those separated from the rolls.
   b. Assure the accuracy of the hours worked.
   c. Control the mechanics of calculating net and gross pay.
   d. Protect against misuse of check stock and signature plates.
2. Review legislation concerning various deductions.
3. Analyze distribution of labor costs to operating or overhead areas.
4. Examine wage rates and related matters defined in the union agreement.

In contrast, an imaginative theory of the audit might include:[1]

1. An examination of the payroll department's assignment of duties, organization, staffing, and work flow. Payroll work is subject to peak loads followed by sharp dips in activity. There is generally a tendency to staff for the peaks. The valleys will see overstaffing, lowered efficiency, and loss of morale. Lowered efficiency will affect the peaks, calling for still further staffing. The cycle could be vicious.

2. An analysis of overtime payments — the incidence and the factors behind them. Why, for example, should a man work 35 hours in one week and 45 hours the next? Does this happen often? Does this happen in a number of departments? Are there indications of poor planning and manloading?

---

[1]Evans, E. R., "Approach — The Key to Operational Auditing," *The Internal Auditor*, Spring 1966, p. 30.

3. An evaluation of labor turnover — whether it is high, low, or average for the industry and what reasons are advanced or determined for high turnover.

4. A check of night premium payments. Why, for instance, are only 20 per cent of the maintenance people on night premium when 70 per cent of routine maintenance can be dealt with more effectively after the operating departments are shut down?

In a way, giving serious consideration to the theory of the audit at the outset — the very decision to think about it — has a tendency to raise the auditor's sights.

Objectives and Controls

In audits of operations — be they financial or other operations — the key to the perceptive, meaningful program is an understanding of the objectives of the operations and the controls needed to see that the objectives are met. In the preliminary survey (Chapter 5) the auditor determines the objectives and the related controls. In preparing the audit program he puts that information to use.

Preparing a program that fails to take those two matters into account fails to get to the marrow of the operation. The resulting program may be a pedestrian schedule of routine verifications — of little interest to higher management.

Management at the policy-making level — one of the levels of management that the auditor is seeking to reach through his reports — is trained to view conditions in the light of company objectives. When it hears from the auditor, it wants to know whether those objectives are being achieved. It wants to know whether the plans devised to meet the objectives are effective and efficient. And it wants to know whether its system of feedback — its reporting system — is providing it with accurate, timely, meaningful information on which to base management decisions.

Programs that seek to accomplish less than that will result in reports which will find indifferent acceptance in the eyes of management. Programs that hit the mark will most likely ensure management interest in the audit report and management's respect for the auditor.

That is why it is vital for the auditor to make sure that the true objectives — the missions that management had in mind when it assigned and funded the activities being audited — are thoroughly understood before the program is prepared. Those objectives represent the lodestar by which the auditor will guide his audit. If he hasn't identified them he is in danger of straying from the course which leads him to one of his own principal objectives: service to executive management.

As an example, consider the audit of the purchasing operation.[2] Stated succinctly, the principal objectives of the purchasing function are to obtain for the company the right product, at the right price, in the right quantity, at the right time. These are the prime purposes for which the purchasing department was organized, staffed, and funded. If it does not accomplish these assignments effectively and efficiently, it is not carrying out its mission. So these are the matters about which management wishes either assurance of accomplishment or recommendations for improvement.

The desired purchasing controls must be keyed to the major objectives. Take one of the objectives as an example: obtaining services and supplies at the right price. The controls — which are to be covered in the audit program — may be represented by the following provisions:

1. A system of pricing targets for major procurements, and material budgets for specific programs — with a system of measurement against the pricing standards set.

2. A system of competitive bids; and where large amounts are involved, a system of written bids mailed and received by someone other than the buyer.

3. Provision for the bidders' list for a particular purchase to be subjected to supervisory review to ensure inclusion of all qualified bidders.

4. Provision for the receipt of cost breakdowns for large purchases and the objective analysis of the cost data by desk or field review.

5. Provision for the negotiation of the final price with the successful bidder.

6. Consideration of market trends. Perhaps purchasing minimum quantities now in anticipation of lower prices — or an extra quantity in anticipation of higher prices.

7. Provision for knowledgeable decisions on whether to make the product in the company or to purchase it from the outside.

8. A system for reviewing periodically all sole source procurements and making plans to obtain competitive sources.

These are far from all the related controls the auditor will consider in his program, but they illustrate the point being made. Each

---

[2]Sawyer, L. B., "The Anatomy of Control," *The Internal Auditor*, Spring 1964, p. 19.

control is closely tied to the objective of the operation being audited — and each provides ample reason for an audit test.

PREPARING THE PROGRAM

There is no one form of program which will fit all needs. The form must fill the audit requirements and the conditions peculiar to the organization and the particular audit.

Some organizations remain in a constant state of flux. A program that accommodates to change must be structured for each audit. Some organizations remain stable over periods of time or contain numerous branch activities of almost an identical nature. For them a pro forma program may be the best answer. We shall discuss and illustrate both. We wish it understood, however, that no special form of program is advocated here and that the illustrations shown do not purport to be complete and immutable. They are merely representative of some forms in actual use. The innovative auditor will follow the dictates of his audit objectives in structuring his individual audit programs.

Individual Programs

Individual programs, tailor-made for the particular examination, work well if they contain the following information:

■ A statement of the objectives of the activity

■ A listing of the existing or needed controls

■ Suggestions for what to test

■ Allocations of audit budget for the audit steps

■ Provision for brief comments on the results of tests, to give a continuous overview of what has been encountered in the audit

Exhibit 6-1 (at end of chapter) provides excerpts from an actual program for the audit of the activities of a Traffic Department.[3] The exhibit presents a listing of some of the segments of the audit, showing the objectives for each operation. It sets forth the control points, man-days, and proposed steps for several of the segments to illustrate the format.

It will also be observed that the program is not developed as a rigid strait jacket for the auditor. He must be permitted flexibility to adjust to the conditions met during the actual audit — conditions which were not or could not be anticipated during the prelim-

[3]The *Operational Auditing Handbook*, written by Bradford Cadmus and published by The Institute of Internal Auditors, New York, 1964, provides complete programs for traffic audits.

inary survey. Hence, the program provides guidelines and does not set forth detailed audit steps. Those steps will be listed in the Scope sections of the working papers dealing with the individual audit segments. The subject of working papers will be covered thoroughly in Chapter 10.

Pro Forma Programs

Pro forma programs, as we have previously mentioned, are developed for various purposes. They may be prepared to collect similar or identical information at many different localities, thus facilitating the preparation of an overall report. Or they may seek to obtain similar or identical kinds of information over a period of time so as to provide information on trends and changes.

Exhibit 6-2 (at end of chapter) consists of excerpts from an actual program developed by a financial institution to audit the safe deposit departments in its various branches. The program is very specific, providing for coverage of all key operations. The excerpts from the program show the general information furnished to the auditor, the purpose of the audit, and the audit procedures.

Exhibit 6-3 (at end of chapter) is a combination verification program and internal control questionnaire for an industrial organization. The same program is used periodically and is applied at three different locations, referred to as A, B, and C.

The excerpts from the program show some of the audit objectives, instructions to the auditor, some of the essential controls, flowcharting instructions, the detailed audit steps for one segment, and a listing of the remaining segments. Also included are some excerpts from the internal control questionnaire.

Selections from Illustrative Programs

An audit will rarely be truly successful unless the auditor applies imagination, ingenuity, and intelligence. But no competent auditor will overlook the experience of others, their different outlooks, and their different audit thrusts and aims.

One of the steps in preparing the program, therefore, is to research the internal auditing literature to see how others have attacked the same problems or operations. The pages of *The Internal Auditor* are a treasure trove of audit approaches and suggestions. The experiences and the ideas of practicing internal auditors are recorded there for all to see. In many cases, the audit approaches discussed there give a new slant or a management viewpoint to audits that may have been done in the same routine way for years.

For purposes of illustration, we will examine selections from the audit approaches used in the examination of matters not often reviewed by internal auditors — although we should add that some organizations perform these audits as a matter of course. The programs to be discussed include the acquisition of new EDP equipment, the acquisition of other companies, budgets for research and development projects, the marketing function, company objectives and plans, and company organization.

The questions and the audit steps suggested indicate the kind of management thinking desirable in all audits.

1. Acquiring New EDP Equipment[4]

a. Are the reasons for acquisition specific in justifying costs — or are they vague statements, such as "improve reporting," "eliminate manual accounting," or "handle increased volume of work"?

b. Has adequate consideration been given to lease or buy?

c. Have alternative systems been carefully considered?

d. Does the proposal spell out the functions of the group involved in the inception and development of the plan?

e. Do the proposals relate the new system to the company's overall plans and goals?

f. Do the proposals show all necessary elements, such as cost, obsolescence, and timing?

g. Do examinations of past proposals and acquisitions involving the same proposers generate confidence in the validity of their proposals?

2. Acquisitions of Other Companies[5]

The source material from which the following audit steps were taken provides a detailed check list to use in the review of proposed acquisitions and mergers, and it points to these areas as being most productive for the internal auditor:

a. Evaluation of inventory.

b. Analysis of product lines with comparisons of gross profit ratios.

c. Analysis of profit trends and comparability of reporting.

d. Review of industry data on competition and the potential for increased markets.

---

[4]Nigra, Alphonse L., "Auditing Acquisitions of Data Processing Equipment," *The Internal Auditor*, January/February 1970, p. 27.
[5]"Education and Practice," *The Internal Auditor*, July/August 1969, p. 64.

   e. Verification of fixed assets and depreciation methods.

   f. Preparation of a pro forma statement.

   g. Evaluation of management policies and the administrative controls.

   h. Interviews with bankers, lawyers, and accountants.

3. **Budgets for Research and Development Projects[6]**

   a. Are standard procedures and forms used in all of the budget forecasts ?

   b. Are individual project budgets for direct labor broken down by hours for each period and by each department which will furnish the labor ?

   c. Are the types of equipment and materials anticipated to be used spelled out in the project's initial technical estimates ?

   d. Are space needs shown in initial project estimates ?

   e. Are other direct expenses, such as travel, consultants, and printing costs, supported by such information as number of trips, days of consultant services required, and pages of technical reports to be printed ?

   f. Do project estimates show the scope of the activity to be undertaken ? Do they show what has already been accomplished and what further accomplishments are expected ?

   g. Are rates of labor, overhead, and material handling — based on actual costs — adjusted for anticipated increases or decreases ?

   h. Have the budget documents been approved at appropriate levels of management ?

   i. Are the dates indicated for each phase of the project in compliance with due dates established by procedures ?

   j. Is there a system of periodic reporting of actual versus budgeted costs ?

---

[6]Knutila, Chester, "An Auditor Looks at Research and Development Budgeting," *The Internal Auditor*, Summer 1962, p. 21.

4. Marketing[7]

a. Costs. Are studies made to determine:

(1) The break-even point for accounts or transactions to avoid taking unprofitable orders?

(2) The optimum level of inventories and related warehouse, layout, and space requirements?

(3) Whether distribution costs are reasonable?

(4) Whether sales compensation is well planned and working effectively?

b. Marketing Research. Has reliable data been used and does it provide for all major users and customers:

(1) Their outstanding characteristics and needs?

(2) The major and secondary factors influencing their buying decisions?

(3) Their assessment of the desirability of the end product?

(4) Reliable warnings of changes or trends in the buying patterns?

c. Marketing Strategy. Are there formal plans, constantly reviewed in relation to competitors' performance, for:

(1) Desirable point-of-market entry?

(2) Impact and timing of promotion effort?

(3) Timing and frequency of new-product introduction?

(4) Product pricing, trade discounts, payment terms, contribution to gross margin?

(5) Keeping product technology abreast or ahead of the competition?

(6) Protection of sales channels and the actual and relative costs of servicing such channels?

(7) Product review, to enable the orderly phasing out of products with falling contribution margins?

(8) Avoiding sales concentration on too limited a number of customers; always keeping in mind Pareto's law — 20% of the customers will probably provide 80% of the worthwhile sales activity?

---

[7]Stewart, Dudley, "The Internal Auditor of the Future," *The Internal Auditor,* March/April 1970, p. 49.

5. Objectives[8]

   a. Are they clear and understandable ?

   b. Are they sufficiently inclusive, or have major areas been overlooked ?

   c. Are they reasonable and do they properly reflect the company's responsibilities to stockholders, employees, community, and government ?

   d. Have they been communicated to operating personnel ?

   e. Are they compatible and in proper balance with each other ?

   f. Are they sufficiently divided and subdivided to make them more clearly understood and more easily followed ?

   g. Are they being changed so often that confusion and frustration result ?

6. Plans

   a. Is the subject matter sufficiently important to warrant formal plans ?

   b. Are the plans compatible with company objectives ?

   c. Do the plans help improve the coordination of reliable company objectives ?

   d. Do the plans anticipate problems and difficulties ?

   e. Do the plans permit proper delegation of responsibilities ?

   f. Do the plans capitalize on the ability and ideas of individuals in a way that will build morale and ensure attainment of objectives and goals ?

   g. Do the plans assist in achieving uniformity of action in the various branches of the company ?

   h. Do the benefits more than offset the cost of preparing the plans ?

   i. Are the plans properly communicated ?

   j. Are the plans made measurable to determine success or failure ?

7. Organization[9]

   a. Is the structure so organized as to be in consonance with the objectives and plans of the company, branch, or department ?

---

[8]Seiler, R. E., "The Internal Auditor's Appraisal of Company Objectives and Plans," *The Internal Auditor*, Winter 1960, p. 9.
[9]Zimmerman, R. R., "Auditing the Organization Structure," *The Internal Auditor*, Fall 1965, p. 59.

b. Does the structure permit authority to be commensurate with responsibility ?

c. Have clean lines of responsibility been established which extend from the top of the organization to the bottom level of supervision ?

d. Is there provision for reasonable spans of management ?

e. Is there provision for unity of command, with each person reporting to no more than one supervisor ?

f. Does the organization clearly define responsibility for every manager ?

g. Are compatible functions grouped together ?

h. Are operating responsibilities assigned to individual managers rather than to groups ?

i. Is the organization properly balanced — no function being too weak or too dominant ?

WHEN TO PREPARE THE PROGRAM

The tailored audit program should be prepared immediately after the preliminary survey. It should not be delayed. It is at that point that the audit which follows must be structured and given form. It is as unreasonable to delay preparing the program until later in the audit as it is for the navigator to first look at his charts well into his voyage when he is concerned chiefly with the running of his ship.

Immediately after the survey, when the objectives of the operation are fresh in mind, the audit program should be carefully and deliberately developed. This form of planning requires unhurried thought, for nothing of significance should be omitted. Later, in the often feverish careening through the actual examination, the air of deliberation will have dissipated; and programs prepared at that time may turn out to be marred by gaps and inadequacies.

The pro forma program used on repeated audits of similar operations often evolves over a period of years, gradually accommodating itself to the problems encountered in the field. At other times these programs may be developed in advance to obtain particular information at many localities or to fit new or changed circumstances.

New pro forma programs which are to be followed at many locations should — if at all possible — be prepared sufficiently in advance to permit them to be purged of errors, unreasonable demands, and unnecessary steps. What is conceived in the ivory tower often fails in the arena. Consequently, to prevent confusion on many fronts, such pro forma programs should be given field trials or pilot runs. The trials permit defects to surface early and to be corrected before the programs are sent out for actual use.

The experienced auditor keeps something else in mind as well when he prepares his program: the audit report. The time of program preparation is none too early to give serious thought to what he will want to say in his report. The report structure may be but dimly formed at that time; but if it is kept in mind as a measure of scope and purpose, it can offer a practical gauge to appraise the relevance and significance of the program steps.

If, for example, the auditor says to himself, "This step just won't fit into a report on the audit of the calibration of test equipment — it's more like the receiving of equipment," then he will eliminate the step and save himself time in the field and agony in the report writing.

One of the chief difficulties in writing the report is that it is often left as a necessary evil — unheeded, unweighed, and unwanted — until the auditor finally picks up his pen to write it. If the report's form and scope are considered early on, the actual writing becomes less of a burden and the report itself becomes a more cohesive whole.

SUMMARY

A thoughtful audit program is essential to the success of the audit project. The auditor should give serious consideration to the "theory of the audit" and base it on current conditions, the style and capability of operating management, and his own particular talents.

All audit programs should be developed to determine whether management's objectives are being carried out and whether adequate and effective controls will provide reasonable assurance that objectives will be met.

The auditor should review existing internal auditing literature to obtain the benefit of the ideas of experienced practitioners before completing his program. He should keep the final report in mind as he prepares the program, and he should raise his sights to make sure his program is management-oriented.

Individual programs should be developed immediately after the preliminary survey. Pro forma programs for repetitive audits should be given trial runs to purge them of errors, impractical requirements, and inconsistencies.

Exhibit 6-1a. EXCERPTS FROM AUDIT PROGRAM FOR A TRAFFIC DEPARTMENT
Source: Major Manufacturing Company

Audit segment: Analysis of Recurring Shipments

Objective of operation: To analyze shipments of a constantly recurring nature so as to reduce costs by consolidating shipments whenever possible and by initiating rate proposals.

Programmed Man-days: 3

Optimum means of control	Audit tests	W/P ref.	Comments
1. A means of obtaining input of recurring shipments, and a system of review and analysis when recurring shipments reach a predetermined level.	Determine the number of analyses made and select at random a representative sample to see whether:		
2. Provision for preparing adequate records of analyses, and supervisory review of the decisions reached.	1. Recurrent shipments are documented and are in fact being analyzed.		
3. Provision for initiating rate proposals after the analyses have been approved.	2. Adequate and accurate records are maintained, showing dates of preparation, the people preparing them, and evidence of supervisory review.		
4. A means of follow-up after proposals have been made.	3. Prompt rate proposals were made after the analyses were approved.		
5. A system of reporting on activities.	4. Steps were taken to follow up disposition of proposals.		
	5. Reports to management indicate proposals initiated, in process, and completed.		

Exhibit 6-1b. EXCERPTS FROM AUDIT PROGRAM FOR A TRAFFIC DEPARTMENT

Audit segment: Routine Inbound and Outbound Shipments

Objective of operation: To select carriers and routes which will provide the most economical and timely shipments of supplies and finished goods.

Programmed man-days: 8

Optimum means of control	Audit tests	W/P ref.	Comments
Inbound Shipments	Select at random documents covering a representative number of routings and determine whether:		
1. Provision for close coordination with the Purchasing Department and for review by Traffic personnel of requests to purchase.	1. Routing was approved by Traffic.		
2. Requirement for special approvals for premium transportation.	2. Premium traffic was properly authorized.		
3. Provision to consolidate shipments to obtain carload rates.	3. Items received in large quantities, and subject to carload rates, were received in carload lots and not LCL (less than carload).		
4. Standard time spans for the ordering of commodities to allow adequate time for nonpremium routings.	4. Sufficient time was allowed by the ordering and purchasing departments between shipping and required dates.		
5. Preparation by Traffic for Purchasing of information on routing and rates for major suppliers of principal purchased commodities.	5. Suppliers made allowances for transportation costs when purchase orders provided for carload shipments and part of the shipment was LCL.		

Exhibit 6-1c. EXCERPTS FROM AUDIT PROGRAM FOR A TRAFFIC DEPARTMENT

Optimum means of control	Audit tests	W/P ref.	Comments
Outbound Shipments	Select at random documents covering a representative number of shipments and determine whether:		
1. Provision for Traffic to specify means of shipment.	1. Routing was specified by Traffic.		
2. Maintenance of current routing and rate guides.	2. Routing and rate guides were up to date.		
3. Provision to charge customer for more expensive routing when such routing is requested.	3. Customer was billed for more expensive routings which he requested.		
4. Provision for adequate support for premium shipments.	4. Premium rates were supported by:		

5. Provision to review and report on the use of premium shipments.	a. Reason for the routing.
	    b. Authorization for premium shipment.
	    c. Appropriate accounting distribution.		

	5. Results anticipated by premium transportation were actually gained.		

Exhibit 6-1d. EXCERPTS FROM AUDIT PROGRAM FOR A TRAFFIC DEPARTMENT

(Editor's Note: The following portions show only the audit segments, objectives of the operation, and programmed man-days, as an indication of how the program can be prepared.)

Audit segment: Demurrage

Objective of operation: To maintain adequate records and surveillance over equipment so as to minimize demurrage charges

Programmed man-days: 1

Audit segment: Travel of Personnel and Transportation of Household Effects

Objective of operation: To make travel and moving arrangements that will ensure the economical and timely transportation of personnel and household effects

Programmed man-days: 4

Audit segment: Audit, Approval, and Recording of Freight Charges

Objective of operation: To see that payments of freight charges are correct and timely and that freight expenses are charged to the proper accounts

Programmed man-days: 7

Audit segment: Processing Freight Claims

Objective of operation: To see that prompt and full payment is received for all shortages, damages, and over-charges involving freight shipments

Programmed man-days: 5

Exhibit 6-1e. EXCERPTS FROM AUDIT PROGRAM FOR A TRAFFIC DEPARTMENT

Audit segment: Licenses and Clearances for Export and Import Shipments

Objective of operation: To obtain promptly the necessary licenses and clearances for shipments to and from foreign countries.

Programmed man-days: 2

Audit segment: Preparation of Export and Import Documents

Objective of operation: To prepare all required export and import documents in an accurate and timely manner

Programmed man-days: 3

Audit segment: Switching

Objective of operation: To control movement of traffic on company-owned property so as to keep switching charges to a minimum

Programmed man-days: 1

Exhibit 6-2. EXCERPTS FROM AUDIT PROGRAM FOR
SAFE DEPOSIT DEPARTMENT

Source: Large Banking Institution

General Information

Boxes are rented to customers for the safekeeping of personal property. Each safe deposit box has two separate locks. The box can be opened only when the key to each of these locks is used at the same time. When a box is rented, two keys to one of these locks are given to the customer. There are no duplicates available. The keys to the other lock, which are called "Guard Keys," are kept by the bank. No customer can gain admittance to a box without proper identification.

Purpose of Audit

1. To determine whether all boxes that are supposed to be rented are actually rented and that proper rental fees are being received.
2. To determine whether there is strict adherence to operating procedures.
3. To determine whether rental collections are credited to the proper income account.

Lease Agreements

1. Review exceptions noted in the last audit.
2. Prepare a list of all safe numbers in the vault. If a prepared list is included with the working papers, make a visual check to verify the numbers.
3. Review lease agreements for rented boxes. Place audit mark opposite the number on the list for each agreement held.
4. If the agreement is new since the previous audit, check for proper completion and correctness of form used. Initial and yeardate on the agreement to the left of the safe number. (An alteration of safe number on the rental agreement should be initialed by the renter.)
5. Check all court orders of guardianship and trusteeship covering new lease agreements.
6. If a box is subject to restricted access because of a deceased depositor, two or more should be present or, if there is an attachment, list the number on a work sheet.
   a. Check to see that the agreement card is jacketed.
   b. Check to see that there is a plug in the lock of the customer's box.
   c. Test-check access slips, for boxes requiring two or more to be present, by comparing signatures with the agreement card.
7. Review customer access procedure with the safe deposit attendant.
   a. Ask attendant to outline procedure followed in admitting customer to box.
   b. Review current access slips for proper processing and filing.
8. At offices where a separate audit is made of the safe deposit department, indicate on the office rating sheet the number of boxes available and number of boxes rented. For example: "Of the 5,268 total number of boxes, 4,183 were rented on the date of our audit."

Keys ■ Annual Rental Cards ■ Contents of Drilled Boxes ■ Storage ■ Night Depository ■ Articles Found on Bank Premises ■ Vacant Boxes.

Exhibit 6-3.   EXCERPTS FROM AUDIT PROGRAM FOR ORDERING, PRODUCTION, AND BILLING

Source: Large Mill

Objectives:

To determine that the procedures followed provide adequate internal control to give practical assurance that:

1. Orders received for processing are properly accounted for and filed in the sequence received, consistent with good operating practice.

2. Orders placed to produce required quantities according to specification requirements are handled expeditiously and in a good business manner.

3. Accurate order identification is maintained for all material at all stages of processing.

4. Loss of material in process and material not meeting order specifications are properly accounted for and classified.

5. Commodities are produced and shipped in accordance with specifications.

6. The customer is billed for the product exactly as shipped unless specific deviations are prescribed.

7. All products shipped are billed.

8. All credit memos issued are properly authorized.

9. Customers receive prompt and dependable service, and quality products are shipped.

THROUGHOUT THIS AUDIT, THE AUDITORS SHOULD BE ALERT TO DETECT AND EXPLORE ANY CONDITION OR PRACTICE IN WHICH A CHANGE MAY PROVIDE FINANCIAL OR OTHER BENEFITS.

The program section titled Examination of Transactions and Detailed Records is intended to provide the means to determine whether internal control is adequate to achieve the stated objectives. Determination of the accuracy of information is important, but the degree of accuracy is not in itself a measure of the adequacy of internal control. Excessive errors indicate that controls may be inadequate, but risks may exist because of inadequate controls even if no errors are detected.

Essentials of Internal Control:

1. Order process scheduling must conform with operating practices to effect economies. The placement of orders for production should be done by the production planning function. The responsibility for the sequence of order placement is fixed and the sequence should be supported by adequate authorizations.

2. Responsibility must be fixed for the ordering of materials to produce the product as ordered. Records of past performance should be used to properly control material requirement orders.

3. Order identification of all material in process should be maintained. Identifications such as company tags, tabulating cards, tickets, or markings should be used and should be readily accessible and legible.

Exhibit 6-3. (Cont.)

4. Complete records should be available to show quantities rejected by order number, at each processing operation. Records, such as order tracing cards, production progress reports, etc., manual or mechanical, should be used.

5. Records of the disposition, including reapplication of all material or products rejected during each stage of processing, should be maintained.

6. Adequate weighing facilities should be maintained to weigh those products billed on an actual weight basis. Procedures should be in effect to ship all products strictly in accordance with the order requirements. All shipments should be supported by formal shipping notices, bills of lading, passout slips, etc. Any products produced in excess of order quantity requirements should be accounted for.

7. All billings to customers should be supported by shipping tallies, and all invoices should be checked against the mill order.

8. Tonnage billed should be reported in billing number sequence on daily reports of shipments.

9. All debit or credit memorandums issued should be supported by proper authorizations, and all credit memorandums covering returned goods should be supported by adequate receiving records.

Preparation for the Audit:

1. The auditor will select a representative number of completed orders on file in the producing unit under audit for a period of a month. The number of orders selected for check will be at the auditor's discretion. The selection should cover a range of customers and product classifications.

   The orders selected will be followed through all processes to final billing or manifesting. The auditor will determine the control over and the disposition of rejected or over-produced quantities.

2. Flow Charts
   a. Prepare a flow chart of the order control, production planning, production, shipping, and invoicing functions. Revise the flow chart during subsequent examinations if changes in procedures have been made.

   b. In completing the audit steps outlined in this program, determine that work actually accomplished by employees of the unit is that which is set forth in the flow chart and applicable manuals.

   c. The extent and areas of electronic data processing operations should be clearly set forth and adequately described.

   d. Differences in departmental practices between branches should be reported in a functional audit report if there is no compelling reason for the differences.

Exhibit 6-3. (Cont.)

Examination of Transactions and Records:

The auditor will survey for proper controls and make the following examinations:

A. Orders

B. Material Requirement Orders

C. Production Records

	19___		19___		19___	
	Schedule	Auditor	Schedule	Auditor	Schedule	Auditor

1. Check mill order detail with the operating schedules for accuracy of quantities and specification.

A_____ _____ _____ _____ _____ _____
B_____ _____ _____ _____ _____ _____
C_____ _____ _____ _____ _____ _____

2. Procure copies of order tracing records, schedules, or other records that indicate quantities produced by each processing operation.

A_____ _____ _____ _____ _____ _____
B_____ _____ _____ _____ _____ _____
C_____ _____ _____ _____ _____ _____

3. Losses indicated between operations should be noted and checked against the production records to determine the classification of the loss. Losses should fall into the classifications of scrap, rejected secondary product, or reclassified prime product.

A_____ _____ _____ _____ _____ _____
B_____ _____ _____ _____ _____ _____
C_____ _____ _____ _____ _____ _____

4. Rejections classified as secondary product or reclassified prime product should be traced back to the mill order records to determine disposition.

A_____ _____ _____ _____ _____ _____
B_____ _____ _____ _____ _____ _____
C_____ _____ _____ _____ _____ _____

5. Attention should be given to elapsed time between operations, and any unreasonable delays should be investigated.

A_____ _____ _____ _____ _____ _____
B_____ _____ _____ _____ _____ _____
C_____ _____ _____ _____ _____ _____

6. Review scale inspection reports to determine that attention is paid to scale accuracy. Determine that test weights used are accurate.

A_____ _____ _____ _____ _____ _____
B_____ _____ _____ _____ _____ _____
C_____ _____ _____ _____ _____ _____

7. Review procedure for reordering quantities rejected on orders. Determine if proper control is maintained over order quantities in process.

A_____ _____ _____ _____ _____ _____
B_____ _____ _____ _____ _____ _____
C_____ _____ _____ _____ _____ _____

Exhibit 6-3. (Cont.)

D. Shipping
E. Billing
F. Material Shipped for Further Processing
G. General

| | 19____ | | 19____ | | 19____ | |
	Answer	Auditor	Answer	Auditor	Answer	Auditor
No suggestions	_____	_____	_____
Suggestions submitted	_____	_____	_____

Internal Control Questionnaire:

1. Is the order booking, order service, and scheduling substantially as set forth in applicable manuals?

A						
B						
C						

2. Is scheduling done on the most economical operating basis consistent with good operating practices?

A						
B						
C						

3. Are order status or tracer records updated currently and maintained in sufficient detail to answer requests for information?

A						
B						
C						

4. Is manual and electronic data processing work coordinated so that wasteful duplication of effort is eliminated?

A						
B						
C						

5. Is material ordering consistent with good operating practices and sufficiently coordinated to reduce excesses?

A						
B						
C						

6. Are production records adequate for the purpose intended?

A						
B						
C						

7. Is an effort made to apply operational stock or slow moving stock to incoming orders if possible?

A						
B						
C						

8. Are unenterable orders withheld from booking and processing until approved by the Product Division?

A						
B						
C						

9. Is metallurgical or production planning overgrading subject to approval by the Product Division?

A						
B						
C						

Exhibit 6-3. (Cont.)

10. Is the description of all processes shown on invoices in sufficient detail to alert pricing personnel to all chargeable extras?

A_____ ____ ____ ____ ____
B_____ ____ ____ ____ ____
C_____ ____ ____ ____ ____

11. Are controls on material shipped for further processing adequate to insure that the customer is ultimately invoiced?

A_____ ____ ____ ____ ____
B_____ ____ ____ ____ ____
C_____ ____ ____ ____ ____

12. Are gate passes or shipping documents received by Plant Protection officers sent directly to the billing department and compared with the completed invoice or traced to the report of trucks forwarded?

A_____ ____ ____ ____ ____
B_____ ____ ____ ____ ____
C_____ ____ ____ ____ ____

13. Is the report of railroad cars forwarded compared with the railroad's interchange report to determine that all cars shipped are recorded?

A_____ ____ ____ ____ ____
B_____ ____ ____ ____ ____
C_____ ____ ____ ____ ____

14. Are "No bills" (railroad cars pulled out of the mill to the mainline railroad before bills of lading are prepared) adequately controlled?

A_____ ____ ____ ____ ____
B_____ ____ ____ ____ ____
C_____ ____ ____ ____ ____

15. Are scales checked at regular intervals?

A_____ ____ ____ ____ ____
B_____ ____ ____ ____ ____
C_____ ____ ____ ____ ____

16. Are tables of theoretical weights, used where scale weights are not available, accurate?

A_____ ____ ____ ____ ____
B_____ ____ ____ ____ ____
C_____ ____ ____ ____ ____

17. Are claim files supported by receiving reports if the material was returned and do they show other disposition if the material was not returned?

A_____ ____ ____ ____ ____
B_____ ____ ____ ____ ____
C_____ ____ ____ ____ ____

Based on your audit and review of internal control, have you any suggestions for improvement of the internal control, procedures, or accounting system in these areas of responsibility?

No suggestions _____ ____ ____ ____

Suggestions submitted _____ ____ ____ ____

seven ■

SAMPLING

INTRODUCTION

Scientific sampling isn't all that hard. There's really no great trick to understanding it. In fact, the biggest barrier to becoming familiar with it is probably the name it goes under: statistical sampling. That name conjures up visions of formidable formulas and abstruse mathematical concepts. It needn't but it does. So for our purposes let us call the subject sampling — just sampling. And this is something the auditor has been doing all his professional life.

Sampling, in essence, is the process of learning about a lot by looking at a little. In auditing it is used mostly to help form an opinion or recommend action on a macrocosm (the population) by examining a microcosm (a sample of the population). Sampling, then, is just another tool that the auditor uses to shape his opinion. It is not an end in itself. It is only a means toward an end. The sample and the sample results are merely raw data. And that data must be weighed and sifted. It must be analyzed for materiality, for reasons, for causes, and for effects. The sample is but the first step on the road to an informed audit opinion.

Sometimes that opinion cannot be formed without a little help from mathematics. But the mathematics need not be difficult. In fact, once the closed mind is opened to permit a clear view of some basic principles, the vista becomes rather inviting. Indeed, the feeling of satisfaction and accomplishment is worth the little trouble it takes to cross the threshold of distrust and find understanding.

The veteran auditor with thousands of samplings behind him may well ask, "I've done all right so far, so why do I have to learn this scientific mumbo jumbo?" That question, in today's environment, is readily answered: The samples he used couldn't be defended. Most likely nobody knew enough to dispute his samples — samples which may not have been representative of the population sampled, whose results could not be objectively measured, or, indeed, which might have been excessive, wasting both the auditor's and the client's time and patience. There is little doubt that a shrewd challenge to many of the veteran's samples could have left him floundering and defenseless.

Modern managers are becoming mathematically literate. Included in that competence today is a good grounding in probability theory — on which all scientific sampling is based. Let the auditor attack their operations with the brittle lance of an unscientific sample and the knowledgeable operating managers will easily shatter the lance and discomfit the lancer.

Moreover, executive management may look to the auditor when faced with problems related to or generated by sampling. Their own assistants may present proposals for courses of action based on samples or sampling theory. On the surface the proposals may hold promise; but the executive, a pragmatist, is sure to ask, "How good are they, really?" The executive may not be able to tell of his own knowledge. So he will naturally turn for assistance to the auditor, his objective advisor; for shouldn't the auditor be an expert on sampling?

Also, auditors from governmental agencies or from prime contractors, auditing the company's transactions, may assert claims or allege discrepancies on the strength of samples. Whom does the manager turn to for his shield? His own auditor, of course.

If the auditor has a firm grasp of some of the basic principles of scientific sampling, he can provide the assistance management feels it has a right to expect of him. And once he has charted those basic principles, it becomes easier and easier for him to sail deeper into the sea of probability theory without getting lost. Let us then explore these principles.

To begin with, the beast is easier to grasp if one understands that audit sampling stands on three legs: Selecting the sample items. Deciding how many to select. Evaluating the sample results.

In this chapter we shall talk of all three. We shall not, however, explore the many variations of each — volumes have been written on that subject. For our purpose, a survey of the key sampling techniques and plans will suffice — together with a discussion of the evaluation of population proportions and approximations, a helpful audit technique.

For a more detailed discussion, I recommend the *Sampling Manual for Auditors* (1967) and the *Supplement to the Sampling Manual for Auditors* (1970) both developed by Lockheed Aircraft Corporation and published by The Institute of Internal Auditors, and the *Handbook of Sampling for Auditing and Accounting* (1963) by Herbert Arkin, New York: McGraw-Hill Book Company.

Also, where long-range, complex scientific sampling plans are undertaken — as, for example, substituting sampling for the complete examination of inventories — it is wise to coordinate the sampling program with such people as the company's public accountant, the cognizant EDP manager, the financial operations manager, and/or a qualified statistician.

SAMPLE SELECTION
General

When an auditor selects a sample, he may take at least two paths. The first is toward the "directed" sample; the second is toward the "random" sample.

The "directed" or "purposive" sample is used when the auditor suspects serious error or manipulation and wants either to obtain evidence to buttress his suspicion or to find as many of the suspected items as he can. This has nothing to do with scientific sampling. It is pure detective work. And the better a sleuth the auditor is, the better his sample will be. But he may not draw conclusions about the population from a directed sample. Such conclusions are completely unwarranted. And the reasons will become more apparent as we discuss the random sample.

The random sample seeks to represent, as closely as possible, the population from which it was taken. When the auditor takes a random sample he is trying to take a picture in miniature of the great mass of records or data that make up the population from which the sample is selected. The better the selection the better the picture — the more closely the sample is a good depiction of the population. In audit argot the sample is termed representative.

There are certain rules for taking a representative sample. They are quite reasonable rules and make good sense. Unfortunately, many auditors flout the rules and wind up making unwarranted assumptions about the population they have sampled. Here are two fundamental rules of selection:

■ Know your population, because audit opinions may be based only on what has been sampled.

■ Let every item in the population have an equal chance of being selected.

Let us examine just what these rules imply.

The mass of data, records, or documents from which the auditor selects his sample is variously referred to as population, universe, and field. They all mean the same thing. They also imply something that is central to good sampling: Know what you are testing.

The first thing that an auditor must do when he takes a sample is to decide what he is taking it from. His initial question must be "What is my population?" It is a most significant question, having as much to do with good audit practice as with statistics. Yet many auditors consistently violate this principle in their sampling. Such violations lay their tests open to serious question on technical grounds; and their opinions are without objective support.

Consider, for example, the auditor who wishes to estimate the annual fuel consumption of the company's automotive fleet. The fleet is made up of:

50 — 12-wheel trucks

100 — pick-up trucks

100 — fork lift trucks

200 — passenger cars

<u>300</u> — motor scooters

750 — pieces of automotive equipment

Let us assume in this example that the fleet has been well maintained and that there are no "gas eaters" within each group. Since the motor scooters were the most numerous, the auditor decided to select a sample of 50 motor scooters, examine fuel consumption for those 50, and project his findings to all 750 pieces of equipment. Stated this way the results are clearly ludicrous. Yet auditors fall into similar traps in their sampling every day. For example:

- They might select a sample of invoices from all those paid in July and use that test to form an opinion of all invoices paid during the year.

- They might select a sample of travel vouchers for local travel only and project their findings to a population which includes foreign travel as well.

- They might select a sample of purchase orders from a population which excludes all orders under $5,000 and express opinions on all purchase orders issued by the purchasing department — from $1 on up.

- They might sample inventory records in one tool crib and express an opinion on the records of tool cribs in all the many locations within the company.

Each of these opinions and projections — unless properly qualified — is without support and just plain wrong. In the case of the motor vehicles, the auditor either should have sampled from all the various types of equipment or should have restricted his opinion to scooters alone.

Hence, the auditor must always remember to *define the population* before starting to take his sample. He must always consider the nature of the population in terms of his audit objectives. For example, the population of the 750 vehicles can have a different meaning, depending on the audit objective. If the audit objective were to determine whether all vehicles are being maintained regularly — and let us assume that every item of equipment, be it scooter or truck, must be periodically maintained — the population assumes a different character than if the audit objective were to estimate fuel consumption. When the population is improperly defined, in the light of the audit objective, the result is bad sampling and bad auditing. When the population is properly defined — and this may take some hard thinking and a lot of questioning — the whole audit thrust and approach improve.

The principles on which scientific sampling are based operate *only* if the sample is selected at random. And to select a random sample each item in a population must have an equal chance of being selected. There are several ways in which random selection can be accomplished. Each method has its advantages and its drawbacks. We shall discuss four. The first two are generally referred to as random sampling and interval sampling. The second two, cluster sampling and stratified sampling, are refinements of the first two.

Random Number Sampling

Random number sampling is generally considered the most likely to result in a random sample. It makes use of tables of digits that have been scientifically "randomized." The tables provide substantially complete assurance that every item in the population has an equal chance of being selected. Many such tables have been compiled. One is the "Table of 105,000 Random Decimal Digits," developed by the Interstate Commerce Commission. Appendix A contains the first six pages from that table.

The line numbers of the random digits are indicated at the left margin. Column numbers are shown in parentheses across the top of the page. The digits have been arranged in groups of 5 by 5, only because the eye would become confused if no spaces were allowed. The spaces are for eye appeal only. They do not mean that the tables are made up of 5-digit numbers.

The tables are easy to use if some simple rules are followed:

- Enter the tables by opening them at random and, with eyes averted, place a pencil point on the page. Start the number selection with the digit closest to the pencil point.
- Use as many digits in a line as there are digits in the reference numbers of the documents being selected. For example, if receiving memos being tested have a maximum of 7 digits in their numbers, use 7 adjoining numbers from the tables.
- Once a starting point has been selected, proceed through the tables in a predetermined order — down the columns or across the columns — without deviation, because deviation implies personal bias.
- If an applicable number does not appear, continue on to the next.

For example, assume a population of rejection memos numbered from 50 to 500. The auditor wishes to select a sample of 5 from that population. The point of his pencil rests on the number 6 in column 5, line 6, of Appendix A-1. He had decided beforehand that the number on which his pencil fell would be the first digit of the number he would select and that he would proceed down the columns. Number 653 is inapplicable, being outside the range of 50 to 500. Thus the first applicable number is 231 (2 from column 5, line 7, and 31 from column 6, line 7). The columns considered, the five numbers he will select, and the numbers he will reject, are as follows:

Columns Considered		Inapplicable Numbers	Applicable Numbers
27756	53498	653	
98872	31016		231
18876	20922	620	
17453	18103		318
53060	59533		059
70997	79936	779	
49626	69445	669	
88974	33488		433
48237	52267	752	
77233	13916		313

The reader will observe that:

■ Inapplicable numbers — those outside the range of 50 to 500 — are skipped.

■ Three digits are consistently used, so 059 becomes 59.

The numbers selected can then be arranged in numerical order for ease in locating the documents bearing those numbers . . . assuming the documents themselves are filed in numerical sequence.

Random number sampling can sometimes be difficult to use. Documents may be unnumbered or may resist ready identification. In these cases, another selection method may be more appropriate, such as interval sampling — sometimes referred to as systematic sampling.

Interval Sampling

Interval sampling simply means selecting items at intervals. It is a relatively simple method. But in using it, the auditor must remember his basic selection principles:

■ Because the audit opinion may be based only on the population sampled, no items should be missing from the population.

■ Because every item must have an equal chance of being selected, the first item in the selection process must be picked *at random.*

Another rule also applies when using interval sampling:

■ Because no pattern in the population should affect the selection, the auditor may have to make two or more passes through the population, each with a random start.

Let us look at a simplified example of interval selection. We will assume that the items in the population are unnumbered. The population does contain some items not applicable to the audit purpose. We shall indicate the applicable items by an x and the inapplicable items by an o. The auditor wishes to select 8 items from a mixed population of 60. Since he knows from a scanning of the population that there are some inapplicable numbers, he will select every 5th item to make sure he selects enough items for his examination, because some items may have to be rejected. If he selects too many, he will eliminate the excess, as we shall explain later.

From a table of random numbers he has determined his random start to be 4. From that 4th item he then selects every 5th item, proceeding horizontally — the selected items are underscored — as follows:

x	x	x	x̲	x	o	o	x	x̲	x
o	x	x	o̲*	x	x	o	o	x̲	x
x	x	x	x̲	o	x	x	x	o̲*	o
x	x	x	x̲	o	x	x	o	x̲	x
x	x	x	o̲*	x	x	x	o	x̲	o
x	o	o	x̲	x	x	o	o	x̲	x

*Inapplicable item found at selection point.

It will be observed that when the interval ends with an inapplicable item (o) the count for the next interval begins again by using the item immediately after the inapplicable item as the point of new departure. If not, a fundamental principle would be violated: Every item must have an equal chance of being selected.

Recall that the auditor needed only 8 items for his sample. The one excess item may be excluded; but at *random*. A simple method of deciding which item to exclude is through the use of the random number tables. The selected items may be given numbers as follows:

1   2   3   4   5   6   7   8   9

From the random number table select a digit at random, using the pencil-point method. If the selected digit were to be 2, for example, the second item in the sample could be excluded.

Interval sampling is the simplest selection technique to use; and if it is used with care, it can provide adequate assurance that the sample has been selected at random.

Stratified Sampling

Stratified sampling helps arrange the population so as to make the sample results more reliable. In every population the auditor should look for wide variations in size, amount, or characteristics of the items making up the population. When he sees wide variations he should consider stratification.

Stratified sampling means separating the population into two or more strata — in effect separate populations — and then taking samples from each. Auditors have always used the principles of stratification. Usually, they set aside the largest or most expensive or most significant items in a population for complete examination and then select a sample from the remainder.

It may sometimes be desirable to allocate the population to many strata so as to reduce the number of items needed, in order to obtain a representative sample of the population. And, as we shall see later, it is variability in the population, not its size, that causes sharp increases in the samples needed to give a good picture of the population.

Obviously, if the population were composed of identical items, a sample of only one of them would be representative of the whole. For example, if the auditor wished to estimate fuel consumption for a fleet of 1,000 cars, and each automotive unit in the fleet was exactly the same as the others, all he would need to do is study the consumption of one unit and multiply by 1,000. He would have fairly good assurance that the projection would be a pretty reliable indicator of the true condition. If, however, the fleet were made up of tiny scooters, huge trailer trucks, and many different types of units in between, he would have to select samples from each type — in other words, he would have to stratify the population.

In real life situations the quality of the population usually varies widely. And the more the quality or character of the individual items differ — in the characteristic under study, of course — the greater the number of items the auditor must select to obtain a fair representation of the population. The auditor is seeking to obtain a good picture of the population through his sample. The picture tends to get distorted by unusual items or wide swings of variability. Sometimes — in fact, usually — the only way to get that picture is through stratification.

Stratification, then, helps the auditor in two important ways: It removes distortion and it permits smaller sample sizes.

Just how to stratify, how many strata to develop, and what items to group together, call for audit judgment. It can be done mathematically, and the methods are described in the *Sampling Manual for Auditors* and in the *Supplement to the Sampling Manual*. In most cases, however, sound audit judgment will suffice. Any reasonable stratification is better than none.

Once stratification is accomplished, the selection of the sample items can be accomplished through random number sampling or through interval sampling, depending on the circumstances.

Cluster Sampling

Cluster sampling is a recognition of the shortness of life. Sometimes documents or records are so scattered or dispersed that it is beyond the available audit budget to use straight random number or interval sampling. Thus, they may be used in combination with cluster sampling which simplifies the selection process even though it does reduce somewhat the reliability of sample results which could have been obtained from random number or interval sampling exclusively.

Cluster sampling is what the name implies. Clusters of items are selected at random. Then, the clusters are either examined in their entirety or are themselves sampled. The latter method is referred to as multistage sampling. So long as each selection is at random — first the clusters and then, if necessary, the items within the clusters — no rules are violated, since each item has been afforded an equal chance of being selected.

Clusters may be "natural," that is, all the documents in a file cabinet drawer or in a bundle of records. Or the clusters may be "artificial," that is, the auditor may decide that each half-inch group of file cards represent a cluster; and he will select such a cluster at, say, 10-inch intervals.

Cluster sampling can be used to select:

- A sample of tool cribs and then a sample of the tools in each crib.
- A sample of stock rooms and a sample of the inventory records in each of the rooms.
- A sample of file drawers and all or some of the documents filed in those drawers.
- A sample of months, weeks, or days, and a sample of the documents processed during those periods.

Mechanized Sampling

The various selection techniques just discussed can also be employed by means of data processing equipment. With so many records today on punched cards, tape, or other machine media, the selection of samples by mechanical means is becoming increasingly popular. Programs can be purchased or developed to select samples mechanically. Both the *Sampling Manual* and the *Supplement* discuss such techniques. Chapter 8 of this book provides examples of the use of the computer for sampling.

SAMPLE SIZES

General

Sample sizes can be determined practically or statistically. The decision depends on the audit objective.

In many audit situations a large audit sample or a statistically determined sample is unnecessary. Often, after a preliminary survey, the auditor may be so impressed with the quality of a control system that he will be content with the review of a few hand-picked items to assure himself that the system is actually in operation.

In such circumstances, how many items should the auditor examine? If the system is being used to process three separate types of transactions, for example, the auditor can walk one sample of each of the three types through the system, touching each of the control points. He can then declare that the system does indeed have the purported control points and that they are indeed operating. Since the system satisfied him that errant items would be detected and corrected automatically, further sampling may be wasteful.

Suppose, however, that he wishes some further assurance. He wants to feel reasonably sure within his own mind that the system is working with substantial effectiveness. What is the smallest sample he can take to give him that assurance? That is hard to say without knowing the system and the quality of the population; but he should not place undue reliance on a sample of under 30 items. Only at 30 may the sample begin to adopt the characteristics of the population. In many situations, a sample of 30 or 40 items will give sufficient assurance that the system is working with reasonable effectiveness.

But what if the auditor wishes to be able to measure objectively the reliability of his sample results? Now he is making a quantum jump. Now he must be willing to step into scientific sampling. But if he keeps an open mind and learns a few basic concepts, he will soon find that he can have a fairly sure grasp of this important subject.

Statistical Theory Simplified

The auditor must understand that when he deals with sampling, he is seeking a reliable estimate, not an exact answer. For instance, let us say an auditor examines 100 items out of a population of 1,000 — a sample of one-tenth of the population. Let us assume that he has found 5 errors. May he then multiply the number of errors by 10 and say with certainty that the population contains 50 errors? No! He *may* say — if his selection was at random — that he has a certain mathematical degree of confidence that his estimate, his projection, comes within a certain range or tolerance — that is, plus or minus some determinable percentage.

This brings us to two concepts that are pivotal to an understanding of scientific sampling:

- Confidence level
- Precision

These concepts sometimes go under other names, but to avoid confusion we shall use no other names in this book.

Confidence level is the degree to which we are justified in believing that the estimate based on a sample drawn at random will fall within a specified range. A confidence level is usually expressed as a percentage. For instance, a confidence level of 95% means that there are 95 chances out of 100 that the sample results will not vary from the true characteristics of the whole population by more than a certain specified amount; there are 5 chances out of 100 that they will.

The confidence level for a sample can be as high as 99.9%. It can never be 100%. For that degree of confidence the auditor will have to examine the entire population.

Precision is the range within which the estimate of the population characteristics will fall at the stipulated confidence level. Precision, being a range or tolerance, is usually expressed as a plus-or-minus percentage, such as ±2%.

Thus, the estimate obtained from a sample may permit the auditor to say, for example, that he is 95% confident that the value of a population is X number of dollars, ±2%.

Confidence level and precision are integral parts of the same mechanism. Each has an effect on the other. And the meaning of sample results cannot be understood without understanding that relationship. A simple example will go much further in showing this relationship than any definitions.

Assume that a baseball pitcher is given 100 balls and is asked to throw them over the center of home plate. Home plate is 17 inches wide and looks like this:

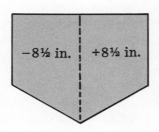

Let us assume that the pitcher can regularly get 95 of the 100 balls over the plate. It could then be said that he has a 95% chance (confidence level) of getting a ball over the center line ±8½ inches (precision).

But then let us say that we widen the plate to 20 inches, like this:

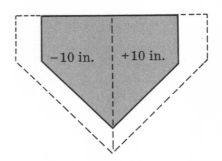

Now, with a broader range, the confidence level improves. Most likely the pitcher could get 98 or 99 balls over the center of the plate ±10 inches.

Pursuing the analogy further, let us reduce the size of the plate to 10 inches.

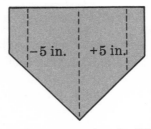

Now perhaps the pitcher can get only 80 balls over the center of the plate ±5 inches. The analogy is rough, but it points out the relationship between confidence level and precision.

Another concept that must be understood in determining sample size is variability.

More than anything else, variability determines how large the sample must be to be representative of the population. Many auditors have long believed that the size of the sample must have a direct relationship to the size of the population. In earlier days the percentage usually employed was 10%. Under that theory, a population of 100 would call for a sample of 10, and a population of a million would call for a sample of 100,000. In truth, in the first example a sample of 10 would be too small; in the second example the sample of 100,000 would be much too large.

This concept will be discussed further in mathematical terms later on. But another simple example will bring the picture into sharper focus. Assume three lengths of cloth, each with a different design. The owner wishes to take a swatch from each so as to match them at the store and purchase more cloth of the same designs. This is how the lengths of cloth look:

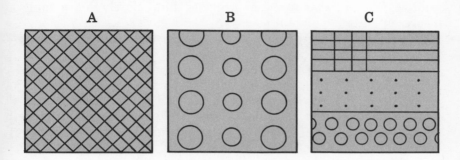

It becomes immediately apparent that although all three lengths are the same size, different sample sizes will have to be taken from each to obtain a good representation of the total length — in effect, the population. From *A* a very small sample will be representative. From *B* a much larger sample would be necessary to represent the total design. From *C*, unless a sample is taken from each of the four design patterns – in effect, stratification – a very large sample would be needed.

So sample size depends on three factors:

1. Confidence level
2. Precision
3. Population variability

The first two are under the control of the auditor. He, in his audit judgment, must decide how much reliability he needs from his sample. This calls for sound judgment, based on the audit objectives and the nature of the associated system of internal control.

Although the auditor may sometimes reduce variability by stratifying the population, variability is outside his control once the population to be sampled has been defined. It is part of the nature and character of the population he must deal with. And one of the basic priciples in sampling is "know your population." With that knowledge there are ways of measuring that variability. This measurement — so fundamental to scientific sampling — will be dealt with shortly.

Once the confidence level and precision have been decided on and once the variability of the population has been measured, the auditor is in a good position to determine how large a sample he will need to give him sample results which are sufficiently reliable for his purpose. In other words, he will be able to predict how close to the true population values (determined precisely only by examining the entire population) are the values of his sample. Put another way, he will see how closely his sample represents his population.

This ability to predict is based on principles that have been developed mathematically. The principle states, roughly, that the measurements of the values of many similar objects — when arrayed according to value or size — tend to take the shape of a bell, also known as the normal curve. And if one were to select from any population, at random, an infinite number of samples of the same size (of about 30 or more units), the frequency distribution of the means (averages) of all those samples would *inevitably* take the shape of a bell-shaped curve — no matter how the values of the population were distributed. Further, the mean of all the sample means would be the same as the population mean. This latter concept is important because it permits a prediction of population values based on sample values.

To pictorialize — so as to show how natural that shape is — assume a huge funnel, closed at the bottom and filled with gravel, suspended over a flat surface.

As the gravel is released from the funnel, it will invariably assume a shape somewhat as follows:

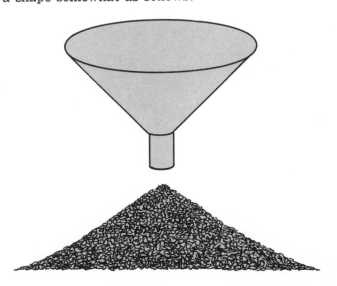

Viewed in silhouette, the pile of sand seems to have a bell-shaped curve. This shape seems natural to the viewer. Any other shape under the same circumstances might seem unnatural.

And that is how the measurements of a great number of objects could be pictured. Assume the measurement of the shoe sizes of 2,000 men selected at random, plotted on a graph. The results could be as follows:

Number of
measurements

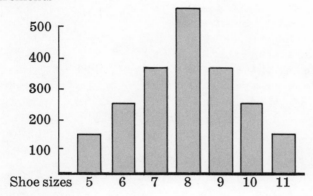

Again we see the frequency of the measurements tending to take the form of a bell-shaped curve. And the shape of the curve will depict the variability of the population: A high, narrow curve will illustrate little variability; a flat, wide curve will illustrate great variability.

Variability within a population can be measured. Just as coal can be weighed by the ton, speed can be measured by miles per hour, length can be measured by yards, and time can be measured by hours . . . so can variability be measured by what is known as the "standard deviation." This formidable term means simply the measure of the variability of a particular population or of a sample from that population.

Let us break it down into its components. The standard deviation, technically, is the square root of the average of the squared deviations from the mean. It is portrayed in the following formula:

$$s = \sqrt{\frac{\Sigma\,(x - \bar{x})^2}{n - 1}}$$

s = standard deviation
Σ = the sum of
x = each observation — the characteristic or value of each sample item
$\bar{x}$ = the average (arithmetical mean) of the sample item values
n = the size of the sample

To determine the standard deviation:

■ Obtain the mean (average) of the sample items
■ Subtract the mean from each item
■ Square the results and sum them
■ Divide that sum by the number of sample items — minus 1
■ Extract the square root

The result is the standard deviation of the sample . . . the measure of variability of the sample . . . and hence an estimate of the variability of the population.

Let us determine the standard deviation, through this method, of two groups of numbers. Each has the same mean, but different variability. The resulting standard deviations will show how this measure portrays variability whereas the mean or average does not:

A				B			
Sample values	Mean*	Difference	Difference squared	Sample values	Mean*	Difference	Difference squared
17 − 20	=	−3	9	11 − 20	=	−9	81
20 − 20	=	0	0	20 − 20	=	0	0
23 − 20	=	+3	9	29 − 20	=	+9	81
3)60 = 20*			2)18 = 9	3)60 =20*			2)162 = 81
$\sqrt{9} = 3$				$\sqrt{81} = 9$			

Note: Sample size of 3 minus 1 = 2

Although both groups of numbers have a common mean, the standard deviation of the one with the greater variability is three times that with the smaller variability.

The relationship between the bell curve, or normal distribution, and the standard deviation is an interesting one. It has been determined that in any normal distribution, the mean of the distribution, plus or minus one standard deviation, includes about 68% of the area under the normal curve; the mean plus or minus two standard deviations includes about 95.5% of the area; and the mean plus or minus three standard deviations includes about 99.7% of the area.

Unlike fixed units of measurement, such as an inch or a minute, the standard deviation will be different for each sample or each population, because the standard deviation is the measure of variability of individual samples or populations. But regardless of the nature of the population, if we select at random a large number of samples of the same size, the distribution of the means of all those samples approximates a normal curve . . . and the average of the sample averages equals the average of the population.

The relationship between standard deviations and the curve can be shown as follows:

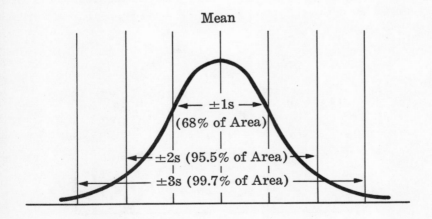

Now let us see how this helps us in a sampling problem. Based on the principles of the normal curve, we could say that any item selected at random would fall — 68% of the time — within the range measured by the sample mean, plus or minus one standard deviation. Let us put it another way: Assuming a sample of invoices — "normally distributed" — with an arithmetic mean of $100 and a standard deviation of $10, we could say that 68% of the sampling units will fall within the value of $100 plus or minus one standard deviation of $10 — from $90 to $110 at a confidence level of 68%.

If we wished to increase our confidence level to 95.5%, we must now be satisfied with a wider range — plus or minus two standard deviations. Thus:

$80 to $120 at a confidence level of 95.5%

If we wished to increase our confidence level still further to 99.7%, we would have to be satisfied with a still wider range — plus or minus three standard deviations. Thus:

$70 to $130 at a confidence level of 99.7%

Or if we wished a confidence level of 95% — plus or minus 1.96 standard deviations, our range would be as follows:

$80.40 to $119.60 at a confidence level of 95%

On the normal curve, the results just enumerated could be pictured as follows:

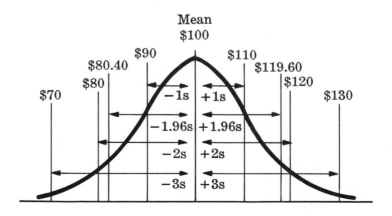

Recapitulating, then, the sample size is largely dependent on:

- The confidence level the auditor wants
- The precision he wants
- The variability he finds in the population

One other factor affects sample size: the audit objective . . . what the auditor is seeking to determine by his tests. His objective may call for any one of several plans.

In the following subsections we shall furnish a brief overview of four statistical sampling plans. The first two constitute estimation sampling and are usually referred to as sampling for attributes and sampling for variables. Sampling for attributes provides answers to the question "How many?" (that is, how many of this or that attribute or characteristic). Sampling for variables provides answers to the question "How much?" (that is, how much in terms of dollars or other variable values). The third plan is referred to as stop-or-go sampling and is an economical way of obtaining certain information about a population. The fourth is called discovery or exploratory sampling and is used to obtain evidence of a single item of impropriety, assuming there was more than one such impropriety in the population. A fifth sampling plan, which does not provide for statistical measurement but which is regularly used in auditing — judgment sampling — is also discussed.

Sampling for Attributes

This plan calls for yes-or-no, black-or-white answers. It is usually applied to testing systems of internal control. It is concerned with estimating the number of errors or other characteristics in a population.

It can provide an estimate of the number of engineering drawings received late by production people. But it will not give an estimate of how late — that is the function of variables sampling.

It can provide an estimate of the number of purchase orders issued to sole sources. But it will not give an estimate of their value — that too is the function of variables sampling.

Determining sample sizes is relatively easy when tables are used, and the method of using the tables is set forth in the *Sampling Manual for Auditors*. Briefly stated, the auditor first determines:

1. The population size
2. The desired confidence level
3. The desired precision
4. The expected error rate

We have not yet discussed the expected error rate. But the principle has been touched on in our discussion of variability. As we have seen, the more variable the items in a population the greater the sample size needed. Obviously, there is no great variability in a situation where the characteristic of interest is either "yes" or "no." And if all the characteristics were "yes" it would take a test of only one to then predict that all the other items in the population were also "yes." But the more "no's" — up to 50% of the items — that are sprinkled throughout the population, the larger the sample needed to obtain a good representation of that population.

Estimating the error rate calls for judgment. But there are methods available to the auditor to give him a reasonably sound basis for his estimate. Here are some of the things he can do:

■ Examine a pilot sample of about 30 or 40 items.

■ Review prior working papers for past experience.

■ Discuss the estimated number of errors being encountered, with knowledgeable people.

■ Estimate the percentage of error it would take to automatically alert management that something was wrong.

Once he has made the necessary decisions the auditor can proceed to the tables without difficulty, finding the one that shows the population size, confidence level, precision, and expected error rate in which he is interested.

The same results can be obtained by using a fairly simple formula and the standard deviation factors just discussed. Here we shall call them Z factors for use in the formula. One of the benefits of the formula is that it can accommodate any population size, any sample size, any confidence level and precision stipulated, and any error rate estimated. It would take an inordinately large number of tables to do the same.

The formula, which can be solved through simple arithmetic and requires no extraction of square roots, is as follows:

$$n = \frac{Z^2 \times N \times p\,(1-p)}{(A^2 \times N)\ +\ (Z^2 \times p\,(1-p)\,)}$$

The symbols have the following meaning:

n = sample size
N = population size
p = expected error rate
A = desired precision
Z = factor for the desired confidence level

A list of the factors for desired confidence levels will be found in Appendix B. The reader will observe that the factors are based on the normal curve, just discussed.

Assuming a population of 1,000 (N), a desired precision of ±2% (A), a confidence level of 95% (Z), and an error rate not to exceed 5% (p), the sample size required would be 313, computed as follows:

$$n = \frac{1.96^2 \times 1000 \times .05\,(1-.05)}{(.02^2 \times 1000) + (1.96^2 \times .05\,(1-.05))}$$

$$n = \frac{3.8416 \times 1000 \times .05 \times .95}{(.0004 \times 1000) + (3.8416 \times .05 \times .95)}$$

$$n = \frac{3841.6 \times .0475}{.4 + (3.8416 \times .0475)}$$

$$n = \frac{182.476}{.4 + .182476}$$

$$n = \frac{182.476}{.582476}$$

$$n = \mathbf{313}$$

If the auditor examines the sample of 313 items and finds that there is indeed an error rate of 5%, then he can declare that he is 95% sure that his population of 1000 contains 950 error-free items, plus or minus 2% of 1000, or plus or minus 20 items. In other words, the number of satisfactory items in the population can be estimated to be anywhere from 930 to 970.

If it turned out that the error rate in his sample is actually much higher — say 10% or 15% — the auditor would recompute the formula, using the new error rate, and determine how many more items he would have to examine to obtain an estimate with the required confidence level and precision.

Sampling for Variables

This form of sampling is sometimes called dollar estimation, since it usually deals with dollar values. It can also be used for any other kinds of variable values, like time periods and weights.

Variables sampling can be used to obtain estimates — based on a sample — of the value of inventories, the value of disallowances of travel vouchers, the value of aged accounts receivable, and the like. And computing sample sizes and sample results is simplified by the use of tables. Such tables can be found in the sampling manuals referred to previously.

In this chapter we shall make use of an alternative set of tables which allows a certain degree of flexibility that may be desirable in computing sample sizes.

To establish suitable sample sizes, the auditor must determine, as he did for attributes sampling, the population size, the desired confidence level, and the desired precision. Instead of an expected error rate, however, he must determine the standard deviation.

As we pointed out before, the expected error rate is a measure of variability, used in attributes sampling, that is needed to work out the formulas for sample sizes. In variables sampling the standard deviation does the same thing.

Accordingly, for the first step in establishing the sample size needed to provide the desired degree of reliability, the auditor must estimate the standard deviation of the population. He does that by determining the standard deviation of the sample. Just as he may take a pilot sample in attributes sampling to estimate the error rate, so he must take a pilot sample in variables sampling to determine the standard deviation.

The sample for that purpose should not be fewer than 100 units. Fewer than that number may not be representative of the population and therefore may not give a correct reading. The sample must be drawn at random, and even though it is termed a pilot sample, all the items selected can be used as a part of the additional sample items that may be required to achieve desired sample reliability.

In dealing with so many numbers, it is best to use a simplified computation in determining the standard deviation. This computation does not require subtracting the mean from the value of each sample item. The results are the same as those obtained from the formula described earlier in this chapter.

The simpler formula (easier to compute even though it looks more complicated) is as follows:

$$s = \sqrt{\frac{\Sigma\,(x^2) - (\Sigma x)^2/n}{n - 1}}$$

The meanings of the symbols are as follows:
s = standard deviation of the sample
Σ = sum of
x = value of each sample item
n = sample size

Using one of the examples shown on page 194, the standard deviation can be computed as follows from the formula:

Sample values	A Sum of squared sample values	B Square of sum of sample values divided by sample size	A - B divided by sample size minus 1	Square root of difference
11	121	11		
20	400	20	1362	
29	841	29	−1200	
	1362	60	2 ⟌ 162 = 81	√81 = 9

$$60^2 = 3600$$

$$3600 \div 3 = 1200$$

The standard deviation from this formula, just as it was when we used the other formula, is 9.

Once the standard deviation has been determined, the tables can be entered to determine the precision obtained through the sample. Let us first explain, however, what the tables have to offer.

Appendix C provides a list of precision factors for sample sizes from 30 to 300 and then at graduated intervals up to 10,000. The factors are shown at confidence levels of 80%, 90%, 95%, and 99%. A column of square roots is also provided to assist in the extraction of the square root in computing standard deviations.

The table is computed for infinite — very large — populations. Thus, if the population is not very large, it is necessary to adjust the precision by a factor which takes into account the relationship between the sample size and the population size. If the population is small, and the sample represents a large percentage of the population, then the precision obtained from Appendix C would have to be adjusted to a considerable degree. Appendix D provides the adjustment factors.

The easiest way to explain the use of the two appendices is through an example. Let us assume the following premises:

Population size	5,000
Population value	$500,000
Standard deviation determined from a sample of 100 items selected at random	$80
Desired confidence level	90%
Desired precision	±4%
Computation of precision per unit of population:	
±4% of $500,000	±$20,000
±$20,000 ÷ 5,000	±$4

The auditor therefore needs a precision of plus or minus $4 per unit before he will be satisfied with the reliability of his sample.

Appendix C-2 shows a precision factor of ±.1660 for a sample size of 100 and a confidence level of 90%.

The ratio of sample (100) to population (5,000) is .02. The finite universe correction factor in Appendix D-1 shown for .02 is .99. The precision obtained from the sample of 100 is thus the result of the following computation:

$$\$80 \text{ x } \pm.1660 \text{ x } .99 = \pm\$13.15$$

Since the sampling precision does not meet the auditor's standards, he will have to sample further. Instead of seeking to compute precise sample sizes, he may increase his initial sample of 100 in increments of 50 or 100, recomputing the precision at each increment, until he has obtained a precision range which will satisfy him. Tables to determine exact sample sizes are available in the *Sampling Manual for Auditors*.

Let us restate the problem we have just discussed, but this time let us give it some audit meaning. With the principles understood, it should be simple to follow the steps required to work out an actual audit problem.

The auditor is asked to estimate the value of an inventory having a book value of $500,000 and composed of 5,000 line items. The average line item — kind of item, which may be composed of a number of units — therefore has a book value of $100.

The auditor has examined 200 line items, comparing the number of units shown on the books with the actual number of units for each line item in his sample. The results are as follows:

Book value	$20,000
Value determined by physical inventory	$18,000

Through simple arithmetic the auditor estimates the actual value of the entire inventory. Since he examined 200 items and found their total value to be $18,000, their average value would be $90 ($18,000 ÷ 200). Since there are 5,000 items in inventory, the estimated actual inventory would be $450,000. This compares with the book value of $500,000.

Can the auditor be satisfied with this estimate, based on simple arithmetic? The answer is *No*. He does not yet know how reliable that estimate is.

But he can measure that reliability through statistical means. First he will determine the standard deviation of the sample of 200 items. Let us assume that it is $40. He determines the precision factor for a sample of 200 at a 90% confidence level by consulting Appendix C-5. The factor is ±.1168. He then determines the finite universe correction factor. First he divides the sample size by the population size. The result is .04. By consulting Appendix D-1 he finds that the related factor is .97985. The computation is therefore:

$$\$40 \text{ x } \pm.1168 \text{ x } .97985 = \pm\$4.58$$

The amount of ±$4.58 is the precision for a single item. For the population of 5,000 items the precision is ±$22,900 (5000 x ±$4.58).

The inventory can thus be valued at $450,000 plus or minus $22,900; that is between $427,100 and $472,900. The auditor observes, however, that the precision of ±$22,900 is over ±5% of the estimated inventory value, while his objective had been ±4%. He therefore examines another 100 items.

Let us assume that the auditor has found the standard deviation and the differences to be substantially the same. What is his precision now?

The factor from Appendix C-7 for a sample of 300 at a 90% confidence level is ±.0954. The sampling fraction is 300/5,000 or .06, providing a correction factor of .96958. Hence:

$$\$40 \text{ x } \pm.0954 \text{ x } .96958 = \pm\$3.70$$

For the entire population (5,000 x ±$3.70) the precision would be ±$18,500, and the estimate of the corrected inventory value would be $450,000, plus or minus $18,500 or between $431,500 and $468,500.

The precision at a 90% confidence level is just about ±4%. Having substantially met his goals, the auditor may cease sampling, satisfied with the reliability of his estimate.

Stop-or-Go Sampling

Stop-or-go sampling was devised by the Air Force to permit audit decisions with statistical reliability that are based on relatively small samples. It applies to attributes sampling. It also applies, by and large, to fairly "clean" populations — those in which the auditor wants to do as little sampling as possible. Based on his knowledge of the system, the auditor may conclude that the population is relatively error-free; but he wants to prove it statistically without extensive testing.

So if he can examine a small sample and find few or no errors, he will have a measurable assurance that he can discontinue his tests and accept the reasonable accuracy of the population.

Appendix E is an excerpt from the tables used in stop-or-go sampling. The first column shows the size of the sample examined. The second column shows the number of errors brought to light by the auditor's analysis of the sample. The other columns are headed by various possible maximum error rates. The columns under each of the error rates show different levels of probability (the number of times out of 100) that the true error rates in the population will be less than the indicated maximum error rates in the headings. A simple example can show how stop-or-go sampling works. Let us say that the auditor is interested in whether receiving memorandums bear evidence that the materials received have been inspected. We shall assume that all items must be inspected. The absence of an inspector's stamp indicates no inspection.

Employees appear to be well trained. Supervisors watch the operations carefully. The manager periodically checks completed receiving memos to see that the rules are being followed. Clearly, under such a system, extensive testing would be wasteful. The auditor takes a sample of 50 items out of a population of 20,000. He stipulates that he would be satisfied if he has adequate assurance that the population has an error rate no higher than 5%.

Let us say that the auditor examines the 50 items and finds no errors. The condition is therefore as shown in the first line of the table: a 92.31% assurance (probability) that the population contains no more than a 5% error rate. If he is satisfied with that assurance, he could discontinue his tests.

But let us say that he found 1 error in his sample of 50. Now the condition is as in the second line: 72.06% assurance that the population contains no more than a 5% error rate. If this does not satisfy him, he might take a sample of 20 more receiving memos — a total of 70. Assume that he finds no more errors. The condition is then as in the second line for a sample size of 70: 87.03% assurance. If the auditor considers that to be adequate — taking into account the excellent system of internal control — he may discontinue his test. Otherwise he will take additional samples.

If the errors keep showing up, however, the auditor should not continue with stop-or-go sampling for sample sizes in excess of the sizes needed for attributes sampling. At that point, the auditor will want to obtain an estimate of the error rate in the population within a plus or minus range of precision at an appropriate confidence level.

Discovery Sampling

Discovery sampling is used when the auditor is examining populations where he suspects the existence of fraud or gross error. Such populations might include fictitious employees on the payroll, duplicate payments, unauthorized shipments of goods, or nonexistent collateral for loans.

The auditor is not trying to express an opinion on the population as a whole. He is trying, through sampling, to find at least one item with a particular characteristic, assuming a stipulated number of those items in the population. The stipulation is significant. The population would require examination item by item until the one such item was found. There would be no other choice if the item of interest were a single unique unit. But if the auditor is willing to specify some limited assumed number of items, he may use discovery sampling to obtain a measurable assurance that he will find at least one of that number, if the actual quantity in the population is equal to or greater than the assumed quantity.

Tablés have been developed for that purpose. Appendix F contains several key pages from the Air Force's table on discovery (exploratory) sampling.

Here is how the tables are used. Assume that the auditor is examining the company records on conflict of interest. Every employee is required to complete a record designed to disclose any such conflicts. There are 10,000 employees on the rolls and he wants to be 95% certain that he would locate at least one instance of impropriety — no record, wrong record, or an uninvestigated record of potential conflict.

By consulting Appendix F-4, for a population size of 10,000, he sees that if he were to stipulate 50 errors in the population he would have to examine a sample of 600 items to be 95.5% sure that his sample would include one of the erroneous items.

If his sample contained none of the errors he would be 95.5% sure that the population included less than 50 erroneous items.

How many erroneous items to stipulate is a matter of judgment, taking into account the seriousness of the errors under consideration. The only alternative to discovery sampling is the examination of each item until an example has been found or the entire population has been examined. Hence the auditor will have to evaluate the impact of the undiscovered errors in the population.

Judgment Sampling

Judgment sampling usually receives poor notices wherever statisticians deign to speak of it. But auditors have used it from time immemorial and still find that it performs signal service when statistical sampling is neither needed nor warranted.

Judgment sampling remains a significant part of the auditor's sample selection and evaluation procedures. But he should know when and how to use it.

Judgment sampling may be used to select examples of deficiencies to support the auditor's contention that the system is weak. He may make a purposive search for defective or improperly processed items to confirm his suspicions or buttress his position that the system is capable of producing improprieties. This is a valid use of judgment sampling. But it should not be used to estimate the number or value of such items in the total population. The auditor had not given every item in the population an equal chance of selection. His test was subjective; not objective.

Judgment sampling can be used where it is known that the population has no variability. For example, in an EDP system each item may be treated exactly the same by the computer. The transactions would be either all wrong or all right. The examination of a single judgment sample will provide the auditor with adequate assurance of the propriety or impropriety of all the items the computer processed.

Judgment sampling can provide the auditor with some clues as to whether to proceed with a statistical sample. If he encounters a well-designed, well-controlled system, good management, well-trained employees, and a feed-back mechanism that highlights errors, it would be extravagant to spend a great deal of time performing extensive transaction tests. A small sample — too small for stop-or-go sampling, but nevertheless selected at random to obtain some reasonable representation of the population — might suffice. If he finds no errors, he may be able to say that he sees no basis for examining the population further or for suspecting any material error. He may *not* say that he has adequate assurance that the population is truly error-free or even reasonably error-free. He has no statistical basis for such a statement. But what he *can* say, about the functioning of the system, may be sufficient for his audit purposes.

Judgment sampling has its place, so long as the auditor is aware of its limitations. Where his audit objectives are fully met by a judgment sample, there would be no valid reason to insist on the discipline of added statistical support.

EVALUATING SAMPLE RESULTS

The internal auditor cannot content himself with the mathematical results of his audit samples. True, they will provide him with a measurable assurance that his sample is a facsimile, in miniature, of the audited population. They will provide him with an objective estimate of the number of errors in the population or of the true value of the population.

In most cases, however, this is not necessarily what management needs. When variances occur management wants to know *why* they occurred. If the book value of an inventory is $500,000 and the auditor can demonstrate that the physical inventory represented by the books is only $450,000, management wants to know — or should want to know — where the $50,000 went.

Scientific sampling helps provide the auditor with assurance that he has found out what has happened. It cannot tell him why it happened. Thus, when samples point to differences the auditor must first determine whether the differences are material. And then he must determine how they happened and what can be done to prevent their recurrence.

The audit objective of the modern internal auditor transcends mere scorekeeping — the number of erroneous items he finds in his sample. His objective is to determine what the score means ... whether it indicates a system failure ... whether it points to poor supervision ... whether it is highlighting adverse trends ... or whether it hints of manipulation.

So unless the sample results provide assurance of satisfactory conditions, the sample is merely a prologue to the real audit task.

A shrewd appraisal of the audit results and surrounding circumstances may give those results an entirely different character. Also, the appraisal may point to the direction the audit report should take. Here are some examples:

- An examination of 200 items discloses only one error. But that error represents a significant item of a material amount. The sample results may not portray a trend; but the individual matter is of sufficient materiality to require reporting to management without reference to the sample. In other words, management may be told that the control system is functioning adequately, although this one matter needs correcting.

- An examination of 100 items discloses 10 errors. The errors resulted from a control breakdown. The sample, taken from a population of 20,000, does not provide good statistical reliability. The auditor, however, feels that his job has been performed and proposes to test no further. The report to management should emphasize the control aspect, buttressed by the fact that 10% of the items were in error. There should be no implication that the error rate may reliably be projected to the entire population.

- An examination of 150 items discloses only 3 errors. But each of the errors is traced to one clerk who has not been adequately trained. The auditor may then make a purposive test, in addition to his random sample, examining a substantial number of the transactions processed by that clerk to determine the seriousness of the deficiency. The results of the purposive test should not be combined with those of the random sample for the purpose of projecting results to the entire population.

- An auditor selects and examines an attributes sample of 796 items out of a population of 10,000 items and finds a 10% error rate. His projection of that rate to the total population carries a 95% confidence level with a precision of ±2%. This is extremely high reliability. The errors can be attributed to poor supervision. The auditor feels that the population should be purged of error. Management is not mathematically sophisticated and has no conception of the measurement of sample reliability. The auditor may recommend an operating review of the entire population, stating that in his opinion the population contains approximately 1,000 erroneous items.

But he would be well advised not to discuss confidence levels and precision, since this may do little more than complicate an issue that is better left simple.

POPULATION PROPORTIONS

The auditor may have occasion to estimate the proportion of a population that possesses some property of interest. He is not concerned with error rates or sample variability. He merely wishes to project the item or items of interest, found in a sample, to the entire population with some measurable degree of reliability.

For example, let us assume that certain purchases are made only after the receipt of competitive bids. Others are not. Still others are made from selected suppliers at the direction of the company's customers. It may be significant to estimate for management — with adequate reliability — what the proportions are.

There are a variety of formulas which will provide the measure of reliability for such estimates. The use of the binomial probability distribution, or the hypergeometric probability distribution for finite universes would define the confidence limits with maximum accuracy. But confidence limits based on these distributions would involve computations so complex that they would not ordinarily be feasible without the use of a computer. Fortunately, the formula for the standard deviation of the binomial distribution can readily be used by the auditor to determine the confidence limits with a reasonably acceptable degree of accuracy. We shall discuss here two formulas based on the standard deviation of the binomial distribution. The first applies when the size of the population is known. The second applies when it is not.

Known Populations

Let us assume a population of 40,000 purchase orders. Let us further assume that the auditor selected a sample of 4,000 purchase orders — every 10th order with a random start — and distributed them to the three categories just enumerated. The results of the sample are as follows:

A. Competitive bids	2,000	50%
B. No competitive bids	1,600	40%
C. Customer direction	400	10%
	4,000	100%

By a simple projection, or "blow-up" (multiplying each sample group by 10) the auditor estimates that the population contains 20,000 of A, 16,000 of B, and 4,000 of C. But how reliable is the estimate? In other words, what is the precision range for the estimate at a stipulated confidence level?

The auditor can obtain that statement of reliability through the following formula:[1]

$$A = ZN \sqrt{\frac{N - n}{N \times n}} \times \sqrt{p (1 - p)}$$

A = Precision
Z = Normal deviate for the desired level of
    confidence (Appendix B)
N = Population size
n = Sample size
p = Proportion of items of interest to sample

The computation of the range of precision, assuming a stipulated confidence level of 95.5%, is as follows:

Number in Population	40,000
Number in Sample	4,000
Z (Appendix B) at 95.5 Confidence Level	2.000
Proportion of items with a particular characteristic	
A. 2,000/4,000	.50
B. 1,600/4,000	.40
C. 400/4,000	.10

First solve:

$$ZN \sqrt{\frac{N - n}{N \times n}}$$

$$2 \times 40,000 \sqrt{\frac{40,000 - 4,000}{40,000 \times 4,000}}$$

[1]Cochran, William G., *Sampling Techniques*, John Wiley & Sons, Inc., New York, 1963, p. 63.

$$80{,}000 \quad \sqrt{\dfrac{36{,}000}{160{,}000{,}000}}$$

$$80{,}000 \quad \sqrt{.000225}$$

$$80{,}000 \times .015 = 1200$$

Then solve, for each class:

$$\sqrt{p(1-p)} \times 1{,}200$$

Class	p	x	1 − p	= p(1 −p)	$\sqrt{p(1-p)}$	Precision (±) at 95% Confidence Level
A	.50	.50	.25	.5000	±600
B	.40	.60	.24	.4900	588
C	.10	.90	.09	.3000	360

Estimated Proportions
And Reliability Statements

	Sample		Estimated	Precision (±) at 95% Confidence Level	
Classification	P.O.s	% of total	P.O.s in population	P.O.s	%
A. Competitive bids	2,000	50%	20,000	±600	± 3.0%
B. No competitive bids	1,600	40	16,000	588	3.7
C. Customer direction	400	10	4,000	360	9.0

It will be observed that the formula provides the best reliability when the item of interest represents a relatively high proportion of the sample.

Unknown Populations

Let us assume a large but unknown population of purchased tools. The auditor wishes to estimate with reasonable reliability how many cost $100 and over.

Assume he has taken a sample of 400 tools and finds the division as follows:

Under $100	320
$100 and over	80
	400

Without an idea of population size, the auditor will be unable to estimate how *many* tools cost $100 or more. But he can estimate the *proportion* of items of interest. In this case he can estimate that 20% of the population contains tools costing $100 or more. He will then seek to determine the reliability of that estimate to help him decide whether he has taken a large enough sample for his purposes.

The formula used to determine the precision of the estimated proportion is as follows:[2]

$$A = Z \pm \sqrt{\frac{p\,(1-p)}{n}}$$

A = Precision
p = Proportion
n = Sample size
Z = Normal deviate for the desired level of confidence (Appendix B)

The computation of the reliability statement for the estimate of tools at a 95% confidence level is as follows:

$$A = \pm 1.96 \sqrt{\frac{.20\,(1-.20)}{400}}$$

$$A = \pm 1.96 \sqrt{\frac{.20 \times .80}{400}}$$

$$A = \pm 1.96 \sqrt{\frac{.16}{400}}$$

$$A = \pm 1.96 \sqrt{.0004}$$

$$A = \pm 1.96 \times .02$$

$$A = \pm .0392$$

---

[2]Arkin, H., *Handbook of Sampling for Auditing and Accounting*, McGraw-Hill Book Company, Inc., New York, 1963, p. 606.

Thus, the precision is .20 ±.0392, or approximately from 16% to 24%. In other words, at a 95% confidence level, between 16% and 24% of the tools cost $100 or more.

If the auditor wishes a more precise result, he might increase his sample size. Assuming that the sample size is doubled to 800 and the sample results remain the same, the precision would be computed as follows:

$$A = \pm 1.96 \sqrt{\frac{.20\,(1 - .20)}{800}}$$

$$A = \pm 1.96 \sqrt{\frac{.16}{800}}$$

$$A = \pm 1.96 \sqrt{.0002}$$
$$A = \pm 1.96 \times .01414$$
$$A = \pm .0277$$

Now the precision, at a 95% confidence level, is ±2.77%, and the range is approximately from 17% to 23%. If this is sufficient reliability in the auditor's judgment, he may stop sampling.

SUMMARY

In dealing with audit sampling, the auditor should keep these ten commandments in mind:

1. Know the principles of scientific sampling — but use them only when they best fit the audit objectives.
2. Know the population, and base audit opinions only on the population sampled.
3. Let every item in the population have an equal chance of being selected.
4. Do not let personal bias affect the sample.
5. Do not permit patterns in the population to affect the randomness of the sample.

6. The purposive (directed) sample has its place; but do not draw conclusions about the entire population from it.

7. Base estimates of maximum error rates on what is reasonable in the real world — try to determine at what point alarms would automatically go off.

8. Stratify wherever it would appear to reduce variability in the sample.

9. Do not set needlessly high reliability goals (confidence level and precision). Controls, supervision, feedback, self-correcting devices, and management awareness and surveillance should all be considered in seeking to reduce the extent of the audit tests.

10. Do not stop with the statistical results — know why the variances occurred.

In deciding which selection technique or sampling plan to use, the auditor should consider these applications:

Recommended Selection Technique	Character of the Population
Random Numbers	Where each of the items in the population is or can readily be numbered or is included in lists or registers which are or can be numbered.
Interval	Where items are not or cannot readily be numbered or where random number sampling would be excessively expensive. Steps must be taken to avoid any bias that may be introduced by patterns in the population or by items missing from the population.
Stratification	Where the population is composed of items which vary considerably in value or other characteristic of interest. Where sample size can be reduced by separating the population into groups of items with reasonably similar values or characteristics.

Cluster or Multistage	Where the population is so dispersed that random number or interval sampling would be burdensome. It must be remembered that there usually may be a loss of sample reliability when cluster or multistage sampling is used, as compared with random number or interval sampling, and that a larger sample size may usually be required to offset that loss.
Mechanized	Where the population is, or readily can be, recorded on punched cards, magnetic tape, or other machine media.

Recommended Sampling Plan	Purpose of the Audit
Attributes	To estimate the attributes or characteristics of a population — obtaining "yes or no" answers — with a measurable degree of reliability.
Variables	To estimate the value of a population — dollars, weights, time spans, or other variable values — with a measurable degree of reliability.
Stop-or-Go	To estimate error rates or similar attributes from the smallest possible sample — discontinuing the sampling when a definitive answer is obtained.
Discovery	To identify through sampling at least one suspected item — assuming some given number of such items in the population—and discontinuing sampling when the one item is identified.
Judgment	To use samples for the purpose of obtaining information that need not be attributed to the entire population with measured reliability.

COMPUTER AUDITING

INTRODUCTION
The Auditor's Responsibility

The expanding universe of electronic data processing is gradually surrounding all of the internal auditor's world. It is a changing, unending universe; and it cannot be ignored. The old ways are going or gone. The new ways are here and now and are getting even more difficult to deal with in the accustomed manner.

Some auditors have plunged eagerly into the exploration of this new world. Some have timidly refrained, still standing in their accustomed places, fearful of mysteries that are not really all that mysterious. But every auditor is in one way or another affected. And as the computer and its generations proliferate, the internal auditor must become involved or leave the arena to the more venturesome.

Computer-related expenses in many companies are already the largest single item of overhead. Computers are being more extensively used because of decreases in equipment cost, increased awareness of computer capabilities, and the constantly expanding scope of computer applications being made available to potential users.[1] Comprehensive business systems are becoming the rule. Management is relying more and more on the computer for furnishing and storing information. The spreading tentacles of this automated octopus probe into every nook in large organizations and will find more and more footholds in small ones.

---

[1] Kaufman, Felix, "The Computer, the Accountant, and the Next Decade," *The Journal of Accountancy*, August 1971, p. 33.

And just as management looks to the auditor to assure it of the adequacy, effectiveness, and efficiency of its other operating controls, so will management, with greater anxiety — because of the mystery that surrounds EDP — look to the auditor to assure it of satisfactory EDP operations and alert it to dangers and pitfalls. The executives and operating managers, hemmed in with the day-to-day problems requiring constant attention, rarely have the time to become knowledgeable and fluent in this new medium with its puzzling and arcane language. Yet they must rely upon EDP and deal with it. Their need for the strong right arm of the modern internal auditor is increased a hundred-fold as computers take over the information systems within the company. Because of the breadth and scope of his approach, his knowledge of intracompany operations, and his independence, the internal auditor is in a unique position to provide such assistance to management.

And where does management need the auditor's help in dealing with the computer? Everywhere: From the first decision to buy a computer to the controls designed to safeguard the system and prevent fraud. More precisely:

- In the evaluation of the benefits to be gained through computer installation. Many an expensive computer was bought on management impulse when a clean-up of the manual system might have been more practical and far more economical.
- In the appraisal of the desirability of using the computer in a particular application. Many of the starry-eyed claims of savings have been puffed up, gone unsupported, and never been realized.

- In the building of controls when a new computer application is being investigated and the computer program is being prepared. To wait until the system is in effect is wasteful and far too late.
- In the monitoring and safeguarding of the computer complex. The accidental or deliberate destruction of equipment or data stored in magnetic files can bankrupt companies that use the computer for extensive data processing. The threat from such loss can be minimized by adequate security for the equipment and by provision for recreating important files that may be destroyed.
- In the establishment of controls over unauthorized access to the computer. The computer can be the embezzler's darling and can help steal the company blind.

Some Areas for Audit Surveillance

The computer is still in its infancy, as business systems go, but it has already built up a chilling record of areas that need surveillance. Here are several examples.

- A manager in a brokerage firm programmed the computer to siphon $250,000 from a company account to two customer accounts — his own and his wife's. The computer was also programmed to show that the money went to buy stock for those two accounts. The manager accomplished the theft by going to the office Sunday mornings to punch new computer cards and feed them into the machine. The manager ran the whole show and could by-pass all systems. After the fraud was detected, and when only a fraction of the money was recovered, the system was revamped and quarterly internal audits were inaugurated.[2]
- A computer system includes numerous equipment components. The components are expensive and contribute heavily toward total data processing costs. Until recently, the components (such as core storage, magnetic tape units, and magnetic disk drives) were available only from the manufacturer of the computer system. Increasing numbers of independent manufacturers, however, are offering compatible components that can be used in place of the like equipment supplied by the computer manufacturer. The independent manufacturer's equipment is usually less costly to lease or to purchase,

[2]*The Wall Street Journal*, April 5, 1968.

and he can provide maintenance service as well.[3] Internal auditors can assist management in identifying such areas of cost reduction and can be instrumental in keeping data processing costs at the lowest practical level.

■ Critical data stored on magnetic devices must be made secure. One security hazard facing a processing installation is related by Chu in a recent article[4] which says in part:

"... a disgruntled employee or an innocent-looking saboteur from outside, armed with a magnet the size of a quarter, could quietly wipe out thousands of reels of magnetic tape that may contain vital corporate data and probably cost millions of dollars to collect."

Magnetically recorded data may also be seriously damaged or destroyed by accident, by dropping a reel of magnetic tape, by improper handling, and by fire, flood, or other catastrophe. By seeing that security gaps are closed, the auditor may relieve his company of the staggering expense of recreating lost data files. Closing the security gap consists in part of duplicating files of critical data and storing them outside the data processing facility.

■ Output from the data processing installation is frequently crucial to the uninterrupted flow of company operations. Automated billing of voluminous accounts receivable files is one example. Because continued and prolonged equipment usage is important, the data processing equipment should be adequately protected. The protection ranges from restricting access to the computer room to provisions to minimize the threat of fire, flood, and accidental damage. By observing people who enter the data processing facility, the auditor can judge whether access is being properly restricted. Other dangers, such as fire and flood, are not so readily detected. Some suggestions for evaluating overall security are discussed in a later section of this chapter.

■ The lack of adequate documentation to support operational computer programs is a common problem within data processing installations. The documentation is important because it is frequently needed by management, by any programmer who has to alter the related computer program, and by other

---

[3]Talbot, J. E., "Adding to and Replacing IBM Core Memory," *Data Dynamics*, August-September 1971, p. 25, and Chu, Albert L. C., "Does the Computer Know Who Made the Peripherals?" *Business Automation*, November 1971, p. 26.
[4]Chu, Albert L. C., "Computer Security: The Corporate Achilles Heel," *Business Automation*, February 1, 1971, p. 33.

interested people. The reasons for referring to computer program documentation are varied. Some examples are: Management's desire to determine the functional adequacy of specific programs; the auditor's need to review program controls; and the programmer's need to make changes in the program being used. In the absence of adequate documentation, it is not uncommon to find: (1) complex and expensive computer programs that had to be substantially rewritten to introduce only minor changes in data; (2) knowledge of the details of what the program does held by only one or two persons, usually the programmers who originally wrote the program; and (3) management being denied the information it might need to review the adequacy of specific computer programs. The auditor can isolate instances of inadequate documentation and can assist management in making sure the important computer programs are sufficiently explained in writing.

These examples cite only a few areas within a data processing installation that cry for audit surveillance. There are many other examples — limited only by the auditor's imagination. As we mentioned, the auditor is in a good position to provide an objective review of computer operations. Of course, such a review could also be made by knowledgeable and technical personnel assigned to the data processing installation. But their independence may be seriously questioned. Hence, executive management must be able to turn to the internal auditor, and he must maintain sufficient competence to warrant management's trust.

Scope of This Discussion

In a general-purpose book such as this, it will be impossible to deal in depth with computers and their operations. Books by the hundred and articles by the thousand have been and are being written on the subject. The use of the computer in auditing is dealt with in the *Sampling Manual for Auditors* and its *Supplement*. The audit of EDP is covered in depth in the repeatedly updated manual, *Internal Auditing of Electronic Data Processing Systems*, published by The Institute of Internal Auditors. We will not seek to duplicate that coverage here. But it will be helpful to provide a nontechnical overview of the computer and its relationship to the auditor, as a stepping stone to more serious studies. Also, some facets of the subject are of special interest to the auditor and so deserve special mention.

Accordingly, we shall in turn touch on:

■ Computer Acquisition and System Design

- Computer Security and Disaster Control
- Computer Controls
- Fast Response Systems
- Mini-Computers
- Operational Audits of the Computer
- Scheduling
- Using the Computer in Auditing
- Training for Internal Auditors

Also, appended to this chapter are, first, a summary of computer control objectives, minimum standards, and techniques which can be used as a check list in computer auditing; and second, an explanation of computer documentation.

COMPUTER ACQUISITION AND SYSTEM DESIGN

The Auditor's Involvement

Acquiring computers and designing computer systems cannot safely be left entirely to the computer specialists. There is too much at stake. Too large a percentage of the company's assets may be devoted to computers to let them escape the close attention of senior management.

The mystery enveloping computers, the terms associated with them, and the complex interrelationships of the different items of computer hardware tend to put senior managers off — tend to make them abdicate their responsibilities to the computer specialists. This can be grievous error. The computer must be used to meet company objectives — not the more parochial goals of specialists. And so executive management, assisted by the objective, knowledgeable, control-oriented internal auditor, must take an active part in the decisions affecting computer acquisition and system design.

The auditor must also step up to his own responsibilities. He must be part of the management team that is concerned with feasibility studies and the design of new systems. The time-hallowed precept that the auditor should not participate in the selection or design of the system he will audit must be reconsidered in the face of computer technology.[5]

The Dangers of Delay

Waiting on the sidelines to make post audits can prove disastrous. The auditor has too much to offer, and he should not hold

[5]Gage, R. G., "EDP — A leadership opportunity for the internal auditor," *The Internal Auditor,* July/August 1970, p. 52.

back at the critical junctures of early decision-making. Where the computer specialist is concerned with equipment, programs, and efficient computer performance, the auditor can offer a rich background that speaks of company objectives and goals, and of company needs that must be satisfied. He can provide a stabilizing influence that takes into account the entire company — not just data processing.

So the caveat that bars the auditor from participating in the development of new systems should not be applied to EDP. The dangers are too great. The corrections are too expensive. Two examples will illustrate the point.[6]

- In one large railroad company, the auditors decided that it would be a good idea to have the computer reject inaccurate data — after the EDP system involving freight car records had been in effect for some time. The auditors worked up an audit test deck. Essential data was deliberately omitted. Incorrect data was deliberately added. For example, the test deck showed cars interchanged with the L & N when the railroad had no interchange at all with the L & N. The test deck showed interchanges with nonexistent railroads, with nonexistent car numbers, and in one instance a car interchanged on May 53rd. Any self-respecting computer program with appropriate edit routines would have screamed TILT when the test deck was introduced. But this program happily processed and printed out all invalid (among valid) transactions, including 22 days extra per diem for the car interchanged on May 53rd.

- The same auditors examined the computer application for the payroll. Employee pay was being machine-calculated by matching the clock numbers that were listed on the current time sheets with a purportedly "active" employee file. The auditors discovered to their horror that many of the employees on the "active" file had left the company as long as three years before. So if the number of the terminated employee appeared (or was placed) on the time report, there was nothing to prevent the preparation of a pay check.

The obvious solutions in those two cases were to (1) reprogram the computer in the freight application to recognize and reject erroneous or incomplete data, and (2) purge the "active" file of data on terminated employees and establish a fool-proof procedure for adding and deleting data from the master file.

---

[6]Pauley, C. A., "Audit Responsibilities in the Design of Computerized Systems," *The Internal Auditor*, July/August 1969, p. 22.

These eminently reasonable suggestions were taken to the data processing people. They immediately talked of the "man-years" required to reprogram — of the thousands upon thousands of dollars it would take to put into the programs the controls that should have been there from the start, the controls a knowledgeable internal auditor would have insisted upon.

As a result of this traumatic experience, the auditors learned these sad lessons:

- Effective controls should be designed into a system — not tacked on afterwards.
- System designers and computer programmers do not always include all of the necessary controls in a new computer application. Controls designed into computer applications require time to conceive and implement. Sometimes they may be omitted for the sake of expedience. But the results can be costly and exasperating.
- Auditors *must* be equipped to be able to participate in the evaluation of system acquisition and system design. The expense of correcting faulty systems is much too high.

The Institute of Internal Auditors has recognized this need. And its 1971 *Statement of Responsibilities* points out that the auditor's "objectivity need not be adversely affected ... by his determination and recommendation of the standards of control to be applied in the development of systems and procedures under his review."

Conditions of Involvement

The development of an EDP system demands a long, complex, and expensive study. As we have demonstrated, the auditor must get involved at the very beginning. His successful involvement, however, will be dependent on certain conditions, and he should be abundantly aware of them.

- He should be able to count on management support. Of what use are cogent, well-buttressed suggestions that are ignored or overruled?
- He and the people who design and implement the system must be able to cooperate. If complete and sincere cooperation is lacking, the auditor will have a lonely, frustrating road to walk. Good working relations are needed at the highest levels of the auditing and the EDP organizations.
- The systems people must be control-oriented. Programmers who write the programs to be executed by the computer should also understand the importance of adequate controls

within their programs. This means salesmanship — demonstrating the heavy penalties for inadequate controls.

■ The auditor must know what he's talking about. He must know the EDP argot. He must be familiar with the EDP hardware. He must have a working knowledge of programming. In short, he must be able to converse on a level with the systems and programming people.

■ The auditor must evaluate the needs of the company — not just those of the requesting department. Somebody must be able to ensure appropriate balance. Somebody must make sure that the demands of Department A will not be filled at the expense of Department B. Department A cannot be expected to be completely objective. It has its own needs to satisfy. The auditor, tuned to the overall company goals, must see to it that local demands do not create control vacuums and adversely affect interdepartmental functions.

Audit Questions

Patently, the auditor's role in the feasibility and system study is not an enviable one. He is dealing with specialists in a very specialized and often esoteric undertaking. He must be knowledgeable, tactful, helpful, and yet watchful of the company's broader goals. After all, he is probably the sole unbiased emissary of management on the team. Not always will he be able to carry out his own function as he wishes, but he will do it much better if he has a definite plan of action in mind. Here are some of the things he should try to find out when he participates in and reviews the feasibility and system study:

■ Is the study made by a team — a team composed of representatives of all departments whose interests must be considered?

■ Is at least one member of the team an expert in the capabilities of EDP equipment?

■ Did the study start with a thorough analysis of the pre-existing manual or automated system? Sometimes the only thing wrong with the prior system is that it needed to have its problems identified and corrected.

■ Was consideration given to the audit deficiencies cited against the pre-existing system?

■ Were specifications for the new system so restricted as to slant them toward only one equipment manufacturer?

■ Are workload projections realistic? Do they improperly show current volume only, without giving consideration to contemplated growth?

- Has consideration been given to recruiting and retraining personnel?

- Has an effective orientation plan for operating personnel been devised to ease the trauma of the new installation?

- Is the basis for equipment selection well supported? Has consideration been given to lowest cost, program and system reliability, and service?

- Has a study been made of new equipment, new operating systems, new programming languages, multiprogramming uses, time sharing, data banks, telecommunications, and progress in the standardization of source language?

- Has appropriate consideration been given to lease or purchase, including provision for (or calculation of):
    Depreciation?
    Cost of capital?
    Cash flow?
    Timing? (Lease implies steady disbursement over the years — purchase implies large initial cash outlay.)
    Obsolescence?
    Preparing the site?
    Providing power facilities, air conditioning, humidity control, soundproofing, raised floors to house cables and wiring, reinforced floors and foundations, and security?
    Storage facilities for tapes, punched cards, and programs?
    Standby equipment in the event of equipment failure?
    Adequate protection, such as off-site storage of vital information so that it can be reproduced if necessary?

- Does the study establish objectives for:
    Cost savings?
    Efficiency?
    Improved information?

- Have time-phased plans been established for:
    Site preparation?
    Equipment delivery?
    Development of operating procedures?
    Programming and testing?
    Personnel recruitment and training?

- Have effective controls been designed into the system?

- Do the people performing the application study have a basic knowledge of system design and programming? Did they use standard operating and documentation procedures?

■ Have provisions been made for the multiple use of common source data? Will source data be converted to machine language at the earliest practical point? Has provision been made for management by exception?

■ Does the planning package contain information on:
   The objectives and goals of the system?
   Systems flow charts?
   Descriptions of both clerical and mechanical functions?
   The general (macro) logic of the programs for the new application?
   A description of the input data?
   Copies of source documents?
   A description of the output of the new system?
   A catalogue of the controls to be included?
   Exception reporting and the action to be taken on exceptions?
   A list of the files to be maintained — documents, cards, magnetic tapes?
   Retention schedules?
   Minimum documentation standards for computer programs?

Close involvement in the feasibility and systems studies will bring many more questions to the mind of the auditor. But the steps just outlined form an adequate foundation.[7]

We shall discuss disaster controls and machine controls in the section that follows.

COMPUTER SECURITY AND DISASTER CONTROL

Businessmen are awakening to the fact that a blow to their computer center can be like a bullet in the brain. A computer disaster can, as one writer put it, induce "total corporate amnesia."[8] This is not high-flown theorizing. One dissatisfied computer employee managed to destroy practically every file and program in his company. It was not known whether enough information could be reconstructed to keep the company in business.[9] At Sir George Wil-

---

[7]Sources: Reynolds, A. L., "Evaluating EDP Management," *The Internal Auditor*, Summer 1967, p. 26; Stewart, Dudley, "The internal auditor of the future," *The Internal Auditor*, March/April, 1970, p. 46; and Nigra, A. L., "Auditing Acquisitions of Data Processing Equipment," *The Internal Auditor*, January/February 1970, p. 19.
[8]Weiss, Harold, "The Danger of Total Corporate Amnesia," *Financial Executive*, June 1969, p. 63.
[9]Allen, Brandt, "Danger ahead! Safeguard your computer," *Harvard Business Review*, November/December 1968, p. 97.

liams University in Montreal in February 1969, students completely destroyed the computer center, hurling cards and tapes from the windows.[10]

More and more companies are taking steps to guard their computers as carefully as a bank guards depositors' funds. It has become plain that every company depending on computers must have a detailed security and disaster plan. The plan should make provision for the safety of the computer room, the protection of records, the steps to follow in emergencies, and recovery procedures.

People without a clear right and need should be kept out of computer rooms. Many companies disregard this simple precaution. They proudly regard their computer installations as showplaces and conduct visitors through them. But it takes only one determined visitor to commit an act of sabotage.

With the infinite variety of misfortunes that can befall a computer installation, total protection is probably a chimera. But the rules that follow should go a long way toward providing substantial security.[11]

Computer Room Protection

1. The computer area should not be located near open courts, stairwells, receiving docks, or manufacturing areas containing manufacturing processes capable of explosion.
2. The computer room should be barred to all people not clearly authorized to be there.
3. The computer room air conditioning system should be separate from the regular system.
4. Each individual computer system should be insulated by a fire-proof partition.
5. Generators and transformers should be located outside the computer room.
6. Machine cables and wiring should not pass through an area containing combustible material.
7. Portable fire extinguishers should be installed and their locations should be clearly marked.
8. Smoking should be prohibited in the computer area.
9. The area should be monitored regularly by night watchmen.
10. Fire department and Civil Defense telephone numbers should be prominently posted.

[10]Wasserman, J. J., "Plugging the leaks in computer security," *Harvard Business Review* September/October 1969, p. 119.
[11]Norris & Gottfried, Inc., Consultants, Los Angeles, California, "Checklists for Emergency Planning," 1971.

Record Protection

1. Duplicates of vital data files should be stored at off-site and protected locations, or should be separately stored and adequately protected within the EDP facility.*

2. There should be a separate data file storage area, under library control. The procedures should provide for logging data files in and out; keeping a current list identifying persons who are authorized to receive data files; keeping records to show the precise locations of all data files at all times; performing follow-up to retrieve issued data files not returned to the storage area within prescribed time limits; and identifying data files that are no longer needed, in accordance with established file expiration dates.

3. Only personnel who are specifically designated as custodians of data files should be allowed access to the storage area where the files are kept when not in use.

4. All data files should be clearly labeled, showing the name of the file, the file number and the jobs for which it is used. If the files are magnetic (tape or disk), they should be kept in closed containers when not in use.

5. Special care should be exercised over data files that represent vital computer programs. The programs are usually kept on magnetic tape or disk. It is a good idea to keep duplicate programs in card form.

6. Data files should be brought to the computer room for processing only; they should then be immediately returned to the storage area after processing.

7. Header labels should be recorded on magnetic tapes to prevent them from being used on jobs other than the ones for which they were created.

COMPUTER CONTROLS

The Need for Controls

With so much going on beneath the surface, with so much data being processed, with so many companies keeping a substantial portion of their vital records on magnetic devices, and with the computer's blind, amoral willingness to do anyone's bidding, controls over the computer must be an integral part of its operation.

---

*Offsite tape units connected through telecommunications lines to the computer installation may make the maintenance of such duplicates easier. But even with duplicate copies of computer programs and information files, it may be very difficult for a computer installation to recover from a disaster. Therefore, computer room protection is of prime importance.

Many functions previously dispersed throughout the company become concentrated within the EDP facility. The dangers once guarded against through separation of duties and manual checks and balances, arise again — just as real and just as perilous.

Management, therefore, should not relax its focus of attention on the computer after the feasibility study is adopted and the computer has been installed. Management must then make sure that the necessary controls have been established to prevent the use of the computer for unauthorized or improper purposes, to reduce the incidence of error, and to obtain optimum results from computer operations. These controls can be divided into three groups.[12]

- Organizational
- Administrative
- Procedural

Organizational Controls

Controls through division of authority are as important in EDP systems as in any other business functions.

The EDP organization should be free of the domination of the organization it serves. If it is a part of the accounting function it may be required to provide computer time and systems and programming efforts for accounting matters that are disproportionate to what is allowed for other organizations. The same would be true if the computer were under the control of production or engineering functions. Normally, it is desirable for the EDP manager to report to a director or vice president of administration who is independent of the company's operating departments.

In most large and well-run companies, the buyer does not originate requirements. For similar reasons, the EDP organization should not originate requests for EDP services. The theory of separation of responsibilities demands that requests for EDP services be initiated by organizational components outside the EDP department. Similarly, all source documents to be processed by the computer should originate in outside organizations.

Within the EDP department itself there should likewise be an appropriate separation of duties. The people designing systems and developing programs should be separate from the people charged with the responsibility of computer operations. As we pointed out earlier, if a programmer is allowed to lay hands on the devices that control the computer's operations he could manip-

[12]John, R. C., and Nissen, T. J., "Evaluating Internal Control in EDP Audits," *The Journal of Accountancy*, February 1970, p. 31.

ulate output to his own uses. And, as we have also pointed out, data files should be controlled by a librarian who should issue files only to individuals authorized to obtain them, and keep a record of file name, date, and the name of the person who received the material. The library should not be accessible to anyone other than the librarian, thereby preventing misfiling of records and unauthorized changes.

Using departments should participate in the study and implementation stages of computer systems. They should be required to approve the final system, since they will suffer the most if the system does not meet their needs.

Management must also take an active part, through a computer steering committee, and should make sure that written performance standards have been set for systems design, programming, and computer operations. Management may not be able to appraise the technical adequacy of the standards, but it should make sure that they have been developed. Here are some of the standards the steering committee would want to see established:

System documentation standards. These standards cover the nature of the documentation required, how revisions should be explained, flowcharting techniques, decision tables, coding, and the particular terms used in the industry.

Programming documentation standards. These include instructions on documenting changes to the original computer program and any subsequent changes. The standards could include logic diagrams, decision tables, coding, and a glossary of terms. Appended to this chapter are 12 categories of documentation that could be used to support computer programs. (See Exhibit 8-2) All 12 categories may be used in those companies which want to include all documentation in one package with little or no need to refer to other sources. Minimum documentation, for the reasons cited in the exhibit, are the four categories of "System Flow Chart," "Logic Flow Chart," "Source Program," and "Computer Run Sheet."

Operating documentation standards. These standards encompass changes in documentation, methods of documenting messages and halts, reconstruction and restart procedures, and procedures governing the end of the job.

Library of file documentation standards. These account for documentation changes, labeling, tape, disk, and card historical records, file numbering and dating, and file storage.

Keypunching or other conversion standards. These cover documenting revisions, identifying codes for machine-readable records, and rules for algebraic signs, blank spaces, and other matters requiring standardized techniques.

Documentation standards for control groups. These standards include contents and format of reports and other output; methods of revision of documentation; the correction, re-entry, and control of previous errors; and period and cut-off arrangements.[13]

Administrative Controls

The administrative controls embrace the means used to ensure consistency and continuity of programming and program testing.

One cannot look at a computer and determine whether the program that it is executing has been properly and completely prepared. The alternative is a well-documented trail showing how the program was prepared and describing any changes in it.

The initial control, therefore, would be a manual of programming standards which lays down specific rules on the initial preparation as well as changes in all computer programs. The manual should be followed religiously so that there is assurance that programs will be documented in an acceptable manner no matter who prepares them.

The test of good documentation is whether a typical programmer can tell what the program is supposed to do and will do, without the need for supplementary explanations. And that requirement is no different from what would be expected of an auditor himself when he documents his audit examination in his working papers.

Program test procedures should likewise be governed by written instructions and should involve common sense precautions. For example:

- The final testing should make use of actual data to be sure the program will be faced with a variety of conditions, including those not specifically provided for in the program.

---

[13]The Canadian Institute of Chartered Accountants, "Computer Control Guidelines," 1970, p. 88.

- The test should go beyond a single cycle so as to expose the master file — a file usually required to be kept current — to updating procedures.
- The test should include improper data or data which deliberately seeks to violate the programmed controls, to see whether the controls are indeed functioning as intended.
- The testing should include a series of related or interlocking programs to see whether any difficulties of interelationships will become apparent.

Modifications to programs need special controls. Few programs go for long without modification, so management should anticipate changes and provide assurance that they will be handled in a formal, controlled fashion. Besides, it is often through program modification that the EDP system is improperly manipulated.

Hence, all changes should be formally authorized, documented, and tested. No change should be made without supervisory review and without being recorded. All changes should be checked out to see that they do not have unanticipated side effects. The volume of changes may make it difficult to control all of them so completely. But, certainly, major changes should be under stringent controls; and procedures should specify the forms of control to be accorded the various types of changes.

Procedural Controls

The procedural controls stand guard over the actual processing of data. They may be subdivided into input controls, processing controls, and output controls.[14] Special controls relating to fast response systems will be discussed later in this chapter.

Input controls. These controls help strengthen the weak link in the chain of EDP events. All manner of checks and balances can be built into a program to assure proper processing, storage, and retrieval of data. But all of this is to no avail if the computer is presented with erroneous or incomplete data at the outset. Nevertheless, some input controls can be devised to help.

First, there should be assurance that whatever is received by the machine is complete. If controls are established close to the point of preparation of the transactions, losses will be minimized. A system of "batch" controls can provide assurance that no data is lost as it travels from place to place before it reaches the computer. One way of obtaining batch control is to process all transactions for a specified period of time, total their values on an adding machine tape, and record and reconcile those totals on logs at different transfer points.

Second, the program should provide for edit checks to reject inaccurate, incomplete, or unreasonable data. For example, the edit routine could reject all items over a certain amount — limit checks. It could reject items on the basis of past experience, like comparing the reasonableness of utility bills with the amount of consumption over a period of 12 months — the historical comparison. It could compare a receivable with a cash receipt to make sure the latter does not exceed the former — the check for logical relationships. It can check for completeness of information, like a billing transaction coded for a new customer, calling for a check to see if the name and address is on the input record — the field check. It can check to see that alphabetic data is not included in fields reserved for numeric data — the numeric check. It can check to see that charges to nonexistent or closed work orders are rejected — the validity check.

Third, there should be some method of ensuring the re-entry of rejected and corrected material.

Processing controls. These controls apply to the machine room. The object here is to prevent or discourage the improper manipulation of data and to ensure the continued, satisfactory operation of equipment.

Access to the computer should be limited to those authorized to operate the equipment. Object programs should be accessible only to the equipment operators. But the source programs should not be available to operators. This separation renders it difficult to make unauthorized modifications to the program. Similarly, programmers should not have access to the computer locations, its files, and its records. Their knowledge of EDP programs makes data manipulation particularly easy.

Nor should operators have unlimited access to the machine. They should be allowed access only to that program information needed to set up the equipment and respond to programmed halts. The data processing supervisor should respond to any unprogrammed halts for programs that have already been tested and approved for use.

Any operator intervention should be made a matter of record. And because of the everpresent possibility of wrongful manipulation, these further precautions should be considered:

- Requiring the presence of at least two trained operators during equipment operation.

14John, R. C., and Nissen, T. J., "Evaluating Internal Control in EDP Audits," The Journal of Accountancy, February 1970, p. 33.

■ Rotating assignments among operators.

Provision should be made for periodic preventive maintenance. The equipment should be maintained in accordance with schedules established by the manufacturer. Environmental controls should be provided to ensure proper temperature, humidity, and electrical power. Equipment can deteriorate when the conditions exceed the environmental ranges set by the manufacturer. Similarly, the machine room should be reasonably dust-free, since dust can affect the accuracy of computer tapes.

Information concerning computer equipment should be maintained in daily computer logs and periodic equipment utilization reports. No matter what controls have been built into the hardware, machine malfunction can occur and result in errors in the processing. Thus, manual and programmed edit procedures should be provided and used to compensate for missing hardware controls or to supplement those in use.

Output controls. These controls govern the accuracy and reasonableness of the information processed. In batch processing systems the totals of records processed should agree with the totals of records input. Prenumbered forms can help control output since they can be accounted for. For example, the number of payroll check forms can be checked against input records. Konrath points out that the effectiveness of internal control varies, depending on the absence of personnel, on the degree of motivation, and on other factors. The result is a large number of different states of nature of the internal controls during an audit period.[15] By using sampling techniques, the auditor can evaluate the processing of the output documents. In effect, the sample forms a test deck which should be representative of all the states of nature of the internal controls and of all conditions of processing during the period under audit. The sample, however, can evaluate only those transactions which were processed. Hence, the sample may not reveal the lack of limit checks or other operational checks designed to see if the input data is valid and proper.

Output controls include the proper handling of exceptions. When valid data is rejected, the fault may lie with machine malfunction or with operator error. Console typewriter sheets — a form of output — should be maintained to show the reason for rejecting valid data and the steps taken to correct the errors.

---

[15]Konrath, L. F., "The CPA's Risk in Evaluating Internal Control," *The Journal of Accountancy*, October 1971, p. 53.

The customer is responsible for correcting errors, listed on exception reports, which are the result of inaccurately submitted data. The EDP department should submit the exception reports to a high enough level to ensure action by appropriate supervision. Complete resubmission of all corrected errors can be assured by using a tape inventory of errors. All errors can be shown on tape according to date. Resubmitted data may be posted against this inventory before they are reprocessed through the system. Periodically, a listing from this tape could be provided to show those errors which are still uncorrected.

Procedures should provide assurance that all output reports are delivered on time and to the prescribed destinations. Where delays are anticipated, the users should be promptly notified. Procedures should also provide that users will be periodically queried as to their continued need for reports.

FAST RESPONSE SYSTEMS
What They Are

Fast response systems are assuming ascendency in the world of computers. In these systems, all the elements, including remote terminals, are connected with the computer and are under its control. The need for special controls and for special means of auditing these systems, because of the possible absence of conventional audit trails, warrants giving them special mention.

Fast response systems have also been called on-line, real-time systems. An on-line system is one in which the input data enters the computer directly from the point of origin and/or the output data is transmitted directly to where it is used. A real-time system is one that controls an environment by receiving data, processing it, and returning the results with sufficient speed to affect the functioning of the environment at that time.[16]

If the conventional audit trail is lost, the auditor will find it difficult — often impossible — to audit around the computer; that is, comparing final output with source documents. He will be unable to rely on independent confirmations of physical observations. He may be required to be constantly available for the surveillance

---

[16]Martin, James, "Programming Real-Time Computer Systems," Prentice-Hall, Inc., Englewood Cliffs, New Jersey, 1965, p. 376.

of the on-going process. The new technique may well be the continuous audit.[17]

Another technique might be to continuously copy the transactions submitted from remote sites onto magnetic tape or other medium. Then, the transactions could be tested by the auditor at his own convenience.

Controls

The controls needed for fast response systems include those required on any EDP system:[18]

- Separation of duties
- Procedures covering the reporting of source data
- Procedures covering the processing of source data
- Intermediate reviews of documents and records
- Review of interpretation of end results

But fast response systems render obsolete some controls used in batch processing. These controls include transcription controls and control totals. The first is obsolete because data is directly entered into the system at point of origin; the second, because data is rarely accumulated and processed in logical transaction groups — and control totals cannot be applied *before* the processing occurs.

Fast response systems make use of on-line remote terminals. Messages are transmitted through these terminals to and from the computer. It becomes necessary, therefore, to make sure that all data transmitted will be properly received and processed. To prevent loss, these additional controls are needed.[19]

- Message identification — ensuring proper flow and processing.
- Message transmission control — ensuring the receipt of all messages sent.
- Detection of transmission errors — determining the correctness of the information received.

---

[17]Bruno, J. D., "Auditing On-Line Real-Time Electronic Data Processing Systems." Dissertation submitted to the Graduate Faculty of the Louisiana State University and Agricultural and Mechanical College, August 1964, p. 14.
[18]Bruno, *op. cit.* p. 69.
[19]Bruno, *op. cit.* p. 70.

Information in the memory of the fast response system is available to terminal operators on request. Unfortunately, personnel who are not authorized to do so may make use of the information. They may destroy it or they may process it improperly through carelessness.

Controls are therefore needed to eliminate any possibility of unauthorized data usage, incorrect file updating, or other improper actions.

Unauthorized usage can be prevented by using lockwords and authority lists.[20] Lockwords, otherwise known as "keywords" or "passwords," are made up of several characters in a data file which the input message must match before access to the file will be permitted. Authority lists provide for identifying the person transmitting from the remote terminal. After the terminal operator has made contact and has identified himself, the computer checks to determine what type of information the individual is authorized to send and receive.

These controls provide adequate protection only if the code systems remain unbroken. There have, however, been instances of broken codes or stolen codes. More exotic controls, such as the use of voice prints or fingerprints, may have to be the answer. In addition to the use of codes, a monitoring routine is advisable. Under such a routine, the number of unsuccessful attempts to enter the system are counted. After some predetermined number of attempts have failed, the downline station is signaled so that an investigation may be instituted.

Fast response systems generally operate continually. It will be necessary, therefore, to install controls which insure continuance of the system when malfunctions occur.

Auditing Fast Response Systems

In fast response systems record-testing is de-emphasized. The system becomes the focus of attention. To that end, test decks have become one audit technique. Test decks have limitations, however. And the limitations stem primarily from the fact that they cannot be expected to evaluate the complete system of control. Konrath[21] states that "... internal control ... is only a part of a broader system of control and cannot safely be considered independent of the

---

[20]Moloney, R. F., "New Generation EDP Controls," *Management Services*, March/April 1968, p. 17.

[21]Konrath, *op. cit.* p. 55.

overall control situation." The internal auditor is concerned with the adequacy of all controls, and the limitation of a test deck in making such evaluations should be kept in mind. The test deck evaluates controls and programs as of a point in time. There is no assurance that the same controls and programs were in effect through the complete audit period. Moreover, it may be difficult to process all conditions which the test deck should be designed to test.

A statistical sample of the transactions of the audit period can serve to evaluate controls and programs that were in effect during the entire audit period. But there is this limitation: The lack of controls may be disclosed only if invalid or improper transactions were processed.

Test decks are composed of sets of punched cards designed by the auditor to test computer programs. The decks are made up of imaginary transactions — often intermingled with actual transactions. The imaginary transactions may include erroneous items to detect the effectiveness of the programmed controls. The auditor predetermines the correct answers for the tests and then compares them with the computer results.

When he develops and uses test decks, the auditor should take certain factors into account and make certain provisions.[22]

- The exact point in the system where the test decks are to be entered.

- The types of transactions to be included in the test decks.

- When to obtain the master records to process against the test transactions and to compute the predetermined results for a comparison with the output that resulted from the test processing.

- What effects the test transactions will have on the normal processing of transactions.

- Obtaining the regular processing programs to make sure that the program is used to process actual as well as test data.

- Making the necessary arrangements to get the data prepared and processed and to get the output in the desired form.

---

[22]Porter, W. T., "Evaluating Internal Controls in EDP Systems," *The Journal of Accountancy*, August 1964, p. 36.

Another technique is the use of generalized computer programs to perform the audit tasks.[23] These programs offer considerable opportunity for increased audit effectiveness and efficiency. Examples of the audit tasks carried out by the programs are:

- Testing extensions and footings.
- Summarizing data and performing analyses useful to the auditor.
- Examining records for completeness, consistency, invalid conditions, and the like.
- Selecting and printing confirmations.
- Selecting and printing audit samples.
- Comparing the same data maintained in different files.
- Comparing audit data with company records.

There are two principal ways of using computer audit programs. One involves adding a loop of instructions to the regular program. The special audit routine can then be put into operation by means of a program alteration switch. The routine could make a series of tests to check both the accuracy of the data being processed and the data internally stored. The other is the use of the generalized programs just discussed.

The benefit of the audit loop is that it does not require an additional computer run to use the program. The benefit of the generalized program is the flexibility it gives the auditor. He may decide when he wants to use it. He does not have to carry out his audit when the operating program is being processed. He does not have to confine his tests to the data processed at that time. He can retain his program under his own control. Further examples of the use of these techniques are shown in this chapter under the heading "Using the Computer in Auditing."

MINI-COMPUTERS
Background

According to testimony given before the U. S. House of Representatives, the use of mini-computers — computers costing less than $50,000 — is increasing rapidly. The testimony points out that present-day mini-computers have more computing capability than did the first "large" computers built in the early 1950's. The testimony provides data on mini-computer deliveries. In 1969

---

[23]Porter, W. T., "Generalized Computer-Audit Programs," *The Journal of Accountancy*, January 1969, p. 54.

about 600 were delivered. The increase by 1971, according to the testimony, would exceed 30,000.[24] Mini-computers are used in a wide variety of applications, including engineering, science, and business.[25] Their use can be expected to increase still further because of their capabilities and their low price. For example, one source estimates that a basic 4,000-word (16-bit) memory machine that cost $25,000 in 1965 will cost about $2,600 in 1975.[26]

When the auditor is confronted with the mini-computer he should adapt his audit approach to fit the specific application for which the equipment is being used. Adapting audit approaches to provide for local circumstances is nothing new to the internal auditor. He tailors his work to unique circumstances on nearly every audit he performs. Computer audit concepts already discussed apply as forcibly to the mini as they do to larger computer systems, with appropriate modification to fit local conditions.

At present, the internal auditor will frequently find that mini-computers are dedicated to performing specialized tasks. The minis can be expected to be used for more and more of the general purpose applications as technology advances. But regardless of how mini-computers are used, they are nothing more than devices which are capable of performing tasks that could also be done by larger computer systems.

The following guides should assist the internal auditor in planning his review of mini-computers and their uses. The guides are not intended to be exhaustive, but they do illustrate that mini-computer audits take on many of the characteristics of audits that are directed toward larger computer systems. The topics discussed are the same as those already commented upon for large computers.

Acquisition and System Design

Previous remarks about the acquisition and system design of large computer systems apply, to a great extent, to mini-computers. The small unit cost of minis can be misleading. For example, a company may need several mini-computers but only one

---

[24]Hearing before a subcommittee of the Committee on Government Operations, House of Representatives, Ninety-Second Congress, First Session, May 20, 1971, on "Automatic Data Processing," p. 39.

[25]Ellis, D. R., "Programming and Mini-Computer Costs," *Computers and Automation*, May 1971, p. 13; "Mini Computers in Action," Data Systems, June 1971, p. 28; and Gross, A. C., "Accessibility and the Small Computer," *Datamation*, November 15, 1971, p. 42.

[26]Theis, D. J., and Hobbs, L. C., "The Minicomputer Revisited," *Datamation*, May 15, 1971, p. 24.

large system. As the minis become increasingly popular for their business data processing capabilities, the auditor will find more of them located throughout the company centers of operation. Therefore, the comparatively low unit price turns into a substantial cost when the total quantity of minis in the company is considered.

The internal auditor can provide special assistance to management by making sure that the mini-computer programming alternatives are considered. The programming costs could be significant and could substantially increase the total cost of using the mini. Normally, the advertised prices of mini-computers do not include programming costs.[27] Thus, alternatives are available which deserve careful consideration. These alternatives include having the manufacturer do the programming, doing it in-house, or contracting to have a third party do it. The auditor does not have to be an expert to determine whether or not all reasonable alternatives are thoroughly studied.

Computer Security and Disaster Control

The small size of the minis is no reason to assume that they should not be properly protected. In many instances, however, it is not feasible to exercise the same degree of security over the minis as is exercised over larger computer facilities. One reason, of course, is that minis are commonly dispersed throughout various company offices. However, computer files (programs and data) used by minis should be controlled strictly and should be given the same protection afforded comparable files for large computers. The consequences of lax security have already been discussed.

Computer Controls

The type of computer controls that should be exercised over minis is dependent on the way the equipment will be used. If the mini is assigned for the exclusive use of one department, it would be proper for the department to decide on the computer's use. But separation of duties within that department is important. For example, if the mini accumulates daily stock issues, the same person should not approve issues, authorize adjustments to totals accumulated by the computer, and also operate the equipment. System, program, and operating standards, similar to those discussed for large computers, should also be prepared for mini-computer operation. As already mentioned, mini-computer files should be controlled. If mini-computer programs are prepared by company pro-

[27]Ellis, D. R., "Programming and Mini-Computer Costs," *Computers and Automation*, May 1971, p. 13.

grammers, a manual of programming standards should be prepared and enforced. The programs should be as carefully documented as other programs used on large computers. Because a mini is small does not mean that its programs can be rewritten in a short time.

If the mini is used for business applications, the procedural controls (input, processing, and output) already discussed should be followed for minis as well. The degree of application would depend on the specific type of input, processing, and output, and the kind of work to which the mini is assigned.

OPERATIONAL AUDITS OF THE COMPUTER

When the uninitiated auditor thinks of auditing computer operations, visions of flashing lights, cores, tapes, programs, and transistors becloud the mind and affect his thinking. But he doesn't have to feel that way. Of course, some audit approaches would require a strong computer background, including the ability to read programs. Yet management can sometimes be served with no more of a background than that possessed by any competent, modern internal auditor.

The internal auditor can make some reviews of computer operations that could provide management with assurance of adequate control or disclose waste and inefficiency without ever probing into the computer itself. His audits can be concerned solely with the administration of the computer operations and will require no dependence on a knowledge of programming methods. It is not feasible to include every area of interest in a work as restricted as this chapter. Yet some examples of the audit steps taken through an operational audit approach — many of which echo the controls just discussed — are as follows:[28]

Querying Users

The users of the computer output may not know how the computer works, but they certainly should know what they need from it and whether they are receiving the benefits they hoped for.

The auditor can prepare a questionnaire which he can send or take around to a representative sample of users. The questions may include those that follow:

- Are the reports you received from the EDP department accurate?
- Do you receive them when they are due?

[28]Heeschen, P. E., "Auditing data processing administrative activities — operational auditing applied to EDP," *The Internal Auditor*, November-December 1970, p. 55.

- Is their format satisfactory?
- Are the reports really needed?
- Do you receive more copies than you absolutely need?

The auditor may recommend that the EDP organization itself make periodic surveys to determine user satisfaction and needs.

Requests for Services

The auditor should satisfy himself that EDP services are requested under formal procedures and are not provided to just anyone who asks for them. The services should be requested on a prescribed form. The requests should be supported by background information showing the need for the services and should contain well-documented cost estimates. The requests should be reviewed by a committee made up of different disciplines. They should have the authority to demand adequate support for requests and they should apply mutually acceptable criteria in evaluating the results.

The auditor should review a representative sample of approved requests for services and evaluate the propriety of the justification offered by the requesters.

The auditor should also review the scheduling of data processing jobs, the reasons for assigning priorities, and the means used to control backlogs. Since scheduling work for the computer is an especially significant aspect of computer work, it will be discussed further under a separate segment of this chapter.

Documentation

Documentation is the auditor's business. He can understand the reason for the adequacy of documentation even though it relates to data that is processed by electronic means. Instructions on documentation should be specific. Therefore, administrative manuals and job descriptions should be developed for the EDP organization. If they have not been developed, the auditor should recommend their preparation as an essential feature of internal control.

Such procedural instructions must include directives on the documentation needed to describe and support an EDP program. With the manuals as a guide, the auditor can then look for such documents as flow charts, program listings, and the like. Documentation is especially needed for program changes. If the auditor finds that documentation is not properly prepared and filed, then he would want to know why and make suitable recommendations for their preparation and retention.

The auditor can request the EDP organization to prepare print-outs of the source program decks and tapes and compare them with the source program listings on file. This is one test for the adequacy with which changes in the source programs have been documented and controlled.

Equipment Utilization

The auditor should examine controls over equipment use and verify the records of machine usage. At one company, controls over daytime usage were satisfactory, but those over swing shift usage were not. When output was compared with recorded usage it became apparent that unauthorized use was being made of the computer — somebody was bringing in programs from the outside and running them on the company machines.

The auditor will want to know whether those who approve rental billings for EDP equipment have adequate information on which to make their decisions. By becoming familiar with the contracts for equipment, the equipment itself, and the usage records, the auditor can be alert to billings which are inapplicable or unreasonable.

The auditor will also be concerned with provisions for periodic reviews of the appropriateness of configurations of the machines currently in use. Have changed conditions rendered them obsolete ? Are new types of equipment available which will provide capabilities sorely needed ? Are current maintenance arrangements the most economical ?

Moreover, the auditor will want to know whether efficiency is being measured. Measurements can run the gamut from keystrokes per hour to comparisons of actual computer processing with established standards. In addition, he would want to review reports that monitor and control the effective use of computer time. Information in these reports can help improve scheduling and machine utilization.

SCHEDULING

The enormous sums invested in computer hardware, software, and personnel demand well-controlled deployment of these resources. Just as inept production control can escalate manufacturing costs, so can poor scheduling erode the hoped-for benefits from the computer system or increase the costs of running it.

The scheduling function should be separate from other data processing activities and should not be under the domination of one particular user. The scheduling supervisor should be in a position to balance equipment capability with the user's demands on the equipment. At the same time he must be aware of broad company needs to make sure essential jobs, like payroll or production control, are not shunted aside for rush jobs having less company-wide emphasis.

The auditor will want to satisfy himself that the rules regarding scheduling have been reduced to writing and that they are well understood and uniformly applied by all schedulers.

The records, logs, and other documentation should support and justify scheduling decisions. They should establish conformance to scheduling procedures and demonstrate whether or not scheduling objectives have been met.

The auditor will want to know how well actual schedules agree with forecasted needs. He will be particularly interested in the basis for accepting nonscheduled work, and how often established schedules are disrupted by special jobs.

The auditor does not have responsibility or authority for *installing* scheduling systems. But he should be aware of advanced methods which show promise to improve both the scheduling and the costing of computer jobs. One such system is now in use at a university and is being investigated by others for business applications.[29]

The basic thesis of the system is that the scheduling decision and the costs of computer jobs should be put squarely in the hands of the users. Every potential user is given certain credits each year for his computer jobs. Higher priorities require the expenditure of more credits. Similarly, as the demands for programming, key-punching, machine run time, and reports go up, so does the amount of the credits required to obtain those services. Thus the user will expend his credits according to his needs and resources. Computer personnel need make no Solomon-like choices among competing users.

USING THE COMPUTER IN AUDITING

The auditor has three major ways of using the computer to help him in his regular audits:[30]

---

[29]SMART (acronym for System Management and Allocation of Resources Technique): An Advanced Installation Management System of Virginia Polytechnic Institute and State University Computer Center, January 1, 1972.

[30]Weiss, Harold, "Reflections on computers and auditing in the 1970s," *The Internal Auditor*, July-August 1971, p. 12.

First, the audit routines can be included in the application programs themselves. Instead of making a special run of a file to select samples or to pull off confirmations, the computer can spill off the samples or other lists as a part of its regular processing of data.

Second, the computer can be used to simulate problems. This can be done off-line or on-line. In the first case, for example, test data can be used to check payroll programs when they are not in operation. In the second case, tests can be made when the programs are in actual operation. The second technique is especially applicable to real-time systems.

Third, there is software available to the auditor in the form of commercial audit programs. These are used for such purposes as printing files or programs, comparing tapes, stringing test data, and providing cross-reference listings. The so-called utility programs can perform many audit functions which the auditor has always had to do by hand: extract data, select samples, perform mathematical verifications, make comparisons, and sort data — to mention a few. These programs have been prepared by some of the large accounting firms, by computer manufacturers, and by some of the software companies. Such programs can also be prepared by in-house programming staffs or by the auditor himself.

Some actual uses of the computer in auditing are as follows:

Accounts Payable and Purchasing

The computer was used to detect duplicate payments. When suppliers submit invoices in duplicate, some of the copies can be processed in error along with the originals. One such comparison disclosed 21 duplicate payments totaling $28,000 in a 15-month period.

Billing

The computer was used in a service organization to verify rental billings and services rendered. It was found that several items of equipment were being serviced but that the services were not being billed. The computer was also used to compare contract rates with the rates billed. In several instances the rates billed did not agree with those in the contracts.

Inventories

Using a general computer program developed by one of the large accounting firms, but modifying it to particular purposes, the auditors had the computer:

- Extend unit prices and quantities on hand for more than 100,000 line items of inventory.
- Select inventory samples.
- Evaluate sample results.
- Obtain a variety of statistical data.

Using the same general computer **program**, unmodified, the auditors analyzed 21,000 items of shop stores by having the computer:

- Compute the amount of excess material included in inventory.
- Compute timeliness in filling requisitions from stores.
- Determine the number and percentage of overdue, unfilled requisitions.
- Select a sample to determine the effect of unfilled requisitions.
- Determine the volume of premature purchases of stores items.
- Determine the length of time items of material had been in storage more than 30, 60, 90, 120, and 360 days, and show the related values.

Machines — Lease or Buy

The computer was used to analyze the costs of leasing versus purchasing certain business machines. Without the computer, the analysis for a single machine presented a formidable problem. With it, costs were accumulated, amortization schedules were produced from a few numbers applied to formulae, and extrapolations were shown for successive years.

Payroll

By using the computer to compare labor charges for certain operations over a two-month period, the auditor was able to suggest increasing production run quantities on 78 parts to reduce the number of expensive machine set-ups.

The computer was used to detect overstatements of parts produced by employees working on a piecework basis. The computer compared production quantities on an operation-by-operation basis for all parts worked on by the employees and reported as having been produced.

Receivables

Using a computer program developed by a large accounting firm, the auditor sampled 2 million receivable records to obtain a 95%

reliability in estimating true values of the universe within ±2%. The computer was used to analyze the receivables according to (a) date in which the receivable (overpayment) was discovered, (b) the type of organization involved, and (c) the overpayment cause — among other things.

Services

By devising a COBOL program, the auditors selected from 27 million entries a sample of 1,395 records to determine whether certain services had actually been rendered and had been paid for at correct rates.

Transportation

Selecting and arraying information from freight bills — shipment dates, weights, locations, rates and total cost, destinations and modes of shipment — provided information that resulted in rescheduling, consolidating shipments to obtain better rates, and determining the most efficient mode of transportation.

Vehicles

Through another COBOL program, records of six classes of vehicles were examined. The computer (a) determined cumulative maintenance costs for each vehicle class, (b) compared cost per mile for each class to determine whether efficient use was being made of vehicles, and (c) compared cost of in-house versus contractor-supplied maintenance care.

TRAINING FOR INTERNAL AUDITORS

Obviously, not all the auditors in an internal auditing organization will acquire a detailed knowledge of computer science. All should have a general knowledge, however, if for no other reason than to pierce the veil of mystery that has often surrounded computers. To this end all auditors should take some of the basic courses in EDP equipment. The internal auditing department itself should provide training seminars to keep the auditors' knowledge up to date and to help maintain an easy relationship with computers.

Some auditors in the department will undoubtedly wish to go further. They should be encouraged and helped to do so. Thus the internal auditing department will maintain a strong cadre of specialists who are equipped to deal with any auditing problems involving the computer.

Indeed, a special committee of the Canadian Institute of Chartered Accountants has suggested that every candidate for certification have: [31]

- A good working knowledge of computer equipment.

- A good working knowledge of programming languages so that the candidate could prepare specifications for and supervise the preparation of a computer program.

- An *expert* knowledge of systems design based on the ability to *analyze* and chart an information system of modest complexity.

- An *expert* knowledge of audit techniques for the computer systems.

- A general knowledge of computer capabilities in such fields as statistics, real-time operations, and time sharing.

A recent survey showed that 62 per cent of the schools which belong to the American Association of Collegiate Schools of Business now require their students to have some computer programming proficiency before graduation. Four years earlier only 11 per cent of the business schools had a programming requirement.[32]

How much more the EDP specialist in internal auditing should know will probably change as computer technology changes. But it would seem that he should be conversant with the standard controls and checks that are prescribed for EDP applications. For example, he should be able to evaluate such checks and controls as these:[33]

1. Hardware and Software Checks
   a. Parity checks
   b. Read-after-write checks
   c. Field overflow checks
   d. Validity checks
   e. Synchronization checks
   f. Dual reads and read-compares
   g. Echo checks
   h. Hole counts and double punch blank column detection
   i. Input/output interlocks and storage protection
   j. Priority routines
   k. File protection rings

---

[31]*Canadian Chartered Accountant,* Special Issue, August 1967.
[32]Weis, *op. cit.,* p. 27.
[33]Wasserman, J. J., "Control in an EDP Environment," *The Internal Auditor,* September-October 1970, p. 43.

2. Input Checks
   a. Limit and reasonableness checks
   b. Check points and restarts
   c. Edit and validity checks
   d. Interrun controls

3. Processing Checks
   a. Record counts, dollar counts, logic checks
   b. Character checks — plus, minus, or blank
   c. Field overflow checks
   d. Restricted or blocked access — memory, tables, program
   e. Limit and reasonableness checks
   f. Internal file labels
   g. Transfer checks
   h. Automatic halts
   i. Intrarun controls

4. Output Checks
   a. Crossfoot and balance checks
   b. Limit and reasonableness checks
   c. Field content checks — size, blank, alpha, or numeric
   d. Record counts
   e. Balances to predetermined totals

5. Checks and Controls for Fast Response Systems
   a. Reconciliation of master files
   b. Prevention of duplicate processing when a system returns to checkpoint
   c. Recovery procedures
   d. Provision for recovery upon hardware or programming failure
   e. Prevention of "concurrent updating"
   f. Limitation of remote terminals through which files can be changed
   g. Restricted access to terminals permitting changes or extraction of data
   h. Identification and authorization codes for employees to use the system.
   i. Validity checks for authorization codes
   j. Changes of identification codes when employees leave the company

The internal auditor cannot be blind or deaf to anything of significance that touches the company. And computers are assuming a significance of prodigious proportions. All internal auditors should know enough about EDP to feel no misgivings when their audits bring them into contact with the computer. Some internal auditors in each auditing organization should have a thorough-going familiarity with data processing systems. No internal auditor should bury his head in the sands of apathy and indifference and hope the computer will go away. It won't. All that will vanish is the internal auditor's image as the eyes and ears of management.

SUMMARY

The auditor has a responsibility to his management to be sufficiently familiar with EDP to assist management in the many activities concerned with data processing.

He should become involved in the acquisition process to make sure that proper consideration is given to company needs and goals, and in the system design process to make sure that proper controls will be incorporated in the system. Post audits are too late.

He must make sure that adequate controls have been developed for computer security and disaster control, because a large part of the company's capital is tied up in the computer, and critical records are entrusted to it.

Organizational, administrative, and procedural controls must be subject to the auditor's review to prevent improper manipulation of the computer and to ensure the integrity of data processing.

He should acquaint himself with the new and burgeoning fast-response systems that are gradually taking over computer operations, and with the new mini-computers.

He should, at the very least, perform operational audits of the administration of computer operations — such audits can be made and can be effective without any in-depth knowledge of computer hardware; but they must be considered as only the initial step toward comprehensive audits of computers.

He should be watchful of the scheduling process, because there can be an inadequate return on the investment in the computer if its resources are not properly deployed.

He should make use of the computer in his own audits, because the enormous number of transactions being processed today can be most effectively and efficiently reviewed through the computer.

Finally, he should keep abreast of the complex and expanding technology that makes up computer operations, through continual training and study.

Exhibit 8-1. EDP CONTROLS

Control objectives	Minimum control standards	Control techniques	Description
			Pre-installation Controls
A			To ensure that a computer is ordered only if it is likely to produce greater benefits than other processing alternatives.
	A1		There should be some method of ensuring that costs, savings, benefits and processing methods resulting from the introduction of computer processing can be determined approximately before the decision to acquire a computer is made.
		A1-1	*A Management Committee should be formed with responsibility for initiating, guiding and reviewing results of the Preliminary Survey.*
		A1-2	*Terms of Reference for the Preliminary Survey should be prepared by the Management Committee.*
		A1-3	*A Preliminary Survey should be carried out and a Survey Report prepared in accordance with the Terms of Reference.*
		A1-4	*A Computer Steering Committee should be formed with responsibility for initiating, guiding and reviewing a Feasibility Study.*
		A1-5	*Terms of Reference for the Feasibility Study should be prepared by the Computer Steering Committee.*
		A1-6	*A Feasibility Study should be carried out and a report prepared in accordance with the Terms of Reference.*
B			To ensure selection of suitable facilities and services.
	B1		Appropriate equipment selection criteria should be established and identified and made available to potential suppliers.
		B1-1	*A list of appropriate selection criteria should be prepared and given to each potential supplier.*
	B2		Selection criteria should be utilized in the evaluation of suppliers' proposals.
		B2-1	*The selection criteria should be set out in the form of a chart on which the evaluation of suppliers' proposals should be entered.*

Source: The Canadian Institute of Chartered Accountants, "Computer Control Guidelines," 1970.

Exhibit 8-1. (Cont.)

Control objectives	Minimum control standards	Control techniques	Description
		B2-2	*Bench mark problems may be submitted to the equipment supplier and the resulting programs evaluated.*
		B2-3	*Packaged simulation programs may be used to evaluate manufacturers' proposals.*
		B2-4	*Contractual arrangements should be carefully reviewed prior to making the final equipment selection and signing the contract.*
C			To ensure that a pre-installation plan is prepared against which results and progress can be measured.
	C1		Pre-installation tasks or activities should be identified and defined.
		C1-1	*A listing of all activities or tasks and their dependencies should be prepared.*
	C2		All tasks or activities should be incorporated into a pre-installation plan.
		C2-1	*The tasks or activities should be presented in a form which shows their interdependency and a time relationship.*

Organizational Controls

Control objectives	Minimum control standards	Control techniques	Description
D			To provide effective organizational control over the concentration of functions in the EDP department.
	D1		The EDP department should be separated from non-compatible functions within the organization.
		D1-1	*There should be a separation of the functions of (i) initiation and authorization of transactions (ii) recording of transactions and (iii) custody of assets.*
	D2		There should be a segregation of duties within the EDP department.
		D2-1	*The functions of system design and programming should be separated from computer operations.*
		D2-2	*A data control group, independent of the other operating functions, should be established.*
		D2-3	*A computer file library should be set up.*

Exhibit 8-1. (Cont.)

Control objectives	Minimum control standards	Control techniques	Description
	D3		Normal separation of duties for control purposes should be retained in the source and user departments.
E			To ensure that management exercises effective control over deployment of computer resources.
	E1		The EDP department should report to senior management.
		E1-1	*The EDP department should report to an executive who has sufficient authority to ensure that the department will receive adequate support and effective management.*
		E1-2	*A Computer Steering Committee should play a prominent role in the systems development work.*
	E2		There should be active participation by management, user departments and auditors in the development, design, and maintenance of systems.
	E3		Management should exercise control over methods and performance standards.

Development Controls

Control objectives	Minimum control standards	Control techniques	Description
F			To ensure that an application is converted to the computer only if it will produce greater benefits than any other alternatives.
	F1		There should be some method of ensuring that costs, savings, benefits and methods resulting from the introduction of computer processing can be determined approximately before the decision to acquire a computer, or to add an application to the computer, is made.
		F1-1	*An effective Feasibility Study should be conducted.*
		F1-2	*Senior management should approve the conclusions of the various study groups.*
	F2		Long-term plans should be made as a guide to subsequent systems design.
G			To ensure the development of effective systems and programs.
	G1		There should be active participation by representatives of the user departments, including the accounting department.
	G2		There should exist a segregation of duties and assignment of responsibilities commensurate with non-compatible functions and skill required.

Exhibit 8-1. (Cont.)

Control objectives	Minimum control standards	Control techniques	Description
		G2-1	*Programming and operating functions should be segregated.*
		G2-2	*The EDP department should not have control over assets or over the origination of transactions.*
	G3		Standard systems design and programming procedures and techniques should be established.
		G3-1	*Systems design standards should be established, documented, and enforced.*
		G3-2	*Programming standards should be established, documented, and enforced.*
	G4		Authorization and approval should be required at each major phase of development.
		G4-1	*Each system should be reviewed and approved by senior management and applicable user departments prior to the commencement of systems design.*
		G4-2	*A system of progress review and comparison to schedules should be established.*
		G4-3	*Final approval should be obtained prior to operation of new system.*
	G5		Systems and programs must be sufficiently tested to ensure reliability in accordance with original specifications.
		G5-1	*User/EDP department cooperation should exist in testing of systems.*
		G5-2	*Final tests should include all phases of the system, including manual and computer.*
	G6		Effective control is required over the conversion of data and the initial operations.
		G6-1	*Conversion of master files should be controlled to prevent unauthorized changes and to ensure accurate and complete results.*
H			To ensure that systems and programs are effectively maintained.
	H1		Changes to systems and programs should be subjected to the same controls as for new systems.

Exhibit 8-1. (Cont.)

Control objec- tives	Mini- mum control stand- ards	Contro tech- niques	Description
		H1-1	*Costs of making changes should be allocated to the user departments.*
		H1-2	*Authorization should be obtained before a change is initiated.*
		H1-3	*Operators should not be authorized to make changes, however minor these changes may be.*
		H1-4	*Testing and final approval of changes should be controlled.*
		H1-5	*The operations section should accept only properly approved changes.*
	H2		Adequate control should be maintained in the operations section to prevent unauthorized changes.
Operations Controls			
I			To prevent or detect accidental errors occurring during processing by the EDP department.
	I1		There should be some method to ensure data is complete, accurate, and authorized when received for processing.
		I1-1	*A control group should be established to receive all data for processing, assume responsibility to see that all errors detected during processing are corrected, and to ensure that all output is properly distributed.*
		I1-2	*The computer edit programs should be used to the extent possible to check the completeness, accuracy, and proper authorization of the data and to complement the control group functions.*
	I2		Standard procedures should be used for all operations and a review should be made to ensure these procedures are followed.
		I2-1	*Manuals of systems and procedures should be provided for all functions in computer operations.*
		I2-2	*The method by which the computer controls its own operations should be evaluated in terms of the overall control requirements.*
		I2-3	*The procedures followed should be reviewed by the operations supervisor.*

Exhibit 8-1. (Cont.)

Control objectives	Minimum control standards	Control techniques	Description
I3			There should be some method to ensure correct files are mounted, switches are correctly set, and output files are properly allocated.
		I3-1	*Computer files should be labelled both internally and externally.*
		I3-2	*All computer files should be controlled by the library.*
		I3-3	*Operators' manuals should be used for all required actions by computer operator.*
		I3-4	*The computer operating system (or programs) should be used to the extent possible to check machine and file set-up procedures.*
I4			There should be some method to ensure early detection of errors and hardware malfunctions.
		I4-1	*Totals on input, master, and output files should be predetermined and periodically balanced during processing.*
		I4-2	*Where possible, the computer should be used to edit for errors.*
		14-3	*There should be some method of ensuring that the hardware is performing accurately.*
	Other desirable controls		
		I5-1	*Scheduling of all computer processing.*
		15-2	*Limitation of access to the computer room.*
		I5-3	*Maintenance of an orderly operation in the computer room.*
J			To prevent or detect fraudulent manipulation of data during processing by the EDP department and to prevent misuse of classified information.
J1			The EDP department should be separated from the source and user departments within the organization.
J2			Control should be exercised over the various functions within the EDP department.
		J2-1	*The programming and operating functions should be separated.*

Exhibit 8-1. (Cont.)

Control objectives	Minimum control standards	Control techniques	Description
		J2-2	It is desirable that the program knowledge of the operator be restricted.
		J2-3	Computer operations should be effectively supervised.
		J2-4	There should be a planned program of rotation of operators and joint operation on sensitive applications.
		J2-5	Machine utilization logs and console print-outs should be reviewed.
		J2-6	Access to the computer room should be restricted.
		J2-7	A librarian should be appointed to control the issuance and storage of computer files.
		Other desirable controls	
		J3-1	Key EDP personnel should be bonded.
K			To provide security against accidental destruction of records and to ensure continuous operation.
	K1		There should be standard procedures to prevent or detect accidental errors caused by operator error or machine or program malfunction.
	K2		There should be some method to reconstruct files after minor processing errors or minor destruction of records.
		K2-1	Procedures should be established to detect errors as early as possible.
		K2-2	Explicit operator instructions on error and halt conditions should be prepared.
		K2-3	Back-up files should be maintained.
		K2-4	Checkpoint and restart procedures should be included with each program which runs for more than thirty minutes.
		K2-5	Built-in equipment and file duplication should be used on critical systems.
	K3		There should be physical safeguarding of files.

Exhibit 8-1. (Cont.)

Control objec- tives	Mini- mum control stand- ards	Control tech- niques	Description
		K3-1	*Environmental control should exist against excesses of humidity, temperature, or other atmospheric conditions.*
		K3-2	*The computer room should be protected against fire.*
		K3-3	*Off-premise storage facilities should be used.*
	K4		There should be some method to ensure continuity of operation after major destruction of files, or hardware breakdown.
		K4-1	*There should be off-premise storage of files.*
		K4-2	*Back-up computer facilities should be available.*
		K4-3	*Procedures to be followed in emergency conditions should be documented.*
		K4-4	*Adequate insurance should be carried.*
	Other desir- able controls		
		K5-1	*Statistics and performance reviews.*

Processing Controls

Control objec- tives	Mini- mum control stand- ards	Control tech- niques	Description
L			To ensure the completeness of data processed by the computer.
	L1		There should be some method of ensuring that all data is initially recorded and identified.
		L1-1	*Each transaction should be initially recorded on a specially designed form which should bear an identification code and be filed in such a manner that subsequent reference can be made to it.*
		L1-2	*Where possible, the computer should be programmed to anticipate each transaction and to detect missing input (anticipation control).*
		L1-3	*Employees responsible for input preparation, or having access to unused source documents, should not also be responsible for, or have access to, the related assets or the computer programs or the computer itself.*
	L2		Control should be established close to the source of the transaction.

Exhibit 8-1. (Cont.)

Control objectives	Minimum control standards	Control techniques	Description
		L2-1	*Input data should be batched close to the point of preparation and batch control totals should be taken; batch header forms should be used containing an identification code and record of the batch control total.*
	L3		Output should be reconciled to input.
		L3-1	*Output control totals should be reconciled back to input control totals by the control group.*
		L3-2	*As an alternative, output control totals should be reconciled to input totals by the computer.*
		L3-3	*Overall control totals should be reconciled from output to input by the source or user departments.*
		L3-4	*In some applications, output should be listed and visually checked in detail to input documents.*
	L4		There should be some method of ensuring that all corrections are re-entered into the system for all identified errors.
		L4-1	*All data rejected from the processing cycle should be entered in an error log by the control group and corrections should be marked off in this log when they are re-entered; open items should be investigated regularly.*
		L4-2	*As an alternative, records of rejected data awaiting correction and re-entry should be maintained by the computer; reports should be generated regularly of items which have remained outstanding in these records for more than a specified length of time.*
		L4-3	*A well-defined system should be established for correcting errors and re-entering corrections as input; and fixed responsibilities for this function should be assigned.*
	L5		The timing of input submission and output distribution should be properly coordinated with processing.
		L5-1	*Control total reconciliations should be reviewed at cut-off dates to ensure that all input information has been received for processing.*

Exhibit 8-1. (Cont.)

Control objectives	Minimum control standards	Control techniques	Description
		Other desirable controls	
		L6-1	*It is normally desirable for the control group to log data through the processing cycle and to balance controls at sufficiently frequent intervals in order to provide the most efficient means of error correction and file reconstruction.*
M			To ensure the accuracy of data processed by the computer.
	M1		There should be procedures to prevent errors in the preparation of input or source data, and to detect and correct any significant errors which do occur.
		Preventive	
		M1-1	*Each transaction should be initially recorded on a specially designed form.*
		M1-2	*Procedures governing preparation of source documents should be specifically described in written manuals.*
		M1-3	*Adequate training and supervision should be given to all persons associated with preparation of data for subsequent computer processing.*
		M1-4	*Whenever possible and practical, information on source documents should be preprinted and/or pre-coded.*
		M1-5	*Employees responsible for input preparation or having access to unused source documents, should not also be responsible for, or have access to, the related assets or the computer programs or the computer itself.*
		Detective	
		M1-6	*A control group should be established to receive all data for processing, assume responsibility to see that all errors detected during processing are corrected, and ensure that all output is properly distributed.*
		M1-7	*In the absence of other controls, key identification codes should utilize the self-checking digit technique to identify coding errors.*
		M1-8	*Computer capabilities should be used wherever practical to edit or screen the input data for accuracy.*

Exhibit 8-1. (Cont.)

Control objectives	Minimum control standards	Control techniques	Description
		M1-9	*Manual editing should be used wherever appropriate to edit or scrutinize the input data for accuracy.*
	M2		There should be procedures to prevent errors arising on conversion of data to machine-processable form and to detect and correct any significant errors which do occur.
		Preventive	
		M2-1	*Each transaction should be initially recorded on a specially designed form.*
		M2-2	*Whenever possible and practical, information on input documents should be pre-coded in machine-sensible form.*
		M2-3	*As an alternative, data should be coded simultaneously with the recording of the original transaction.*
		M2-4	*There should be written manuals, adequate training and supervision of staff, and division of duties.*
		M2-5	*In the absence of any other controls, key identification codes should utilize the self-checking digit technique to identify coding errors.*
		Detective	
		M2-6	*Except where otherwise controlled, important keypunched data should be keyverified.*
		M2-7	*Computer capabilities should be used wherever practical to edit or screen the input data for accuracy.*
		M2-8	*Manual editing should be used wherever appropriate to edit or scrutinize the input data for accuracy.*
		M2-9	*In the absence of other effective controls, key fields should be verified by the use of control totals.*
		M2-10	*A control group should be established to receive all data for processing, assume responsibility to see that all errors detected during processing are corrected, and to ensure that all output is properly distributed.*
		M2-11	*Data conversion equipment selected should contain adequate hardware controls.*
	M3		There should be procedures to ensure that data is transmitted accurately to the computer center.

Exhibit 8-1. (Cont.)

Control objectives	Minimum control standards	Control techniques	Description
		Preventive	
		M3-1	*In the absence of other effective controls, key fields should be verified by the use of control totals.*
		M3-2	*Input terminal control logs should be maintained.*
		M3-3	*Particularly sensitive data in on-line transmission should be controlled by answer-back procedures.*
		M3-4	*Data transmission devices selected should contain adequate hardware controls.*
M4			Procedures should be in effect to ensure that the computer equipment is functioning correctly and that malfunctions and resulting data errors are detected.
		Preventive	
		M4-1	*Manufacturers' recommended preventive maintenance procedures should be followed with respect to equipment.*
		M4-2	*Manufacturers environment specifications should be maintained.*
		Detective	
		M4-3	*Computer equipment selected should have adequate hardware controls.*
		M4-4	*Output control totals should be reconciled back to input control totals.*
		M4-5	*Control information should be reconciled within individual runs.*
		M4-6	*Computer editing and manual editing procedures should be used where appropriate to edit for a possible machine malfunction.*
M5			Procedures should ensure that only valid files are used.
		Preventive	
		M5-1	*Proper conversion controls should be maintained.*
		M5-2	*Adequate training of staff, operator manuals, and supervision of operations should be provided.*

Exhibit 8-1. (Cont.)

Control objectives	Minimum control standards	Control techniques	Description
		M5-3	*Computer files should be labelled externally.*
		M5-4	*All computer files should be controlled by the library.*
		Detective	
		M5-5	*Computer files should be labelled internally.*
		M5-6	*Where in use, the computer operating system should be utilized to determine the validity of the files being used.*
		M5-7	*Computer editing and manual editing procedures should be used where appropriate to edit for a possible machine malfunction.*
	M6		Controls must ensure that the accuracy of data is maintained during processing.
		Preventive	
		M6-1	*Computer programming should be accurate.*
		M6-2	*Computer equipment selected should have adequate hardware controls.*
		Detective	
		M6-3	*Adequate software control procedures should be employed.*
		M6-4	*Output control totals should be reconciled back to input control totals.*
		M6-5	*Control information should be reconciled within individual runs.*
		M6-6	*Computer editing and manual editing procedures should be used where appropriate to edit for a possible machine malfunction.*
	M7		Procedures should ensure that program computations are performed correctly.
		Preventive	
		M7-1	*Computer programming should be accurate.*
		M7-2	*Computer equipment selected should have adequate hardware controls.*

Exhibit 8-1. (Cont.)

Control objectives	Minimum control standards	Control techniques	Description
		Detective	
		M7-3	*Computer capabilities should be used wherever practical to edit or screen the input data for accuracy.*
		M7-4	*Crossfooting, arithmetic and overflow tests should be used to the fullest extent possible.*
	M8		There should be a system of control over the physical operation of the computer system.
		M8-1	*Adequate training of staff, operator manuals, and supervision of operations should be provided.*
		M8-2	*Access to the computer room should be restricted to authorized personnel.*
		M8-3	*It is desirable that the program knowledge of the operator be restricted.*
		M8-4	*There should be a planned program of rotation of operators and joint operation on sensitive applications.*
		Detective	
		M8-5	*Adequate software control procedures should be employed.*
		M8-6	*Machine utilization logs and console print-outs should be reviewed.*
		M8-7	*Output control totals should be reconciled back to input control totals.*
		M8-8	*Computer editing and manual editing procedures should be used where appropriate to edit for a possible machine malfunction.*
	M9		There should be procedures to ensure that all significant errors which have been identified at various stages in the system have been corrected, re-entered, and properly reflected in the output.
	M10		There should be procedures to ensure that all required output reports are delivered to the proper user departments.
		Preventive	
		M10-1	*The control group should ensure that all output is properly distributed.*

Exhibit 8-1. (Cont.)

Control objectives	Minimum control standards	Control techniques	Description
		Detective	
		M10-2	*User departments should anticipate the return of output from the computer center.*
N			To ensure that all data processed by the computer is authorized.
	N1		The EDP department should be separated from non-compatible functions within the organization and there should be a segregation of duties within the EDP department.
		N1-1	*There should be a separation of the functions of (i) initiation and authorization of transactions; (ii) recording of the transactions; and (iii) custody of assets.*
		N1-2	*Access to critical forms should be restricted to individuals responsible for the initiation function.*
		N1-3	*Access to the computer and computer files and programs should be restricted to designated employees.*
	N2		To ensure that only authorized data is processed, input documents should bear evidence of authorization and should be reviewed by the control group for such evidence.
		N2-1	*In a batch processing system, clerical procedures should be established to authorize input and subsequently scrutinize it for proper authorization.*
		N2-2	*To the extent practical, computer routines should be utilized to authorize input and subsequently scrutinize it for proper authorization.*
O			To ensure the adequacy of management trails.
	O1		There should be some method of identifying and locating the component file records and input/output documents involved in the processing of a given transaction or in the accumulation of a given total.
		O1-1	*Each document and machine-sensible file record should have a unique identification.*
		O1-2	*Each document and machine-sensible file record should be filed in a significant and planned sequence to facilitate its accessibility.*

Exhibit 8-1. (Cont.)

Control objectives	Minimum control standards	Control techniques	Description
		O1-3	*Methods of tracing specific items of data backwards and forwards through the processing cycle should be an integral part of the systems design.*

Documentation Controls

Control objectives	Minimum control standards	Control techniques	Description
P			To ensure that adequate documentation exists and is effectively controlled.
	P1		There should be some method to ensure that all documentation is prepared in accordance with predetermined standards.
		P1-1	*Systems documentation standards should be established, published, and enforced.*
		P1-2	*Programming documentation standards should be established, published, and enforced.*
		P1-3	*Operating documentation standards should be established, published, and enforced.*
		P1-4	*Library or file control documentation standards should be established, published, and enforced.*
		P1-5	*Keypunching or other data conversion documentation standards should be established, published, and enforced.*
		P1-6	*Documentation standards for the preparation of instructions to persons responsible for the control over computer input and output (control group and user groups) should be established, published, and enforced.*
Q			To ensure that all systems are adequately documented.
	Q1		There should be some method of ensuring that a problem to be solved is clearly and accurately stated.
		Q1-1	*For each processing problem or general application area, a Problem Definition should be prepared.*
	Q2		There should be some method of ensuring that a system designed to solve a problem is clearly and accurately presented.
		Q2-1	*Systems documentation should be prepared for each application.*
	Q3		There should be some method of ensuring that the control functions and responsibilities for any system are clearly defined and the appropriate control procedures clearly and completely documented.

Exhibit 8-1. (Cont.)

Control objectives	Minimum control standards	Control techniques	Description
		Q3-1	*Systems documentation should include clear and complete statements of control functions, responsibilities, and procedures.*
R			To ensure that all programs are adequately documented.
	R1		There should be some method of ensuring that all documents and records necessary for the complete understanding of each program are prepared.
		R1-1	*Adequate program documentation should be prepared for each program.*
S			To ensure that instructions to all data processing and user personnel are adequately documented.
	S1		There should be some method of ensuring that all information required by the computer operator for the performance of his responsibilities is available.
		S1-1	*Operating instructions should be prepared for each program.*
		S1-2	*Standing operating instructions should be prepared for each computer installation.*
	S2		There should be some method of ensuring that all information necessary for a complete understanding of file maintenance and file protection operations is available.
		S2-1	*File control instructions should be prepared for each system and made available to the person responsible for safeguarding of files.*
		S2-2	*Standing file protection instructions should be prepared for each computer installation.*
	S3		There should be some method of ensuring that all information required by persons responsible for data conversion operations is available.
		S3-1	*Data conversion instructions should be prepared for each system and made available to the persons responsible for these operations.*
	S4		There should be some method of ensuring that all information required by persons responsible for controlling input to, and output from, a computer is available.

Exhibit 8-1. (Cont.)

Control objectives	Minimum control standards	Control techniques	Description
		S4-1	*Data control instructions should be prepared for each system and made available to the persons responsible for data control.*
	S5		There should be some method of ensuring that all information required by departments submitting data to, or receiving information from, a computer is available.
		S5-1	*User department instructions should be prepared for each system and made available to the appropriate departments.*

Outside Data Center Controls

T			To ensure that a commitment for data center services is made only if they are likely to produce greater benefits than any other processing alternatives.
	T1		A need for computer processing facilities must be established.
		T1-1	*A preliminary survey of computer processing requirements should be made.*
		T1-2	*A feasibility study should be carried out.*
	T2		The benefits to be gained from using data center facilities must be clearly demonstrated.
		T2-1	*A detailed comparison of the procedures, costs and benefits of various "in-house" computer systems and data centers must be made.*
U			To ensure selection of suitable data center facilities.
	U1		Selection criteria should be determined and used to evaluate and rank available data center services.
		U1-1	*An evaluation chart should be prepared showing the selection criteria and providing spaces for entering an evaluation of each data center for each of the selection criteria.*
V			To ensure the adequacy of customer and data center organizational and procedural arrangements.
	V1		There should be a proper division of duties among all persons involved in data processing operations, both in the customer and in the data center organizations.

Exhibit 8-1. (Cont.)

Control objec-tives	Mini-mum control stand-ards	Control tech-niques	Description
		V1-1	*Job descriptions snould be written for all the customer's staff concerned with data processing.*
		V1-2	*Data center organizational structure should be reviewed.*
		V1-3	*All dealings with the data center on a day-to-day basis should be coordinated through one person.*
	V2		Data processing procedures at the customer's premises and at the data center must be developed to meet manage-ment's needs and provide the most efficient operation, and all responsibilities must be clearly defined.
		V2-1	*All existing data processing procedures at the customer's premises must be reviewed and revised where neces-sary; and conversion procedures should be developed and fully documented.*
W			To ensure that all data processed is complete, accurate, and authorized.
X			To ensure the adequacy of management and audit trails.
Y			To ensure the adequacy of security and protection over customer data, records, and reports.
	Y1		There should be some method of ensuring that only author-ized persons have access to customer's data, records, and reports.
		Y1-1	*Access to the data center should be limited to author-ized personnel.*
		Y1-2	*Data center employees should be required to sign a se-crecy agreement as a condition of employment.*
		Y1-3	*When dealing with confidential data, codes should be used instead of descriptions.*
		Y1-4	*Customer employees should be in attendance for confi-dential processing operations.*
	Y2		There should be adequate protection of documents, re-ports, and files against theft, fire or other damage or destruction.
		Y2-1	*Documents, reports and files should be placed in ade-quate storage facilities when not in use.*
		Y2-2	*Customers should have adequate insurance against loss of data and to cover file reconstruction costs.*

Exhibit 8-2. COMPUTER PROGRAM DOCUMENTATION

Opinions vary on what constitutes adequate and complete documentation of operational computer programs. It is generally agreed, however, that at least four categories of documentation are required if long and complex programs are to be significantly changed or subjected to other scrutiny.

The four categories are system flow charts, detailed program flow charts, source programs, and computer runsheets. Still other categories of documentation may be found when the auditor embarks on an audit of documentation supporting computer programs. The documentation may be placed in 12 different categories. They are explained here to show the relationship of various forms of documentation to the four first mentioned. The auditor is cautioned, however, that each EDP installation may not place the documentation in the precise categories described here. Some of the 12 categories may have been combined, others may have been eliminated or omitted, and still others may have been added.

1. Cover Sheet. The purpose of the cover sheet is to identify the computer program by giving such information as program name, program number, purpose (a brief nontechnical description of the problem solved by the program), source language used (such as COBOL or FORTRAN), EDP configuration that the program was designed for, programmer's name, and date of the program. Even though helpful, the cover sheet is not an absolute necessity because the information it contains is usually shown elsewhere in the documentation or is easily obtained.

2. Forms Layout. The purpose of this section is to show the content of input and output documents and reports. If it is not included in the documentation, it is usually available from other sources, such as current reports and currently used input documents.

3. Definitions. The purpose of this section is to define all symbolic names used anywhere in the program documentation. Symbolic names are abbreviated terms that are used in place of longer names, terms, or titles. For example, one of the input documents in the forms layout section may show a form space and identify its contents as "TAXDED." Reference to the definitions section might show that "TAXDED" means "Tax Deduction." This section may also contain any tables or other information the programmer feels should be defined. A table might show, for example, the number of dependents in one column and the applicable tax deduction in an adjacent column.

Like the forms layout section, the definitions may be available from other sources if they are not defined in a separate section of documentation. As an example, definitions may be recorded on system flow charts and detailed program flow charts (explained later) or defined in the comments contained in the source program. Of course, the symbolic names used may have an obvious or easily determinable meaning. In that case, the definitions may not be essential.

4. System Flow Chart. The purpose of the system flow chart is to show the flow of work, documents, and reports in a specific data processing job. It is designed to demonstrate how the data processing job is organized from beginning to end. It is general in nature because it does not specify the detailed and specific computer steps that are necessary for a particular processing run. (This detail is a function of the detailed program flow chart described later.)

Exhibit 8-2. (Cont.)

Special data processing symbols are used in a system flow chart, along with symbolic names, previously described, and English language statements to describe flow of work, documents, and reports. By referring to the system flow chart, programmers and others can find out how the overall data processing job is organized, the source and type of input records, the point at which input records are introduced into the computer for processing, the sequence of the overall processing, all resulting output — such as printed reports — and the ultimate destination of the output.

This type of information is not usually available from another source unless it can be recalled by the people who worked on the program or unless it can be reconstructed from other detailed data processing records or current practices. Reconstruction can take a great deal of time if the data processing job is a lengthy one. Besides, it is not a good practice to rely on an individual's memory, because some important details may be forgotten or the individual may leave the company.

5. Detailed Program Flow Chart. Like the system flow chart, the detailed program flow chart uses special data processing symbols, symbolic names, and English language statements. Unlike the system flow chart, however, the detailed program flow chart shows a step-by-step sequence in implementing a data processing job so that it can be made operational.

It is from the detailed program flow chart that the programmer prepares the actual computer program (called a source program) to be compiled and executed by the computer. Unless the source program is simple and only a few source program steps are required, a current detailed program flow chart is a valuable tool to the programmer in making necessary changes at a later date.

Because of its extremely detailed nature, it is important that the detailed program flow chart be kept current. Otherwise, important and minute details may be forgotten and the programmer may find it difficult or impossible to make changes in the related source program when the need arises. This is particularly true if the changes are to be made by a programmer other than the one who initially prepared the detailed program flow chart and source program. For some complex source programs, the programmer may prepare several program flow charts, each becoming progressively more detailed until one of them possesses the detail that is necessary for writing the source program. When making program changes, the detailed program flow chart is almost always used in conjunction with the source program, which is described in item 7.

6. Program Description. This section describes how the logic of the source program was developed, using the higher-level language (such as COBOL or FORTRAN) and the computer. It is a detailed flow chart in prose form. Sometimes, because COBOL is near to English, this section is not prepared for source programs written in COBOL. If it is not prepared, the same information is almost always available from the detailed program flow chart or the source program, except without the detailed and sometimes lengthy prose statements which explain why specific procedures were followed.

7. Source Program. This section contains the actual program as it is written in such higher-level languages as COBOL or FORTRAN. By comparing the detailed program flow chart with the actual source program, the programmer or others can trace each step of the computer through to a final conclusion. In reviewing

Exhibit 8-2. (Cont.)

and making changes in the programs, the programmer must generally refer to the source program to determine precisely how the higher-level language statements were used before the current review and change became necessary.

The detailed program flow chart is useful in determining the purpose of specific source program statements. Some EDP installations may also follow the practice of requiring programmers to include English language comments in the source program to briefly explain the purpose of each program step. Such comments are useful and, together with the detailed program flow chart, can provide a clear audit trail that shows the step-by-step procedure that was followed in developing the source program.

Sometimes, English language comments in the source program are sufficient to permit an accurate review of or change in the computer program. This, of course, depends upon the extent and clarity of the English language comments, the length and complexity of the source program, and the extent of the required review or program changes.

If a current copy of the source program is not formally kept as documentation, it can usually be obtained from punched cards that were used to introduce the source program into the computer or from other storage devices, such as magnetic tape, that may be used to hold the information.

8. List of Test Data. This section identifies the test data used by the programmer in testing the source program after it was written. The results are shown in the Test Report, described in item 10.

9. Sample Output. This section contains sample output resulting from the source program. Examples of output include reports and punched cards. If this information is not included in the documentation it is usually easily obtained by referring to recent output that resulted from EDP processing runs.

10. Test Report. This section explains the results that were obtained when the source program was tested to determine whether it was operational. If test data and test reports are not included in the documentation, the programmer can prepare other test data to determine the current effectiveness of the source program.

11. Deck Setup. This section gives the order of the source program card deck. It is similar to the source program (see item 7), but it is not in as much detail. The source program is an exact duplication of the computer program in the higher-level language. The deck setup shows the order of the related card deck, but it is usually subdivided by major category and does not outline each program step.

This section may include such other information as requirements for peripheral equipment (magnetic tape drives, card readers, and card punchers), the time limit for the computer program when it is being executed by the computer, and special control cards needed for a successful run of the job. This information is also available from the programmer.

12. Computer Run Sheet. This section contains information needed by the console operator for running the computer program, such as the magnetic tapes or disks to be mounted, the names and usage of all input files, any Central Processing Unit (CPU) console messages that may appear during the run, and any operator action to be taken as a result of these messages. This information is also usually available from retained copies of the CPU console messages and from programmers responsible for maintaining the source program.

FIELD WORK

THE NATURE OF FIELD WORK

Field work, as considered here, encompasses all the efforts of the internal auditor to accumulate, classify, and appraise information so as to enable him to form an opinion and to make any needed recommendations for improvement. It includes collecting, arraying, and analyzing data and records anywhere inside or outside the company. It consumes by far the greatest part of the auditor's time.

Field work, when reduced to its barest essentials, is largely measurement and evaluation. These terms are an echo of what is said in the *Statement of Responsibilities of the Internal Auditor*, published by The Institute of Internal Auditors. The second sentence of the Statement says that internal auditing "is a managerial control which functions by *measuring* and *evaluating* the effectiveness of other controls." (Emphasis supplied.)

The concept of measurement has a special significance for the internal auditor. When he has fully grasped this concept, he can successfully examine virtually any operation in the company. But he must understand that he cannot audit an operation in a vacuum. He cannot observe a process and make an off-hand decision that it is good or bad. He must look at the operation in terms of units of measurement and standards. The units of measurement are the discrete elements that apply to the operation — the dollars, days, pounds, degrees, people, documents, machines, or other quantifiable things — and by which its success or failure can be objectively gauged. The standards are those qualities of acceptability with which the measured things will be compared.

So each audit subject must be approached with the thought that it can be dealt with by —

- Determining its size, extent, or other quality in terms of units of measurement, and
- Comparing the results with acceptable standards.

Then the auditor can measure objectively and intelligently. But where he cannot measure, he had better tread lightly, because he will be able to produce only a subjective observation — not an objective opinion.

An example of a routine examination will illustrate the concept of audit measurement. Suppose the auditor wishes to evaluate the promptness with which materials clear through receiving inspection. The unit of measurement is an hour or a day. The standard may be what management considers acceptable, as stated in job instructions. It may be the needs of the production departments, as set out in production schedules. Or it may be some other logical criterion that is keyed to a company objective. The auditor will apply the unit of measurement to each transaction — to each delivered shipment in his sample. He will then compare the results with the standard. Finally, he will determine whether the sum total of his findings portrays a good or bad condition, by evaluating the results of his measurement.

Now let us take a more esoteric audit situation. Assume that the auditor wishes to determine whether a test pilot is calling out defects in the aircraft when he should. Pilots use check sheets which they fill in as they fly the plane and read the instruments. Some entries relate to pressure readings. The pressure instruments are calibrated in terms of pounds per square inch. The pilot is asked to read a particular instrument at a given altitude and power setting and to enter the reading on his check sheet. If the reading is outside acceptable limits, the pilot must prepare a "squawk" sheet which will trigger an investigation of the reason for the unacceptable reading.

The auditor, to make his determination, will read the pilot's check sheet. His units of measurement are there — the pounds per square inch shown on the instruments and on the pilot's check sheet. Yet if he were to examine the pilot's readings without reference to a standard he would be wasting his time. He could draw no supportable conclusions. A reading of 80 or 100 or 120 might all seem equally appropriate.

But if the auditor reviewed engineering specifications and found, for example, that fuel pressure at 20,000 feet and a power setting of 85% should be between 90 and 110 pounds, he now has a standard. If the pilot's entry on the check sheet is 100, the auditor can be quite satisfied that no action was needed. But if the entry were 130 pounds, then the auditor would expect to see a squawk sheet. If one had not been prepared, he would record a deficient condition. And he could do so confidently.

So to make a meaningful examination, the auditor looks for a unit of measurement and then for a standard. The standards can be found in job instructions, company directives, budgets, product specifications, trade practices, minimum standards of internal control, generally accepted accounting principles, contracts, statutes, sound business practices, or even in the multiplication tables. Then, by comparing his findings of fact with the standards, he can arrive at an objective conclusion.

As the auditor wades deeper and deeper into the stream of operations, and as he begins evaluating management functions for which standards have not been established, he may find himself faced with the need to establish his own. This may not be an easy path to take. But if it is traveled with care it may lead to audit results often thought beyond the auditor's reach.

The standards should match the objectives of the operation reviewed. And if the subject is technical, the standards should be validated by one who is technically qualified. An example of this approach involved an audit of a company's safety and security controls. Since no standards existed, the auditor constructed them. Then, to obtain adequate assurance that the standards were reasonable, and proper, he asked a representative of the National Safety Council to review them. Once validated, the auditor was able to use those standards with confidence in making his measurements.

Relevant excerpts from the resulting audit report demonstrate the auditor's methods:

"To evaluate the adequacy of the organizational structure as a means for dealing with potential disasters and with matters of safety, we constructed a set of criteria to use as a yardstick in measuring the adequacy of the control system. Our criteria covered matters of both industrial security and safety and were as follows:

"1. Committee structure, composition, and operation.

   a. Have appropriate committees been constituted to provide policy guidance and direction over disaster and safety control?
   b. Are the line organizations which are responsible for industrial security and safety operations adequately represented on the committees?
   c. Are committee activities carried out in a businesslike manner, including the advance scheduling of meetings, the provision for detailed agendas, the recording, assigning, and resolution of action items, and the preparation and distribution of minutes?
   d. Is there assurance that safety problems at the hourly employee level will receive proper attention and will be followed to a satisfactory conclusion?
   e. Is there a means of obtaining interface among the various committees for handling related problems?

"2. Plans, programs, practices, and implementing instructions.

   a. Have emergency and/or disaster plans been developed and have appropriate instructions been issued to implement the plans?
   b. Have industrial safety programs been established for the promotion of safety through accident prevention?
   c. Have adequate provisions been made for the implementation of the requirements of the Occupational Safety and Health Act which became effective April 28, 1971?

"3. Monitoring, inspecting, and reporting activities.
   a. Have specific hazards been identified and has provision been made to monitor them?
   b. Are physical inspections of plants and facilities being made and are reports on the inspections being distributed?
   c. Is the workmen's compensation insurance company with which our company deals represented at general safety meetings and is the insurance company being provided with minutes of all safety meetings and reports of the inspections?
   d. Is corrective action being taken on deficiencies reported as a result of inspections?

"To obtain assurance that our criteria have provided us with adequate yardsticks, we submitted them to the occupational safety director of the local chapter of the National Safety Council. He informed us that in his judgment our criteria were both reasonable and complete and that an organizational structure together with appropriate plans and programs, which measure up to those criteria, would represent an adequate system of control."

But measurement is only one of the two faces of field work. Having made his measurements, the auditor must then evaluate the results. He will now determine what his opinions and recommendations should be by evaluating the data produced by his measurements.

Evaluation suggests an intent to arrive at a mathematically correct judgment; to express that judgment in terms of what is known. It seldom suggests the determination of a thing's monetary worth — but rather to find its equivalent in other and more familiar terms, such as the evaluation of the timeliness with which invoices are being processed, or the evaluation of the promptness with which receipts are inspected, or the evaluation of the correctness of a pilot's records.

The mathematical connotation permits measurement and evaluation to walk side by side down the audit trail with perfect compatibility. Thus, measurement and evaluation constitute the key to field work.

There are many modes and approaches to field work, and the auditor should understand when each one applies. He should be able to decide when to use surveys — reviews of systems and controls with minimal checking of transactions — and when to do detailed transaction verifications, the examination of representative samples of total populations. He should be conversant with the many forms field work takes: observing, questioning, analyzing, verifying, investigating, and evaluating.

He should understand the difference between functional and organizational audits and the uses of each. He should understand how to use or develop "tip sheets" that point to aberrant conditions or suspicious trends. And as he gathers data for his measurements, he should have a working knowledge of the rules of evidence as they apply to auditing.

But throughout all his field work, as he applies standards, the auditor should not fail to evaluate the standards themselves. The fact that they have been established and approved does not necessarily make them sacrosanct. Standards developed yesterday may not be applicable today. Changing circumstances may require new or revised statutes, contracts, procedures, or instructions. In other words, standards too should be measured, and the measuring stick is the applicability of the standards in the real world of today and their adequacy in meeting the organization's objectives and goals.

The auditor's measurements will normally be directed to three aspects of an operation: quality, cost, and schedule. As a simple example, assume that the auditor is examining controls over the preparation and release of engineering drawings. Included among his measurements will be those that follow:

Quality

- See whether drawings have been independently checked in the manner prescribed in drafting instructions and whether errors and variances disclosed by the checkers have been corrected.

- Examine drawings for evidence of a prescribed technical review that is designed to determine whether the drawings will produce products that will meet contract specifications.

Cost

- Compare the number of man-hours spent on the drawings with the number of man-hours budgeted.

- Find out the extent and cost of product changes required because the products designed did not work as intended, and compare the extent and cost with established norms.

Schedule

- Measure the various spans involved in the checking and approving processes against prescribed time spans, and identify any unreasonable delays.

- Compare the dates blueprints were released to the shop with the dates they were promised.

THE FORMS OF FIELD WORK

The form the field work takes depends on the subject of the examination and the circumstances of the particular situation. Under some circumstances, detailed verification of transactions is essential. In other circumstances, surveys with minimal verification will suffice.

If the auditor foresees high risks and serious consequences from the improper functioning of an activity, he should seek thorough and detailed support for his opinion. The survey form of examination in such a situation may not be enough. A substantial verification of transactions would be needed to provide him with requisite assurance. For example:

- In an audit of compliance with conflict of interest programs, the auditor must understand that even one conflict might present management with serious problems. Determining that adequate controls have been provided is not enough. The auditor would most likely want to examine a very large sample to provide reasonable assurance that he will detect instances of possible conflict. And if suspicions are aroused, he may have to look under every stone.

- Sales of scrap traditionally present problems and can represent significant amounts. The auditor would wish to examine in detail representative samples of transactions before he would express an opinion that the system is working as intended.

On the other hand, the subject may not be fraught with high risk, or self-checking devices may have been installed to highlight defects and alert management to control breakdowns. Then the auditor may be willing to place reliance on the system and concentrate on the checking devices to determine that they are operating effectively. For example:

- A stock room has a system of self-checks. Supervisors are required to make periodic tests of stores and the related records. They are responsible for reporting their tests and results in writing to the department manager. He provides evidence of his review of their tests and of his follow-through of action items. Here the auditor may reduce his tests. He may evaluate the adequacy of the check lists, the frequency of the tests, and the correction of observed defects. These reviews, together with minimal tests of transactions to provide assurance that the system is indeed functioning as prescribed, should give the auditor adequate support for an opinion on the operations.

■ A document security department is subject to quarterly reviews by government inspectors who provide written reports of all defects. Besides, department personnel use a comprehensive check list to make examinations of every document control station in the company once a year. Personnel charged with the conduct of the document control stations are provided with indoctrination and periodic reindoctrination courses. In such circumstances, the auditor's review may be restricted to providing assurance that the control system is functioning and that all prescribed self-checks are being made.

Between the two extremes of surveys on the one hand and the detailed tests on the other are a multitude of variations. The auditor must dip into his store of audit techniques for the appropriate instrument to make his measurement and obtain his assurances.

He achieves audit objectives by a process referred to as testing. Testing implies placing activities or transactions on trial, putting them to the proof, and revealing their inherent qualities or characteristics. We shall now discuss the subject of testing and the various methods used to accomplish tests.

TESTING

Testing, to the auditor, connotes the measurement of selected transactions or processes and the comparison of the results of those measurements with established standards. The purpose is to form an audit opinion.

The audit test usually implies the evaluation of transactions, records, activities, functions, and assertions, by examining all or part of them. In today's complex world, the examination of an entire entity in detail is usually impractical or uneconomical. But testing — when viewed as putting something to the proof — does not necessarily exclude a complete examination. It is anything which supplies the auditor with the proof he needs to support his audit opinion.

Circumstances will vary the steps to be taken in this audit function. But usually the steps include:

1. Determining standards.
2. Defining the population.
3. Selecting a sample of transactions or processes.
4. Examining the selected transactions or processes.

Determining the Standards

Standards are explicit or implicit. They are explicit when they are set forth clearly in directives, job instructions, specifications, or laws.

Instructions may state categorically, for example, that time spans shall not exceed five days, or that competitive bids must be obtained for all procurements over $1,000, or that production lots shall be rejected when error rates exceed 5%, or that engineering drawings must conform strictly to a design handbook. The auditor in such cases has a well-calibrated measuring stick for his comparisons — units of measurement and established standards.

Standards are implicit when management may have established — or may be working toward — objectives and goals, but has not set forth with particularity how they will be achieved. In those cases the auditor, after reviewing the objectives and goals and determining the controls established or needed, will have to consult with management on what it considers to be satisfactory performance. To make tests without coming to agreement on units of measurement and on standards of acceptability may result in wasted work and fruitless argument.

It must be emphasized that without standards there can be no meaningful measurement. And without measurement, field work becomes conjecture and not fact.

Defining the Population

The population to be tested must be considered in terms of the audit objectives. If the objective is to form an opinion on the transactions which took place since the last audit, the totality of such transactions since then represents the population. If the objective is to form an opinion on the adequacy, effectiveness, and efficiency of existing systems of control, the population may be more restricted. Under the latter circumstances, management is not interested in past history. It is concerned with the here and now: Is the system working the way it should? If not, how can we improve it?

In either event, the auditor should seek to obtain a reasonable idea of the number of transactions involved — purchase orders, receiving memos, invoices, billings, shipping tickets, shop orders, rejections, sales slips, contracts, travel vouchers, blueprints, change orders, manifests, etc.

He should seek to determine the character and location of the population, to see if any documents can be missing, and to help him decide on the appropriate selection plan. How are the documents filed? Are they in random order? Are files receipts supposed to be substituted for all items removed from the files? Is there good control over the files? Are the transactions stratified according to value or other quality? Are the documents serially numbered?

Selecting the Sample

The selection should follow the plan which fits the audit objective — judgmental or statistical — knowledgeably determined. It is best to make the selection from a listing which is separate from the records of transactions themselves. In that way there is better assurance that items abstracted from the files will not be overlooked. The method of selecting samples was discussed in Chapter 7.

Examining Transactions

The auditor examines transactions — or processes — to get at the truth and to reach conclusions. The alpha of the audit measurement and the omega of the audit evaluation are both encompassed in the term examination. The auditor has many techniques at his disposal to help him achieve this audit objective. Just what those techniques should be called is a moot point among auditors. But for our purposes we shall group them under six headings which can carry the auditor from the alpha to the omega of his field work.

We have given these terms definitions that are sometimes more relevant to audit examinations than to their common usage. But they should serve our purposes here. We have termed the six forms of field work as follows:

- Observing
- Questioning
- Analyzing
- Verifying
- Investigating
- Evaluating

The first five may be considered as part of the measurement process. The last — evaluation — gives meaning to the information that the auditor has gathered.

Observing. To the auditor, observing means seeing, noticing, and not passing over. It implies a careful, knowledgeable look at people and things. It means a visual examination with a purpose . . . a mental comparison with standards . . . an evaluative sighting.

It differs from analysis, because analysis implies setting down and arraying data. Observation, on the other hand, means seeing and making mental notes, mental judgments. Since all auditing, including observing, is largely measurement, proper observation is probably one of the most difficult of audit techniques. For the auditor is measuring what he sees with what he has in his mind. The broader his experience, the more standards he retains, the more alert he is to deviations from the norm, the better an observer he can become.

While observing is important, it is generally preliminary to other techniques. It usually requires confirmation through analysis or investigation. It takes place during the preliminary survey when the auditor familiarizes himself with the physical plant and with systems and processes. But it can also take place during questioning and interviewing when the auditor notes the reactions and behavior of those he deals with. And it can take place, as well, when he is obtaining impressions of work tempo, facilities, staffing, and plant conditions.

Observations can be useful in noting clerical filing practices or work flow for unnecessary effort or tortuous routing. The auditor can observe the condition of rejected material, as a start to backtracking for causes. He can tour a plant and observe idle equipment or idle facilities. He can observe security precautions on the perimeter of a plant or inside a bank or store. He can observe dangerous conditions and safety violations. He can observe cluttered stock rooms and evidence of backlogs. He can observe poorly stored or dangerously stacked materials. He can observe storerooms left unlocked. He can observe lack of adequate maintenance. He can observe trucks leaving the plant without being halted by guards. The list is without end.

Knowledgeable observations can provide keen insights. But the auditor must be careful how he uses them in citing deficient conditions. If such visual examinations are reported without confirmation, they should be clearly labeled observations and impressions. They will seldom withstand a frontal attack by the auditee. But they need not be followed up with detailed analysis if the auditee agrees with the observations and takes corrective action.

Questioning. Questioning is probably the most pervasive technique of the auditor who is reviewing operations. Questioning is carried on throughout the audit and may be oral or written.

Oral questions are usually the most common, yet probably the most difficult to pose. Obtaining information orally can be raised to the level of an art. To get the truth and to do so without upsetting the auditee is sometimes not an easy task. If the auditee detects an inquisitorial tone or perceives a cross-questioning attitude, he may promptly raise his defenses and be loath to part with the truth. The information he then gives may be wrong or incomplete; or answers may not be forthcoming at all. So if the auditor can understand how the average auditee sees him — as a potential threat — and can then modify his manner to allay fears, his chances of obtaining adequate information are considerably enhanced.

At the same time, the auditor's concern for the auditee's feelings should not deter him from insisting on the truth. To that end, he should not put words in the auditee's mouth. A question such as this will usually produce an affirmative response, true or not: "Do you always keep the doors to the storeroom locked?" A question like "How do you protect stores?" might bring a different answer. And a good rule to follow when audit decisions will be based on answers to oral questions is to confirm the questions by putting the same question to at least two people.

Questions may sometimes be the most satisfactory way of determining how well or how poorly an activity is being performed. For example, the test of whether or not a service is acceptable rests on the opinions of those served. This is especially true of technical operations, where only the technicians are qualified to evaluate the manner in which a service or product meets their expectations or standards.

One example is the usefulness of reports. The auditor could prepare a questionnaire along the following lines:

- Do you receive the report on time for it to be of value to you?
- Does the report seem readily understandable?
- Does it give you the information you need?
- What use do you make of the report?
- When is the last time you used it to help you accomplish your own objectives?
- Have you ever found the report inaccurate or misleading?
- If so, what did you do about it?
- What would you do if you no longer received the report?

Questions such as these can be submitted in writing, used as a poll over the telephone, or asked face to face.

Analyzing.   Analyzing implies a detailed examination. It stresses dividing a complex entity for the purpose of determining its true nature. It contemplates laying bare the inner workings of some function, activity, or mass of transactions and determining the relationships of the individual parts.

Analyzing suggests the intent to discover or uncover qualities, causes, effects, motives, and possibilities — often as a springboard for further investigation or as a basis for a judgment. Justus von Liebig, the German chemist, by analyzing foodstuffs of every kind, came to the conclusion that the principal elements of food are protein, fats, and carbohydrates. By analyzing an account, the financial auditor separates, arrays, and spreads out the individual elements that constitute the account. In this way he can see which elements are significant, which recur, which are minimal, and which need further attention.

The internal auditor who examines operations does much the same. The principles are no different — only the subject matter. And whatever the subject matter, the auditor can see significant relationships and make precise measurements by parading before his audit microscope the individual elements that make up the activity he examines. In contrast, when the entities are examined as a whole, the mind cannot perceive the intricate interrelationships of the diverse and varied elements that make up a complex function or a large population.

In audits of operations, the subject matter can span a broad spectrum. Here are some of the subjects the modern internal auditor may be concerned with in making his evaluations:

The auditor can list a sample of purchase orders on a spread sheet and analyze each one in terms of bids, sole source procurement, approvals, past history of particular purchases, routing, cost analysis, schedules, purchase order preparation in accordance with instructions, and a host of other qualities.

Similarly, the auditor can analyze a directive, a statute, or a contract. Here too, he spreads the document out, reads each word, underlines what is significant, measures it in terms of good business practice or real-world conditions, or measures existing practices in terms of the documents. A simple reading is not enough. The auditor must identify and highlight significant elements and determine what they mean.

Also, the auditor may analyze the company's safety program. In most large companies the safety program is conducted by numerous committees operating independently or in relation to each other. The auditor may analyze the program by arraying the functions of the significant committees in a matrix which shows for each one (1) where the committee gets its authority, (2) what its precise functions are, (3) who the chairman is, (4) to whom it reports, (5) how often it meets, (6) who prepares the minutes and what happens to them, (7) how action items are assigned and monitored, and (8) how the various committees interface. In this way the auditor can observe administrative failings, decide whether there is overlap among committees, and see whether some essential function has somehow been overlooked.

In analyzing the function of tool cribs, the auditor might examine a sample of cribs by studying each one and recording his findings on work sheets. The work sheets might show: (1) an appraisal of physical conditions — whether tools are neatly stored in properly identified compartments; (2) whether inventories are promptly taken and variances are reconciled and adjusted; (3) whether the inventory records are current; (4) whether all tools are recorded; (5) whether a tool is accounted for by its physical presence, by a tool repair order, or by a tool check (surrendered by a worker when he borrows a tool) ; and (6) whether the crib operator "ages" the surrendered tool checks and follows up those that have been on hand for excessive periods of time.

Any composite can be analyzed by division, by breaking it into its elements, and by observing trends, making comparisons, and isolating aberrant transactions or conditions. The auditor does it by arraying data on work sheets, verifying its validity, and evaluating the results. This is the heart and the marrow of the auditor's art. And he steps into modern internal auditing when he applies these techniques to operating matters which are a far cry from account analysis. This precise appraisal, this ability to see the elements through his audit microscope, this ability to isolate, identify, quantify, and measure, makes the audit results useful, sound, and unassailable.

Verifying. Verifying suggests attesting to the truth, accuracy, genuineness, or validity of something. It is the auditor's oldest tool. It is most often used in establishing the correspondence of the actual facts or details to those that are given in an account, or statement, or the like. It implies the deliberate efforts to establish the accuracy or truth of some affirmation by putting it to the test — such as a comparison with ascertainable facts, with an original, or with some standard.

Verification includes corroboration, when statements of one person are confirmed by discussions with others. It also includes confirmation, which implies the removal of all doubts through independent validations by objective parties.

The auditor verifies an accounting entry by comparing it with supporting detail. He verifies an amount due by confirming it with a creditor. He verifies an approval by consulting authorized directives establishing levels of approval and by comparing the approval signature with that on a signature card. He verifies the propriety of a purchase by assuring himself that the requirement for the purchased item was established by someone other than the buyer; that the number of items procured did not exceed those called for in a bill of materials; that the items were procured on time, but not in advance of need, by reference to production schedules; that the items were actually received, by reference to a receiving memo, a visit to stores, or an examination of the end product.

Verifying has not only certain unique qualities of its own, but also has some of the attributes of the other audit techniques the auditor uses.

Investigating. Investigating is a term that generally applies to an inquiry which has for its aim the uncovering of the facts and the establishing of the truth. It implies a systematic tracking down of something that the auditor hopes to discover or needs to know. It includes, but is not limited to, probing, which applies to investigations that search deeply and extensively with the intent to detect wrong-doing.

Investigations may occur as a part of or as a result of other audit techniques. When comparisons disclose excessive variations, the auditor will investigate to find reasons or determine causes. When analyses disclose aberrant conditions, the auditor will track them down to determine their extent and their effect. When observations disclose potential weaknesses or improprieties, the auditor will extend his audit work to obtain full information.

Investigations are not restricted to improprieties. They are generally concerned with establishing the truth about a transaction or a series of transactions. They have more pointed direction, however, than analyses, which imply the examination of data having relatively unknown qualities until examined.

Probes are related to wrong-doing. And here the auditor must be careful not to go beyond his depth. Probes often involve legal and criminal considerations; and after obtaining some inkling of serious impropriety, the auditor should refer the matter to those who are experienced in interrogations of such matters. The auditor who does not heed warnings may find himself violating an individual's rights and laying his company open to prosecution for libel, slander, defamation of character, malicious prosecution, or false imprisonment. He should therefore refer such matters to his company's security people or to legal counsel.

Evaluating. Evaluating, as well as its kindred term "appraising," implies estimating worth. In auditing it means arriving at a judgment. It conveys the thought of weighing what has been analyzed and determining its adequacy, its effectiveness, and its efficiency. It is the step between analysis and verification on the one hand and the audit opinion on the other. It represents the conclusions the auditor draws from the facts he has accumulated.

Evaluation implies professional judgment, and it is the thread that runs through the entire fabric of the audit. In the early stages of the audit, the auditor must evaluate the risk of eliminating an activity from his review in terms of the cost of covering it. In his program he must evaluate the need for detailed tests in place of a survey or a walk-through. In his sampling procedures he must evaluate the precision and confidence level he must have to achieve the degree of sample reliability he believes he needs. As he compares a transaction with a standard and finds a variance, he must evaluate the significance of the difference and determine whether corrective action is necessary. As he summarizes the results of his audit examination he must evaluate what those results imply.

Fact-finding without evaluating becomes a clerical function. Proper evaluations lift the audit from what may be a detailed check to a management appraisal. As has been said, the auditor first observes the facts through the bottom of his bifocals — the verification half — and then evaluates them through the top part — the management half.

No auditor can become a full professional until he evaluates everything he looks at in terms of objectives and standards. Arrayed data, no matter how artfully arranged, is merely base metal and ore until it has been transmuted into something of value through evaluation.

Every auditor who finishes an analysis of transactions and who has methodically summarized the results, must understand that his task is not complete until he has evaluated what he has gathered together.

Evaluation, obviously, calls for judgment. The mature, experienced auditor, the veteran of many audit examinations, the participant of many a report draft review, the wise observer of the company's course and objectives, evaluates his audit findings almost intuitively, and usually is correct. But even he can benefit from a structured, organized approach to the evaluation of what his findings mean. For example, in evaluating deviations from the norm — the failures to meet standards — he might ask himself these questions:

1. How significant are these deviations?
2. Have they prevented the organization or function from achieving its objectives and goals?
3. Who or what has been hurt?
4. How badly?
5. If corrective action is not taken, is the deviation likely to recur?
6. Why did the deviation occur in the first place?
7. What is the cause or causes? What event or combination of events threw the process off its track?
8. Has the cause been truly ascertained and precisely described? Will the event or combination of events cause the observed result every time? Does the cause satisfactorily explain every aspect of the deviation?

We shall discuss later the auditor's recommendations for corrective action to cure deficient conditions. But patently the auditor's mind is bound to turn to thoughts of how to cure the difficulties as he evaluates them. He might as well ponder his proposals in an organized manner. Some of the questions he might ask himself in that connection are:

1. What course of action will most practically and economically cure the defect?
2. What objectives should he keep in mind in recommending corrective action? What should management be trying to achieve in setting forth an improved course of action?
3. What choices are open? How do they measure up when compared with the objectives?
4. What tentative alternate has been selected and what injurious side effects might be expected?
5. Which is the best choice with the least unsatisfactory side effects?
6. What mechanism should be suggested to control the corrective action after it is taken? How can one make sure that the corrective action is taken . . . that it will be carried to a conclusion . . . that future deviations will be referred back to

someone authorized to remove impediments from the proper fulfilment of the suggested course of action?

The auditor owes management a duty not only to suggest corrective action to cure defects, but also to point the way to ensuring continued efficacy of that action.

AUDIT MODES

The techniques of observing, questioning, analyzing, comparing, investigating, and evaluating are applied under varied circumstances. They are used whenever the auditor performs an examination. By and large, however, they are applied within broad frameworks, or audit modes, which indicate the direction or scope of the audit. The end results are the same: an audit opinion and recommendations for improvement. But the approach to the audit will differ, according to the auditor's particular plan of attack.

Most audit projects will be carried out under one of three audit modes: the functional audit, the organizational audit, and the management study. We shall discuss all three.

Functional Audits

As used here, a functional audit is one which follows a process from beginning to end, crossing organizational lines. Functional audits tend to concentrate more on operations and processes than on administration and people. They seek to determine how well all the organizations concerned with a function will interface and cooperate to see that it is carried out effectively and efficiently.

Some functional audits that can be of value in an organization are:

- Scrap accumulation, segregation, and sale
- The incorporation of changes into products
- Ordering, receiving, and paying for materials and supplies
- Safety controls and practices
- The classification of employees as direct or indirect
- Programs designed to detect conflicts of interest

Functional audits present special difficulties because of their breadth and scope. The auditor is required to define the parameters of the job, keeping it within reasonable bounds, yet covering all significant aspects of the function. He must deal with a number of organizations, each perhaps with objectives which might be in conflict with the objectives of downstream or upstream organizations.

Yet functional audits can provide special benefits to management. Varying viewpoints can be identified. Bottlenecks can be exposed. Differing objectives can be reconciled. Duplications can be highlighted. Cooperation between auditor and auditee can be made to replace hostility and misunderstanding.

An example of the benefits of the functional audit is given in the following case history.

A manufacturing company had developed procedures and assigned responsibilities for the accumulation, segregation, and sale of scrap metals. In general, the responsibilities were as follows:

- The machine shops where the scrap metal was generated were responsible for segregating the scrap according to types of metals.

- The Reclamation Department was charged with supplying carts bearing signs to show the categories of scrap to be deposited in the carts. Reclamation was to ticket the carts when they were ready to be transported to the salvage sales yards or to truck bodies which had been supplied by scrap dealers under contract with the company.

- The Transportation Department was responsible for transporting the carts either to the company's Salvage Sales yard (for mixed metals) or to the truck bodies (for large volumes of metal turnings or chips).

- Plant Protection guards were directed to verify the documentation for scrap leaving the plant and to record the time that the truck drivers for the scrap dealers left the production departments on their way to the company's Salvage Sales yard for weighing.

- The Salvage Sales yard was held responsible for obtaining the best prices for scrap and for rejecting those carts which contained improperly segregated scrap, returning the carts with the mixed scrap to the scrap-generating departments.

- The Procurement Department was to issue reports on sales of different types of scrap, showing the prices received for each.

The auditor followed the process from the point of scrap generation to the point of sale. He examined scrap placed in the carts, rode in trucks, talked to people, and compared the amounts received for scrap with prices listed in a technical publication dealing with metals. As he carried on his examination, he became aware of a considerable amount of parochialism, with excessive concern for individual departmental goals and with indifference to or lack of understanding for the needs of other organizations or of the company's overall goals. For example:

- At scrap generating points, production supervisors gave little thought to the need for scrap segregation. They were not aware of the value of properly segregated scrap as compared with the value of contaminated scrap. They were resentful of having to segregate scrap when Reclamation refused to accept carts with contaminated scrap or when Salvage Sales returned carts containing improperly mixed metals.

- Reclamation supplied carts, but was not always careful to supply the identifying signs that would facilitate segregation.

- Guards were indifferent to the need to record the time that truck drivers left the scrap-generating department on the way to Salvage Sales for weighing.

- Salvage Sales was concerned solely with the highest dollar return for scrap and rejected any carts which carried contaminated scrap.

- The Procurement Department prepared reports of scrap sales, but submitted the reports to its own management only.

As a result of conflicting goals, lack of good communication, and the failure to understand the goals of others and the objectives of the company as a whole, the auditor found the following conditions:

- The cost of segregation in some instances exceeded the value of the segregated metals.

- Rejected carts were shuttled back and forth because Salvage Sales was concerned only with cash returns and not with the cost of resegregating scrap.

- Guards were not always recording the time that trucks left the plant because they had not been instructed as to the purpose of the recording. They had never been informed that if the drivers were not controlled they could stop off before arriving at Salvage Sales and dump some of the scrap metals for their personal gain.

- Since Procurement sent reports of sales receipts to its own management only, others were not aware of the amounts of return that could be received for properly segregated scrap as against contaminated scrap.

At the conclusion of the audit, the auditor held meetings with the managers responsible for the processing and sale of scrap metals. As a result the following corrective action was taken:

- Company procedures were revised to emphasize company objectives and to establish reasonable rules for scrap segregation, accumulation, and sale.
- Carts were properly identified.
- Generating departments were supplied with reports of scrap sales and were given the authority to segregate or not segregate metals, based on the volume of scrap generated and the potential return.
- The shuttling back and forth of the carts was discontinued; but to keep generating departments informed of their derelictions, Salvage Sales would send them memos informing them of the losses in revenue that were suffered because of improperly segregated scrap.
- The guards were instructed on just why the recording of time was important on documents accompanying scrap.

The auditor managed to resolve conflicts, reconcile differences, and generate a better *net* return for scrap. He made a follow-up review about six months after the new procedures went into effect. He was amazed at the turnabout in attitude, cooperation, and results. People were willingly following policies that made sense to them. The system was functioning smoothly, effectively, and economically.

The functional audit can achieve similar results for other systems and processes in the company, so long as the auditor keeps his eye on overall company objectives and manages to bridge the gaps between the various organizations concerned with the function.

Organizational Audits

Organizational audits are concerned not only with the activities performed within an organization but also with the administrative controls used to make sure they will be carried out. The auditor is interested, therefore, with how well the organization's manager is meeting the objectives of the organization with the resources at his disposal. An incisive organizational approach can often provide insights into operations which transcend those obtained solely by tests of transactions that are aimed at seeing how well actions follow procedures.

Especially in large organizations with a multiplicity of operations and functions, the auditor is better advised to determine how well management is managing than how well transactions flow or trickle through the organization's pipeline. The auditor's measuring stick, then, the standards he applies in appraising an organization's operations, are constructed from the elements that make up acceptable principles of administrative control.

It is a rare organization indeed that is so managed that it operates in accordance with all or even most of the theoretical precepts of good administrative control. Yet the auditor, in performing an organizational audit should have those precepts in mind. Often an unsatisfactory condition can be the direct result of the violation of an accepted principle of good administration. A capsule rule of proper administration may be considered to be:

Feedback, Follow-up, and No Surprises

If a manager has so constituted his organization and so indoctrinated his people that he is aware of what is going on, if he keeps on top of what is going on, and if he is alerted to problems before they become critical so that he can take timely action, then he is probably doing a good job of managing.

If the auditor keeps these guides in mind, he will begin to function at the management level. Obviously, however, these guides are but a hint of what good administration embraces. And if the auditor is to perform organizational audits in depth he should have more than a hint of what good administration is all about.

He should have a working knowledge of administrative, or management control within a business. We first discussed management control in Chapter 5, "Performing the Preliminary Survey." As the auditor carries out an organizational audit, he will be putting the principles of management control to work. He should be able to flesh out the skeletal structure delineated in Chapter 5. A clear, crisp picture of the completed structure, engraved on the mind's eye, can have a profound effect on how the auditor views the administration of the organization when he performs his audit, and on the questions he asks. And the nature of those questions will contribute mightily to increasing his stature in the eyes of operating management.

The auditor should be conversant with the principle of planning — with setting objectives, assigning responsibility, maintaining continuity, and reappraising plans and goals in the light of changed conditions.

He should be conversant with the principle of organizing — with the means of achieving objectives, discharging responsibility, developing staff, and periodically reappraising organization and operation.

He should be conversant with the principle of controlling — with setting standards; maintaining standards; training personnel to comply with standards; prescribing an approval system; ensuring compliance with standards; devising systems of records, reports, and master control; and monitoring the entire ongoing process.

Exhibit 9-1 provides a chart depicting one view of the hierarchy of management controls implicit in a management control system.

The organizational audit functions best when it operates at the management level. If the manager is doing his job effectively and efficiently, then there is a good chance that the department's output is going to be effective and efficient. And if the auditor can satisfy himself that the manager is a good administrator who has established a smoothly functioning organization operating under reasonable controls, then tests of transactions can be sharply reduced. When the auditor sees a lopsided organization chart, a lack of planning, an absence of follow-up and feedback, and a poor reporting system, then he knows that he must pick up his audit spade and dig deeply.

Patently, the auditor who is skilled in scientific management principles will more successfully be able to evaluate the capacity of the organization's manager to administer effectively and efficiently. The scope of this book, however, does not contemplate a study in depth of scientific management. Yet there are some key questions the auditor can ask himself about the organization which may prove revealing.

Administrative Control

Without attempting to be all-encompassing, the following questions — geared to some extent to the hierarchy of management controls depicted in Exhibit 9-1 — may lead to helpful answers.

I. Planning

  A. Setting objectives

    1. Are annual objectives set down in writing, and have the commitments been submitted to higher management? Do these objectives contain provision for:

      a. Improvements in the organization's operations?

      b. Improvement of the organization's image?

      c. Cost reduction?

      d. Personal development of the manager and all his subordinates?

    2. Has a workable budget system been established? Does the system provide for:

      a. Actual plans and expectations, rather than ideal goals?

      b. Logical, supportable, mathematically correct premises and standards?

Exhibit 9-1. MANAGEMENT CONTROLS WITHIN THE COMPANY STRUCTURE

I. Planning

Defining what should be done and how, where, and when it should be done. Planning includes:

A. Setting objectives and devising plans and budgets;

B. Assigning responsibility to carry out the plans and achieve the objectives, under budget constraints;

C. Maintaining needed continuity for the plans; and

D. Reappraising objectives and plans periodically in the light of changing conditions.

II. Organizing

Providing the plant, capital, staff, and materials required to achieve the objectives, and setting the basic guidelines within which the plans should be pursued. Organizing includes the establishment of a structure and a system which are designed to:

A. Achieve the objectives;

B. Discharge the assigned responsibility for carrying out the established plans;

C. Maintain continuity of organization and responsibility; and

D. Periodically reappraise the structure and system to ensure their continued effectiveness.

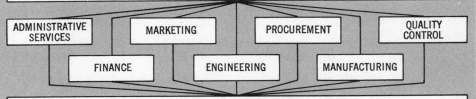

III. Controlling

Directing, coordinating, constraining, and regulating action in accordance with the requirements of the plans for the accomplishment of objectives. Controlling includes:

A. Setting basic standards for cost, quality, and timeliness;

B. Maintaining the standards to meet changing conditions;

C. Training personnel to comply with the standards;

D. Prescribing a system of approvals to maintain management control over operations;

E. Ensuring compliance with the standards;

F. Devising systems of records, reports, and master control over all activities; and

G. Monitoring all ongoing processes, obtaining feedback, and achieving improvement.

   c. Adequate documentation in support of proposals by subordinate organizations ?
   d. Flexibility — the capability of rebuilding budgets quickly and accurately when plans change?
   e. Comparisons between budgeted and actual amounts or other goals?
   f. Explanations of significant variances between budgets and actuals?
   g. Exclusion of those items over which the manager has no control or which are not sufficiently significant to warrant budgetary control?
   h. Differentiation between budget goals and enterprise goals, and an understanding that enterprise goals are not to be sacrificed for budget alone?
   i. Periodic examination of standards and premises to make sure they do not hide inefficiencies by perpetuating prior overruns ?
   j. Permitting the participation in setting budgets by those who must live with them ?
   k. Giving reasons to participants in the budget-setting when they are overruled?
B. Assigning responsibility
   1. Is there a proper delegation of responsibility that provides for accountability to higher authority for the activities assigned, while at the same time capitalizing on the ideas and abilities of individuals?
   2. Do the plans provide goals that are subject to measurement, and do they also provide for reports on periodic measurements to ensure the proper discharging of the responsibility assigned?
C. Maintaining continuity
   1. Are there long-range and short-range plans ? Do the long-range plans provide for continuity of effort on major programs ? Do the short-range plans concentrate on achieving interim milestones or accomplishing less extensive programs?
   2. Do plans provide for a personal development plan for each employee, encompassing not only company training programs but also outside study and development ?
D. Reappraising objectives
   1. Are the organization's plans, objectives, policies, and proce

dures reappraised periodically to make sure they remain consistent with the overall plans and objectives of the company, that they achieve uniformity among related organizations, and that their benefits outweigh their costs?

II. Organizing

A. Achieving objectives

1. Is the organizational structure in harmony with the objectives of the company or division?
2. Is the organizational structure designed to accomplish its particular objectives without an overlapping of functions and a duplication of effort?

B. Discharging assigned responsibilities

1. Are the functions, responsibilities, authority, and relationships of each significant position in the organization defined in writing?
2. Does the organization chart set forth the major areas of responsibility?
3. Is authority so delegated as to permit decisions to be made at the lowest practicable levels of management?
4. Does the organizational structure provide for unity of command — each person reporting to no more than one superior?
5. Does the organizational structure provide for authority to be commensurate with responsibility, while providing reasonable spans of management — not too much or too little?
6. Do the lines of responsibility extend from the top of the organization to the lowest level of supervision — without gaps?
7. Are compatible functions grouped together, and do all functions have proper balance — no function being excessively weak or excessively dominant?

C. Maintaining continuity

1. Does the organization provide for continuing training to develop qualified personnel for higher positions?
2. Are replacement charts prepared, and are they periodically reviewed at appropriate levels of management?
3. Does management give consideration to an appropriate mix of ages so that retirements will not adversely affect the functioning of the organization?

D. Periodically reappraising the organization

1. Is the organization flexible and capable of adjusting to changing conditions? Are periodic reviews made to determine the need for adjustment?

2. Are periodic — at least annual — reviews made to appraise functions, manpower, and facilities so as to reaffirm their justification in terms of the organization's objectives, to improve techniques and efficiency, and to eliminate all unessential matters?

III. Controlling

A. Setting standards

1. Have measurable, quantitative goals been established for all subordinate groups and, where applicable, for individuals, in the areas of cost, quality, and schedule?

2. Have estimated man-hours and schedule spans been established for repetitive work?

3. Has the manager provided for estimated man-hours and specific due dates to be assigned to each job or increment? Does he make sure that these standards are understood by all personnel affected?

4. Are the standards established by management based on a balanced set of criteria, so as not to sacrifice any one factor (quality, cost, or schedule) for another?

5. Are the performance requirements reasonable — not so minutely controlled as to result in excessive costs, overcontrol, and interference with the work of subordinate supervision?

6. Does the system of control provide for feedback of significant information to the manager which will enable him to evaluate the continued validity of the standards and his success or failure in meeting them?

7. Is there provision for establishing and disseminating new standards of performance when the old ones are found to be inadequate or ineffective?

B. Maintaining standards

1. Are directives and job instructions periodically reviewed to ensure their continued validity and appropriateness and to determine whether or not the system can be improved upon?

2. Are standard man-hours and schedule spans reviewed periodically to determine their correctness and applicability?

3. Are the needs of serviced organizations reviewed and are their opinions solicited as to the quality of services or products furnished?

4. Do all job instructions, procedures, and policies reflect the latest performance requirements of the company, the customers, and the organization?

5. Are continuing efforts made to eliminate or reduce the causes of exceptions and deviations rather than accepting the variances as "normal" and covering them with specially designed procedures?

6. Are employees told how their performance will be measured?

C. Training personnel

1. Have employees been adequately instructed? Have they been provided with check lists when they are asked to consider numerous factors as they perform their tasks?

2. Does employee training include instruction on the requirements, functions, and responsibilities of their positions and of the organization's objectives, standards, policies, procedures, and means of measuring performance?

3. Does management disseminate, interpret, and explain to its people the pertinent policies, procedures, specifications, regulations, and other requirements originated by other organizations?

4. Are personnel informed of management's cost, quality, and schedule standards for work and product requirements, and is information on changes communicated promptly?

5. Are the people affected required to initial or sign controlled copies of disseminated information, job instructions, procedures, and the like, to evidence their reading and understanding of them? Are the copies retained in the files?

6. Are employees kept informed of the results of the feedback from downstream organizations?

7. Are employees promptly reinstructed when what they do prevents the accomplishment of plans?

8. Does management encourage employees to improve their capabilities by taking advantage of company training programs and outside courses?

D. Prescribing approvals

1. Has an approval system been provided and do the approval levels appear to be commensurate with the significance of the transactions or programs?

2. Is planned and scheduled work supported by valid requests or authorizations? Are the requests related to the functions of the requesting organization?

3. Are incoming or self-generated jobs reviewed at a sufficiently high level to determine whether they should be performed at all and what priority should be assigned to them?

4. Are the requesters notified of the additional cost of special or more exacting work before the work is scheduled?

5. Are activities coordinated with interfacing organizations and, where necessary, approved by them, so as to promote cooperative and efficient performance?

6. Is the assignment of personnel to activities or individual jobs approved at appropriate levels?

7. Are up-to-date lists maintained of authorized signatures for all applicable documents, stating the limits or other criteria for which the authorizations are valid?

8. Can a job be rescheduled or rebudgeted without the approval of specifically designated management?

9. When policies and procedures are not working, must approval for changes be at the same level of authority where those policies were prescribed in the first place?

E. Ensuring compliance

1. Are methods established for reviewing and passing upon completed work, so as to make sure it meets established standards?

2. Is work (assigned and in process) reviewed to make sure it is being performed on schedule?

3. Has provision been made to have the failure of coordination and the breakdown of communication between interdependent organizations disclosed to management so as to permit corrective action?

4. Does the control system provide for subordinates to be informed of responsibilities and standards and for methods of fixing responsibility for any deviations from such standards? Is work that does not meet acceptable standards returned to the originator?

5. Is provision made for the prompt expediting and feedback of information to management on variances between established budgets and schedules and actual accomplishment?

6. Is provision made for periodic spotchecks — in addition to normal monitoring — of work in process and completed work, to ensure conformity to the established requirements?

F. Devising records and reports and establishing master control

1. Does the manager have the records and reports he needs to translate his duties and the organization's objectives into action, and to operate and control his organization effectively?

2. Does the manager maintain adequate and current statistics on the volume of work and the accomplishment of objectives, so that he can plan efficiently for the future?

3. Does the system of control provide for an interchange of reports among interdependent organizations?

4. Are reports made to management on contacts with customers or potential customers to keep management current on the quality of service rendered, the company's or organization's image, and the reasons for unsuccessful bids?

5. Does the manager constructively question the quality of his own reports to make sure they present a fair picture:
   a. To himself of his operations?
   b. Of his people's contributions?
   c. To his superiors and to others who rely upon his reports?

6. Have primary (or master) records been established — charts, control accounts, work orders, or other appropriate devices — to ensure overall control of the organization's activities and to see that no significant matters are overlooked?

7. Are records maintained of the dates that jobs are received and started, the dates appropriate milestones are reached, and the dates the jobs are completed and delivered?

8. Does the scheduling system of control provide assurance that the oldest and/or most important jobs will receive priority attention?

9. Does management maintain a master control record of the jobs or activities to which personnel are currently assigned? Does management at the appropriate level always know what each employee is doing?

10. Does management see to it that the total group workload and the priorities of jobs will be periodically reviewed, and that schedules and budgets will be adjusted, as required, to bring results into conformity with plans?

11. Are control records periodically reconciled with subsidiary or detail records where applicable, bringing variances and their reasons to the attention of appropriate levels of management?

G. Monitoring processes

1. Do controls provide for prevention, rather than correction, of deviations and exceptions to the greatest extent possible?

2. Does management provide for monitoring the reports it issues or uses to satisfy itself of their reliability, currentness, and meaningfulness?

3. Does management give attention to exceptions at the most strategic control points in the system, instead of waiting until it is found that the ultimate objective has not been achieved?

4. Is provision made for all complaints and recommendations from customers and serviced organizations to be recorded upon receipt, evaluated, acted upon, and answered?

5. Has provision been made to prevent or eliminate:
   a. Misdirected effort?
   b. Unnecessary and/or unrelated tasks?
   c. Uneven distribution of workload?
   d. Work assignments that are made only because of the improper performance of others?

    e. Complicated or impractical procedures?

    f. Clerical or other routine work being performed by supervision?

    g. Bottlenecks in work flow?

The series of questions just listed for planning, organizing, and controlling should not be used as a questionnaire to be posed to a manager at the outset of an audit project. Such a questionnaire would represent a meaningless exercise that would unfairly tax the time and temper of both the manager and the auditor. Rather, the questions should be considered as a set of standards for the auditor to keep in mind as he makes his organizational review.

When practices disclose negative answers to any of the questions, the auditor should then be alerted to probe further and to see whether a negative answer signals an administrative gap or breakdown.

Management Studies

Functional and organizational audits form the framework of the long-range audit program. The individual audits are generally repeated at appropriate intervals and represent the bread and butter of the auditor's fare. But another aspect of auditing may well be his caviar and champagne. It is directed toward solving problems for management.

Many companies call upon outside consultants to perform studies, make evaluations, and offer recommendations for improvement in problem areas of the business. Some of these companies have benefited from the experience and knowledge that consultants bring to bear on the problems they are asked to solve. Others have not. The disappointments are the result of a number of factors. Some of them are as follows:

■ Employees may regard the consultants as strangers who have no feel for the company's life style or personality. Both employees and managers may be resentful and secretive, preventing the consultants from obtaining a complete understanding of the problems they are engaged to solve.

■ The consultant has a long and expensive training period to go through. No matter how experienced he may be, he still has to learn the company's geography, its organizational structure, its ingrained methods and procedures, and the personalities, strengths, weaknesses, and predilections of its management.

- The outside consultant's recommendations, usually first communicated in an exit interview or in an elaborate report, may get a defensive reaction. Company personnel may spend more time in defending entrenched operations than in implementing what may very well be worthwhile suggestions.

- Outside consultants generally charge sizable fees which in most cases would exceed the cost of using existing talent already in the company.

A top-notch internal audit staff, experienced in audits of operations, familiar with the company's objectives, policies, organization, and people, is a natural source of talent for this kind of consulting work. The internal auditor is already well versed in the techniques needed for problem solving: fact-gathering, analysis, and objective evaluation. He developed those techniques in his regular audits. They are the same that are needed for solving management problems.

Further, he will have developed an understanding of management principles and philosophy, essential to the dissection and evaluation of matters concerning management. And if he has developed a proper image within his company, he has the reputation for objectivity, fairness, and personal concern for the company's interests. He will not feel impelled to generate a host of recommendations — warranted or not — merely to justify a fee.

The internal auditor, then, who feels competent to take on special studies within the company, should accept the opportunity when it is presented to him. Indeed, he should be close enough to the councils of management to know when the opportunity arises and to offer his services in appropriate circumstances and under appropriate conditions.

Of course, the problem should be one that the internal auditor has a chance of solving. Matters that are completely technical or which depend entirely on executive judgment should probably be avoided. They may not yield to the tools the auditor possesses or which are available to him.

On the other hand, the fact that the problem is difficult or extensive should be an inducement and not a deterrent. And if some aspects of the engagement are technical, they may be dealt with through the assistance of technicians assigned to help the auditor over the technical hurdles.

These engagements should be requested and endorsed by executive management. Their scope and breadth will usually require backing at that level. It must be made clear to all employees and operating managers that this is a management project operating under a special management charter. In fact, it will function best as a task force, nominally headed by a vice president or other executive manager, with the audit manager conducting the actual work.

The task force should be staffed by key internal auditors, capable and eager to take on the assignment. Technical assistance should be solicited either on an as-needed basis or for the duration of the assignment. But the auditor must be in charge. The technician is needed to clarify esoteric matters, point toward the areas that need probing, and protect the auditor from being given inaccurate information or self-serving declarations by line personnel. But the technician may not have the ability to gather evidence, array facts, and examine data so as to impel logical conclusions.

The auditor should, from the outset and throughout the engagement, employ all the techniques of salesmanship that he possesses — keeping management informed and selling his recommendations at the grassroots level before presenting them to management.

As soon as possible after he has taken the measure of the situation, he should make a formal presentation to management on how he views the problem and how he proposes to attack it. This presentation can be made through flip charts or view graphs. It should be carefully thought through and it should be carried out in a professional fashion. The presentation of the parameters of the problem, and the theory of the case as the auditor sees it can have several benefits. It may force management to consider the aspect of the problem in a light it had not considered before because the problem had not been laid out visibly and in a logical manner. It can save the auditor from pursuing matters or running down avenues that are of no special interest to management. It can develop better rapport with management and draw executive management more solidly into a problem-solving partnership.

The study itself must be in depth. It cannot be a broad-stroke pass at the problem. It will require extensive reviews and thorough research. It must be able to produce authoritative answers to any relevant questions management poses. It must be able to provide a stout defense for any recommendations that it makes. It must be based on a thorough understanding of the following matters, among others:

- What is the problem? Not necessarily what management thought it was, but what it really is.

- What are the relevant facts? The statistics, the processes, the systems, the procedures, the policies, the organizations, the people, the past, the present, the probable future, what has been written on the subject, and what is being done at other companies.

■ What are the causes? The number and variety of causes. The root causes and the surface causes. When they began to affect the problem.

■ What are the possible solutions? The alternatives, the costs, the answers to associated local problems within affected operating organizations, the solution or solutions to the generic problem with company-wide implications, the possible side effects of proposed solutions.

A management study of broad scope will have a general cleansing effect. As the audit teams probe and query and analyze, they may find systems and performance defects. The audit team should promptly reduce each of these matters to writing, discuss it with the people concerned, and issue a memorandum that identifies the particular problem, provides adequate detail, sets forth the views of those interviewed, and proposes solutions. A format for such a memorandum is shown in Exhibit 9-2. Each such memorandum would identify a particular problem, indicate the people with whom the problem was discussed, set out their views, and offer solutions.

Exhibit 9-2. MANAGEMENT STUDY MEMORANDUM

No:_____

Date:_____

Organizations Concerned:	(Show all the organizations involved in or affected by the condition or its solution.)
Summary of Condition:	(Provide a capsule comment that identifies the condition.)
Details of Condition:	(Describe the condition in sufficient detail to explain its significance, its causes, and its actual or probable effect.)
Proposed Solution:	(Supply the various alternatives that are available to cure the condition.)
Discussed with:	(List the names and identities of all management and supervisory personnel with whom the matter was discussed.)
Results of Discussions:	(Summarize the comments of each person with whom the matter was discussed, indicating whether he agreed with the statement of condition and/or the solution.)
Distributed to:	(Distribute the memo to all management personnel with whom the condition was discussed, and their superiors, as well as to the executives responsible for the task force.)

Each week, or every two weeks, appropriate management personnel should be provided with a summary showing the status of the memorandums, termed here Management Study Memorandums. Separate summaries should be prepared for each major organization. The outline for such a summary — using the Procurement organization as an example — might be as follows:

Record of Management Study Memorandums
Procurement

| | | | Status | | |
MSM No.	Date	Summary of Condition	Initiated	Completed	Under Consideration

The Record of Management Study Memorandums keeps the study in the forefront of management's attention. Those matters requiring action remain flagged until corrected. The study is not permitted to fade into the background.

Every month, the audit manager may give a progress report to executive management on the status of the study. In that report he may:

■ Summarize the number of Management Study Memorandums issued and their status.

■ Show the number of people — both auditors and technicians — who are involved in the study and the number of teams to which they are assigned.

■ Identify the more significant problems that either have been solved or remain unsolved.

■ Discuss in general terms the progress of the work.

■ Provide an estimate of the time required to complete the study.

When the task is completed, the results should be incorporated in a final report. The report should be a professional piece of work, giving the matter the aura of importance that it deserves. It might have a hard cover, comb or spiral bindings, with a double-spaced summary and a single-spaced detail. It should be inviting to read. The detail may very well be a listing of the Management Study Memorandums, as shown in the Records of Management Study Memorandums, minus the final three columns (initiated, completed, under consideration), supported by copies of the memorandums themselves. The report should discuss the matters that have been corrected and those remaining uncorrected.

Well-executed management studies can probably do more for the stature and the image of the Internal Auditing organization than any other effort it undertakes. They are outside the ordinary routine. They answer a particular, current, pressing need of management, and therefore have management's special attention. They prove that the Internal Auditing organization can be a part of a problem-solving partnership with executive management and that the internal auditor can perform more economically and more successfully the function generally considered to be exclusively within the purview of the outside consultant.

TIP SHEETS

Certain analyses of operating data can provide revealing insights into business functions. Such analyses highlight relationships and trends, and permit valuable comparisons. They may form the basis for action or indicate the need for audit investigation and further analysis.

Standard financial analysis (the various Balance Sheet and Income Statement ratios, for example) has long been used to show trends and potential trouble spots. But there are other analyses that are available and useful to the auditor and which involve the operating areas of the company.

Management usually works through a multiplicity of reports. The auditor can use these reports as "Tip Sheets" in identifying existing or potential problems. Some examples are as follows:

Fixed Assets

In examining records of fixed assets, the auditor would want to know whether property has been aged by class and whether each class has been related to its cost of maintenance. Do the reports show where the maintenance people spend the bulk of their time? Have analyses been made of the relative economies of purchase versus lease? Do the records show machine hours between breakdowns? Do they show maintenance hours and cost of major repairs as related to replacement cost? Such analyses may disclose either excessively liberal replacement policies or excessive preventive maintenance.

Personnel Statistics

Reports can be analyzed to show various relationships in numbers of employees and the trends those relationships are taking, as for example, ratios of:

- Hourly to salary personnel
- Direct to indirect personnel
- Sales to nonsales personnel
- Truck drivers to shipping personnel
- Supervisory to nonsupervisory personnel
- Total personnel to sales
- Total personnel to profit

Reports of different branches can be studied to disclose variances in procedures or the efficiency of personnel deployment. The results of the analyses may not be an end in themselves, but rather indicators for more studies in depth.

Inventory Turnover

Turnover is generally reported as a lump figure, often embracing a number of accounts or stores. But even within a single account or store, unfortunate conditions can be hidden. For example, unless inventories are periodically aged by class of item, many individual slow-moving or obsolete items can be overlooked. An overall turnover rate of four times a year, say, may conceal the fact that 30% of the items turn over only two times a year or less.

An analysis of turnover rates, including an examination of the records of specific items, may disclose how many items in inventory are over a year old. It may point to buying errors that are hidden in inventory and are protected by a satisfactory overall turnover ratio.

Employment Costs and Employee Turnover

The cost and time involved for the average hire, by class of employee, is often a matter of interest. Also of interest is the turnover rate by department or branch, and a comparison of the company's turnover rate with that in other companies in the same business.

Rolling Stock

Of interest are computations of the relationship between mileage traveled and the average life of tires, batteries, and plugs; analyses of the comparative cost of using personal versus company cars; and comparisons of manpower or dock and warehouse space with loading and unloading times, standby time, and delivery time between points.

Stationery and Supply Stores

It is often interesting to compare usage and stock balances. Also, it is useful to compare usage with the number of using personnel, particularly where items are attractive for use at home and where physical control over the stock leaves something to be desired.

Material Records

The auditor can analyze reports prepared to show the number of storeroom requisitions processed for the purpose of distributing material costs. In some cases the average unit prices may be too low to warrant the extensive paper flow. Why spend $50,000 to distribute $500,000 worth of material a year when approximations based on samples can accomplish the same results at far less cost ?

Telephones

The auditor could analyze and determine the ratios of the number of telephone instruments to the number of people, the number of outside calls made, the number of toll calls, the average length of calls, and the number of restricted phones in each department. Periodic reports of the results of these analyses to operating management can have a salutary effect in reducing the number and length of calls.

★　　★　　★

The auditor must use caution in making any such analyses. They may produce data which impel false or superficial conclusions. The auditor should seek to measure his findings against norms — norms that may already have been developed in the company or in the industry. Statistics in a vacuum are meaningless. Used, however, to show deviations from norms, variances between similar operations, or adverse trends, they may be significant. And they can then point the way to further investigation to establish causes and effects.

EVIDENCE

In seeking to determine the conditions which exist in the area of his review, the auditor must rely on the evidence his tests and fact-finding adduce. This calls for some knowledge of the anatomy of evidence as it applies to auditing; and this knowledge becomes doubly important if any of the matters covered by the audit become an issue in a legal suit.

Evidence is anything that gives proof. Valid evidence embraces whatever brings to mind an honest belief about the truth or falsity of any proposition at issue. Belief is produced by the consideration of something presented to the mind. The matter thus presented, in whatever shape it may come, is evidence. There are various degrees of evidence. Some of the more pertinent are described in the following paragraphs.

Primary Evidence

Primary evidence affords the greatest certainty of the fact. An original, signed contract, for example, is the best evidence of its existence and its contents.

Secondary Evidence

Secondary evidence is inferior to primary evidence and cannot be given the same reliance. Secondary evidence may include a copy of a contract or oral evidence of its contents. Secondary evidence may be considered acceptable if the primary evidence is destroyed or lost and if it can be shown that the secondary evidence is a proper representation of the primary evidence.

Direct Evidence

Direct evidence proves a fact without inference or presumption. It tends to show a fact or matter in issue without the intervention of proof of any other fact. Evidence is direct when the facts at issue are asserted by those who have actual knowledge of them by having personally witnessed them.

Circumstantial Evidence

Circumstantial evidence tends to establish one fact by proving another collateral fact. Even though true, circumstantial evidence does not conclusively establish the fact. It is founded on experience and observed facts and coincidences, establishing a connection between the known and proved facts and the facts sought to be proved. Short receipts that have been cleared through the Receiving Department may represent circumstantial evidence that the receiving inspector either failed to count the receipts or counted them inaccurately.

Corroborative Evidence

Corroborative evidence is additional evidence, of a different character, to the same point. An oral statement, for example, may corroborate that a purported copy of a document is a true copy.

Legal evidence is based on a body of rules that have grown up over the years and which are designed to help the court and the jury find the truth. Many of the rules have little applicability to the auditor. But there are some that he should be aware of.

One of these rules of evidence is the Hearsay Rule. It renders objectionable any statements not made in court under oath, when those statements are used to prove the truth or falsity of the matter asserted. Stated another way, it refers to any oral or written evidence brought *into* court, which is offered as proof of things said *out* of court.

The reason that hearsay is generally inadmissible is because one of the best ways of getting at the truth or falsity of an assertion is by putting a witness under oath and by cross-examining him about what he personally saw or heard. Cross examination has a way of bringing to light the untrustworthiness and the many possible deficiencies, suppressions, and sources of error that lie under the bare untested assertions of a witness.

The auditor must put himself in the position of the court as he asks questions and examines records. If Smith says to the auditor "I personally saw Jones sign the receiving memo," it is direct evidence and it is not hearsay. Smith is in the presence of the auditor who can "cross-examine" him by asking questions designed to elicit information which will tend to prove the truth or falsity of Smith's statement. The auditor could ask "Do you know Jones when you see him?" "Were you able to see Jones signing the receiving memo?" "How do you know this is the same receiving memo?" "When did he sign it?" and so forth and so on.

But if Smith were to tell the auditor "Thompson told me he saw Jones sign the receiving memo," that is hearsay. Thompson is not there to answer the auditor's questions. The auditor is unable to query Thompson as to the truth or falsity of his statement. All the auditor can satisfy himself of is whether Smith heard Thompson's words exactly: "Is that word-for-word what Thompson said?" "Where were you at the time?" "What brought up the conversation?" "How can you remember so precisely?" As to the truth or falsity of Thompson's statement, however, that is hearsay.

What about a written statement — a sales slip, a purchase order, a discrepancy report, or any of the myriad business documents that are prepared, signed, and processed by people? They too are hearsay. They also represent statements by people not in court (or not in the presence of the auditor) about some transaction. But business documents come under one of the various exceptions to the Hearsay Rule. The exception holds that business records made during the course of business are admissible in court as evidence. That is because records made in the ordinary course of business are usually trustworthy. A sales slip, a purchase order, a discrepancy report are such business entries and are therefore considered admissible evidence.

The trend in the courts today is to follow the methods of ordinary business in assuming the validity of records daily accepted as commercial routine, until they are actually discredited. In other words, the presumption of the validity of the business record is rebuttable. The document is not unassailable merely because it is a so-called business record. With proper proof it can be found to be invalid or incorrect. Thus, where the auditor finds that the document or record represents critical evidence, he would wish to discuss it with the person responsible for preparing it and satisfy himself of its truth or falsity by "cross-examination."

Photographs also represent hearsay evidence. But they will be considered admissible if properly authenticated. Photographs may be authenticated by the testimony of one or more witnesses, familiar with the subject portrayed, that the photograph is a good likeness of the person, place, object, or condition sought to be described. The auditor who observes the act of photography or takes the photograph himself is a competent witness. If he has a photographer take the picture, he should have the photographer record on the reverse of the photograph his signature, the date, the time, a brief description of the subject matter — in fact anything that would help him authenticate the photograph at a later date after memory has grown dim.

Another rule of evidence which may be of interest to the auditor is the Opinion Rule. It holds that witnesses must ordinarily testify to fact only — to what they saw or heard. Thus the auditor, as he seeks the truth, should filter out opinions and gather and evaluate facts only — those matters that tend to prove truth or falsity. Opinions offered by others may be useful to point the auditor in the right direction to gather his facts. But he should not use them as part of the platform on which he will construct his own opinion. Management looks to the auditor for *his* opinion — not for the opinions of others, opinions which may be biased, self-serving, or uninformed.

There is an exception to the Opinion Rule, however. It is called the Expert Testimony Rule. Under it an expert is permitted to offer his own opinion on the facts because it is the only way the jury will understand them — the only way the jury will get to the truth. Some safeguards have been set up about opinion testimony, however. These safeguards require two elements to be present. First, the subject on which the opinion is expressed must be distinctly related to some science, profession, business, or occupation that is beyond the understanding of the average layman. Second, the expert witness himself must have such skill, knowledge, or experience in that field or calling that his opinion will probably help the jurors or the court in their search for the truth.

The auditor should keep the opinion rule in mind when he encounters matters outside his ken. He should understand that the opinions of others are valid when they come within the scope of the Expert Testimony Rule — that they are not valid unless they include the essential elements of (1) a subject beyond what the auditor is expected to understand, and (2) an acknowledged expert in the field. As a practical matter, the auditor should include a third element: freedom from bias. In business situations the expert is usually a company employee. The auditor should, if possible, select one who is outside the department or division involved in the audit. An engineer whose opinion is solicited on a matter involving Project A should be selected from Project B or C. Of course, in some companies the only expert may be working on the project under review. In that case the auditor must take into account the possibility that the expert's testimony may not be completely free from bias.

The auditor's judgment will dictate the degree and probity of the evidence he will rely upon in examining transactions and forming an opinion. While he may not always insist on following the strict rules of evidence, he should be aware of what they are.

APPRAISING THE RESULTS

When the evidence has been gathered and the tests have been completed and summarized, the auditor must then stand back and view the results through the eyes of management.

He must decide whether the operation he reviewed is, by and large, functioning effectively and efficiently. He must determine whether his examination proved the adequacy of the system of control. He must come to a conclusion on the various discrepancies he may have encountered in his tests. Were they material? Will they recur? Do they seriously affect the operation of the activity audited? Who might be hurt? How badly? Are the discrepancies part of the minor human errors that occur in every activity carried out by people, within acceptable tolerance limits, or are they evidence of system weaknesses or supervisory neglect?

On the one hand, the auditor does not wish to be accused of nit-picking. On the other he does not wish to leave uncorrected those matters that need improvement or to fail to point out incipient danger spots.

The auditor must look at the results of his efforts and ask himself: "If this were my company, if I were its president and were appraising the results of my efforts, what would I do about them?" If, as president, he would feel that there has been substantial compliance with procedures and instructions, that the procedures and instructions themselves are reasonably calculated to reflect company goals and objectives, if the operation is functioning in a reasonable manner despite minor imperfections, he would so report. If, however, corrective action is needed, he must press forward and discuss his findings and recommendations at the management levels where corrective action should be taken.

The careful, intelligent appraisal of audit results is the hallmark of the professional auditor. This is what constitutes so-called management auditing — seeing audit results through the eyes of a manager. The eager, inexperienced auditor, in hot pursuit of deficiency findings, gauging his own worth by the quantity of defects he unearths — never mind the quality — is the bane, not the aid of management. Such an auditor must be taught to raise his sights. Anyone can find scattered acorns on the ground. One must look up to see the oak from which they fell.

The kinds of unsatisfactory conditions that the auditor can bring to light are varied and can span the spectrum of business activity. Through the techniques of observing, questioning, analyzing, comparing, investigating, and evaluating, he can perform prodigious acts of service for his company.

Sometimes the audit results are a product of one of these techniques; sometimes a combination of two or more. At any rate, it is easier to give examples of the results of the techniques than to explain them; and a number of examples are shown in Exhibit 9-3 (at end of chapter), identified according to the activities audited. In each instance the reader will observe the results of good, imaginative, professional audit techniques.

OBTAINING CORRECTIVE ACTION

Nothing ever happens until somebody sells something. And the auditor will not see a satisfactory conclusion to the results of his efforts if he does not sell them at appropriate levels. Sometimes it is necessary for his salesmanship to be carried up through the hierarchy of management before the proper ear is reached.

But first the findings should be aired at the operating level. Every unsatisfactory condition or deficiency — fraud excepted, of course — should be discussed with the person responsible for it. Some matters may resolve themselves with ease and be found to be proper transactions. For those that show the need for corrective action, the auditor will have to obtain answers to a number of questions:

- Is the deficiency material? What effect does it have on the functioning of the operation under review?
- What is responsible for the deficiency?
- Would the matter have come to light in the normal functioning of the control system and in the absence of the audit?
- Was the deficiency an isolated error or an indication of control weakness?
- Could the deficiency occur again?
- Was the deficiency a violation of established procedures?
- Did the deficiency indicate the need to clarify or amplify existing instructions?
- How can the deficiency be corrected?

After the audit tests of the particular audit segment have been completed, and after the results have been summarized and appraised in the working papers, the auditor will have to decide whether the discrepancies he found are material and warrant action. If corrective action is in order, if the matter requires action at the management level, the auditor should outline his thoughts and findings in a single document. He can use this document for synthesizing his appraisals, recording his discussions, and referencing supporting documents.

One form of such a document follows. It is called a Record of Audit Findings. It provides space for:

- A capsule comment of the finding.
- An identifying number for the particular finding and a reference to the supporting working papers.
- An indication of whether the finding was a repetition of something found in prior audits.
- A citation to the directives, procedures, or job instructions involved in the finding.
- A summary of the extent of the tests and the incidence of the discrepancy.
- The reason the discrepancy occurred.
- A statement of the corrective action proposed or taken.

RECORD OF AUDIT FINDINGS

RAF No. _____

W/P REF. NO. _____

Organization _____

Nature of Finding:
Same finding disclosed in last audit: Yes_____   No_____

Directives or procedures involved: _____
Tests made:

Population size_____   Sample size_____

Method of selection of sample_____

Discrepancies: No._____   %_____

Causes: _____
Corrective action: _____
Discussions with auditee personnel: _____

	Name	Title	Department	Date	Auditor
(1)	_____	_____	_____	_____	_____
(2)	_____	_____	_____	_____	_____
(3)	_____	_____	_____	_____	_____
(4)	_____	_____	_____	_____	_____

Comments by auditee personnel:
(1)
(2)
(3)
(4)

_____   _____

                     Auditor   Date

■ A record of the discussions with auditee personnel, and space for a record of their comments — usually whether they agree or disagree with the auditor's conclusions and what is the nature of the action, if any, they propose to take.

The form provides flexibility, since a number of Records of Audit Findings can be sorted and re-sorted to facilitate reporting. It provides a ready reference for discussion, since it contains on one sheet most of the information needed to describe the problem.

And it functions as a guide to help the auditor remind himself that he has done all that is necessary to obtain the information he needs for a thoroughly developed finding.

The methods the auditor uses to obtain corrective action will depend on the nature of the finding and the receptiveness of management. Operating management should be the first level of discussion after clearing the matter at the working level. If the matter is critical and significant it should be discussed as soon as the finding has been established and supported. If it does not call for immediate action, the finding may be discussed at the conclusion of the particular audit segment. At that time both the good and the bad may be explained — making the bad more palatable.

The auditor has no responsibility for prescribing the exact path the auditee shall take in correcting or improving conditions. Indeed, he is well advised not to leave the impression that his path is the only one. For once he insists on a particular course of action he becomes sponsor for it and an insurer of its efficacy. On his next audit of the same activity he may be reluctant to reject the action if it has not worked. Also, he will in effect be auditing himself, which is hardly conducive to objectivity.

Nevertheless, the auditee should not be deprived of the auditor's experience and knowledge. And the auditor does owe some duty to propose *a* method — not *the* method — for improvement. Here the auditor can bring into play his approach toward a problem-solving partnership. "Let us work together to see how we can improve things without increasing costs. Let us see how we can reduce costs and improve profits for *our* company."

Also, during the oral discussion, while the auditor is not responsible for insisting on corrective action — that is the responsibility of higher management — he should point out such advantages as (1) improved operations, (2) prompt closure of the finding, (3) the ability to report to higher management that the matter has been taken care of, and (4) the elimination of the requirement for a formal reply to the audit report.

What form of action is relevant depends on the nature of the finding. If an overpayment has been made, then recovery of the amounts and improved controls to prevent recurrence constitute the corrective action. If people have not been adequately instructed, then management should issue new or improved instructions and agree to monitor the process in the future. If the system is weak, then the weak spots must be strengthened by the institution of appropriate controls. If transactions are being processed improperly, then evidence of proper processing will be needed.

There are no limits to the forms of corrective action. But whatever the action required, the deficiency finding should remain open until it is corrected. Some matters can be closed promptly. Others may take investigation and systems work. But no deficiency finding should be closed until the auditor has satisfied himself — by whatever means he considers necessary — that corrective action actually took place.

If the auditor does not follow through, operating management may learn to flood him with innocuous memorandums that purport to correct the problem but fail to do so. Each succeeding audit will see repetitions of discrepant conditions. The efforts of the auditor will go for naught. Operating management will treat his recommendations with indifference. Only when the auditor monitors corrective action and has the support of executive management will his audit efforts bear fruit.

That is why the auditor should communicate his findings to whatever level of management he believes will take or ensure corrective action. Where discussions accomplish the task no other action, prior to the final report, is necessary.

Certainly, the auditor should try to use participative techniques, because then action is taken and harmonious relations are maintained. But it is a sad fact that very often nothing happens in a large company until something is put into writing. Apathy and indifference change to earnest effort when a significant finding is reduced to writing in the form of a progress report to operating management — with copies to appropriate superiors — setting forth the matter at issue and recommending corrective action.

In some cases, copies of the Records of Audit Findings, or an expanded variant, may suffice. In other cases more formal memorandums may be required. These memorandums are issued while the field work is still in progress. But since they are a part of the reporting function, they will be described in the following chapter which deals with audit reports.

SUMMARY

Field work is essentially measurement. It measures what *is* against what *should be*. All field work, then, implies units of measurement and the existence or the development of standards. In making his measurements, the auditor is generally concerned with matters of quality, cost, and schedule.

Field work can be performed through surveys or detailed tests or a combination of the two, depending on the significance of the activity and the adequacy of the systems of control. The auditor performs his field work through the use of a number of different techniques which include observing, questioning, analyzing, comparing, investigating, and evaluating.

The auditor can employ a number of different modes of field work. He may make organizational audits, keeping within the confines of a particular organization. He can perform functional audits, following a process from beginning to end. He can engage in management studies, which represent special examinations to help solve pressing management problems. He can perform quantitive analyses to determine relationships, observe trends, and provide insights into operations or point the way to further reviews, analyses, and investigations.

A considerable part of the field work is spent in gathering data and accumulating evidence. The auditor should have some familiarity with the rules and the forms of evidence, including the hearsay rule and certain exceptions to that rule.

Gathering and arraying data represent only the beginning of the auditor's field work. He must appraise the results of his examinations, decide when he has encountered matters requiring corrective action, and then monitor the action that is taken and see whether it is adequate and effective.

Exhibit 9-3. EXAMPLES OF AUDIT FINDINGS

The following examples have all been taken from the Round Table of *The Internal Auditor,* the journal of The Institute of Internal Auditors. We have abstracted typical examples and have given credit, after each item, to the contributing chapter of The Institute. Also shown, after each item, is the particular issue of *The Internal Auditor* and the page where the original item can be found.

Accounts Payable

The auditor's evaluation of the disbursement function disclosed many duplicate payments. By analyzing a sample of the payments he found a number of apparent system and manual processing problems.

When he brought the matter to the attention of management, a contract was placed with an outside software house to isolate the duplications. The auditor assisted in writing program specifications and analyzing test results.

The auditor evaluated the results of the program, which consisted of a listing of duplicate payments for a 22-month period. Actual payments in the amount of $1.1 million were identified and $850,000 was recovered.

(Detroit Chapter, January/February 1972, p. 65.)

Automotive Equipment

The auditor questioned the transportation manager, seeking the reason why all trucks were equipped with four-wheel drives. The auditor saw no logical reason for such equipment for the entire fleet, since most of the work was being performed on paved roads or flat terrain. As a result of the question, the transportation manager established a policy of equipping 50% of his fleet with two-wheel-drive and 50% with four-wheel-drive vehicles. Savings amounted to $270,000 a year.

(Los Angeles Chapter, November/December 1970, p. 75.)

Cash

The auditor analyzed receipts and disbursements for a two-year period. He wanted to know when surplus cash was available for investment — even for a few days. He found the following conditions:

■ General bank accounts contained several million dollars more than was needed for current operations.

■ Several noninterest-bearing "good will" accounts were no longer needed for that purpose.

■ The company did not take advantage of investment techniques which would produce returns over weekends and for a few days.

■ Investments were in United States government securities even though high-quality commercial paper offered higher yields.

As a result of the auditor's recommendations, income from short-term investments increased by $400,000.

(Pittsburgh Chapter, January/February 1971, p. 75.)

Construction

The auditor investigated a charge from a building contractor for an extension of a foundation. The charge was claimed after the construction work was completed — an unusual circumstance. The auditor could obtain no independent verification from the architect or from his own company. He therefore visited the site — about 500 miles away — and with the help of a local crew drilled test holes which established that the foundation had never been extended. Spurred on, the auditor detected other falsified claims. His audit resulted in recovering $122,000 and in revising procedures and controls calculated to save millions.

(Chicago Chapter, July/August 1971, p. 84.)

The auditor observed a construction site and was struck by the large number of gates allowing ingress and egress. Each gate was dutifully guarded by a security guard. When management accepted the auditor's recommendations to reduce the number of gates, guard-service expense was reduced by $2,000 a month.

(Los Angeles Chapter, July/August 1971, p. 85.)

Disaster Prevention

The auditor verified the propriety of actual practices by comparing them with procedures set forth in a manual dealing with emergency situations. The manual called for specific assignments to individuals designated by name. The auditor found that three of the 25-man squad were no longer employed. Of 10 men questioned, only 2 had adequate knowledge of their responsibilities, and only 5 had copies of the manual. Meetings were to be held every six months to review practices and procedures. Seven of those questioned said that they had never attended a meeting, and three said that there had been no meetings in three years. No one could ever remember a fire drill. The auditor was unable to report savings in terms of dollars, but his report of conditions sent a chill through management and prompted speedy action.

(Central Ohio Chapter, Summer 1965, p. 62.)

Employee Benefits

A personnel manager had failed to analyze an employee benefit plan and was authorizing excessive benefits. Married female employees' benefits did not provide for coverage of husbands and children. But the manager was authorizing payments for such coverage. The auditor's analysis of the plan resulted in savings of about $25,000 a year.

(New York Chapter, January/February 1969, p. 66.)

The auditor's analysis of transactions involving pension plan settlements showed poor handling by both actuary and trustee. The actuary's settlements showed overpayments because of sloppy work. The trustee failed to credit the trust fund with stock received as a result of stock splits — an employee of the trustee had bowed to temptation. The projected savings over a five-year period approximated $120,000.

(Toronto Chapter, Fall 1967, p. 97.)

Files

During his observation of filing practices, the auditor saw numerous instances of the unnecessary retention of duplicate, triplicate, and quadruplicate copies of documents. The annual cost of producing extra copies, providing files, and doing the filing was estimated at about $30,000.

(Southern New England Chapter, November/December 1969, p. 82.)

Group Insurance

The auditor for an insurance company was evaluating statistical analyses printed out by the computer. Claims filed by a vendor under his policy for group creditor insurance showed that 18 of his customers had died leaving unpaid bills for hearing aids. The auditor found that most of the dead people were relatively young — having died violent deaths. The auditor called a hearing aid supplier and found that the bills had been exorbitant. He called some relatives of the deceased young people and found in each case that the deceased had not been deaf. The audit resulted in a restitution of $10,000. But it also pointed to the possibility of using the computer to perform analyses and facilitate evaluations by printing out transactions outside the norm:

■ Instances where claims are relatively high in relation to the number of persons involved in the insurance.

■ Instances where the percentage of violent deaths are relatively high.

■ Instances where the ages of the deceased are relatively low.

Quantitative analyses with the aid of the computer can prove fruitful.

(New England Chapter, May/June 1969, p. 84.)

Inspections

The auditor analyzed inspection costs. He found that they had risen from 10% to 10.5%. He visited the inspection site and observed that the inspectors had substantial idle time and were overinspecting. Savings as a result of his recommendations were estimated at $240,000 for a 5-year period.

(Toronto Chapter, July/August 1971, p. 86.)

Insurance

The auditor analyzed an insurance policy issued in connection with construction work. He looked beyond the computation for Workmen's Compensation and

found that the construction contractor was on a Retrospective Rating Adjustment Plan. The auditor found that the contractor was eligible for refunds that he had never claimed and therefore had not passed on to the auditor's company. The audit finding resulted in refunds of contract charges exceeding $70,000.
(Los Angeles Chapter, September/October 1971, p. 59.)

The auditor analyzed the level of deductibles on insurance policies, comparing them with losses over a period of years. By raising the level of deductibles and by resorting to self insurance for some coverage, savings ranged from $10,000 to $100,000 a year.
(Pittsburgh Chapter, March/April 1970, p. 83.)

Investment Credit

The auditor analyzed the federal tax law dealing with investment credit. The government recaptures the credit if equipment purchased is not held for the required four to eight years. The auditor learned that the recapture is prevented if the disposed-of equipment is replaced within six months with like equipment. This provision had been overlooked throughout the company. The auditor's question saved $6,600 and permitted recovery of about $3,000.
(Michiana Chapter, July/August 1971, p. 86.)

Maintenance

The auditor sought to verify the propriety of janitorial cleaning schedules with those recommended by the American Carpet Institute. His company was vacuuming every two days. The ACI recommended vacuuming every five days. The savings were estimated at $27,000 a year.
(San Francisco Chapter, Fall 1966, p. 77.)

Magnetic Tapes

The auditor questioned why the library of magnetic tapes was building up and what was the basis for the retention of tapes for indefinite periods. A quick survey of tapes permitted programmers to release 200 tapes for reuse. Before the survey the tapes would have been held indefinitely. At $25 a tape, the saving amounted to $5,000, and that was just the beginning.
(Chattanooga Chapter, Fall 1965, p. 81.)

Overtime

The auditor evaluated the company's overtime policy. He found that control was over people and not over hours. He prepared a well-documented presentation showing the inadequacies of the policy. The predetermined ratio of direct to indirect employees had been strictly observed, but no attention had been given to the ratio of the hours worked. The number of direct personnel had been held under the ceilings set, but no restriction had been placed on the number of hours worked. By revising its policies, the company increased staff, improved morale, and reduced overtime to that required for isolated peak loads.
(Toronto Chapter, May/June 1968, p. 82.)

Physical Examinations

The auditor evaluated the need for pre-employment physical examinations. During a period of 18 months, 7,025 examinations were given at a cost of $65,670.

Only 35 applicants were rejected, and 18 of the 35 were rejected for pregnancy and varicose veins. The remaining 17 applicants were rejected for heart trouble and high blood pressure. The medical history questionnaire was expanded to obtain an indication of potentially serious problems, and examinations were required only in those cases. Savings were estimated at $30,000 a year.
(Phoenix Chapter, Summer 1967, p. 79.)

Production-Manufacturing

The auditor verified the gauge of sheet steel by comparing it with the steel mill's specifications. The gauge could come anywhere within certain tolerances. He found that in the mill section, where the steel sold by the hundredweight was being fabricated, the sheet was rolled at a thickness that was within the tolerance, but on the **thin** side. In another section, where the steel was made to be sold by the unit, it was rolled to the **thick** side of the tolerance. The mill was losing out in both cases. Reversing the widths resulted in annual savings of $20,000.
(Toronto Chapter, May/June 1969, p. 86.)

Production-Packaging

The auditor sought to verify the amounts of finished products placed in bags by comparing them with the guaranteed weights. He found that the amounts packaged exceeded those weights. He investigated further and found that the bagging machines were not properly calibrated. His recommendations for recalibration resulted in savings estimated at $12,000 a year.
(St. Louis Chapter, September/October 1971, p. 60.)

Production Control

The auditor investigated production control practices because of production line stoppages. He found that the dispatching of material to the line was not being controlled. For example, materials were being sent to the wrong areas, and nobody was checking bins for adequate supplies until shortages occurred. New orders were being placed to cover line shortages. In his own investigations the auditor was able to locate and put into use parts whose replacement would have cost $22,000. As a result of the auditor's recommendations the production control procedures were overhauled and improved.
(Toronto Chapter, January/February 1970, p. 77.)

Purchasing

While analyzing purchase orders, the auditor saw many which permitted the vendor to ship to a weight tolerance of plus or minus 10%. Most vendors were shipping to the top of the range. He found that there were no procedures to guide buyers on weight tolerances. They were using their own judgment and using plus or minus 10% tolerances where they were not really warranted as, for example, in the purchase of aluminum billets. Procedures were issued which specified the particular commodities where tolerances were applicable.
(San Diego Chapter, July/August 1969, p. 77.)

The auditor appraised the overshipment procedure in the purchasing organization. He found that all overshipments over 10% were to be reviewed by purchasing and production personnel but that few overshipments were ever returned to suppliers. The auditor selected a sample of 57 invoices involving overshipments and found that they resulted in excess expenditures that totaled $29,000.

An inventory analysis of 33 of the receipts revealed:

- The average time that an overshipment remained in inventory was six months.
- The longest time was over 12 months.
- The shortest time was one month.

Some firms were shipping 10 per cent extra on every order. When buyers were asked about the practice, they said they thought it was regular operating procedure to call for 10% extra from the suppliers. Procurement policies and procedures were changed, and the resulting annual savings were estimated at $100,000.

(Chicago Chapter, January/February 1972, p. 65.)

Receiving

Raw chemicals were being received in tank trucks. No verifications were being made that the amounts billed for the chemicals agreed with the amounts received, since it was believed that the unloading equipment could not fully unload the truck. The auditor made his own comparisons of receipts and billings from two different suppliers. One showed variances of less than 1%. The other showed variances of over 8%. Savings of $40,000 were realized as a result of negotiations with the second supplier.

(Philadelphia Chapter, September/October 1971, p. 60.)

Bulk material was being weighed on receipt. Since the tare weight of the trucks was on file, they were not being weighed empty. The auditor observed that on rainy days the wooden weighing platform became heavier because it was wet. By having the added weight determined and taken into account, savings of about $24,000 were realized in the first year.

(Toronto Chapter, January/February 1969, p. 68.)

Rejections

The auditor's observation of rejected material disclosed that expensive assemblies were being scrapped in the last phases of the work. Further investigation brought to light the fact that in this critical phase of the work inexperienced personnel were being used. At the auditor's recommendations only experienced people were used in those stages of assembly where large numbers of man-hours had already been invested in the assemblies. Estimated savings totaled $80,000 in the first year and, because of increased production, about $600,000 over the next 5 years.

(Toronto Chapter, March/April 1971, p. 80.)

Reports

No attempt had been made to question recipients of data processing reports. As a result of the auditor's questions, two reports were discontinued completely. One report of 300 pages, run in quadruplicate, was reduced to an original only, saving some 900 pages each week.

(San Francisco Chapter, July/August 1970, p. 84.)

Scrap

The auditor was evaluating scrap quantities. He found that when stock was drawn from stores and cut, long pieces of scrap were often left over. The auditor discussed the matter with the Purchasing people and found that the material could be purchased at the desired cut lengths and delivered the next day at little extra cost. Savings ran about $3,000 annually.

(Ak-Sar-Ben Chapter, July/August 1968, p. 80.)

Miniaturized components were coated with epoxy before they were incorporated in assemblies. During coating, both epoxy scrap and components dropped to the floor from encapsulating machines and were swept into vacuum chutes. The auditor observed what was happening and requested an analysis of the material in the receptacles at the ends of the chutes. He found that about $14,000 of good parts were being scrapped annually because of the commingling. At the auditor's suggestion, barriers were installed around the machines to prevent further losses.

(Central Penn Chapter, November/December 1968, p. 63.)

The auditor observed that steel scrap was being downgraded because of an occasional piece of plate exceeding a certain length. This one piece could downgrade the entire lot by $7. By cutting such pieces, the scrap could be sold as Grade 1 instead of Grade 2. Annual increased income was estimated at $75,000.

(Toronto Chapter, January/February 1971, p. 73.)

The auditor analyzed property disposition notices and compared the prices recently received for used refrigerator trucks with those received in the past. The prices received seemed low and the trucks were being sold in one area of the country. Intensive investigation disclosed collusion between company employees and used car dealers. The analysis and investigation resulted in recoveries of $200,000 and in tightened salvage sales procedures.

(Chicago Chapter, May/June 1971, p. 71.)

Shipments

During an analysis of invoices for finished goods, the auditor noted that the cartons containing the goods were being invoiced at uniform quantities. He investigated the contents of cartons over a period of time and found that they actually contained about 10% more than the invoiced quantity. As a result, shipping personnel prepared invoices for actual quantities shipped. The annual savings were estimated at $113,000.

(Piedmont-Carolinas Chapter, January/February 1972, p. 66.)

Shipping

The auditor analyzed shipping documents and found numerous errors. He traced the errors to the night shift at the warehouse. Both the day and night shifts used the same procedures. Both supervisors were equally experienced. By observing the work at both shifts, the auditor realized that the light on the night shift was so bad that the numbers on the records were often misinterpreted. Improved lighting resulted in improved accuracy.

(Detroit Chapter, January/February 1969, p. 66.)

Stamps

The auditor questioned why at one location the requests for reimbursement of the cost of stamps were always $35 for 700 five-cent stamps. The postmaster's receipts seemed authentic. Yet close examination showed that the receipts were really for $5. What happened was that a clerk put a "3" in front of the $5.00, a "thirty" in front of the five dollars, and changed the 100 to 700. This was one change which could be made without ready detection. The embezzlement had gone undetected for three years.

(Southern New England Chapter, March/April 1969, p. 77.)

Storage

The quality of expensive vinyl fabrics was down. Technical personnel reviewed the processing and made some recommendations — but they were not effective. The auditors were called in to make a study of conditions. They observed the operation from beginning to end. They found that the problem lay in the handling of the raw material:

- Incoming materials were not tested. Specifications had not been established.
- Drums of raw material were left in the open, contaminated by rain water. Incredibly, drums of raw material were not kept near the batching area because scrap was kept in that space.
- Rolls of vinyl awaiting further processing were stored in the aisles and were being walked on.

With appropriate changes in procedures and practices, the plant manager reported considerable improvement in quality.

(St. Louis Chapter, January/February 1969, p. 67.)

Tool Sharpening

Tools sent out for sharpening were picked up and returned by the vendor's representative. All normal controls for shipping and receiving were by-passed. Receiving memos were prepared by the Receiving Department on the basis of a call from the foreman in charge of the tool cribs. The auditor compared the quantities of tools going out with those being returned and found that the bills showed more tools returned than were sent out. The auditor found that the bills had been inflated to show the sharpening of more tools than were actually returned. Since the returned tools did not clear through Receiving, there was no independent verification which would show that the number of tools billed for and the number actually returned did not agree. Changed procedures plugged the leak.

(Detroit Chapter, Summer 1964, p. 69.)

Travel Expense

Analysis of travel expense showed that less than 20% of the employees who traveled stayed at hotels with which the company had rate agreements. The variance in prices amounted to about $100,000 annually.

(Phoenix Chapter, March/April 1968, p. 75.)

Warranties

The auditor's analysis of warranty expense totaling $350,000 disclosed that many of the items returned to his company as being covered by warranty were in fact out of warranty. The auditor asked the quality control department to make a test of returns for two months. It was determined that 32% of the returned items did not qualify for warranty. Changed procedures resulted in estimated annual savings of $100,000.

(Detroit Chapter, January/February 1972, p. 66.)

WORKING PAPERS

INTRODUCTION

What They Are

Working papers document the audit. They contain the records of preliminary planning and survey, the audit program, and the results of the field work. Working papers are prepared from the time the auditor first launches his assignment until he writes the final report.

Skillfully prepared working papers are the trademark of the professional — of the experienced, seasoned auditor who has learned from past audits how fleeting memory can be. He is rarely distracted by the pressures of field work, of budgets, or of intriguing investigations, from carefully and currently recording his findings and conclusions. Just as the scientist meticulously documents experiments, so does the experienced auditor document his work and the supporting detail for his conclusions and opinions. Scientific method is as much a part of the techniques of the auditor as it is a part of the practices of the research chemist.

What They Do

The auditor prepares working papers for a number of different purposes. He develops and uses his working papers:

- As the repository of the information he obtains through questioning people, reviewing instructions and directives, analyzing systems and processes, and examining transactions.

- To identify and document deficiency findings, accumulating the evidence needed to determine the existence and extent of the deficient conditions.

- To help perform his audit in an orderly fashion, documenting what he has done, indicating what is still to be done, and giving reasons for what he will leave undone.

- To give support for discussions with operating personnel. Operations can be quite complex. Interrelationships of systems and organizations can be difficult to retain in memory. Rules and exceptions to rules can be legion. Well-documented explanations and charts in the working papers, indexed for ready access, can put the auditor on an equal footing with the people who live with the operations and understand them intimately.

- To provide support for the audit report. Well-structured working papers make it easy to transfer the material written during the audit to the pages of the interim and final audit reports. The auditor can develop a discipline that moves both the field work documentation and the audit report on the same assembly line so as to reduce rephrasing and restructuring to a minimum and ease the report writing effort. The experienced auditor has one eye on the report throughout the entire audit project. It helps keep his field work relevant and pointed in the right direction.

■ As a line of defense when his conclusions and recommendations are challenged. Criticism, express or implied, is rarely taken kindly. It leads to challenges from the one criticized. And such challenges must be rebutted with facts and proof. The working papers, properly developed and referenced, readily accessible with a minimum of fumbling, lend stalwart support to the auditor and a warm feeling of security.

■ As a basis for supervisory review of the audit's progress and accomplishment. Supervision of the audit project should be current and continual. The working papers, as evidence of work done and to be done, are a much better index of accomplishment than unsupported oral assertions which may easily become general, distorted, or superficial. The supervisor's review of working papers can be specific and can materially benefit the audit. His review of work progress is seriously diminished in value if based only upon a conversation with the auditor.

■ As a basis for appraising the auditor's technical ability, skill, and working habits. The auditor's proficiency, or his lack of it, are clearly mirrored in the way he documents his work and supports his conclusions. Some auditors give short shrift to working papers. They rely on investigative and inquisitorial tactics to unearth significant findings. Sporadically they may produce a master stroke. But their work has little consistency and cannot, over the long run, match that of the professional who has learned the need to marshal the facts cogently, analyze them, and use them to provide firm support for his findings.

■ As background and reference data for subsequent reviews. Audit projects are usually repeated or followed up. Professional working papers make the repeat audit much easier and more economical. There is no need to plow the same ground and dig the same holes. The subsequent review can build on the earlier one and not have to start from ground zero.

In the sections that follow, we shall explore in detail, with illustrations to supplement the explanations, the subjects of:

■ Documentation, including working paper arrangement
■ Summaries, including records of deficiency findings
■ Indexing and cross-referencing
■ Control of working papers

DOCUMENTATION

Working papers should follow a reasonably consistent form and arrangement. Once the auditor becomes accustomed to a workable format, he can give less thought to how the working papers are laid out and more to what they have to say.

Working papers should be economical — economical to prepare and economical to review. It is easy to dump every scrap of information and every form and procedure into the papers. But they then become a confused mixture of miscellany which is difficult to assimilate and use. Working papers should be spare but complete — a *usable* record of work done. The professional auditor includes in his papers only what is essential, and he will make each worksheet serve a purpose that fits into the audit objective.

Keep Papers Neat

Working papers should be easy on the eye. Preparing neat working papers is a form of discipline which the professional auditor has developed painstakingly because he considers it important — and in the long run, economical. He regards neat working papers as a mirror of neat thinking.

When this discipline is in control, the auditor considers carefully what he wants to say in his papers before he says it. In that way he writes just once. And what he writes is logically set out. Paper is cheaper than the time of both the auditor and his reviewer. So working papers should not be crowded. Many auditors write on every other line of their working papers so that any interlineations subsequently needed can be entered without crowding. It is far better to use more paper in the beginning — leaving parts of sheets unused — than to discard a partially completed sheet and have to start over when it develops that not enough space was allowed.

To avoid confusion and error, all names and titles should be printed, clearly and neatly. Only one side of a work sheet should be used. Material on the reverse side can easily be overlooked.

Keep Papers Uniform

All working papers should be prepared on paper of uniform size and appearance. When it becomes necessary to include pieces of paper that are smaller than the standard size, the small sheet should be fastened to a standard sheet. Larger pieces of paper should be folded in a manner that simplifies their later review.

Forms and directives should be included only when they are relevant to the audit or to the audit findings. Written directives may often contain much information that is not relevant, with but a few lines that are significant to the audit purposes. On the first reading, therefore, the relevant portions should be underlined — in red or in some other contrasting color — so that they stand out on subsequent review.

Keep Papers Economical

The auditor should avoid unnecessary listing and scheduling. To this end he will use copies of client's records or computer printouts as much as possible. He can show by distinctive tick marks what audit steps he carried out and record his comments in the margins.

To keep his papers economical, the auditor should try to cover as many tests as he can on one worksheet, using the same sample for as many analyses as feasible.

Along the same lines, the auditor should not try to answer every conceivable question that can be raised, particularly where the tests indicate satisfactory conditions. Of course, if deficiencies are found, the auditor should be prepared to meet any challenge to his findings.

In line with not writing more than is necessary, the auditor should make full use of the working papers developed in the prior audit. Flow charts, system descriptions, and other data may still be valid, by and large. Those papers which remain useful should be transferred to the current working papers. They should be updated with current information, renumbered, rereferenced, and initialed and dated by the current auditor. The updated working papers are now *his* working papers and he bears full responsibility for them. If there is anything in the prior working papers that does not reflect current conditions, and if there is anything with which the current auditor does not agree, he is charged with the responsibility for making any necessary changes.

Keep Papers Reasonably Complete

The working papers should leave nothing hanging. No questions asked should go unanswered. Nothing is so frustrating as finding a course of inquiry dropped without explanation. If a space has been left for a cross reference, it should be filled in. If a question is raised, it should be answered, or the reason for not answering it should be shown.

The auditor should keep a "to do" list in his papers on which he notes matters still to be covered, new thoughts worth pursuing, and any other items not specifically set out in the program but warranting audit action. Then, each item on the "to do" list should be answered or otherwise commented on.

Every time a supervisor reviews working papers, he should record his review notes or questions — preferably on the left-hand side of a fresh worksheet. The auditor should then record his answering comments on the other side of the sheet. And each review note should be answered. The notes should become a part of the auditor's working papers.

While the working papers should not contain superfluous information, they should not be stripped of relevant material. For example, the auditor should not discard working papers on a course of action initiated and then dropped. Even though the audit in a particular area is discontinued after only a few notes are made, the notes should be retained and the reason for the discontinuance should be recorded. The auditor's thinking and rationale for his decisions can thus be reviewed knowledgeably.

Prior deficiency findings should be followed up. Management is generally quite interested in whether deficiencies previously reported have again come to light. The working papers should contain summaries of prior deficiencies and notes on their current status.

Use a Logical Working Paper Arrangement

Keep the papers arranged in a manner that makes them parallel to the audit program.

The segmentation used in the program should govern the segmentation of the working paper file. The items should be arranged within each section of the papers in a logical sequence so as to afford ready reference during and after the audit.

For each segment of the audit the auditor should provide some general information at the beginning of that section of the papers. Such information should include:

■ The objective of the activity
■ Background information
    Organization
    Statistics
■ The control system

For each audit segment, the auditor should spell out in the working papers the detailed purposes of the audit, as they relate to that segment. These purposes should include, and where necessary expand on, the relevant matters set out in the audit program.

Also, the auditor should explain in the working papers the scope of his audit — what he covered and what he did not cover. In this part of his papers, the auditor will discuss the sample selection methods he used and the size of his sample.

After he has made his tests and analyzed the results, the auditor will record his findings in his working papers. The findings should be restricted to the facts — the good as well as the bad. There should be no intrusion of audit opinion. This is not the point at which to draw conclusions. Rather, it is the time to set down the bald facts, on the basis of which the conclusions will be drawn. The auditor should try to segregate his findings between control and performance, since control defects will generally require different kinds of corrective action than performance defects.

After the statement of the findings the auditor should state his opinion on what he found. Based on the findings as to control and performance — in terms of comparisons with standards — the auditor will state whether the conditions which he found are satisfactory or unsatisfactory. This is a professional opinion based on statistics, materiality, or the need for improved controls or performance. These opinions, in the aggregate, will support the auditor's opinion on the entire organization or function he has reviewed.

Finally, he will propose recommendations to correct the conditions he has found and the corrective action taken by the auditee.

Behind the narrative comments will be the records of the audit — the flow charts of the control system, the schedules of audit tests, and the summaries of the findings.

Each such worksheet should generally contain the following information:

■ *A descriptive heading.* The heading should identify the review and show the nature of the data contained in the paper.

■ *A legend of tick marks and other symbols.* Tick marks should be uniform throughout the audit. They should be small and neatly placed — useful but unobtrusive.

■ *The date of preparation and the auditor's initials.* The date should be the one on which the worksheet was completed. The auditor's initials should appear on each worksheet. A separate sheet in the working papers should list the names of all the auditors on the assignment and their initials — just to make sure illegible initials can be properly identified.

■ *The reference number of the working papers.* Working papers should be referenced as they are prepared and should be kept in logical groupings. There is nothing so discouraging — both to the auditor and his reviewer — as a mass of working papers, unnumbered and uncontrolled.

SAMPLE WORKING PAPERS
Format

Exhibit 10-1 is a sample segment of working papers. The exhibit demonstrates the preparation of papers in an audit of an engineering function. This segment deals with the release of engineering drawings after they have been prepared by the draftsmen.

Under "General Information" will be found the objectives of the activity, background information, and a discussion of the control system. The objectives of the activity will dictate the approach the auditor takes in his review. The background information contains only enough to provide an understanding of the tests. The explanation of the control system is supported by a simple flow chart.

The "Scope" statement shows the source of information or records used in tests and the sample selection technique. The "Purpose" statement can be related to the objectives of the activity, because obviously the auditor is mainly interested in whether the activity's objectives are being carried out.

The "Findings" answer each item in the purpose. They provide factual information only, since it is important in subsequent reviews to distinguish between provable facts and matters of audit judgment. The "Opinion" covers all the findings and provides the auditor's assessment of the findings. The recommendations cover all significant defects found in the audit and indicate the action taken by the auditee to improve conditions requiring correction.

The supporting schedules describe the tests and highlight the deficient items. The schedules are then summarized in workable form. The corrective action is documented at the end of the working papers.

The format and arrangement shown in Exhibit 10-1 may not be applicable in all companies or in all circumstances. Yet such working papers have proved effective in many situations and are easy to prepare after only a little practice.

By following a standard working paper arrangement, the auditor will be able to complete one segment of his audit before going on to another — he will know just what each segment requires. He will leave no trailing ends. He will wrap up each segment completely. And even when he must leave the audit segment for a while, waiting for data not currently available, the practice of completing sections of papers to the extent possible makes the return to them much easier.

Write It Now

The initial statements covering objectives, background, controls, scope, and purpose, can be prepared as soon as the auditor has made an initial review of the activity. He does not have to withhold his writing until the end of his review of the segment, when many aspects have become blurred in his mind.

The findings are summarized right after the tests have been made so that the results are immediately usable in discussions with the auditee.

Keep the Writing Simple

Working paper comments should be simple and readily understandable to an uninitiated reviewer. Jargon should be avoided. If it is used it should be explained in a separate part of the working papers, along with all the other technical and arcane terms used in the activity and in the working papers.

SUMMARIZATION

Although we have touched on summarization briefly, it is worth special mention because of its importance in working paper presentation.

The auditor, in full careen down the audit trail, is reluctant to disrupt the tempo of his audit to summarize. But if he fails to summarize, often and currently, he is making a sad mistake. What he thinks he has grasped fully may be dispelled by the passage of time. The mind can be a rebellious servant — often retaining what it wishes rather than what is.

The process of summarizing provides an objective overview. It hauls back the mind to hard facts. It helps put findings in perspective. It distills the valuable findings from the dross. It focuses on what is significant and relevant and helps put in its proper place what is trivial and irrelevant. The auditor who periodically summarizes his findings — both the good and the bad — retains firm control over his audit project.

There are many ways of summarizing audit results. Here are a few:

Statistical Summaries

The auditor most often uses statistical summaries which bring together the results of audit tests. For an example, refer to the Summary of Tests and List of Discrepant Items in Exhibits 10-1c through 10-1d. The data scattered through the test schedules is built into a cohesive unit which is easy to read and easy to deal with. These summaries should be treated as a pyramid, with the final, compacted data gradually expanding down to the test schedule. The secret of good statistical summaries is the carefulness with which they are structured. From the top summary to the individual test items, the reviewer can go surely and accurately without having to use a pencil to compute or summarize data — the auditor has done it for him.

Summaries of Meetings

Discussions with the auditees should be summarized promptly, giving their observations, agreements, disagreements, and suggestions. These summaries should be recorded immediately to recall things exactly as they were said, not as they filter through diminished recollection. The dates and the hours of the discussion may be valuable, in the event of later dispute.

Summaries in the Audit Program

As the auditor completes a segment of his audit, he should make comment in the program — a comment which encapsulates his conclusions about the related activity. The comment should be brief and explicit. As he moves through his program these comments can keep him aware of the course the audit is taking. It can tell him where he has been and where he still must go. It can help him in controlling the audit. And it can be a cumulative summarization of how he feels about the operation he is reviewing. Some brief examples are as follows:

Program Steps	W/P Ref.	Comments
Examine a representative number of drawings to see whether they are:		
1. Being properly checked	C8	Unsatisfactory at Project A. See RAF-1. Satisfactory at Projects B and C.
2. Meeting specifications	C8	Unsatisfactory at Project A. See RAF-2. Satisfactory at Projects B and C.
3. Meeting schedule	C8	Unsatisfactory at Projects A and C. See RAFs 3 and 4.

The "RAF" refers to the Record of Audit Findings which will be touched upon next.

Summaries of Deficiencies

Perhaps the most important summary is that for deficiency findings. These matters need the most support and result in the most discussion. The summary should place at the auditor's fingertips the relevant and significant facts about a finding. A form for that purpose, "Record of Audit Finding" (RAF for short) was shown in Chapter 9. An example is shown in Exhibit 10-2.

INDEXING AND CROSS-REFERENCING

Good cross-referencing serves many purposes:

- It simplifies the supervisory review of the papers. Although the auditor may have all relevant facts about an issue clearly in mind, the relationship between facts may not be that clear to another.

- It eases the path of the next person who uses the working papers on a follow-up review.

- It simplifies reference to the papers by the auditor himself when he later reviews his papers. In a heated review with the auditee, good cross-referencing helps prevent fumbling and bumbling — those terrible "stage waits" after the auditee has asked a pertinent and pointed question and the auditor frantically flips work sheets back and forth while the whole room sits in impatient silence.

- It improves the final product — the internal audit report. As the auditor prepares the draft of report, the well-referenced papers open up their supporting information readily and helpfully — the ill-referenced papers hide their secrets.

The system of indexing should be simple and flexible. Different kinds of reviews will call for different indexing patterns, but certain principles should apply.

The system to be used in a particular examination should be considered and devised at the outset. The auditor should try to see the audit in his mind's eye and decide how he proposes to index his papers. When he has his system well-defined he will be able to index his papers as he goes along.

In Chapter 4 we discussed a sample table of contents which can be used to launch the audit. The working papers referenced on the table of contents use the letter A for matters needed to control the project and the letter B for questionnaires, statistics, flow charts, records of audit findings, and other matters which do not relate to specific audit segments.

Experience has taught that the simpler the index system the easier it will be to use. One simple form is to use a capital letter to designate broad segments of the audit and Arabic numerals for the worksheets within the segments. Some auditors make use of Roman numerals. This may be satisfactory for extremely broad divisions of a large audit project, but when the numbers go beyond I, II, and III, the auditor, accustomed to Arabic numerals, must translate the Roman numerals to the Arabic numerals in his mind. Indexing and cross-referencing are tedious enough without the added problem of translation.

Thus, capital letters and Arabic numerals are usually sufficient. They stand the test of good indexing systems: simplicity and infinite expansion. The capital letters can be repeated if the alphabet of A, B, C, etc., are exhausted in the first series of segments. For the next series, the auditor can use AA, BB, CC, and so on. The Arabic numerals can also be expanded to infinity. A1 can become A1.1 or A1.1.1 or A.1.1.1.1.

We find this simple system much more preferable to some forms of indexing which can get to look like algebraic formulas. For example:

$$\frac{IX - A - 1 - a}{(a) - (1)}$$

The auditor should constantly strive for simplicity. For example, a complete audit segment can run simply as C1, C2, C3, C4, right through the entire segment. Breakdowns within the segment are seldom necessary. If the auditor needs to add worksheets, the system permits for ready expansion. For example, if a worksheet is to be added between C2 and C3, the C2 becomes C2.1 and the added sheet can be indexed C2.2.

The auditor in charge should expect his assistants to keep their working papers currently referenced. But if they are to do the referencing within the scope of the project, he should assign a symbol to them at the same time they are assigned a task. The number of segments should be planned in the audit program. The letters of the alphabet can be assigned to the segments in the program. When the assistant is given the appropriate symbol, D or D.1, for example, he can then be held responsible for indexing his papers and cross-referencing them within his segment, or a section within the segment.

Cross-referencing within working papers should be complete and accurate. Professional auditors sprinkle their references copiously throughout their working papers. The references are usually in red, or some other contrasting color, so that they will stand out clearly.

Cross-referencing in the margins of the draft audit report can be very valuable. The references readily provide direct access to the working papers. This can be extremely important when the report is reviewed in draft with the auditee. The auditee's request for amplification can be promptly answered if the marginal references can send the auditor directly to the supporting papers. Also, when the auditor is making his painstaking verification of the final report, his marginal references can save him much valuable time and help prevent him from overlooking relevant material.

When the working papers are complete, they should be referenced to an overall table of contents. The initial table of contents set forth in Chapter 4 should be added to so as to provide ready access to any desired section in the papers, and to provide an overview of what the papers contain.

CONTROLLING WORKING PAPERS

The working papers are the auditor's property[1] and they should be kept under his control. He should know exactly where they are during the conduct of his audit. They should be kept in a locked file or a locked desk overnight. They should not be available to people unauthorized to use them. To do so invites people to misuse them, remove information from them, change information in them, or read information not for their eyes.

This does not mean that the auditor is debarred from showing his working papers to auditee personnel under appropriate circumstances. It can sometimes be quite useful for the auditor — where there are no indications of fraud, of course, or any damaging comments — to spread the results of his review before the auditee so that the auditor is helped to evaluate significance, perspective, accuracy, and relevance. But the auditor must always know who has access to his papers.

Audit management must take a direct interest in the control the auditor exercises over his working papers. There have been instances where a set of working papers — in the middle of the audit — have been lost. What a waste of time and money this can entail. Audit management should also be concerned with the ability of a substitute auditor to pick up — with the least disruption to the program — the work done by an auditor who suddenly becomes unavailable. The rule should be: "Keep your working papers so guarded, so organized, and so indexed and cross-referenced that the audit job can be picked up by the next auditor with a minimum of program interruption."

---

[1] *Ipswich Mills* vs. *Dillon & Son*, 157 N.E. 604, 260 Mass. 453 (Massachusetts Supreme Court, 1927).

Working papers should be disposed of when they are of no further use. Some one-time audits of extreme significance may be retained in storage indefinitely. In the main, however, repetitive audits do not require the retention of superseded papers. After the auditor has completed his examination, he should make a determination, approved by his supervisor, as to whether or not the working papers covering the preceding audit should be retained.

SUMMARY

Working papers evidence the audit work. They are the bridge between the examination and the audit report.

Neat, accurate, reasonably complete working papers are the hallmark of the professional auditor.

If working papers are to be useful, they should be prepared as the auditor goes along with his audit examination. They become especially useful when they are well-summarized as the audit progresses. The auditor should summarize the results of his tests, the discussions he holds with auditees, and the deficiencies he detects. In addition, to provide him with a view of where he's been and where he still must go, he should summarize his results briefly in his audit program.

Working papers can be of little value unless they are thoroughly cross-referenced. The person who reads the working papers for the first time — and even the auditor himself, after the passage of time — will not have in mind the various relationships between different sets of papers or different schedules.

Working papers should be kept under strict control. And they should be so maintained and referenced that another auditor could pick up the audit with the least effect on the program if the original auditor becomes unavailable.

Exhibit 10-1. SAMPLE WORKING PAPERS: RELEASE OF ENGINEERING DRAWINGS

SAMPLE WORKING PAPERS

Release of Engineering Drawings
General Information

Objective of Activity

To prepare engineering drawings that are accurate and will meet specification requirements, and to release them in time to meet factory needs.

Background

Three separate engineering project organizations prepare and release drawings: Projects A, B, and C. Each project works under a project engineer. All three project engineers report to the Chief Engineer. A separate Checking Department, under a Chief Checker, also reports directly to the Chief Engineer and is therefor not under the control of the people whose drawings he checks. See organization chart on C8.

LBS 2/1/7x

C1

Each project has its own procedures for controlling the preparation, checking, approval, and release of drawings.

Each project provides for a span of 20 factory days from completion of drawings to release to the factory. [Factory dates are numbered from 1 to 1000 (going back to 1 when they reach 1000) and exclude weekends and holidays.] The 20 days are to cover checking the drawings, correcting them, and obtaining approvals.

LBS 2/1/7x

C2

Control System

1) To assure accuracy of drawings, each one is to be verified by a checker using different color checks: yellow to indicate accuracy, red to indicate an error. All errors are to be corrected or, if not corrected, the reasons for release without correction are to be shown.

2) To make sure that the drawings met contract specifications, they must be approved in writing by the:

Engineering Supervisor
Project Engineer
Production Engineer
Quality Engineer

Projects B and C have a system for reviewing all drawings for evidence of check and approval before release to the shop. Project A does not.

3) To assure the release of drawings in time to meet factory needs, schedules covering

LBS 2/7/7x

C3

Exhibit 10-1. (Cont.)

Card C4:

drafting provide for completion of the drawings within 20 days of factory need dates. Project B has a follow-up system. Projects A and C do not.

4) All projects use registers to record completed drawings. All projects show release dates. Only Project B shows receipt dates. (See flow chart on C9)

Purpose

To determine whether control system is adequate to meet objectives of:

1. Accuracy
2. Meeting specification requirements
3. Meeting schedules

To determine whether performance is effective in that:

- All drawings are checked and corrected
- All drawings bear evidence of

LBG 2/1/7X — C4

Card C5:

approval

All drawings are released within 20 days of completion.

Scope

We took a judgment sample for our preliminary review of drawings released during the last half of 197X. We made a selection at random, using the interval selection technique, from the registers of released drawings maintained at each project. We decided to take a sample of 20 drawings as a preliminary test and expand our test if necessary. Since our findings were conclusive at each project, we decided not to expand the tests.

Control	Findings
1) Accuracy	
2) Meeting Specs	Project A had no
LBG 2/4/7X	provision for reviewing
	C5

Card C9:

drawings before release or for evidence of check and of approvals. Projects B and C did. C9.

Projects A and C had no follow-up system for drawings in process of checking. Project B did. C9.

3) Schedule

Card C6:

Performance

1) Accuracy
2) Meeting Specs

At Project A: 4 drawings by-passed the checking; 3 drawings had a total of 7 uncorrected errors; 3 drawings did not have the signatures of the Production Engineer.

At Projects B & C we found no errors. C10.

At Project A — 5 out of 20 drawings were 21 to 50 days late.

At Project C — 8 out of 50 drawings were 10 to 30 days late.

At Project B — all C6

3) Schedule

LBG 2/4/7X

Card C7:

drawings in sample were released on time C10.

Opinion

Project A — Controls over accuracy, meeting specs and schedule inadequate

Project B — Controls satisfactory

Project C — Controls over schedule inadequate

Recommendations

Install at Projects A and C the same system of control in effect at Project B.

The Project Engineers at A and C agreed with our recommendation. They issued instructions to their administrative assistants to that effect. See C15 and C16.

Subsequent reviews showed that the new controls were in actual operation.

LBG 2/4/7X

C7

Exhibit 10-1a. TEST OF ENGINEERING DRAWINGS FOR
TIMELINESS OF RELEASE AND ADEQUACY
OF CHECK AND APPROVAL

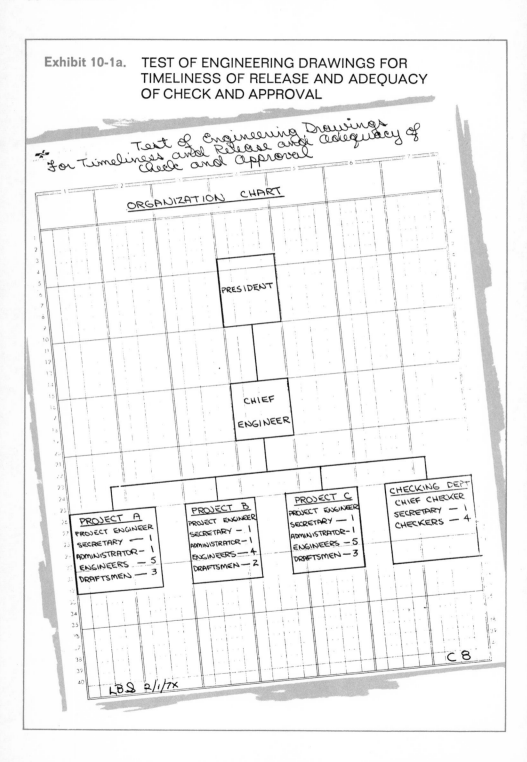

Exhibit 10-1b. RELEASE OF ENGINEERING DRAWINGS

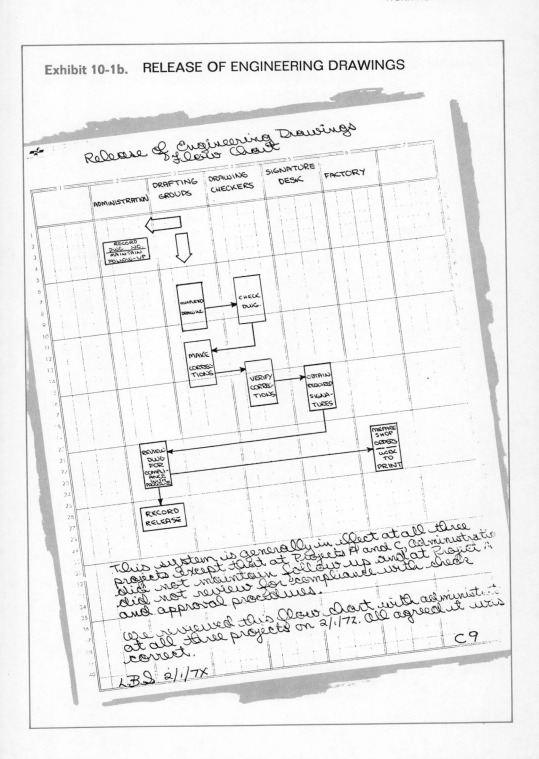

Exhibit 10-1c. TEST OF ENGINEERING DRAWINGS FOR TIMELINESS OF RELEASE AND ADEQUACY OF CHECK AND APPROVAL

Test of Engineering Drawings for Timeliness of Release and Adequacy of Check and Approval

SUMMARY OF TESTS

			A	PROJECTS B	C	TOTAL
						420
POPULATION: DWGS. ISSUED LAST 6 MOS, 197X			150	130	140	
SAMPLE: JUDGMENT SAMPLE, SELECTED AT RANDOM BY INTERVAL SAMPLING FROM DRAWING RELEASE REGISTERS SELECTED EVERY Nth STARTING WITH:			20 #3	20 #6	20 #1	60

DELAYS

				A	B	C	TOTAL
10	TO	20	DAYS LATE	—	—	2	2
21	TO	30	″ ″	1	—	2	3
31	TO	40	″ ″	1	—	3	4
41	TO	50	″ ″	3	—	1	4
				5		8	13

DRAWINGS BY-PASSING CHECK

4

UNCORRECTED ERRORS

NO. DWGS.	NO. ERRORS
3	7

UNOBTAINED SIGNATURES

NO. DWGS.	NO. SIG'S.
3	3

REASONS FOR DEFICIENCIES

DELAYS } PROJECTS A & C HAD NO SYSTEM OF FOLLOW-UP CONTROL
PROJECT B HAD AN EFFECTIVE SYSTEM

BY-PASSING CHECKERS
UNCORRECTED ERRORS } PROJECT A DID NOT PROVIDE FOR A REVIEW OF DRAWINGS BEFORE RELEASE TO FACTORY
NO SIGNATURES } PROJECTS B AND C HAD AN EFFECTIVE SYSTEM

REFER TO C11

C/10

LBP 2/3/7X

Exhibit 10-1d. TEST OF ENGINEERING DRAWINGS FOR TIMELINESS OF RELEASE AND ADEQUACY OF CHECK AND APPROVAL

Test of Engineering Drawings for Timeliness of Release and adequacy of Check and Approval

LIST OF DISCREPANT ITEMS

DELAYS

(DRAWINGS REQUIRING MORE THAN 20 DAYS)

PROJECT A		PROJECT B		PROJECT C	
DRAWING	NO. OF DAYS	DRAWING	NO. OF DAYS	DRAWING	NO. OF DAYS
A-1219	65-20*=45	NONE		C-325	50-20*=30
A-1105-1	62 " =42			C-331	60 " =40
A-1232	58 " =38			C-334	63 " =43
A-1250	70 " =50			C-338	53 " =33
A-1283	50 " =30			C-350	48 " =28
				C-359	30 " =10
				C-376	53 " =33
				C-389	40 " =20

* 20 DAYS CONSIDERED TO BE STANDARD FLOW TIME

DRAWINGS BY-PASSED CHECK

PROJECT A	PROJECT B	PROJECT C
A-1222	NONE	NONE
A-1260		
A-1266		
A-1283		

UNCORRECTED ERRORS

PROJECT A		PROJECT B		PROJECT C	
DRAWING	NO. OF ERRORS	DRAWING	NO. OF ERRORS	DRAWING	NO. OF ERRORS
A-1105-1	2	NONE		NONE	
A-1247	2				
A-1285	3				

SIGNATURES NOT OBTAINED

PROJECT A		PROJECT B		PROJECT C	
DRAWING	MISSING SIG'S	DRAWING	MISSING SIG'S	DRAWING	MISSING SIG'S
A-1227	PROD. ENG.	NONE		NONE	
A-1253	PROD. ENG.				
A-1279	PROD. ENG.				
SEE C 12		SEE C 13		SEE C 14	

C 11

LBQ 2/3/7X

Exhibit 10-1e. TEST OF ENGINEERING DRAWINGS FOR TIMELINESS OF RELEASE AND ADEQUACY OF CHECK AND APPROVAL

Test of Engineering Drawings for Timeliness of Release and Adequacy of Check and Approval

PROJECT A

DRAWING NUMBER	FACTORY DWG. PREP'D.	DATE WAS REL'D.	NO. OF DAYS BETWEEN PREP. & REL.	NO. OF DEFECTS PER CHECKER	NO. CORRECTED	REQUIRED APPROVALS SHOWN	COMMENTS
A-1206	605	615	10	3	3	YES	
A-1219	550	615	65	7	7	YES	DWG. DELAYED IN CHECK
A-1222	600	616	16	0	0	YES	DWG. BYPASSED CHECK IN ERROR
A-1105-1	555	617	62	4	2	YES	DWG. DELAYED IN CHECK, 2 ERRORS UNCORRECTED (NO REASON SHOWN)
A-1227	607	617	10	4	4	NO	PROD. ENG. DID NOT SIGN
A-1232	560	618	58	5	5	YES	DWG. DELAYED IN CHECK
A-1240	604	618	14	3	3	YES	
A-1247	605	618	13	6	4	YES	2 ERRORS UNCORRECTED (NO REASON SHOWN)
A-1250	549	619	70	9	9	YES	DWG. DELAYED IN CHECK
A-1253	612	621	9	2	2	NO	PROD. ENG. DID NOT SIGN
A-1260	614	622	8	0	0	YES	DWG. BYPASSED CHECK IN ERROR
A-1266	612	622	10	0	0	YES	DWG. BYPASSED CHECK IN ERROR
A-1270	610	622	12	3	3	YES	
A-1274	611	622	11	4	4	NO	PROD. ENG. DID NOT SIGN
A-1279	612	624	12	3	3	YES	
A-1283	575	625	50	6	6	YES	DWG. BYPASSED CHECK (NO REASON SHOWN) PROD. ENG. DID NOT SIGN, 3 ERRORS UNCORRECTED (NO REASON)
A-1285	615	625	10	4	1	YES	
A-1290	617	627	10	3	3	YES	
A-1292	618	627	9	3	3	YES	
A-1296	619	628	9	2	2	YES	

ALL DIFFERENCES REVIEWED WITH ADMINISTRATOR JOHN DOE 2/3/72, HE AGREED WITH OUR FINDINGS.

LBS 2/2/7x

C12

Exhibit 10-1f. TEST OF ENGINEERING DRAWINGS FOR TIMELINESS OF RELEASE AND ADEQUACY OF CHECK AND APPROVAL

Test of Engineering Drawings
For Timeliness of Release and Adequacy of
Check and Approval
PROJECT B

DRAWING NUMBER	FACTORY DWG. WAS PREP'D.	DATE REL'D.	NO. OF DAYS BETWEEN PREP & REL.	NO. OF DEFECTS PER CHECKER	COR-RECTED	REQUIRED APPROVALS SHOWN	COMMENTS
B- 614	606	616	10	4	4	YES	
B- 615	614	617	3	5	5	YES	
B- 619	610	620	10	5	5	YES	
B-622	609	620	11	6	6	YES	
B-626	609	620	11	3	3	YES	
B-629	612	623	11	2	2	YES	
B- 632	620	627	7	7	7	YES	
B-639	621	627	6	2	2	YES	
B-642	620	627	7	2	2	YES	
B-645	619	630	11	5	5	YES	
B-647	619	630	11	5	5	YES	
B-649	626	632	6	5	5	YES	
B-661	626	632	6	3	3	YES	
B-662	622	632	10	2	2	YES	
B-671	624	634	10	7	7	YES	
B-680	627	634	7	6	6	YES	
B-692	628	635	7	8	8	YES	
B-693	628	636	8	3	3	YES	
B-695	626	636	10	4	4	YES	
B-698	625	636	11	2	2	YES	

LBS 2/2/7X

C 13

Exhibit 10-1g. TEST OF ENGINEERING DRAWINGS FOR TIMELINESS OF RELEASE AND ADEQUACY OF CHECK AND APPROVAL

Test of Engineering Drawings for Timeliness of Release and adequacy of Check and approval

PROJECT C

DRAWING NUMBER	FACTORY DWG PREP'D	DATE WAS REL'D	NO. OF DAYS BETWEEN PREP & REL.	NO. OF DEFECTS PER CHECKER	DEFECTS COR-RECTED	REQUIRED APPROVALS SHOWN	COMMENTS
C-325	570	620	50	4	4	YES	DELAYED IN CHECK (NO FOLLOW UP)
C-327	610	622	12	4	4	YES	
C-331	562	622	60	7	7	YES	DITTO
C-334	562	625	63	2	2	YES	DITTO
C-338	572	625	53	2	2	YES	DITTO
C-341	606	625	19	4	4	YES	
C-344	612	625	13	3	3	YES	
C-346	615	629	14	6	6	YES	
C-350	581	629	48	5	5	YES	DITTO
C-352	620	630	10	5	5	YES	
C-359	601	631	30	4	4	YES	DITTO
C-365	619	631	12	4	4	YES	
C-370	623	633	10	3	3	YES	
C-372	623	633	10	2	2	YES	
C-376	580	633	53	2	2	YES	DITTO
C-381	617	636	19	3	3	YES	
C-383	620	636	16	4	4	YES	
C-389	596	636	40	4	4	YES	DITTO
C-392	616	636	20	5	5	YES	
C-397	620	640	20	5	5	YES	

ALL DIFFERENCES REVIEWED WITH ADMINISTRATOR RICHARD ROE 2/3/72. HE AGREED WITH OUR FINDINGS.

JBS 2/2/7x

C 14

Exhibit 10-1h.

To: Administrator, Project A

From: Project Engineer, Project A

Subject: Control over Drawings — Check, Approvals, Follow-up

An audit of our operations has disclosed that:

1. Some drawings had by-passed the checkers,
2. Some drawings did not bear all required approvals, and
3. Some drawings had been delayed in check without proper follow-up.

The following procedures will be put into effect immediately, pending the issuance of suitable job instructions covering these matters:

1. All drawings being released to production shall clear over the administrator's desk. He shall initial and date the release document to show that he has reviewed the document for evidence of:

   a. Check

   b. Appropriate approvals

   All documents not checked or approved shall be returned to the responsible individual by a brief memo, with copy to this office.

2. The administrator shall establish and maintain a record of all drawings sent to check, showing the dates of release to and from check. Each week, the administrator shall prepare a report listing all drawings in check for more than 20 days. One copy of the report shall be sent to this office and one copy to the Chief Checker.

/s/ P. Snow
Project Engineer
Project A

C 15

Exhibit 10-1i.

To: Administrator, Project C

From: Project Engineer, Project C

Subject: Control over Drawings in Check

An audit of our administrative procedures has shown that drawings were delayed in the checking process without adequate follow-up.

Please install the following procedures immediately, pending the issuance of a job instruction:

> The administrator shall establish and maintain a record of all drawings sent to check, showing the dates of release to and from check. Each week, the administrator shall prepare a report listing all drawings in check for over 20 days. One copy of the report shall be sent to this office and one copy to the Chief Checker.

/s/T. Blow
Project Engineer
Project C

C 16

Exhibit 10-2. RECORD OF AUDIT FINDING

RAF No. 4
W/P REF. No. C5, C8, C9

Organization: Eng. Branch — Project C Eng. Dep't.

Nature of Finding: No provision had been made to monitor drawings sent to the Checking Dep't. As a result, a large percentage of the drawings included in our test had been held by the Checking Department beyond the prescribed 20-day period.

Same finding disclosed in last audit: Yes_____ No_X___

Directives or procedures involved: Eng. Proc. D-79 permits only 20 working days from drawing completion to release.

Tests made:

Population size _140_   Sample size _20_

Method of selection of sample _Every 7th, with random start_

Discrepancies: No. _8_   % _14_

Causes: Project management had not considered the need for schedule control over drawings sent to check.

Corrective action: Controls were established to monitor drawings sent to check. See C-15 and C-16 .

Discussion with auditee personnel:

Name	Title	Department	Date	Auditor
(1) R. Roe	Administrator	Proj. C Eng.	2/3/7X	LBS
(2) P. Snow	Proj. Engineer	Proj. C Eng.	2/3/7X	LBS
(3)				
(4)				

Comments by auditee personnel:

(1) Roe corroborated the accuracy of our findings and the cause of the delay.

(2) Snow agreed with the need for corrective action. He said he'd install the same kinds of controls as those used in Project B.

(3)

(4)

LBS   2/4/7X
Auditor   **Date**

C 17

eleven ■

REPORTS

WHAT THEY ARE AND WHAT THEY DO

Reports are the auditor's opportunity to get management's undivided attention. That is how he should regard reporting — as an opportunity. He should not see it as dreary drudgery, but rather as a prized opportunity to show management what he has to offer toward business betterment.

Much too often the auditor carelessly throws away this golden chance to open management's eyes . . . to show management what he has accomplished and what he can accomplish . . . to explain what management needs to know and what it needs to do. He throws away his opportunity by pallid prose, by making mountains out of rubbish heaps, by uninviting report formats, by allegations that won't withstand assault, by unsupported conclusions, and by complaints without recommendations.

The auditor should regard his report in the same light that a salesman regards an opportunity to present his product to the president of a company: an opening for a well-rehearsed, well-tested, well-conceived sales presentation. In this light, the audit report has two functions: First, to communicate. Second, to persuade and, when necessary, sound a call to action. As Dudley E. Browne said, "We have, on the whole, an admirable story to tell — buttressed by facts and figures, and supported by analysis and reason — and it surely is one that deserves to be told often and in the right places."[1]

---

[1]Browne, D. E., "Patterns for Progress in Internal Auditing," *The Internal Auditor*, Spring 1966, p. 18.

The auditor's findings and opinions are important to management. His dispassionate, objective conclusions may ease management's mind about well-functioning activities, and his recommendations may alert management to matters needing improvement.

But management must want to read or hear the reports. For communication to be effective, the channels must be clear — the medium must be incisive and easily understood. The story must be worthy of the material; much skillful and constructive audit effort flounders in the murky waters of poor reporting. The auditor who sharpens his auditing techniques but leaves his reporting dull will be unable to penetrate the circles where his story should be told.

And when management gives him his audience he must never forget that he is selling. So he must be consciously persuasive — by the techniques of motivation and by the style he uses. He must highlight what is management-oriented. He must downplay what is immaterial. He must artfully translate the technical into the readily understandable. And he must point skillfully to the need for taking action and the penalties for avoiding action.

Then management will begin to appreciate the significance of the audit product. It will see the valuable insights it can obtain. It will learn to accept the accuracy, the objectivity, and the plain good sense of what the auditor has to say. Then, and not until then, will the audit report become required reading for management. And this will help the auditor achieve one of his own objectives: To be privy to the councils of management and to have access to management's ear.

There is small likelihood that the auditor was born with the word mastery of a Shakespeare or the crisp, lean style of a Hemingway. If he were, he would probably be in the business of writing instead of auditing. But what writing talent he has can be forged into an effective tool — with the right effort, with the right desire, with the right standards, and with the right techniques. To discuss those techniques is the purpose of the remainder of this chapter.

CRITERIA FOR REPORTS

We pointed out in the chapter on Field Work that the concept of measurement implies the presence of standards or criteria. Internal audit reports can be measured, and the standards of measurement have been agreed upon, by and large, by those practitioners who have written about reports. It is generally agreed that reports should be accurate, concise, clear, and timely.[2] To this catalogue of criteria we should like to add that reports should have "tone." Let us now address ourselves to each of these hallmarks of good reporting:

Accuracy

The report must be completely and scrupulously factual. Every categorical statement, every figure, every reference must be based on hard evidence. The internal auditing organization, through unremitting effort, must develop a reputation for reliability. Utter reliability must become the hallmark of the internal audit report. It should be written and documented so as to impel belief and reliance. It should have character. It should speak with authority. Thus, whatever is said, particularly in operating areas outside the auditor's normally accepted scope, must be supported or supportable. The reader must be able to rely upon the report because of its well-documented facts and inescapable logic.

Statements of fact must carry the assurance that the auditor personally observed or validated the fact. If he says there was an excessive backlog of work, it means that he personally knows this to be a fact. It means he knows what backlogs are considered normal and the exact extent of the backlog he personally observed. True, there may be conditions which the auditor has not personally

---

[2]"Internal Audit Report Practices," Research Committee Report No. 10. *The Institute of Internal Auditors,* 1961, p. 19.

observed but which management should be made aware of. A statement to that effect in a report should show the source: "The department manager told us that the backlog was excessive." The reported statement is completely factual — the auditor personally heard the statement from the department manager. But the auditor is not himself certifying to the existence or the extent of the conditions.

Accuracy also implies perspective — the reporting of matters in a proper light — objective observations — refraining from puffing up that which is neither material nor relevant. Executive management generally gives serious attention to audit reports. Conditions reported to be deficient may become the subject of executive wrath. It is a form of inaccuracy, therefore, to hold up as deficient one of a dozen related activities without showing how the one activity fits into the mosaic of the overall function or organization. If an operating manager is fiercely, and by and large successfully, fighting the battle of quality, schedule, and cost in his organization, if he is producing an acceptable product, if he is delivering it on time, if he is making it within his budget constraints, and if he trains his people well and knows what they are doing — wouldn't it be a form of inaccuracy to highlight in an audit report to executive management that written job instructions could stand updating?

So first and foremost, the internal auditing organization must develop within management this feeling of certainty: If the internal auditor has said it, then it must be true, it must be relevant, and it must be in perspective.

Clarity

Clarity implies many things. But chiefly it means putting into the mind of the reader or the listener what was in the mind of the auditor when he wrote or delivered his report. Yet there are a host of impediments to this hoped-for consummation. The auditor must be aware of them, and he must consciously try to remove them.

Lack of clarity in the mind of the auditor is the prime impediment to clear writing. One cannot write clearly what he does not understand clearly. If he does not have a firm grasp of his subject, he is not ready to write. Until the auditor knows precisely what he is talking about, he should do more field work or research before he takes his report-writing pencil in hand.

Dull and tedious writing is an impediment to clarity. Dreary, stilted prose makes the mind turn to other things. Consider: "Reconciliation of the accounts was effected by the accounting personnel." How much clearer it comes through when we say: "The accounting people reconciled the accounts."

Poorly structured reports are impediments to clarity. An orderly procession of ideas enhances clarity. Some auditors start their reports in the middle and then go off in all directions. They may well be hiding excellent findings and recommendations in a morass of tangled sentences and paragraphs. The ideas that management desperately needs may never get communicated. For the want of an outline the audit is lost.

Technical and jargonish terms are impediments. Skillful translations clear the way. This means more than just substituting "rejections by inspectors" for "I-tags." It also means conveying ideas in terms that mean something to the reader. It is one thing to say that receiving memos are not being matched with invoices. It is quite another to say that there was no assurance that the company was receiving the goods it was paying for. The first statement is factual — but it paints no pictures. The second is no more factual — but it will sound sirens and galvanize management into action.

Reporting findings without setting the stage is an impediment. Giving the proper background information is sometimes essential to the understanding of a process or a condition, or to appreciate its significance. If the auditor is recommending a new procedure he should first tell what the existing one is like, what is wrong with it, and the probable effect of its continued use. Then management will be more receptive to the cogency of the auditor's proposal; and yet be in a position to make its own considered decision.

Long discussions of technical matters like the interrelationships of many different amounts are impediments to understanding. Artful schedules, tabulations, charts, and graphs can bring clarity. One picture can make clear what a thousand words can only obscure.

Clarity is the sister of salesmanship. And the report is a sales pitch — with none of the unfortunate connotations that the term carries with it. The purpose of the audit report is to get desired action. It must therefore be effective. And to be effective it must be clear.

Conciseness

Conciseness means cutting out what is superfluous. That does not necessarily mean short, because the subject matter may demand extended discussion. But it does mean eliminating what is irrelevant and immaterial.

Conciseness means eliminating the ideas, the findings, the words, the sentences, and the paragraphs that do not help get across the central theme of the report.

At the same time, conciseness should not become such a fetish that writing is reduced to an abrupt, telegraphic style. There must still be a continuity of thought, an ease of reading, and a comfortable, integrated flow of ideas.

But auditors sometimes fall into the trap of long sentences that leave the reader puzzled and weary. If the auditor really puts his mind to it, he can cut the long sentences into comfortable bite sizes. And he can overcome abruptness through words or thoughts of transition.

Also, conciseness does not mean using only short sentences. An uninterrupted series of short sentences creates its own sameness and dullness. A few well-constructed long sentences, sprinkled among the short ones, give a much-needed variety and tend to avoid tedium.

But one man's conciseness may be another man's lack of information. What is concise enough for the operating manager who needs sufficient detail to know how to correct a condition may be overwordy to the executive who just wants to get the general idea. The report should then supply both sufficient detail for the operating manager and a summary for the executive.

Timeliness

The final, formal report is not designed to be a historical document. It is a call to action. It answers management's needs for current information. Its effect is lost, therefore, if it is not timely. On the one hand, it must be carefully thought out. It must be impregnable. It must be incapable of being misunderstood. And this cannot be done with a stroke of the pen.

These sometimes conflicting needs — thoughtfulness and promptness — must both be met. And the informal progress report, issued while the audit is still going on, may be one answer.

Progress reports convey in writing the need for prompt action. And what is written, in most big companies, gets action where the spoken word may not. As the Chinese proverb has it, "The mouth is wind. The pen leaves tracks."

Progress reports can be brief, addressing themselves to only one or two ideas. They can be labeled progress reports and contain written caveats against accepting them as the final word, thereby permitting expedited action while reserving the right to polish and to revise. Yet they can give operating management an opportunity to get action started or to begin studying the condition.

The transmittal for the progress report can start by saying: "This progress report is designed to provide current information on conditions needing management attention. Our final report will include the matters discussed here, along with such other information obtained during the remainder of our field work."

The progress report can have other salutary results. It can serve to set the auditor straight on his facts or to sharpen his perspective, since the response evoked by the progress report can confirm or deny the auditor's findings to date. And operating management's studies, action, and/or replies may have a significant effect on what the auditor will finally report.

Where the auditing organization employs many young and still unseasoned auditors to perform audits away from headquarters, there may be an understandable concern about permitting them to draft and release progress reports without supervisory review. Yet prompt notice to operating management of deficient conditions — in writing — may be important. In those cases it may be advisable to develop a form, similar to the Record of Audit Findings discussed in Chapter 9, which compels the auditor to cover all significant aspects of a deficient condition: a concise statement of condition, size of the population, size of the sample, extent of the deficiency, causes and effects, applicable written procedures, and discussions with operating personnel.

A draft of such a progress report, specifically labeled as informal, may be of value in providing current, prompt audit information without compromising the final report.

Progress reports notwithstanding, the final report should be timely. The auditing organization should have goals for the prompt issuance of reports. And the auditor should be taught to construct his working papers in such a manner that the information they contain can be readily transformed into a final report with a minimum of restructuring.

Tone

Finally, the audit report must have a proper tone. It should be courteous. It should consider the report's effect upon subordinate operating people. It should not, therefore, identify individuals or highlight the mistakes of individuals. It should eschew pettiness and not concern itself with trivia. It should so speak that it sounds like the voice of management.

It should be dignified without being stodgy. It should avoid slang on the one hand and high-blown language on the other; they do not stand the test of time.

The executive, pressed from all quarters by operating reports and arguments — often self-serving declarations that put the best face on questionable matters — should be able to see in the audit report a calm, objective, thoughtful, dispassionate exposition on which he can rely.

REPORT FORMATS

The format of the report depends much on the kind of report being issued:

- Formal versus informal
- Final versus progress
- Written versus oral
- Overall opinion versus deficiency findings only
- Financial versus operational

The format of the report will also depend on the reader: what the reader expects and how much time he can devote to reading the reports.

The format of the report will further depend on the nature and the seasoning of the auditing activity. An auditing organization just starting on reviews of nonfinancial operating areas, will feel impelled to give abundant support for its opinions and conclusions to overcome a reluctance on the part of the reader to accept audit opinions on matters that are far afield from accounting activities.

Hence, different auditing organizations will employ different report formats and subdivide their reports into different subsections. Whichever format is found most appropriate, it should be used with reasonable consistency. Consistency combats confusion. The reader should know what to expect. He learns where he can readily find whatever interests him most and then can turn to that part of the report without difficulty.

We shall first discuss the formal, final written report. With each auditing organization pursuing its own ideals and objectives, it would be fruitless to define an optimum format for such reports. But the auditor should be acquainted with the different elements of an audit report that are in current use. Some or all of these elements will be found in most reports. A discussion of these various elements follows.

FORMAL REPORTS

The Summary

Summaries come in many shapes and sizes. A summary may be a simple transmittal memorandum that sends the report to the president or other executives of the company. Properly drafted, such a summary may be ideal for the harried, harassed executive who wants to read no more than he absolutely has to while reserving the right to dip into whatever detail he wishes.

Such summaries are useful devices. But they present some pitfalls to the unwary report writer. He must be careful, as he compresses the report into a brief summation, that he does not twist or distort meaning, materiality, or perspective.

An example of a brief transmittal is as follows:

Here is our report on Receiving Department activities. In general the department had provided an adequate system of controls for its receiving functions. Activities were being carried out effectively and efficiently, with the following exception:

No comparisons were being made between chemicals received and billed. Our own comparisons showed that tank cars were not being completely emptied. As a result we found variances of over 8%. After we discussed the matter with operating management, systems were improved and negotiations with the supplier resulted in recoveries of about $40,000.

We shall give examples of extended summaries which include forewords, purpose and scope statements, opinions, and abbreviated findings, later in this chapter.

The Foreword or Introduction

This report section is the first to meet the reader's eye. It should be stated crisply and clearly so as to invite the reader to read further. It is usually a stage-setter and can be used:

- To identify the audit as a regular examination or as the response to a special management request.
- To identify the organizations or functions reviewed.
- To refer to any relevant prior examinations.
- To comment on findings or recommendations discussed in prior reports and on their current status.
- To provide any explanatory information needed to acquaint the reader with the subject under examination. A report on shipping or receiving needs no more introduction than the title of the report itself. A report on special test equipment, however, may deserve some explanatory comment.
- To set forth briefly the value or volume of transactions processed, so as to give the reader an idea of the significance of the function.

An example of a Foreword section is as follows:

We have completed our regular audit of the Engineering Property Control Department. Our 19XX audit reported four deficiency findings. None of the deficient conditions then reported has recurred. The department is responsible for tools and equipment, valued at $7 million, which are used in the Engineering Branch.

The Statement of Purpose

The Purpose describes the audit objectives. It should be in sufficient detail to help the reader understand what to expect from the rest of the report.

When the purpose is spelled out with some preciseness, and when the discussions of findings that follow address themselves to each statement in the Purpose, then it serves as a road map, making it easier for the reader to find his way through the report.

An example of a detailed statement of purpose is as follows:

Our audit was directed toward determining whether an adequate and effective system of control had been provided over the activities of the Credit Department. We were concerned specifically with the following activities of the department:

- *Performing credit investigations and determining the financial responsibility of both suppliers and customers.*
- *Establishing credit terms for sales to commercial customers.*
- *Establishing control over payments to assignees.*
- *Investigating new suppliers.*

The Statement of Scope

The Scope statement is sometimes combined with the Purpose. The Scope can be of particular importance in identifying any limitations of the examination. It should specifically point to areas which were not covered — areas which, because of the very title of the report, the reader would consider covered in the audit unless he is told differently.

The scope is particularly important when normal auditing techniques are dispensed with and other techniques are relied upon.

Examples of two Scope statements are as follows:

We confined our review of receiving activities to those carried out in the central Receiving Department. We did not review controls over direct deliveries, which by-pass central Receiving. We plan on making a separate examination of direct deliveries.

★   ★   ★

Our preliminary survey disclosed an excellent system of control over the Shipping Department's activities. All job in-

structions are up to date. The department's supervisors are required to make periodic examinations of selected transactions and report their findings to the manager. He sees that deficient conditions are corrected. We discussed the shipping activities with representatives of peripheral organizations and found that they uniformly held the shipping operations in high regard. As a result, we reduced considerably the tests of transactions we normally make as a basis for our opinions.

In any event, the auditor should avoid giving a detailed account of the audit steps he takes. For some activities of a "sensitive" nature, such a disclosure may provide some people with a blueprint to follow in manipulating transactions for personal gain.

The Statement of Opinion

The Opinion is the auditor's professional judgment of the activity he has reviewed. It provides a capsule comment of his assessment of the conditions he has found. Not all auditing organizations provide overall opinions on the results of their examinations. The failure to do so, no doubt, deprives management of a significant service.

It would be most natural for a president of a company who meets an auditor after the completion of an audit assignment to ask, "Well, what do you think of the activity?" A responsive answer would represent an overall opinion: "The activity is operating quite well." Or, "I think they're doing a poor job, because . . ." or "Except for some minor matters which they quickly corrected, they're doing a reasonably good job."

Judgments along these lines are what executives expect from their auditing organizations. They are entitled to receive them.

Certainly, the auditor should not express an opinion he is not capable of supporting. And, certainly, he must weigh carefully the factors supporting his opinion. The opinion should say exactly what the auditor means, include only what he can justify, and be adequately supported by the facts. Finally, it should encompass and be responsive to the purposes of the examination he set out in his Purpose statement. Several examples of opinions on audits of operations follow:

Based on the result of our review, we formulated the opinion that an adequate system of control has been established over the activities of the Purchasing Department and that the department's assigned responsibilities were being carried out effectively and efficiently.

★   ★   ★

In our opinion, the activities concerned with the layoff and recall of employees were well controlled and, with one excep-

tion, were being performed effectively and efficiently. The one exception related to inadequate explanation for monetary settlements of grievances resulting from improper layoffs.

★   ★   ★

In our opinion the system designed to ensure the timely calibration of test equipment was inadequate, because no provision had been made to identify all of the equipment subject to calibration.

The auditor, in formulating his opinion should not hesitate to be complimentary, if the compliment is deserved. If he finds a well-controlled, well-organized, well-managed, and smoothly functioning operation, he should say so. It would give evidence to his thesis that he does not seek deficiencies only. He should, of course, have adequate support for a complimentary opinion. He would not wish to see an opinion refuted by activities he did not cover or events he should have foreseen. But if he is certain of his grounds, he should have the courage of his convictions. Here is an example of a richly deserved compliment.

Based on the results of our review, we formed the opinion that adequate controls had been provided over the activities of the Procurement Services Department. We also formed the opinion that the controls were working effectively and efficiently.

In fact, we considered this department to be highly effective in accomplishing its assigned mission. We believe this can be attributed to highly motivated and knowledgeable supervision and key personnel; good communications and feedback between management and subordinates; thorough on-the-job training of the individual employees, reinforced by a rotational assignment policy; up-to-date, comprehensive job instructions; constant vigilance on the part of supervision and alternates to monitor workload schedule and performance and to minimize errors; good rapport and loyalty between the manager and the group supervisors; and the participation of the manager and her supervisors in arriving at management decisions.

Findings

Findings are the source from which all opinions and recommendations flow. Findings are the results of inquiries and investigations. They are the facts produced by the auditor's efforts. They are the product of his field work. Findings may be favorable or unfavorable. They may explain a satisfactory condition that warrants explanation in the report, or they may set forth unsatisfactory conditions that need correcting.

Favorable findings, understandably, will require less explanation in the report. But they do represent an audit determination, and they are backed by the integrity and reputation of the auditor and the audit organization.

Some audit organizations do not report their favorable findings. Whether this is desirable or undesirable is a moot point. Some auditors feel that executive management does not want to be bothered with matters that do not require their action or decision. Others feel that reporting favorable findings shows objectivity and creates a better rapport between them and operating personnel. Also, some managers wish to be told of satisfactory conditions to set their minds at rest about a particular operation. Each view has its merits. This is not the forum at which to make the final judgment. We shall therefore give an example of a favorable finding along with some comments on the elements to consider in drafting the findings. We shall then follow this with an example of an unfavorable finding.

In favorable findings, the elements needed to provide the reader with background and the auditor's reasoning include authority, objectives, conditions, and effect.[3]

Authority. Someone or something must have authorized the function under review. Knowing the authority permits the auditor to determine whether the function is being conducted within bounds or is exceeding its bounds. The authority may be statutory, may come from the board of directors, or may be the result of a management decision, express or implied.

Where the authority is in writing, its intent and scope are more readily ascertainable. If it is oral, the auditor would probably want to discuss it with both the one who granted the authority and the one who received it.

The auditor will ascertain, if at all possible, both the broad authority granted to the entire function and the specific authority granted to that portion of the function which is under his review. For example, assume that the board of directors authorized the establishment of a new plant to make tools. The auditor, however, is concerned solely with the supply department of the plant. He would then seek to ascertain the specific authority granted to the supply department. The Authority portion of the reported findings might be as follows:[4]

The plant at Bethany was established by the board of directors to manufacture small tools. The supply department of the Bethany plant is authorized to maintain enough materials and

[3]Scantlebury, D. L. "The Structure of a Management Audit Finding," *The Internal Auditor*, March/April 1972, p. 10.
[4]*Ibid.* p. 12.

parts to keep the production lines adequately stocked and to purchase such quantities of materials and parts as are needed for that purpose except that, by instruction of the Vice President for Manufacturing Operations, all steel sheets and ingots are to be ordered through the main office so that quantity discounts can be obtained through consolidation of the orders of all plants.

Objectives. Having established authority, the auditor must then address himself to the activity's objectives. Objectives are pivotal to appraisal. To know if something is done well, one must first determine what is sought to be done or what needs to be done. In audits of operations, an appraisal of an activity is often meaningless if it does not take into account the activity's mission, its reason for being.

Normally, audits have several objectives. They may be grouped under the terms effectiveness and economy. Effectiveness implies the production of a satisfactory product — one that meets specifications and standards — using "product" in its broadest sense to include services as well as tangible items. Economy includes efficiency. It implies spending only enough money to achieve other objectives.

Pursuing the audit of the supply department, the discussion of the objectives might be as follows:[5]

The primary objective of the supply department is to maintain sufficient stock on hand to ensure uninterrupted production. A secondary, but almost equally important objective is economy which, for supply purposes, means keeping enough stock on hand to meet production needs but at the same time keeping the investment in inventory as low as practicable.

Certainly, the auditor must not feel precluded from appraising the objectives themselves. If they are in conflict with company aims, this conflict must be brought to light and resolved.

Condition — Favorable. In the context of audit reports, condition means the results of the auditor's appraisal of the ongoing process, through observing, questioning, analyzing, and other audit techniques. The statement of condition should be relevant to the objectives considered in the auditor's examination. In a favorable finding, a simple statement of conclusion should be sufficient for management:

1. *We found that the stock on hand was commensurate with plant needs.*
2. *We also found that systems in effect provided assurance that inventories would be kept to a practical minimum.*

---

[5]Ibid. p. 14.

Some audits of operations cover matters which may be considered by some managements to be outside the scope of the auditor's competence. In such cases the auditor may wish to set forth the criteria he used in appraising the conditions he found and the steps he took in measuring transactions and processes against those criteria.

Condition — Unfavorable. Let us now turn to the discussion of unsatisfactory findings. The auditor can take a slightly different approach to zero in directly on the deficient condition. The statements of such findings will usually include a capsule summary of the finding, the applicable criteria, the conditions found, the significance of the deficiency and its probable or actual effect, the cause of the conditions, the auditor's recommendations, and the corrective action taken.

To illustrate, let us continue with the story of the supply department. Let us assume that the auditor found the supply department's inventory records to be inaccurate and that as a result the department overstocked material.

Summary. The first statement would be a summary, a sort of headline that prepares the reader for what is to follow. Usually, a single sentence, lined to make it stand out, would suffice. For example:

> *Because of inaccurate inventory records, the supply department bought unneeded supplies costing $75,000.*

Criteria. The text of the finding should begin with a statement of the standards against which the audit findings should be measured. Let us assume that the problem in the supply department was the violation of existing procedures. Thus, the procedures — which the auditor found to be reasonable — become the criteria.

> *Established procedures provide that excess materials returned by the production department shall be entered on the records of the supply department to show currently the levels of inventory on hand and available for issuance.*

These criteria are simple and sensible. It would be hard for any businessman to quarrel with them.

Facts. Then come the facts which the auditor adduced — the conditions he observed.

> *Based on our observations and tests, we found that for a period of six months, supplies returned from Production had not been entered on the supply department's records.*

<u>Effect.</u> Unless the effect is shown, and unless that effect is significant, the attitude of management may be "so what?" Hence, the probable or actual effect should be stated:

As a result of the inaccurate inventory records, the company bought unneeded supplies costing about $75,000.

<u>Cause.</u> The next question that would immediately come to the mind of the perceptive reader of the report would be: "How in the world could this happen?" This is a determination the auditor should make for any deficiency finding:

We found that the employees responsible for the posting of returned supplies had not been instructed in their duties. In addition, supervisors had not been monitoring the process.

<u>Recommendation.</u> Finally, the reader will ask: "Very well, Mr. Auditor, you've made your point. Now what shall we do about it?" The report obligingly continues:

We reviewed the conditions with the manager of the supply department, and we recommended that:

1. He bring his inventory records up to date.

2. He issue job instructions spelling out to the workers the need to record returned supplies.

3. He instruct his supervisors to monitor the process in the future and to submit written reports on their periodic reviews.

Before we concluded our examination, the manager took all three steps. Our subsequent spot checks showed that the action was effective. We therefore consider this finding closed.

In sum, the auditor should be aware of the questions that a knowledgeable executive will have in mind when he reads a report of a deficient condition. These questions, recapitulating what we have just discussed, are as follows:

■ What's the general subject we're talking about? Orient me to the problem.

■ What were the people supposed to be doing?

■ What were they actually doing?

■ How badly did we get hurt? How badly could we get hurt?

■ How did all this come about?

■ What do you think should be done about it?

■ What did the operating manager say when you talked to him about these conditions, and what did he do about them? Is there anything that I should do?

With these questions as his own criteria, the auditor should be able to satisfy himself, his own supervisor, operating management, and executive management, that he has done an adequate audit job and viewed things fairly, objectively, and in their proper perspective.

Graphics

Even the most professionally written audit reports can gain from illustrations that clarify concepts and highlight interrelationships. They can provide believability to reported conditions that words could not possibly portray.

Some of the matters that can be appended to reports are:

- Bar charts showing relationships between two or more kindred sets of statistics.
- Flow charts explaining complex processes.
- Pictures showing clearly the existence and extent of hazardous conditions or wasteful practices.

Six such examples follow.

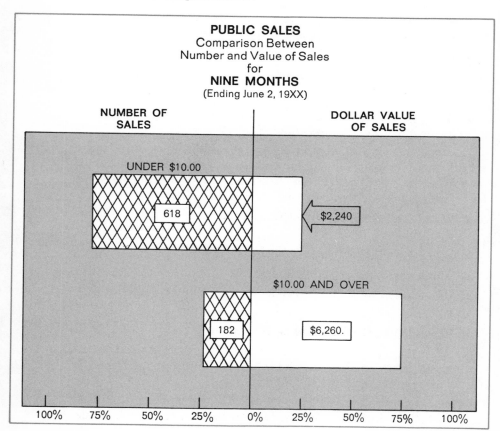

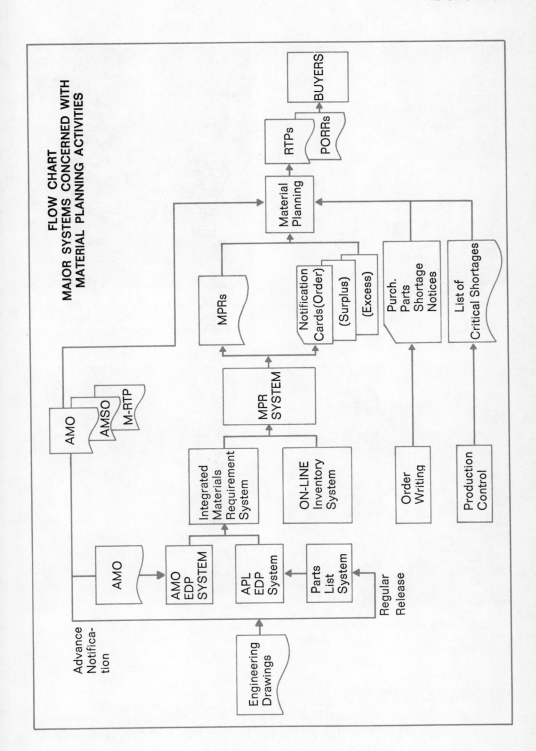

FLOW CHART
MAJOR SYSTEMS CONCERNED WITH
MATERIAL PLANNING ACTIVITIES

Warehouse open to elements (note daylight through open wall). Also, product damaged in handling.

Customer's warehouse containing company's consigned products. Deterioration on the outside indicates conditions inside.

Bulk product stored in tank with evidence of corrosion at top of tank. Impurities can materially damage the product.

Open burning at plant site. Potential violation of pollution standards.

INFORMAL REPORTS

Every auditing department has a need for an informal reporting system to complement its formal reporting system. Matters may be encountered during the audit engagement which:

- Require the prompt attention of management to supplement oral reports on an ongoing project.
- Have no relation to an ongoing project but warrant reporting to management.
- Require the postponement or abandonment of a project.

These and other matters can be made the subject of interim, or progress, informal written reports.

We discussed earlier in this chapter progress reports as a means to keep communications timely. Such reports, along with other informal reports, should occupy an official position in the auditing function. Readers will become accustomed to these informal reports if they follow a regular pattern, are referred to by a common designation, and are subject to some form of numerical control.

They may be designated "Informal Audit Reports" and may be given consecutive numbers for each year. The first report for the year could be designated "IAR XX-1."

The reports may be of any length, depending on the subject to be covered. If they are brief they may be presented on a single typed page. If they exceed one page, it is preferable that the report itself act as a transmittal and briefly outline the fully discussed material contained in an attachment to the informal report.

As an example, assume that the information on the Bethany supply department is being reported informally to management. The full discussion, treated earlier in this chapter, may be incorporated in an attachment. The transmittal report may be as follows:

IAR 7X-10

To: Manager
From: Auditor
Subject: Bethany Supply Department

This informal report is sent to you so that you may be currently informed on a matter which we found in our audit of the Bethany supply department, now in progress.

We found that inventory records were not being kept up to date. As a result, the supply department purchased unneeded material costing $75,000. The matter is discussed in detail in the attachment to this report.

The matter will be covered in our formal report on the Bethany supply department. We would like to acknowledge any corrective action that you take before we issue that report. Please let us know, therefore, of any action you take or intend to take. Our field work will be completed in about two or three weeks.

ORAL REPORTS

Oral reports should not, in our opinion, replace written reports. But they do have their place, and a valuable place it is. And they are being used more and more because:

- They are immediate. They give management prompt assurances or current information for corrective action.
- They evoke face-to-face responses. They can disclose to the auditor attitudes and convictions.
- They permit the auditor to counter arguments and provide additional information that his audience may require.
- They can bring out inaccuracies in the auditor's thinking.
- They can develop improved rapport with the auditee.

Oral reports should not be off the cuff. They should be prepared with care. They should show that the auditor has done his homework — that he did not arrive for a rambling discussion.

That does not mean that the auditor should make gold-plated presentations that go beyond the needs of the subject or the audience. It is possible to present them economically without the appearance of excessively expensive preparation.

Desk-top flip charts for small groups can be eminently effective. The charts can be prepared without too much effort and are extremely effective in:

- Keeping the auditor in charge of the meeting.
- Keeping the auditees focused on what is being said.
- Keeping the auditor himself on track.

The flip charts can be prepared on 8½" x 11" cards and lettered free-hand with felt pens. They should not get wordy, because that only serves to distract attention rather than focus it.

One means of achieving brevity is to print the material first on 3" x 5" slips of paper. There just is not sufficient room for extended comments on them.

A series of charts for the audit of the Bethany supply department giving background, pointing out the problem, and recommending action, might be as follows:

1. Authorization
   - Board of Directors — minutes 3/7/XX
   - Mfr. small tools
   - Supply department —
     Local purchases
     Purchases through central office

2. Objective
   - Keep production lines stocked
   - Keep inventories minimal

3. Conditions
   - Lines well stocked
   - Unneeded stock ordered

4. Procedures
   - Permanent inventory records
   - Record returns

5. Findings
   - Returns not recorded
   - Excessive purchases — $75,000

6. Cause
   - New employees
   - Inadequate job instructions
   - Insufficient monitoring

7. Recommendation
   - Update records
   - Prepare job instructions
   - Monitor process
   - Provide feedback to manager

The informal, desk-top presentation may not always suit the auditor's needs. He may be called upon to make formal oral presentations. His audience may be at a level where he must give considerable thought to his talk and prepare carefully for it. This should not be regarded as a catastrophe — but rather as a splendid opportunity to present another facet of his character: the articulate, practiced speaker.

These presentations deserve effort, and the results should reflect the care with which they were put together. Here are some of the considerations the auditor should take into account.

Flexibility

Keep your options open as you proceed toward your oral presentation. Be capable of cutting the presentation short. Be prepared to skip material, amplify material, and do whatever else is necessary to keep the listener interested.

Conciseness

Wordiness makes the listener's mind wander. Do not embellish or amplify beyond what is essential. Do not bring in what is not germane. When you see your listeners looking at their watches or drumming on the table with their fingers, be prepared to abbreviate the talk.

Completeness

At the same time, do not leave a subject until you have answered the obvious questions. When you say "considerable amount," the audience will not be happy until you tell them just how much. When you say "long time," they will want to know how long. When you say "a number of errors," they will want to know what that number is. When you talk about a condition, they will want to know its cause and its effect.

Currency

Just before the meeting, the auditor should try to get a reading on current conditions. There is nothing more satisfying to a questioner than to hear a response like: "I checked on that just this morning. The condition is still the way I described it."

Preparation

Careful, methodical preparation for the big day will pay off. As in any other endeavor, there are techniques that can help the tyro and remind the expert. Here are some of them:[6]

Establish objectives. Make sure you have determined precisely what your objectives are in this oral presentation. Is it to answer questions? Is it to show progress? Is it to show results? Is it to persuade and motivate toward a certain course of conduct? The objectives must be known and fixed firmly in mind. If not, the presentation may have a tendency to wander from its path and confuse the audience.

---

[6]Seeman, P. G., "Effective Briefing or Oral Presentation," Internal Auditing Research Study, Lockheed-California Company, 1970.

Analyze the audience. A technically perfect presentation may fail its objective if it is directed toward an audience whose likes, dislikes, and backgrounds have not been considered and taken into account. As you prepare your presentation ask yourself these questions:

- What does the audience know about the subject? How much background do they need? How much time can they comfortably give me?
- How receptive will they be to my ideas? How much softening up do they need? How persuasive must I be?
- What are their interests?
    Cost savings?
    Work reduction?
    Staff reduction?
    Improved accuracy?
    Improved schedules?
    Improved controls?
    Greater visibility and feedback?
- What should I avoid for this audience? What are their known biases?

Prepare a preliminary plan. No matter how rough it may be, put something down in writing. It will clarify and order your thinking:

- A title
- The objectives
- The audience
- The main ideas
    The sub ideas
- The order of presentation
- The form of the visual aids

Select the material. Determine what is pertinent. Eliminate what is irrelevant. Make sure there are no gaps. Consider the transitions from one thought to another. In selecting the material, use these criteria:

- Will it contribute to the purpose or objective of the meeting?
- Will it clarify the main ideas?
- Does it relate to this audience?

Organize the material. There are many methods of organizing material. But whatever method you use, the material *must* be organized. Good organization shines through and commands respect. Poor organization casts a gloomy pall and makes the audience restless. So you must decide early on just what form of organization you want:

- Chronological?
- Sequential?
- Comparison or contrast?
- Cause and effect?
- Theory versus practice ?

Make sure the message is clear.   Any presentation is wasted if the message does not come across clearly to the audience. Make sure the audience knows what you're trying to say and what you want of them. Keep in mind the many ways available to clarify the message and the material.

- Analysis
- Definition
- Facts and figures
- Illustrations
- Statistics
- Authority
- Restatement

Plan visual aids.   Visual aids have proved extremely important in getting the message across. They have many benefits: They keep the speaker on track. They save time in getting to the point. They focus attention. They support and clarify ideas. They can clearly show trends and relationships where purely oral statements cause confusion and make the listener struggle with too many concepts at once. They help the listener understand, retain data, and stay interested.

Visual aids include:

- Chalk boards
- Easel displays. Either the notebook-sized easel, previously discussed; the magnetic slap board; or the tripod which holds large cards or sheets.
- Projection equipment:
    Overhead
    35 mm. slides
    Movie: Audio-visual
- Actual physical objects

The visual aids can be used in a variety of ways. The speaker may use any or a combination of the following means:

- Words and phrases
- Graphs
- Tabulations
- Sketches and drawings
- Diagrams and flow charts
- Photographs

Practice the presentation. Practicing the presentation before the meeting is good insurance. If possible, practice in front of several other auditors to get their reactions and suggestions. Since they are auditors, it is safe to say they will have a number of comments and recommendations.

Practice builds confidence as the material becomes more familiar. It will point up flaws and gaps. It will improve the physical handling of the visual aids. It will help timing. The matters to work on include:

- Pauses
- Voice intensity
- Inflections
- Gestures
- Facial expressions (Speaking before a mirror can be invaluable.)
- Body movement
- Summaries

Prepare for questions and answers. If you are going to entertain questions, alert the audience. They will then be prepared to note their questions as the presentation moves along. Show that you are receptive to the questions and anxious to hear them. In answering them, try to be accurate and complete, without being wordy. If you don't know the answer, say so; but add that you will try to get it. When you answer a question, watch the questioner's face to make sure that he appears to be satisfied. If not, ask if his question has been answered. Particularly before large groups, repeat or rephrase the question to make sure you are answering what the questioner had in mind and that the rest of the audience has heard it.

In Sum

S. H. Thomas[7] sums up what the auditor should be concerned about in his oral presentations, as follows:

[7]Thomas, S. H., "Improving the Oral Communication of Internal Auditors," *The Internal Auditor*, Spring 1966, p. 69.

- Think more about your listeners than yourself.

- Cultivate a "lean" economical style — no needless repetition, no evasions, no weakening of force.

- Carefully use transitions to carry the audience from one thought to another.

- Avoid ambiguities. (The audience will be chewing on them as the presentation moves to other things.)

- Speak loudly enough to be heard, clearly enough to be understood, smoothly enough to be welcome.

GOOD WRITING

Let us emphasize once more that good writing calls for good thinking. There is no escaping it. If the auditor's concepts are confused and tangled, if his thoughts are muddy, and if he has established no logical relation between cause and effect, between the important and the insignificant, then the report that rises from this accumulation is bound to be an ineffectual piece of work. So before he starts writing he must straighten out his thinking, put things in place, and get his findings in proper perspective.

Outlines

One way of sorting things out, making sure of a logical and reasonable flow of ideas, is through the report outline. And the drafting of the outline is simplified if the auditing department has developed a reasonably standardized format for its regular reports.

Standardization spells economy. It makes the writer and the reader feel comfortable. Both know the general path the report will take. Filling in the information needed to fit a particular set of circumstances becomes simplified to a considerable extent.

Outlining takes discipline. We have seen many an auditor, instructed to outline his report, present a completed draft with the statement "I started to outline, but when I began writing I just couldn't stop." The compassionate reviewer winds up outlining the report himself. The hard-nosed (and probably the more effective) reviewer tosses the draft back with a terse comment: "When I ask for an outline, I want an outline."

And what the reviewer really wants is a crisp, simple skeleton of the report — a word or a phrase — to make sure that the thoughts flow logically and that nothing has been omitted.

A sample outline, expanding on the Bethany audit and employing the report segments previously discussed, is as follows:

SUMMARY

A. Foreword
   1. First regular audit
   2. Covered supply department
   3. Procures, maintains supplies
      a. Locally
      b. Through headquarters
   4. Total value — $2,500,000

B. Purpose
   Evaluate:
   1. Procurement
   2. Physical inventory
   3. Records

C. Scope
   1. Test purchase documents
   2. Observe inventory-taking
   3. Examine records

D. Opinion
   1. Satisfactory on —
      a. Procurements
      b. Physical inventories
   2. Unsatisfactory on —
      a. Records

E. Findings
   1. Procurements
      a. Written bids
      b. Approvals
      c. Follow-up system
   2. Physical inventories
      a. Security
      b. Arrangement of stock
      c. Bin cards
   3. Records
      a. Perpetual inventory records
      b. Returns from production
         (1) Not recorded
         (2) Overprocurement

DETAILS

A. Summary statement re overprocurement

B. Procedures — criteria
   Enter returns on records

C. Results of tests — facts
   Returns not entered

    D. Effect
       Overprocurement — $75,000
    E. Cause
       Employees not instructed
       Inadequate supervision
    F. Recommendation
       Update records
       Issue instructions
       Monitor performance
    G. Action
       All steps taken

Prior Reports

The auditor should not overlook or fail to take counsel from any prior reports. Much thought probably went into those reports. Shades of meaning were considered. Difficult wording may have been drafted and polished. Reporting policies were probably observed. A proper format was no doubt employed.

But the prior report should be relied upon with discretion. Conditions may have changed. Procedures may have been revised. Reporting styles may have been amended. With these caveats, the prior report may be a great time saver.

The First Draft

No writer who ever held pen or sat before a typewriter did not at one time or another get stuck. His gears slip into neutral and he does not move. The auditor, too, may wait for inspiration, for that perfect beginning which will give character and interest to all that follows.

He may wait forever before that sterling sentence forms itself on paper. Somehow he must develop the discipline that says: "I must write. Therefore I shall."

Andre Gide, in his *Journal,* June 4, 1930, said, "Too often I wait for the sentence to finish taking shape in my mind before setting it down. It is better to seize it by the end that first offers itself, head or foot, though not knowing the rest, then pull: the rest will follow."

The writer therefore needs some spur to getting words down on paper. The outline helps. It shows where to begin and what will come after. The next step is to boldly violate the purity of the blank page with the thrust of the pencil. Some mark, some line, some word. Perhaps the title. Perhaps a heading. But something. That will prime the pump and get the words flowing.

The material is there. The working papers are full of facts and figures. All it takes is a dogged persistence for the draft to grow. Little matter that the first words are trite or poorly phrased. No one waits to cart them away and put them in print. They will be revised and reshaped before they reach their final form. For there is no such thing as good writing. Just good rewriting. The first draft is a lump of clay to be pummeled and mauled — to be cut away here and added to there until it emerges as a monument to the auditor's persistence.

When the first draft has been written, hacked at, and interlineated, have it typed or retyped. In the interim the ideas within the subconscious will marinate and become more palatable. Then when the new draft is received and perused, new thoughts, better thoughts, and better phrases will come. The draft will be seen with new eyes. New ways of getting ideas across will emerge. And gradually the report will take the desired form and give the hoped-for message.

Then, after dozens and dozens of painstakingly written reports, the writing improves, the chore becomes less painful, and the product becomes more professional. But at the beginning the answer lies in good field work, a well-structured outline, and dogged persistence.

Language

No language is easy to master. It takes a long, hard apprenticeship and a flair for words. But as in any craft there are techniques that keep the writing from being inept and amateurish. Three basic rules can help any report writer: Keep your writing simple. Keep your writing clear. Keep your writing alive. And within the compass of these rules are a number of subrules which, if followed, can reward the efforts of even the poorest of writers. We shall now amplify these rules.

Keep your writing simple.

- Use short sentences. It is easy for the reader to get lost in the labyrinth of a long sentence. But add some well-constructed long sentences for variety.

- Use common words. Do not try to send the reader to the dictionary. If an unusual word is the only one that fits, define it.

- Omit needless words.

- Do not include any unnecessary ideas, phrases, or words in a sentence or a paragraph. Keep all the thoughts relevant and related.

- Make the ideas flow in logical succession. Do not force the reader to rearrange the ideas in his mind.

- Avoid contradictory ideas, or thoughts that violate logic. What is said should make sense.

- Avoid beginning a sentence with verb forms. "The completion of our audit occurred in September" is improved by saying "We completed our audit in September."

Keep your writing clear.

- Write to communicate your findings and express your ideas, not to impress someone with your learning.

- Use common words.

Don't use:	When you can use:
terminate	*stop, end*
optimum	*best*
institute	*begin*
initiate	*start*
initial	*first*
purchase	*buy*
facilitate	*ease, simplify*
demonstrate	*show*
subsequent	*next*
expedite	*hasten, speed*
prior to	*before*
numerous, innumerable	*many*
velocity	*speed*
accordingly, consequently	*so*
furthermore	*then, also*
nevertheless	*but, however*
adhere	*stick, follow*
likewise	*and, also*
conducted, effected	*made*
utilize	*use*
informed, indicated	*told*
implemented	*carried out*
reflect	*show*

- Consider the reader's experience. Give him enough information to supply background, but not so much as to belabor the obvious or be patronizing.

■ Express coordinate ideas in similar form. Keep related expressions in parallel. Switching between different forms for comparable thoughts troubles and confuses the reader.

Not: We made our audit by observing receipts, examining documentation, and we interviewed inspectors.

But: *We observed receipts, examined documentation, and interviewed inspectors.*

■ Make it clear which of two or more things just mentioned is being referred to or discussed.

■ Define clearly any technical or unfamiliar subject.

■ Make it clear *when* something happened and *where* it happened.

■ Be specific about quantities. A "substantial percentage" is not as clear as 20 out of 50.

■ Use the right word. Rarely do two English words mean the same. Use the one that best describes what you have in mind.

■ Avoid ambiguous words and phrases. Good writing should be susceptible to only one meaning. If a word or phrase can possibly be misunderstood it most likely will be.

■ Put words in the right place.
"We only wish to improve procedures" is different from "we wish only to improve procedures."

■ Do not omit important details.
If a finding states "The checks did not bear two signatures," it should be shown by what authority two signatures are required.

■ Carry out promises. If an introductory sentence says "We shall discuss three controls over the accuracy of engineering drawings," make sure all three are discussed. On the other hand, if a heading states *"Accuracy of Engineering Drawings,"* do not discuss under that heading the timeliness with which drawings are prepared.

■ Lists of items should include words belonging to the same categories.

■ Do not use the same word in different senses in the same sentence. Avoid, for example, "There was a material amount of rubbish mixed with the scrap material."

■ Avoid ambiguous references. Make sure there can be no doubt about what the referent is when you use such words as "it," "they," "this," "that," "these," and "which."

- Avoid dangling modifiers.

Not: Having discussed our finding, the manager took corrective action.

But: *After we discussed our finding with him, the manager took corrective action.*

Keep your writing alive.

- Use action words. They command attention. They give writing spice. The active voice is preferable, but the passive may sometimes be used for variety.
- Use words that draw pictures. Avoid vague and fuzzy generalities. "Envelopes and writing paper" draws a clearer picture than "stationery."
- Avoid sentences that begin with "As a result of," "Although," "Despite," "In view of," and the like. The sentences tend to get long and dreary.

PHYSICAL CHARACTERISTICS

Appearance

Like any other product on the market, the report should be attractively packaged. It should have a dignified and tasteful appearance. At the same time it should not indicate excessive expense in the preparation. An expensive-looking package is inconsistent with exhortations by the auditor to the addressee to practice greater economy.

Most companies follow fairly consistent formats in their report presentation — consistency in covers and distribution sheets. Some of the reports we have seen are transmitted by memoranda. Others have the distribution sheet as the first page. Some are placed within covers with varying types of bindings.

In the main, audit reports show a good deal of "white space." Paragraphs are generally short. There is an abundant use of headings to indicate what follows and to break up the serried lines.

Some reports are in double space; but the majority of those we have seen are in single space. For still others, the summaries are double spaced and the detail is single spaced.

Length

Reports come in all lengths. But long reports are generally summarized to give executive management the gist of the audit results. Longer reports will generally have tables of contents to make their contents more accessible.

Signatures

Most reports are signed by the auditor and by the head of the auditing department. The signature may appear on the transmittal memorandum, at the end of the summary, or at the end of the entire report. Accepted practice most often calls for the signature to follow rather than to precede any opinions, thereby implying a certification of the auditor's conclusions.

Distribution

Report distributions run the gamut. They can be addressed solely to the executive to whom the manager of auditing reports or they may go to every manager who is in any way involved in the matters reported. In between can be found a host of variations.

Some distributions merely show names of distributees. Others show the departments of the managers and indicate whether the report was reviewed in draft with them and whether they are being asked to take corrective action.

Ratings

Some companies have adopted a plan which calls for an adjective or numerical rating for each organization audited. This idea faces opposition from many auditors. They feel that it is very difficult for the auditor to produce logically comparable ratings for the many diverse operations they review.[8]

In most instances, the rating would merely represent the auditor's subjective opinion, vulnerable to dispute and argument. To be reasonably objective, the following factors should apply:

■ The operations to be rated should be similar. Only under such conditions could standards be developed which are equally applicable to the different operations and equally applied by different auditors in the same auditing department.

■ The conditions should be quantifiable — numbers of errors and differences in inventories are examples. Where audit opinions become the significant factor, ratings may be difficult to apply fairly. This is particularly true in large audit organizations with many auditors, each with different views and audit approaches.

In one company, the first item in the report is a rating, (A, B, C, D) for the current audit and, for purposes of comparison, the

---

[8]Research Report 10, *op. cit.*, p. 22.

rating for the previous audit. An explanation follows these ratings. For example:

Rating for this audit	B Minus
Rating for last audit (June 28, 19XX)	B Plus

This unsatisfactory rating shows a serious deterioration in controls, irregularities in the handling of estimates, and a poor credit routine performance. In additon, the work in a number of other sections is far from satisfactory.

In another firm, Audit Rating Sheets are included in the reports of wholesale sales regions. The sheet lists the activities to be examined and shows for each activity the number of points which indicate the standard for top performance. Another column shows the number of points assigned in the current audit. The third and last column shows the percentage relationship between the current rating and the standard. An overall rating is then developed and is reported in the first paragraph of the transmittal letter.

Titles

Titles of reports deserve careful consideration. They should be sufficiently descriptive to convey clearly the subject matter of the report. They should not be so long as to be a report in themselves. Yet they should not imply coverage that is not contemplated.

For example:

- "Review of Warranties" — This title is so broad that it can be construed to cover both warranties to customers and warranties from suppliers.

- "Review of Warranties from Suppliers" — This title restricts the field, but implies coverage of warranties on productive equipment as well as non-productive equipment, such as typewriters and other office equipment.

- "Reviews of Warranties from Suppliers of Productive Equipment" — This title may accurately convey the entire extent of the audit coverage.

EDITING REPORTS

Reviews

In most companies audit reports are edited with great care. They are drafted by the auditor and then reviewed in detail by an editor, by a supervisor, and/or by an audit manager. This review is made to put reported findings in perspective, to make sure the company's policies are followed, and to ensure accuracy, logic, and acceptable style.

The review may be a training ground for the auditor. It should point up any weaknesses in thought or in the development of facts. It should highlight the matters the auditor ought to keep in mind in his next audit. The reviewer owes it to the auditor to explain the changes and improvements he makes — so that weaknesses can be strengthened. The reviewer should have, therefore, a thorough understanding of the factors that contribute to poor reporting.

Basically, the reviewer is concerned with the report's readability, correctness, and appropriateness. Certainly, the report writer is concerned with the same qualities, and to some extent these qualities were touched on earlier in this chapter. But the need for excellence in finished reports is so vital, that these matters will be reemphasized here.

Readability. The reviewer will look to see how clearly the report will get across to the reader. Does it lay proper foundation and background? Are the sentences well constructed? Are the paragraphs lacking in topic sentences and are they overlong? Is the language clear and free from jargon? Do the thoughts flow freely and logically? Is the message clear?

Correctness. Are the grammar and punctuation correct? Are the department's reporting policies followed? Are the thoughts properly connected? Are ideas and conclusions summarized, yet properly supported? Does the report stick to its purpose? Does it make use of all the significant data accumulated in the field work? Do the working papers support the reported statements?

Appropriateness. Is the tone tactful? Are opinions separated from facts? Is the attitude objective? Are minor deficiencies given too much space — and are major deficiencies given too little? Does the report do a proper job on the ideas that need selling, while not wasting time on matters of little import?

★   ★   ★

Reviewers can use the "performance inventory" which follows in evaluating report drafts. The inventory identifies common reporting mistakes. It clarifies for the reviewer precisely what it is about a particular report that he does not like. When the auditor asks in outrage, "What do you mean, I can't write," the reviewer can answer with authority.[9]

---

[9]Fielden, J. S., "What Do You Mean I Can't Write," *Harvard Business Review*, May-June 1964, p. 147.

WRITTEN PERFORMANCE INVENTORY

I. READABILITY

READER'S LEVEL
- Too specialized in approach
- Assumes too great a knowledge of subject
- So underestimates the reader that it belabors the obvious

SENTENCE CONSTRUCTION
- Unnecessarily long in difficult material
- Subject-verb-object word order too rarely used
- Choppy, overly simple style (in simple material)

PARAGRAPH CONSTRUCTION
- Lack of topic sentences
- Too many ideas in single paragraph
- Too long

FAMILIARITY OF WORDS
- Inappropriate jargon
- Pretentious language
- Unnecessarily abstract

READER DIRECTION
- Lack of "framing" (i.e., failure to tell the reader about purpose and direction of forthcoming discussion)
- Inadequate transitions between paragraphs, thoughts, and conclusions
- Absence of subconclusions to summarize reader's progress at end of divisions in the discussion

FOCUS
- Unclear as to subject of communication
- Unclear as to purpose of message

II. CORRECTNESS

MECHANICS
- Shaky grammar
- Faulty punctuation

FORMAT
- Careless appearance of documents
- Use of unacceptable form

COHERENCE
- Sentences seem awkward owing to illogical and ungrammatical yoking of unrelated ideas
- Failure to develop a logical progression of ideas through coherent, logically juxtaposed paragraphs

SUPPORTING DETAIL
- Inadequate support for recommendations
- Too much undigested detail for busy executive

PREPARATION
- Inadequate thought given to purpose of communication prior to its final completion
- Inadequate preparation or use of data
- Failure to stick to job assigned

ANALYSIS
- Superficial examination of data leading to unconscious overlooking of important evidence
- Failure to draw obvious conclusions from data presented
- Presentation of conclusions unjustified by evidence
- Failure to qualify tenuous assertions
- Failure to identify and justify assumptions used
- Bias, conscious or unconscious, which leads to distorted interpretation of data

III. APPROPRIATENESS

TACT
- Failure to recognize differences in position between writer and receiver
- Impolitic tone — too brusque, argumentative, or insulting
- Context includes unnecessary sharpness or implications
- Overbearing attitude toward subordinates
- Insulting and/or personal references

OPINION
- Adequate research but too great an intrusion of opinions
- Too few facts (and too little research) to entitle drawing of conclusions
- Opinions not clearly identified as opinions

ATTITUDE
- Too obvious a desire to please recipients
- Too defensive in face of authority
- Too fearful of recipients to be able to do best work

PERSUASIVENESS
- Seems more convincing than facts warrant
- Seems less convincing than facts warrant
- Too obvious an attempt to sell ideas
- Lacks action-orientation and managerial viewpoint
- Too blunt an approach where subtlety and finesse called for
- Failure to identify cost/benefit relationship of recommendations

Proofreading

After the report has been reviewed with the auditee — a matter which is covered in the chapter which follows — it will be put in final form. It must then be scrubbed clean of errors. It is unfortunate but true that one relatively insignificant mechanical flaw — a typographical or spelling error — can cruelly blemish and downgrade a well-written, soundly documented report. The very nature of audit reports — finding fault, exposing deficiencies, suggesting changes — magnifies in the eyes of the reader any defects within the report itself.

Typographical errors and other minor mistakes divert the reader's attention from the text and thereby lessen the force of the subject matter. The reader may begin thinking about the writer rather than about what is written. He may begin to wonder whether errors in the text may be an indication of substantive blunders in the documents behind it.

The internal auditor must therefore be exceptionally careful not only in what he says and how he says it, but also in how successfully he has purged his report of niggling errors.

This may not be easy to do. Sometimes we cannot trust our own eyes. In reading our own reports we would *like* to see them without flaws. As a result our eyes may slip over errors because we don't really want to see them.

Also, the intelligence that makes us good internal auditors may be the very thing that blinds us to the blemishes in our own work. The more intelligent a person is the fewer details he needs to perceive the whole. Hence the less likely he is to plod doggedly through the individual words and letters that express a thought — a thought which he has grasped at a glance, or with which he is completely familiar.

The auditor must therefore slow himself down and follow a careful regimen before signing his report and sending it off to the addressees. And the audit manager should establish a routine which makes sure all reasonable steps have been taken to ensure complete accuracy. The following routine can prove helpful:

Comparison.   After it has been typed, the report should be compared with the draft by reading it aloud. The typist who typed the final report should not be the one who holds the report. She should read the rough draft and someone else should read the final report — it is hard to detect a flaw in one's own offspring. Both people who do the proofing should initial the report or a form prepared for the purpose, to evidence their work.

Reference check. The auditor should then "tick" on a carbon of the final report every factual statement, every number, every title, every date. The tick marks bear evidence that each item has been referenced back to basic data — to directives, organization charts, working papers, computations, and the like. The auditor will be helped if his draft carries marginal references to his working papers.

The whole picture. The auditor should then focus his attention on the report's overall organization. This becomes quite simple if he spreads out the pages of the report before him like a game of solitaire. Then, any inconsistencies in format, headings, and indentation will practically leap out at him. It will also simplify the verification of references within the report or between the report and the supporting schedules.

The auditor should then read the report for sense and flow. How often what sounded completely logical and reasonable and what appeared in perfect sequence, when read in rough draft, assumes a most discouraging aspect in final form. The auditor who does his reading aloud may be benefitted by being slowed down and by hearing how the report may sound to others.

The detailed picture. After he has satisfied himself with the organization, sense, and flow of the report, the auditor should then focus on detecting the maddening typographical errors that so easily elude the eye. Here he had better have some assistance: Some device to force him to focus, to keep him from reading too rapidly, to help him concentrate on letters and not on word pictures.

One such device can be made from a sheet of blank paper or cardboard. Cut a strip from the center of the sheet — a strip that is long enough and wide enough to disclose one line of type, but no more.

Lay this scanner over the line and read each line slowly, undistracted by the lines before or after it. Finally, if the report is of such significance that a single typographical or mechanical error is utterly unthinkable, read the report *backwards* through the scanner, thereby focusing on individual words and letters, undiverted by the sense of what was written.

Included in the techniques of the professional proofreader is a mental listing of the kinds of errors that most easily escape detection. With these in the back of his mind, the auditor is less likely to overlook them.

Some of the major ones are: Letters omitted or added, words spelled two ways in the same report, missing or superfluous commas, inconsistent compounding or capitalization, transposition of letters, missing closing parentheses or quotation marks, headings having no relation to the subject matter, lack of agreement between subject and predicate or between pronoun and antecedent, and using the singular and plural when referring to the same noun.

These are a few of the many errors to watch for. Some examples follow:

- Letters omitted (omited) or added (ommitted)
- Doublets or repeaters (alllocable)
- Words spelled two ways in the same report (travelled, traveled)
- Improper or inconsistent capitalization
- Incorrect indentation
- Wrong division of words
- Transposition of letters (form for from)
- Inconsistent compounding ("14-foot extrusions and 7 gauge sheet stock")
- Poor spacing (f. o. b. should be f.o.b.)
- Headings that do not relate to the subject matter
- Showing open quotes or parentheses, but no closed quotes or parentheses.
- Disagreement between subject and predicate in person or number
- Disagreement between pronoun and its antecedent in person or number
- Pronoun with unclear referent
- Using "above" or "below" when matter referred to is on another page (Use foregoing, previously, following.)
- Day of week does not agree with date
- Incorrect use of homonyms (principal, principle; compliment, complement; course, coarse; stationary, stationery)
- Using hyphens between adverbs and adjectives (recently-revised instructions)
- Using percent and % both ways in same text
- Failing to place commas before *and* after etc., e.g., i.e., when they are in the middle of a sentence
- Disagreement between the total of a list of items and the specific number mentioned (we have discussed the following five deficiency findings, etc.)

- Failing to put words in quotations that might otherwise be misunderstood (removing the *bugs* from the system)
- Using both the singular and the plural when referring to the same noun

Joseph Lasky's monumental work on proofreading gives many more.[10]

Style Manual

Every auditing department should have a style manual. It may be developed within the department or it may be a standard work. The Government Printing Office Style Manual is a respected and comprehensive text.

The cost of a good manual can easily be recovered by eliminating the time spent in arguments and differences of opinion on mechanical matters. For those departments embarking on the preparation of a style manual, here are some of the matters that should be included:

A. Report Responsibilities
 1. Preparation
 2. Client Reviews
 3. Distribution
 4. Progress Reports
 5. Checking and Proofreading

B. Report Format
 1. Distribution Sheet
 2. Report Segments
 3. Report Addenda
  a. Exhibits
  b. Appendices
  c. Schedules
 4. Elements of Style
  a. Abbreviations
  b. Apostrophes
  c. Capitalization
  d. Citations
  e. Colons
  f. Commas
  g. Connectives
  h. Dashes
  i. Hyphens

---

[10]Lasky, Joseph, "Proofreading and Copy-Preparation," New York, Mentor Press, 1941, pp. 88-176.

      j. Jargon
      k. Numbers
      l. Paragraphs
      m. Plurals
      n. Prepositions
      o. Quoted Material
      p. Semicolons
      q. Spelling
      r. Miscellaneous
  C. Report Examples

SAMPLE REPORTS

There are audit reports and there are audit reports. They come in every conceivable size and style. There is not, and there probably never will be, a standard form. Some take their present form from a gradual evolution. Others retain their present form because that is what people have become accustomed to and are reluctant to see changed.

We believe that the internal audit report is much too important a document to go on in an accustomed form year after year without considering improvements. New needs, new technology, new insights into what will attract or influence the reader should be periodically evaluated by the audit staff. Not change for change's sake. But change which will further management's needs and the auditor's objectives.

The audit report samples shown as Exhibits 11-1 through 11-7 (appended to this chapter) have been taken from the examples furnished to us by a broad spectrum of audit organizations. They point to interesting variances. It is difficult to say what is good and what is bad. Evidently all of the reports shown are doing their jobs since they come from well-established, forward-looking audit organizations. Each one selected, however, is directed toward a subject considered properly within the purview of modern internal auditing.

Some of the reports have been reproduced in their entirety. From others we have selected representative excerpts. In each of them it can be seen that the auditor is concerned with promoting improved control, improved operations, and improved profits.

★   ★   ★

Research Committee Report No. 10, Internal Audit Reporting Practices, The Institute of Internal Auditors, provides a wide range of reporting practices. The report prints excerpts from 13 reports from diverse businesses and industries. The excerpts illustrate varying reporting styles and methods.

SUMMARY

Reports are the auditor's opportunity to get management's attention. The auditor has an admirable story to tell; he should not throw that opportunity away through inept or unprofessional reporting.

Reports will be evaluated according to their accuracy, clarity, conciseness, timeliness, and tone. Whatever their formats may be — and these formats come in many styles — they will include one or more of these elements: A summary, a foreword or introduction, a purpose, a scope, an opinion, and findings. Statements of findings should themselves contain certain elements. For satisfactory findings: authority, objectives, and conditions. For unsatisfactory findings: a summary, criteria, facts, effect, cause, and recommendation. Graphics can spice a report and add needed illustrations.

An informal reporting system, to supplement his formal system, can be a great help to the auditor. It permits prompt and easy communication. Oral reports are of equal importance. They too present an opportunity for the auditor to display his wares, and they should be prepared with care.

Good writing takes practice and training. But any writing can be improved by certain techniques: Outlines to ensure logical flow. Practice to keep writing simple, clear, and alive.

Reports should present an attractive appearance. They should be easy to read. The auditor should be on the constant lookout for ways of improving his reports and of making reading them an interesting rather than a dreary task.

Reports need careful editing for readability, correctness, and appropriateness. And the auditing organization should install a rigorous proofreading routine to make sure no errors creep into the final copy.

The chapter concludes with examples of a variety of forms and types of written reports.

Exhibit 11-1. AIRPLANE MANUFACTURER

This report covers a number of the multitude of activities carried out by a highway transportation department. The report is reproduced in its entirety to show the overall structure of the report.

The distribution sheet lists all the people having a need to know about the report. It shows with whom the report was reviewed in draft. It also shows who is to take corrective action and who is responsible that action is taken.

The report is in three major parts: A highlight section. A summary which briefly lays the groundwork for the report and then provides a statement of purpose, an opinion of the overall operation, and a brief description of the findings — both satisfactory and unsatisfactory — relating to the matters set forth in the purpose. A supplement which gives the details of the matters requiring corrective action and then summarizes the findings at the end.

Each section is for a different level of reader. The highlight section gives the busy executive an abbreviated commentary on the audit results.

The summary report carries enough information to give the reader at the middle management level all the information needed, in order to know about: (1) the subject under review; the thrust of the audit; the auditor's opinion and an identification of the most serious deficiency, and a brief overview of the audit results.

The summary report is signed by the auditor in charge, his supervisor, and the manager of the internal auditing department.

The supplement to the report is chiefly for operating management and discusses deficiency findings only. Each finding is preceded by headnotes which summarize the deficient conditions. The headnotes are repeated under the summary of findings for ready reference. This summary shows which findings still need action and to whom they are referred for action. The discussions of the findings set forth the conditions, their significance, and the suggested action.

XYZ CORPORATION
INTERNAL AUDIT REPORT

Audit Project R7X-18   Date: August 26, 197X

DISTRIBUTION	TAKE ACTION	SECURE ACTION	INFOR- MATION	REVIEWED PRIOR TO RELEASE
President			X	
Executive Vice President		X	X	
Vice President-Controller			X	
Director of Materiel		X		X
Manager, Procurement	X			X
Manager, Highway Transportation Department	X			X
Director of Industrial Relations				X
Chief, Security Division				X
Chief, Plant Protection				X

Exhibit 11-1. (Cont.)

AUDIT HIGHLIGHTS

Highway Transportation Department
(A Regularly Scheduled Review)

Prior Audit:	No deficiency findings.
Audit Coverage:	1. Equipment maintenance and vehicle dispatching
	2. Fuel, parts, and repair services
	3. General administrative activities.
Overall Opinion:	In general, the operation was functioning in a reasonably satisfactory manner.

We did find some control weaknesses. The most serious involved the lack of separation of duties in the procurement of parts and services. Steps are being taken to correct these weaknesses.

Despite the weaknesses, however, the department's activities were being performed satisfactorily.

Executive
Action Required: None.

SUMMARY REPORT

Foreword

This report covers the results of our regularly scheduled review of the activities of the Highway Transportation Department. Our last review of the Department's activities disclosed no deficiencies.

The department's primary responsibilities are (1) to transport personnel and materials, and (2) to maintain and repair automotive equipment.

At the time of our review there were about 50 employees assigned to the department. Operating costs (not including labor) for equipment rental, repair parts and services, and fuel and oil, are projected to reach about $900,000 for 19XX. Mileage for the year will total about 5 million miles.

During this review we issued one progress report to bring to management's attention certain matters requiring prompt corrective action.

Purpose

We have made an examination of the Highway Transportation Department's principal activities to determine whether they were being controlled adequately and effectively. In performing our review, we examined the system of controls concerned with the following activities:

1. Equipment maintenance and vehicle dispatching, including (a) scheduling preventive maintenance inspections, (b) performing regular maintenance and repairs, and (c) dispatching cars and trucks.
2. Ordering, receiving, and disbursing fuel and parts and obtaining automotive repair services.
3. General administrative activities concerned with (a) property accountability, (b) plant protection, (c) accident reporting, (d) insurable value reporting, (e) gasoline credit cards, and (f) petty cash.

Exhibit 11-1. (Cont.)

Opinions and Findings

We formed the opinion that adequate controls had been provided over the activities we reviewed, except for a lack of separation of duties in the procurement of parts and services. Three other matters of lesser significance likewise involved control weaknesses.

We also formed the opinion that, despite the control weaknesses we had detected, the functions we reviewed were being performed in a generally satisfactory manner.

Our conclusions and findings on each of the three groups of activities covered in our examination are summarized in the following paragraphs.

Equipment Maintenance and Vehicle Dispatching

Adequate controls had been provided which were designed to make sure that (1) automotive equipment would receive inspection and preventive maintenance in accordance with the manufacturers' recommendations, and (2) truck and car dispatching would be accomplished in accordance with established procedures.

We examined preventive maintenance reports and related control records and satisfied ourselves that maintenance was being properly scheduled, monitored, and performed. We also examined documentation supporting vehicle dispatching and observed the dispatching operations; we concluded that dispatching was being adequately controlled and performed.

Ordering, Receiving, and Disbursing Fuel and Parts, and Obtaining Vehicle Repair Services

Controls had been provided which were designed to make sure that fuel, parts, and outside repair services were (1) ordered when needed, (2) recorded upon receipt, and (3) properly approved for payment; and that the disbursement of fuel and parts was adequately documented.

We did find, however, that there was (1) a lack of appropriate separation of duties in the procurement of parts and services, and (2) what we considered to be inadequate surveillance over the withdrawal of gasoline and oil by vehicle operators. These matters are discussed more fully in the Supplement to this Summary Report.

We examined representative samples of (1) reports, records, and blanket purchase orders covering the procurement and receipt of supplies and services; and (2) the logs and records covering fuel withdrawals. Despite the control weaknesses referred to, we concluded on the basis of our tests that the functions were being performed in a reasonably satisfactory manner. We made an analysis of the fuel pump meter records and compared them with the amounts of fuel recorded by vehicle operators. The results showed little variance between the two, indicating that fuel withdrawals were in the main being properly recorded.

General Administrative Activities

Controls had been devised to provide assurance that (1) property accountability records would be complete and accurate, (2) accidents to licensed vehicles would be reported promptly, (3) gasoline credit cards would be used for the purpose issued and only when vehicles were operated away from company-owned fuel supplies, and (4) petty cash would be properly safeguarded and used only for the purpose for which the petty cash fund was established.

Exhibit 11-1. (Cont.)

It did seem to us that the area in which Highway Transportation was located was inadequately protected, and we did find that there was no provision for reporting the insurable values of repair parts inventories. These matters are also discussed further in the Supplement.

We tested, among other things, (1) equipment information cards; (2) facilities location control cards; (3) acquisition and retirement fixed asset work orders; (4) the department's accident register; (5) the company insurance administrator's control number assignment log covering vehicle and other accidents; (6) a gasoline credit card assignment register; (7) credit card delivery tickets; (8) petty cash reimbursement requests; and (9) vouchers covering petty cash disbursements, making a petty cash count as well. Based on our tests, we concluded that except for the lack of reports on insurable values, the activities we examined were carried out in a satisfactory manner.

*　　*　　*

The four deficiency findings previously mentioned are discussed in the Supplement which follows and are summarized at the end of the Supplement, along with the referrals for completion of corrective action.

Before we completed our review, provision was made to report insurable values, and steps were initiated to correct the remaining three control weaknesses.

————————————————————————— Auditor-in-Charge
————————————————————————— Supervising Auditor
————————————————————————— Manager of Internal Auditing

Supplement to
Summary Report

DETAILS OF DEFICIENCY FINDINGS

1. There was no separation of functional authority in the procurement of parts and services, and effective administration of labor-hour agreements was beyond the Highway Transportation Department's resources.

Blanket Purchase Orders (BPOs) have been issued for the procurement of parts and services. The cognizant purchasing department has assigned to the Highway Transportation Department all authority and responsibility for controlling (a) releases of orders under the BPOs to suppliers; (b) receipt, inspection, and acceptance upon delivery; and (c) approvals of invoices for payment.

In practice, all of these functions are performed by the department manager or by one or two people under his direct control and supervision. Thus, there is none of the protection normally afforded by the separation of such functions among personnel of independent departments; such as establishing requirements, ordering, receiving, inspecting, and approving for payment.

There are about 70 currently active BPOs which require suppliers to furnish automotive parts and/or services, as requested. Expenditures for the year are budgeted at about $230,000. Many of the BPOs specify labor-hour rates for the repair of automotive equipment. In effect, these BPOs are Time and Material (T and M) agreements since no fixed number of hours is established for the orders released. Thus, the scope of work is undefined. Yet, the BPOs do not include clauses providing the company with the right of audit, something normally included in T and M agreements.

Exhibit 11-1. (Cont.)

In our opinion, these labor-hour BPOs do not appear to meet the intent of Procurement Instruction 501, in that they do not ensure the establishment of a fixed price for the order involved at the time of delivery. Furthermore, adequate and effective contract administration of these agreements is beyond the present resources of the Highway Transportation Department.

Because of the lack of separation of duties and the nature of the agreements, we made an extensive examination of the system and of transactions, but we found no basis for questioning any of the charges. Nevertheless, we recommend that Branch management review this condition with a view toward implementing some reasonable control through assignment of some of the key functions to other departments. Further, we recommend that management implement appropriate controls to preclude the use of T and M BPOs without an audit clause.

We discussed this matter with management personnel and they informed us that they intended to review the methods used at other major divisions of the company to determine whether any of their practices may warrant adoption.

2. Gasoline and oil were being withdrawn by company employees without adequate surveillance.

Since our last examination, the department reassigned elsewhere the service station attendant who had recorded gasoline and oil disbursements on the form provided for that purpose. Under present practice the vehicle operator serves himself and records his own withdrawals of gasoline and oil, without surveillance. There is no assurance, therefore, that the records are maintained accurately or that the information is always entered. Hence the dangers of misappropriation are increased. We estimate that the total yearly gasoline withdrawal will approximate 300,000 gallons at a cost of about $66,000.

We recognize that there must be a weighing of the benefits versus the costs of control. Nevertheless, we recommend that managment consider some means of surveillance — even on a spot check basis — to provide minimum elements of control.

We discussed this matter with management personnel and they indicated that appropriate surveillance would be conducted over fuel pump operations.

3. The area in which the Highway Transportation Department is located was not adequately protected.

Area 10, the site of the Highway Transportation Department, is used to house vehicles, fuel pumps, oil, repair parts, and the garage. The area is completely fenced. But it has two large gates, one at the northwest corner and one at the southeast corner. At the time we began our review both gates were kept open during the regular and swing shifts. A sign at the southeast gate warned that entrance is for company vehicles only. No such sign appeared at the other gate.

We observed that departmental employees, as well as other company employees, were allowed to park their private vehicles within the area. No guards were posted at the gates. Plant Protection personnel informed us that guards were not available for that purpose.

Exhibit 11-1.   (Cont.)

Supplement to
Summary Report

After we discussed this matter with the department manager, he closed the northwest gate to strengthen security somewhat. We believe that further action should be considered, however. While there is an adequate number of employees on hand during the day shift to provide some protection for property, it is doubtful that the reduced swing shift staff can do the same. Also, permitting private cars in the area violates the posted instructions and increases the danger of losses.

We recognize that the unavailability of Plant Protection guards creates some problems. But we believe that management should consider some substitute safeguards, particularly on swing shift.

During discussions with management personnel they indicated that additional measures to strengthen plant protection would be considered.

4. The insurable value of repair parts on hand was not being reported.

We found that the value of the repair parts on hand in the Highway Transportation Department had not been reported for insurance purposes since the inventory records were decontrolled in 19VV. The value of these repair parts is about $4,500.

We called the matter to the attention of the Insurance Administrator, and he requested the Highway Transportation Department to report the estimated dollar value as of the end of June 19XX. He has also taken action to revise the Company Insurance Manual to show this requirement.

The Highway Transportation Department informed the Insurance Administrator of the insurable value on July 16, 19XX. Corrective action on this matter is considered complete.

SUMMARY OF FINDINGS REQUIRING CORRECTIVE ACTION

The four matters requiring corrective action are summarized as follows:

1. There was no separation of functional authority in the procurement of parts and services, and effective administration of labor-hour agreements was beyond the Highway Transportation Department's resources.

2. Gasoline and oil were being withdrawn by company employees without adequate surveillance.

3. The area in which the Highway Transportation Department is located was not adequately protected.

4. The insurable value of repair parts on hand was not being reported.

Finding 1 is referred jointly to the manager of the Procurement Department and the manager of the Highway Transportation Department for completion of corrective action. Findings 2 and 3 are referred to the manager of the Highway Transportation Department for completion of corrective action. Finding 4 has been corrected.

Exhibit 11-2. UNIVERSITY

This report was in response to a management request and is so stated in the statement of purpose and scope. The auditor's general observations follow immediately.

Attachments to the report — not included in this sample — are discussed under a "Summary of Survey Responses."

Suggestions for improvement are divided between those requiring immediate consideration and those warranting long-range consideration. Each suggestion is followed by a brief statement of condition.

The report ends with a general conclusion and a referral to designated individuals to take action. Since the statements of conditions are quite brief, the report ends with the comment that "our workpapers contain data (including cost comparisons) which we will be glad to discuss with anyone interested in more details covering the study."

COPIER STUDY — ABC UNIVERSITY

Purpose and Scope

This study was made at the request of the Director of Business Services. The primary purpose was to gather information concerning the use and control of copying equipment on the campus.

General Comments

In our opinion, a controlled and economical approach to the "copying problem" can only be achieved by a more centralized administration of copier facilities and services. Our studies indicate that, short of centralization, cost savings available through more economical usage would constitute such small divisional increments that little, if any, motivation is provided. The gross saving to the university might not be worth the sacrifice of existing convenience. However, something needs to be done to stem the trends indicated by the following conditions:

- The number of copying machines on campus has about tripled in the last four years, from 11 machines to 31 machines.
- The monthly volume of copies increased during the 6-month period July 19XX through December 19XX from 273,000 copies to 359,000 copies. This averages 18,000 copies (a stack about seven feet high) produced each working day.
- Despite the better pricing policies negotiated in 19XX, copier expense has shown an average increase in excess of 10 per cent a year since fiscal year 19XX. This year the total will run over $110,000.
- Nine of the 31 copier machines the university is currently leasing are not sufficiently used to meet minimum price break requirements.
- Two of the academic divisions provide sophisticated copier capabilities which the central Graphic Arts facility has not been able to afford.

Summary of Survey Responses

Schedule I, which accompanies this report, reflects cognizance, average usage, accounts charged, and cross-charging practices. Schedule II indicates the volume necessary to achieve reduced pricing. Schedule III depicts the physical location of existing equipment. Schedule IV lists the contributors to this study. The following suggestions are based upon discussions concerning (and our interpretation of) the data shown in the schedules.

Exhibit 11-2. (Cont.)

Suggestions

For Immediate Consideration

1. Purchasing should discontinue buying the current brand of toner and developer.

    Tests made on campus indicate that there is no sacrifice of quality in certain selected lower priced competing products. Projections made by Purchasing indicate a savings of $4,000 to $5,000 a year at our present usage level.

    Action has been promised on this point.

2. Purchasing should take the initiative in developing an administrative procedure covering the servicing and repair of copier equipment.

    Most requests for the servicing of copying equipment are processed through Purchasing, but there are a few persons who still contact the supplier's repair center directly. In the interest of more efficient scheduling and better record keeping, this operation should be centralized.

3. All organizations should consider going to a standard rate for cross-charging.

    At prevailing prices in some of the divisions, the paper-work could cost more than the actual copying. To prevent "shopping" and the existence of "discount shops," all facilities should charge the same amount for given services.

4. Graphic Arts should develop a set of guidelines covering ways to economize in the copying process. Such information should be communicated through the medium of the new Secretary's Manual now being prepared in Personnel.

    Guidelines are needed in such areas as cheaper methods of copying, appropriate use of carbon copies, routing of information copies vs. copies for all, cost recovery of bad copies, proper dial settings for self-operated machines, and the like.

For Long-Range Consideration

5. Accounting should investigate the possibility of centralized budget coverage (in the Graphic Arts budget) for copying expense.

    The effect on indirect cost rates if these costs were handled as General Institutional Expense should be explored. Centralized budgeting and accounting may be the only way to get sufficient visibility to control the total.

6. Purchasing should take the initiative in developing an administrative procedure which prescribes that all requisitions for new or upgraded copier equipment be reviewed by Graphic Arts before being processed by Purchasing.

    Centralized assessment of the need for and the appropriateness of the equipment requested is desirable. Eventually, no copying equipment should be acquired, upgraded, moved or returned without central coordination.

7. Graphic Arts should develop a long-range plan for the eventual reduction of the number of machines.

    Inherent in such a plan would be centralized budgeting, surveillance, and administration of an optimum number of appropriately decentralized "satellite" operations.

Exhibit 11-2. (Cont.)

Conclusion

Existing conditions are not really serious, but the trend in copying expenditures is alarming. Some immediate savings can be realized in the cost of supplies. Any appreciable reduction beyond that point will depend upon the degree to which centralized coordination can be achieved.

We would appreciate receiving a reply within 30 days from the Director of Business Services concerning suggestions Number 1, 2, 4, 6, and 7; and a reply from the Director of Financial Services concerning suggestions Number 3 and 5. Our working papers contain data (including cost comparisons) which we will be glad to discuss with anyone interested in more details concerning the study.

Staff Consultant

Director, Internal Auditing and
    Consulting Staff

Exhibit 11-3. THE LEGISLATIVE AUDIT BUREAU FOR A
STATE GOVERNMENT

This report covered an audit of records for one of the departments of the state government. It was bound in black leatherette covers and was addressed to an official in the state capitol.

The transmittal sets forth the scope of the audit. The first two pages of the report — not included here — contain detailed financial information on appropriations, revenues, and expenditures. The text of the report is headed "Comments and Recommendations." Each subheading sets forth the need for certain action or a brief statement of conditions. The discussions are quite brief and are generally restricted to recommendations for improvement or corrective action.

The excerpts shown here cover the first three pages of the text of the report.

COMMENTS AND RECOMMENDATIONS

Need to Improve Internal Accounting and Management Report Systems

We urge the Department of Public Instruction (DPI) to give top priority to improving internal accounting and management reports in its plan to develop a management information system.

Present financial information from DPI's office and the Department of Administration is not timely and does not meet the needs of different management levels.

In developing the management information system, the department should:

■ Determine management's needs before the system is designed.

■ Evaluate financial information which the Department of Administration can provide. If DPI needs to use its own computer to get this information, they should arrange for an exchange of input data to prevent duplication of effort.

■ Make sure documentation is provided to support the allocation of expenditures, especially salaries and related expenses which represent 60-65% of total operating costs.

Exhibit 11-3. (Cont.)

■ Study the present accounting system to determine which changes are necessary to promote more efficient use of personnel and provide essential information. The present partially decentralized system of hand-kept records is costly to maintain and does not promote the orderly flow of information required for efficient administration.

Review of Surplus Food Commodity Distribution Program

Practices and procedures used to administer the surplus food commodity program need revision. We recommend that the department:

■ Centralize surplus food commodity accounting functions under DPI's fiscal officer.

■ Study the feasibility of putting commodity inventory records on the computer.

■ Use input control totals to check computer output. At present, each computer-generated billing statement is reconciled manually, with supporting notices of allocation and receipt, before it is mailed.

■ Reduce the time lag between dates commodities are shipped and the dates handling charges are billed. This will speed collections and increase interest earnings. The practice of billing schools and institutions semiannually resulted in lost interest earnings estimated at $3,800 during the last fiscal year.

■ Reduce the time required to deposit receipts. It now takes as long as 16 days for the food service section to process and turn receipts over to the fiscal office, and an additional one to five days to deposit the same receipts with the state treasurer.

■ Periodically inspect warehouse to insure that required standards are maintained.

■ Physically inventory commodities at least once each year.

Need to Review Functions of the Staff Services Section

The department is implementing our recommendation to:

■ Study the feasibility of transferring to the payroll section some of the functions now performed by staff services.

■ Update the records supporting employees' authorizations for payroll deductions.

■ Update employees' statements of exemptions claimed. (W-4s).

Capital Equipment Accounting

The fiscal officer is implementing our recommendations to:

■ Centralize responsibility for equipment accounting.

■ Establish guidelines for capitalizing equipment.

■ Take a physical inventory of acquisitions and disposals.

Cost Reduction in Tape-Controlled Typewriter Rentals Possible

Four tape-controlled typewriters are rented at a cost of $986 a month for the four. Our analysis of machine usage, for the three months ended November 30, 19XX, disclosed that these machines are idle 51% of the time and are used 20%

Exhibit 11-3. (Cont.)

of the time for reproduction work which can be done more efficiently by other means. We recommend:

■ The creation of a machine pool so that tape-controlled machines and operators are used to full capacity.

■ A study of clerical tasks to define those which can be done more efficiently on tape-controlled machines and to make sure that all such work is channeled to the operators of those machines.

■ All machines not needed to take care of valid workload be returned to the supplier. Each machine not needed costs the department about $3,000 a year.

Exhibit 11-4. HEAVY INDUSTRY

The audit was concerned with the costs of a division of the company. The report is transmitted to the Vice President-Finance by a memorandum which summarizes the auditor's comments. The report is restricted to deficiency findings. It carries underlined headnotes which summarize the auditor's recommendations, followed by detailed analyses of the conditions.

The transmittal memo and some excerpts from one of the findings are reprinted here.

TO: VICE PRESIDENT-FINANCE

FROM: DIRECTOR, INTERNAL AUDIT DEPARTMENT

SUBJECT: Cost Audit of XYZ Division

The Internal Audit Department has reviewed cost accounting records and related procedures at the XYZ Division. Records for May 19XX were audited in detail and tests were made in other months as deemed necessary.

Details of the following comments are attached:

1. Charges for outside services should be verified in detail to avoid overpayments.
2. Control weaknesses have resulted in duplicate payroll payments.
3. Performance efficiency of operations should be evaluated through engineered standards.
4. Allocation of power costs at some plants should be reviewed.
5. Waste heat credit is not computed on a current cost basis.
6. Foremen approve their own petty cash slips.

We have discussed other recommendations with the Division Comptroller concerning (1) account 401 supply costs to be charged through M & S inventory, and (2) improved journal voucher descriptions. Remedial action is to be taken.

This report has been reviewed with XYZ Division's General Superintendent, Comptroller, and Division Chief Engineer. Their comments are included in the detailed report.

Internal Audit Department

Exhibit 11-4. (Cont.)

3. Performance Efficiency of Operations Should be Evaluated Through Engineered Standards

3.1 Observations:

Field observations and discussions with operating personnel indicate that control over labor cost could be improved through engineered standards, thereby affording a means to measure efficiency and productivity on front line foreman levels.

A. A field test (August 2) of five men assigned to repair Station 21 showed that:

1. Repair time of eight hours per man was charged.
2. Station 21 was unattended during the field observation which was made at 11:10 a.m.
3. No repair tools were in evidence.
4. The five men were sitting in a tool truck nearby.
5. The foreman made no physical check of the crew. Communication was by radio only.

A subsequent field test on swing shift showed that one man was sleeping at the controls of an operating drill.

B. Equipment utilization percentage, an important operational measurement, is currently determined from several foremen's casual observations during a normal shift. "Utilized" time includes idle and delay time. Equipment cards prepared by equipment operators, which show idle time, are not considered in arriving at efficiency utilization of equipment.

[The report continues with a statistical analysis and further discussion of the conditions found in the audit]

3.2 Recommendations:

We recommend that the division consider a small scale test program to establish engineered standards.

Standards could initially be established in production areas that are easily defined and amenable to measurement.

All information pertinent to the determination of efficiencies should be considered in arriving at manpower or equipment utilization.

3.3 Comments of Division Comptroller:

Engineered standards have been considered before. They did not prove effective and the study was discontinued.

3.4 Comments of General Superintendent:

We have inaugurated a maintenance standard system at two of our plants. They are based primarily on historical data and an effectiveness system. Both are pilot programs. If they work out well we intend to expand.

Exhibit 11-5. LARGE MANUFACTURER

This is a report on a personnel department. The report is in two separate parts, both of which were individually bound. The first report was entitled Interim Recommendation Report. It was issued before the final report and contained 12 recommendations.

The final report is addressed to the person who will take action — the personnel director. Copies are sent to appropriate officials.

The final report is seven pages long and is in the form of a letter. It is subdivided as follows:

FOCUS — Extent of the department's operation and its budget. Scope of the audit assignment.

OVERALL ASSESSMENT — The auditor's general conclusions of what he found.

MAJOR RECOMMENDATIONS — An abbreviated discussion of seven of the twelve recommendations included in the interim report.

The interim report discusses each recommendation in detail. The first item is a brief one-sentence statement of the recommendation. This is the same as the statement in the final report. Following the recommendations are:

FACTS — Set forth in some detail.

CONCLUSION — Giving the auditor's opinion.

OTHER COMMENTS — Discussing the auditor's general feelings about the operation.

SPECIFIC RECOMMENDATION — Setting forth the detailed steps the auditor believes should be taken.

INVESTMENT REQUIRED TO IMPLEMENT RECOMMENDATIONS — The cost of carrying out the auditor's suggestions.

BENEFITS TO BE REALIZED ON INVESTMENT — The beneficial effects the recommendations should achieve.

TIME REQUIRED TO IMPLEMENT RECOMMENDATIONS — The period that will elapse before the changes will be made.

The excerpts that follow include the general statements in the final report and the discussion about one of the recommendations. Also excerpted are the lead sentences of the remaining seven recommendations and the closing sentences of the final report.

Exhibit 11-5. (Cont.)

CORPORATE OPERATIONS ANALYSIS DEPARTMENT
SUMMARY LETTER REPORT

Personnel Director
ABC Company
Dear Bob,

Our analysis of your Personnel Department is now completed. This report summarizes our findings and recommendations.

Focus

Personnel services 2,200 office and technical employees who are located in five different divisions or operating units within the metropolitan area. Approximately one-half of these employees are in the XYZ Division.

The department has 36 people and operates on a budget of about $600,000 annually.

Our analysis was confined to the three major Personnel functional responsibilities of Placement, Manpower Development/Training, and Compensation Practices.

Overall Assessment

XYZ Personnel provides service to operating management on an "as requested" basis; when provided, our review revealed this service to be generally adequate.

However, XYZ Personnel's role in the management of office and technical personnel is mainly passive. As such, most personnel practices are handled by the operating people, who are not technically trained in personnel administration.

Further, the Personnel Department is not knowledgeable in the extent, quality, and consistency of personnel administration practices performed by the operating people.

Finally, we believe that Personnel concentrates too much of its efforts and resources on activities that are of low priority in the management of human resources.

The department's whole approach to the acquisition, development and retention of people does not assure operating management of optimum use of their investment in manpower.

Major Recommendations

1. Analyze and Define the Role of the Residential Personnel Department

The Personnel Department does not play a major role in the administering of personnel practices upon employees. Personnel does not know either the extent, quality, or consistency (and inconsistency) of these practices among the many managers and departments.

Many important personnel practices are the complete prerogative of individual operating managers.

Examples of these practices are:

A. Manpower requirement forecasting.
B. Employee performance appraisals.
C. Career counseling and career development.
D. Determination of specific individual training needs and training received.
E. Early identification of "marginal" and "failing" employees. Establishment of corrective action programs.

Exhibit 11-5. (Cont.)

   F. Analysis of absenteeism levels and control.

   G. Information flow to employee's Personnel jackets.

Personnel usually does not participate in, or monitor, these activities. We contribute this passive role to two factors:

■ The lack of a formally defined charter from top management.

■ A low level of expertise among departmental employees, below the managerial positions, due to an aggressive job rotation policy. (Department management considers this necessary to keep employees challenged.)

Several steps are required before Personnel can undertake a more aggressive, employee-oriented service role.

■ Develop a formal written charter of operations, approved by top divisional management. Describe areas of personnel administration where the Personnel Department has sole responsibility. Delineate those areas where Personnel should play an advisory or monitoring role.

■ Discontinue the rapid rotation practice. Develop greater vertical growth potential within the Personnel Department.

■ Gradually implement the above charter through assignments of specific action programs to individual department employees.

The major benefit of this effort will be to give assurance that the biggest investment — the investment in people — is always being well managed.

2. Improve the Accuracy of the Manpower Forecast.

3. Implement a Disciplined Program for Job Description Development and Maintenance.

4. Assist and Monitor Operating Management in the Employee Appraisal Function. Utilize Appraisal Information.

5. Guide and Monitor Personnel Training Activities.

6. Compile and Utilize Statistical Information to Improve Effectiveness and Efficiency in Personnel Activities.

7. Improve the Quality and Completeness of Employee Personnel Information.

8. Investigate the Desirability of an Organizational Realignment.

We believe that implementation of our recommendations will substantially increase and improve the level of service now being offered by the Personnel function to operating management. Furthermore, the company will have greater assurance that their biggest investment — the investment in people — is being well managed.

The specific details supporting these and other recommendations are contained in the Interim Recommendation Reports which have been furnished you.

                              Manager

                              Lead Analyst

Exhibit 11-6. LARGE MILL

This report covers the audit of a knitting division of the mill. The auditing department addresses its report to the president of the division being audited. Copies of the report are sent to the Corporate President, the Treasurer, and the Corporate Controller. The report is sent by a brief memorandum of transmittal.

The report begins with the scope of the examination and indicates a broad audit coverage. Immediately thereafter, the findings are briefly summarized and are divided between items on which action has been taken and those on which action is still required.

The summary is followed by brief discussions of the findings, grouped according to functional activity. The report is signed by the head of the audit department.

The excerpts that follow are from the summary of findings and the related detailed findings and recommendations.

INTERNAL AUDIT REPORT
AUDIT OF THE KNIT DIVISION

Scope of Examination

Our review covered the analysis of operations at the E.F.G. Plant, the Customer Service Center and the Sales Office. We examined the policies and procedures followed in order-booking, invoicing, shipping, receiving, claims, purchasing, payroll, waste control, quality audit, and production scheduling and control.

Summary of Findings

A. *Items on Which Action Has Been Taken*

1. Revised procedures covering packing, shipping, and billing of retail sales items expected to result in additional income of $129,000 a year.
2. Elimination of overtime amounting to $14,000 annually.
3. Collection of $3,000 excessive freight paid due to failure to deduct proper allowances on yarn invoices.
4. Revised handling of unclaimed wages to conform to company policy.
5. Discontinue allowing Sales personnel to charge personal telephone calls to the company.

B. *Items on Which Action Is to be Taken*

1. Improved control over cash received for retail sales.
2. Improved control in accounting for and safeguarding purchase orders.
3. Establish procedures to insure that quantities of materials and supplies received agree with quantities paid for.
4. Improved control over bills of lading to insure that all goods shipped are billed.
5. Establish control routines governing use of company truck and gasoline purchases.
6. Require medical examinations for new employees.
7. Proper authorization for employee insurance deductions.

Exhibit 11-6. (Cont.)

8. Compare number of dependents claimed for tax withholding with those used in computing net pay.

9. Process leaves of absence and terminations in accordance with company policy.

10. Follow company policy on:
    a. Approval of time orders
    b. Travel expenses paid from petty cash
    c. Preparation of exit interview forms
    d. Wage and work notices
    e. Bulletin board notices

11. Eliminate unnecessary copies of reports and use multilith instead of more expensive copier service; savings of approximately $4,750 annually.

12. Improve control over and accounting for movement of inventories, and eliminate duplicate grey goods inventory maintained in Sales Office.

13. Consolidate mail between plants; estimated savings of about $1,300 annually.

14. Establish preventive maintenance program and control over spare parts to provide accurate maintenance and supply costs for each machine.

15. Install program for accurately determining and reporting waste generated by each production operation.

16. Have department managers approve time sheets in accordance with company policy.

17. Have plant employees charge reimbursable mileage from plant base for better control.

18. Develop written operating procedures for training employees, defining problems, and coordinating activities.

19. Exclude nonbusiness visitors from enclosed parking lot to prevent possible company liability for personal injury and to provide better plant security.

20. Proper and timely follow-up of late purchase orders.

Detailed Findings and Recommendations

1. Retail Sales

A. Tests revealed that approximately 10 per cent of goods shipped were not being billed because of quantity differences between shipping documents and invoices and because of errors in measuring the quantities packed. The adoption of procedures to make sure that all quantities are billed will result in additional income of about $129,000 annually based on current sales volume projections. Procedures to insure accurate packing, shipping, and billing have been adopted.

B. Internal control of cash receipts for retail sales is weakened by the fact that the person receiving cash also prepares original sales documents and by the further fact that the sales documents are not accounted for numerically.

Exhibit 11-7. CARD COMPANY

This is a brief report on a specific subject — the adequacy of controls over salesmen's cars.

A memorandum submitting the report explains the scope of the examination. The report itself begins with a "Report Summary and Follow-up Request." This is followed by the findings and recommendations. The report is double-spaced. The findings are indented so that they command attention. The report is supported by two graphs to emphasize certain data.

The excerpts that follow include the transmittal memorandum, the summary, and the first two findings.

AUDIT AND OPERATIONS REVIEW

February 3, 19XX

To:

cc:

SUBJECT: Fleet Cars (Project No. 72-30)

We made a review to determine the adequacy of controls over salesmen's and other fleet cars. Included in the review were a comparison of our lease plan with other available plans, the controls over unassigned cars in open territories, controls over maintenance of cars, insurance costs, and guidelines for determining the appropriate number of cars.

Prepared: _____

Reviewed by: _____

Manager

Fleet Cars (Project No. 72-30)

Report Summary and Follow-up Request

72-30/1   An analysis of the three available leasing plans showed that the Open-End Lease presently used is the most economical. (Section 5)

72-30/2   A breakeven chart of the three forms of mileage compensation to salesmen showed that an annual savings of $41,000 could be realized if all leased cars driven less than 1,400 miles per month were eliminated and the $12.50 per week plus 6¢ a mile system were used. However, Sales Management feels that the leased car is a part of the salesman's compensation and that it maintains the company image. (Section 4)

[Manager] Please Follow Up

72-30/3   In 14 open territories reviewed, an average of 1,600 miles were driven without being accounted for. Sales Management, in conjunction with Fleet Expense Department, should require salesmen and district man-

Exhibit 11-7. (Cont.)

agers to account for mileage driven on cars in open territories. (Section 1)

[Manager] Please Follow Up

72-30/4 In 60 of 78 instances of repairs in excess of the Sales Department $25 limit, no evidence of authorization was found. While some of these instances were authorized by telephone, some written record of authorization of repairs should be maintained by Fleet Expense Department. (Section 2)

A & OR
72-30

Findings and Recommendations

1. Mileage was reviewed in 14 open territories. In two instances no mileage was driven during the open period. In the remaining 12 instances a total of 22,455 miles were recorded but never accounted for. This is an average of 1,800 miles per occurrence.

   Sales Management, in conjunction with Fleet Expense Department, should require salesmen and district managers to account for mileage driven on cars in open territories.

2. A review was made of 22 car folders to determine if authorization is given for repairs. The sales policy states that any repair in excess of $25 must be authorized by Fleet Expense Department. There were 78 instances of repairs in excess of $25 for the 22 cars sampled. Of the 78 instances, 60 had no evidence of prior authorization. Some of these repairs may have been authorized by phone, but no written record is maintained.

   Instances were noted where Fleet Expense Department had informed the salesmen that repairs were not authorized. In addition, several of the messages from Fleet Expense Department indicated that unauthorized repairs had resulted in additional expense to the company. Some examples follow:

   a. The Sales Reference Manual requires all major repairs to be made at an authorized dealership. In several cases, repairs were made at a place other than an authorized dealership. The work would have been covered under warranty at any authorized dealership. In one other case, work was performed at an unauthorized establishment and had to be done over again because of the inferior quality of the repairs.

   b. Tires were purchased without authorization and without using available discounts.

   c. Excessive periodic maintenance, such as tune-ups, were made without prior authorizations.

      Some written record of authorization of repairs should be maintained by Fleet Expense Department.

twelve ■

AUDIT REPORT
REVIEWS AND REPLIES

INTRODUCTION

Reviewing report drafts with auditees is a form of insurance as well as a form of courtesy. And due concern for replies to published audit reports is an assumption of a proper audit responsibility. We shall discuss both these matters in this chapter.

Some audit organizations — albeit a minority — still refrain from reviewing drafts of audit reports with auditees before issuing the reports in final form. This is a kind of arrogance. It assumes omniscience on the part of the auditor. And one thing the auditor is certainly not, particularly in operational matters, is omniscient.

The auditor spends in the field but a minute portion of the time spent there by the auditee. The auditor can, within that short span, isolate and identify problems. But he cannot possibly be aware of all the nuances, the historical reasons, the oral executive mandates, the delicate interfaces with peripheral organizations, and the conflicting forces throughout the company that are usually involved in some of the conditions found during the audit. Also, he may have resolved problems at the working levels during his development of his audit findings — or he may think he has. But he may not have obtained the views of line management or middle management.

People at those levels may have significant information to offer that can give perspective or a new view to reported findings. They may add an ingredient to the finding that the auditor may not himself be able to supply: the mature experience of the managers involved — their thorough understanding of the many facets of the problem.

Also, if he cannot be omniscient, the auditor can at least be courteous. And showing line and middle management the draft of the report which will find its way to the executive desk is a gesture of courtesy. The auditor does not owe it to the auditee to be soft and tender. He may not gloss over what is adverse and significant. But he does owe fairness, candor, and courtesy.

Often, the very way the auditee regards the auditor will affect his reaction to what is said about him in the draft report. If he sees in the auditor a fair, honest, competent individual, doing his job without rancor or an axe to grind — then he may gulp and accept the description of the most serious of findings; his sole response will be to take corrective action. But if he sees the findings in print for the first time when he reads the final report, and if he does not regard the auditor personally in a favorable light, he may be resentful, defensive, and arbitrary; and he may respond to the report with denials and excuses instead of with constructive corrective action.

So aside from any considerations of the auditee's feelings, the auditor must regard draft reviews in the light of his own self interest — as a way of getting his audit job done without unfortunate repercussions.

The auditor must assume — with executive blessing — the responsibility for obtaining, reviewing, and assessing the adequacy of written replies to those reports requiring replies. If written replies are not mandated by executive management, busy line management may see no reason to take the time to consider them and respond to them.

And clearly, the auditor who has reported the condition and made the recommendation is surely in the best position to assess the reasonableness of the response. Certainly, he has no right to dictate line management's course of action. But he does have the responsibility for seeing that the condition is corrected irrespective of whether his own recommendations are followed to the letter. Put simply, then, the objectives of report reviews are:

- To resolve conflicts.
- To reach agreement on the facts.
- To prevent disputatious replies.
- To permit the auditee to see in advance the written word — which sometimes will look different from the spoken word.

The objectives of the right to obtain written replies to reports and to review and evaluate them are:

- To ensure the auditee's proper consideration of the auditor's findings and recommendations.
- To provide assurance that matters reported remain monitored until corrected.

REPORT REVIEWS

With Whom to Review Drafts

Who will review report drafts will depend on the nature of the report itself and on the interest or concern of the individual managers and executives.

Draft reviews of a completely satisfactory report, with no deficiency findings or recommendations, and covering some relatively small and well-defined area or function, can be held to the line manager and his superior. Some people may believe that such reports (1) either should not be written at all, or (2) do not warrant the review time. We disagree. We believe that even completely satisfactory findings should be put in writing, no matter how briefly. Such reports demonstrate audit objectivity. They give credit where due. They raise the auditor from the level of deficiency finder to that of objective analyst. They present a permanent record of audit coverage that management can see. They bring management and auditor together under pleasant circumstances. They cement the understanding between the two. Therefore, the time devoted to drafting such a report and reviewing the draft with the auditee is time well spent.

Thus, once the satisfactory report is drafted, the draft review becomes compulsory. It is insurance — to make sure the report has not overlooked significant aspects of the operation under audit. The draft review may point up needs for shifts of emphasis of which the auditor himself is unaware. It may raise questions on the nature of the audit coverage. It may provide needed face-to-face discussions between auditor and management to establish good rapport for the future when different circumstances may make that rapport a significant foundation on which to build. And it may construct a desirable image of the auditor in the eyes of management.

The reviews of the report describing deficient conditions call for different considerations. It should be reviewed with anyone who may be able to object with validity to its contents. It should be reviewed with anyone required to take action. It should be reviewed with anyone having responsibility for the area or condition needing corrective action — whether or not he personally would take that action or would be affected by the action.

Where the conditions are restricted to specific areas, the matter presents relatively few problems. Then the reviews would include the manager responsible for taking action and his superior. But in functional audits crossing many lines, and in organizational audits bringing extensive defects to light or calling for massive system overhauls, the report may require reviews that go through many organizations and to the executive level.

It is well for the auditing organization to furnish its staff with written instructions on draft reviews. In large organizations it may be easy to forget who should review what and in what order the reviews should take place. Exhibit 12-1 is an example of such an instruction.

In general, reviews should be made with the auditee manager and his superior. Yet some branch directors may wish to see all drafts of reports affecting their branches. The auditor should be glad to comply; but he should also tactfully point to the need for promptness, so that the reviews will not delay the issuance of the final report.

Reports calling for systems changes should be reviewed with the procedures people or with systems analysts — such as the industrial engineers or EDP analysts.

In instances where the auditor has conducted his review at the line level, it may be well to ask whether reviews at higher levels are necessary. The auditee generally has a good idea how his superior or superiors regard audit reports. His views on whether or not to go higher should be given full consideration. And where line or middle management people say that no further reviews are needed,

**Exhibit 12-1. ABC CORPORATION INTERNAL
AUDITING DEPARTMENT**

REVIEWS OF DRAFT REPORTS

Policy

It is the policy of Internal Auditing to review drafts of audit reports with the management personnel responsible for the activities examined — in advance of the formal release of the reports.

Order

The review should begin with responsible line management and proceed, as necessary, through the branch level of management. As a minimum, the draft should be reviewed with the manager responsible for the activity and with his superior. Reviews may be held at levels beyond the branch director when circumstances warrant. Such reviews should be approved in advance by the audit manager.

Form of Review

The individual drafts should be reviewed to the extent necessary — in whole or in part; or through the oral or the written word, or a combination of the two. To this end the auditor should remember that the purpose of these reviews is to obtain agreement on the facts and to make sure management people understand the key statements in the report: The report is the responsibility of the auditor, not the auditee; hence, the review process is designed to ensure a proper interpretation of what the auditor has written, not what the auditee would like to see written.

Disagreement as to facts is another matter. The auditor should make an earnest effort to resolve such disagreements. But if after all reasonable attempts at reconciling differences have proved fruitless, the report should clearly set forth the positions of both the auditor and the operating manager for the benefit of higher management.

those comments should be carefully recorded in the working papers. These records can defend the auditor from irate accusations of withholding information. After the final report is issued the auditor may receive a call from higher management asking why the report was not reviewed in draft at that level. If he has taken the proper steps, the auditor can respond by (1) explaining normal practices, and (2) stating exactly who told him that further reviews were unnecessary, giving the time and date of the statement, and offering to ensure higher management reviews in the future — if the manager so wishes.

Experienced auditors are usually aware of those people with whom they have trouble in draft reviews. The reviews may be dreaded and the sessions may be unpleasant experiences. Sometimes these confrontations just cannot be helped. But they may be alleviated. For example, the auditor may try to include in the review conference the superior of the troublesome individual. This may have a salutary tendency to keep the meeting on a less turbulent keel.

In all cases the report reviews should be carefully documented. The results of the review should be recorded in the working papers immediately after the conference so that no significant matter, comment, or decision is lost. These notes can be very important in the event of later dispute.

Timing the Reviews

Obviously, the greater the number of draft reviews the longer the delay in issuing the final report. This places the auditor in a dilemma. On the one hand he wishes to afford all those with a "need to know" the opportunity to review the draft. On the other hand, he is aware of the urgency for current reporting.

The problem is not insuperable, however. But it does require pressure and setting deadlines, both for the auditor and the reviewer. After the auditor drafts his report he should prepare his list of distributees. Together with his supervisor, he should decide which people should review the report in draft and the order of those reviews.

The order is important. The list of draft reviewers should begin with those who are most closely involved in or affected by the report. They are the ones most likely to have suggestions for changes, objections to phrasing, or disputes as to facts. They are the ones with whom the report should be reviewed face to face, if possible, to iron out differences and to get agreement on the facts.

Thereafter, the draft can be duplicated and sent to all others concerned for review. The transmittal memo should identify the report, indicate with whom it has been reviewed, offer to discuss it in person, and set a date for its return. For example:

To: Draft Reviewer

From: Auditor

Subject: Draft Report — Review of Controls Over Conflicts of Interest

The subject report draft is forwarded for your review. It has already been reviewed with A. B. See, E. F. Gee, and H. I. Jay. They were in agreement with the matters described in the draft which reflects changes resulting from their reviews.

If you have any questions on the draft or wish to discuss it, please call me. Otherwise, kindly have your secretary return the draft after your review.

We would appreciate your giving the draft your prompt attention, since we plan to put it in final form on Wednesday, July 10, 197X.

_____ Internal Auditor

This memorandum can be used to submit draft reports to reviewers in other cities. Distance should not prevent draft reviews. Reviewers in other cities should be afforded the same courtesy as those in the central offices.

The Review Conference

The draft review can be either a grim confrontation or an open and courteous discussion. True, the auditor presumably has discussed all findings with the auditee. But a comprehensive written draft, showing distribution to executive management, somehow has a different impact from informal reports or oral discussions.

It is the auditor's conference. He can and should influence its course. No matter how serious are the findings, the auditor who is sensitive to the feelings of others can put the draft in a perspective that takes much of the harshness out of it.

No draft review should be started abruptly. There should be a setting of the stage. There should be an attempt to bring about a pleasant atmosphere. The more critical the report, the more attention is needed for proper preliminaries. Somehow, in some way, there should be developed the feeling that what is reported is not said in rancor but in the spirit of correcting unfortunate conditions. Here are some of the matters to consider in orally setting the stage:

- The scope of the examination.
- The significance of the matters reviewed.
- An acknowledgment of the difficulties which face the auditee in carrying out his responsibilities.
- The cooperation obtained during the audit.
- The fact that the report contains no surprises — that all findings were discussed during the field work. (If the auditor has

not done so, he has no one but himself to blame for antagonism during the draft review.)

■ Comments on how many matters are already corrected, how many are in process of correction, and how many are still to be corrected.

■ A willingness to discuss all matters in whatever detail is necessary.

Avoiding and Resolving Conflicts

It would be wishful thinking for the auditor to expect every draft review to be conducted without conflict, no matter how well-accepted Internal Auditing is in the company. Indeed, the stronger the auditor's position, the greater the auditee's concern with what the report has to say to his superiors.

The auditor must therefore be prepared — thoroughly prepared — for conflict and dispute. He must be able to retrieve information, support facts, and amplify findings without difficulty or delay. It is embarrassing to the auditor and unnerving to his supervisor to see an aimless fumbling through volumes of audit working papers when it becomes necessary to buttress reported statements. The room is hushed. The conversation has ceased. All eyes are on the hapless auditor as he flips the papers, passing by the desired documents time and again in his confusion.

The auditor brings these awful moments upon himself. He should be aware that every critical comment may evoke objection and a call for additional proof. He can rise to the challenge with forethought and preparation. His own copy of the draft should be copiously annotated in the margin with references to the supporting detail. This simple preparation will pay big dividends.

Suppose the auditee says, "I can't believe that this particular function that you're talking about is my responsibility." The prepared auditor, looks for the proper marginal notation in his draft. He then turns immediately to the copy of the appropriate directive in his working papers. There, underlined in red — if he has done his homework — for all to see, is the particular statement which assigned responsibility to the auditee.

Suppose the auditee asks, "Are you sure there are no instructions on the subject?" The auditor — again, if he has done his homework — promptly turns to a work sheet which records that on a particular date he spoke to the individual responsible for preparing such instructions and learned that indeed no instruction had been issued, and why.

References to Records of Audit Findings (See Chapter 9) showing all relevant details of deficiencies can be invaluable. They can give ready information on the population sampled, the manner of sample selection, the proof that the sample was representative, the citations to directives, the causes, the effects, and the people with whom the conditions were discussed.

When the auditor must go through an agony of fumbling for each piece of data he needs to support his position, his credibility and the credibility of his report declines. When, on the other hand, he is able to answer each question promptly and fully, when his working papers appear to be a readily accessible storehouse of easily retrieved information, then the stream of objections and questions gradually dries up.

But serious disagreements are bound to occur. The draft makes a statement. The auditee makes a contradictory statement. The auditor disagrees with it. An impasse occurs. How, then, to resolve the disagreement and go on with the business of the review?

The auditor must recognize that the auditee is on the defensive. Somehow that defensive barrier must be removed and agreement reached. Here are some simple rules that may help:

- **Have Good Manners.** It is just plain bad manners to say bluntly "I disagree with you" or "You're wrong." It is worse manners to use such words as "idiotic," "ridiculous," or "nonsense." Besides, it is poor judgment. Under this kind of attack, the auditee either lashes back or withdraws. More important, communication is destroyed and the auditor's objectives cannot be met.

- **Use Nonpersonal Phrases.** In disagreeing, avoid starting a sentence with "You." That implies disagreeing with the individual rather than with the concept or idea. Use neutral phrases: "It might be worth considering . . ." "There might be a possibility that . . ." "Perhaps it might be useful to explore . . ." These phrases, being impersonal, seldom arouse emotions — certainly not the emotions aroused by "You haven't thought of . . ." "You've forgotten . . ." "You don't realize . . ." "You don't know about . . ." Never underestimate the emotional impact of certain words.

- **Get on Common Ground.** Where an impasse appears to be reached, step back until some point can be agreed upon — even if it is just agreement that the problem is not an easy one to solve. Stand on that ground until tempers are calmed and the auditee is comfortable enough to be willing to discuss reasonably the matters at issue.

- **Don't Back Anyone into a Corner.** Do not press the auditee for a clear statement that he has reversed himself. If he finally goes along with a point, resist the temptation. Don't say something like "I'm glad you finally see things my way." The auditor's objective is to get his conclusions and recommendations across. It doesn't really matter whether or not the auditee changed his mind.
- **Don't Mistake Airing of Views with Disagreement.** Often all that is necessary is to let the auditee talk himself out. Perhaps he does not really disagree but merely wants a chance to justify his position or to explain the reasons for the conditions that the auditor found. After he has made his point, the auditee might be perfectly willing to let the wording of the draft stand as written.

At the same time, when there is irreconcilable disagreement, when no mutual grounds can be found, the auditor has a responsibility to give the auditee's views equal prominence with his own. The auditor may then observe that he must report matters as he sees them, but that he will record the auditee's views as well.

In some situations, the mere offer to quote the auditee will reconcile the disagreement. If the auditee secretly realizes that he is in an untenable position, he would not want that position paraded before his superiors in the body of an audit report. But when there is an honest disagreement on interpretations — never on the facts; they *must* be agreed upon — the auditee's views should be incorporated in the report.

It is common courtesy, of course, to ask the auditee to read the added material to make sure he will not feel he was misquoted.

Reaching Agreement

The auditor should not be inflexible. He must recognize that people are understandably defensive. He must recognize that his report may visit executive wrath on the head of the auditee. He must understand that words mean different things to different people. He must be sufficiently realistic to recognize that it is possible for him to be wrong. Hence, he should be willing to substitute words and phrases that do not destroy the meaning he wishes to convey, if by so doing he will be making the auditee feel more comfortable.

He should also heed the auditee in matters of perspective or relevance. It may well be that what the auditor considers to have gone to the heart of a function was really only a side issue. It may also be that what the auditor was told at the working level failed to take into account matters not known at that level.

These things happen. The auditor must be prepared to adjust accordingly. He must try to maintain a reputation for fairness, for objectivity, and for concern solely with what is factual and significant. To that end he should not be averse to changes that make for a better report.

Audit Opinions

There are some suggestions for changes with which the auditor cannot agree. They affect his audit opinion. That opinion cannot be delegated. It cannot be compromised. It can be only what the auditor can defend and support and is willing to attest to by his signature. He cannot substitute someone else's opinion for his own.

The professional opinion of the auditor cannot be negotiated. It is either what he honestly believes, based on what he has seen, or it is nothing. Thus, it must be clearly understood that while the auditor will discuss facts and the meaning of facts, his audit opinion is not subject to give and take.

Cause and Effect

Executive management is vitally concerned with the causes and effects of the conditions the auditor reports. The understanding of cause and effect may be a significant factor in making executive decisions. It is well, therefore, for the auditor to explore these matters during the draft review. Very often line management is in the best position to advance the reasons for the deficient conditions; and the manager's views on the subject should be sought and carefully considered.

The auditor should probe for the reasons so that he can be sure that proposed corrective action is aimed at the causes. For example:

- Was management aware of the problem?
- Was the problem traceable to inadequate instruction or insufficient training of personnel?
- Did the condition occur because supervisors were not adequately monitoring the ongoing process?
- Were improper priorities assigned?
- Were insufficient resources provided?
- Did the need for controls go unrecognized?

- Was there a lack of coordination with interfacing organizations?
- Were conditions caused by human error?
- Were the defects attributable to the attitude of the employees? Of the supervisors? Of the manager?

One source of conflict is the auditor's statement in the audit report of the effect of deficient conditions. The auditor's estimate of the amounts of money lost or potentially lost can be a source of irritation to the auditee whose superiors readily understand such numbers; and if the auditee considers them inflated, it will just be another point of conflict and dispute. Hence, it is important during the draft reviews to get agreement on the effects of deficiencies. In that vein, the auditor should come to the draft review prepared to demonstrate the validity of his estimates and assessments.

Reviewing Revisions

As the draft report goes through its course of reviews, some changes may be made. Their significance becomes a matter of judgment. So does the need to review the changed wording with those who have not seen the revisions.

Certainly, if the auditee is now called upon to take action that he was unaware of in the first review, he is entitled to see the draft again as modified. Similarly, if as a result of subsequent reviews the draft places the auditee in a less favorable light or quotes the auditee or attributes something to the auditee, then he should have the same opportunity.

Sometimes the changes can be communicated by telephone. The auditor, in the interest of prompt report release, should try that method first. If he is unsuccessful, he will have to let the auditee see the changes. Sometimes the changes are merely word substitutions. These often do not call for reviews. The chief criterion must be the maintenance of the auditor's reputation for fairness and objectivity and the assurance that he takes no sides.

REPLIES TO REPORTS

The auditing department which does not have the authority to demand replies to its reported findings and evaluate the adequacy of the corrective action is a tiger without teeth.

Management directives or policy statements must spell out clearly that audit reports calling for corrective action must be responded to in writing. Usually these directives and statements set forth the time limits within which replies are to be submitted. The distribution sheet in one company bears this statement regarding replies[1].

> An "x" following your name in the column "For Securing Action" means that you are responsible for seeing that satisfactory action is taken with respect to the findings which are referred for action to persons under your jurisdiction.
>
> Management Directive XX requires you to see that an adequate reply, describing the action taken, is sent to the Vice President Finance and Controller within thirty days after the Audit Report release date. If action cannot be completed within this time limit, the Vice President Finance and Controller should be informed of the reason for the delay and when the final report may be expected.

It is desirable for each operating branch or division to have its own instructions regarding replies to audit reports. These instructions should state:

- Who should prepare the reply.
- Who should sign it.
- That the reply should be straightforward, addressing itself to the findings and not trying to justify the status quo.
- What steps should be taken if corrective action canot be completed within the established time span.

The auditors should let it be known that they will be willing to discuss corrective action and review drafts of replies. At the same time, the auditors should scrupulously respect the difference between staff and line. The line people must live with the corrective action they take. The auditor is responsible for pointing out defects and recommending *a* course of action — not *the* course of action. Still, he must have the right to point out that the course selected is inadequate.

Reports should remain open until the auditing organization considers the replies satisfactory. Some auditing organizations will not be satisfied solely with the statement of corrective action in a reply from the auditee. They may wish to see copies of revised directives. They may wish to return to the audit site to satisfy themselves that effective action has indeed been taken. They may schedule interim examinations within a period of six months or a year to make sure the reported deficiencies have not recurred.

When replies are unsatisfactory, and agreement cannot be reached orally with the auditee, the reply should be formally rejected by memorandum. The memorandum should spell out specifically in what respects the reply is deficient. Copies of the reply

---

[1]Research Committee Report No. 10, *Internal Audit Reporting Practices,* p 32.

should be addressed to whatever level of management is needed to see that the matter is satisfactorily resolved.

The auditing department should have a formal method of closing reports that have been satisfactorily responded to. This may be in the form of a memorandum to the director of auditing over the signature of the auditor. The memorandum should state that the auditor is satisfied with the response and that the report may now be closed. Exhibit 12-2 is an example of such a memorandum.

Exhibit 12-2.

To: Director of Internal Auditing
From: Auditor
Subject: Replies to report dated _____, Project No. _____
          Title _____
Ref: Replies:

Date	From
_____	_____
_____	_____

We have received the referenced replies describing the action taken on findings discussed in the subject report. Our evaluation of this action is as follows:

| | Reference to |
Evaluation	Findings

Considered an Interim Reply

Appears satisfactory. Awaiting final reply.
Does not appear satisfactory. We are investigating.

Considered a Final Reply

Appears satisfactory. Finding considered closed.
Appears satisfactory; but the action described needs confirmation before the finding can be considered closed.
Appears unsatisfactory; needs further investigation.

The action indicated in the referenced replies does _____ does not _____ constitute completion of satisfactory action on all the findings described in the subject report. Accordingly, we recommend that Project No. _____ be_____ not be _____ closed at this time.

_____
                    Auditor

Different companies follow different reporting practices. But there seems to be a uniform feeling about the need for follow-up procedures — with management's interest and support. Exhibit 12-3 is an example of a procedure covering replies to audit reports.

Exhibit 12-3. ABC CORPORATION
INTERNAL AUDITING DEPARTMENT

REPLIES TO AUDIT REPORTS

Policy

It is the policy at ABC that auditors may regard their responsibility discharged when they make their report. The responsibility for seeing that unsatisfactory conditions reported are properly corrected is assigned to operating management.

But to have some assurance that operating managers will take corrective action promptly, they are asked in the instructions on the report distribution sheet to reply to the executive vice president in writing when there are findings requiring corrective action. The reply must outline action taken to correct the unsatisfactory conditions reported and must bear the approval of all persons responsible for securing action. If any of the corrective action described in the reply is merely proposed and not completed, or is deferred to some future date, the reply should indicate the date when corrective action will be completed. A final reply should be made when all the corrective action has been completed.

Action Required

When replies are received they will be reviewed by the auditor in charge, the supervisor concerned, and by the audit manager. If the reply seems likely to dispose satisfactorily of the findings reported, the in-charge auditor should inform the director of internal auditing on the form provided for that purpose. The auditor should describe any matters subsequently discussed with operating management, such as action taken which is not clearly described in the reply, or action which does not conform to our recommendations but which we feel is worth a trial. This form should close the project.

If the corrective action described in the reply does not seem likely to correct the conditions reported, further action on the part of the in-charge auditor or supervisor is necessary. This may take the form of discussion with the operating manager in order to:

■ Clear up any questions or misunderstandings which may not have been cleared up in the review of the draft report.

■ Clear up any questions regarding action taken or to be taken which may not have been expressed clearly enough in the reply.

In any event, the objective is to secure some agreement or understanding as to an acceptable course of action with a minimum of further correspondence. It is therefore important to have clearly in mind what we mean by an acceptable course of action. We do not necessarily mean the adoption of all the recommendations made in a report in precisely the manner we have set forth. As operating management has the responsibility for correcting unsatisfactory conditions it also has been given the authority to decide how it should be done. Accordingly, in the absence of considerations of such importance as to cause the executive vice president or other members of top management to intervene, operating management will be free to accept, to accept with modifications, or to reject, any recommendations we have made. What we mean then is some course which at least does not seem so objectionable that it should not be given a trial.

Where no action is taken or the action taken or proposed seems clearly unsatisfactory and operating management seems unwilling to take any action which

Exhibit 12-3. (Cont.)

will satisfactorily dispose of the matter, a letter should be prepared for the signature of the executive vice president. It should state our position on the unsatisfactory conditions. These letters should be addressed to branch managers.

Monitoring Replies

The audit manager will delegate to the secretary or to a member of the staff the responsibility for keeping a record of replies required but not received.

When a reply has not been received within one month after the date of the report, the person responsible for keeping the record will notify the supervisor responsible. The supervisor will then make, or will have the auditor make, whatever inquiries seem to be necessary to determine when the reply might be expected. Thereafter, he will make further inquiries at intervals until he reaches a point where he and the audit manager think different action is desirable.

At this point it may be desirable for the supervisor to write a formal letter of inquiry for the signature of the executive vice president. That letter should be addressed to the person from whom the auditor's report requested the reply and should be forwarded through the director of internal auditing for the signature of the executive vice president. From that point on, the nature of any further action will depend on the kind of response received from operating management, or on the nature of any instructions received from the executive vice president.

The audit manager will submit a monthly report not later than the tenth of each month showing the status of replies. Copies should be provided for the executive vice president, the director of internal auditing, and the audit manager.

SUMMARY

Report reviews are both insurance for the auditor and courtesy to the auditee. They are important in resolving conflicts, establishing facts, and preventing disputatious replies.

The right to obtain and review replies to reports ensures proper consideration of the auditor's findings and recommendations and sees to it that deficient conditions are monitored until corrected.

The auditor must carefully consider the people with whom the reports should be reviewed and the order of the consecutive reviews. During the review conference he should try to set the stage for a calm and friendly discussion. He must be aware of potential conflicts and be prepared to resolve them. He must be amply equipped to present prompt and unequivocal support for his findings. He should be flexible in making word changes, but he must be adamant in seeing that his audit opinion is completely his own.

Executive management is vitally interested in the causes and effects of deficient conditions. The causes and effects should be explored and their description agreed upon in draft review.

The auditor must be given final responsibility for deciding on the adequacy of replies to audit reports. Management directives should spell out the auditor's authority to evaluate replies.

SUMMARY REPORTS TO MANAGEMENT

WHAT THEY DO

Summary reports to management have two separate functions. They tell management what the auditor has accomplished in comparison with what he had planned. And they summarize the auditor's conclusions about what he has seen. Both types of reports can be made quarterly, semiannually, or annually. Because both are extremely important, they deserve the auditor's best effort.

Reports of Accomplishment

The auditor issues internal audit reports during the year — reports that have brought significant findings and recommendations to management's attention. These reports may individually have been of inestimable value to management. But they are like yesterday's newspaper — they are obscured by the rush of time and events. They need to be summarized — to present a totality of what the auditor has done and accomplished.

The auditor's accomplishments can sometimes be identified by a dollar sign. This is salutary. When the auditor consistently and validly recovers or saves more than the amount that management pays for his services, the comparison of expense with savings is a potent reason to retain or expand the auditor's services. The auditor, then, should give prominent place to the amounts he has recovered or saved for his company.

Dollar return, however, is but one of the auditor's accomplishments. Often it is the least of them. And when a dry year passes with minimal or no recovery, he must look elsewhere to bring to management's eyes the significance of his other accomplishments.

The auditor must periodically call to management's attention summaries of his accomplishments — monetary or other — to demonstrate constantly the value of his efforts. And when he puts his mind to it, he can report an impressive array of things done and matters accomplished.

Reports of Audit Conclusions

The financial statements are a source of important information to management. They show in terms of dollars the position of the business and what it accomplished in the preceding period. They constitute the financial thermometer of the enterprise. They are indicators of its financial health or illness. They point to strengths and weaknesses. They display financial trends. They highlight danger spots. They represent *the* required reading of the businessman.

But with the expansion of audits directed toward operations that span an enterprise, businessmen are finding in these audits a source for other forms of business reports. These too can be objective and useful, because they are prepared by objective and competent professionals — the internal auditors. And these too can be relied upon.

Some internal auditing organizations have been issuing summary reports that appraise the company's administrative health or illness. But such reports are relatively new. Some managements are unaccustomed to them. They do not know if they can rely upon them. And therefore they do not know how to make use of them. Such reports take boldness, innovativeness, and persistence on the part of the internal auditor. In time these reports will be accepted.

The raw data is already available to the auditor. It is found in his working papers, his audit reports, and his records of observations around the entire audit course. All he has to do is learn how to summarize the data in a provocative and meaningful fashion.

Once accepted by management, these summaries — like financial reports — can also provide a sensitive thermometer, one that registers management's administrative health and provides a useful temperature chart for the corporate body.

In this chapter we shall discuss both these types of reports and the kinds of records that should be kept to prepare them.

REPORTS OF ACCOMPLISHMENT

These reports come in many forms. The precise form will depend on the skill of the director of auditing and how he sees the needs of those who receive his reports.

In some companies, internal auditing is firmly entrenched, and management's prime concern is over the extent of audit coverage. In other companies, the internal auditor must be constantly on the alert to justify his existence; and here the auditor will wish to concentrate on the results of audits and audit effectiveness.

Some of the reports can be simple and relatively brief. Some may be extensive and supported by charts and visual aids. The common denominators in these reports might be:

■ Comparison of work programmed with work accomplished
■ Number of areas covered
■ Number of reports issued
■ Number of communications to management
■ Cost of operating the auditing department
■ Amounts of recoveries and savings

The auditing department must develop and maintain administrative records which accumulate these data. For example:

Comparisons of Work Programmed with Work Accomplished

For each project, comparisons can be made between man-days programmed and man-days expended. Programmed man-days can be taken from the long-range program (see Exhibits 3-1 and 3-2). Man-days expended can be summarized by project on registers posted from individual time reports, such as that shown on Exhibit 4-3.

Areas Covered

This data can be accumulated on forms prepared for each completed audit project. The form has many purposes. It provides spaces for overall audit opinions for the entire project, yet it provides for segmented opinions also. Each project is often subdivided into specific operating functions or areas. This is particularly true in functional audits. There, the audit may cross many organizational lines. Each organization, therefore, may be considered separately, even though the several organizations were involved in the same project.

Also, some large organizational audits embrace a number of significant activities. Each such activity may itself be larger than some activities which constitute a single audit project. Hence, to achieve some measure of equality, the form should provide for a subdivision of the discrete elements covered by the audit project.

The form should also permit a classification of audit findings between major and minor. This information, as well as information on audit opinions, will be discussed in more detail later in this chapter.

A suggested form is shown as Exhibit 13-1. The data in the form can be used both for reports on audit activities and for reports on the company's operations.

Number of Reports Issued and Communications to Management

These can be summarized from data in Exhibit 13-1 and from registers of informal reports.

Costs of Operating the Department

These costs can be accumulated by recording salaries, fringe benefits, and allowances for vacations and estimated sick leave. The added overhead rate can be negotiated each year with the Budget Department.

Amounts of Recoveries and Savings

These amounts should be accumulated on a special record which identifies the project and analyzes the recoveries and savings. The record would show estimated recoveries at the end of the reporting period and actual recoveries after they have been finally determined.

Exhibit 13-1. CLASSIFICATION OF REPORT OPINIONS
AND DEFICIENCIES

Audit Project No. _____ Report Date _____

Title _____

	Opinions	**OVERALL**	**OPINIONS**		
		Controls		Performance	
		Sat.	Unsat.	Sat.	Unsat.
	Overall	___	___	___	___
Organization	Function	Detailed Opinions			

	Deficiencies	**Controls**		**Performance**	
		Major	Minor	Major	Minor
Organization	Finding No. (R)				

Totals
Open Findings _____
(R) Repeat Findings _____

_____

Date   Supervisor

In the following pages, we shall discuss and illustrate excerpts from four different reports of accomplishment. The first is a brief informal report. The second is a more extended narrative of accomplishments. The third is a selection of some graphs and charts taken from a report of accomplishment. The fourth is a brief report summarizing the year in retrospect and plans for the future.

A Textile Mill (Exhibit 13-2).   This semiannual report begins with a listing of the projects completed.

The summary of activities sets forth budgeted versus actual audit hours. The cost of operations shows the total expense of the auditing department, less costs billed to other organizations.

The report goes on to set forth the auditing department's most significant accomplishments, including cost recoveries. The report concludes with its goals for the following year. Two schedules support the report.

Exhibit 13-2a.   SUMMARY REPORT

TEXTILE MILL

Memorandum to: Mr. John Doe

Subject: Review of Audit Department Activity
                               Six Months Ended July 3, 19XX

                               Services performed during the period were:

Internal Auditing

Accounts Payable and Invoice Processing
Personnel Department
Commissary and Cafeteria
Computer Information Services
Purchasing Procedures
Credit Department
Bleachery Lot System
Group Annuity Dividend Statement
Kitchen Cotton and Bath Operations
Knit Division
Leases and Agreements
Mortgages Serviced by Trust Companies
Physical Inventories
Plant Payrolls
Plant Supply Rooms
Project Authorizations
Royalties and License Agreements
Traffic Department
Transportation Department
Travel Expenses

External Auditing

Six Credit Associations

Special Projects

Expedite X Orders
Assistance to Consumer Division — Inventory Controls
Budget for Sample Card Plant
Comparison of Rental Costs for Transportation Department
Nonoperative Assets
Annuity Dividend
XYZ Project

Exhibit 13-2b. SUMMARY OF ACTIVITIES

Schedule A shows total and chargeable hours compared with budget and with the periods ended January 2, 19XX and July 4, 19WW. Total staff time employed was 3,642 less than the last half of 19WW. Time spent on vacations, holidays, illness, staff training, etc., decreased 1,601 hours, leaving a net decrease of 2,041 hours charged to projects.

Time spent on company projects as a per cent of total time increased 2% with a corresponding decrease in external audits. Distribution of the increase is as follows:

	Hours	Per Cent
Audits	989	25%
Inventories	(1,881)	(17)
Special Projects	(914)	(6)
	(1,806)	2

The shift in time from inventories and special projects to audits is due to the fact that most inventories were taken in the last half of the year and that we completed the expediting of X Orders in January.

The department entered the first half of the year with a staff of 11 men. One man transferred to the Personnel Department, three men terminated, one man was acquired from the Management Intern Program, and one man was acquired from outside, leaving a staff level of eight men at mid-year.

Cost of Operations

The net cost to the company for operations of the Audit Department was as follows:

Total Cost	$81,359
Less: Services billed	4,500
	$76,859

Exhibit 13-2c.

Accompanying Schedule B shows department costs for the current period compared with budget and with the periods ended January 2 ,19XX and July 4, 19WW. Total cost per chargeable hour for the current period was $XX. This is $X more than the last half of 19WW and $X more than the budgeted cost per hour. Total costs decreased $5,190 from the last half of 19WW and were $12,000 less than budgeted costs. Major areas of cost per hour increases were salaries, clerical labor, and related payroll costs.

Significant Results Achieved

Significant results achieved due to our work in the first half of 19XX were concerned with improved procedures and controls in the following areas:

- Time Reporting and Payrolls
- Supply Rooms
- Traffic Department
- Knit Division
- Personnel
- Accounts Payable and Invoice Processing
- Transportation Department
- Consumer Division Inventory Controls

The adoption and implementation of Audit Department recommendations made during the first half of 19XX will result in approximate savings and /or additional income to the company as follows:

Transportation Department	$ 41,000
Credit Department	4,000
Accounts Payable	5,146
X Payroll	5,683
Y Payroll	24,959
Knit Division	152,050
Commissary and Cafeterias	524
	$233,362

Exhibit 13-2d.

The savings we have listed represent 3.04 times the net cost of $76,859 for the operation of the Audit Department.

General

Our present staff evaluation system and promotion policies appear to be adequate for the immediate future.

The status of the goals which we set for 19XX is as follows:

1. Intensify training in and use of statistical sampling. This has been accomplished. We are also using an EDP program to obtain our samples, and evaluate them where applicable.

2. Complete EDP training and include EDP audits as part of overall departmental audit coverage. This includes both operational audits of EDP Department and reviews of individual systems on a selected basis. The audit of the EDP Department has been completed. We are currently reviewing systems applicable to the Carpet Division.

3. Adoption of Audit Department Policy Statement. This has been submitted for approval but no action has been taken.

4. Increase audit coverage to include marketing efforts and selected area sales offices and warehouses. The only area covered to date is the Knit Division operations in the X Office.

5. Review staff salary levels for the purpose of remaining competitive. This has been accomplished through the director of compensation and benefits.

6. Send selected staff members to seminars for further development of their proficiency. This has not been accomplished because of budget reductions. We are, however, sending one senior auditor to a seminar in October.

Manager, Audit Department

SCHEDULE A

Exhibit 13-2e. SUMMARY OF ACTIVITIES

UVW Company — Audit Department
Six Months Ended July 3, 19XX

	Six Months Ended					
	July 3, 19XX		Jan. 2, 19XX		July 4, 19WW	
	Hours	%	Hours	%	Hours	%
Total Staff Hours	8,794	100.0%	12,436	100.0%	10,236	100.0%
Less: Vacations, Holidays, Military, Illness, etc.	741	8.4	1,402	11.3	1,001	9.8
Total Hours Available	8,053	91.6%	11,034	88.7%	9,235	90.2%
Less Training and General Office	263	3.0	1,203	9.7	968	9.5
Total Hours Charged to Projects	7,790	88.6%	9,831	79.0%	8,267	80.7%
Budgeted Hours	10,518		11,520		11,520	
% Budget Achieved		74 %		85 %		72 %
% Available Time Charged to Projects		97 %		89 %		90 %
Average Manpower	7.2		10.1		9.5	
Average Work Week (Hours)	40.6		41.0		43.1	

Distribution of Chargeable Hours

	Six Months Ended					
	July 3, 19XX		Jan. 2, 19XX		July 4, 19WW	
	Hours	%	Hours	%	Hours	%
Area Served						
UVW Company						
Audits	5,530	71%	4,541	46%	4,844	59%
Inventories	749	10	2,630	27	2,195	27
Special Projects	1,018	13	1,932	19	461	5
Total	7,297	94%	9,103	92%	7,500	91%
External Audits	493	6	728	8	767	9
Total Chargeable Hours	7,790	100%	9,831	100%	8,267	100%

SCHEDULE B

Exhibit 13-2f. OPERATING COST COMPARISONS

UVW Company — Audit Department

———————————— Six Months Ended ————————————

	July 3, 19XX				Jan. 2, 19XX		July 4, 19WW	
	Budget		Actual		Actual		Actual	
	Total	Hour	Total	Hour	Total	Hour	Total	Hour
Staff Salaries and Wages	$68,762	$6.54	$58,282	$ 7.48	$71,104	$7.23	$57,504	$6.96
Overhead:								
Clerical Labor Related	6,318	.60	6,010	.77	5,695	.58	3,306	.40
Payroll Costs	6,201	.59	5,196	.67	4,580	.47	4,718	.57
P.S.C.D. & Paid Holidays	318	.03	351	.05	274	.03	171	.02
Overtime Premium	- 0 -		- 0 -		35		- 0 -	
Supplies & Repairs	157	.02	88	.01	141	.01	118	.01
Traveling	8,269	.79	6,124	.79	7,805	.79	5,143	.62
Dues & Subscriptions	25		105	.01	293	.03	256	.03
Miscellaneous	345	.03	2,239	.29	3,294	.34	1,909	.23
Rent Expense	2,964	.28	2,964	.38	3,328	.34	3,328	.40
Total Overhead	$24,597	$2.34	$23,077	$ 2.97	$25,445	$2.59	$18,949	$2.28
Total Operating Costs	$93,359	$8.88	$81,359	$10.45	$96,549	$9.82	$76,453	$9.24

Gain (Loss) from Budget

	Dollars	Hours	Cost/Hour
Budget	$93,359	10,518	$ 8.8761
Actual	81,359	7,790	10.4440
	$12,000	2,728	($ 1.5679)

Excess of Budgeted Hours Over Actual (2,728 @$8.8761 Per Hour)	$24,214
Excess Cost Per Hour — Actual Over Budget (7,790 Hours @ $1.5679 Per Hour)	(12,214)
Net Budget Cost Over Actual Cost	$12,000

A Manufacturing Company Working Closely with a Government Agency (Exhibit 13-3). The report is formally transmitted by letter to the manager of finance. The text of the report covers four separate areas.

The first speaks of improvements in the audit function. It includes an upgrading from departmental to divisional status, improved relations with government auditors, an expansion in services to management, the preparation of a brochure on internal auditing for the benefit of management, and the action taken on certain government audit findings.

The second area reports on workloads, staff levels, salary increases, audit reports issued, and audit findings.

The third highlights improvements that include greater emphasis on operational auditing techniques, the use of audit findings as a basis for merit increases*, and potential computerization.

The fourth discusses several problem areas. One involves a difficulty unique to this company. Since the company works closely with the government, it is required to use certain audit programs; and the programs are difficult to apply. Another matter is the difficulty of scheduling work. Finally, the report points to the failure of some managers to accept internal auditing as a management tool.

Exhibit 13-3a. SUMMARY REPORT

A MANUFACTURING COMPANY WORKING CLOSELY WITH A GOVERNMENT AGENCY

1. IMPROVEMENTS IN THE AUDITING FUNCTIONS

Auditing Department Becomes Auditing Division

Fiscal year 19XX was a particularly memorable one for the audit function because as of April 1, 19XX, the Central Auditing Department of the General Accounting and Finance Division became the Auditing Division. We have already noted an improvement in the effectiveness of our operations as a result of this tangible and graphic evidence of the support of top management for auditing.

Improved Government Audit Reporting Procedure

Fiscal year 19XX brought a distinct improvement in the government's audit reporting procedure. Under this new procedure government audit representatives sit down with company representatives and discuss their audit findings in much the same way we have done for years. At these meetings, the company representatives make commitments for action they will take on the audit findings, and government representatives accordingly close the audit items so that they do not become follow-up items. Actually, this new system went into effect in the latter part of fiscal year 19WW prior to the time the bulk of the fiscal year 19WW reports were issued. Thus, the drastic reduction in number of follow-up items began in fiscal year 19WW as is demonstrated in the following listing of follow-up items generated during the past three fiscal years:

Year	No. of Items
Fiscal Year 19VV	86
Fiscal Year 19WW	5
Fiscal Year 19XX	2

---

*This is an extremely controversial point. Some people believe this system may set loose a task force of fault finders on operating managers. Others feel it is a frank acknowledgement of the auditor's reason for being.

Exhibit 13-3b.

Management Services Work Expands

During 19XX we engaged in several difficult management services projects; we believe the customers were quite satisfied with the results of this work. [The Appendix listing these jobs is not shown here.] We feel that this work is perhaps the most important and satisfying work we do, because we are working on live, active problems which are plaguing management and on which they really need objective, professional assistance.

Brochure on Internal Auditing Printed

We have prepared a handsome brochure explaining the internal auditing function for the benefit of installation management and others. We are in process of preparing a similar brochure describing our management services function to be used in informing plant management of this available service.

II. WORKLOAD AND STAFF LEVELS

Difficult to Evaluate Subcontract Audit Workload

The UVW project and the XYZ program pose staffing problems for the Auditing Division. Periodically, we hold discussions with the Purchasing Division to try to establish reasonable estimates of potential contract auditing workload for six months to a year in the future. The latest such reviews in FY 19XX with the Purchasing Division were during July 19WW and March 19XX and resulted in a requisition for increase in staff by one professional auditor.

Staff Level Increased by Six in Past Two Years

The staff level of the Auditing Division has been increased in the past two years by six permanent employees. This is due to three principal reasons. First, the need for contract auditing services for the Purchasing Division. We give this work top priority and feel we must be in a position to provide this service. Second, the government-wide audits of recent years have consumed an unusual amount of time.

Third, we have broadened our services by undertaking selected and important management service assignments at management's request. These operational-type assignments are needed; if we don't do them someone else (such as an outside consultant) will do them. We feel qualified to do this work because of our objectivity, independence, and the investigative training and capabilities of our staff.

Exhibit 13-3c.

Audit Staff at Full Strength First Time in Two Years

The last 12 months was the year of the "nursery." We have no less than 10 new, young, well-educated people who have been on the payroll less than two years. Some of these young people have already demonstrated outstanding qualities and will be real assets to the company before too long. 19XX saw the audit staff at full strength for the first time in two years. Until recently, it has been difficult to obtain qualified applicants for professional audit openings because our salary levels were not sufficiently attractive for the top graduates. Probably the recent general slowdown in the economy has boosted our chances of getting qualified applicants.

In fiscal year 19WW we received authorization to increase the professional staff by four because of the significant increase in the contract auditing workload. While these requisitions were all filled in fiscal year 19WW, we also lost four men and were only able to hire two replacements in fiscal year 19WW. Thus, at July 1, 19WW we had two open requisitions for professional auditors.

In fiscal year 19XX, we received authorization to increase the professional staff by one, and to increase the clerical staff by one. Both of these requisitions, plus the two held over from fiscal year 19WW, were filled in fiscal year 19XX, so that at June 30, 19XX, we were at full staff for the first time in several years.

Exhibit 13-3d.

278 Auditing Division Reports Issued in FY 19XX

While good solid audit findings are our principal product, the results of the audit work are summarized in informal hard copy lists of findings, and then in formal audit reports, together with management comments. During fiscal year 19XX, we published the following number of reports in the categories indicated.

Internal audit reports and hard copies	34
Special reports	23
Interim contract reports of audit trips	36
Advisory accounting reports to Purchasing	20
Fixed-price subcontract reports	4
Final contract audit reports	44
Monthly subcontract accounting reports	108
Annual subcontract accounting reports	9
Total	278

We are constantly striving to improve the quality of our formal audit reports to make them more readable and effective for management.

Exhibit 13-3e.

Significant Audit Findings

Approximately 40 significant findings resulted from the year's activity. There were many times that number of findings of lesser importance. We deem an audit finding to be significant when it:

■ Represents a breakdown in approved internal management controls.

■ Represents absence of an internal control which we feel is needed.

■ Represents significant procedure violations.

■ Represents poor or inefficient practice, such as an inordinate number of human errors.

■ Represents an irregularity.

■ Is indicative of poor management.

It is difficult or impossible to place a dollar value on these types of audit findings. Indeed, some findings can result in more initial cost, as where we recommend the institution of an internal control which we feel is badly needed to prevent future excessive costs.

Our analysis of these significant findings reveals that they fall into these general categories:

Strengthening internal controls	5
Organizational changes	1
Improved efficiency of operations	9
Procedural violations (major)	8
Procedures needing revision	2
Recommended decisions for management	5
Contract costs inaccurate, resulting in recoveries or savings	9
	39

Generally, these findings represent significant value to the company and good production from the auditing function. However, we anticipate that, with added emphasis on findings resulting from our forthcoming seminar on audit findings and our "incentive" plan for audit findings, fiscal year 19YY will bring forth even more audit findings than fiscal year 19XX. This should by no means be interpreted as indicating that the company is in bad shape. Quite the contrary, the administrative and service type functions particularly are on the whole well-managed and efficiently operated, in our opinion.

Exhibit 13-3f.

III. IMPROVEMENTS IN PROCESS

FY 19YY Audit Emphasis to be on Operational Auditing Techniques

At the urging of the government agency's assistant controller for auditing, our fiscal year 19YY plans include increased use of operational auditing techniques in all of our planned audits. Under this concept, searching questions will be asked which have been avoided in the past under more traditional (financial) auditing techniques. In all audits, an attempt will be made to ascertain objectives of the functions being reviewed and what progress has been made in achieving the objectives.

Whereas the traditional financial audit concluded when the auditor satisfied himself that assets were accounted for or cost was properly charged, the operational audit really begins at this point. The auditor may ask such questions as: Is this investment in assets really needed? Does it enhance the objectives of the function?

Exhibit 13-3g.

Quality and Resolution of Audit Findings to Be Used for Merit Increases

The disclosure and resolution of audit findings is the principal reason for the existence of the audit function. Management obviously expects us to discover audit findings if they exist.

There is a definite correlation between an auditor's ability and the findings he discovers, follows through, and successfully resolves. It is relatively easy to disclose a "half-baked" finding; i.e., one which looks on the surface like it might be a finding. It is much more difficult to follow the finding through and to get all the facts below the surface. When auditors give management "half-baked" findings, it is really a disservice and the auditors themselves are making negative points with management.

Starting July 1, 19XX, we are going to keep confidential records on findings discovered, studied in depth and resolved by our staff. This record will be a major factor in the awarding of merit increases in fiscal year 19YY.

Exhibit 13-3h.

Feasibility of Computerization of Subcontract Records Being Studied

We are currently studying the feasibility of computerizing our cost-type subcontract accounting, record-keeping and reporting. The study should be completed in about a month.

The volume of transactions in this function is large; and if computerization proves feasible, there should be some saving of clerical effort.

IV. PROBLEM AREAS

Government Audits Are Time Consuming

One of the least satisfying facets of our work is the government agency audits. There are several reasons for this. First, the audit programs are prepared centrally to be applied at all installations, both large and small. While we have tried to faithfully apply these programs at the four installations, we find that it usually consumes an enormous amount of audit time for what we feel is very little return on investment of this time. [The report shows a schedule of fiscal years, descriptions of the audits, and the man-hours consumed.] Another criticism of these audits is that many of them are statistical gathering jobs which could, in our opinion, be done at less cost by line personnel.

Scheduling the Workload Difficult

The reason that scheduling our work is so difficult is that we control less than half of our own time. We have always given top priority to requests for assistance by the Purchasing Division. Sometimes we receive very little notice (like a day) of an urgent trip to some distant city to review a strange accounting system or to aid purchasing personnel in negotiations with a vendor. Our work for the Purchasing Division consumes approximately one-third of our time.

We give second priority to requests by company management for management services work, depending upon its urgency and need for our services. We also give lower priority to government audits. These two types of work constitute about another one-third of our workload.

Therefore, lowest priority is given to our regularly scheduled internal audits, constituting the remaining one-third of our total workload. In other words, if necessary, we pull men off these assignments to put on contract assignments, government audits or management services jobs.

Exhibit 13-3h. (Cont.)

Government representatives are constantly asking us why we cannot put more men on our internal audits in order to assure getting them done on schedule. We always answer that other matters of greater urgency have come up (as they always do), and we had to pull men off our internal audit and assign them to the more urgent jobs.

Is There Too Much Auditing?

A rule of thumb to judge the size of an internal auditing function is about one auditor per 1,000 employees. This rule of thumb is the result of studies conducted nationwide by two independent organizations — the National Industrial Conference Board and The Institute of Internal Auditors. If one eliminates our equivalent audit personnel engaged in contract auditing, real estate and management services (15¾ people), one comes up with a figure of 13¼ equivalent internal auditors on our staff. This seems to be in line with the one auditor per thousand employees criteria.

Unwarranted Fear by Auditees

Certain management personnel never seem to have learned to accept auditing as a management tool and aid. They continually express fear and apprehension, probably that the results of the audits will place them in a bad light with their superiors. It is too bad that these individuals do not learn to accept audits and understand that our internal auditors have the same objectives as management, i.e., improved operations. The only thing management has to fear from our audit is the consequences of not acting upon valid audit recommendations.

On the other hand, the majority of auditees have learned to accept auditing and really benefit from it. Also, a growing number of auditees request management services help on some of their knotty problems. [The report is supported by a number of appendixes not recorded here.]

A Large Manufacturer. In the annual audit report, the auditing organization provides several charts. We have adapted two. One, Exhibit 13-4, shows the level of audit effort in terms of man-days, and compares it with the programmed man-days. The second, Exhibit 13-5, shows the number of written audit communications — both formal (Internal Audit Reports) and informal (Internal Audit Memos) — as an indicator of audit effort.

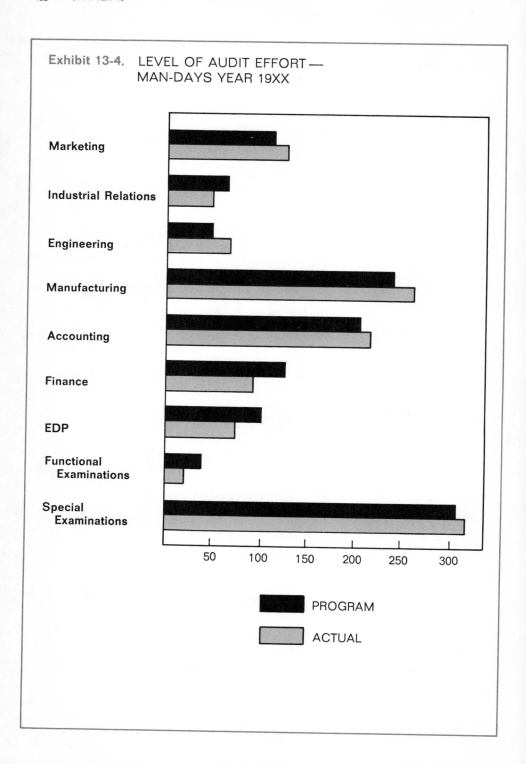

Exhibit 13-4. LEVEL OF AUDIT EFFORT —
MAN-DAYS YEAR 19XX

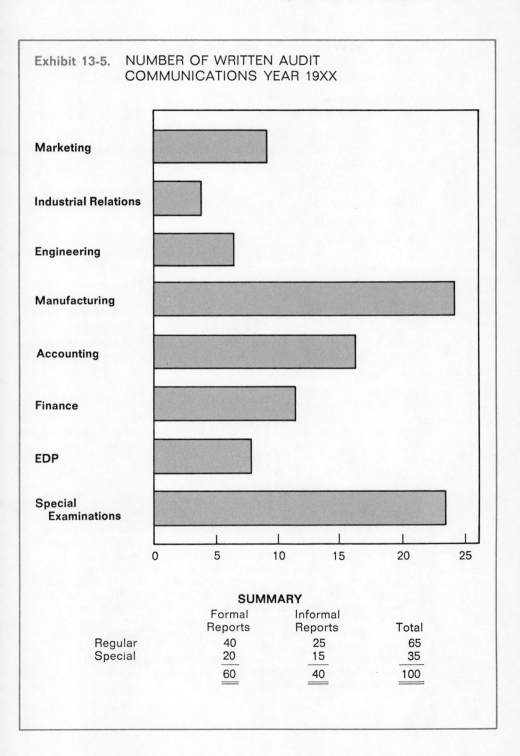

Exhibit 13-5. NUMBER OF WRITTEN AUDIT COMMUNICATIONS YEAR 19XX

SUMMARY

	Formal Reports	Informal Reports	Total
Regular	40	25	65
Special	20	15	35
	60	40	100

The various status reports, not reproduced here, cover such matters as:

- Expanded use of EDP
- Use of oral and visual presentations
- Application of management techniques to solve management problems
- Study of how to classify deficiency findings according to cause
- Staff training sessions
- Professional activities
- Conferences with executive management
- Contacts with external auditors
- Cost savings
- Titles of audit projects completed

A Financial Institution (Exhibit 13-6). This is an excerpt from a longer report. The excerpted portions show the highlights of activities for the preceding year, plans for the following year, including objectives for the year and strategies for accomplishing the objectives.

Exhibit 13-6. SUMMARY REPORT

FINANCIAL INSTITUTION

19XX in Retrospect

The year 19XX was a period of adjustment and reorganization for the Auditing Department. During the year, the department was relocated in its new permanent headquarters. A new Directors' Committee on Examinations and Audits was appointed; a new general auditor was elected; an accounting firm was engaged to audit the _____ for the first time, and the _____ was examined by the National Bank Examiners for the first time.

Many changes were made in the departmental organization, and a number of new audit programs were initiated. The most important of these was the development of a direct confirmation program of all of the bank's deposit and loan classifications. The bank's overseas office was audited for the first time, as were several new offices.

Exhibit 13-6.   (Cont.)

The department's audit of systems and data processing activities was strengthened by the addition of an experienced EDP auditor and an audit programmer to the staff. All members of the field crews were given the opportunity to take an elementary EDP correspondence course.

A high degree of coordination and cooperation between the department and the external auditors was achieved fairly soon after their employment. As expected, the integration of procedures and the required expansion of audit programs were time consuming for both parties during this first year. However, the time and effort spent in doing so substantially improved our audit program and will yield continuing benefits in the future.

Good rapport was also reached with the National Bank Examiners during their initial examinations of the bank. Few operating exceptions, and none of a general nature, were noted in their first consolidated reports which were circulated to all members of the Committee on Examinations and Audits.

Plans for 19YY

The authorized staff for the department is 120 persons, including 50 field crew auditors. At present, the department is near quota, as it has been during most of the year. During the coming year the department expects to add a five-man field crew to serve other areas and two internal auditors in the headquarters office. At the head office, staff additions will include an additional investigator and a clerk typist in the Investigation Section and two reconcilement clerks in the Bank Reconcilement Section.

Discussions have been held with the Bank's Training Department and the external auditing company on the development of a training program for the Auditing Department. It is hoped that such a program will begin within the year. We will make use of the seminar programs offered by the Bank Administration Institute and The Institute of Internal Auditors.

During 19WW the department was asked to submit its long-range plan for the period 19XX-19ZZ. The objectives and strategies outlined in the plan were as follows:

Objectives

The 19XX-19ZZ objectives of the Auditing Department are to assist all levels of management in the effective discharge of their responsibilities by furnishing them with objective analyses, recommendations and pertinent comments concerning offices, departments, and activities audited. The overall goal of the department is service to management.

Exhibit 13-6. (Cont.)

The primary means used to attain these objectives will be:

- Reviewing and appraising the soundness, adequacy, and application of the bank's accounting, financial, and operating controls.
- Ascertaining the extent of compliance with established policies, plans, and procedures.
- Ascertaining the extent to which company assets are accounted for, and safeguarded from losses of all kinds.
- Ascertaining the reliability of accounting and other data developed within the organization.
- Appraising the quality of performance in carrying out assigned responsibilities.

Strategies

1. Consult with our outside auditors and the National Bank Examiners in identifying areas of weak or inadequate audit coverage and providing corrective action.
2. Expand significantly our EDP audit staff and increase EDP training of other audit staff.
3. Expand the number of field crews, in keeping with the branch expansion program.
4. Step up our staff training program, utilizing the facilities of the Training Division, outside seminars and courses.
5. Recruit staff at a higher level of competency from both internal and external sources, particularly when recruiting for specialist positions.

Judiciously prepared, reports of accomplishment cannot help but benefit the auditor. They tell management that the auditor is evaluating himself and measuring his own accomplishment against approved standards. They point out that the auditor is carefully weighing what he has done and where he is going. They can be written in a light and simple style to make reading easy. They can be dressed up with charts and diagrams to improve understanding.

These reports are not easy to devise or prepare. They encroach upon the busy auditor's schedule of making audits. They may be started with a flourish, but abandoned after a few trials because they are onerous to keep up. But the auditor must remember that, artfully prepared, they *will* be read by management, and they will keep the auditor's efforts and accomplishments before management's eyes.

Reports on Company Operations

Reports on the operational health of the enterprise can be of absorbing interest to management. They can be a powerful instrument, and hence they must be used with discretion.

Management will see them as an indicator of administrative well-being or company malaise. Thus they must be soundly based. Conclusions drawn from a scattering of data can be misleading. A few random numbers will give incomplete and random data. But the stability provided by large numbers can be the strong foundation on which the auditor can build when he constructs and presents his reports on company operations.

It is true that executive management receives from operating management operating reports that provide information on production, schedules, quality, backlogs, staffing, and the like. But these may be self-serving declarations. What executive management needs is an objective, educated, professional evaluation of what all the auditor's efforts have brought to light in terms of administering the company's affairs.

This does not imply the direct evaluation of individuals. That is much too rock-strewn a path to walk. Such evaluations are difficult to support and easy to dispute. What it does imply is the accumulation of individual findings and conclusions and the depiction of trends and variations. There are several units of measurement — denominators — for such reports. We shall concentrate on two: Audit opinions. Audit deficiency findings.

Summarizing Audit Opinions

To be able to summarize and report to executive management on audit opinions, one must first set some ground rules.

Such opinions should be set out in the reports themselves. In that way, through the report draft reviews, the operating manager is acquainted with the auditor's opinion. He is given an opportunity to clarify, question, or dispute the audit opinion and be aware of the auditor's position. The fact that the opinion covers conditions and not individuals should make it easier to reach agreement.

Put in the simplest terms, audit opinions are satisfactory or unsatisfactory. There may be gradations, of course — highly satisfactory, satisfactory, qualified, poor, unsatisfactory. But that is a mere quibble. From management's point of view, the operation either measured up to standards or it didn't. The job was either being done or it wasn't.

Summarizing Deficiency Findings

The pivotal question is: What makes an unsatisfactory opinion? That, of course, depends on the deficiency findings. It is the deficiency finding that causes an otherwise satisfactory opinion to become an unsatisfactory one. And deficiency findings must also be divided into two classifications: major and minor. So guidelines must be set for these categories as well. And there can be endless hairsplitting on what constitutes a major finding and what constitutes a minor one. The director of auditing will have to define them, and all reports will have to follow the definitions if there is to be stability in the reports on operations. Here are some usable definitions:

A *major deficiency finding* is one which prevents an activity, function, or organization from meeting a substantial part of its significant goals or objectives, and changes a satisfactory opinion to an unsatisfactory one.

A *minor deficiency finding* is one which warrants reporting and which requires corrective action but which cannot be considered as preventing the accomplishment of a significant goal or objective. Of itself it will not impel an unsatisfactory opinion — although a number of such findings may.

Clearly, such rules need consistent and judicious interpretation. All deficiency findings, therefore, should be submitted for evaluation to the audit manager to ensure consistency and due deliberation at the appropriate level.

Deficiencies need one further breakdown if they are to be used effectively. Put in simple terms, management has two basic responsibilities in carrying out its operations. The first is to tell its people what needs to be done. The second is to motivate them to do it and do it right. Implicit in the first is providing systems, standards, directives, procedures, job instructions, and other means that come under the generic heading of control. Implicit in the second is carrying out activities in accordance with these systems, standards, directives, procedures, job instructions, and other means of control; and this comes under the generic heading of performance.

Deficiency findings, therefore, may be major or minor, and they may affect control or performance. Let us give some simple examples of each.

Control-Major

The procurement organization does not require competitive bids. Such a dereliction could seriously and adversely prevent the organization from reaching one of its primary objectives of getting required products at the best price. It affects control, rather than performance, since there is nothing to *prevent* buyers from obtaining bids. And even if, without being told to do so, experienced buyers were obtaining bids, this would not minimize the seriousness of the deficiency. New buyers might enter the procurement organization and, in the absence of rules to the contrary, give all their orders to favored suppliers. And any buyers might succumb to the blandishments of unscrupulous suppliers.

Performance-Major

Procedures required competitive bids. Yet 50% of the 200 purchase orders examined, representing a substantial portion of the amounts committed for materials, were not bid competitively, and the failure to obtain bids was not justified or otherwise documented. This is a performance deficiency because activities were not carried out in accordance with existing instructions. There may be a related control deficiency if the procurement instruction did not require supervisory review of the orders placed. But essentially we have a performance defect which prevents the accomplishment of an important procurement objective.

Control-Minor

Instructions on preparing a statistical report to executive management on procurement commitments did not provide for an independent verification of the figures. It is assumed that supervisory review of the report would prevent gross errors from being reported to management. But the missing control violates precepts of good administration and should be corrected.

Performance-Minor

Although instructions called for an independent verification of the commitment report to executive management, we found a number of errors in the report, none of which exceeded $100. Employees should be cautioned to exercise greater care. The person who signs the report should make periodic tests of the report to ensure its accuracy. Certainly, the performance deficiency needs correcting — but it cannot be said that the errors adversely affected a significant goal or objective.

With these definitions and guidelines known by all, reports on the volume of deficiency findings can be of significant interest to management and can indicate either deterioration or improvement in the administration of the company's activities. The information furnished can prompt management to take corrective action.

Trends in opinions and deficiency findings can be charted and can provide a useful indicator of the company's administrative health. Exhibit 13-7 contains charts that set out graphically the records of unsatisfactory opinions. The opinions follow the definitions of deficiency findings and are shown separately for controls and performance. A final chart shows the combination of the two. The charts indicate a gradual deterioration of administration. They show a need to search for basic causes and to prompt management to take the action needed to reverse an unsatisfactory trend.

At the foot of the chart is set forth the number of audit segments. This provides information as to the base on which the charts were constructed. Obviously, the base should be substantial enough to validate the report.

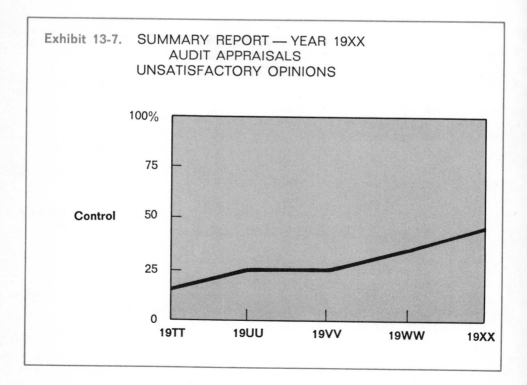

Exhibit 13-7. SUMMARY REPORT — YEAR 19XX
AUDIT APPRAISALS
UNSATISFACTORY OPINIONS

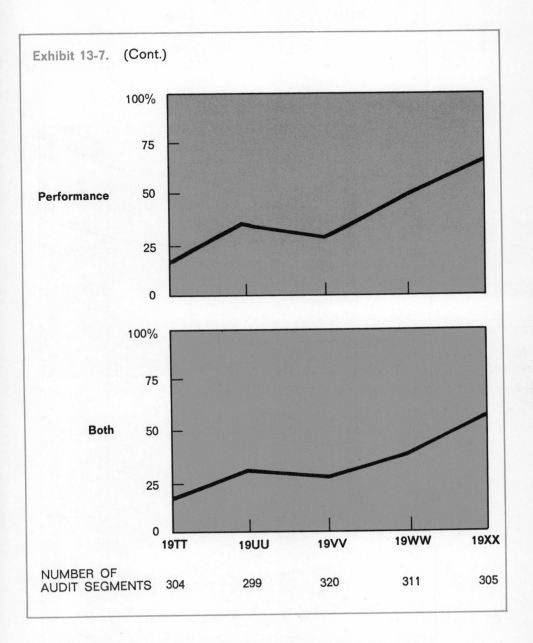

Exhibit 13-7. (Cont.)

Exhibit 13-8 shows a similar chart. This one portrays the number of deficiency findings over a period of five years and shows a condition which parallels that shown on the charts of opinions. The charts differentiate between (1) control and performance, and (2) major and minor deficiencies.

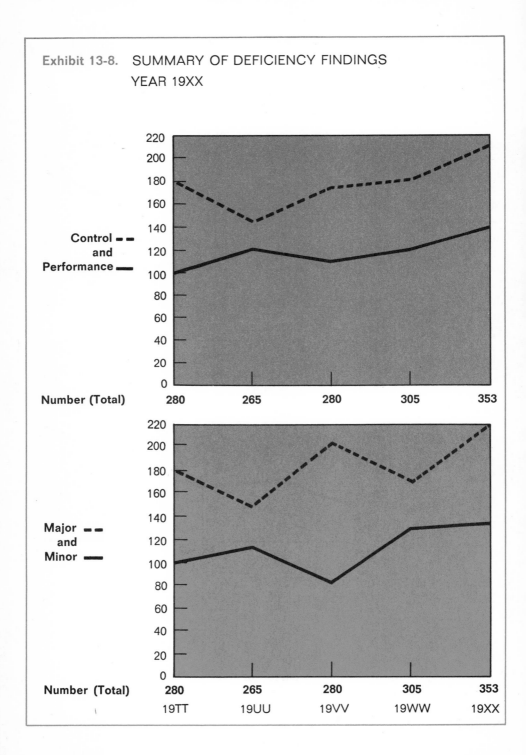

Exhibit 13-8. SUMMARY OF DEFICIENCY FINDINGS
YEAR 19XX

Summarizing Causes

But knowing that things are bad is not enough. Management should know why. Probably the most helpful information the auditor can provide management concerns causes of deficiencies. Know the cause and it is easier to prescribe the cure. Reports of deficient conditions and unsatisfactory opinions can provide management with reason for concern. But they can also be frustrating. The executive looks at the assessment of operational weakness and says, "I agree with you, Mr. Auditor, that things look bad. But *why* are they bad ? Until I know the causes I'm not sure I can make things better."

A good system of determining and reporting causes of deficiencies can go a long way toward helping the executive take broad corrective action. The individual reports set forth specific deficiencies which are then corrected. But the individual deficiencies do not spell out tendencies. They do not provide management with the spotlight which brings a condition into focus, which relates it to other deficiencies, and which shows the groups of deficient conditions deserving the most attention.

Spelling out causes takes painstaking work and much planning. The first step is to identify potential causes of defects. This is a matter of judgment. A dozen seasoned auditors presented with the problem could argue ad infinitum on the subject and never come to full agreement. Each auditing organization, working in entirely or slightly different environments might find certain causes more relevant than others. We shall point out some possibilities. The individual director of auditing or audit manager must make his own decision on what best suits his organization.

Here is one set of causes, keyed to the hierarchy of management controls in Exhibit 9-1:

A. Failure to devise suitable objectives and plans.

B. Failure to provide suitable resources of manpower or materials.

C. Failure to set standards.

D. Failure to train personnel.

E. Failure to provide an approval system.

F. Failure to provide a master (central) control.

G. Failure to ensure compliance with standards.

H. Failure to monitor the ongoing process.

I. Failure to devise a satisfactory system of records and reports.

These causes are directed exclusively to the manager or supervisor of an activity. There is some validity to this hierarchy of causes because when all is said and done, the superb manager can make anything happen under any circumstances. He is restricted solely by the resources at his disposal. When these restrictions seriously affect him and are beyond his control, the cause will most likely be Item A — failure (by executive management) to devise suitable objectives and plans, and B — failure to provide suitable resources. The remaining causes cover matters generally under the operating manager's control.

Here is another set of causes which encompass the efforts of organizations, managers, and individuals. These causes are segregated according to the major headings in Exhibits 9-1 and, in a general way, encompass the concepts in that exhibit.

A. Planning and Organizing
    1. Need for controls not recognized.
    2. Management decision not to take the required action.
    3. Failure to update.
    4. Failure to assign appropriate authority.
    5. Failure to assign appropriate priority.
    6. Failure to assign sufficient personnel.
    7. Failure to provide adequate basic training.
    8. Failure to provide adequate equipment.
    9. Failure to provide for coordination.
    10. Failure to assign responsibility.
    11. Other.

B. Controlling
    1. Failure to set or meet schedule.
    2. Failure to provide adequate instruction.
    3. Failure to see that standards are met.
    4. Failure to obtain feedback about the ongoing process.
    5. Failure to take prompt corrective action.
    6. Insufficient management attention.
    7. Insufficient supervisory attention.
    8. Management or supervisory attitude.
    9. Employee attitude.
    10. Human error.
    11. Other.

SUMMARY REPORTS TO MANAGEMENT ■ 465

In addition to defining the cause, it becomes necessary to determine the nature of the deficiency. True, the cause may be, for example, the failure to take prompt corrective action. But this defect could happen all the time, or part of the time. The action could be not timely or inaccurate. Finally, the action could be inconsistent. So along with the cause it is of interest to know whether the control or performance was:

a. Incomplete
b. Lacking
c. Not timely
d. Inaccurate
e. Inconsistent

It becomes abundantly clear, as efforts are made to assign causes, that like boxes within boxes within boxes, there are causes behind causes behind causes. One can easily get lost in philosophical theorizing about the cause behind the cause. Carried far enough it winds up with man's first fall from grace. But the essential cause — the cause that operating management is preoccupied with — is the cause whose removal most directly corrects the condition. Hence, it is significant, in assigning causes, to look to the action which line management took to correct the reported condition and to the nature of the deficiency.

This brings us to the use of a form that will help the auditor accumulate the data he needs to prepare analyses of deficiencies for management's use. Exhibit 13-9 is one example of such a form. It provides for identifying the deficiency for purposes of control. The identification can be made at the conclusion of each audit project. It also provides spaces for showing the project number and title, the date of the report which described the deficiency, and the supervisor and auditor-in-charge responsible for it. The functional area would be the broad organizational unit concerned, usually at the branch level of Finance, Administration, Procurement, Manufacturing, and Quality Control, to name a few. Some organizations, however, will require further breakdowns. For example, Manufacturing may be subdivided among Production Control, Tooling, and Production.

Exhibit 13-9. CAUSES OF DEFICIENCIES
CLASSIFICATION RECORD

Def. No. _____

Project No. _____ Title _____

Report Date _____ Supervisor _____ AIC _____

Functional Area _____

Deficiency: _____

_____

_____

_____

_____

_____

Corrective Action: _____

_____

_____

_____

_____

_____

Auditor's Statement of Underlying Cause: _____

_____

_____

_____

_____

_____

_____

	Major	Minor	Nature	Cause
Control	_____	_____	_____	_____
Performance	_____	_____	_____	_____

The deficiency would be stated essentially as it was summarized in the report. The corrective action would be that taken or proposed. The cause would be a narrative exposition of how the auditor — the one closest to the problem — perceived the cause of the condition.

The identification of the finding helps accumulate statistical data on whether the finding concerned control or performance and whether it is considered major or minor. If the same finding involves both control and performance, individual forms should be prepared for each category, to make summarization easy. This is proper since both the cause and the corrective action may be different.

For example: If an instruction was lacking on competitive bids in the procurement organization, the corrective action is to issue one. The cause is (A-1) the failure to recognize the need, and the nature is (b) lacking. If, however, some buyers — because they were experienced and did not need to be told — were obtaining competitive bids while others were not, the entire situation changes. The corrective action — after the instruction has been issued — is closer supervisory control. The cause is (B-7) insufficient supervisory attention, and the nature is (a) incomplete.

When these forms are faithfully prepared they can readily be summarized into a report to management. Exhibit 13-10 is an example of a report of the auditor's analysis of deficiencies. We have used the second set of causes, just listed, in the sample report.

Exhibit 13-10. ANALYSIS OF DEFICIENCY FINDINGS/YEAR 19XX

| | Total | | | | | |
	Number	Per Cent	Contr.	Perf.	Major	Minor
Nature of Deficiency						
Control or Performance:						
Incomplete	138	39	117	57	82	61
Lacking	110	31	72	38	76	32
Not timely	55	16	11	17	30	21
Inaccurate	36	10	6	18	10	9
Inconsistent	14	4	5	12	22	10
	353	100	211	142	220	133

Exhibit 13-10. (Cont.)	TOTAL					
	Number	Per Cent	Contr.	Perf.	Major	Minor
Cause of Deficiency						
Planning and Organizing						
Need not recognized	78	22	110	14	60	24
Unauthorized decision by line management	37	11	22	20	30	12
Failure to update	18	5	21	—	12	4
Failure to assign appropriate priority	18	5	2	12	10	3
Failure to provide for coordination	14	4	6	4	5	5
Failure to assign responsibility	14	4	6	4	6	3
Failure to assign sufficient personnel	11	3	1	2	7	4
Failure to provide adequate training	11	3	2	3	10	5
Failure to provide adequate facilities	3	1	1	1	—	—
Subtotal	204	58	171	60	140	60
Controlling						
Insufficient supervisory attention	75	21	16	32	31	37
Insufficient management attention	25	7	13	18	22	15
Failure to provide adequate instruction	21	6	3	16	8	3
Management/Supervisory attitude	11	3	3	4	4	4
Employee attitude	7	2	2	3	6	6
Human error	3	1	2	5	5	4
Other	7	2	1	4	4	4
Subtotal	149	42	40	82	80	73
Total	353	100	211	142	220	133

The various administrative activities and reports just discussed may seem burdensome. When the auditor works feverishly to meet the deadlines for such reports he may bewail his task and berate his taskmaster. But the rewards are worth the effort. As he examines these reports, the executive manager sees the auditor as a continuing source of information that will help in the guidance of the enterprise. The auditor becomes more — not less — valued. And he moves one step closer toward his goal of being a rightful member of the councils of executive management.

SUMMARY

The auditor's efforts are displayed primarily and initially in his individual audit reports. But these reports do not inform management of the sum total of his efforts. The auditor, therefore, owes management summary information on two fronts: (1) the extent and measure of his own efforts to provide adequate audit coverage and to maintain his technical ability to cope with business problems; and (2) his evaluation of the administrative competence of the enterprise.

The first front involves all the auditor has done to carry out his job in a professional way and to make sure he is able to continue doing so. The second is more difficult. It seeks to tell management how the auditor diagnoses the administrative health of the enterprise.

With careful preparation and planning, the auditor can provide management with significant information on trends, problem areas, and the causes of the problems. Such information elevates the auditor from a finger-pointer to a source of constructive information and to a member of the problem-solving team.

appendices

subject index

APPRAISING
OPERATIONS
FOR
MANAGEMENT

THE
PRACTICE
OF MODERN
INTERNAL
AUDITING

appendices

Appendix A-1

Table of 105,000 Random Decimal Digits, Statement 4914, Interstate Commerce Commission, May 1949. Reproduced with the permission of Bureau of Transport Economics and Statistics, Interstate Commerce Commission, Washington.

Line / Col.	(1)	(2)	(3)	(4)	(5)	(6)	(7)	(8)	(9)	(10)	(11)	(12)	(13)	(14)
1														
2														
3														
4														
5														
6														
7														
8														
9														
10														
11														
12														
13														
14														
15														
16														
17														
18														
19														
20														
21														
22														
23														
24														
25														
26														
27														
28														
29														
30														
31														
32														
33														
34														
35														
36														
37														
38														
39														
40														
41														
42														
43														
44														
45														
46														
47														
48														
49														
50														

Appendix A-2

Line\Col.	(1)	(2)	(3)	(4)	(5)	(6)	(7)	(8)	(9)	(10)	(11)	(12)	(13)	(14)
51	16408	81899	04153	53381	79401	21438	83035	92350	36693	31238	59649	91754	72772	02338
52	18629	81953	05520	91962	04739	13092	97662	24822	94730	06496	35090	04822	86774	98289
53	73115	35101	47498	87637	99016	71060	88824	71013	18735	20286	23153	72924	35165	43040
54	57491	16703	23167	49323	45021	33132	12544	41035	80780	45393	44812	12515	98931	91202
55	30405	83946	23792	14422	15059	45799	22716	19792	09983	74353	68668	30429	70735	25499
56	16631	35006	85900	98275	32388	52390	16815	69298	82732	38480	73817	32523	41961	44437
57	96773	20206	42559	78985	05300	22164	24369	54224	35083	19687	11052	91491	60383	19746
58	38935	64202	14349	82674	66523	44133	00697	35552	35970	19124	63318	29686	03387	59846
59	31624	76384	17403	53363	44167	64486	64758	75366	76554	31601	12614	33072	60332	92325
60	78919	19474	23632	27889	47914	02584	37680	20801	72152	39339	34806	08930	85001	87820
61	03931	33309	57047	74211	63445	17361	62825	39908	05607	91284	68833	25570	38818	46920
62	74426	33278	43972	10119	89917	15665	52872	73823	73144	88662	88970	74492	51805	99378
63	09066	00903	20795	95452	92648	45454	09552	88815	16553	51125	79375	97596	16296	66092
64	42238	12426	87025	14267	20979	04508	64535	31355	86064	29472	47689	05974	52468	16834
65	16153	08002	26504	41744	81959	65642	74240	56302	00033	67107	77510	70625	28725	34191
66	21457	40742	29820	96783	29400	21840	15035	34537	33310	06116	95240	15957	16572	06004
67	21581	57802	02050	89728	17937	37621	47075	42080	97403	48626	68995	43805	33386	21597
68	55612	78095	83197	33732	05810	24813	86902	60397	16489	03264	88525	42786	05269	92532
69	44657	66999	99324	51281	84463	60563	79312	93454	68876	25471	93911	25650	12682	73572
70	91340	84979	46949	81973	37949	61023	43997	15263	80644	43942	89203	71795	99533	50501
71	91227	21199	31935	27022	84067	05462	35216	14486	29891	68607	41867	14951	91696	85065
72	50001	38140	66321	19924	72163	09538	12151	06878	91903	18749	34405	56087	82790	70925
73	65390	05224	72958	28609	81406	39147	25549	48542	42627	45233	57202	94617	23772	07896
74	27504	96131	83944	41575	10573	08619	64482	73923	36152	05184	94142	25299	84387	34925
75	37169	94851	39117	89632	00959	16487	65536	49071	39782	17095	02330	74301	00275	48280
76	11508	70225	51111	38351	19444	66499	71945	05422	13442	78675	84081	66938	93654	59894
77	37449	30362	06694	54690	04052	53115	62757	95348	84299	96196	87517	48708	34195	52924
78	46515	70331	85922	38329	57015	15765	97161	17869	45349	67189	84147	31791	44164	48612
79	30986	81223	42416	58353	21532	30502	32305	86482	05174	07901	54339	58861	74818	46942
80	63798	64995	46583	09785	44160	78128	83991	42865	92520	83531	80377	35909	81250	54238
81	82486	84846	99254	67632	43218	50076	21361	64816	51202	88124	43086	56613	91511	75928
82	21885	32906	92431	09060	64297	51674	64126	62570	85072	01511	34347	15125	23642	57031
83	60336	98782	07408	53458	13564	59089	26445	29789	85205	41001	12535	12133	14645	23541
84	43937	46891	24010	25560	86355	33941	25786	54990	71899	15475	95434	98277	36288	95386
85	97656	63175	89303	16275	07100	92063	21942	18611	47348	20203	18623	88579	27982	53402
86	03299	01221	05418	38982	55758	92237	26759	86367	21216	98442	08303	56613	91511	75928
87	79626	06486	03574	17668	07785	76020	79924	25651	83325	88428	45476	93932	58200	35402
88	85636	68335	47539	03129	65651	11977	02510	26113	99447	68645	34327	15152	55230	93448
89	18039	14367	61337	06177	12143	46609	32989	74014	64708	00533	35398	58408	13261	47908
90	08362	15656	60627	36478	65648	16764	53412	09013	07832	41574	17639	82163	60859	75567
91	79556	29068	04142	16268	15387	12856	66227	38358	22478	73373	88732	09443	82558	05250
92	92608	82674	27072	32534	17075	27698	98204	63863	11951	34648	13873	81008	35960	15087
93	23982	25835	40055	67006	12293	02753	14827	23235	35071	99704	37543	11601	35503	85171
94	09915	96306	05908	97901	28395	14186	00821	80703	70426	75647	76310	88717	37890	40129
95	59037	33300	26695	62247	69927	76123	50842	43834	86654	70959	79725	93872	28117	19233
96	42488	78077	69882	61657	34136	79180	97526	43092	04098	73571	80799	76536	71255	64239
97	46764	86273	63003	93017	31204	99968	24205	32758	57506	55043	15243	17099	47625	88684
98	03237	45430	55417	63282	90816	17349	88072	22999	36058	43788	21216	30057	46356	90038
99	86591	81482	52667	61583	14972	90053	89534	76036	49199	43716	97548	04379	46370	28672
100	38534	01715	94964	87288	65680	43772	39560	12918	86537	62738	19636	51132	25739	56947

Appendix A-3

Line	(1)	(2)	(3)	(4)	(5)	(6)	(7)	(8)	(9)	(10)	(11)	(12)	(13)	(14)
101	13284	16834	74151	92027	24670	36665	00770	22878	02179	51602	07270	76517	97275	45960
102	97459	99887	91065	90453	46809	76324	17564	17560	91547	91604	07954	91607	07436	24120
103	35240	38640	81065	64464	62729	80432	65787	83287	14141	63248	05948	97257	35848	91983
104	38980	64060	34759	38867	87836	94624	98535	57185	67501	77661	33336	97819	70401	11019
105	60578	06483	28673	37867	07936	98710	89539	27186	31237	80612	44448	98122	29812	95419
106	36247	27850	73958	20673	37800	63815	71051	54288	39296	37318	65724	90412	96104	62077
107	99638	66980	99746	72438	11174	42159	19202	17564	30867	12635	88607	01458	89578	50413
108	07913	94740	14637	81845	60571	80434	90628	19324	68574	92445	33236	11450	30240	52630
109	22403	15774	43857	99805	61365	96399	59993	59062	30404	13198	59966	70404	29812	37126
110	24038	48605	85788	55835	88835	53761	37790	37790	39404	13198	59966	70404	29812	83126
111	74976	14631	35908	28821	39470	63835	12854	30166	52432	22342	36878	17456	96104	18327
112	35565	71628	70189	26436	63426	42159	92038	55359	52527	26936	36270	42737	86725	96805
113	41275	67523	43155	82389	42016	80834	06203	20639	37414	85170	07648	98553	43968	82524
114	49651	30688	45046	23189	02460	63599	13780	32816	37404	39520	49455	50955	34698	37286
115	45234	65551	45173	09	91060	89	23925							32286
116	76509	47069	76869	41797	11910	49672	12854	97966	09073	75887	36878	00268	97121	57676
117	17894	60868	43967	21357	72485	11899	92038	63708	80807	44014	32704	95331	89572	21059
118	32751	05338	79945	61596	01360	63594	10628	57120	58855	89560	07648	56314	72736	73344
119	54604	22688	37946	13960	67637	59411	59993	32035	58559	39221	46747	50558	34698	67662
120	25944	29950	59180	65204	41737	59577	17891	86464	01434	39221	46747	50558	34698	71800
121	99035	34202	02743	92503	30098	63362	56625	92265	24102	00789	05822	26760	58975	30761
122	52024	45744	98100	26309	06127	61030	97001	93145	65889	05373	01908	95409	57355	72862
123	78752	45404	68110	85197	83102	33240	26361	01045	58712	58146	09080	79531	53271	97775
124	25282	67106	89685	60413	67737	14080	05427	71845	86809	21545	10429	75035	36699	53464
125	25282	67106	89685	60413	17127	14080	05542	71845	86809	21545	10429	75035	36699	55580
126	11959	90928	90226	92503	70725	90262	56073	00661	73102	60278	15261	06969	44294	07672
127	10630	31936	98105	01428	57117	35577	59984	03170	22197	15269	43087	34736	19308	83614
128	83516	19363	68110	85197	24325	14278	82637	81547	23500	53042	30364	95847	96142	53354
129	55338	66666	89600	60806	02810	43609	12224	35543	60184	17337	35857	54289	80090	18118
130	55338	66666	89600	60806	02810	43609	12224	35543	60184	17337	35857	54289	80090	18118
131	78017	90928	02730	92503	83375	51811	12998	76847	73321	14436	53891	31915	97764	54149
132	44760	31936	98105	01428	54316	09744	55583	05176	31516	16308	22811	79800	07322	60388
133	83163	19363	68110	85197	51685	46532	35426	83090	37952	53417	30307	54293	80504	60735
134	41347	46666	89600	60806	07824	14360	66819	84164	66036	66311	85851	41258	14631	09251
135	41347	46666	89600	60806	71020	83658	12224	33322	66036	26311	66851	41258	14631	55251
136	78017	90928	02730	92503	83375	51811	74399	76847	05320	29169	53891	70204	15428	75091
137	44760	31936	98105	01428	43188	29674	28456	05188	47700	46138	22811	39034	30642	80534
138	83163	19363	68110	85197	51685	45619	35426	83090	08931	34822	85851	42387	42601	96447
139	41347	46666	89600	60806	71020	14007	58317	84164	68131	98712	66851	16308	78286	90473
140	41347	46666	89600	60806	71020	83658	12224	33322	66036	98712	66851	16308	78286	84473
141	78017	90928	02730	92503	83375	51811	74399	76847	84567	29169	53891	53357	15428	84476
142	44760	31936	98105	26309	43188	69744	28456	05188	94138	46138	22811	39034	30642	94451
143	83163	19363	68110	85197	51685	46532	35426	83090	84628	34822	85851	42387	42601	33676
144	41347	46666	89600	60806	71020	14007	58317	37726	46036	98712	66851	16308	29167	29015
145	41347	46666	89600	60413	71020	83658	33322	33322	66036	98712	66851	16308	28413	05417
146	78017	90928	02730	92503	83375	51811	74399	76847	84567	29169	53891	53357	15428	86932
147	44760	31936	98105	26309	43188	69744	28456	05188	94138	46138	22811	39034	30642	12645
148	83163	19363	68110	85197	51685	46532	35426	83090	84628	34822	85851	42387	42601	29167
149	41347	46666	89600	60806	71020	14007	58317	37726	46036	98712	66851	16308	29167	29167
150	41347	46666	82961	60413	71020	83658	32415	33322	66036	98712	66851	16308	28413	05417

Appendix A-4

Line	Col. (1)	(2)	(3)	(4)	(5)	(6)	(7)	(8)	(9)	(10)	(11)	(12)	(13)	(14)
151	38128	51178	75056	13606	16111	73533	42564	59874	29399	67834	91055	89917	51096	89011
152	60952	60455	29830	96118	50717	73826	32160	78274	25399	37011	91285	33917	54273	49326
153	90524	07326	67160	96118	75792	23537	09446	24960	80523	39828	93174	95597	97567	30814
154	49899	18278	29526	81010	75750	23537	01426	59605	80247	19293	02018	47908	02853	05819
155	18499	99209	81060	19488	65596	55987	47939	91225	94768	43608	00438	05548	09443	82897
156	65373	72984	30171	37741	70203	94094	87261	30056	54124	70131	18936	02138	59372	09075
157	40653	12843	04213	70925	50760	50317	61709	61776	25472	81162	52817	51597	54273	49033
158	51326	22238	56344	44580	83231	50488	74541	07116	25447	41602	77318	15102	57515	07633
159	69742	99302	62578	83570	30337	09482	65412	17106	47538	13452	22620	24260	40015	74716
160	58013	74072	67488	74580	47992	96419	58624	13624	47538	13452	22620	24260	40015	74716
161	18334	19855	42887	08279	43206	47077	42637	45603	09011	20662	14642	49984	94509	56380
162	59618	09193	58063	29080	62734	72658	70572	91363	72757	26969	13954	14632	24168	74648
163	75668	28623	39210	70061	54463	52890	98059	67204	76818	01859	13487	14663	87603	89713
164	13964	77802	69101	86418	54468	34519	80572	13756	72757	02185	34837	35934	80603	97701
165	96656	06490	36741	84518	34463	86432	15417	41375	76886	19008	66877	35934	59801	00497
166	03363	50769	15942	14549	38324	87094	19069	67590	11087	68574	22591	20894	85915	91499
167	70367	25057	12925	25496	13254	73467	91407	49120	07302	76074	29567	67042	38698	65708
168	47870	08636	72761	16042	32873	53709	31204	73120	48009	76074	95605	23097	16698	14557
169	79504	21875	22761	10518	28375	73898	00552	76684	77366	32276	04697	76148	48779	26776
170	46967	21416	50920	54673	20628	98995	30162	89561	76199	42257	11647	76148	48779	97907
171	14558	11128	35444	59019	87516	48193	02945	00922	48189	04724	21263	17226	92955	91251
172	12449	61853	01133	30412	28150	66587	17701	10097	54236	67788	20856	20420	53892	53892
173	32290	16853	06819	31049	39520	25998	87315	99166	93126	62703	76538	51068	21468	36920
174	13261	54174	72761	17982	51508	55798	34428	93131	45124	32000	25748	45869	96831	30651
175	47663	61089	59571	56992	20628	21798	65177	63133	72699	82000	41569	76148	21124	21128
176	16948	57839	76164	78311	47547	58003	64630	45817	67867	18062	87453	17226	72904	73117
177	21258	13986	65181	57760	72061	59392	45460	96015	66552	20444	59662	20420	39201	58740
178	99015	74712	49586	70749	85004	62880	34189	25034	49959	25788	56104	51068	04188	27954
179	08759	67420	23706	65599	33925	03004	16398	31384	37553	55209	34651	45869	22835	13311
180	67323	32031	35303	32994	33925	03004	63938	98	404	60	52	04	81	26
181	36304	40944	88292	65784	21245	63377	64536	98373	48971	75442	95592	06141	45096	73117
182	15887	61399	54137	57649	72261	38255	54660	90527	52306	36563	25410	05824	46430	58740
183	78934	61678	50967	41363	85004	16663	15634	78731	45289	39612	56693	30173	63026	27954
184	17624	89421	03612	63645	62620	85212	62363	29566	00519	84545	24587	84617	44682	13311
185	27418		09623	80725		84162	12929					79121	18929	13445
186	67392	40944	37566	80019	21245	69377	13305	94523	55263	57910	78870	36538	14513	82118
187	04910	10283	48530	59244	23055	13845	10474	10723	65287	63058	95588	57809	37305	81062
188	19445	20302	63762	23701	15553	40781	92196	87561	74538	65227	90791	15132	62578	96176
189	21406	13512	46189	76311	24299	87212	67460	20637	57166	91206	16817	79121	37329	14521
190	23995	20912		23751		27024		09471		35026			18929	
191	04910	24681	55977	16412	01101	69341	13305	94303	80703	57910	78770	36593	14513	18091
192	19445	01958	11325	11325	02861	43803	10748	69507	17689	63958	95588	21057	37305	39170
193	21406	96688	42205	72882	56167	42855	07296	06422	10689	88818	90791	57851	62578	29288
194	23995	06643	41478	58897	56249	27024	21460	20563	40937	16961	16817	78744	18929	10628
196	09866	24681	55977	16412	01101	69341	13305	94303	80703	57910	78770	36593	42546	03060
197	46041	01958	11325	11325	02861	43803	10748	69507	17689	63958	42857	21057	09781	58160
198	19911	96688	42205	72882	56167	42855	07296	06422	10689	88818	66885	57851	64533	27040
199	23995	06643	41478	58897	56249	27024	21460	20563	40937	16961	35893	78744	46707	21983
200											26053			

Appendix A-5

Line\Col.	(1)	(2)	(3)	(4)	(5)	(6)	(7)	(8)	(9)	(10)	(11)	(12)	(13)	(14)
201	78995	36244	02673	25475	84953	61793	50243	63423	69303	80308	49977	18075	43227	08266
202	04908	58450	06684	93935	84887	73059	60826	57003	69331	87895	47651	79532	29510	41695
203	46580	33570	33630	86719	86194	46736	60461	80349	44738	33996	47147	75493	51427	41958
204	29240	91792	98680	05175	07194	46772	22803	09607	01851	62711	31170	74373	68150	17956
205	68010	81333	97090	06280	78944	20228	22080	09607	10251	62711	16200	43733	35820	78966
206	17156	02182	82504	19840	93747	80910	78260	25136	62018	62918	73800	57197	97305	70597
207	50711	94789	59171	12611	99299	80755	79913	18302	84280	16702	97855	79936	84544	72916
208	39612	52739	75916	77362	39976	93275	37931	09044	29107	04643	88536	68651	09405	80510
209	75620	82726	36113	72657	58181	03075	01154	14442	04107	17493	19334	25619	97435	89491
210	01020	55151	34027	51175	13215	30735	04467	35427	25257	93614	39928	52519	34368	02114
211	08337	89989	24260	08618	66794	25889	52860	57715	46763	45319	18027	14270	27305	56535
212	76808	42269	19705	30509	69431	96234	08734	52086	82294	49039	15290	40387	87505	72561
213	39830	30641	08670	49018	95814	74304	91404	72662	30636	75579	25082	40388	09515	65930
214	85990	55817	55647	75105	06442	30575	11640	15084	74466	32701	90108	44118	40650	40507
215	85990	51371	56070	54075	94367	20228	23802	03711	25257	06121	39928	55295	34368	57574
216	62936	33074	76718	08618	21597	47386	45553	08754	46763	95315	23157	15116	18017	42730
217	31588	94289	67309	12611	13574	36628	08434	23434	82294	73413	52761	10673	21836	56274
218	07380	30549	00510	47890	46558	14200	11640	09124	30636	53737	76431	23867	00331	85186
219	45600	68729	05852	47792	91004	07218	24807	15184	74465	82182	03412	13217	14313	70593
220	31600	55151	34027	51175	11534	07218	23802	03584	25257	06121	03412	13217	14313	70593
221	01452	03423	23917	53017	16026	47286	78411	95107	38036	30177	89117	32054	44015	61149
222	37012	92693	67993	52890	90816	07996	36449	24354	05294	77348	65908	32590	17010	55765
223	51919	54893	44608	34837	90924	99547	44703	89373	79219	38647	65200	32696	60545	60308
224	67338	87291	38248	74854	13363	21605	41806	16832	99211	46182	96111	60913	35623	29812
225	16198	46893	14608	15677	79365	14200	03705	85584	08774	46182	96111	60913	35623	29812
226	18755	67545	76498	09761	22661	39610	07965	02628	10783	48806	44612	06830	27848	87597
227	61901	95975	07082	23997	96071	03456	13085	06830	10635	01630	64675	09644	07442	92472
228	94714	95970	38261	25095	96601	34560	36526	15336	06336	94548	07509	36447	23010	17006
229	03466	60899	07428	47854	76521	03630	03796	13248	09211	06547	30299	30014	23057	17175
230	52692	43030	58256	41175	78099	18835	05947	03821	09518	06547	37110	39013	27890	17006
231	18751	25352	25556	09761	94441	96100	20035	66592	78261	24503	73518	70635	99088	66369
232	19914	56155	07082	23998	97739	13166	60382	07442	73161	01277	44274	76355	07471	61445
233	19111	95976	07082	25999	75180	91304	60288	80354	49528	17517	42765	04192	12103	64138
234	82224	46089	58126	41175	06498	54190	03121	28165	05317	48779	60266	30010	21789	77506
235	55405	43693	09644	51075	64498	54190	03121	28165	05317	48779	60266	30010	21789	77506
236	94170	44467	76498	09761	09441	43294	20328	37879	01825	11453	18047	95095	08649	25047
237	21850	55155	07082	55897	97735	09581	50780	15069	08817	35456	04771	50787	35238	58313
238	55864	95976	07471	55056	37518	35948	60288	80354	49666	14456	12765	25014	40312	76187
239	22944	24083	13294	50894	64498	09825	69286	32911	79666	52959	12760	66793	10543	06807
240	36840	42092	52075	83926	42875	71500	69216	01350	02132	97393	44080	60342	08232	80102
241	—	—	—	—	—	—	—	—	21825	11453	29585	70067	09471	16319
242	—	—	—	—	—	—	—	—	18817	35456	01177	69687	10543	57652
243	—	—	—	—	—	—	—	—	79666	52959	91685	83341	24991	39377
244	—	—	—	—	—	—	—	—	79666	52959	87545	66342	22422	80101
245	—	—	—	—	—	—	—	—	—	—	—	—	—	37379

Appendix A-6

Line / Col.	(1)	(2)	(3)	(4)	(5)	(6)	(7)	(8)	(9)	(10)	(11)	(12)	(13)	(14)
251	89429	26726	15563	94972	99991	44419	60523	31022	23728	76417	16477	11177	68376	56874
252	24197	25401	25568	91976	78736	47101	06231	45632	90252	18152	41192	11469	27085	62291
253	81858	21958	51840	80136	74481	01755	83846	78021	69632	31813	27562	14640	40282	60115
254	51049	12846	02646	80636	67808	09116	63682	92227	63212	81816	93657	16439	80247	33922
255	73891	47025	40937	71907	26827	98065	36882	25715	26662	92141	89357	87800	61521	60600
256	40938	73894	40854	15997	55299	95033	31736	75064	91314	75293	04895	39355	54837	72003
257	59057	43567	24892	69890	57345	96050	62540	73642	57805	17223	35604	35604	50205	95334
258	59774	29158	16904	39883	57345	60528	25410	01446	54636	01723	94603	29727	07731	99476
259	39765	07548	09013	89841	95440	13610	51420	70446	13760	94635	85521	95244	79795	10742
260	38901	64502	24770	29209	89140	06610	94418	66214	26001	78605	69117	72446	79783	22305
261	25642	27100	56128	62145	82388	45197	76462	83994	01126	71717	32855	58679	97165	02810
262	31871	74120	60806	63092	17846	31615	17981	13193	05344	49293	33185	52477	00733	27085
263	81171	75630	66588	85693	04840	36910	49682	12031	59445	32358	94729	90013	24324	93670
264	69874	31231	43144	49563	48446	26269	47864	11604	39964	13360	13771	94152	38744	56047
265	27848	31107	05761	02015	53911	61486	31189	32225	11155	08144	49011	23061	07795	95047
266	69407	69736	25918	42915	45847	87401	13339	19864	34931	06601	67478	45218	27887	93049
267	38221	03091	42340	78175	43356	59760	28287	16550	24985	46251	52477	60847	23937	68481
268	24631	31231	41039	50252	67516	41146	49682	65409	39393	89265	53361	58400	94631	09979
269	81185	33796	42830	74544	52210	90567	72801	25759	47630	22865	13584	31650	96901	79961
270	45275	16885	56229	02151	13010	61448	31189	53346	41155	08144	11987	33250	44611	95047
271	97260	09552	22829	66403	73837	73445	86663	15929	32052	06601	15785	99708	58678	95967
272	00031	65214	21468	51997	06348	24117	51958	19511	50780	51396	24147	50372	60580	27800
273	24631	45214	41038	99530	41006	68097	94198	25709	04087	89286	76309	75340	60205	15850
274	81185	79442	84803	00550	51165	03197	94260	35033	38667	25037	30210	64017	46890	53850
275	34101	87189	56289	00170	13010	61486	31186	55334	11155	02211	01899	33250	41011	53850
276	77186	93097	27005	30265	18176	03254	06079	85467	08237	06601	15785	10060	58675	95967
277	23148	01498	10851	16704	76557	53147	21487	95591	35047	56251	24147	45245	60485	07800
278	11863	03935	16313	25035	59657	58189	65857	19511	31131	89265	43031	73740	66493	21686
279	51189	14254	09383	04457	89457	01757	64260	28013	04087	25030	09107	01899	27102	99968
280	27587	84772	56207	54341	72829	36097	72801	53346	41155	02211	09507	33250	53850	53850
281	42116	86593	22829	11422	90687	23726	11212	30418	41804	49222	46560	51060	33157	83948
282	39654	61400	21420	42088	02654	87251	73912	30447	30947	51376	42431	45245	79928	78783
283	53549	31231	11400	69978	41680	75382	53010	83447	30047	89265	43031	90822	70022	17141
284	25910	76150	98445	00550	62962	10707	34124	01487	02098	51030	09651	74756	00147	21686
285	91106	86450	84455	54341	72962	08172	37822	25187	24098	34946	50106	12116	27102	99968
286	37133	89234	27008	13067	90254	23726	48534	16955	25754	95645	03148	10602	15660	86520
287	13983	28517	10088	16702	91759	10383	89531	10757	02000	16733	39193	90297	66457	61938
288	62663	36187	16313	25003	78555	33539	56310	08026	06309	51714	12886	57112	66499	88034
289	65575	08125	08388	24693	54043	63113	79968	15635	28440	03141	62864	58112	27102	87334
290	65925	95455	08385	24641	72962	33477	37822	54187	34034	06844	14251	58112	71702	88415
291	97978	74676	44229	54895	51592	71196	48534	48092	77568	51123	34199	31176	06238	15973
292	01945	14524	06157	86630	91759	10383	89531	91306	58550	11805	50553	20520	71705	81487
293	68560	14811	34779	60248	78555	35539	56310	08672	39051	50554	42331	43743	41702	45264
294	54530	31672	03888	41803	53440	63113	87968	74189	61147	13177	62887	73712	54182	84115
295	79954	69601	83557	99067	83235	48663	31503	54829	54723	13177	15387	26073	68915	84115
296	55479	01059	44229	56975	06785	80930	92443	48920	77568	51123	34199	31176	06238	15973
297	38761	00330	16157	86680	06212	97821	70601	91306	58550	05744	50553	20520	71705	81487
298	31776	06540	64779	60248	54056	69613	19602	74189	39051	50554	45827	73712	54182	45264
299	31710	70640	36772	41803	33455	53164	19603	74192	61147	13177	15387	26073	41182	84115
300	77532	87188	83557	99067	83235	48663	31503	54829	54723	13177	15387	26073	68915	84115

Appendix B FACTORS REQUIRED TO ACHIEVE GIVEN CONFIDENCE LEVELS

(Confidence levels in percentages converted to standard deviation units, based on the normal distribution curve.)

Confidence level	Factor
99.9	3.2905
99.7	3.0000
99.5	2.8070
99.0	2.5758
98.0	2.3263
95.5	2.0000
95.0	1.9600
90.0	1.6449
85.0	1.4395
80.0	1.2816
75.0	1.1503
70.0	1.0364
68.3	1.0000
60.0	0.8416
50.0	0.6745
40.0	0.5244
30.0	0.3853
20.0	0.2534
10.0	0.1257

Appendix C-1 SQUARE ROOT OF SAMPLE SIZE AND PRECISION FOR MEAN VALUES IN STANDARD DEVIATION UNITS FOR AN INFINITE UNIVERSE

Reprinted with permission of Department of Defense, Defense Contract Audit Agency.

Sample Size (n)	Square Root of Sample Size	Precision for Confidence Level of: [*]			
		80%	90%	95%	99%
30	5.4772	+ .2394	+ .3102	+ .3734	+ .5032
31	5.5678	.2351	.3046	.3662	.4930
32	5.6569	.2312	.2996	.3599	.4836
33	5.7446	.2275	.2949	.3539	.4770
34	5.8309	.2240	.2900	.3484	.4685
35	5.9161	.2208	.2857	.3431	.4604
36	6.0000	.2175	.2815	.3380	.4548
37	6.0828	.2144	.2775	.3331	.4463
38	6.1644	.2115	.2737	.3283	.4396
39	6.2450	.2087	.2698	.3238	.4336
40	6.3246	.2060	.2663	.3196	.4276
41	6.4031	.2036	.2628	.3154	.4218
42	6.4807	.2009	.2595	.3114	.4163
43	6.5574	.1986	.2564	.3075	.4110
44	6.6332	.1962	.2533	.3038	.4060
45	6.7082	.1939	.2503	.3002	.4010
46	6.7823	.1917	.2476	.2968	.3910
47	6.8556	.1896	.2448	.2935	.3915
48	6.9282	.1876	.2421	.2903	.3871
49	7.0000	.1856	.2393	.2871	.3829
50	7.0710	.1837	.2370	.2841	.3787
51	7.1414	.1818	.2346	.2812	.3747
52	7.2111	.1800	.2323	.2783	.3708
53	7.2801	.1783	.2300	.2755	.3670
54	7.3485	.1766	.2277	.2728	.3632
55	7.4162	.1749	.2256	.2702	.3598
56	7.4833	.1733	.2235	.2677	.3564
57	7.5498	.1717	.2215	.2652	.3529
58	7.6158	.1702	.2195	.2628	.3497
59	7.6811	.1687	.2177	.2605	.3466
60	7.7460	.1673	.2157	.2582	.3434
61	7.8102	.1658	.2139	.2560	.3403
62	7.8740	.1645	.2121	.2539	.3374
63	7.9373	.1631	.2103	.2517	.3346
64	8.0000	.1619	.2086	.2497	.3319
65	8.0623	.1606	.2068	.2477	.3292
66	8.1240	.1593	.2054	.2457	.3266
67	8.1853	.1582	.2038	.2437	.3240
68	8.2462	.1569	.2022	.2418	.3215
69	8.3066	.1558	.2007	.2399	.3190
70	8.3666	.1547	.1992	.2383	.3165

[*]Multiply applicable factor by standard deviation computed from sample. The result is the precision at the indicated confidence level.

Appendix C-2

Sample Size (n)	Square Root of Sample Size	Precision for Confidence Level of: 80%	90%	95%	99%
71	8.4261	± .1535	± .1978	± .2366	± .3143
72	8.4853	.1525	.1963	.2349	.3120
73	8.5440	.1514	.1949	.2332	.3097
74	8.6023	.1504	.1936	.2316	.3075
75	8.6602	.1494	.1923	.2300	.3053
76	8.7178	.1484	.1910	.2284	.3032
77	8.7750	.1474	.1897	.2269	.3011
78	8.8318	.1464	.1885	.2254	.2990
79	8.8882	.1454	.1872	.2240	.2970
80	8.9443	.1445	.1860	.2225	.2951
81	9.0000	.1435	.1847	.2211	.2932
82	9.0554	.1427	.1836	.2198	.2913
83	9.1104	.1418	.1825	.2183	.2894
84	9.1651	.1409	.1814	.2170	.2876
85	9.2195	.1401	.1806	.2157	.2858
86	9.2736	.1392	.1795	.2145	.2840
87	9.3274	.1385	.1785	.2131	.2823
88	9.3808	.1376	.1774	.2119	.2807
89	9.4340	.1369	.1761	.2107	.2790
90	9.4868	.1361	.1752	.2094	.2774
91	9.5394	.1353	.1741	.2083	.2758
92	9.5917	.1346	.1732	.2070	.2742
93	9.6436	.1338	.1722	.2059	.2726
94	9.6954	.1331	.1713	.2048	.2712
95	9.7468	.1324	.1704	.2038	.2696
96	9.7980	.1317	.1694	.2026	.2681
97	9.8489	.1310	.1685	.2016	.2666
98	9.8995	.1303	.1677	.2005	.2652
99	9.9499	.1296	.1668	.1995	.2640
100	10.0000	.1290	.1660	.1984	.2626
101	10.0499	.1284	.1651	.1974	.2613
102	10.0995	.1277	.1643	.1964	.2600
103	10.1489	.1271	.1635	.1955	.2587
104	10.1980	.1265	.1627	.1945	.2574
105	10.2469	.1259	.1619	.1936	.2562
106	10.2956	.1253	.1611	.1927	.2550
107	10.3441	.1247	.1604	.1918	.2537
108	10.3923	.1241	.1596	.1908	.2525
109	10.4403	.1236	.1589	.1899	.2514
110	10.4881	.1230	.1581	.1891	.2502

Appendix C-3

Sample Size (n)	Square Root of Sample Size	Precision for Confidence Level of:			
		80%	90%	95%	99%
111	10.5356	± .1224	± .1574	± .1882	± .2490
112	10.5830	.1219	.1567	.1874	.2479
113	10.6301	.1214	.1560	.1865	.2468
114	10.6771	.1208	.1553	.1857	.2457
115	10.7238	.1203	.1546	.1848	.2445
116	10.7703	.1198	.1539	.1840	.2434
117	10.8166	.1193	.1533	.1832	.2424
118	10.8628	.1188	.1526	.1825	.2414
119	10.9087	.1183	.1520	.1817	.2403
120	10.9544	.1178	.1514	.1809	.2393
121	11.0000	.1173	.1507	.1801	.2383
122	11.0454	.1168	.1501	.1794	.2373
123	11.0905	.1163	.1495	.1786	.2362
124	11.1355	.1158	.1489	.1779	.2353
125	11.1803	.1153	.1483	.1772	.2343
126	11.2250	.1148	.1476	.1765	.2334
127	11.2694	.1144	.1470	.1756	.2324
128	11.3137	.1139	.1465	.1751	.2315
129	11.3578	.1134	.1459	.1744	.2306
130	11.4018	.1130	.1453	.1737	.2297
131	11.445	.1126	.1448	.1730	.2287
132	11.4891	.1122	.1442	.1723	.2279
133	11.5326	.1118	.1437	.1717	.2270
134	11.5758	.1114	.1431	.1710	.2262
135	11.6189	.1109	.1426	.1704	.2252
136	11.6619	.1105	.1421	.1698	.2244
137	11.7047	.1101	.1416	.1692	.2236
138	11.7473	.1097	.1410	.1685	.2228
139	11.7898	.1093	.1405	.1679	.2220
140	11.8322	.1089	.1400	.1672	.2211
141	11.8743	.1086	.1395	.1667	.2203
142	11.9164	.1081	.1390	.1661	.2195
143	11.9583	.1078	.1385	.1655	.2188
144	12.0000	.1074	.1380	.1649	.2179
145	12.0416	.1070	.1375	.1643	.2172
146	12.0830	.1067	.1371	.1638	.2164
147	12.1244	.1063	.1366	.1631	.2157
148	12.1655	.1060	.1361	.1626	.2149
149	12.2066	.1056	.1357	.1620	.2141
150	12.2474	.1052	.1352	.1615	.2134

Appendix C-4

Sample Size (n)	Square Root of Sample Size	Precision for Confidence Level of: 80%	90%	95%	99%
151	12.2882	± .1048	± .1348	± .1610	± .2127
152	12.3288	.1045	.1343	.1604	.2119
153	12.3693	.1041	.1339	.1599	.2112
154	12.4097	.1038	.1334	.1594	.2106
155	12.4499	.1035	.1330	.1588	.2098
156	12.4900	.1031	.1326	.1583	.2091
157	12.5300	.1028	.1322	.1578	.2085
158	12.5698	.1025	.1317	.1573	.2077
159	12.6095	.1021	.1313	.1568	.2071
160	12.6491	.1018	.1309	.1563	.2064
161	12.6886	.1015	.1305	.1558	.2058
162	12.7279	.1012	.1301	.1552	.2051
163	12.7671	.1009	.1296	.1549	.2045
164	12.8062	.1006	.1292	.1544	.2038
165	12.8452	.1003	.1288	.1538	.2032
166	12.8841	.1000	.1285	.1534	.2026
167	12.9228	.0997	.1281	.1529	.2020
168	12.9615	.0994	.1277	.1524	.2013
169	13.0000	.0991	.1273	.1520	.2007
170	13.0384	.0988	.1269	.1515	.2001
171	13.0767	.0985	.1266	.1510	.1992
172	13.1149	.0982	.1262	.1506	.1989
173	13.1529	.0979	.1258	.1502	.1983
174	13.1909	.0976	.1255	.1497	.1977
175	13.2288	.0974	.1250	.1493	.1971
176	13.2664	.0970	.1247	.1489	.1965
177	13.3041	.0967	.1243	.1484	.1960
178	13.3417	.0965	.1240	.1480	.1943
179	13.3791	.0962	.1236	.1476	.1949
180	13.4164	.0959	.1233	.1472	.1942
181	13.4536	.0957	.1229	.1467	.1937
182	13.4907	.0954	.1226	.1463	.1932
183	13.5277	.0951	.1223	.1459	.1926
184	13.5647	.0949	.1219	.1455	.1920
185	13.6015	.0946	.1216	.1451	.1915
186	13.6382	.0944	.1213	.1447	.1910
187	13.6748	.0941	.1210	.1444	.1905
188	13.7113	.0939	.1206	.1440	.1899
189	13.7477	.0936	.1202	.1436	.1894
190	13.7840	.0934	.1199	.1431	.1889

Appendix C-5

Sample Size (n)	Square Root of Sample Size	Precision for Confidence Level of: 80%	90%	95%	99%
191	13.8203	+ .0931	+ .1196	+ .1428	+ .1884
192	13.8564	.0929	.1193	.1424	.1879
193	13.8924	.0926	.1190	.1420	.1874
194	13.9284	.0924	.1187	.1417	.1869
195	13.9642	.0922	.1184	.1413	.1864
196	14.0000	.0919	.1181	.1409	.1859
197	14.0357	.0917	.1178	.1406	.1854
198	14.0712	.0915	.1175	.1402	.1849
199	14.1067	.0912	.1172	.1399	.1845
200	14.1421	.0909	.1168	.1394	.1839
201	14.1774	.0907	.1165	.1391	.1835
202	14.2127	.0904	.1162	.1387	.1830
203	14.2478	.0903	.1159	.1384	.1826
204	14.2829	.0900	.1157	.1381	.1820
205	14.3178	.0898	.1154	.1377	.1816
206	14.3527	.0896	.1151	.1374	.1811
207	14.3875	.0894	.1148	.1371	.1807
208	14.4222	.0892	.1145	.1367	.1803
209	14.4568	.0890	.1143	.1364	.1798
210	14.4914	.0887	.1140	.1361	.1794
211	14.5258	.0885	.1137	.1358	.1790
212	14.5602	.0883	.1135	.1354	.1786
213	14.5914	.0881	.1132	.1351	.1782
214	14.6287	.0879	.1129	.1348	.1777
215	14.6629	.0877	.1127	.1345	.1772
216	14.6969	.0875	.1124	.1342	.1768
217	14.7309	.0873	.1121	.1339	.1764
218	14.7648	.0871	.1119	.1336	.1760
219	14.7986	.0869	.1116	.1333	.1756
220	14.8324	.0867	.1114	.1330	.1752
221	14.8661	.0865	.1111	.1326	.1748
222	14.8997	.0863	.1109	.1324	.1744
223	14.9332	.0861	.1106	.1321	.1740
224	14.9666	.0859	.1104	.1318	.1737
225	15.0000	.0857	.1101	.1315	.1733
226	15.0333	.0855	.1099	.1312	.1729
227	15.0665	.0853	.1096	.1309	.1725
228	15.0997	.0852	.1094	.1306	.1721
229	15.1327	.0850	.1092	.1303	.1717
230	15.1657	.0848	.1089	.1300	.1713

Appendix C-6

Sample Size (n)	Square Root of Sample Size	Precision for Confidence Level of:			
		80%	90%	95%	99%
231	15.1987	+ .0846	+ .1087	+ .1297	+ .1709
232	15.2315	.0844	.1085	.1295	.1706
233	15.2643	.0842	.1082	.1292	.1702
234	15.2971	.0841	.1080	.1289	.1698
235	15.3297	.0839	.1078	.1286	.1695
236	15.3623	.0837	.1075	.1284	.1691
237	15.3948	.0835	.1073	.1280	.1688
238	15.4278	.0834	.1071	.1278	.1684
239	15.4596	.0832	.1069	.1275	.1680
240	15.4919	.0830	.1066	.1272	.1676
241	15.5242	.0828	.1064	.1270	.1673
242	15.5563	.0827	.1062	.1267	.1669
243	15.5885	.0825	.1060	.1264	.1666
244	15.6205	.0823	.1058	.1262	.1663
245	15.6525	.0822	.1055	.1259	.1659
246	15.6844	.0820	.1053	.1257	.1656
247	15.7162	.0818	.1051	.1254	.1652
248	15.7480	.0817	.1049	.1252	.1649
249	15.7797	.0815	.1047	.1249	.1646
250	15.8114	.0813	.1045	.1247	.1642
251	15.8430	.0812	.1043	.1244	.1639
252	15.8745	.0810	.1041	.1242	.1635
253	15.9060	.0808	.1039	.1239	.1632
254	15.9374	.0807	.1036	.1237	.1629
255	15.9687	.0805	.1035	.1234	.1626
256	16.0000	.0804	.1033	.1232	.1622
257	16.0312	.0802	.1030	.1229	.1619
258	16.0624	.0801	.1028	.1227	.1616
259	16.0935	.0799	.1026	.1225	.1613
260	16.1245	.0797	.1025	.1222	.1609
261	16.1555	.0796	.1023	.1220	.1606
262	16.1864	.0794	.1021	.1218	.1603
263	16.2173	.0793	.1019	.1215	.1600
264	16.2481	.0791	.1017	.1213	.1597
265	16.2788	.0790	.1015	.1211	.1594
266	16.3095	.0788	.1013	.1208	.1591
267	16.3401	.0787	.1011	.1206	.1588
268	16.3707	.0785	.1009	.1204	.1585
269	16.4012	.0784	.1007	.1202	.1582
270	16.4317	.0783	.1005	.1199	.1579

Appendix C-7

Sample Size (n)	Square Root of Sample Size	Precision for Confidence Level of: 80%	90%	95%	99%
271	16.4621	+ .0781	+ .1004	+ .1197	+ .1576
272	16.4924	.0780	.1002	.1195	.1573
273	16.5227	.0778	.1000	.1193	.1570
274	16.5529	.0777	.0998	.1191	.1567
275	16.5831	.0775	.0996	.1189	.1564
276	16.6132	.0774	.0994	.1186	.1561
277	16.6433	.0773	.0993	.1184	.1559
278	16.6733	.0771	.0991	.1182	.1556
279	16.7033	.0770	.0989	.1180	.1553
280	16.7332	.0769	.0987	.1178	.1550
281	16.7631	.0767	.0985	.1176	.1547
282	16.7929	.0766	.0984	.1174	.1544
283	16.8226	.0764	.0982	.1172	.1541
284	16.8523	.0763	.0980	.1170	.1539
285	16.8819	.0762	.0979	.1167	.1536
286	16.9115	.0760	.0977	.1165	.1533
287	16.9411	.0759	.0975	.1163	.1531
288	16.9706	.0758	.0973	.1161	.1528
289	17.0000	.0756	.0972	.1159	.1525
290	17.0294	.0755	.0970	.1157	.1522
291	17.0587	.0754	.0968	.1155	.1519
292	17.0880	.0753	.0967	.1153	.1517
293	17.1172	.0751	.0965	.1151	.1514
294	17.1464	.0750	.0963	.1149	.1512
295	17.1756	.0749	.0962	.1147	.1509
296	17.2046	.0747	.0960	.1145	.1507
297	17.2337	.0746	.0959	.1143	.1504
298	17.2627	.0745	.0957	.1141	.1501
299	17.2916	.0744	.0955	.1139	.1498
300	17.3205	.0742	.0954	.1137	.1496
325	18.0278	.0713	.0916	.1092	.1437
350	18.7083	.0686	.0882	.1052	.1384
375	19.3649	.0664	.0852	.1016	.1337
400	20.0000	.0642	.0825	.0983	.1294
425	20.6155	.0623	.0800	.0954	.1255
450	21.2132	.0605	.0777	.0927	.1220
475	21.7945	.0589	.0757	.0902	.1187
500	22.3607	.0574	.0737	.0879	.1156
525	22.9129	.0560	.0719	.0858	.1129
550	23.4521	.0547	.0703	.0838	.1103

Appendix C-8

Sample Size (n)	Square Root of Sample Size	Precision for Confidence Level of:			
		80%	90%	95%	99%
575	23.9792	± .0535	± .0687	± .0819	± .1078
600	24.4949	.0524	.0673	.0802	.1055
625	25.0000	.0513	.0659	.0786	.1034
650	25.4951	.0503	.0646	.0770	.1014
675	25.9808	.0494	.0634	.0756	.0995
700	26.4575	.0485	.0623	.0742	.0977
725	26.9258	.0476	.0611	.0729	.0960
750	27.3861	.0468	.0601	.0717	.0944
775	27.8388	.0461	.0592	.0705	.0928
800	28.2843	.0454	.0582	.0694	.0913
825	28.7228	.0447	.0573	.0684	.0899
850	29.1548	.0440	.0565	.0674	.0886
875	29.5804	.0434	.0557	.0664	.0873
900	30.0000	.0428	.0549	.0654	.0861
925	30.4138	.0422	.0542	.0645	.0849
950	30.8221	.0416	.0534	.0637	.0838
975	31.2250	.0411	.0527	.0628	.0827
1000	31.6228	.0405	.0520	.0620	.0816
1100	33.1662	.0387	.0496	.0592	.0778
1200	34.6410	.0370	.0475	.0566	.0745
1300	36.0555	.0356	.0450	.0544	.0716
1400	37.4166	.0343	.0440	.0524	.0690
1500	38.7298	.0331	.0425	.0507	.0666
1600	40.0000	.0321	.0411	.0490	.0645
1700	41.2311	.0311	.0399	.0476	.0625
1800	42.4264	.0302	.0388	.0462	.0608
1900	43.5890	.0294	.0378	.0450	.0592
2000	44.7214	.0287	.0368	.0438	.0576
2500	50.0000	.0256	.0329	.0392	.0516
3000	54.7723	.0234	.0300	.0358	.0471
3500	59.1608	.0217	.0278	.0332	.0436
4000	63.2455	.0203	.0260	.0310	.0408
4500	67.0820	.0191	.0245	.0292	.0384
5000	70.7107	.0183	.0233	.0277	.0365
5500	74.1620	.0173	.0222	.0264	.0348
6000	77.4597	.0165	.0212	.0253	.0333
6500	80.6226	.0159	.0204	.0243	.0320
7000	83.6660	.0153	.0197	.0234	.0308
7500	86.6025	.0148	.0190	.0226	.0299
8000	89.4427	.0143	.0184	.0219	.0288
8500	92.1954	.0139	.0178	.0213	.0280
9000	94.8683	.0135	.0173	.0207	.0272
9500	97.4679	.0132	.0169	.0201	.0264
10000	100.0000	.0128	.0164	.0196	.0253

Appendix D-1   FINITE UNIVERSE CORRECTION FACTOR

Reprinted with permission of Department of
Defense, Defense Contract Audit Agency.

Sampling Fractions n/N	Finite Universe Correction Factor	Sampling Fractions n/N	Finite Universe Correction Factor	Sampling Fractions n/N	Finite Universe Correction Factor
		(Read Table Across)			
.0001	1.00000	.0005	.99980	.0010	.99955
.0015	.99930	.0020	.99905	.0025	.99880
.0030	.99855	.0035	.99830	.0040	.99805
.0045	.99780	.0050	.99755	.0055	.99730
.0060	.99705	.0065	.99780	.0070	.99654
.0075	.99629	.0080	.99604	.0085	.99579
.0090	.99554	.0095	.99529	.0100	.99504
.0105	.99479	.0110	.99454	.0115	.99428
.0120	.99403	.0125	.99378	.0130	.99353
.0135	.99328	.0140	.99303	.0145	.99277
.0150	.99252	.0155	.99227	.0160	.99202
.0165	.99177	.0170	.99151	.0175	.99126
.0180	.99101	.0185	.99076	.0190	.99050
.0195	.99025	.0200	.99000	.0205	.98975
.0210	.98949	.0215	.98924	.0220	.98899
.0225	.98874	.0230	.98848	.0235	.98823
.0240	.98798	.0245	.98772	.0250	.98747
.0255	.98722	.0260	.98696	.0265	.98671
.0270	.98646	.0275	.98620	.0280	.98595
.0285	.98570	.0290	.98544	.0295	.98519
.0300	.98494	.0305	.98468	.0310	.98443
.0315	.98417	.0320	.98392	.0325	.98367
.0330	.98341	.0335	.98316	.0340	.98290
.0345	.98265	.0350	.98239	.0355	.98214
.0360	.98188	.0365	.98163	.0370	.98138
.0375	.98112	.0380	.98087	.0385	.98061
.0390	.98036	.0395	.98010	.0400	.97985
.0405	.97959	.0410	.97933	.0415	.97908
.0420	.97882	.0425	.97857	.0430	.97831
.0435	.97806	.0440	.97780	.0445	.97755
.0450	.97729	.0455	.97703	.0460	.97678
.0465	.97652	.0470	.97627	.0475	.97601
.0480	.97575	.0485	.97550	.0490	.97524
.0495	.97499	.0500	.97473	.0505	.97447
.0510	.97422	.0515	.97396	.0520	.97370
.0525	.97345	.0530	.97319	.0535	.97293
.0540	.97267	.0545	.97242	.0550	.97216
.0555	.97190	.0560	.97165	.0565	.97139
.0570	.97113	.0575	.97087	.0580	.97062
.0585	.97036	.0590	.97010	.0595	.97934
.0600	.96958	.0605	.96933	.0610	.96907
.0615	.96881	.0620	.96855	.0625	.96829
.0630	.96804	.0635	.96778	.0640	.96752
.0645	.96726	.0650	.96700	.0655	.96674
.0660	.96649	.0665	.96623	.0670	.96597
.0675	.96571	.0680	.96545	.0685	.96519
.0690	.96493	.0695	.96467	.0700	.96441

Appendix D-2

Sampling Fractions · n/N	Finite Universe Correction Factor	Sampling Fractions n/N	Finite Universe Correction Factor	Sampling Fractions n/N	Finite Universe Correction Factor
		(Read Table Across)			
.0705	.96415	.0710	.96390	.0715	.96364
.0720	.96338	.0725	.96312	.0730	.96286
.0735	.96260	.0740	.96234	.0745	.96208
.0750	.96182	.0755	.96156	.0760	.96130
.0765	.96104	.0770	.96078	.0775	.96052
.0780	.96026	.0785	.96000	.0790	.95974
.0795	.95948	.0800	.95921	.0805	.95895
.0810	.95869	.0815	.95843	.0820	.95817
.0825	.95791	.0830	.95765	.0835	.95739
.0840	.95713	.0845	.95687	.0850	.95660
.0855	.95634	.0860	.95608	.0865	.95582
.0870	.95556	.0875	.95530	.0880	.95504
.0885	.95477	.0890	.95451	.0895	.95425
.0900	.95399	.0905	.95373	.0910	.95346
.0915	.95320	.0920	.95294	.0925	.95268
.0930	.95241	.0935	.95215	.0940	.95189
.0945	.95163	.0950	.95136	.0955	.95110
.0960	.95084	.0965	.95057	.0970	.95031
.0975	.95005	.0980	.94978	.0985	.94952
.0990	.94926	.0995	.94899	.1000	.94873
.1005	.94847	.1010	.94820	.1015	.94794
.1020	.94768	.1025	.94741	.1C30	.94715
.1035	.94688	.1040	.94662	.1045	.94636
.1050	.94609	.1055	.94583	.1060	.94556
.1065	.94530	.1070	.94503	.1075	.94477
.1080	.94451	.1085	.94424	.1090	.94393
:1095	.94371	.1100	.94345	.1105	.94318
.1110	.94292	.1115	.94265	.1120	.94239
.1125	.94212	.1130	.94185	.1135	.94159
.1140	.94132	.1145	.94106	.1150	.94079
.1155	.94053	.1160	.94026	.1165	.93999
.1170	.93973	.1175	.93946	.1180	.99920
.1185	.99893	.1190	.99866	.1195	.93840
.1200	.93813	.1205	.93786	.1210	.93760
.1215	.93733	.1220	.93706	.1225	.93680
.1230	.93653	.1235	.93626	.1240	.93600
.1245	.93573	.1250	.93546	.1255	.93519
.1260	.93493	.1265	.93466	.1270	.93439
.1275	.93412	.1280	.93386	.1285	.93359
.1290	.93332	.1295	.93305	.1300	.93279
.1305	.93252	.1310	.93225	.1315	.93198
.1320	.93171	.1325	.93144	.1330	.93118
.1335	.93091	.1340	.93064	.1345	.93037
.1350	.93010	.1355	.92983	.1360	.92955
.1365	.92929	.1370	.92902	.1375	.92976
.1390	.92849	.1385	.92822	.1390	.92795

Appendix D-3

Sampling Fractions n/N	Finite Universe Correction Factor	Sampling Fractions n/N	Finite Universe Correction Factor	Sampling Fractions n/N	Finite Universe Correction Factor
		(Read Table Across)			
.1395	.92768	.1400	.92741	.1405	.92714
.1410	.92687	.1415	.92660	.1420	.92633
.1425	.92606	.1430	.92579	.1435	.92552
.1440	.92525	.1445	.92498	.1450	.92471
.1455	.92444	.1460	.92417	.1465	.92390
.1470	.92363	.1475	.92336	.1480	.92309
.1485	.92281	.1490	.92259	.1495	.92227
.1500	.92200	.1505	.92173	.1510	.92146
.1515	.92119	.1520	.92092	.1525	.92064
.1530	.92037	.1535	.92010	.1540	.91983
.1545	.91956	.1550	.91929	.1555	.91901
.1560	.91874	.1565	.91847	.1570	.91820
.1575	.91792	.1580	.91765	.1585	.91738
.1590	.91711	.1595	.91683	.1600	.91656
.1605	.91629	.1610	.91602	.1615	.91574
.1620	.91547	.1625	.91520	.1630	.91492
.1635	.91465	.1640	.91438	.1645	.91410
.1650	.91383	.1655	.91356	.1660	.91328
.1665	.91301	.1670	.91273	.1675	.91246
.1680	.91219	.1685	.91191	.1690	.91164
.1695	.91136	.1700	.91109	.1705	.91081
.1710	.91054	.1715	.91027	.1720	.90999
.1725	.90972	.1730	.90944	.1735	.90917
.1740	.90889	.1745	.90862	.1750	.90834
.1755	.90807	.1760	.90779	.1765	.90751
.1770	.90724	.1775	.90696	.1780	.90669
.1785	.90641	.1790	.90614	.1795	.90586
.1800	.90558	.1805	.90531	.1810	.90503
.1815	.90476	.1820	.90448	.1825	.90420
.1830	.90393	.1835	.90365	.1840	.90337
.1845	.90310	.1850	.90282	.1855	.90254
.1860	.90227	.1865	.90199	.1870	.90171
.1875	.90143	.1880	.90116	.1885	.90088
.1890	.90060	.1895	.90032	.1900	.90005
.1905	.89977	.1910	.89949	.1915	.89921
.1920	.89893	.1925	.89866	.1930	.89838
.1935	.89810	.1940	.89782	.1945	.89754
.1950	.89726	.1955	.89698	.1960	.89671
.1965	.89643	.1970	.89615	.1975	.89587
.1980	.89559	.1985	.89531	.1990	.89503
.1995	.89475	.2000	.89447	.2005	.89419
.2010	.89391	.2015	.89363	.2020	.89335
.2025	.89307	.2030	.89279	.2035	.89251
.2040	.89223	.2045	.89195	.2050	.89167
.2055	.89139	.2060	.89111	.2065	.89083
.2070	.89055	.2075	.89027	.2080	.88999
.2085	.88971	.2090	.88943	.2095	.88915
.2100	.88886	.2105	.88858	.2110	.88830

Appendix E-1 TABLES OF PROBABILITIES FOR USE IN STOP-OR-GO SAMPLING

PROBABILITY THAT ERROR RATE IN UNIVERSE SIZE OF OVER 2000 IS LESS THAN:

SIZE OF SAMPLE EXAMINED	NO. OF ERRORS FOUND	1%	2%	3%	4%	5%	6%	7%	8%	9%	10%	12%	14%	16%	18%	20%
50	0	39.50	63.58	78.19	87.01	92.31	95.47	97.34	98.45	99.10	99.49	99.83	99.95	99.96	100.00	100.00
	1	8.94	26.42	44.47	59.95	72.06	81.00	87.35	91.73	94.68	96.62	98.69	99.52	99.83	99.94	99.98
	2	1.38	7.84	18.92	32.33	45.95	58.38	68.92	77.40	83.95	88.83	94.87	97.79	99.10	99.65	99.87
	3	0.16	1.78	6.28	13.91	23.96	35.27	46.73	57.47	66.97	74.97	86.55	93.30	96.88	98.64	99.43
	4	0.02	0.32	1.68	4.90	10.36	17.94	27.10	37.11	47.23	56.88	73.21	84.72	91.92	96.01	98.15
	5		0.05	0.37	1.44	3.78	7.76	13.51	20.81	29.28	38.39	56.47	71.86	83.23	90.71	95.20
	6		0.01	0.07	0.36	1.18	2.89	5.83	10.19	15.96	22.98	39.35	56.16	70.81	81.99	89.66
70	0	50.52	75.69	88.14	94.26	97.24	98.69	99.38	99.71	99.86	99.94	99.99	100.00	100.00	100.00	100.00
	1	15.53	40.96	62.47	77.51	87.03	92.81	96.10	97.93	98.92	99.45	99.86	99.97	99.99	100.00	100.00
	2	3.34	16.50	35.08	53.44	68.63	79.87	87.59	92.60	95.72	97.58	99.28	99.80	99.95	99.99	100.00
	3	0.54	5.19	15.87	30.71	46.61	61.15	73.07	82.10	88.53	92.88	97.48	99.19	99.76	99.93	99.98
	4	0.07	1.32	5.93	14.85	27.21	41.13	54.77	66.80	76.61	84.12	93.36	97.51	99.16	99.74	99.92
	5		0.28	1.86	6.12	13.72	24.27	36.58	49.24	61.06	71.28	85.94	93.92	97.64	99.17	99.73
	6		0.05	0.50	2.18	6.04	12.61	21.75	32.70	44.40	55.82	74.98	87.57	94.50	97.81	99.20
	7			0.12	0.68	2.34	5.80	11.54	19.54	29.33	40.12	61.33	78.13	89.04	95.08	98.00
	8			0.02	0.19	0.80	2.38	5.49	10.54	17.59	26.37	46.66	66.03	80.85	90.36	95.63
	9				0.05	0.25	0.88	2.36	5.14	9.60	15.86	32.88	52.46	70.10	83.23	91.55
100	0	63.40	86.74	95.25	98.31	99.41	99.80	99.93	99.98	99.99	100.00	100.00	100.00	100.00	100.00	100.00
	1	26.42	59.67	80.54	91.28	96.29	98.48	99.40	99.77	99.91	99.97	100.00	100.00	100.00	100.00	100.00
	2	7.94	32.33	58.02	76.79	88.17	94.34	97.42	98.87	99.52	99.81	99.97	100.00	100.00	100.00	100.00
	3	1.84	14.10	35.28	57.05	74.22	85.10	92.56	96.33	98.27	99.22	99.86	99.98	100.00	100.00	100.00
	4	0.34	5.08	18.22	37.11	56.40	72.32	83.68	90.97	95.26	97.63	99.47	99.90	99.98	100.00	100.00
	5	0.05	1.55	8.08	21.16	38.40	55.93	70.86	82.01	89.55	94.24	98.48	99.66	99.93	99.99	100.00
	6	0.01	0.41	3.12	10.64	23.40	39.37	55.57	69.68	80.60	88.28	96.33	99.03	99.78	99.96	99.99
	7		0.09	1.06	4.75	12.80	25.17	40.12	55.29	68.72	79.40	92.39	97.67	99.39	99.86	99.97
	8		0.02	0.32	1.90	6.31	14.63	26.60	40.74	55.06	67.91	86.14	95.08	98.53	99.62	99.91
	9			0.09	0.68	2.82	7.75	16.20	27.80	41.25	54.87	77.44	90.78	96.84	99.08	99.77
	10			0.02	0.22	1.15	3.76	9.08	17.57	28.82	41.68	66.63	84.40	93.93	98.00	99.43
	11				0.07	0.43	1.68	4.69	10.29	18.76	29.70	54.58	75.91	89.39	96.05	98.74
	12				0.02	0.15	0.69	2.24	5.59	11.38	19.82	42.39	65.66	82.97	92.89	97.47
	13					0.05	0.26	0.99	2.82	6.45	12.39	31.14	54.36	74.69	88.19	95.31
	14					0.01	0.09	0.41	1.33	3.41	7.26	21.60	42.94	64.90	81.77	91.96
	15						0.03	0.16	0.59	1.69	3.99	14.15	32.27	54.20	73.70	87.15

Appendix E-2

PROBABILITY THAT ERROR RATE IN UNIVERSE SIZE OF OVER 2000 IS LESS THAN:

SIZE OF SAMPLE EXAMINED: 120

No. of Errors Found	1%	2%	3%	4%	5%	6%	7%	8%	9%	10%	12%	14%	16%	18%	20%
0	70.06	91.15	97.41	99.25	99.79	99.94	99.98	100.00	100.00	100.00	100.00	100.00	100.00	100.00	100.00
1	33.77	69.46	87.82	95.53	98.45	99.48	99.83	99.95	99.98	99.99	100.00	100.00	100.00	100.00	100.00
2	11.96	43.13	70.16	86.28	94.25	97.75	99.17	99.71	99.90	99.97	100.00	100.00	100.00	100.00	100.00
3	3.30	22.00	48.67	71.13	85.56	93.40	97.19	98.87	99.60	99.84	100.00	100.00	100.00	100.00	100.00
4	0.74	9.38	29.24	52.67	72.18	85.27	92.83	96.75	98.61	99.44	99.92	99.99	100.00	100.00	100.00
5	0.14	3.41	15.29	34.83	55.85	73.23	85.23	92.47	96.42	98.40	99.72	99.96	99.99	100.00	100.00
6	0.02	1.07	7.03	20.57	39.37	58.50	74.26	85.35	92.26	96.18	99.21	99.87	99.98	99.99	100.00
7		0.30	2.86	10.90	25.24	43.20	60.81	75.25	85.57	92.16	98.08	99.62	99.94	99.98	100.00
8		0.07	1.04	5.21	14.74	29.39	46.51	62.85	76.21	85.86	95.89	99.05	99.82	99.97	99.99
9		0.02	0.34	2.26	7.86	18.43	33.12	49.44	64.70	77.14	92.18	97.89	99.53	99.91	99.99
10			0.10	0.89	3.85	10.66	21.93	36.49	52.06	66.39	86.56	95.79	98.94	99.78	99.96
11			0.03	0.32	1.73	5.70	13.50	25.23	39.56	54.45	78.90	92.39	97.80	99.48	99.90
12			0.01	0.11	0.72	2.83	7.75	16.33	28.33	42.39	69.41	87.35	95.83	98.88	99.75
13				0.03	0.28	1.31	4.15	9.91	19.11	31.27	58.66	80.53	92.71	97.78	99.44
14				0.01	0.10	0.56	2.07	5.64	12.13	21.82	47.45	72.05	88.17	95.95	98.86
15					0.03	0.23	0.97	3.01	7.26	14.40	36.66	62.30	82.06	93.10	97.82
16					0.01	0.09	0.43	1.51	4.10	8.99	26.99	51.88	74.42	89.00	96.12
17						0.03	0.18	0.72	2.18	5.31	18.93	41.50	65.52	83.49	93.53
18						0.01	0.07	0.32	1.10	2.97	12.64	31.84	55.82	76.57	89.81

SIZE OF SAMPLE EXAMINED: 150

No. of Errors Found	1%	2%	3%	4%	5%	6%	7%	8%	9%	10%	12%	14%	16%	18%	20%
0	77.86	95.17	98.96	99.78	99.95	99.99	100.00	100.00	100.00	100.00	100.00	100.00	100.00	100.00	100.00
1	44.30	80.39	94.15	98.41	99.60	99.90	99.98	100.00	100.00	100.00	100.00	100.00	100.00	100.00	100.00
2	19.05	57.91	83.07	94.16	98.19	99.48	99.86	99.96	99.99	100.00	100.00	100.00	100.00	100.00	100.00
3	6.47	35.28	66.16	85.42	94.52	98.14	99.42	99.81	99.95	99.99	100.00	100.00	100.00	100.00	100.00
4	1.80	18.30	46.93	72.04	87.44	95.01	98.20	99.40	99.81	99.95	100.00	100.00	100.00	100.00	100.00
5	0.42	8.19	29.57	55.76	76.56	89.17	95.52	98.31	99.41	99.81	99.99	100.00	100.00	100.00	100.00
6	0.08	3.20	16.60	39.37	62.71	80.16	90.66	96.03	98.45	99.44	99.98	100.00	100.00	100.00	100.00
7	0.02	1.11	8.34	25.32	47.72	68.34	83.12	91.94	96.20	98.60	99.82	99.99	99.99	100.00	100.00
8		0.34	3.78	14.85	33.62	54.84	72.98	85.58	93.04	96.50	99.52	99.98	99.97	100.00	100.00
9		0.10	1.55	7.97	21.91	41.26	60.93	76.85	85.45	94.00	98.89	99.94	99.94	100.00	100.00
10		0.02	0.58	3.93	13.22	29.03	48.15	66.16	80.13	89.40	97.66	99.74	99.82	100.00	100.00
11		0.01	0.20	1.79	7.40	19.09	35.90	54.32	70.66	82.91	95.54	99.26	99.61	99.99	100.00
12			0.06	0.75	3.85	11.74	25.23	42.40	59.82	74.55	92.19	98.25	99.35	99.97	100.00
13			0.02	0.29	1.87	6.77	16.70	31.39	48.43	64.70	87.34	96.70	98.70	99.92	99.99
14				0.11	0.85	3.66	10.42	22.03	37.41	53.98	80.86	94.25	98.25	99.77	99.97
15				0.04	0.36	1.86	6.13	14.64	27.53	43.18	72.85	90.62	97.58	99.52	99.92
16				0.01	0.14	0.89	3.40	9.22	19.28	33.06	63.64	85.63	95.78	99.05	99.83
17					0.05	0.40	1.79	5.51	12.86	24.19	53.74	79.24	93.07	98.24	99.65
18					0.02	0.17	0.89	3.13	8.16	16.92	43.76	71.54	89.26	96.92	99.31
19					0.01	0.07	0.42	1.68	4.93	11.30	34.31	62.84	84.21	94.90	98.72
20						0.03	0.19	0.86	2.84	7.21	25.87	53.56	77.92	92.01	97.76
21						0.01	0.08	0.42	1.56	4.40	18.74	44.22	70.50	88.08	96.28
22							0.03	0.20	0.82	2.56	13.04	35.29	62.22	83.02	94.10
23							0.01	0.09	0.41	1.43	8.72	27.20	53.43	76.84	91.07
24								0.04	0.20	0.76	5.60	20.24	44.58	69.66	87.06

Appendix E-3

PROBABILITY THAT ERROR RATE IN UNIVERSE SIZE OF OVER 2000 IS LESS THAN:

SIZE OF SAMPLE EXAMINED: 180

NO. OF ERRORS FOUND	1%	2%	3%	4%	5%	6%	7%	8%	9%	10%	12%	14%	16%	18%	20%
0	83.62	97.37	99.58	99.94	99.99	100.00	100.00	100.00	100.00	100.00	100.00	100.00	100.00	100.00	100.00
1	53.84	87.69	97.27	99.45	99.90	99.98	100.00	100.00	100.00	100.00	100.00	100.00	100.00	100.00	100.00
2	26.91	70.01	90.86	97.65	99.46	99.89	99.98	100.00	100.00	100.00	100.00	100.00	100.00	100.00	100.00
3	10.77	48.61	79.10	93.20	98.10	99.52	99.89	99.98	100.00	100.00	100.00	100.00	100.00	100.00	100.00
4	3.56	29.28	63.01	84.99	94.93	98.50	99.60	99.90	99.98	100.00	100.00	100.00	100.00	100.00	100.00
5	1.00	15.39	45.49	72.95	89.05	96.21	98.84	99.68	99.92	99.98	100.00	100.00	100.00	100.00	100.00
6	0.24	7.13	29.69	58.32	80.02	91.93	97.16	99.11	99.75	99.93	100.00	100.00	100.00	100.00	100.00
7	0.05	2.93	17.54	43.17	68.21	85.15	94.03	97.88	99.32	99.80	99.99	100.00	100.00	100.00	100.00
8	0.01	1.08	9.41	29.51	54.77	75.79	88.92	95.57	98.42	99.49	99.96	100.00	100.00	100.00	100.00
9		0.36	4.61	18.64	41.26	64.37	81.58	91.72	96.70	98.82	99.88	99.99	100.00	100.00	100.00
10		0.11	2.07	10.89	29.09	51.90	72.13	86.00	93.81	97.55	99.71	99.98	100.00	100.00	100.00
11		0.03	0.86	5.90	19.20	39.61	61.13	78.32	89.38	95.37	99.35	99.94	100.00	100.00	100.00
12		0.01	0.33	2.98	11.86	28.56	49.48	68.91	83.21	91.96	98.65	99.84	99.99	100.00	100.00
13			0.12	1.40	6.87	19.44	38.14	58.33	75.33	87.06	97.42	99.65	99.96	100.00	100.00
14			0.04	0.62	3.74	12.50	27.96	47.36	66.03	80.57	95.42	99.27	99.92	99.99	100.00
15			0.01	0.25	1.92	7.59	19.48	36.81	55.86	72.59	92.41	98.58	99.81	99.98	100.00
16				0.10	0.92	4.36	12.90	27.34	45.48	63.44	88.17	97.43	99.60	99.96	100.00
17				0.04	0.42	2.38	8.12	19.40	35.57	53.63	82.59	95.62	99.23	99.90	99.99
18				0.01	0.18	1.23	4.87	13.11	26.70	43.77	75.69	92.95	98.57	99.79	99.98
19					0.08	0.60	2.78	8.51	19.22	34.42	67.68	89.25	97.52	99.59	99.95
20					0.03	0.28	1.51	5.26	13.27	26.06	58.89	84.40	95.89	99.22	99.89
21					0.01	0.13	0.78	3.11	8.78	18.98	49.75	78.39	93.54	98.62	99.78
22						0.05	0.39	1.76	5.57	13.30	40.74	71.31	90.29	97.66	99.59
23						0.02	0.18	0.96	3.40	8.96	32.31	63.40	86.05	96.21	99.25
24						0.01	0.08	0.50	1.99	5.81	24.78	54.97	80.76	94.13	98.69
25							0.04	0.25	1.12	3.62	18.38	46.41	74.47	91.27	97.83
26							0.02	0.12	0.60	2.18	13.17	38.10	67.34	87.54	96.54
27							0.01	0.06	0.31	1.26	9.12	30.39	59.58	82.87	94.70
28								0.02	0.16	0.70	6.11	23.52	51.51	77.27	92.19
29								0.01	0.08	0.38	3.95	17.67	43.45	70.82	88.90

Appendix E-4

PROBABILITY THAT ERROR RATE IN UNIVERSE SIZE OF OVER 2000 IS LESS THAN:

SIZE OF SAMPLE EXAMINED: 220

NO. OF ERRORS FOUND	1%	2%	3%	4%	5%	6%	7%	8%	9%	10%	12%	14%	16%	18%	20%
0	89.04	98.83	99.88	99.99	100.00	100.00	100.00	100.00	100.00	100.00	100.00	100.00	100.00	100.00	100.00
1	64.69	93.55	99.04	99.87	99.98	100.00	100.00	100.00	100.00	100.00	100.00	100.00	100.00	100.00	100.00
2	37.76	81.77	96.21	99.35	99.90	99.99	100.00	100.00	100.00	100.00	100.00	100.00	100.00	100.00	100.00
3	17.99	64.30	89.84	97.75	99.58	99.93	99.99	100.00	100.00	100.00	100.00	100.00	100.00	100.00	100.00
4	7.15	44.96	79.15	94.15	98.66	99.74	99.95	99.99	100.00	100.00	100.00	100.00	100.00	100.00	100.00
5	2.42	27.91	64.88	87.67	96.58	99.21	99.84	99.97	99.99	100.00	100.00	100.00	100.00	100.00	100.00
6	0.71	15.43	49.06	77.99	92.66	97.99	99.53	99.90	99.98	100.00	100.00	100.00	100.00	100.00	100.00
7	0.19	7.65	34.10	65.67	86.34	95.61	98.81	99.72	99.94	99.99	100.00	100.00	100.00	100.00	100.00
8	0.04	3.43	21.78	51.99	77.48	91.57	97.38	99.30	99.83	99.97	100.00	100.00	100.00	100.00	100.00
9	0.01	1.39	12.81	38.57	66.51	85.50	94.83	98.43	99.59	99.90	100.00	100.00	100.00	100.00	100.00
10		0.52	6.95	26.77	54.32	77.32	90.79	96.85	99.07	99.76	99.99	100.00	100.00	100.00	100.00
11		0.18	3.50	17.38	42.07	67.35	84.98	94.21	98.09	99.45	99.98	100.00	100.00	100.00	100.00
12		0.06	1.63	10.57	30.84	56.27	77.36	90.22	96.40	98.85	99.92	100.00	100.00	100.00	100.00
13		0.02	0.71	6.03	21.39	44.96	68.19	84.67	93.72	97.78	99.81	99.99	100.00	100.00	100.00
14			0.29	3.23	14.03	34.28	57.98	77.53	89.82	96.02	99.59	99.97	100.00	100.00	100.00
15			0.11	1.63	8.71	24.92	47.43	69.00	84.51	93.35	99.18	99.94	100.00	100.00	100.00
16			0.04	0.78	5.13	17.26	37.25	59.50	77.78	89.54	98.46	99.86	99.99	100.00	100.00
17			0.01	0.35	2.86	11.40	28.06	49.59	69.80	84.46	97.28	99.71	99.98	100.00	100.00
18				0.15	1.52	7.18	20.26	39.87	60.89	78.09	95.47	99.43	99.95	100.00	100.00
19				0.06	0.77	4.31	14.02	30.89	51.53	70.57	92.85	98.94	99.90	100.00	100.00
20				0.02	0.37	2.48	9.29	23.04	42.22	62.17	89.25	98.15	99.80	99.99	100.00
21				0.01	0.17	1.36	5.91	16.53	33.46	53.29	84.58	96.93	99.61	99.97	100.00
22					0.07	0.71	3.60	11.42	25.61	44.36	78.82	95.12	99.29	99.93	100.00
23					0.03	0.36	2.11	7.59	18.94	35.81	72.06	92.59	98.76	99.86	100.00
24					0.01	0.17	1.19	4.85	13.52	28.02	64.49	89.21	97.93	99.74	99.98
25						0.08	0.64	2.99	9.31	21.23	56.40	84.90	96.69	99.52	99.95
26						0.04	0.33	1.78	6.20	15.58	48.12	79.63	94.93	99.17	99.91
27						0.02	0.17	1.02	3.98	11.06	40.01	73.47	92.51	98.62	99.83
28						0.01	0.08	0.56	2.47	7.60	32.39	66.56	89.34	97.78	99.69
29							0.04	0.30	1.48	5.06	25.51	59.11	85.34	96.56	99.45
30							0.02	0.15	0.86	3.26	19.54	51.39	80.49	94.85	99.09
31							0.01	0.08	0.48	2.03	14.24	43.69	74.83	92.56	98.52
32								0.04	0.26	1.23	10.52	36.28	68.46	89.58	97.69
33								0.02	0.14	0.72	7.40	29.41	61.54	85.86	96.50
34								0.01	0.07	0.41	5.05	23.26	54.30	81.37	94.86
35									0.04	0.23	3.36	17.94	46.97	76.13	92.69
36									0.02	0.12	2.17	13.49	39.80	70.21	89.90

Appendix E-5

PROBABILITY THAT ERROR RATE IN UNIVERSE SIZE OF OVER 2000 IS LESS THAN:

SIZE OF SAMPLE EXAMINED	NO. OF ERRORS FOUND	1%	2%	3%	4%	5%	6%	7%	8%	9%	10%	12%	14%	16%	18%	20%
240	0	91.04	99.22	99.93	99.99	100.00	100.00	100.00	100.00	100.00	100.00	100.00	100.00	100.00	100.00	100.00
	1	69.31	95.38	99.44	99.94	99.99	100.00	100.00	100.00	100.00	100.00	100.00	100.00	100.00	100.00	100.00
	2	43.08	86.01	97.60	99.66	99.96	99.99	100.00	100.00	100.00	100.00	100.00	100.00	100.00	100.00	100.00
	3	22.06	70.85	93.10	98.75	99.81	99.97	100.00	100.00	100.00	100.00	100.00	100.00	100.00	100.00	100.00
	4	9.49	52.52	84.85	96.49	99.34	99.90	99.99	100.00	100.00	100.00	100.00	100.00	100.00	100.00	100.00
	5	3.49	34.86	72.81	90.04	98.19	99.66	99.94	99.99	100.00	100.00	100.00	100.00	100.00	100.00	100.00
	6	1.12	20.75	58.23	84.79	95.80	99.06	99.82	99.97	99.99	100.00	100.00	100.00	100.00	100.00	100.00
	7	0.32	11.12	43.15	74.69	91.60	97.78	99.51	99.91	99.98	100.00	100.00	100.00	100.00	100.00	100.00
	8	0.08	5.40	29.57	62.44	85.16	95.40	98.83	99.74	99.95	99.99	100.00	100.00	100.00	100.00	100.00
	9	0.02	2.39	18.74	49.27	76.43	91.49	97.50	99.38	99.87	99.98	100.00	100.00	100.00	100.00	100.00
	10		0.97	11.00	36.60	65.82	85.73	95.20	98.65	99.68	99.93	100.00	100.00	100.00	100.00	100.00
	11		0.36	6.00	25.56	54.14	78.04	91.58	97.33	99.28	99.83	99.99	100.00	100.00	100.00	100.00
	12		0.12	3.05	16.78	42.40	68.67	86.38	95.14	98.53	99.62	99.98	100.00	100.00	100.00	100.00
	13		0.04	1.45	10.37	31.57	58.17	79.51	91.79	97.24	99.20	99.96	100.00	100.00	100.00	100.00
	14		0.01	0.64	6.04	22.33	47.32	71.13	87.07	95.16	98.46	99.90	100.00	100.00	100.00	100.00
	15			0.27	3.32	15.00	36.88	61.63	80.88	92.07	97.21	99.77	99.99	100.00	100.00	100.00
	16			0.11	1.72	9.57	27.50	51.57	73.32	87.76	95.25	99.54	99.97	100.00	100.00	100.00
	17			0.04	0.85	5.81	19.62	41.60	64.65	82.15	92.39	99.11	99.94	99.99	100.00	100.00
	18			0.01	0.40	3.36	13.39	32.30	55.32	75.28	88.45	98.40	99.87	99.99	100.00	100.00
	19				0.18	1.85	8.74	24.11	45.83	67.34	83.33	97.26	99.74	99.98	100.00	100.00
	20				0.07	0.97	5.46	17.31	36.72	58.66	77.06	95.55	99.50	99.96	100.00	100.00
	21				0.03	0.49	3.27	11.94	28.42	49.66	69.75	93.10	99.09	99.93	100.00	100.00
	22				0.01	0.23	1.87	7.92	21.23	40.81	61.66	89.77	98.43	99.85	99.99	100.00
	23					0.11	1.03	5.06	15.31	32.51	53.15	85.47	97.42	99.72	99.98	100.00
	24					0.05	0.55	3.10	10.65	25.09	44.59	80.17	95.92	99.49	99.96	100.00
	25					0.02	0.28	1.84	7.15	18.74	36.38	73.92	93.82	99.12	99.92	100.00
	26					0.01	0.14	1.05	4.64	13.56	28.84	66.88	90.99	98.52	99.85	99.99
	27						0.06	0.57	2.90	9.49	22.19	59.27	87.34	97.63	99.72	99.98
	28						0.03	0.30	1.76	6.43	16.58	51.37	82.82	96.33	99.51	99.96
	29						0.01	0.16	1.03	4.22	12.01	43.50	77.44	94.53	99.17	99.92
	30							0.08	0.58	2.68	8.45	35.95	71.28	92.11	98.64	99.85
	31							0.04	0.32	1.65	5.77	28.98	64.48	88.99	97.86	99.73
	32							0.02	0.17	0.98	3.82	22.76	57.26	85.11	96.74	99.54
	33							0.01	0.09	0.57	2.45	17.43	49.85	80.45	95.19	99.24
	34								0.04	0.32	1.53	12.99	42.50	75.05	93.12	98.78
	35								0.02	0.17	0.93	9.44	35.46	68.99	90.45	98.10
	36								0.01	0.09	0.55	6.67	28.94	62.42	87.11	97.14
	37									0.05	0.31	4.60	23.08	55.52	83.06	95.81
	38									0.02	0.17	3.08	17.99	48.50	78.32	94.04
	39									0.01	0.09	2.02	13.70	41.57	72.92	91.74
	40										0.05	1.28	10.18	34.94	66.97	88.86

Appendix E-6

PROBABILITY THAT ERROR RATE IN UNIVERSE SIZE OF OVER 2000 IS LESS THAN:

SIZE OF SAMPLE EXAMINED	NO. OF ERRORS FOUND	1%	2%	3%	4%	5%	6%	7%	8%	9%	10%	12%	14%	16%	18%	20%
260	0	92.67	99.48	99.96	100.00	100.00	100.00	100.00	100.00	100.00	100.00	100.00	100.00	100.00	100.00	100.00
	1	73.42	96.70	99.67	99.97	100.00	100.00	100.00	100.00	100.00	100.00	100.00	100.00	100.00	100.00	100.00
	2	48.23	89.36	98.50	99.83	99.98	100.00	100.00	100.00	100.00	100.00	100.00	100.00	100.00	100.00	100.00
	3	26.36	76.48	95.39	99.31	99.91	99.99	100.00	100.00	100.00	100.00	100.00	100.00	100.00	100.00	100.00
	4	12.16	59.59	89.20	97.93	99.68	99.96	99.99	100.00	100.00	100.00	100.00	100.00	100.00	100.00	100.00
	5	4.82	41.94	79.39	94.99	99.06	99.86	99.98	100.00	100.00	100.00	100.00	100.00	100.00	100.00	100.00
	6	1.66	26.64	66.51	89.79	97.67	99.57	99.93	99.99	100.00	100.00	100.00	100.00	100.00	100.00	100.00
	7	0.51	15.30	52.05	81.92	92.02	98.92	99.81	99.97	100.00	100.00	100.00	100.00	100.00	100.00	100.00
	8	0.14	7.99	37.91	71.34	90.60	97.60	99.50	99.91	99.99	100.00	100.00	100.00	100.00	100.00	100.00
	9	0.03	3.81	25.67	59.44	84.09	95.24	98.86	99.77	99.96	99.99	100.00	100.00	100.00	100.00	100.00
	10	0.01	1.67	16.16	46.79	75.49	91.46	97.64	99.46	99.89	99.98	100.00	100.00	100.00	100.00	100.00
	11		0.67	9.48	34.80	65.21	85.98	95.55	98.85	99.75	99.95	100.00	100.00	100.00	100.00	100.00
	12		0.25	5.19	24.44	53.97	78.72	92.30	97.74	99.44	99.88	99.99	100.00	100.00	100.00	100.00
	13		0.09	2.66	16.21	42.69	69.88	87.63	95.90	98.87	99.74	99.99	100.00	100.00	100.00	100.00
	14		0.03	1.28	10.15	32.22	59.92	81.42	93.09	97.88	99.45	99.98	100.00	100.00	100.00	100.00
	15		0.01	0.58	6.01	23.18	49.50	73.76	89.07	96.26	98.93	99.94	100.00	100.00	100.00	100.00
	16			0.25	3.38	15.89	39.31	64.94	83.73	93.82	98.04	99.88	99.99	100.00	100.00	100.00
	17			0.10	1.80	10.39	29.98	55.40	77.05	90.35	96.62	99.74	99.99	100.00	100.00	100.00
	18			0.04	0.91	6.48	21.94	45.71	69.22	85.71	94.49	99.49	99.97	100.00	100.00	100.00
	19			0.01	0.44	3.86	15.40	36.42	60.54	79.87	91.47	99.07	99.94	100.00	100.00	100.00
	20				0.20	2.19	10.37	28.00	51.45	72.91	87.44	98.36	99.88	99.99	100.00	100.00
	21				0.09	1.19	6.71	20.75	42.42	65.05	82.31	97.27	99.77	99.99	100.00	100.00
	22				0.04	0.62	4.16	14.82	33.88	56.60	76.12	95.64	99.56	99.97	100.00	100.00
	23				0.01	0.31	2.48	10.21	26.21	47.95	69.01	93.35	99.22	99.95	100.00	100.00
	24					0.15	1.42	6.78	19.61	39.50	61.21	90.27	98.67	99.89	99.99	100.00
	25					0.07	0.78	4.34	14.20	31.62	53.02	86.29	97.83	99.80	99.99	100.00
	26					0.03	0.42	2.68	9.94	24.57	44.80	81.40	96.59	99.64	99.98	100.00
	27					0.01	0.21	1.60	6.74	18.53	36.89	75.61	94.83	99.37	99.95	100.00
	28						0.11	0.92	4.42	13.55	29.57	69.05	92.46	98.94	99.91	99.99
	29						0.05	0.51	2.80	9.62	23.06	61.88	89.37	98.30	99.83	99.99
	30						0.02	0.28	1.72	6.62	17.50	54.37	85.49	97.35	99.71	99.98
	31						0.01	0.14	1.03	4.42	12.91	46.76	80.81	96.00	99.50	99.96
	32							0.07	0.59	2.87	9.26	39.33	75.36	94.17	99.17	99.93
	33							0.04	0.33	1.81	6.46	32.34	69.23	91.77	98.68	99.87
	34							0.02	0.18	1.10	4.38	25.97	62.56	88.70	97.96	99.77
	35							0.01	0.09	0.66	2.89	20.36	55.56	84.94	96.93	99.61
	36								0.05	0.38	1.85	15.58	48.43	80.46	95.52	99.36
	37								0.02	0.21	1.16	11.64	41.40	75.28	93.65	98.99
	38								0.01	0.12	0.70	8.48	34.69	69.51	91.24	98.44
	39									0.06	0.42	6.03	28.47	63.24	88.22	97.66
	40									0.03	0.24	4.18	22.88	56.65	84.57	96.57
	41									0.02	0.13	2.83	17.99	49.91	80.26	95.12
	42									0.01	0.07	1.87	13.85	43.21	75.34	93.23
	43										0.04	1.20	10.42	36.75	69.85	90.84

Appendix E-7

PROBABILITY THAT ERROR RATE IN UNIVERSE SIZE OF OVER 2000 IS LESS THAN:

SIZE OF SAMPLE EXAMINED: 300

NO. OF ERRORS FOUND	1%	2%	3%	4%	5%	6%	7%	8%	9%	10%	12%	14%	16%	18%	20%
0	95.10	99.77	99.99	100.00	100.00	100.00	100.00	100.00	100.00	100.00	100.00	100.00	100.00	100.00	100.00
1	80.24	98.34	99.89	99.99	100.00	100.00	100.00	100.00	100.00	100.00	100.00	100.00	100.00	100.00	100.00
2	57.79	93.98	99.43	99.96	100.00	100.00	100.00	100.00	100.00	100.00	100.00	100.00	100.00	100.00	100.00
3	35.28	85.15	98.01	99.80	99.98	100.00	100.00	100.00	100.00	100.00	100.00	100.00	100.00	100.00	100.00
4	18.39	71.77	94.76	99.32	99.93	99.99	100.00	100.00	100.00	100.00	100.00	100.00	100.00	100.00	100.00
5	8.29	55.59	88.80	98.14	99.77	99.98	100.00	100.00	100.00	100.00	100.00	100.00	100.00	100.00	100.00
6	3.28	39.37	79.74	95.72	99.34	99.92	100.00	100.00	100.00	100.00	100.00	100.00	100.00	100.00	100.00
7	1.15	25.46	67.97	91.49	98.40	99.77	99.98	100.00	100.00	100.00	100.00	100.00	100.00	100.00	100.00
8	0.36	15.07	54.64	85.03	96.59	99.41	99.92	99.99	100.00	100.00	100.00	100.00	100.00	100.00	100.00
9	0.10	8.18	41.26	76.30	93.50	98.68	99.79	99.97	100.00	100.00	100.00	100.00	100.00	100.00	100.00
10	0.03	4.10	29.22	65.71	88.77	97.32	99.50	99.92	99.99	100.00	100.00	100.00	100.00	100.00	100.00
11	0.01	1.90	19.40	54.07	82.20	95.03	98.93	99.82	99.97	100.00	100.00	100.00	100.00	100.00	100.00
12		0.82	12.09	42.40	73.88	91.50	97.91	99.59	99.93	99.99	100.00	100.00	100.00	100.00	100.00
13		0.33	7.08	31.63	64.17	86.52	96.19	99.15	99.85	99.98	100.00	100.00	100.00	100.00	100.00
14		0.12	3.90	22.42	53.70	80.00	93.54	98.37	99.67	99.94	100.00	100.00	100.00	100.00	100.00
15		0.04	2.03	15.11	43.19	72.07	89.74	97.08	99.33	99.87	100.00	100.00	100.00	100.00	100.00
16		0.01	1.00	9.69	33.34	63.05	84.64	95.08	98.74	99.74	100.00	100.00	100.00	100.00	100.00
17			0.46	5.91	24.67	53.43	78.23	92.17	97.76	99.48	99.99	100.00	100.00	100.00	100.00
18			0.21	3.43	17.50	43.77	70.65	88.19	96.24	99.03	99.98	100.00	100.00	100.00	100.00
19			0.09	1.90	11.91	34.63	62.18	83.05	94.01	98.29	99.92	100.00	100.00	100.00	100.00
20			0.03	1.01	7.76	26.43	53.22	76.78	90.91	97.13	99.84	100.00	100.00	100.00	100.00
21			0.01	0.51	4.86	19.45	44.23	69.51	86.82	95.42	99.69	99.99	100.00	100.00	100.00
22				0.25	2.92	13.79	35.65	61.49	81.69	93.01	99.43	99.98	100.00	100.00	100.00
23				0.12	1.68	9.44	27.84	53.06	75.56	89.77	99.01	99.95	100.00	100.00	100.00
24				0.05	0.94	6.22	21.05	44.60	68.56	85.61	98.34	99.90	100.00	100.00	100.00
25				0.02	0.50	3.96	15.42	36.47	60.92	80.51	97.33	99.82	99.99	100.00	100.00
26				0.01	0.26	2.43	10.93	29.00	52.92	74.52	95.88	99.67	99.99	100.00	100.00
27					0.13	1.44	7.50	22.41	44.90	67.76	93.87	99.43	99.97	100.00	100.00
28					0.06	0.83	4.99	16.82	37.16	60.44	91.20	99.04	99.94	100.00	100.00
29					0.03	0.46	3.21	12.26	29.99	52.81	87.78	98.46	99.90	100.00	100.00
30					0.01	0.25	2.00	8.68	23.58	45.16	83.57	97.59	99.81	99.99	100.00
31						0.13	1.21	5.97	18.05	37.75	78.57	96.36	99.68	99.98	100.00
32						0.06	0.71	3.99	13.46	30.83	72.84	94.69	99.47	99.97	100.00
33						0.03	0.40	2.59	9.77	24.58	66.49	92.47	99.12	99.94	100.00
34						0.02	0.22	1.63	6.91	19.14	59.69	89.63	98.61	99.90	100.00
35						0.01	0.12	1.00	4.75	14.53	52.65	86.12	97.87	99.82	99.99
36							0.06	0.60	3.19	10.77	45.57	81.92	96.84	99.70	99.98
37							0.03	0.35	2.08	7.79	38.69	77.03	95.44	99.50	99.97
38							0.02	0.20	1.32	5.49	32.20	71.53	93.59	99.21	99.94
39							0.01	0.11	0.82	3.78	26.25	65.51	91.22	98.77	99.90
40								0.06	0.50	2.54	20.96	59.12	88.28	98.15	99.83
41								0.03	0.29	1.66	16.38	52.52	84.73	97.29	99.72
42								0.02	0.17	1.06	12.53	45.90	80.56	96.12	99.56
43								0.01	0.09	0.67	9.39	39.43	75.79	94.57	99.31
44									0.05	0.41	6.88	33.27	70.49	92.60	98.94
45									0.03	0.24	4.93	27.58	64.74	90.13	98.42
46									0.01	0.14	3.46	22.44	58.68	87.12	97.70
47										0.08	2.38	17.91	52.43	83.56	96.72
48										0.04	1.60	14.03	46.16	79.43	95.42

Appendix E-8

PROBABILITY THAT ERROR RATE IN UNIVERSE SIZE OF OVER 2000 IS LESS THAN:

SIZE OF SAMPLE EXAMINED	NO. OF ERRORS FOUND	1%	2%	3%	4%	5%	6%	7%	8%	9%	10%	12%	14%	16%	18%	20%
400	0	98.20	99.97	100.00	100.00	100.00	100.00	100.00	100.00	100.00	100.00	100.00	100.00	100.00	100.00	100.00
	1	90.95	99.72	99.99	100.00	100.00	100.00	100.00	100.00	100.00	100.00	100.00	100.00	100.00	100.00	100.00
	2	76.34	98.69	99.95	100.00	100.00	100.00	100.00	100.00	100.00	100.00	100.00	100.00	100.00	100.00	100.00
	3	56.75	95.91	99.79	99.99	100.00	100.00	100.00	100.00	100.00	100.00	100.00	100.00	100.00	100.00	100.00
	4	37.12	90.27	99.30	99.97	100.00	100.00	100.00	100.00	100.00	100.00	100.00	100.00	100.00	100.00	100.00
	5	21.41	81.15	98.10	99.88	99.99	100.00	100.00	100.00	100.00	100.00	100.00	100.00	100.00	100.00	100.00
	6	10.96	68.91	95.65	99.65	99.98	100.00	100.00	100.00	100.00	100.00	100.00	100.00	100.00	100.00	100.00
	7	5.02	54.85	91.38	99.10	99.94	100.00	100.00	100.00	100.00	100.00	100.00	100.00	100.00	100.00	100.00
	8	2.08	40.74	84.90	97.99	99.83	99.99	100.00	100.00	100.00	100.00	100.00	100.00	100.00	100.00	100.00
	9	0.78	28.21	76.16	95.97	99.58	99.97	100.00	100.00	100.00	100.00	100.00	100.00	100.00	100.00	100.00
	10	0.27	18.21	65.60	92.67	99.06	99.92	99.99	100.00	100.00	100.00	100.00	100.00	100.00	100.00	100.00
	11	0.08	10.97	54.01	87.80	98.10	99.80	99.98	100.00	100.00	100.00	100.00	100.00	100.00	100.00	100.00
	12	0.02	6.19	42.40	81.23	96.45	99.56	99.96	100.00	100.00	100.00	100.00	100.00	100.00	100.00	100.00
	13	0.01	3.27	31.68	73.05	93.86	99.10	99.91	99.99	100.00	100.00	100.00	100.00	100.00	100.00	100.00
	14		1.62	22.52	63.63	90.10	98.28	99.79	99.98	100.00	100.00	100.00	100.00	100.00	100.00	100.00
	15		0.76	15.23	53.53	85.01	96.95	99.57	99.96	99.99	100.00	100.00	100.00	100.00	100.00	100.00
	16		0.34	9.80	43.40	78.56	94.90	99.18	99.90	99.99	100.00	100.00	100.00	100.00	100.00	100.00
	17		0.14	6.01	33.87	70.88	91.94	98.50	99.80	99.98	100.00	100.00	100.00	100.00	100.00	100.00
	18		0.06	3.51	25.42	62.29	87.93	97.42	99.61	99.96	100.00	100.00	100.00	100.00	100.00	100.00
	19		0.02	1.96	18.34	53.20	82.78	95.78	99.27	99.91	99.99	100.00	100.00	100.00	100.00	100.00
	20		0.01	1.04	12.72	44.09	76.51	93.43	98.71	99.81	99.98	100.00	100.00	100.00	100.00	100.00
	21			0.53	8.49	35.41	69.27	90.23	97.83	99.65	99.96	100.00	100.00	100.00	100.00	100.00
	22			0.26	5.45	27.54	61.32	86.08	96.52	99.37	99.91	100.00	100.00	100.00	100.00	100.00
	23			0.12	3.37	20.73	52.97	80.95	94.64	98.91	99.83	99.99	100.00	100.00	100.00	100.00
	24				2.00	15.10	44.60	74.88	92.07	98.20	99.69	99.98	100.00	100.00	100.00	100.00
	25				1.15	10.65	36.56	68.02	88.72	97.14	99.46	99.99	100.00	100.00	100.00	100.00
	26				0.64	7.27	29.16	60.56	84.50	95.63	99.08	99.98	100.00	100.00	100.00	100.00
	27				0.34	4.80	22.62	52.79	79.43	93.56	98.51	99.96	100.00	100.00	100.00	100.00
	28				0.18	3.07	17.06	44.99	73.56	90.83	97.65	99.93	100.00	100.00	100.00	100.00
	29				0.09	1.90	12.51	37.47	67.01	87.37	96.43	99.87	100.00	100.00	100.00	100.00
	30				0.04	1.14	8.92	30.46	59.96	83.14	94.76	99.78	100.00	100.00	100.00	100.00
	31				0.02	0.67	6.18	24.17	52.65	78.15	92.54	99.62	99.99	100.00	100.00	100.00
	32				0.01	0.38	4.16	18.71	45.31	72.45	89.70	99.37	99.98	100.00	100.00	100.00
	33					0.21	2.73	14.12	38.20	66.17	86.18	98.99	99.97	100.00	100.00	100.00
	34					0.11	1.74	10.40	31.53	59.47	81.95	98.43	99.95	100.00	100.00	100.00
	35					0.06	1.08	7.47	25.46	52.53	77.04	97.64	99.91	100.00	100.00	100.00
	36					0.03	0.65	5.23	20.11	45.58	71.51	96.54	99.84	100.00	100.00	100.00
	37					0.01	0.38	3.57	15.53	38.81	65.47	95.07	99.74	99.99	100.00	100.00
	38						0.22	2.38	11.73	32.42	59.05	93.15	99.58	99.99	100.00	100.00
	39						0.12	1.55	8.66	26.55	52.44	90.72	99.33	99.98	100.00	100.00

Appendix E-9

PROBABILITY THAT ERROR RATE IN UNIVERSE SIZE OF OVER 2000 IS LESS THAN:

SIZE OF SAMPLE EXAMINED	NO. OF ERRORS FOUND	1%	2%	3%	4%	5%	6%	7%	8%	9%	10%	12%	14%	16%	18%	20%
400 (Cont)	40						0.07	0.98	6.25	21.31	45.80	87.73	98.97	99.96	100.00	100.00
	41						0.04	0.61	4.41	16.77	39.33	84.15	98.45	99.94	100.00	100.00
	42						0.02	0.37	3.04	12.92	33.18	79.98	97.73	99.89	100.00	100.00
	43						0.01	0.22	2.05	9.76	27.49	75.24	96.75	99.83	100.00	100.00
	44							0.13	1.36	7.21	22.37	70.00	95.46	99.72	99.99	100.00
	45							0.07	0.88	5.23	17.86	64.35	93.80	99.56	99.99	100.00
	46							0.04	0.55	3.71	14.00	58.40	91.71	99.33	99.98	100.00
	47							0.02	0.34	2.58	10.76	52.29	89.15	98.99	99.96	100.00
	48							0.01	0.21	1.76	8.12	46.16	86.09	98.52	99.93	100.00
	49								0.12	1.17	6.01	40.16	82.51	97.88	99.89	100.00
	50								0.07	0.77	4.36	34.42	78.41	97.01	99.82	99.99
	51								0.04	0.49	3.11	29.04	73.84	95.89	99.72	99.99
	52								0.02	0.31	2.17	24.12	68.84	94.45	99.57	99.98
	53								0.01	0.19	1.49	19.71	63.50	92.65	99.35	99.97
	54									0.12	1.00	15.85	57.91	90.45	99.05	99.96
	55									0.07	0.66	12.54	52.18	87.81	98.62	99.93
	56									0.04	0.43	9.75	46.44	84.71	98.06	99.89
	57									0.02	0.27	7.46	40.80	81.15	97.30	99.82
	58									0.01	0.17	5.62	35.38	77.14	96.32	99.73
	59										0.11	4.16	30.25	72.71	95.08	99.59
	60										0.06	3.03	25.51	67.91	93.52	99.39
	61										0.04	2.17	21.21	62.82	91.62	99.12
	62										0.02	1.52	17.38	57.52	89.34	98.75
	63										0.01	1.06	14.04	52.10	86.65	98.25
	64											0.72	11.18	46.67	83.54	97.59
	65											0.48	8.76	41.32	80.01	96.74
	66											0.32	6.77	36.15	76.08	95.67
	67											0.21	5.15	31.24	71.78	94.32
	68											0.13	3.86	26.65	67.16	92.68
	69											0.08	2.86	22.45	62.28	90.70
	70											0.05	2.08	18.67	57.21	88.36

Appendix E-10

PROBABILITY THAT ERROR RATE IN UNIVERSE SIZE OF OVER 2000 IS LESS THAN:

SIZE OF SAMPLE EXAMINED	NO. OF ERRORS FOUND	1%	2%	3%	4%	5%	6%	7%	8%	9%	10%	12%	14%	16%	18%	20%
500	0	99.34	100.00	100.00	100.00	100.00	100.00	100.00	100.00	100.00	100.00	100.00	100.00	100.00	100.00	100.00
	1	96.02	99.95	100.00	100.00	100.00	100.00	100.00	100.00	100.00	100.00	100.00	100.00	100.00	100.00	100.00
	2	87.66	99.74	100.00	100.00	100.00	100.00	100.00	100.00	100.00	100.00	100.00	100.00	100.00	100.00	100.00
	3	73.64	99.02	99.92	100.00	100.00	100.00	100.00	100.00	100.00	100.00	100.00	100.00	100.00	100.00	100.00
	4	56.04	97.19	99.75	100.00	100.00	100.00	100.00	100.00	100.00	100.00	100.00	100.00	100.00	100.00	100.00
	5	38.40	93.43	99.30	99.99	100.00	100.00	100.00	100.00	100.00	100.00	100.00	100.00	100.00	100.00	100.00
	6	23.71	87.24	98.32	99.98	100.00	100.00	100.00	100.00	100.00	100.00	100.00	100.00	100.00	100.00	100.00
	7	13.23	78.25	96.46	99.94	100.00	100.00	100.00	100.00	100.00	100.00	100.00	100.00	100.00	100.00	100.00
	8	6.71	66.95	93.31	99.82	99.99	100.00	100.00	100.00	100.00	100.00	100.00	100.00	100.00	100.00	100.00
	9	3.11	54.33	88.52	99.56	99.98	100.00	100.00	100.00	100.00	100.00	100.00	100.00	100.00	100.00	100.00
	10	1.32	41.70	81.93	99.03	99.95	100.00	100.00	100.00	100.00	100.00	100.00	100.00	100.00	100.00	100.00
	11	0.52	30.21	73.62	98.05	99.89	99.99	100.00	100.00	100.00	100.00	100.00	100.00	100.00	100.00	100.00
	12	0.19	20.65	63.97	96.38	99.74	99.99	100.00	100.00	100.00	100.00	100.00	100.00	100.00	100.00	100.00
	13	0.06	13.33	53.59	93.77	99.45	99.97	100.00	100.00	100.00	100.00	100.00	100.00	100.00	100.00	100.00
	14	0.02	8.14	43.19	89.98	98.92	99.93	100.00	100.00	100.00	100.00	100.00	100.00	100.00	100.00	100.00
	15	0.01	4.70	33.44	84.87	98.01	99.85	100.00	100.00	100.00	100.00	100.00	100.00	100.00	100.00	100.00
	16		2.57	24.85	78.42	96.57	99.69	99.99	100.00	100.00	100.00	100.00	100.00	100.00	100.00	100.00
	17		1.34	17.73	70.76	94.41	99.40	99.98	100.00	100.00	100.00	100.00	100.00	100.00	100.00	100.00
	18		0.66	12.14	62.20	91.35	98.90	99.96	100.00	100.00	100.00	100.00	100.00	100.00	100.00	100.00
	19		0.31	7.98	53.16	87.28	98.10	99.83	100.00	100.00	100.00	100.00	100.00	100.00	100.00	100.00
	20		0.14	5.04	44.09	82.12	96.87	99.67	99.98	100.00	100.00	100.00	100.00	100.00	100.00	100.00
	21		0.06	3.06	35.46	75.91	95.07	99.40	99.95	100.00	100.00	100.00	100.00	100.00	100.00	100.00
	22		0.02	1.79	27.62	68.79	92.58	98.95	99.90	100.00	100.00	100.00	100.00	100.00	100.00	100.00
	23		0.01	1.01	20.84	61.01	89.26	98.25	99.82	100.00	100.00	100.00	100.00	100.00	100.00	100.00
	24			0.55	15.22	52.86	85.06	97.20	99.67	99.97	100.00	100.00	100.00	100.00	100.00	100.00
	25			0.28	10.76	44.71	79.96	95.71	99.42	99.95	100.00	100.00	100.00	100.00	100.00	100.00
	26			0.14	7.37	36.86	74.00	93.65	99.02	99.90	99.99	100.00	100.00	100.00	100.00	100.00
	27			0.07	4.89	29.61	67.33	90.92	98.42	99.82	99.99	100.00	100.00	100.00	100.00	100.00
	28			0.03	3.14	23.17	60.13	87.46	97.54	99.68	99.97	100.00	100.00	100.00	100.00	100.00
	29			0.02	1.96	17.65	52.65	83.22	96.28	99.46	99.95	100.00	100.00	100.00	100.00	100.00
	30			0.01	1.18	13.09	45.16	78.21	94.57	99.11	99.90	100.00	100.00	100.00	100.00	100.00
	31				0.69	9.44	37.91	72.50	92.32	98.60	99.82	100.00	100.00	100.00	100.00	100.00
	32				0.40	6.64	31.13	66.19	89.45	97.85	99.70	100.00	100.00	100.00	100.00	100.00
	33				0.22	4.54	24.99	59.46	85.90	96.38	99.50	100.00	100.00	100.00	100.00	100.00
	34				0.12	3.03	19.61	52.49	81.67	95.38	99.21	99.99	100.00	100.00	100.00	100.00
	35				0.06	1.96	15.03	45.52	76.78	93.50	98.77	99.98	100.00	100.00	100.00	100.00
	36				0.03	1.24	11.26	38.74	71.27	91.10	98.14	99.97	100.00	100.00	100.00	100.00
	37				0.02	0.77	8.24	32.33	65.27	88.13	97.26	99.95	100.00	100.00	100.00	100.00
	38				0.01	0.46	5.90	26.46	58.92	84.55	96.07	99.91	100.00	100.00	100.00	100.00
	39					0.27	4.12	21.23	52.37	80.35	94.50	99.85	100.00	100.00	100.00	100.00
	40					0.16	2.81	16.69	45.81	75.56	92.49	99.75	100.00	100.00	100.00	100.00
	41					0.09	1.88	12.85	39.40	70.26	89.99	99.61	99.99	100.00	100.00	100.00
	42					0.05	1.23	9.70	33.32	64.52	86.95	99.39	99.99	100.00	100.00	100.00

Appendix E-11

PROBABILITY THAT ERROR RATE IN UNIVERSE SIZE OF OVER 2000 IS LESS THAN:

SIZE OF SAMPLE EXAMINED	NO. OF ERRORS FOUND	1%	2%	3%	4%	5%	6%	7%	8%	9%	10%	12%	14%	16%	18%	20%
500 (Cont)	43					0.02	0.78	7.17	27.68	58.47	83.35	99.07	99.98	100.00	100.00	100.00
	44					0.01	0.49	5.19	22.59	52.26	79.20	98.62	99.97	100.00	100.00	100.00
	45						0.30	3.68	18.11	46.04	74.53	98.01	99.96	100.00	100.00	100.00
	46						0.18	2.56	14.25	39.96	69.40	97.17	99.93	100.00	100.00	100.00
	47						0.10	1.75	11.01	34.14	63.88	96.07	99.88	100.00	100.00	100.00
	48						0.06	1.17	8.35	28.71	58.10	94.65	99.81	100.00	100.00	100.00
	49						0.03	0.76	6.22	23.76	52.18	92.87	99.70	100.00	100.00	100.00
	50						0.02	0.49	4.55	19.34	46.24	90.68	99.55	99.99	100.00	100.00
	51						0.01	0.31	3.26	15.49	40.42	88.04	99.32	99.99	100.00	100.00
	52							0.19	2.30	12.19	34.84	84.94	99.00	99.98	100.00	100.00
	53							0.12	1.59	9.44	29.59	81.36	98.57	99.96	100.00	100.00
	54							0.07	1.08	7.19	24.77	77.32	97.98	99.94	100.00	100.00
	55							0.04	0.72	5.38	20.42	72.86	97.21	99.91	100.00	100.00
	56							0.02	0.47	3.96	16.58	68.02	96.21	99.86	99.98	100.00
	57							0.01	0.30	2.87	13.26	62.87	94.94	99.78	99.97	100.00
	58								0.19	2.04	10.44	57.52	93.96	99.67	99.96	100.00
	59								0.12	1.43	8.10	52.05	91.43	99.51	99.99	100.00
	60								0.07	0.98	6.18	46.57	89.12	99.29	99.98	100.00
	61								0.04	0.67	4.65	41.17	86.42	98.99	99.97	100.00
	62								0.03	0.44	3.44	35.97	83.30	98.58	99.96	100.00
	63								0.02	0.29	2.50	31.03	79.76	98.03	99.93	100.00
	64								0.01	0.19	1.80	26.44	75.84	97.32	99.90	100.00
	65									0.12	1.27	22.23	71.55	96.42	99.84	100.00
	66									0.07	0.88	18.45	66.95	95.28	99.77	100.00
	67									0.05	0.60	15.11	62.10	93.88	99.66	99.99
	68									0.03	0.41	12.22	57.08	92.18	99.50	99.99
	69									0.02	0.27	9.74	51.95	90.16	99.29	99.98
	70									0.01	0.18	7.67	46.82	87.78	99.00	99.97
	71										0.11	5.95	41.76	85.04	98.62	99.95
	72										0.07	4.56	36.84	81.93	98.13	99.93
	73										0.04	3.44	32.16	78.46	97.49	99.89
	74										0.03	2.56	27.75	74.64	96.68	99.84
	75										0.02	1.88	23.68	70.51	95.67	99.76
	76										0.01	1.37	19.98	66.11	94.42	99.66
	77											0.98	16.65	61.50	92.92	99.51
	78											0.69	13.72	56.73	91.14	99.31
	79											0.48	11.17	51.88	89.05	99.05
	80											0.33	8.99	47.02	86.63	98.70
	81											0.22	7.14	42.22	83.88	98.25
	82											0.15	5.61	37.54	80.79	97.68

Appendix F-1 TABLES OF PROBABILITIES FOR USE IN EXPLORATORY SAMPLING

Reprinted with permission of
the United States Air Force Auditor General.

PROBABILITY, IN PER CENT, OF FINDING AT LEAST ONE ERROR IF TOTAL NO. OF ERRORS IN UNIVERSE IS AS INDICATED

TOTAL ERRORS IN UNIVERSE SIZE OF 1000

SAMPLE SIZE	2	3	4	5	10	15	20	25	30	40	50	75	100	200	300	500	1000	2000
5.	1.0	1.5	2.0	2.5	4.9	7.3	9.6	11.9	14.2	18.5	22.7	32.3	41.0	67.3	83.3	96.9	100.0	—
10.	2.0	3.0	3.9	4.9	9.6	14.1	18.4	22.5	26.4	33.6	40.3	54.3	65.3	89.4	97.2	99.9	100.0	—
15.	3.0	4.4	5.9	7.3	14.1	20.4	26.3	31.8	36.9	46.0	53.9	69.2	79.7	96.6	99.5	100.0	100.0	—
20.	4.0	5.9	7.8	9.6	18.4	26.3	33.5	40.0	45.9	56.2	64.5	79.3	88.1	98.9	99.9	100.0	100.0	—
25.	4.9	7.3	9.6	11.9	22.5	31.8	40.0	47.3	53.7	64.4	72.7	86.1	93.0	99.7	100.0	100.0	100.0	—
30.	5.9	8.7	11.5	14.2	26.4	36.9	45.9	53.7	60.4	71.2	79.0	90.7	96.0	99.9	100.0	100.0	100.0	—
35.	6.9	10.1	13.3	16.3	30.1	41.6	51.3	59.4	66.2	76.6	83.9	93.8	97.7	100.0	100.0	100.0	100.0	—
40.	7.8	11.5	15.1	18.5	33.6	46.0	56.2	64.4	71.2	81.1	87.6	95.8	98.6	100.0	100.0	100.0	100.0	—
45.	8.8	12.9	16.8	20.6	37.0	50.1	60.5	68.8	75.4	84.7	90.6	97.2	99.2	100.0	100.0	100.0	100.0	—
50.	9.8	14.3	18.6	22.7	40.3	53.9	64.5	72.7	79.0	87.6	92.8	98.2	99.6	100.0	100.0	100.0	100.0	—
55.	10.7	15.6	20.3	24.7	43.4	57.5	68.1	76.1	82.1	90.1	94.5	98.8	99.7	100.0	100.0	100.0	100.0	—
60.	11.6	17.0	22.0	26.7	46.3	60.7	71.3	79.1	84.8	92.0	95.8	99.2	99.9	100.0	100.0	100.0	100.0	—
65.	12.6	18.3	23.6	28.6	49.1	63.8	74.3	81.8	87.1	93.6	96.8	99.5	99.9	100.0	100.0	100.0	100.0	—
70.	13.5	19.6	25.2	30.5	51.8	66.6	76.9	84.1	89.0	94.8	97.6	99.7	99.9	100.0	100.0	100.0	100.0	—
75.	14.4	20.9	26.8	32.3	54.3	69.2	79.3	86.1	90.7	95.8	98.2	99.8	100.0	100.0	100.0	100.0	100.0	—
80.	15.4	22.2	28.4	34.1	56.7	71.6	81.4	87.9	92.1	96.7	98.6	99.8	100.0	100.0	100.0	100.0	100.0	—
85.	16.3	23.4	29.9	35.9	59.0	73.9	83.4	89.5	93.3	97.3	99.0	99.9	100.0	100.0	100.0	100.0	100.0	—
90.	17.2	24.7	31.5	37.7	61.2	76.0	85.1	90.8	94.3	97.9	99.2	99.9	100.0	100.0	100.0	100.0	100.0	—
95.	18.1	25.9	33.0	39.4	63.3	77.9	86.7	92.0	95.2	98.3	99.4	100.0	100.0	100.0	100.0	100.0	100.0	—
100.	19.0	27.1	34.4	41.0	65.3	79.7	88.1	93.0	96.0	98.6	99.6	100.0	100.0	100.0	100.0	100.0	100.0	—
125.	23.4	33.0	41.4	48.8	73.9	86.7	93.3	96.6	98.3	99.6	99.9	100.0	100.0	100.0	100.0	100.0	100.0	—
150.	27.8	38.6	47.9	55.9	80.5	91.4	96.3	98.4	99.3	99.9	100.0	100.0	100.0	100.0	100.0	100.0	100.0	—
175.	32.0	43.9	53.7	61.9	85.5	94.5	98.0	99.2	99.7	100.0	100.0	100.0	100.0	100.0	100.0	100.0	100.0	—
200.	36.0	48.8	59.1	67.3	89.4	96.6	98.9	99.7	99.9	100.0	100.0	100.0	100.0	100.0	100.0	100.0	100.0	—
225.	40.0	53.5	64.0	72.1	92.3	97.9	99.4	99.8	99.9	100.0	100.0	100.0	100.0	100.0	100.0	100.0	100.0	—
250.	43.8	57.9	68.4	76.2	94.5	98.7	99.7	99.9	100.0	100.0	100.0	100.0	100.0	100.0	100.0	100.0	100.0	—
275.	47.5	61.9	72.4	80.0	96.1	99.2	99.8	100.0	100.0	100.0	100.0	100.0	100.0	100.0	100.0	100.0	100.0	—
300.	51.0	65.7	76.1	83.1	97.2	99.5	99.9	100.0	100.0	100.0	100.0	100.0	100.0	100.0	100.0	100.0	100.0	—
325.	54.5	69.3	79.3	86.1	98.1	99.7	100.0	100.0	100.0	100.0	100.0	100.0	100.0	100.0	100.0	100.0	100.0	—
350.	57.8	72.6	82.2	88.5	98.7	99.8	100.0	100.0	100.0	100.0	100.0	100.0	100.0	100.0	100.0	100.0	100.0	—
375.	61.0	75.6	84.8	90.5	99.1	99.9	100.0	100.0	100.0	100.0	100.0	100.0	100.0	100.0	100.0	100.0	100.0	—
400.	64.0	78.4	87.1	92.3	99.4	100.0	100.0	100.0	100.0	100.0	100.0	100.0	100.0	100.0	100.0	100.0	100.0	—
425.	67.0	81.0	89.1	93.8	99.6	100.0	100.0	100.0	100.0	100.0	100.0	100.0	100.0	100.0	100.0	100.0	100.0	—
450.	69.8	83.4	90.9	95.0	99.8	100.0	100.0	100.0	100.0	100.0	100.0	100.0	100.0	100.0	100.0	100.0	100.0	—
475.	72.5	85.6	92.4	96.0	99.8	100.0	100.0	100.0	100.0	100.0	100.0	100.0	100.0	100.0	100.0	100.0	100.0	—
500.	75.0	87.5	93.8	96.9	99.9	100.0	100.0	100.0	100.0	100.0	100.0	100.0	100.0	100.0	100.0	100.0	100.0	—
550.	79.8	90.9	95.9	98.2	100.0	100.0	100.0	100.0	100.0	100.0	100.0	100.0	100.0	100.0	100.0	100.0	100.0	—
600.	84.0	93.6	97.5	99.0	100.0	100.0	100.0	100.0	100.0	100.0	100.0	100.0	100.0	100.0	100.0	100.0	100.0	—
650.	87.8	95.7	98.5	99.5	100.0	100.0	100.0	100.0	100.0	100.0	100.0	100.0	100.0	100.0	100.0	100.0	100.0	—
700.	91.0	97.3	99.2	99.8	100.0	100.0	100.0	100.0	100.0	100.0	100.0	100.0	100.0	100.0	100.0	100.0	100.0	—
750.	93.8	98.5	99.6	99.9	100.0	100.0	100.0	100.0	100.0	100.0	100.0	100.0	100.0	100.0	100.0	100.0	100.0	—
800.	96.0	99.2	99.8	100.0	100.0	100.0	100.0	100.0	100.0	100.0	100.0	100.0	100.0	100.0	100.0	100.0	100.0	—
850.	97.8	99.7	99.9	100.0	100.0	100.0	100.0	100.0	100.0	100.0	100.0	100.0	100.0	100.0	100.0	100.0	100.0	—
900.	99.0	99.9	100.0	100.0	100.0	100.0	100.0	100.0	100.0	100.0	100.0	100.0	100.0	100.0	100.0	100.0	100.0	—
950.	99.8	100.0	100.0	100.0	100.0	100.0	100.0	100.0	100.0	100.0	100.0	100.0	100.0	100.0	100.0	100.0	100.0	—
1000.	100.0	100.0	100.0	100.0	100.0	100.0	100.0	100.0	100.0	100.0	100.0	100.0	100.0	100.0	100.0	100.0	100.0	—
1100.	—	—	—	—	—	—	—	—	—	—	—	—	—	—	—	—	—	—
1200.	—	—	—	—	—	—	—	—	—	—	—	—	—	—	—	—	—	—
1300.	—	—	—	—	—	—	—	—	—	—	—	—	—	—	—	—	—	—
1400.	—	—	—	—	—	—	—	—	—	—	—	—	—	—	—	—	—	—
1500.	—	—	—	—	—	—	—	—	—	—	—	—	—	—	—	—	—	—
1600.	—	—	—	—	—	—	—	—	—	—	—	—	—	—	—	—	—	—
1700.	—	—	—	—	—	—	—	—	—	—	—	—	—	—	—	—	—	—
1800.	—	—	—	—	—	—	—	—	—	—	—	—	—	—	—	—	—	—
1900.	—	—	—	—	—	—	—	—	—	—	—	—	—	—	—	—	—	—
2000.	—	—	—	—	—	—	—	—	—	—	—	—	—	—	—	—	—	—

Appendix F-2

PROBABILITY, IN PER CENT, OF FINDING AT LEAST ONE ERROR IF TOTAL NO. OF ERRORS IN UNIVERSE IS AS INDICATED

TOTAL ERRORS IN UNIVERSE SIZE OF 3000,

SAMPLE SIZE	1	2	3	4	5	10	15	20	25	30	40	50	75	100	200	300	500	1000	2000
5	0.2	0.3	0.5	0.7	0.8	1.7	2.5	3.3	4.1	4.9	6.5	8.1	11.9	15.6	29.2	41.0	59.6	86.9	99.6
10	0.3	0.7	1.0	1.3	1.7	3.3	4.9	6.5	8.0	9.6	12.6	15.5	22.4	28.8	49.9	65.2	83.9	98.3	100.0
15	0.5	1.0	1.5	2.0	2.5	4.9	7.3	9.6	11.8	14.0	18.3	22.3	31.7	39.9	64.6	79.5	93.6	99.8	100.0
20	0.7	1.3	2.0	2.6	3.3	6.5	9.6	12.6	15.5	18.3	23.6	28.6	39.8	49.3	75.0	87.9	97.4	99.8	100.0
25	0.8	1.7	2.5	3.3	4.1	8.0	11.8	15.5	18.9	22.3	28.6	34.4	47.0	57.3	82.3	92.9	99.0	100.0	100.0
30	1.0	2.0	3.0	3.9	4.9	9.6	14.0	18.3	22.3	26.1	33.3	39.8	53.4	64.0	87.5	95.8	99.4	100.0	100.0
35	1.2	2.3	3.5	4.6	5.7	11.1	16.2	21.0	25.6	29.8	37.7	44.2	59.0	69.7	91.2	97.6	99.8	100.0	100.0
40	1.3	2.6	3.9	5.2	6.5	12.6	18.3	23.6	28.6	33.3	41.8	49.2	63.9	74.5	93.8	98.6	99.9	100.0	100.0
45	1.5	3.0	4.4	5.9	7.3	14.0	20.3	26.2	31.6	36.6	45.6	53.3	68.3	78.5	95.6	99.2	100.0	100.0	100.0
50	1.7	3.3	4.9	6.5	8.1	15.5	22.3	28.6	34.4	39.8	49.2	57.1	72.1	81.9	96.9	99.5	100.0	100.0	100.0
55	1.8	3.6	5.4	7.1	8.8	16.9	24.3	31.0	37.2	42.8	52.5	60.7	75.5	84.8	97.8	99.7	100.0	100.0	100.0
60	2.0	4.0	5.9	7.8	9.6	18.3	26.2	33.3	39.8	45.6	55.7	63.9	78.4	87.2	98.4	99.8	100.0	100.0	100.0
65	2.2	4.3	6.4	8.4	10.4	19.7	28.1	35.6	42.3	48.3	58.6	66.9	81.1	89.2	98.9	99.9	100.0	100.0	100.0
70	2.3	4.6	6.8	9.0	11.1	21.1	29.9	37.7	44.7	50.9	61.4	69.6	83.4	90.9	99.2	99.9	100.0	100.0	100.0
75	2.5	4.9	7.3	9.6	11.9	22.4	31.7	39.9	47.0	53.4	63.9	72.1	85.4	92.4	99.4	99.9	100.0	100.0	100.0
80	2.7	5.3	7.8	10.3	12.6	23.7	33.4	41.9	49.3	55.7	66.3	74.4	87.2	93.6	99.6	100.0	100.0	100.0	100.0
85	2.8	5.6	8.3	10.9	13.4	25.0	35.1	43.8	51.4	58.0	68.6	76.5	88.7	94.6	99.7	100.0	100.0	100.0	100.0
90	3.0	6.0	8.7	11.5	14.1	26.3	36.7	45.7	53.4	60.1	70.7	78.5	90.1	95.5	99.8	100.0	100.0	100.0	100.0
95	3.2	6.2	9.2	12.1	14.9	27.6	38.4	47.6	55.4	62.1	72.6	80.3	91.3	96.2	99.8	100.0	100.0	100.0	100.0
100	3.3	6.6	9.7	12.7	15.6	28.8	39.9	49.3	57.3	64.0	74.5	81.9	92.4	96.8	99.9	100.0	100.0	100.0	100.0
125	4.2	8.2	12.0	15.7	19.2	34.7	47.3	57.4	65.6	72.3	82.0	88.3	96.1	98.7	100.0	100.0	100.0	100.0	100.0
150	5.0	10.0	14.3	18.6	22.6	40.2	53.8	64.2	72.4	78.7	87.3	92.5	98.0	99.4	100.0	100.0	100.0	100.0	100.0
175	5.8	11.3	16.5	21.4	26.0	45.2	59.5	70.1	77.9	83.7	91.1	95.2	99.0	99.7	100.0	100.0	100.0	100.0	100.0
200	6.7	12.9	18.7	24.1	29.2	49.9	64.6	75.0	82.3	87.5	93.8	96.9	99.5	99.8	100.0	100.0	100.0	100.0	100.0
225	7.5	14.4	20.9	26.8	32.3	54.2	69.0	79.1	85.9	90.5	95.7	98.0	99.7	99.9	100.0	100.0	100.0	100.0	100.0
250	8.3	16.0	23.0	29.4	35.3	58.2	73.0	82.6	88.7	92.7	97.0	98.8	99.9	100.0	100.0	100.0	100.0	100.0	100.0
275	9.2	17.5	25.1	31.9	38.2	61.9	76.4	85.5	91.1	94.5	97.9	99.2	100.0	100.0	100.0	100.0	100.0	100.0	100.0
300	10.0	19.0	27.1	34.4	41.0	65.2	79.0	87.9	92.9	95.8	98.6	99.5	100.0	100.0	100.0	100.0	100.0	100.0	100.0
325	10.8	20.5	29.1	36.8	43.7	68.1	81.3	89.9	94.2	96.8	99.0	99.7	100.0	100.0	100.0	100.0	100.0	100.0	100.0
350	11.7	22.0	31.1	39.1	46.2	70.9	83.3	91.3	95.2	97.6	99.3	99.8	100.0	100.0	100.0	100.0	100.0	100.0	100.0
375	12.5	23.4	33.0	41.4	48.7	73.7	85.2	92.5	96.1	98.2	99.5	99.8	100.0	100.0	100.0	100.0	100.0	100.0	100.0
400	13.3	24.9	34.9	43.6	51.1	76.1	86.6	93.4	96.5	98.2	99.5	99.8	100.0	100.0	100.0	100.0	100.0	100.0	100.0
425	14.2	26.3	36.8	45.7	53.4	78.3	88.0	94.3	97.2	98.7	99.7	99.9	100.0	100.0	100.0	100.0	100.0	100.0	100.0
450	15.0	27.8	38.6	47.8	55.7	80.4	89.3	95.2	97.8	99.0	99.8	99.9	100.0	100.0	100.0	100.0	100.0	100.0	100.0
475	15.8	29.2	40.4	49.8	57.8	82.1	90.4	95.8	98.3	99.4	99.9	100.0	100.0	100.0	100.0	100.0	100.0	100.0	100.0
500	16.7	30.6	42.1	51.8	59.8	83.9	91.5	96.5	98.7	99.6	99.9	100.0	100.0	100.0	100.0	100.0	100.0	100.0	100.0
550	18.3	33.3	45.5	55.1	63.7	86.8	93.6	97.7	99.1	99.8	100.0	100.0	100.0	100.0	100.0	100.0	100.0	100.0	100.0
600	20.0	36.0	48.8	58.4	67.3	89.2	95.2	98.3	99.4	99.8	100.0	100.0	100.0	100.0	100.0	100.0	100.0	100.0	100.0
650	21.7	38.6	51.9	61.8	70.5	91.3	96.4	98.9	99.6	99.9	100.0	100.0	100.0	100.0	100.0	100.0	100.0	100.0	100.0
700	23.3	41.2	54.9	64.8	73.5	93.0	97.4	99.3	99.8	99.9	100.0	100.0	100.0	100.0	100.0	100.0	100.0	100.0	100.0
750	25.0	43.8	57.8	68.4	76.3	94.4	98.1	99.5	99.8	100.0	100.0	100.0	100.0	100.0	100.0	100.0	100.0	100.0	100.0
800	26.7	46.2	60.6	71.1	78.8	95.5	98.7	99.6	99.9	100.0	100.0	100.0	100.0	100.0	100.0	100.0	100.0	100.0	100.0
850	28.3	48.6	63.3	73.6	81.1	96.4	99.1	99.8	99.9	100.0	100.0	100.0	100.0	100.0	100.0	100.0	100.0	100.0	100.0
900	30.0	51.0	65.7	76.0	83.2	97.2	99.4	99.9	100.0	100.0	100.0	100.0	100.0	100.0	100.0	100.0	100.0	100.0	100.0
950	31.7	53.3	68.1	78.2	85.1	97.8	99.5	99.9	100.0	100.0	100.0	100.0	100.0	100.0	100.0	100.0	100.0	100.0	100.0
1000	33.3	55.6	70.4	80.3	86.9	98.3	99.7	100.0	100.0	100.0	100.0	100.0	100.0	100.0	100.0	100.0	100.0	100.0	100.0
1100	36.7	59.9	74.6	83.9	89.9	99.1	99.9	100.0	100.0	100.0	100.0	100.0	100.0	100.0	100.0	100.0	100.0	100.0	100.0
1200	40.0	64.0	78.4	87.1	92.2	99.4	100.0	100.0	100.0	100.0	100.0	100.0	100.0	100.0	100.0	100.0	100.0	100.0	100.0
1300	43.3	67.9	81.8	89.7	94.2	99.7	100.0	100.0	100.0	100.0	100.0	100.0	100.0	100.0	100.0	100.0	100.0	100.0	100.0
1400	46.7	71.6	84.8	91.9	95.7	99.8	100.0	100.0	100.0	100.0	100.0	100.0	100.0	100.0	100.0	100.0	100.0	100.0	100.0
1600	50.0	75.0	87.5	94.2	97.4	99.9	100.0	100.0	100.0	100.0	100.0	100.0	100.0	100.0	100.0	100.0	100.0	100.0	100.0
1800	53.3	78.2	89.8	95.3	97.8	100.0	100.0	100.0	100.0	100.0	100.0	100.0	100.0	100.0	100.0	100.0	100.0	100.0	100.0
1900	56.7	81.2	91.9	97.4	98.5	100.0	100.0	100.0	100.0	100.0	100.0	100.0	100.0	100.0	100.0	100.0	100.0	100.0	100.0
2000	60.0	84.0	93.1	98.8	99.6	100.0	100.0	100.0	100.0	100.0	100.0	100.0	100.0	100.0	100.0	100.0	100.0	100.0	100.0

Appendix F-3

PROBABILITY, IN PER CENT, OF FINDING AT LEAST ONE ERROR IF TOTAL NO. OF ERRORS IN UNIVERSE IS AS INDICATED

TOTAL ERRORS IN UNIVERSE — SIZE OF 5000.

SAMPLE SIZE	1	2	3	4	5	10	15	20	25	30	40	50	75	100	200	300	500	1000	2000
5.	0.1	0.2	0.3	0.4	0.5	1.0	1.5	2.0	2.5	3.0	3.9	4.9	7.3	9.6	18.5	26.6	41.0	67.2	92.2
10.	0.2	0.4	0.6	0.8	1.0	2.0	3.0	3.9	4.9	5.8	7.7	9.6	14.0	18.3	33.5	46.2	65.2	89.3	99.4
15.	0.3	0.6	0.9	1.2	1.5	3.0	4.4	5.8	7.3	8.6	11.4	14.0	20.3	26.2	45.8	60.5	79.5	96.5	100.0
20.	0.4	0.8	1.2	1.6	2.0	3.9	5.8	7.7	9.6	11.4	14.9	18.2	26.1	33.3	55.9	71.1	87.9	98.9	100.0
25.	0.5	1.0	1.5	2.0	2.5	4.9	7.3	9.6	11.8	14.0	18.2	22.3	31.5	39.7	64.1	78.8	92.9	99.6	100.0
30.	0.6	1.2	1.8	2.4	3.0	5.8	8.6	11.4	14.0	16.6	21.5	26.1	36.5	45.5	70.7	84.5	95.8	99.9	100.0
35.	0.7	1.4	2.1	2.8	3.5	6.8	10.1	13.1	16.1	19.1	24.6	29.7	41.2	50.8	76.2	88.6	97.5	99.9	100.0
40.	0.8	1.6	2.4	3.2	3.9	7.7	11.4	14.9	18.2	21.6	27.6	33.2	45.5	55.6	80.6	91.7	98.5	100.0	100.0
45.	0.9	1.8	2.7	3.6	4.4	8.7	12.7	16.6	20.3	23.8	30.4	36.5	49.5	59.9	84.2	93.9	99.1	100.0	100.0
50.	1.0	2.0	3.0	3.9	4.9	9.6	14.0	18.2	22.0	26.1	33.2	39.6	53.2	63.8	87.1	95.5	99.5	100.0	100.0
55.	1.1	2.2	3.3	4.3	5.4	10.5	15.3	19.9	24.2	28.3	35.9	42.6	56.6	67.3	89.5	96.7	99.7	100.0	100.0
60.	1.2	2.4	3.6	4.7	5.8	11.6	16.6	21.5	26.1	30.5	38.4	45.5	59.8	70.5	91.5	97.6	99.8	100.0	100.0
65.	1.3	2.6	3.9	5.1	6.3	12.3	17.8	23.1	28.0	32.5	40.9	48.2	62.8	73.3	93.1	98.3	99.9	100.0	100.0
70.	1.4	2.8	4.1	5.5	6.8	13.2	19.1	24.6	29.8	34.6	43.2	50.8	65.5	75.9	94.1	98.7	99.9	100.0	100.0
75.	1.5	3.0	4.4	5.9	7.3	14.0	20.3	26.1	31.5	36.5	45.5	53.2	68.1	78.3	95.4	99.1	100.0	100.0	100.0
80.	1.6	3.2	4.7	6.2	7.8	14.9	21.5	27.6	33.2	38.4	47.7	55.3	70.4	80.4	96.3	99.3	100.0	100.0	100.0
85.	1.7	3.4	5.0	6.6	8.2	15.8	22.7	29.1	34.9	40.3	49.8	57.8	72.6	82.3	97.0	99.5	100.0	100.0	100.0
90.	1.8	3.6	5.3	7.0	8.7	16.6	23.9	30.5	36.6	42.1	51.8	59.9	74.7	84.0	97.5	99.6	100.0	100.0	100.0
95.	1.9	3.8	5.6	7.4	9.1	17.5	25.0	31.9	38.2	43.9	53.7	61.9	76.5	85.6	98.0	99.7	100.0	100.0	100.0
100.	2.0	4.0	5.9	7.8	9.6	18.3	26.2	33.3	39.7	45.5	55.6	63.8	78.3	87.0	98.4	99.8	100.0	100.0	100.0
125.	2.5	4.9	7.3	9.6	11.9	22.4	31.6	39.8	47.0	53.3	63.8	72.0	85.2	92.3	99.4	100.0	100.0	100.0	100.0
150.	3.0	5.9	8.7	11.5	14.1	26.3	36.7	45.7	53.4	60.0	70.6	78.4	90.0	95.4	99.8	100.0	100.0	100.0	100.0
175.	3.5	6.9	10.1	13.3	16.3	30.0	41.4	51.0	59.1	65.8	76.1	83.3	93.2	97.3	99.9	100.0	100.0	100.0	100.0
200.	4.0	7.8	11.5	15.1	18.5	33.5	45.8	55.9	64.1	70.7	80.6	87.1	95.4	98.4	100.0	100.0	100.0	100.0	100.0
225.	4.5	8.8	13.0	16.8	20.6	36.9	49.8	60.3	68.5	75.0	84.3	90.1	96.9	99.0	100.0	100.0	100.0	100.0	100.0
250.	5.0	9.8	14.3	18.6	22.6	40.2	53.7	64.2	72.3	78.6	87.3	92.4	97.9	99.4	100.0	100.0	100.0	100.0	100.0
275.	5.5	10.7	15.6	20.3	24.6	43.2	57.2	67.8	75.8	81.8	89.7	94.2	98.6	99.7	100.0	100.0	100.0	100.0	100.0
300.	6.0	11.6	16.9	21.9	26.6	46.0	60.5	71.1	78.8	84.5	91.7	95.5	99.1	99.8	100.0	100.0	100.0	100.0	100.0
325.	6.5	12.6	18.3	23.6	28.6	49.0	63.6	74.0	81.4	86.8	93.3	96.6	99.4	99.9	100.0	100.0	100.0	100.0	100.0
350.	7.0	13.5	19.6	25.2	30.4	51.6	66.4	76.6	83.8	88.7	94.6	97.4	99.6	99.9	100.0	100.0	100.0	100.0	100.0
375.	7.5	14.4	20.9	26.8	32.3	54.2	69.0	79.0	85.8	90.4	95.6	98.0	99.7	99.9	100.0	100.0	100.0	100.0	100.0
400.	8.0	15.4	22.2	28.4	34.1	56.6	71.4	81.1	87.6	91.9	96.5	98.5	99.8	99.9	100.0	100.0	100.0	100.0	100.0
425.	8.5	16.3	23.4	29.9	35.9	58.9	73.7	83.1	89.2	93.1	97.2	98.8	99.9	100.0	100.0	100.0	100.0	100.0	100.0
450.	9.0	17.2	24.8	31.4	37.6	61.1	75.7	84.9	90.6	94.1	97.7	99.1	99.9	100.0	100.0	100.0	100.0	100.0	100.0
475.	9.5	18.1	25.9	32.9	39.3	63.2	77.7	86.5	91.8	95.0	98.2	99.3	99.9	100.0	100.0	100.0	100.0	100.0	100.0
500.	10.0	19.0	27.1	34.4	41.0	65.2	79.5	87.9	92.9	95.8	98.5	99.5	100.0	100.0	100.0	100.0	100.0	100.0	100.0
550.	11.0	20.8	29.5	37.3	44.0	68.9	82.6	90.3	94.6	97.0	99.1	99.7	100.0	100.0	100.0	100.0	100.0	100.0	100.0
600.	12.0	22.6	31.9	40.0	47.2	72.2	85.2	92.3	95.9	97.9	99.4	99.8	100.0	100.0	100.0	100.0	100.0	100.0	100.0
650.	13.0	24.3	34.2	42.7	50.2	75.2	87.4	93.9	97.0	98.5	99.6	99.9	100.0	100.0	100.0	100.0	100.0	100.0	100.0
700.	14.0	26.0	36.4	45.3	53.0	77.8	89.4	95.1	97.7	98.9	99.7	99.9	100.0	100.0	100.0	100.0	100.0	100.0	100.0
750.	15.0	27.8	38.6	47.8	55.6	80.3	90.9	96.2	98.3	99.2	99.8	100.0	100.0	100.0	100.0	100.0	100.0	100.0	100.0
800.	16.0	29.4	40.7	50.2	58.2	82.5	92.7	97.0	98.7	99.4	99.9	100.0	100.0	100.0	100.0	100.0	100.0	100.0	100.0
850.	17.0	31.1	42.8	52.6	60.6	84.5	93.9	97.6	99.1	99.6	99.9	100.0	100.0	100.0	100.0	100.0	100.0	100.0	100.0
900.	18.0	32.8	44.9	54.8	62.8	86.0	94.8	98.1	99.3	99.7	100.0	100.0	100.0	100.0	100.0	100.0	100.0	100.0	100.0
950.	19.0	34.4	46.9	56.9	65.1	87.3	95.8	98.5	99.5	99.8	100.0	100.0	100.0	100.0	100.0	100.0	100.0	100.0	100.0
1000.	20.0	36.0	48.8	59.1	67.2	89.3	96.5	98.8	99.6	99.9	100.0	100.0	100.0	100.0	100.0	100.0	100.0	100.0	100.0
1100.	22.0	39.2	52.6	63.0	71.1	91.7	97.6	99.3	99.8	99.9	100.0	100.0	100.0	100.0	100.0	100.0	100.0	100.0	100.0
1200.	24.0	42.2	56.1	66.7	74.1	93.5	98.3	99.5	99.9	100.0	100.0	100.0	100.0	100.0	100.0	100.0	100.0	100.0	100.0
1300.	26.0	45.2	59.5	70.1	77.8	95.1	98.9	99.7	99.9	100.0	100.0	100.0	100.0	100.0	100.0	100.0	100.0	100.0	100.0
1400.	28.0	48.2	62.7	73.0	80.1	96.3	99.3	99.8	100.0	100.0	100.0	100.0	100.0	100.0	100.0	100.0	100.0	100.0	100.0
1500.	30.0	51.0	65.7	76.0	83.2	97.2	99.5	99.9	100.0	100.0	100.0	100.0	100.0	100.0	100.0	100.0	100.0	100.0	100.0
1600.	32.0	53.8	68.6	78.6	85.5	97.9	99.7	99.9	100.0	100.0	100.0	100.0	100.0	100.0	100.0	100.0	100.0	100.0	100.0
1700.	34.0	56.4	71.3	81.0	87.6	98.4	99.8	100.0	100.0	100.0	100.0	100.0	100.0	100.0	100.0	100.0	100.0	100.0	100.0
1800.	36.0	59.0	73.8	83.2	89.3	98.9	99.8	100.0	100.0	100.0	100.0	100.0	100.0	100.0	100.0	100.0	100.0	100.0	100.0
1900.	38.0	61.6	76.2	85.2	90.9	99.2	99.9	100.0	100.0	100.0	100.0	100.0	100.0	100.0	100.0	100.0	100.0	100.0	100.0
2000.	40.0	64.0	78.4	87.1	92.2	99.4	99.9	100.0	100.0	100.0	100.0	100.0	100.0	100.0	100.0	100.0	100.0	100.0	100.0

Appendix F-4

PROBABILITY, IN PER CENT, OF FINDING AT LEAST ONE ERROR IF TOTAL NO. OF ERRORS IN UNIVERSE IS AS INDICATED

TOTAL ERRORS IN UNIVERSE SIZE OF 10000.

SAMPLE SIZE	1	2	.3	4	5	10	15	20	25	30	40	50	75	100	200	300	500	1000	2000
5.	0.1	0.1	0.1	0.2	0.2	0.5	0.7	1.0	1.2	1.5	2.0	2.5	3.7	4.9	9.6	14.1	22.6	41.0	67.2
10.	0.1	0.2	0.3	0.4	0.5	1.0	1.5	2.0	2.5	3.0	3.9	4.9	7.3	9.6	18.3	26.3	40.1	65.1	89.3
15.	0.2	0.3	0.4	0.6	0.7	1.5	2.2	3.0	3.7	4.4	5.8	7.2	10.7	14.0	26.2	36.7	53.7	79.4	96.5
20.	0.2	0.4	0.6	0.8	1.0	2.0	3.0	3.9	4.9	5.8	7.7	9.5	14.0	18.2	33.2	45.7	64.2	87.9	98.9
25.	0.3	0.5	0.7	1.0	1.2	2.5	3.7	4.9	6.1	7.2	9.5	11.8	17.2	22.2	39.7	53.3	72.3	92.8	99.6
30.	0.3	0.6	0.9	1.2	1.5	3.0	4.4	5.8	7.2	8.6	11.3	14.0	20.2	26.1	45.5	60.0	78.6	95.8	99.9
35.	0.4	0.7	1.0	1.4	1.7	3.4	5.1	6.8	8.4	10.0	13.1	16.1	23.2	29.7	50.8	65.6	83.4	97.5	100.0
40.	0.4	0.8	1.2	1.6	2.0	3.9	5.8	7.7	9.5	11.3	14.8	18.2	26.2	33.2	55.2	70.5	87.2	98.5	100.0
45.	0.5	0.9	1.3	1.8	2.2	4.4	6.5	8.6	10.7	12.7	16.5	20.2	28.8	36.5	59.2	74.7	90.1	99.1	100.0
50.	0.5	1.0	1.5	2.0	2.5	4.9	7.2	9.5	11.8	14.0	18.2	22.2	31.4	39.6	63.7	78.3	92.4	99.5	100.0
55.	0.6	1.1	1.6	2.2	2.7	5.4	7.9	10.5	12.9	15.3	19.8	24.2	34.2	42.6	67.2	81.4	94.1	99.7	100.0
60.	0.6	1.2	1.8	2.4	3.0	5.8	8.6	11.3	14.0	16.5	21.4	26.0	36.4	45.4	70.4	84.0	95.4	99.8	100.0
65.	0.7	1.3	1.9	2.6	3.2	6.3	9.3	12.2	15.1	17.8	23.0	27.9	38.8	48.1	73.2	86.3	96.5	99.9	100.0
70.	0.7	1.4	2.1	2.8	3.5	6.8	10.0	13.1	16.1	19.0	24.5	29.7	41.1	50.6	75.8	88.2	97.3	99.9	100.0
75.	0.8	1.5	2.2	3.0	3.7	7.2	10.7	14.0	17.2	20.2	26.0	31.4	43.3	53.1	78.1	89.7	97.9	99.9	100.0
80.	0.8	1.6	2.4	3.2	4.0	7.7	11.4	14.9	18.2	21.6	27.5	33.1	45.4	55.1	80.4	91.3	98.4	100.0	100.0
85.	0.9	1.7	2.5	3.4	4.2	8.2	12.0	15.7	19.2	22.6	29.0	34.8	47.4	57.6	82.2	92.2	98.7	100.0	100.0
90.	0.9	1.8	2.7	3.5	4.7	8.6	12.7	16.6	20.3	23.8	30.8	38.0	49.4	59.7	83.9	93.6	99.0	100.0	100.0
95.	1.0	1.9	2.8	3.7	4.7	9.3	13.3	17.4	21.3	24.9	31.8	38.0	51.3	61.7	85.5	94.5	99.3	100.0	100.0
100.	1.0	2.0	3.0	3.9	4.9	9.6	14.0	18.2	22.0	26.0	33.2	39.6	53.1	63.6	86.9	95.3	99.4	100.0	100.0
125.	1.3	2.5	3.7	4.9	6.1	11.8	17.2	22.3	27.0	31.5	39.6	46.8	61.2	71.8	92.1	97.8	99.9	100.0	100.0
150.	1.5	2.9	4.4	5.8	7.3	14.0	20.3	26.1	31.7	36.5	45.4	54.1	67.9	78.1	95.3	98.9	100.0	100.0	100.0
175.	1.8	3.5	5.2	6.8	8.5	16.2	23.2	29.7	35.7	41.1	51.3	58.7	73.5	83.0	97.2	99.4	99.8	100.0	100.0
200.	2.0	4.0	5.9	7.8	9.6	18.3	26.2	33.3	39.7	45.5	55.5	63.7	78.1	86.9	98.3	99.8	100.0	100.0	100.0
225.	2.3	4.5	6.6	8.7	10.8	20.4	28.9	36.6	43.4	49.5	59.8	68.0	82.0	89.8	99.0	99.9	100.0	100.0	100.0
250.	2.5	4.9	7.3	9.6	11.9	22.4	31.6	39.8	46.9	53.3	63.7	71.9	85.1	92.1	99.4	99.9	100.0	100.0	100.0
275.	2.8	5.4	8.0	10.6	13.0	24.3	34.2	42.8	50.2	56.7	67.3	75.3	87.7	93.9	99.6	100.0	100.0	100.0	100.0
300.	3.0	5.9	8.7	11.5	14.1	26.3	36.7	45.7	53.3	60.0	70.5	78.3	89.9	95.3	99.8	100.0	100.0	100.0	100.0
325.	3.3	6.4	9.4	12.4	15.2	28.1	39.1	48.4	56.3	62.9	73.4	80.9	91.7	96.4	99.9	100.0	100.0	100.0	100.0
350.	3.5	6.9	10.1	13.3	16.3	30.0	41.7	51.0	59.0	65.7	76.0	83.2	93.2	97.2	99.9	100.0	100.0	100.0	100.0
375.	3.8	7.4	10.8	14.2	17.4	31.8	43.7	53.7	61.6	68.3	78.6	85.3	94.4	97.9	100.0	100.0	100.0	100.0	100.0
400.	4.0	7.8	11.5	15.1	18.5	33.6	45.8	56.0	64.0	70.9	81.7	87.1	95.4	98.3	100.0	100.0	100.0	100.0	100.0
425.	4.3	8.3	12.2	15.9	19.5	35.2	47.9	58.1	66.3	72.9	82.5	89.0	96.2	98.7	100.0	100.0	100.0	100.0	100.0
450.	4.5	8.7	12.9	16.8	20.6	36.9	49.9	60.2	68.4	74.0	84.2	90.1	96.6	98.9	100.0	100.0	100.0	100.0	100.0
475.	4.8	9.3	13.6	17.7	21.6	38.5	51.8	62.3	70.4	76.8	85.8	91.3	97.4	99.2	100.0	100.0	100.0	100.0	100.0
500.	5.0	9.8	14.2	18.6	22.6	40.1	53.7	64.2	72.2	78.6	87.4	92.4	97.9	99.4	100.0	100.0	100.0	100.0	100.0
550.	5.5	10.7	15.6	20.3	24.6	43.2	57.2	67.8	75.7	81.7	89.6	94.1	98.6	99.7	100.0	100.0	100.0	100.0	100.0
600.	6.0	11.6	16.9	21.9	26.6	46.2	60.5	71.0	78.7	84.4	91.6	95.5	99.1	99.8	100.0	100.0	100.0	100.0	100.0
650.	6.5	12.5	18.3	23.6	28.5	49.0	63.5	74.0	81.2	86.7	93.2	96.6	99.4	99.9	100.0	100.0	100.0	100.0	100.0
700.	7.0	13.5	19.6	25.2	30.4	51.6	66.4	76.6	83.5	88.7	94.5	97.4	99.6	99.9	100.0	100.0	100.0	100.0	100.0
750.	7.5	14.4	20.9	26.8	32.3	54.2	69.0	79.0	85.6	90.4	95.6	98.0	99.7	100.0	100.0	100.0	100.0	100.0	100.0
800.	8.0	15.4	22.1	28.4	34.1	56.6	71.4	81.2	87.6	91.8	96.5	98.5	99.8	100.0	100.0	100.0	100.0	100.0	100.0
850.	8.5	16.3	23.4	29.9	35.9	58.9	73.6	83.4	89.2	93.1	97.0	98.8	99.9	100.0	100.0	100.0	100.0	100.0	100.0
900.	9.0	17.2	24.6	31.4	37.6	61.1	75.7	84.9	90.6	93.8	97.7	99.1	99.9	100.0	100.0	100.0	100.0	100.0	100.0
950.	9.5	18.1	25.9	32.9	39.3	63.2	77.7	86.4	91.8	95.1	98.2	99.2	99.9	100.0	100.0	100.0	100.0	100.0	100.0
1000.	10.0	19.0	27.1	34.4	41.0	65.1	79.4	87.9	92.8	95.8	98.5	99.3	100.0	100.0	100.0	100.0	100.0	100.0	100.0
1100.	11.0	20.8	29.5	37.3	44.2	68.8	82.6	90.3	94.4	97.0	99.0	99.7	100.0	100.0	100.0	100.0	100.0	100.0	100.0
1200.	12.0	22.6	31.9	40.1	47.2	72.2	85.5	92.3	95.8	97.8	99.3	99.8	100.0	100.0	100.0	100.0	100.0	100.0	100.0
1300.	13.0	24.3	34.2	42.7	50.2	75.2	87.6	93.8	96.7	98.4	99.6	99.9	100.0	100.0	100.0	100.0	100.0	100.0	100.0
1400.	14.0	26.0	36.4	45.3	53.0	77.9	89.6	95.1	97.5	98.9	99.8	99.9	100.0	100.0	100.0	100.0	100.0	100.0	100.0
1500.	15.0	27.8	38.6	47.8	55.6	80.3	91.3	96.1	98.1	99.2	99.9	100.0	100.0	100.0	100.0	100.0	100.0	100.0	100.0
1600.	16.0	29.4	40.7	50.2	58.2	82.5	92.7	96.9	98.7	99.4	99.9	100.0	100.0	100.0	100.0	100.0	100.0	100.0	100.0
1700.	17.0	31.1	42.8	52.5	60.6	84.5	93.9	97.6	99.0	99.6	99.9	100.0	100.0	100.0	100.0	100.0	100.0	100.0	100.0
1800.	18.0	32.8	44.9	54.8	62.9	86.3	94.9	98.1	99.3	99.8	100.0	100.0	100.0	100.0	100.0	100.0	100.0	100.0	100.0
1900.	19.0	34.4	46.9	57.0	65.1	87.9	95.8	98.5	99.5	99.9	100.0	100.0	100.0	100.0	100.0	100.0	100.0	100.0	100.0
2000.	20.0	36.0	48.8	59.0	67.2	89.3	96.5	98.9	99.6	99.9	100.0	100.0	100.0	100.0	100.0	100.0	100.0	100.0	100.0

Appendix F-5

PROBABILITY, IN PER CENT, OF FINDING AT LEAST ONE ERROR IF TOTAL NO. OF ERRORS IN UNIVERSE IS AS INDICATED

TOTAL ERRORS IN UNIVERSE SIZE OF 15000.

SAMPLE SIZE	1	2	3	4	5	10	15	20	25	30	40	50	75	100	200	300	500	1000	2000
5.	0.0	0.1	0.1	0.1	0.2	0.3	0.5	0.7	0.8	1.0	1.3	1.7	2.5	3.3	6.5	9.6	15.6	29.2	51.1
10.	0.1	0.1	0.2	0.3	0.3	0.7	1.0	1.3	1.7	2.0	2.6	3.3	4.9	6.5	12.6	18.3	28.8	49.5	76.1
15.	0.1	0.2	0.3	0.4	0.5	1.0	1.5	2.0	2.5	3.0	3.9	4.9	7.2	9.5	18.2	26.2	39.9	64.5	88.2
20.	0.1	0.3	0.4	0.5	0.7	1.3	2.0	2.6	3.3	3.9	5.2	6.5	9.5	12.5	23.6	33.7	49.3	74.9	94.3
25.	0.2	0.3	0.5	0.7	0.8	1.7	2.5	3.3	4.1	4.9	6.5	8.0	11.8	15.4	28.5	39.7	57.2	82.4	97.2
30.	0.2	0.4	0.6	0.8	1.0	2.0	3.0	3.9	4.9	5.8	7.7	9.5	14.0	18.2	33.2	45.5	63.9	87.4	98.6
35.	0.2	0.5	0.7	0.9	1.2	2.3	3.4	4.6	5.7	6.7	8.8	11.0	16.1	20.9	37.5	50.7	69.5	91.1	99.3
40.	0.3	0.5	0.8	1.1	1.3	2.6	3.9	5.2	6.4	7.7	10.1	12.5	18.2	23.5	41.6	55.5	74.3	93.7	99.7
45.	0.3	0.6	0.9	1.2	1.5	3.0	4.4	5.8	7.2	8.6	11.3	14.0	20.2	26.0	45.4	59.8	78.3	95.5	99.8
50.	0.3	0.7	1.0	1.3	1.7	3.3	4.9	6.5	8.0	9.5	12.5	15.4	22.2	28.5	48.9	63.6	81.7	96.8	99.9
55.	0.4	0.7	1.1	1.5	1.8	3.6	5.4	7.1	8.8	10.4	13.7	16.8	24.1	30.8	52.3	67.1	84.6	97.8	100.0
60.	0.4	0.8	1.2	1.6	2.0	3.9	5.8	7.7	9.5	11.3	14.8	18.2	26.0	33.1	55.4	70.3	87.0	98.5	100.0
65.	0.4	0.9	1.3	1.7	2.1	4.3	6.3	8.3	10.3	12.2	16.0	19.5	27.9	35.3	58.3	73.2	89.0	99.0	100.0
70.	0.5	0.9	1.4	1.9	2.3	4.6	6.8	8.9	11.0	13.1	17.1	20.9	29.7	37.5	61.0	75.8	90.7	99.2	100.0
75.	0.5	1.0	1.5	2.0	2.5	4.9	7.2	9.5	11.8	14.0	18.2	22.2	31.4	39.5	63.6	78.1	92.2	99.4	100.0
80.	0.5	1.1	1.6	2.1	2.6	5.2	7.7	10.1	12.5	14.8	19.3	23.5	33.1	41.5	65.9	80.2	93.4	99.6	100.0
85.	0.6	1.1	1.7	2.2	2.8	5.5	8.2	10.7	13.3	15.7	20.4	24.8	34.8	43.5	68.2	82.1	94.4	99.7	100.0
90.	0.6	1.2	1.8	2.4	3.0	5.8	8.6	11.3	14.0	16.5	21.4	26.0	36.4	45.3	70.2	83.9	95.3	99.8	100.0
95.	0.6	1.3	1.9	2.5	3.1	6.2	9.1	11.9	14.7	17.4	22.4	27.3	38.0	47.1	72.2	85.4	96.0	99.9	100.0
100.	0.7	1.3	2.0	2.6	3.3	6.5	9.5	12.5	15.4	18.2	23.5	28.5	39.5	48.9	74.0	86.8	96.7	99.9	100.0
125.	0.8	1.7	2.5	3.3	4.1	8.0	11.8	15.4	18.9	22.2	28.5	34.2	46.7	56.8	81.0	92.1	98.6	100.0	100.0
150.	1.0	2.0	3.0	3.9	4.9	9.6	14.0	18.2	22.2	26.1	33.2	39.5	53.0	63.5	86.0	95.2	99.4	100.0	100.0
175.	1.2	2.3	3.5	4.6	5.7	11.1	16.2	20.9	25.4	29.7	37.5	44.4	58.6	69.2	90.0	97.1	99.7	100.0	100.0
200.	1.3	2.6	3.9	5.2	6.5	12.6	18.2	23.6	28.5	33.2	41.6	48.9	63.6	74.0	93.3	98.3	99.9	100.0	100.0
225.	1.5	3.0	4.4	5.9	7.3	14.0	20.3	26.1	31.5	36.5	45.4	53.1	67.9	78.1	95.2	99.0	99.9	100.0	100.0
250.	1.7	3.3	4.9	6.5	8.1	15.5	22.3	28.6	34.3	39.6	49.0	56.9	71.7	81.5	96.6	99.4	100.0	100.0	100.0
275.	1.8	3.6	5.4	7.1	8.8	16.9	24.2	30.9	37.0	42.6	52.3	60.4	74.2	84.4	97.5	99.6	100.0	100.0	100.0
300.	2.0	4.0	5.9	7.8	9.6	18.3	26.1	33.2	39.7	45.5	55.5	63.6	78.1	86.9	98.2	99.8	100.0	100.0	100.0
325.	2.2	4.3	6.4	8.4	10.4	19.7	28.0	35.5	42.2	48.2	58.4	66.6	80.6	88.8	98.7	99.9	100.0	100.0	100.0
350.	2.3	4.6	6.8	9.0	11.1	21.0	29.8	37.6	44.6	50.7	61.1	69.3	82.9	90.6	99.1	99.9	100.0	100.0	100.0
375.	2.5	4.9	7.3	9.6	11.9	22.4	31.6	39.7	46.9	53.2	63.7	71.9	85.1	92.1	99.4	100.0	100.0	100.0	100.0
400.	2.7	5.3	7.8	10.2	12.6	23.7	33.3	41.8	49.1	55.5	66.1	74.2	86.9	93.4	99.6	100.0	100.0	100.0	100.0
425.	2.8	5.6	8.3	10.9	13.4	25.0	35.0	43.7	51.3	57.8	68.4	76.3	88.5	94.4	99.7	100.0	100.0	100.0	100.0
450.	3.0	5.9	8.7	11.5	14.1	26.3	36.7	45.6	53.3	59.9	70.5	78.2	89.9	95.3	99.8	100.0	100.0	100.0	100.0
475.	3.2	6.2	9.2	12.1	14.9	27.5	38.3	47.5	55.3	62.0	72.4	80.0	91.1	96.0	99.8	100.0	100.0	100.0	100.0
500.	3.3	6.6	9.7	12.7	15.6	28.8	39.9	49.3	57.2	63.9	74.3	81.7	92.2	96.7	99.9	100.0	100.0	100.0	100.0
550.	3.6	7.1	10.6	13.9	17.0	31.2	42.2	52.6	60.7	67.4	76.8	84.6	94.0	97.6	99.9	100.0	100.0	100.0	100.0
600.	4.0	7.8	11.5	15.1	18.5	33.5	45.8	55.8	64.0	70.6	80.5	87.1	95.4	98.3	100.0	100.0	100.0	100.0	100.0
650.	4.3	8.5	12.4	16.2	19.9	35.8	48.5	58.8	66.9	73.6	83.0	89.1	96.4	98.8	100.0	100.0	100.0	100.0	100.0
700.	4.7	9.1	13.4	17.4	21.2	38.0	51.2	61.6	69.7	76.2	85.3	90.8	97.2	99.2	100.0	100.0	100.0	100.0	100.0
750.	5.0	9.7	14.3	18.5	22.6	40.1	53.7	64.2	72.3	78.5	87.4	92.3	97.9	99.4	100.0	100.0	100.0	100.0	100.0
800.	5.3	10.4	15.2	19.7	23.9	42.2	56.1	66.6	74.6	80.7	88.8	93.5	98.4	99.6	100.0	100.0	100.0	100.0	100.0
850.	5.7	11.0	16.1	20.8	25.3	44.2	58.3	68.9	76.7	82.6	90.3	94.6	98.7	99.7	100.0	100.0	100.0	100.0	100.0
900.	6.0	11.6	16.9	21.9	26.6	46.1	60.5	71.0	78.7	84.4	91.6	95.5	99.0	99.8	100.0	100.0	100.0	100.0	100.0
950.	6.3	12.3	17.8	23.0	27.9	48.0	62.5	73.0	80.5	86.0	92.7	96.2	99.3	99.9	100.0	100.0	100.0	100.0	100.0
1000.	6.7	12.9	18.7	24.1	29.2	49.8	64.5	74.8	82.2	87.4	93.7	96.8	99.4	99.9	100.0	100.0	100.0	100.0	100.0
1100.	7.3	14.1	20.4	26.3	31.7	53.3	68.1	78.2	85.1	89.8	95.2	97.8	99.7	100.0	100.0	100.0	100.0	100.0	100.0
1200.	8.0	15.4	22.1	28.4	34.1	56.6	71.4	81.1	87.6	91.8	96.4	98.5	99.8	100.0	100.0	100.0	100.0	100.0	100.0
1300.	8.7	16.6	23.8	30.4	36.4	59.6	74.3	83.7	89.6	93.4	97.3	98.9	99.9	100.0	100.0	100.0	100.0	100.0	100.0
1400.	9.3	17.8	25.5	32.4	38.7	62.5	77.0	85.9	91.4	94.7	98.0	99.3	99.9	100.0	100.0	100.0	100.0	100.0	100.0
1500.	10.0	19.0	27.1	34.4	40.9	65.1	79.4	87.8	92.8	95.8	98.5	99.5	100.0	100.0	100.0	100.0	100.0	100.0	100.0
1600.	10.7	20.2	28.7	36.3	43.1	67.6	81.6	89.5	94.0	96.6	98.9	99.6	100.0	100.0	100.0	100.0	100.0	100.0	100.0
1700.	11.3	21.4	30.3	38.2	45.2	70.0	83.5	91.0	95.1	97.3	99.2	99.8	100.0	100.0	100.0	100.0	100.0	100.0	100.0
1800.	12.0	22.6	31.9	40.0	47.2	72.2	85.3	92.2	95.9	97.8	99.4	99.8	100.0	100.0	100.0	100.0	100.0	100.0	100.0
1900.	12.7	23.7	33.4	41.8	49.2	74.2	86.9	93.3	96.6	98.3	99.6	99.9	100.0	100.0	100.0	100.0	100.0	100.0	100.0
2000.	13.3	24.9	34.9	43.6	51.1	76.1	88.3	94.3	97.2	98.6	99.7	99.9	100.0	100.0	100.0	100.0	100.0	100.0	100.0

Appendix F-6

PROBABILITY, IN PER CENT, OF FINDING AT LEAST ONE ERROR IF TOTAL NO. OF ERRORS IN UNIVERSE IS AS INDICATED

TOTAL ERRORS IN UNIVERSE SIZE OF 25000.

SAMPLE SIZE	2	3	4	5	10	15	20	25	30	40	50	75	100	200	300	500	1000	2000
5.	0.0	0.1	0.1	0.1	0.2	0.3	0.4	0.5	0.6	0.8	1.0	1.5	2.0	3.9	5.9	9.6	18.5	34.1
10.	0.0	0.1	0.1	0.2	0.4	0.6	0.8	1.0	1.2	1.6	2.0	3.0	3.9	7.7	11.4	18.3	33.5	56.6
15.	0.1	0.2	0.2	0.3	0.6	0.9	1.2	1.5	1.8	2.4	3.0	4.4	5.8	11.4	16.6	26.1	45.8	71.1
20.	0.1	0.2	0.3	0.4	0.8	1.2	1.6	2.0	2.4	3.2	3.9	5.8	7.7	14.8	21.6	33.3	55.8	81.1
25.	0.2	0.2	0.4	0.5	1.0	1.5	2.0	2.5	3.0	3.9	4.9	7.2	9.5	18.2	26.1	39.7	64.0	87.5
30.	0.2	0.3	0.5	0.6	1.2	1.8	2.4	2.9	3.5	4.7	5.8	8.6	11.3	21.4	30.5	45.5	70.6	91.8
35.	0.3	0.4	0.6	0.7	1.4	2.1	2.8	3.4	4.1	5.5	6.8	10.0	13.1	24.5	34.5	50.7	76.1	94.6
40.	0.3	0.5	0.6	0.8	1.6	2.4	3.2	3.9	4.7	6.2	7.7	11.3	14.8	27.5	38.3	55.5	80.5	96.4
45.	0.4	0.5	0.7	0.9	1.8	2.7	3.5	4.4	5.3	7.0	8.6	12.7	16.5	30.4	41.9	59.7	84.1	97.7
50.	0.4	0.6	0.8	1.0	2.0	3.0	3.9	4.9	5.8	7.7	9.5	14.0	18.2	33.1	45.4	63.6	87.0	98.5
55.	0.4	0.7	0.9	1.1	2.2	3.3	4.3	5.4	6.4	8.4	10.4	15.2	19.8	35.7	48.6	67.1	89.4	99.0
60.	0.5	0.7	1.0	1.2	2.4	3.6	4.7	5.8	7.0	9.2	11.3	16.5	21.4	38.3	51.6	70.3	91.4	99.3
65.	0.5	0.8	1.0	1.3	2.6	3.8	5.1	6.3	7.5	9.9	12.2	17.8	23.0	40.7	54.1	73.1	93.0	99.6
70.	0.6	0.8	1.1	1.4	2.8	4.1	5.5	6.8	8.1	10.6	13.1	19.0	24.5	43.1	57.1	75.7	94.3	99.7
75.	0.6	0.9	1.2	1.5	2.9	4.4	5.8	7.2	8.6	11.3	14.0	20.2	26.0	45.3	59.6	78.1	95.3	99.8
80.	0.6	1.0	1.3	1.6	3.2	4.7	6.2	7.7	9.2	12.0	14.8	21.4	27.5	47.5	62.0	80.2	96.2	99.9
85.	0.7	1.0	1.4	1.7	3.3	5.0	6.6	8.2	9.7	12.7	15.7	22.6	28.9	49.5	64.2	82.1	96.9	99.9
90.	0.7	1.1	1.4	1.8	3.5	5.3	7.0	8.6	10.3	13.4	16.5	23.7	30.3	51.5	66.3	83.8	97.5	99.9
95.	0.8	1.1	1.5	1.9	3.7	5.6	7.3	9.1	10.8	14.1	17.3	24.9	31.7	53.4	68.3	85.4	98.0	100.0
100.	0.8	1.2	1.6	2.0	3.9	5.8	7.7	9.5	11.3	14.8	18.2	26.0	33.1	55.3	70.2	86.8	98.3	100.0
125.	1.0	1.5	2.0	2.5	4.9	7.2	9.6	11.8	14.0	18.2	22.2	31.4	39.5	63.5	78.0	92.0	99.1	100.0
150.	1.2	1.8	2.4	2.9	5.8	8.6	11.4	14.0	16.5	21.4	26.0	35.8	45.3	67.0	83.7	95.2	99.6	100.0
175.	1.4	2.1	2.8	3.5	6.8	10.0	13.2	16.2	19.0	24.5	29.6	40.0	50.5	73.0	88.0	97.1	99.8	100.0
200.	1.6	2.4	3.2	3.9	7.7	11.4	15.0	18.4	21.6	27.8	33.1	43.0	55.3	75.6	91.1	98.3	99.9	100.0
225.	1.8	2.7	3.6	4.4	8.6	12.7	16.5	20.2	23.8	30.4	36.4	45.3	59.6	80.1	93.5	99.0	99.9	100.0
250.	2.0	3.0	3.9	4.9	9.6	14.0	18.2	22.2	26.0	33.1	39.5	47.5	63.5	81.7	95.1	99.4	100.0	100.0
275.	2.2	3.3	4.4	5.4	10.5	15.3	19.9	24.2	28.3	35.8	42.5	56.4	67.0	86.7	95.5	99.6	100.0	100.0
300.	2.4	3.6	4.7	5.9	11.4	16.6	21.5	26.1	30.5	38.3	45.4	58.6	70.2	89.2	96.5	99.8	100.0	100.0
325.	2.6	3.8	5.1	6.3	12.3	17.8	23.0	27.9	32.5	40.8	48.1	62.6	73.0	91.1	97.4	99.8	100.0	100.0
350.	2.8	4.1	5.5	6.8	13.2	19.1	24.6	29.7	34.6	43.1	50.6	65.5	75.7	92.8	98.0	99.9	100.0	100.0
375.	3.0	4.4	5.9	7.3	14.0	20.3	26.1	31.5	36.5	45.6	53.1	67.9	78.0	94.1	98.6	99.9	100.0	100.0
400.	3.2	4.7	6.2	7.7	14.9	21.5	27.6	33.2	38.4	47.6	55.4	70.2	80.1	95.2	99.0	99.9	100.0	100.0
425.	3.4	5.0	6.6	8.2	15.8	22.7	29.0	34.9	40.2	49.7	57.6	72.4	82.1	96.1	99.2	100.0	100.0	100.0
450.	3.6	5.3	7.0	8.7	16.6	23.9	30.5	36.5	42.0	51.7	59.7	74.4	83.8	96.8	99.4	100.0	100.0	100.0
475.	3.8	5.6	7.4	9.2	17.5	25.0	31.9	38.1	43.8	53.6	61.7	76.3	85.4	97.4	99.6	100.0	100.0	100.0
500.	4.0	5.9	7.8	9.6	18.3	26.1	33.2	39.7	45.5	55.5	63.6	78.1	86.8	97.9	99.7	100.0	100.0	100.0
550.	4.4	6.5	8.5	10.5	19.9	28.4	35.8	42.5	48.7	59.0	67.2	81.2	89.2	98.6	99.8	100.0	100.0	100.0
600.	4.7	7.0	9.3	11.4	21.6	30.5	38.5	45.5	51.8	62.4	70.4	83.9	91.2	99.1	99.9	100.0	100.0	100.0
650.	5.1	7.6	10.0	12.3	23.2	32.7	41.0	48.3	54.7	65.5	73.2	86.2	92.9	99.4	99.9	100.0	100.0	100.0
700.	5.5	8.1	10.7	13.2	24.7	34.7	43.3	50.9	57.4	68.4	75.7	88.2	94.2	99.6	100.0	100.0	100.0	100.0
750.	5.9	8.7	11.5	14.1	26.3	36.7	45.6	53.3	59.9	71.0	78.2	89.9	95.3	99.8	100.0	100.0	100.0	100.0
800.	6.3	9.3	12.2	15.0	27.8	38.6	47.8	55.7	62.3	73.5	80.4	91.3	96.2	99.8	100.0	100.0	100.0	100.0
850.	6.7	9.9	13.0	15.9	29.2	40.5	49.9	57.9	64.6	75.8	82.3	92.6	96.9	99.9	100.0	100.0	100.0	100.0
900.	7.1	10.4	13.8	16.8	30.7	42.3	52.0	60.0	66.7	77.9	84.0	93.7	97.5	99.9	100.0	100.0	100.0	100.0
950.	7.5	11.0	14.4	17.6	32.1	44.1	53.9	62.1	68.7	79.9	85.6	94.6	97.9	100.0	100.0	100.0	100.0	100.0
1000.	7.8	11.5	15.1	18.3	33.5	45.8	55.9	64.0	70.6	81.7	87.0	95.3	98.3	100.0	100.0	100.0	100.0	100.0
1100.	8.6	12.6	16.5	20.1	36.2	49.1	59.1	67.4	74.1	85.0	89.5	96.5	98.9	100.0	100.0	100.0	100.0	100.0
1200.	9.4	13.7	17.9	21.8	38.9	52.2	62.6	70.8	77.2	87.6	91.5	97.5	99.3	100.0	100.0	100.0	100.0	100.0
1300.	10.1	14.8	19.2	23.4	41.4	55.1	65.4	73.7	80.0	89.4	93.1	98.2	99.5	100.0	100.0	100.0	100.0	100.0
1400.	10.9	15.9	20.6	25.0	43.8	57.9	68.2	76.3	82.3	91.1	94.4	98.7	99.7	100.0	100.0	100.0	100.0	100.0
1500.	11.6	16.9	21.9	26.5	46.1	60.5	70.5	78.7	84.5	92.5	95.5	99.0	99.8	100.0	100.0	100.0	100.0	100.0
1600.	12.4	18.0	23.2	28.2	48.4	62.9	73.4	80.9	86.3	93.5	96.3	99.3	99.8	100.0	100.0	100.0	100.0	100.0
1700.	13.1	19.0	24.6	29.7	50.6	65.2	75.6	82.9	87.9	94.6	97.1	99.5	99.9	100.0	100.0	100.0	100.0	100.0
1800.	13.9	20.1	25.8	31.2	52.6	67.4	77.6	84.6	89.4	95.3	97.6	99.6	99.9	100.0	100.0	100.0	100.0	100.0
1900.	14.6	21.1	27.1	32.8	54.6	69.5	79.4	86.2	90.7	96.0	98.1	99.7	99.9	100.0	100.0	100.0	100.0	100.0
2000.	15.4	22.1	28.4	34.1	56.6	71.4	81.1	87.6	91.8	96.4	98.5	99.8	100.0	100.0	100.0	100.0	100.0	100.0

Appendix F-7

PROBABILITY, IN PER CENT, OF FINDING AT LEAST ONE ERROR IF TOTAL NO. OF ERRORS IN UNIVERSE IS AS INDICATED

TOTAL ERRORS IN UNIVERSE SIZE OF 50000.

SAMPLE SIZE	1	2	3	4	5	10	15	20	25	30	40	50	75	100	200	300	500	1000	2000
5	0.0	0.0	0.0	0.0	0.0	0.1	0.1	0.2	0.2	0.3	0.4	0.5	0.7	1.0	2.0	3.0	4.9	9.6	18.5
10	0.0	0.0	0.1	0.1	0.1	0.2	0.3	0.4	0.5	0.6	0.8	1.0	1.5	2.0	3.9	5.8	9.6	18.3	33.5
15	0.0	0.1	0.1	0.1	0.1	0.3	0.4	0.6	0.7	0.9	1.2	1.5	2.2	3.0	5.8	8.6	14.0	26.1	45.8
20	0.0	0.1	0.1	0.2	0.2	0.4	0.6	0.8	1.0	1.2	1.6	2.0	3.0	3.9	7.7	11.3	18.2	33.2	55.8
25	0.1	0.1	0.1	0.2	0.2	0.5	0.7	1.0	1.2	1.5	2.0	2.5	3.7	4.9	9.5	14.0	22.2	39.7	64.0
30	0.1	0.1	0.2	0.2	0.3	0.6	0.9	1.2	1.5	1.8	2.4	3.0	4.4	5.8	11.3	16.5	26.0	45.5	70.6
35	0.1	0.1	0.2	0.3	0.3	0.7	1.0	1.4	1.7	2.1	2.8	3.4	5.1	6.8	13.1	19.0	29.7	50.7	76.0
40	0.1	0.2	0.2	0.3	0.4	0.8	1.2	1.6	2.0	2.4	3.2	3.9	5.8	7.7	14.8	21.4	33.1	55.4	80.5
45	0.1	0.2	0.3	0.4	0.4	0.9	1.3	1.8	2.2	2.7	3.5	4.4	6.5	8.6	16.5	23.7	36.4	59.7	84.1
50	0.1	0.2	0.3	0.4	0.5	1.0	1.5	2.0	2.5	3.0	3.9	4.9	7.2	9.5	18.2	26.0	39.5	63.6	87.0
55	0.1	0.2	0.3	0.4	0.5	1.1	1.6	2.2	2.7	3.2	4.3	5.4	7.9	10.4	19.8	28.2	42.5	67.1	89.4
60	0.1	0.2	0.4	0.5	0.6	1.2	1.8	2.4	3.0	3.5	4.7	5.8	8.6	11.3	21.4	30.3	45.3	70.2	91.4
65	0.1	0.3	0.4	0.5	0.6	1.3	1.9	2.6	3.2	3.8	5.1	6.3	9.3	12.2	22.9	32.4	48.0	73.1	93.0
70	0.1	0.3	0.4	0.6	0.7	1.4	2.1	2.8	3.4	4.1	5.4	6.8	10.0	13.1	24.5	34.4	50.5	75.7	94.3
75	0.1	0.3	0.4	0.6	0.7	1.5	2.2	3.0	3.7	4.4	5.8	7.2	10.7	13.9	26.0	36.3	52.9	78.0	95.3
80	0.2	0.3	0.5	0.6	0.8	1.6	2.4	3.2	3.9	4.7	6.2	7.7	11.3	14.8	27.4	38.2	55.3	80.1	96.2
85	0.2	0.3	0.5	0.7	0.8	1.7	2.5	3.3	4.2	5.0	6.6	8.2	12.0	15.6	28.9	40.1	57.4	82.0	96.9
90	0.2	0.4	0.5	0.7	0.9	1.8	2.7	3.5	4.4	5.3	7.0	8.6	12.6	16.5	30.3	41.8	59.5	83.8	97.5
95	0.2	0.4	0.6	0.8	0.9	1.9	2.8	3.7	4.6	5.5	7.3	9.1	13.3	17.3	31.7	43.6	61.5	85.3	97.9
125	0.2	0.5	0.7	1.0	1.2	2.5	3.7	4.9	6.1	7.2	9.5	11.8	17.1	22.1	39.4	52.9	71.5	92.0	99.4
150	0.3	0.6	0.9	1.2	1.5	3.0	4.4	5.8	7.2	8.6	11.3	13.9	20.2	25.9	45.2	59.5	77.9	95.2	99.8
175	0.3	0.7	1.0	1.4	1.7	3.4	5.1	6.8	8.4	10.0	13.1	16.1	23.1	29.6	50.4	65.1	82.8	97.1	99.9
200	0.4	0.8	1.2	1.6	2.0	3.9	5.8	7.7	9.5	11.3	14.8	18.1	25.9	33.0	55.1	70.0	86.6	98.2	100.0
225	0.4	0.9	1.3	1.8	2.2	4.4	6.5	8.6	10.6	12.6	16.5	20.2	28.7	36.3	59.4	74.2	89.6	98.9	100.0
250	0.5	1.0	1.5	2.0	2.5	4.9	7.2	9.5	11.8	13.9	18.1	22.1	31.3	39.4	63.3	77.8	91.9	99.4	100.0
275	0.5	1.1	1.6	2.2	2.7	5.4	7.9	10.4	12.9	15.2	19.8	24.1	33.8	42.3	66.8	80.9	93.7	99.6	100.0
300	0.6	1.2	1.8	2.4	3.0	5.8	8.6	11.3	13.9	16.5	21.3	25.9	36.3	45.2	70.0	83.6	95.1	99.8	100.0
325	0.6	1.3	1.9	2.6	3.2	6.3	9.3	12.2	15.0	17.7	22.9	27.8	38.5	47.8	72.8	85.9	96.2	99.9	100.0
350	0.7	1.4	2.1	2.8	3.4	6.8	10.0	13.1	16.1	18.9	24.5	29.5	40.9	50.4	75.4	87.8	97.0	99.9	100.0
375	0.7	1.5	2.2	3.0	3.7	7.2	10.6	13.9	17.1	20.2	25.9	31.3	43.0	52.8	77.8	89.5	97.7	99.9	100.0
400	0.8	1.6	2.4	3.1	3.9	7.7	11.3	14.8	18.1	21.3	27.4	33.0	45.1	55.1	79.9	91.0	98.2	100.0	100.0
425	0.8	1.7	2.5	3.3	4.2	8.1	12.0	15.6	19.1	22.6	28.9	34.6	47.2	57.3	81.8	92.2	98.6	100.0	100.0
450	0.9	1.8	2.7	3.5	4.4	8.6	12.6	16.5	20.2	23.7	30.2	36.3	49.1	59.4	83.5	93.3	98.9	100.0	100.0
475	0.9	1.9	2.8	3.7	4.6	9.1	13.3	17.3	21.1	24.8	31.6	37.8	51.0	61.4	85.1	94.3	99.2	100.0	100.0
500	1.0	2.0	3.0	3.9	4.9	9.5	13.9	18.1	22.1	25.9	33.0	39.4	52.8	63.3	86.5	95.1	99.3	100.0	100.0
550	1.1	2.2	3.2	4.3	5.4	10.4	15.2	19.8	24.1	28.1	35.6	42.3	56.2	66.7	89.0	96.3	99.6	100.0	100.0
600	1.2	2.4	3.5	4.7	5.8	11.3	16.5	21.3	25.9	30.2	38.1	45.1	59.4	69.9	91.0	97.3	99.8	100.0	100.0
650	1.3	2.6	3.8	5.1	6.3	12.2	17.7	22.9	27.8	32.3	40.6	47.8	62.3	72.8	92.6	98.0	99.9	100.0	100.0
700	1.4	2.8	4.1	5.4	6.8	13.1	18.9	24.4	29.5	34.3	42.9	50.4	65.0	75.4	94.0	98.5	99.9	100.0	100.0
750	1.5	3.0	4.4	5.8	7.2	13.9	20.2	25.9	31.3	36.2	45.1	52.8	67.6	77.7	95.1	98.9	100.0	100.0	100.0
800	1.6	3.1	4.7	6.2	7.7	14.8	21.3	27.4	33.0	38.1	47.3	55.1	69.9	79.8	96.0	99.2	100.0	100.0	100.0
850	1.7	3.3	5.0	6.6	8.1	15.6	22.5	28.8	34.6	40.0	49.4	57.3	72.1	81.8	96.7	99.4	100.0	100.0	100.0
900	1.8	3.5	5.3	6.9	8.6	16.5	23.7	30.2	36.2	41.7	51.4	59.4	74.1	83.5	97.3	99.6	100.0	100.0	100.0
950	1.9	3.7	5.5	7.3	9.1	17.3	24.8	31.6	37.8	43.5	53.3	61.4	76.0	85.1	97.8	99.7	100.0	100.0	100.0
1000	2.0	3.9	5.8	7.7	9.5	18.1	25.9	33.0	39.4	45.1	55.1	63.2	77.7	86.5	98.2	99.8	100.0	100.0	100.0
1100	2.2	4.3	6.4	8.4	10.4	19.8	28.1	35.6	42.3	48.3	58.5	66.7	80.8	88.9	98.8	99.9	100.0	100.0	100.0
1200	2.4	4.7	6.9	9.2	11.3	21.3	30.2	38.1	45.1	51.3	61.7	69.9	83.5	91.0	99.2	99.9	100.0	100.0	100.0
1300	2.6	5.1	7.5	9.9	12.2	22.9	32.3	40.6	47.8	54.2	64.7	72.8	85.8	92.6	99.5	100.0	100.0	100.0	100.0
1400	2.8	5.4	8.1	10.6	13.1	24.4	34.3	42.9	50.4	56.8	67.4	75.4	87.8	93.9	99.6	100.0	100.0	100.0	100.0
1500	3.0	5.8	8.6	11.3	13.9	25.9	36.2	45.1	52.8	59.4	69.9	77.7	89.5	95.1	99.8	100.0	100.0	100.0	100.0
1600	3.1	6.2	9.2	12.0	14.8	27.4	38.1	47.3	55.1	61.7	72.2	79.8	90.9	95.9	99.8	100.0	100.0	100.0	100.0
1700	3.3	6.6	9.7	12.7	15.6	28.8	40.0	49.4	57.3	64.0	74.4	81.7	92.2	96.7	99.9	100.0	100.0	100.0	100.0
1800	3.5	6.9	10.2	13.4	16.5	30.2	41.7	51.3	59.4	66.1	76.3	83.5	93.3	97.3	99.9	100.0	100.0	100.0	100.0
1900	3.7	7.3	10.8	14.1	17.3	31.6	43.5	53.3	61.4	68.0	78.1	85.1	94.2	97.8	100.0	100.0	100.0	100.0	100.0
2000	3.9	7.7	11.3	14.8	18.1	33.0	45.1	55.1	63.2	69.9	79.8	86.5	95.0	98.2	100.0	100.0	100.0	100.0	100.0

Appendix F-8

PROBABILITY, IN PER CENT, OF FINDING AT LEAST ONE ERROR IF TOTAL NO. OF ERRORS IN UNIVERSE IS AS INDICATED

TOTAL ERRORS IN UNIVERSE SIZE OF 100000.

SAMPLE SIZE	1	2	3	4	5	10	15	20	25	30	40	50	75	100	200	300	500	1000	2000
5	0.0	0.0	0.0	0.0	0.0	0.0	0.1	0.1	0.1	0.1	0.2	0.2	0.4	0.5	1.0	1.5	2.5	4.9	9.6
10	0.0	0.0	0.0	0.0	0.0	0.1	0.1	0.2	0.2	0.3	0.4	0.5	0.7	1.0	2.0	3.0	4.9	9.6	18.3
15	0.0	0.0	0.0	0.1	0.1	0.1	0.2	0.3	0.4	0.4	0.6	0.7	1.1	1.5	3.0	4.4	7.2	14.0	26.1
20	0.0	0.0	0.1	0.1	0.1	0.2	0.3	0.4	0.5	0.6	0.8	1.0	1.5	2.0	3.9	5.8	9.5	18.2	33.2
25	0.0	0.0	0.1	0.1	0.1	0.2	0.4	0.5	0.6	0.7	1.0	1.2	1.9	2.5	4.9	7.2	11.8	22.2	39.7
30	0.0	0.1	0.1	0.1	0.1	0.3	0.4	0.6	0.7	0.9	1.2	1.5	2.2	3.0	5.8	8.6	14.0	26.0	45.5
35	0.0	0.1	0.1	0.1	0.2	0.3	0.5	0.7	0.9	1.0	1.4	1.7	2.6	3.4	6.8	10.0	16.1	29.6	50.7
40	0.0	0.1	0.1	0.2	0.2	0.4	0.6	0.8	1.0	1.2	1.6	2.0	3.0	3.9	7.7	11.3	18.2	33.0	55.4
45	0.0	0.1	0.1	0.2	0.2	0.4	0.7	0.9	1.1	1.3	1.8	2.2	3.3	4.4	8.6	12.6	20.2	36.4	59.7
50	0.0	0.1	0.1	0.2	0.2	0.5	0.7	1.0	1.2	1.5	2.0	2.5	3.7	4.9	9.5	14.0	22.2	39.5	63.6
55	0.1	0.1	0.2	0.2	0.3	0.5	0.8	1.1	1.4	1.6	2.2	2.7	4.0	5.4	10.4	15.2	24.1	42.5	67.1
60	0.1	0.1	0.2	0.2	0.3	0.6	0.9	1.2	1.5	1.8	2.4	3.0	4.4	5.8	11.3	16.5	26.0	45.3	70.3
65	0.1	0.1	0.2	0.3	0.3	0.6	1.0	1.3	1.6	1.9	2.6	3.2	4.8	6.3	12.2	17.7	27.8	48.0	73.1
70	0.1	0.1	0.2	0.3	0.3	0.7	1.0	1.4	1.7	2.1	2.8	3.4	5.1	6.8	13.1	19.0	29.6	50.5	75.7
75	0.1	0.1	0.2	0.3	0.4	0.7	1.1	1.5	1.9	2.2	3.0	3.7	5.5	7.2	13.9	20.2	31.3	52.9	78.0
80	0.1	0.2	0.2	0.3	0.4	0.8	1.2	1.6	2.0	2.4	3.2	3.9	5.8	7.7	14.8	21.4	33.0	55.2	80.1
85	0.1	0.2	0.3	0.3	0.4	0.8	1.3	1.7	2.1	2.5	3.3	4.2	6.2	8.2	15.7	22.5	34.7	57.4	82.1
90	0.1	0.2	0.3	0.4	0.4	0.9	1.3	1.8	2.2	2.7	3.5	4.4	6.5	8.6	16.5	23.7	36.3	59.5	83.6
95	0.1	0.2	0.3	0.4	0.5	0.9	1.4	1.9	2.3	2.8	3.7	4.6	6.9	9.1	17.3	24.8	37.9	61.5	85.3
100	0.1	0.2	0.3	0.4	0.5	1.0	1.5	2.0	2.5	3.0	3.9	4.9	7.2	9.5	18.2	26.0	39.4	63.4	86.8
125	0.1	0.2	0.4	0.5	0.6	1.2	1.9	2.5	3.1	3.7	4.9	6.1	9.0	11.8	22.1	31.3	46.6	71.5	92.0
150	0.1	0.3	0.4	0.6	0.7	1.5	2.2	3.0	3.7	4.4	5.8	7.2	10.6	13.9	25.9	36.3	52.8	77.8	95.2
175	0.2	0.3	0.5	0.7	0.9	1.7	2.6	3.4	4.3	5.1	6.8	8.4	12.3	16.1	29.6	40.9	58.4	82.8	97.1
200	0.2	0.4	0.6	0.8	1.0	2.0	3.0	3.9	4.9	5.8	7.7	9.5	13.9	18.1	33.0	45.2	63.3	86.6	98.2
225	0.2	0.4	0.7	0.9	1.1	2.2	3.3	4.4	5.5	6.5	8.6	10.6	15.5	20.2	36.3	49.1	67.6	89.6	98.9
250	0.2	0.5	0.7	1.0	1.2	2.5	3.7	4.9	6.1	7.2	9.5	11.8	17.1	22.1	39.4	52.8	71.4	91.9	99.4
275	0.3	0.5	0.8	1.1	1.4	2.7	4.0	5.4	6.6	7.9	10.4	12.9	18.6	24.1	42.4	56.2	74.8	93.7	99.6
300	0.3	0.6	0.9	1.2	1.5	3.0	4.4	5.8	7.2	8.6	11.3	13.9	20.2	25.9	45.1	59.4	77.8	95.1	99.8
325	0.3	0.6	1.0	1.3	1.6	3.2	4.8	6.3	7.8	9.3	12.2	15.0	21.6	27.8	47.8	62.3	80.4	96.2	99.8
350	0.3	0.7	1.0	1.4	1.7	3.4	5.1	6.8	8.4	10.0	13.1	16.1	23.1	29.6	50.4	65.1	82.7	97.0	99.9
375	0.4	0.7	1.1	1.5	1.9	3.7	5.5	7.2	9.0	10.6	13.9	17.1	24.5	31.3	52.8	67.6	84.8	97.7	99.9
400	0.4	0.8	1.2	1.6	2.0	3.9	5.8	7.7	9.5	11.3	14.8	18.1	25.9	33.0	55.1	70.0	86.5	98.2	100.0
425	0.4	0.8	1.3	1.7	2.1	4.2	6.2	8.2	10.1	12.0	15.6	19.2	27.3	34.6	57.3	72.1	88.1	98.6	100.0
450	0.4	0.9	1.3	1.8	2.2	4.4	6.5	8.6	10.6	12.6	16.5	20.2	28.6	36.3	59.4	74.1	89.5	98.9	100.0
475	0.5	0.9	1.4	1.9	2.3	4.6	6.9	9.1	11.2	13.3	17.3	21.2	30.0	37.8	61.4	76.0	90.8	99.2	100.0
500	0.5	1.0	1.5	2.0	2.5	4.9	7.2	9.5	11.8	13.9	18.1	22.1	31.3	39.4	63.3	77.8	91.8	99.3	100.0
550	0.5	1.1	1.6	2.2	2.7	5.4	7.9	10.4	12.9	15.2	19.7	24.0	33.8	42.3	66.7	80.9	93.6	99.6	100.0
600	0.6	1.2	1.8	2.4	3.0	5.8	8.6	11.3	13.9	16.5	21.3	25.9	36.3	45.1	69.9	83.5	95.1	99.8	100.0
650	0.6	1.3	1.9	2.6	3.2	6.3	9.3	12.2	15.0	17.7	22.9	27.8	38.6	47.8	72.8	85.8	96.2	99.9	100.0
700	0.7	1.4	2.1	2.8	3.4	6.8	10.0	13.1	16.1	19.0	24.4	29.6	40.9	50.4	75.4	87.8	97.0	99.9	100.0
750	0.7	1.5	2.2	3.0	3.7	7.2	10.6	13.9	17.1	20.2	25.9	31.3	43.0	52.8	77.7	89.5	97.7	99.9	100.0
800	0.8	1.6	2.4	3.1	3.9	7.7	11.3	14.8	18.1	21.3	27.4	33.0	45.1	55.1	80.0	91.0	98.2	100.0	100.0
850	0.8	1.7	2.5	3.3	4.2	8.2	12.0	15.6	19.2	22.5	28.8	34.6	47.1	57.3	81.9	92.3	98.6	100.0	100.0
900	0.9	1.8	2.7	3.5	4.4	8.6	12.6	16.5	20.2	23.7	30.2	36.3	49.1	59.4	83.6	93.3	98.9	100.0	100.0
950	0.9	1.9	2.8	3.7	4.6	9.1	13.3	17.3	21.2	24.8	31.6	37.8	51.0	61.4	85.1	94.2	99.1	100.0	100.0
1000	1.0	2.0	3.0	3.9	4.9	9.5	13.9	18.1	22.1	25.9	33.0	39.4	52.8	63.4	86.5	95.1	99.3	100.0	100.0
1100	1.1	2.2	3.2	4.3	5.4	10.4	15.2	19.7	24.0	28.1	35.6	42.3	56.2	66.7	88.9	96.3	99.6	100.0	100.0
1200	1.2	2.4	3.5	4.7	5.8	11.3	16.5	21.3	25.9	30.2	38.1	45.1	59.4	69.9	91.0	97.3	99.8	100.0	100.0
1300	1.3	2.6	3.8	5.1	6.3	12.2	17.7	22.9	27.8	32.3	40.6	47.8	62.3	72.8	92.6	98.0	99.9	100.0	100.0
1400	1.4	2.8	4.1	5.4	6.8	13.1	18.9	24.4	29.6	34.3	42.9	50.4	65.0	75.4	93.9	98.5	99.9	100.0	100.0
1500	1.5	3.0	4.4	5.8	7.2	13.9	20.2	25.9	31.3	36.3	45.1	52.8	67.6	77.7	95.0	98.9	100.0	100.0	100.0
1600	1.6	3.1	4.7	6.2	7.7	14.8	21.3	27.4	33.0	38.1	47.3	55.1	69.9	79.8	95.9	99.2	100.0	100.0	100.0
1700	1.7	3.3	5.0	6.6	8.2	15.6	22.5	28.8	34.6	40.0	49.3	57.3	72.1	81.7	96.7	99.4	100.0	100.0	100.0
1800	1.8	3.5	5.3	6.9	8.6	16.5	23.7	30.2	36.3	41.7	51.3	59.4	74.1	83.5	97.3	99.6	100.0	100.0	100.0
1900	1.9	3.7	5.5	7.3	9.1	17.3	24.8	31.6	37.8	43.5	53.3	61.3	76.0	85.1	97.8	99.7	100.0	100.0	100.0
2000	2.0	3.9	5.8	7.7	9.5	18.1	25.9	33.0	39.4	45.1	55.1	63.3	77.7	86.5	98.2	99.8	100.0	100.0	100.0

Appendix F-9

PROBABILITY, IN PER CENT, OF FINDING AT LEAST ONE ERROR IF TOTAL NO. OF ERRORS IN UNIVERSE IS AS INDICATED

TOTAL ERRORS IN UNIVERSE SIZE OF 150000.

SAMPLE SIZE	1	2	3	4	5	10	15	20	25	30	40	50	75	100	200	300	500	1000	2000
5.	0.0	0.0	0.0	0.0	0.0	0.0	0.1	0.1	0.1	0.1	0.1	0.2	0.2	0.3	0.7	1.0	1.7	3.3	6.5
10.	0.0	0.0	0.0	0.0	0.0	0.1	0.1	0.1	0.2	0.2	0.3	0.3	0.5	0.7	1.3	2.0	3.3	6.5	12.6
15.	0.0	0.0	0.0	0.0	0.1	0.1	0.1	0.2	0.2	0.3	0.4	0.5	0.7	1.0	2.0	3.0	4.9	9.5	18.2
20.	0.0	0.0	0.0	0.1	0.1	0.1	0.2	0.3	0.3	0.4	0.5	0.7	1.0	1.3	2.6	3.9	6.5	12.5	23.5
25.	0.0	0.0	0.1	0.1	0.1	0.2	0.2	0.3	0.4	0.5	0.7	0.8	1.2	1.7	3.3	4.9	8.0	15.4	28.5
30.	0.0	0.0	0.1	0.1	0.1	0.2	0.3	0.4	0.5	0.6	0.8	1.0	1.5	2.0	3.9	5.8	9.5	18.2	33.1
35.	0.0	0.0	0.1	0.1	0.1	0.2	0.3	0.5	0.6	0.7	0.9	1.2	1.7	2.3	4.6	6.8	11.0	20.9	37.5
40.	0.0	0.1	0.1	0.1	0.1	0.3	0.4	0.5	0.7	0.8	1.1	1.3	2.0	2.6	5.2	7.7	12.5	23.5	41.6
45.	0.0	0.1	0.1	0.1	0.1	0.3	0.4	0.6	0.7	0.9	1.2	1.5	2.2	3.0	5.8	8.6	14.0	26.0	45.3
50.	0.0	0.1	0.1	0.1	0.2	0.3	0.5	0.7	0.8	1.0	1.3	1.7	2.5	3.3	6.5	9.5	15.4	28.4	48.9
55.	0.0	0.1	0.1	0.1	0.2	0.4	0.5	0.7	0.9	1.1	1.5	1.8	2.7	3.6	7.1	10.4	16.8	30.8	52.2
60.	0.0	0.1	0.1	0.2	0.2	0.4	0.6	0.8	1.0	1.2	1.6	2.0	3.0	3.9	7.7	11.3	18.2	33.1	55.3
65.	0.0	0.1	0.1	0.2	0.2	0.4	0.6	0.9	1.1	1.3	1.7	2.2	3.2	4.2	8.3	12.2	19.5	35.3	58.2
70.	0.0	0.1	0.1	0.2	0.2	0.5	0.7	0.9	1.2	1.4	1.9	2.3	3.4	4.6	8.9	13.1	20.9	37.4	60.9
75.	0.1	0.1	0.1	0.2	0.2	0.5	0.7	1.0	1.2	1.5	2.0	2.5	3.7	4.9	9.5	13.9	22.2	39.5	63.5
80.	0.1	0.1	0.2	0.2	0.3	0.5	0.8	1.1	1.3	1.6	2.1	2.7	3.9	5.2	10.1	14.8	23.4	41.4	65.8
85.	0.1	0.1	0.2	0.2	0.3	0.6	0.8	1.1	1.4	1.7	2.3	2.8	4.2	5.5	10.7	15.7	24.7	43.4	68.1
90.	0.1	0.1	0.2	0.2	0.3	0.6	0.9	1.2	1.5	1.8	2.4	3.0	4.4	5.8	11.3	16.5	26.0	45.2	70.1
95.	0.1	0.1	0.2	0.3	0.3	0.6	0.9	1.3	1.6	1.9	2.5	3.1	4.6	6.1	11.9	17.3	27.2	47.0	72.1
125.	0.1	0.2	0.2	0.3	0.4	0.8	1.2	1.6	2.1	2.5	3.3	4.1	6.1	8.0	15.4	22.1	34.1	56.7	81.3
150.	0.1	0.2	0.3	0.4	0.5	1.0	1.5	2.0	2.5	3.0	3.9	4.9	7.2	9.5	18.1	26.0	39.4	63.4	86.7
175.	0.1	0.2	0.3	0.5	0.6	1.2	1.7	2.3	2.9	3.4	4.5	5.6	8.4	11.0	20.8	29.6	44.3	69.0	90.5
200.	0.1	0.3	0.4	0.5	0.7	1.3	2.0	2.6	3.3	3.9	5.1	6.4	9.5	12.5	23.4	33.0	48.7	73.8	93.2
225.	0.2	0.3	0.4	0.6	0.7	1.5	2.2	2.9	3.7	4.4	5.7	7.0	10.7	13.9	25.9	36.3	52.8	77.8	95.1
250.	0.2	0.3	0.5	0.7	0.8	1.7	2.5	3.3	4.1	4.9	6.4	7.9	11.8	15.4	28.4	39.4	56.6	81.2	96.5
275.	0.2	0.4	0.5	0.7	0.9	1.8	2.7	3.6	4.5	5.3	7.0	8.6	12.9	16.8	30.7	42.4	60.1	84.1	97.5
300.	0.2	0.4	0.6	0.8	1.0	2.0	3.0	3.9	4.9	5.8	7.7	9.5	13.9	18.1	33.0	45.2	63.3	86.6	98.2
325.	0.2	0.4	0.7	0.9	1.1	2.2	3.2	4.2	5.3	6.3	8.3	10.2	15.0	19.5	35.2	47.9	66.3	88.7	98.7
350.	0.2	0.5	0.7	0.9	1.2	2.3	3.4	4.6	5.7	6.7	8.9	11.0	16.1	20.8	37.3	50.4	69.0	90.4	99.1
375.	0.3	0.5	0.8	1.0	1.3	2.5	3.7	4.9	6.1	7.2	9.5	11.7	17.1	22.2	39.4	52.8	71.5	91.9	99.4
400.	0.3	0.5	0.8	1.1	1.3	2.7	3.9	5.2	6.4	7.7	10.1	12.4	18.2	23.4	41.4	55.1	73.7	93.1	99.5
425.	0.3	0.6	0.9	1.1	1.4	2.8	4.2	5.5	6.8	8.1	10.7	13.2	19.2	24.7	43.3	57.3	75.9	94.2	99.7
450.	0.3	0.6	0.9	1.2	1.5	3.0	4.4	5.8	7.2	8.6	11.3	13.9	20.2	26.0	45.2	59.4	77.8	95.1	99.8
475.	0.3	0.6	1.0	1.3	1.6	3.1	4.7	6.1	7.6	9.1	11.9	14.6	21.2	27.2	47.0	61.4	79.6	95.8	99.8
500.	0.3	0.7	1.0	1.3	1.7	3.3	4.9	6.5	8.0	9.5	12.5	15.3	22.2	28.4	48.7	63.3	81.2	96.5	99.9
550.	0.4	0.7	1.1	1.5	1.8	3.6	5.4	7.1	8.8	10.4	13.7	16.8	24.1	30.7	52.1	66.8	84.1	97.5	99.9
600.	0.4	0.8	1.2	1.6	2.0	4.0	5.9	7.7	9.5	11.3	14.8	18.0	26.0	33.0	55.2	70.0	86.6	98.2	100.0
650.	0.4	0.9	1.3	1.7	2.2	4.3	6.3	8.3	10.3	12.2	15.9	19.4	27.8	35.2	58.1	72.9	88.6	98.7	100.0
700.	0.5	0.9	1.4	1.9	2.3	4.6	6.8	8.9	11.0	13.1	17.1	20.9	29.6	37.4	60.8	75.5	90.4	99.1	100.0
750.	0.5	1.0	1.5	2.0	2.5	4.9	7.2	9.5	11.7	13.9	18.2	22.2	31.3	39.4	63.3	77.8	91.9	99.3	100.0
800.	0.5	1.1	1.6	2.1	2.6	5.2	7.7	10.1	12.5	14.8	19.3	23.5	33.0	41.4	65.7	79.9	93.1	99.5	100.0
850.	0.6	1.1	1.7	2.2	2.8	5.5	8.2	10.7	13.2	15.7	20.3	24.7	34.7	43.4	67.9	81.9	94.2	99.7	100.0
900.	0.6	1.2	1.8	2.4	3.0	5.8	8.6	11.3	13.9	16.5	21.4	26.0	36.3	45.2	70.0	83.6	95.1	99.8	100.0
950.	0.6	1.3	1.9	2.5	3.1	6.2	9.1	11.9	14.7	17.3	22.4	27.2	37.9	47.0	72.0	85.2	95.8	99.8	100.0
1000.	0.7	1.3	2.0	2.6	3.3	6.5	9.6	12.5	15.4	18.2	23.5	28.4	39.5	48.8	73.8	86.6	96.5	99.9	100.0
1100.	0.7	1.5	2.2	2.9	3.6	7.1	10.5	13.7	16.8	19.8	25.5	30.8	42.4	52.1	77.1	89.0	97.5	99.9	100.0
1200.	0.8	1.6	2.4	3.2	4.0	7.7	11.4	14.8	18.2	21.4	27.5	33.1	45.3	55.2	80.0	91.0	98.2	100.0	100.0
1300.	0.9	1.7	2.6	3.4	4.3	8.3	12.2	16.0	19.6	23.0	29.4	35.3	48.0	58.1	82.5	92.7	98.7	100.0	100.0
1400.	0.9	1.9	2.8	3.7	4.6	9.0	13.1	17.1	20.9	24.5	31.3	37.4	50.5	60.9	84.7	94.0	99.1	100.0	100.0
1500.	1.0	2.0	3.0	4.0	4.9	9.6	14.0	18.2	22.2	26.0	33.1	39.5	52.9	63.4	86.6	95.1	99.3	100.0	100.0
1600.	1.1	2.1	3.2	4.2	5.2	10.2	14.9	19.3	23.5	27.5	34.9	41.5	55.3	65.8	88.3	96.0	99.5	100.0	100.0
1700.	1.1	2.3	3.4	4.5	5.6	10.8	15.7	20.4	24.8	29.0	36.6	43.4	57.5	68.0	89.8	96.7	99.7	100.0	100.0
1800.	1.2	2.4	3.6	4.7	5.9	11.4	16.6	21.5	26.1	30.4	38.3	45.3	59.6	70.1	91.1	97.3	99.8	100.0	100.0
1900.	1.3	2.5	3.8	5.0	6.2	12.0	17.4	22.5	27.3	31.8	39.9	47.1	61.6	72.1	92.2	97.8	99.8	100.0	100.0
2000.	1.3	2.6	3.9	5.2	6.5	12.6	18.2	23.5	28.5	33.1	41.5	48.9	63.5	73.9	93.2	98.2	99.9	100.0	100.0

Appendix F-10

PROBABILITY, IN PER CENT, OF FINDING AT LEAST ONE ERROR IF TOTAL NO. OF ERRORS IN UNIVERSE IS AS INDICATED

TOTAL ERRORS IN UNIVERSE SIZE OF 200000.

SAMPLE SIZE	1	2	3	4	5	10	15	20	25	30	40	50	75	100	200	300	500	1000	2000
5.	0.0	0.0	0.0	0.0	0.0	0.0	0.0	0.1	0.1	0.1	0.1	0.1	0.2	0.2	0.5	0.7	1.2	2.5	4.9
10.	0.0	0.0	0.0	0.0	0.0	0.0	0.1	0.1	0.1	0.2	0.2	0.3	0.4	0.5	1.0	1.5	2.5	4.9	9.6
15.	0.0	0.0	0.0	0.0	0.1	0.1	0.1	0.2	0.2	0.2	0.3	0.4	0.6	0.7	1.5	2.2	3.7	7.2	14.0
20.	0.0	0.0	0.0	0.1	0.1	0.1	0.2	0.2	0.3	0.3	0.4	0.5	0.7	1.0	2.0	3.0	4.9	9.5	18.2
25.	0.0	0.0	0.1	0.1	0.1	0.2	0.2	0.3	0.3	0.4	0.5	0.6	0.9	1.2	2.5	3.7	6.1	11.8	22.2
30.	0.0	0.0	0.1	0.1	0.1	0.2	0.3	0.3	0.4	0.5	0.6	0.7	1.1	1.5	3.0	4.4	7.2	14.0	26.0
35.	0.0	0.0	0.1	0.1	0.2	0.2	0.3	0.4	0.4	0.5	0.7	0.9	1.3	1.7	3.4	5.1	8.4	16.1	29.7
40.	0.0	0.0	0.1	0.1	0.2	0.2	0.3	0.4	0.5	0.6	0.8	1.0	1.5	2.0	3.9	5.8	9.5	18.2	33.1
45.	0.0	0.0	0.1	0.2	0.2	0.3	0.3	0.5	0.6	0.7	0.9	1.1	1.7	2.2	4.4	6.5	10.7	20.2	36.4
50.	0.0	0.1	0.1	0.2	0.2	0.3	0.4	0.5	0.6	0.7	1.0	1.2	1.9	2.5	4.9	7.2	11.8	22.2	39.5
55.	0.0	0.1	0.1	0.2	0.3	0.3	0.5	0.6	0.7	0.8	1.1	1.4	2.0	2.7	5.4	7.9	12.9	24.1	42.5
60.	0.0	0.1	0.1	0.2	0.3	0.4	0.6	0.6	0.7	0.9	1.2	1.5	2.2	3.0	5.8	8.6	13.9	26.0	45.3
65.	0.0	0.1	0.1	0.2	0.3	0.4	0.6	0.7	0.8	1.0	1.3	1.6	2.4	3.2	6.3	9.3	15.0	27.8	48.0
70.	0.0	0.1	0.1	0.2	0.3	0.5	0.7	0.7	0.9	1.0	1.4	1.7	2.6	3.4	6.8	10.0	16.1	29.6	50.5
75.	0.0	0.1	0.1	0.2	0.4	0.6	0.7	0.9	1.0	1.1	1.5	1.9	2.8	3.7	7.2	10.6	17.1	31.3	52.9
80.	0.0	0.1	0.1	0.2	0.4	0.6	0.8	1.0	1.0	1.2	1.6	2.0	3.0	3.9	7.7	11.3	18.2	33.0	55.3
85.	0.0	0.1	0.2	0.3	0.4	0.6	0.8	1.1	1.1	1.3	1.7	2.1	3.1	4.2	8.2	12.0	19.2	34.7	57.4
90.	0.0	0.1	0.2	0.3	0.4	0.7	0.9	1.1	1.2	1.4	1.7	2.2	3.3	4.4	8.6	12.6	20.2	36.3	59.5
95.	0.0	0.1	0.2	0.3	0.5	0.7	0.9	1.2	1.3	1.4	1.9	2.3	3.5	4.6	9.1	13.2	21.2	37.9	61.5
100.	0.1	0.1	0.2	0.4	0.6	0.7	1.0	1.2	1.5	1.5	2.0	2.5	3.7	4.9	9.5	13.9	22.1	39.4	63.4
125.	0.1	0.2	0.2	0.4	0.6	1.2	1.3	1.6	1.6	1.9	2.5	3.1	4.6	6.1	11.8	17.1	26.9	46.6	71.5
150.	0.1	0.2	0.3	0.5	0.7	1.4	2.0	1.9	2.3	2.3	3.0	3.7	5.6	7.2	12.9	20.1	31.3	52.9	77.9
175.	0.1	0.2	0.4	0.6	0.8	1.5	2.2	2.6	3.0	3.4	4.3	4.4	6.4	8.4	16.1	23.1	35.5	58.4	82.8
200.	0.1	0.2	0.4	0.8	1.0	1.7	2.4	3.0	3.0	3.9	4.9	4.5	8.1	10.6	18.1	25.9	39.4	63.3	86.6
225.	0.1	0.2	0.3	0.4	0.6	1.1	1.7	2.2	2.8	3.1	4.4	5.5	8.7	11.0	20.2	28.7	43.1	67.6	89.6
250.	0.1	0.2	0.4	0.5	0.6	1.2	1.9	2.5	3.1	3.7	4.9	6.1	9.0	11.8	22.1	31.3	46.5	71.5	91.9
275.	0.1	0.3	0.4	0.6	0.7	1.4	2.0	2.7	3.3	4.0	5.4	6.6	9.8	12.9	24.1	33.8	49.8	74.8	93.7
300.	0.2	0.3	0.4	0.6	0.8	1.5	2.2	3.0	3.7	4.4	5.8	7.2	10.6	13.9	25.9	36.3	52.8	77.8	95.1
325.	0.2	0.3	0.5	0.7	0.8	1.6	2.4	3.2	4.0	4.7	6.3	7.8	11.5	15.0	27.8	38.6	55.7	80.4	96.2
350.	0.2	0.3	0.5	0.7	0.9	1.7	2.6	3.4	4.3	5.1	6.8	8.4	12.3	16.1	29.6	40.9	58.4	82.7	97.0
375.	0.2	0.4	0.6	0.8	1.0	1.9	2.8	3.7	4.6	5.5	7.2	9.0	13.1	17.1	31.3	43.2	60.9	84.8	97.7
400.	0.2	0.4	0.6	0.8	1.0	2.0	3.0	3.9	4.9	5.8	7.7	9.5	13.9	18.1	33.0	45.3	63.3	86.6	98.2
425.	0.2	0.4	0.6	0.8	1.1	2.1	3.1	4.2	5.2	6.2	8.2	10.1	14.7	19.2	34.7	47.3	65.5	88.1	98.6
450.	0.2	0.4	0.7	0.9	1.1	2.2	3.3	4.4	5.5	6.5	8.6	10.7	15.5	20.2	36.3	49.1	67.6	89.5	98.9
475.	0.2	0.5	0.7	0.9	1.2	2.3	3.5	4.6	5.8	6.9	9.1	11.2	16.3	21.2	37.9	51.0	69.6	90.8	99.2
500.	0.3	0.5	0.7	1.0	1.2	2.5	3.7	4.9	6.1	7.2	9.5	11.8	17.1	22.1	39.4	52.8	71.4	91.9	99.3
550.	0.3	0.5	0.8	1.1	1.4	2.7	4.0	5.4	6.7	7.9	10.4	12.9	18.7	24.1	42.4	56.3	74.8	93.7	99.6
600.	0.3	0.6	0.9	1.2	1.5	3.0	4.4	5.8	7.3	8.6	11.3	14.0	20.2	26.0	45.2	59.4	77.8	95.1	99.8
650.	0.3	0.6	1.0	1.3	1.6	3.2	4.8	6.3	7.8	9.3	12.2	15.0	21.7	27.8	47.9	62.4	80.4	96.2	99.8
700.	0.4	0.7	1.0	1.4	1.7	3.4	5.1	6.8	8.4	10.0	13.1	16.1	23.1	29.6	50.4	65.1	82.7	97.0	99.9
750.	0.4	0.7	1.1	1.5	1.9	3.7	5.5	7.2	9.0	10.7	14.0	17.1	24.6	31.3	52.8	67.6	84.8	97.7	99.9
800.	0.4	0.8	1.2	1.6	2.0	3.9	5.8	7.7	9.5	11.3	14.8	18.2	26.0	33.0	55.2	70.0	86.6	98.2	100.0
850.	0.4	0.8	1.3	1.7	2.1	4.2	6.2	8.1	10.1	12.0	15.7	19.2	27.3	34.7	57.4	72.2	88.1	98.6	100.0
900.	0.5	0.9	1.3	1.8	2.2	4.4	6.5	8.6	10.7	12.7	16.5	20.2	28.7	36.3	59.4	74.2	89.5	98.9	100.0
950.	0.5	0.9	1.4	1.9	2.4	4.6	6.9	9.1	11.3	13.3	17.3	21.2	30.0	37.9	61.4	76.1	90.8	99.2	100.0
1000.	0.5	1.0	1.5	2.0	2.5	4.9	7.2	9.5	11.8	14.0	18.2	22.2	31.3	39.4	63.3	77.8	91.9	99.3	100.0
1100.	0.6	1.1	1.6	2.2	2.7	5.4	8.0	10.5	12.9	15.3	19.8	24.1	33.9	42.4	66.8	80.9	93.7	99.6	100.0
1200.	0.7	1.2	1.8	2.4	3.0	5.8	8.6	11.3	14.0	16.5	21.4	26.0	36.7	45.2	70.0	83.6	95.1	99.8	100.0
1400.	0.7	1.4	2.1	2.8	3.5	6.8	10.0	13.2	16.2	19.0	24.5	29.6	41.0	50.5	75.5	87.9	96.9	99.9	100.0
1500.	0.8	1.5	2.2	3.0	3.7	7.3	10.7	14.0	17.2	20.2	26.0	31.4	43.1	52.9	77.8	89.6	97.7	99.9	100.0
1600.	0.8	1.6	2.4	3.2	3.9	7.7	11.4	14.9	18.2	21.4	27.5	33.1	45.3	55.2	80.0	91.0	98.2	100.0	100.0
1700.	0.9	1.7	2.5	3.4	4.2	8.2	12.0	15.7	19.2	22.6	28.9	34.7	47.3	57.4	81.9	92.3	98.6	100.0	100.0
1800.	0.9	1.8	2.7	3.6	4.4	8.6	12.7	16.5	20.2	23.8	30.3	36.4	49.2	59.5	83.6	93.4	98.9	100.0	100.0
1900.	1.0	1.9	2.8	3.7	4.7	9.1	13.3	17.4	21.2	24.9	31.7	38.0	51.1	61.5	85.2	94.3	99.2	100.0	100.0
2000.	1.0	2.0	3.0	3.9	4.9	9.6	14.0	18.2	22.2	26.0	33.1	39.5	52.9	63.4	86.6	95.1	99.3	100.0	100.0

Appendix G

STATEMENT OF RESPONSIBILITIES
of the Internal Auditor

NATURE

Internal Auditing is an independent appraisal activity within an organization for the review of operations as a service to management. It is a managerial control which functions by measuring and evaluating the effectiveness of other controls.

OBJECTIVE AND SCOPE

The objective of internal auditing is to assist all members of management in the effective discharge of their responsibilities, by furnishing them with analyses, appraisals, recommendations and pertinent comments concerning the activities reviewed. The internal auditor is concerned with any phase of business activity where he can be of service to management. This involves going beyond the accounting and financial records to obtain a full understanding of the operations under review. The attainment of this overall objective involves such activities as:

- Reviewing and appraising the soundness, adequacy, and application of accounting, financial, and other operating controls, and promoting effective control at reasonable cost.
- Ascertaining the extent of compliance with established policies, plans, and procedures.
- Ascertaining the extent to which company assets are accounted for and safeguarded from losses of all kinds.
- Ascertaining the reliability of management data developed within the organization.
- Appraising the quality of performance in carrying out assigned responsibilities.
- Recommending operating improvements.

RESPONSIBILITY AND AUTHORITY

The responsibilities of internal auditing in the organization should be clearly established by management policy. The related authority should provide the internal auditor full access to all of the organization's records, properties, and personnel relevant to the subject under review. The internal auditor should be free to review and appraise policies, plans, procedures, and records.

The internal auditor's responsibilities should be:

- To inform and advise management, and to discharge this responsibility in a manner that is consistent with the Code of Ethics of The Institute of Internal Auditors.
- To coordinate his activities with others so as to best achieve his audit objectives and the objectives of the organization.

In performing his functions, an internal auditor has no direct responsibility for nor authority over any of the activities which he reviews. Therefore, the internal audit review and appraisal does not in any way relieve other persons in the organization of the responsibilities assigned to them.

INDEPENDENCE

Independence is essential to the effectiveness of internal auditing. This independence is obtained primarily through organizational status and objectivity:

- The organizational status of the internal auditing function and the support accorded to it by management are major determinants of its range and value. The head of the internal auditing function, therefore, should be responsible to an officer whose authority is sufficient to assure both a broad range of audit coverage and the adequate consideration of and effective action on the audit findings and recommendations.
- Objectivity is essential to the audit function. Therefore, an internal auditor should not develop and install procedures, prepare records, or engage in any other activity which he would normally review and appraise and which could reasonably be construed to compromise his independence. His objectivity need not be adversely affected, however, by his determination and recommendation of the standards of control to be applied in the development of systems and procedures under his review.

The Statement of Responsibilities of the Internal Auditor was originally issued by The Institute of Internal Auditors in 1947. The continuing development of the profession has resulted in two revisions, in 1957 and 1971. The current statement embodies the concepts previously established and includes such changes as are deemed advisable in light of the present status of the profession.

Appendix H

THE INSTITUTE OF INTERNAL AUDITORS, INC.
CODE OF ETHICS

INTRODUCTION: Recognizing that ethics are an important consideration in the practice of internal auditing and that the moral principles followed by members of **The Institute of Internal Auditors, Inc.** should be formalized, the Board of Directors at its regular meeting in New Orleans on December 13, 1968, received and adopted the following resolution:

WHEREAS, the members of **The Institute of Internal Auditors, Inc.** represent the profession of internal auditing; and

WHEREAS, managements rely on the profession of internal auditing to assist in the fulfillment of their management stewardship; and

WHEREAS, said members must maintain high standards of conduct, honor and character in order to carry on proper and meaningful internal auditing practice;

THEREFORE BE IT RESOLVED that a Code of Ethics be now set forth outlining the standards of professional behavior for the guidance of each member of **The Institute of Internal Auditors, Inc.**

In accordance with this resolution, the Board of Directors further approved of the principles set forth.

INTERPRETATION OF PRINCIPLES: The provisions of this Code of Ethics cover basic principles in the various disciplines of internal auditing practice. A member shall realize that individual judgment is required in the application of these principles. He has a responsibility to conduct himself so that his good faith and integrity should not be open to question. While having due regard for the limit of his technical skills, he will promote the highest possible internal auditing standards to the end of advancing the interest of his company or organization.

ARTICLES:

I. A member shall have an obligation to exercise honesty, objectivity and diligence in the performance of his duties and responsibilities.

II. A member, in holding the trust of his employer, shall exhibit loyalty in all matters pertaining to the affairs of the employer or to whomever he may be rendering a service. However, a member shall not knowingly be a part to any illegal or improper activity.

III. A member shall refrain from entering into any activity which may be in conflict with the interest of his employer or which would prejudice his ability to carry out objectively his duties and responsibilities.

IV. A member shall not accept a fee or a gift from an employee, a client, a customer or a business associate of his employer without the knowledge and consent of his senior management.

V. A member shall be prudent in the use of information acquired in the course of his duties. He shall not use confidential information for any personal gain or in a manner which would be detrimental to the welfare of his employer.

VI. A member, in expressing an opinion, shall use all reasonable care to obtain sufficient factual evidence to warrant such expression. In his reporting, a member shall reveal such material facts known to him, which, if not revealed, could either distort the report of the results of operations under review or conceal unlawful practice.

VII. A member shall continually strive for improvement in the proficiency and effectiveness of his service.

VIII. A member shall abide by the Bylaws and uphold the objectives of **The Institute of Internal Auditors, Inc.** In the practice of his profession, he shall be ever mindful of his obligation to maintain the high standard of competence, morality and dignity which **The Institute of Internal Auditors, Inc.** and its members have established.

subject index

Q

R